MESSAGES, ADDRESSES, AND PUBLIC PAPERS
OF
LUTHER HARTWELL HODGES

Luther Hartwell Hodges

MESSAGES, ADDRESSES, AND PUBLIC PAPERS

of

LUTHER HARTWELL HODGES

GOVERNOR OF NORTH CAROLINA

1954-1961

Volume III

1959-1960

Edited by

James W. Patton
Professor of History and Director of the
Southern Historical Collection
UNIVERSITY OF NORTH CAROLINA

Raleigh
Council of State
State of North Carolina
1963

iii

FOREWORD

Following the same pattern set in the two preceding volumes of this series, published in 1960 and 1962 respectively, this volume covers the last two years of Governor Hodges' six-year tenure as chief executive of North Carolina.

During this period the Governor made approximately 210 full-length speeches, of which 164 are preserved in typescript form among his official papers in the State Department of Archives and History at Raleigh. For reasons of space, as was true of the preceding volumes, only a limited number of those speeches are here printed. Fifty-four addresses, considered to be among the more important and less repetitious, are included in their entirety; seventy are described in brief summaries; and the remainder are listed by date, title, and place of delivery. For similar reasons, only selections are included from the numerous proclamations, greetings, statements, and other public papers that emanated from the governor's office during this period. The list of appointments includes only those made by Governor Hodges during the years 1959-1960.

The funds for printing this volume have been supplied by the Council of State of North Carolina, as has been done for previous volumes of the governors' papers. The editor has continued to work under the general supervision of a committee consisting of Dr. Christopher Crittenden, chairman, Professor Hugh T. Lefler, and Messrs. E. A. Resch, Edward L. Rankin, Jr., and Harold Makepeace, the last two of these having been successively the private secretaries of Governor Hodges during his tenure of office. Mrs. Geraldine Shunk Hall and Mrs. Ellen Ragan Strong typed the manuscript; Mrs. Elizabeth Dantzler Geer assisted in various phases of the editorial work; and Mrs. Ida Killough McQueen made the index.

James W. Patton

Chapel Hill, North Carolina
August 1, 1963

TABLE OF CONTENTS

vii

LIST OF ILLUSTRATIONS

THE HODGES ADMINISTRATION, 1959-1960

As was true of the years covered by the two preceding volumes of these papers, Governor Hodges continued during 1959-1960 to maintain the same busy schedule which he had set for himself at the beginning of his first term in office. In so far as the Governor was concerned the most time consuming events of the last two years of his administration were the 1959 session of the General Assembly and a prolonged strike at the Harriet-Henderson cotton mills in Vance County.

To the last legislature of his term Hodges announced the most ambitious and far-reaching set of goals ever presented by a North Carolina governor. Significant among the proposals to which the legislature gave favorable action were: a state minimum wage law which gave North Carolina the distinction of being the first state in the South to enact such a law; extension of unemployment security benefits to such a level as to make North Carolina's rank among the best in the nation in this respect; compulsory polio vaccination for children; reorganization and improvement of various state agencies, thereby continuing a trend which had begun with the 1955 General Assembly; uniform assessment and periodic and systematic revaluation of property for tax purposes; a new Department of Water Resources; and a new building for the General Assembly to replace the congested and inadequate quarters in which that body was forced to operate in the State Capitol.

With reference to the biennial budget, traditionally and naturally one of the most complex legislative problems with which the executive department has to deal, the General Assembly went along with the recommendations of Governor Hodges and the Advisory Budget Commission for spending $1,200,000,000 during the biennium 1959-1960, this being an increase of $50,500,000 in General Fund appropriations over expenditures of the preceding two years. The legislature also adopted the Governor's proposal that a "windfall" in the form of a tax withholding plan and an anticipated increase in tax revenues would provide for the increased appropriations without resorting to any new taxes—which proved to be true.

Of the Governor's proposals which failed to gain legislative approval the most important were: repeal of the absentee ballot law; incentive funds to supplement local school support on a matching basis; and plans for a uniform court system and revision of the state constitution. For the first time in a number of years the Governor did not call for a state-wide liquor referendum.

In contrast to the measure of success which he experienced in his relations with the legislature, the Governor's involvement in the Henderson textile strike was the least successful of any of his activities during his entire administration. This conflict, beginning in November, 1958, and lasting until August, 1959, was characterized by recalcitrance on both sides and violence to such an extent that the Governor felt called upon to assign highway patrolmen to assist in maintaining law and order and eventually to call out the National Guard. Throughout the controversy his efforts at mediation were so sabotaged by both management and labor as to cause him to describe the strike and its aftermath as "the most tragic single matter to confront me during my administration as governor."

Continuing his efforts to raise the per capital income of North Carolina by attracting new industries to the state, Governor Hodges in May and October, 1960, led industry hunting missions to New York and Chicago, respectively, where he told "The North Carolina Story" of economic opportunity to various groups of businessmen in each of these cities. In November, 1959, he headed a sixty-eight member trade and industry mission which spent fourteen days in five European countries seeking business contacts and expounding the commercial opportunities of North Carolina. This venture, during which the Governor made eight major speeches in as many European cities, marked a new departure in American-European trade relations, as it was the first time an individual state had sent a trade and industry mission abroad.

Another activity in which Governor Hodges played his favorite role of "Businessman in the Statehouse" was his continued interest in and support of the Research Triangle which he had helped to establish in the Durham-Raleigh-Chapel Hill area. Still other activities of the same nature included numerous speeches to business, banking, and industrial groups, both within and without the state, addresses welcoming new industries to the state, speeches at ground breaking ceremonies for new industrial plants, and various other appearances of a similar character.

During the calendar year 1959 Governor Hodges broke his own record as the state's most travelled chief executive by logging a total of 67,252 miles. This included 58,159 miles by air, 7,857 miles by automobile, 1,177 miles by train, and 70 miles by bus. In addition to the trade and industry mission which he led to Europe in this year, he also went in June, 1960, with eight other governors on a three-week tour of Soviet Russia. Statistics on the Governor's travel for 1960 are not readily available, but it appears that the total mileage for this year would approximate that of previous years. The total number of his speeches for 1959-1960 was somewhat smaller than that of previous two-year periods: 209 as compared with 243 in 1957-1958 and 284 in 1955-1956.

Interested as he was primarily in bringing business-type management to the operations of government, Luther Hodges was inclined to neglect political power-building and to show an indifference to Democratic Party organization. Unfettered by political ties himself, he was able to ignore the various factions in state politics and appoint to state offices men whose first loyalty was a personal one to him or to the office to which they were appointed. This led to some exceptionally good appointments, including a large number of career state workers elevated to top positions. But it also led to a neglect of party organization which on at least one occasion caused county chairmen to complain that they were not consulted about appointments.

Thus when the time came to pick his successor Hodges was unable to add much strength to the candidacy of Malcolm B. Sewell whom he supported unsuccessfully in a four-way race for the Democratic gubernatorial nomination. At the Democratic National Convention, to which he was a delegate, at Los Angeles in July, 1960, his first choice among the available candiates for the Democratic nomination for president was Lyndon B. Johnson rather than John F. Kennedy. But on the national as well as the state level, when the lines were drawn between the two major parties, he campaigned for the Democrats with so much vigor and enthusiasm that many observers give him much credit for the Democratic victory in 1960.

After this, it was only natural to assume that he would be in line for a high appointment in the National Democratic administration. On December 3, 1960, he was called to Palm Beach, Florida, for a conference with President-elect John F. Kennedy, immediately after which his appointment as Secretary of Commerce in the Kennedy administration was announced. The remainder of the Hodges administration was a busy prelude to his going to Washington, ending on January 5, 1961, when he turned the keys to the mansion and the Great Seal of the State of North Carolina over to the Honorable Terry Sanford and took off the white carnation which had been the symbol of his administration for eight years—twenty-two months as lieutenant governor and six years and two months as governor, longer than any other man in the history of North Carolina since it became a state.

MESSAGES TO THE GENERAL ASSEMBLY

MESSAGES TO THE GENERAL ASSEMBLY

[The messages of February 5, February 9, and March 12 were delivered by the Governor in person and are printed in the *Journal of the Senate of the General Assembly of the State of North Carolina, Session 1959*, pp. 12-25, 28-41, and 110-18; and also in the *Journal of the House of Representatives of the General Assembly of the State of North Carolina, Session 1959*, pp. 19-34, 45-60, and 206-16. Two messages of a routine nature, transmitting appointments, were sent, one to a joint session of the two houses on May 21 and one to the Senate on May 22. These appear in the *Journal of the Senate*, 1959, pp. 404-406 and 416-17, and in the *Journal of the House*, 1959, pp. 714-16.]

BIENNIAL MESSAGE TO THE GENERAL ASSEMBLY

February 5, 1959

[This fifty-minute "State of the State" message was addressed to the 170 members of the General Assembly and full galleries in the Hall of the House of Representatives, and was also carried over radio and television networks. The Governor, facing the last legislature of his term, announced the most ambitious and far-reaching set of legislative goals ever presented by a North Carolina governor. Many of his requests were shaped from proposals made by study commissions or boards which he had appointed. The address was comprehensive in nature and did not spell out the details of the specific policies which the Governor had in mind. This he would do in a special message on the budget to be delivered four days later.]

Mr. President, Mr. Speaker, and Members of the General Assembly of North Carolina:

May I express my personal welcome and cordial best wishes to each of you.

From every part of our beloved North Carolina you have come, chosen by the people to represent them. The legislative responsibilities vested in you by the people are great, and the opportunities available to you to chart a sound and enduring course for the present and future progress of our state are without limit.

I gratefully acknowledge the privilege and honor that is mine as governor in addressing this General Assembly today. This is the third consecutive occasion, upon the convening of a regular legislative session, that I have had this opportunity. I am also mindful of the fact that this is the last time that I shall have the duty and honor of presenting a biennial message to the General Assembly of North Carolna.

Many of the problems and issues which will press forward for your attention in the days ahead are not new but are recurring ones. Revenues and appropriations, for example, are major issues at each biennial session. I propose to deal with these matters in detail in my budget message next Monday.

Other major questions which will come before you for determination arise primarily because of the normal growth and change in our economy and in the life of our state and nation. Our very best efforts are required merely to meet the challenge of the unfolding present. And certainly our challenge as we face the future is how we can provide North Carolina with better public schools and colleges, more adequate health and welfare services, more roads and highways, a diversified agriculture and industry, a greatly improved system of courts, continued improvement in the organization and operation of state government, improved tax laws, and other laws to enable our people to take full advantage of their opportunities in the growing years ahead.

We are particularly fortunate that the 1957 Session of the General Assembly authorized appointment of special study commissions and committees to give intensive, careful thought to some of our most pressing problems, and to report to this session.

The able and dedicated citizens who served on these study commissions gave generously of their time and energies, and many of them are members of this General Assembly or have served in previous legislative sessions. I make this observation merely to emphasize that these studies and recommendations come to you from capable and devoted citizens. Their reports are worthy of your serious consideration. All of us appreciate the time and effort given by these commission members, and I am confident their studies will be of great assistance to you in your own deliberations.

THE STATE'S ECONOMY—AGRICULTURE AND INDUSTRY

Since the day more than four years ago that the duties of this office were placed upon me, I have devoted much time and travel to the economic problems of our state. Further diversification and development in agriculture and industry have been among the major objectives of this administration. I firmly believe that we can and should carry out a well-conceived program to improve the economic opportunities available to our people, and to increase their per capita income, which means just plain "better living"!

In my message to the 1957 General Assembly I said that we must develop more industry, both manufacturing and agricultural, and that we must remove insofar as possible whatever roadblocks now exist to our further industrial development.

Certain changes made in the tax laws by the 1957 General Assembly removed one of the roadblocks to our industrial progress. Since then, we have been able to carry the message far and wide that North Carolina has a reasonable and fair method of taxing business income earned in this state. The temporary loss in corporate tax revenues has been less than one-half of the $14,000,000 which was estimated two years ago. It is now evident, even after this short time, that the outlook for future revenues gained from industry and agricultural processing locating or expanding in our state will be many times our limited and temporary decreases.

During the calendar year 1957 our state experienced its greatest annual industrial growth up to that time, with a total for new and expanded plants in excess of $191,000,000. The 1957 record has now been shattered by a new high in accomplishment for the year 1958 during which a total of $253,000,000 was committed to new plants and expansions.

These figures are more meaningful when we realize that the new plants and expansions in 1958 alone are expected to furnish employment for more than 21,750 people, with an annual payroll of at least $72,633,000. Furthermore, this economic progress for North Carolina was achieved largely during a period of economic recession, at a time when other less fortunate areas of our nation were experiencing pronounced economic distress.

Let me mention a significant and impressive comparison. While the nation as a whole invested 17.4 per cent *less* in new plants and expansions during 1958, North Carolina had an *increase* of

32.5 per cent. This means our state was 50 per cent better than
the national average!

I do not mean to imply at all that the good industrial progress
we have enjoyed during the past two years is attributable solely
to a change in our tax laws. The important factor, in my opinion,
is the attitude and spirit of our people and our state. This is
revealed in the energy and enthusiasm of countless citizens—
businessmen, farmers, professional people and others—throughout
North Carolina who have joined hand-in-hand in this great effort
to make our state a better place in which to live; it is exemplified
by the action of the legislature in setting tax policy; and it is
demonstrated by officials and employees of the executive branch
who have labored long hours in this great endeavor.

I want to pay tribute to the agencies of state government,
to the more than one hundred local development groups, both
old and new, and to our many fine chambers of commerce for
their effective cooperation in achieving these goals.

The direct impact of agriculture—and indeed one agricultural
crop—on the income of our state is graphically revealed by what
happened in 1957. The decrease in tobacco farm income alone
during 1957, over the previous year amounted to $137,313,000,
or a drop of 27.1 per cent. This serious drop was due to several
factors, including acreage reductions and adverse weather conditions. Had our tobacco farm income held its own during that
year, we would have had $1,352 in per capita income, with a na-
tional ranking of forty-fourth. Instead, because of the farm income loss in 1957, our per capita income was only $1,317 and our
standing dropped from forty-fourth to forty-fifth in the nation.

Happily, 1958 was, by comparison, a banner year in agricultural prices and production, and according to present estimates
our farm income in 1958 was at least 8 per cent over 1957. This
encouraging development in our farm income, together with
new industrial payrolls of more than $72,000,000, including excit-
ing growth in food processing, certainly adds up to a good improvement in our over-all economy.

Last spring I appointed a Governor's Farm Advisory Committee which has been most helpful in providing a better understanding of some of the state and national problems we face on our

farms. This committee has made many helpful suggestions and I want to pay warm tribute to all its members.

CONSERVATION AND DEVELOPMENT OF OUR RESOURCES

Our state is favored with many natural resources. Their full significance to our present and our future well-being is not, I fear, generally appreciated.

Our forests comprise one of our most precious resources and hold promise of greater economic benefit to our people. Having constantly emphasized this potential, I am encouraged with the progress we are beginning to make. For example, in 1954, a total of 17,000,000 seedlings were distributed throughout the state from the state forest tree nurseries. In 1958, there were 84,000,000 made available to landowners in North Carolina.

In 1958, a new geological map of the state was issued, which will greatly assist our citizens in the exploration and development of mineral resources. This was the first complete map of this type issued since 1875.

Our future industrial and agricultural progress is dependent upon an adequate supply of water. Although North Carolina has an annual rainfall considerably higher than the national average, the demands for water as our population increases have substantially reduced our margin of safety. We should not forget the recent periods of drought when many cities and towns throughout the state were in serious trouble because of a lack of adequate water reserves.

The Reorganization Commission which was appointed following the 1957 legislative session has given further careful study to this problem, and in a report already made available to each of you, it is recommended that a Department of Water Resources be created, to which could be transferred the responsibilities scattered among the various state agencies now involved in water resource activities. The report further recommends that as part of this new agency, the State Stream Sanitation Committee be continued, until July 1, 1965, to complete its project on classification of streams. I heartily endorse the recommendations contained in the report and urge their adoption.

The Outer Banks of North Carolina form a protective barrier for our sounds and inland cities and counties against a ravaging ocean. If present rates of deterioration of the Outer Banks continue, they will be destroyed in a few short years. Time will not permit a full discussion of the problem, but I want to say with great earnestness that the state must meet this growing problem with vision, courage, and determination. A sensible program must be begun and continued, with the aid of federal agencies, to stabilize our inlets and dunes and to restore the Banks as vital dikes for the protection of our coastal area. The state, with local cooperation, must take the lead and I urge your serious attention to the problem. I shall have specific recommendations in my budget message.

PUBLIC EDUCATION AND SCHOOL FINANCE

We all recognize that education is one of the most important functions of government. We allocate more of our taxes to the support of education than to all other governmental activities combined. For the current biennium, 76 per cent of total General Fund appropriations is for education, and 67 per cent of the General Fund is for public schools alone.

North Carolina has in the past, considering our resources, made a good effort in support of our public schools. Notwithstanding our effort, however, we still rank near the bottom in per pupil expenditure for education, and our ranking in teachers' salaries continues to be comparatively low, although our national rank in teacher pay is substantially better than our national income rank.

The 1957 General Assembly expressly recognized that we should have a "more thorough understanding of the problems involved in financing public education in this state." Accordingly, the General Assembly authorized appointment of a Committee for the Study of Public School Finance. The report of that committee has already been made public, and each of you has a copy.

A major recommendation from this committee is an incentive plan to encourage local supplementary support for the public schools. The committee found that several of the administrative school units in the state have voted local taxes with which to supplement state appropriations, yet a majority furnish no supplement. The present plan of school support in North Carolina contemplates that the state shall furnish the basic support for the operation of the nine-months' school term, with this basic support being supplemented at the local level. Our present and long-standing approach on public school finance—basic state support with local effort to supplement—is, in my judgment, sound.

However, to enable us better to meet our school needs, it is proposed that the state establish an incentive fund, which would be distributed to the counties which make matching contributions in accordance with their economic ability. This would be entirely voluntary. The formula governing the distribution of the incentive fund would take into account the number of pupils and the taxable resources in the county.

I, for one, do *not* desire to see the state "unload" the burden of public school financing on the counties. The report of the Committee on the Study of Public School Finance does *not* make any such recommendation.

We need to do more for public education in North Carolina, both in the total number of dollars we provide and in the comparative effort that we put forth. Our future economic growth and strength will depend on how well we do in our educational efforts at all levels.

The people of North Carolina want to improve our public schools and want to see them made more modern and effective with more attention being given to fundamental learning. Our people will pay for good schools if given the opportunity. There is a popular interest in an improved and more serious curriculum, as well as improved teaching. I am happy to report excellent progress on a major curriculum study which has been underway for several months.

I endorse the principle implicit in the incentive plan proposed by the School Finance Study Committee, and I urge that you enact suitable legislation to give effect to this approach. In my opinion, such legislation will mean much to the future of our public schools. In my later message to you on the state budget, I shall submit for your consideration specific dollar amounts recommended for inclusion in the state's appropriations for the coming biennium.

HIGHER EDUCATION

Enrollments in our state-supported institutions of higher education continue to increase rapidly. In the fall of 1958, a total of 29,500 full-time students were enrolled in our nine state-supported colleges and in the three branches of the University. By the middle 1960's, we shall have an enrollment of about 37,000, and by 1969 an enrollment of 50,000 or more.

Notwithstanding these prospective increases in numbers, North Carolina still stands in a regrettably low position in the nation in the ratio of college enrollment. For the nation as a whole, 31 per cent of the college-age group attends college. In North Carolina, only 17 per cent of this group is enrolled in college.

We should not, of course, attempt to enroll more college students just to attain a more favorable statistical position. Nor should we maintain colleges for students who want to go to college simply because "it is the thing to do." And we should be sure that our colleges are offering opportunities for a *genuine* higher education.

This leads us to the subject of admission standards for our state-supported institutions of higher education. I do not suggest any blind and unreasoned adherence to an admission test as a sole criterion to judge admission to an institution of higher education. Rather, admission tests should constitute a useful tool. They should provide an objective appraisal, both of our students and of our high schools from which they graduate; and proper tests in colleges will go a long way toward raising the standards in our high schools.

You probably know that since the fall term of 1957 preadmission tests have been used as a criterion for admission of students to the Consolidated University. I compliment our University leadership for this step and I would like to see every state-supported institution of higher education announce that, effective no later than the fall term of 1961, preadmission tests will be required of all applicants for purposes of guidance and measurement of aptitudes and qualifications of the student. I hope the General Assembly will seriously interest itself in this matter.

In the ten-year period 1947-1957, appropriations by the General Assembly of North Carolina for capital improvements in

Left to right: Dean John H. Lampe, North Carolina State College School of Engineering, Governor Hodges, Professor C. R. McCullough, and Colonel R. P. Rosengren, federal highway official, at a State Highway Conference in Raleigh, January 21, 1959.

Raleigh Boy Scouts presenting to the Governor a report of the past year's activity, February 10, 1959. *Left to right:* Jack Shutt, David Williams, Tom Welch, Kent Cobb, Governor Hodges, Nickey Dombalis, Bobby Wrenn.

our state-supported institutions of higher education amounted to $105,000,000. In this decade, enrollments in these institutions increased *16 per cent*, from 24,300 in 1947 to 28,400 in 1957. Recently the Board of Higher Education completed a study of probable capital needs for our colleges for the ten-year period 1959 through 1969, a decade in which enrollments are expected to increase *66 per cent*, from about 30,000 to about 50,000. The board has concluded that the reasonable needs of our institutions during the next ten-year period can be met with a substantially less capital expenditure than was appropriated for the 1947-1957 decade. The capital improvements approach suggested by the board, and for the most part approved by the institutions, involves renovation and alteration of present facilities, a moderate increase in instructional and dormitory facilities, an increased use of present space, an increased use of facilities in the summer months, and provision for the expansion of community colleges. In my budget message, I shall have specific recommendations for a capital improvement program for our higher education institutions.

During the past two years we have had notable advances in the important field of community colleges. Colleges in Asheville, Charlotte, and Wilmington are now fully qualified under the Community College Act of 1957, and the state appropriations for capital improvements at these colleges have already been more than matched by bond issues approved in local elections.

The present accomplishments of our various institutions of higher education are good and commendable. Our potentials for future achievement are unlimited. The challenge that confronts our state is immense, and we will need a continued full measure of dedication to higher education on the part of the trustees, the officers, the faculties, and students of each separate institution to meet the great task that lies ahead.

We will also need the vital contribution of a vigorous and fearless Board of Higher Education which can assist us in charting that course which will give to the state a program of higher education which is strong in all parts, and which in its total result gives to North Carolina the best of which our state is capable, with a minimum of overlapping programs and with the least possible waste of public funds.

As you are aware, a very satisfactory agreement has been reached with respect to certain differences between the University Trustees and the Board of Higher Education, and recommended changes in present statutes, which I endorse, are supported by the presidents and governing boards of other state institutions of higher learning and by the Board of Higher Education.

WELFARE AND HEALTH

We must always remember the obligation of government to provide assistance for those who cannot assist themselves. Many of our citizens, for reasons beyond their control, must rely on the help given to them under our welfare program. These citizens include those who are too old, too young, too disabled, or too ill to work, and who are without private means of financial support.

North Carolina has continued to maintain a good record in the administration of its public welfare program, its public health program, and its hospital program. Our welfare activities, insofar as possible, are designed to help individuals attain a position of self-support. In some instances, the welfare officials are hampered by a lack of proper laws in developing policies that are needed to improve administration. I urge your careful consideration of proposals which will be presented to you, including such matters as strengthening our support laws and making possible better control over welfare payments, especially those dealing with illegitimate children.

Outstanding results have been achieved during the past two years in the control and prevention of polio epidemics. In 1957, only 233 cases of polio were reported in North Carolina and in 1958 only seventy-four cases were reported. More than 3,500,000 doses of Salk polio vaccine, made available under the federal program, have been administered to more than 1,000,000 children in North Carolina, with most of these voluntary immunizations administered during the past two years. However, it is estimated that more than 20 per cent of our children and young people through age 19 (the age group most susceptible to polio) have never received any polio vaccination.

I believe the General Assembly should consider a law providing for mandatory polio vaccination, especially for younger children.

EMPLOYMENT SECURITY

Our state for many years has maintained a soundly-operated employment security program. Our weekly benefit payments, in comparison with average weekly earnings in this state, are approximately equal to the national average. We have maintained sufficient reserve balances in our unemployment insurance fund so that tax rates have been commensurate with those in adjoining states, and at the same time our reserved have been sufficient to meet normally anticipated unemployment conditions. During 1958, unemployment was abnormally high through the nation. In North Carolina alone more than 200,000 workers received unemployment benefits, meaning that this number was out of work one or more weeks during the year.

Many other states experienced far more drastic unemployment than did North Carolina. You will recall that several months ago there was a strong movement in Congress to enact substantial changes in the federal laws governing the unemployment insurance program. Some people even went so far as to suggest, in effect, the complete federalization of the employment security programs, with the federal government prescribing minimum benefit payments, minimum number of weeks for which benefits would be paid, and so on.

In my opinion, many such proposals were prompted by conditions in other states which were attributable in part to a less actuarially sound administration of their own state programs, and in part to a governmental philosophy with which I basically disagree.

I do not think that the employment security program should be administered from Washington. I do believe that the states should always have a sound and adequate program of unemployment insurance benefits. In my opinion, the states should take the lead in this matter and should do whatever is necessary to cope adequately with periods of prolonged unemployment such as that experienced during 1958.

I think that our own state should give consideration to statutory changes which would, under unemployment emergencies expressly described by statute, enable state officials to extend by executive action the number of weeks for which benefits would be available. I, therefore, recommend that this session of the General Assembly approve legislation which would authorize the governor, under emergency conditions specified by law, to extend the benefit period for *an additional thirteen weeks*. This would permit payment of unemployment benefits for as much as thirty-nine weeks at the very time—and only then—when unemployment benefits would be most needed.

MINIMUM WAGE

More than 90,000 North Carolinians receive a wage of less than 75 cents an hour. We should have a state law requiring a minimum wage of at least 75 cents an hour. I could talk at great length on this matter but I think it is enough to say that employers can afford it, employees deserve it, and the state's economic progress demands it. I strongly recommend enactment of a state minimum wage law.

STATE PERSONNEL

Our many state employees, teachers, and officials continue to render devoted service, and I wish to express to all of them, on behalf of the people of this state, our sincere appreciation. It has been a distinct and enjoyable experience working with our state employees. In my budget message I shall have recommendations to make regarding several phases of employee relations.

NATIONAL GUARD

Just recently our North Carolina National Guard was reorganized under modern military concepts, and in keeping with new requirements set forth by the Department of Defense. I am happy to report that because of the good work of our adjutant general and his general officers in reaching an agreement with the Pentagon, we will be able to maintain our Guard at practically the same strength as before.

HIGHWAYS

The reorganization of the State Highway Commission, which was authorized by the 1957 General Assembly and placed into effect on July 1 of that year, has already achieved in this short time outstanding results which prove the wisdom of these organizational changes. The smaller State Highway Commission has operated as a state-wide policy-making board. The responsibility for day-to-day execution and direction of the highway program has been fulfilled by an able director and his assistants. New accounting procedures will provide an adequate system of accrual accounting which enables us to keep a closer check and control on all expenditures and costs.

Within the Highway Commission we have established a department of secondary roads, and complete secondary road plans for the present biennium, for all one hundred counties, have been approved by the respective boards of county commissioners and the Highway Commission.

The Highway Commission has put into effect a new right-of-way policy which provides for independent appraisals of all properties taken for highway purposes and proper and adequate notification by certified mail to all property owners. Every effort is made to deal fairly and justly with the property owner.

The State Highway Commission has held a record total of twenty-five meetings outside the city of Raleigh in various sections of the state. It has received and carefully considered countless requests from cities, counties, groups of citizens, and individuals. At least two meetings between county commissioners of each county and secondary road officials have been held, and in many instances there has been a third or fourth meeting to work out highway plans with local officials.

A few persons have claimed that our highway work has been centralized and moved away from the people. The exact opposite is the case. The Highway Commission is more responsive to *all* the people, and our highways and roads are now being built according to established need, without special favors to anyone, and with closer cooperation with local officials and local communities than we have had for many years.

During the period July 1, 1957 to December 31, 1958, projects totaling more than $106,000,000 have been placed under contract. North Carolina continues in the forefront in the entire nation in progress on the interstate highway program. During this same period, approximately 1,200 miles of secondary roads have been paved and more than 1,400 miles have been improved at a total cost in excess of $24,000,000. By December 1959, an additional 817 miles of secondary roads will be paved and 616 miles will be improved, at an additional expenditure of almost $16,0000,000.

In cooperation with the Municipal Government Study Commission and with local officials, the Highway Commission has carefully studied its policies relating to urban streets and highways. Some modification of present laws which will further aid our municipalities will be submitted for your consideration.

HIGHWAY SAFETY

Since 1947 motor vehicle registrations in North Carolina have doubled. In the past year, we registered more than 1,700,000 vehicles. Larger registrations are, of course, to be anticipated in the years ahead.

Since 1930 more than 27,000 people have lost their lives in traffic accidents in North Carolina. Each year in our state more than 1,000 persons are killed in highway accidents. To this tragic loss of life, we must add the staggering toll of injured and maimed and the enormous economic loss in property damage.

Our Department of Motor Vehicles has received national acclaim for its program in highway safety. Yet, highway safety is a never-ending problem. We cannot relax in our concern, and in truth we must intensify our efforts and assure that our officials have available every reasonable and practicable method for better traffic-law enforcement.

The Department of Motor Vehicles will place before you suggestions for legislation which it feels will advance the cause of traffic safety. I urge that you give careful consideration to these proposals, and keep in mind the great value of just one life which may be saved by improving our highway safety program.

ADMINISTRATION OF THE PRISON SYSTEM

Commendable improvements in prison administration have been achieved during the current biennium. Many of these are attributable to the legislation enacted by the 1957 General Assembly vesting control of the state's prison system in an independent Prison Department. Control of its own affairs has enabled the Prison Department to achieve economies while improving the quality and effectiveness of its programs for custody, employment, and rehabilitation of prisoners.

Unlike most other states, North Carolina has responsibility at the state level for all persons receiving a prison sentence, whether for a long term or a short term. Current figures show that of approximately 11,000 prisoners in the state's prison system, 7,300, or 66 per cent, are serving six months or less. Sixty-five per cent of the total prison population is comprised of repeaters, most of whom were convicted of drunken offenses.

As of December, 1958, there were 10,930 men and 426 women imprisoned by the state. It is estimated that the number of male prisoners will increase to 13,000 by 1965, and to 15,000 by 1970, with corresponding increases in the number of women prisoners. Faced with these increasing numbers, it is imperative that we make the maximum use of probation and parole consistent with the public safety and conducive to the rehabilitation of the offender. Rehabilitation programs of the Prison Department must be expanded and improved and new prison facilities both for lodging and work must be provided. The budget includes appropriations for these purposes.

In view of the increase in prison population that seems inescapable in spite of all that we may do to slow its rate, new legislation is urgently needed to enable the Prison Department to provide constructive employment for additional prisoners. Bills will be introduced for your consideration which will implement these recommendations. I also recommend that the work-release law, enacted in 1957, be amended so as to permit an increased flow of suitable prisoners to this proven program. I hope that your appropriate committees will give intensive study to the entire problem of prisoners and their rehabilitation.

ELECTION LAWS

The State Board of Elections has informed me that several changes in our statutes are desirable so as to improve our election procedures and to eliminate some legal questions and ambiguity. Also, the board has suggested that the date of our primary election should be advanced from May to the last Tuesday in June. I endorse this suggestion. In addition, may I repeat with all emphasis possible the previous recommendations concerning the civilian absentee-ballot law. Because of the widespread abuses under this law, it should, in the public interest, be repealed.

THE SCHOOL SEGREGATION PROBLEM

More than four years ago the United States Supreme Court handed down its decision in the "school segregation cases," drastically revising its previous interpretation of the Federal Constitution. North Carolina has moved with calmness to meet the great problem forced upon us by an interpretation of the Federal Constitution with which interpretation most of our citizens profoundly disagree. In reposing trust and confidence, and authority, in the people themselves at the local level, I believe our state has dealt wisely with this issue. No one has suggested a better approach than the one of local control and local responsibility. If in the future it becomes evident that a better course of action for North Carolina should be devised, I shall take appropriate steps to bring the matter before the General Assembly.

REORGANIZATION OF STATE AGENCIES

The Commission on Reorganization of State Government has submitted a total of eleven separate reports. Each report deals with some aspect of state government organization or administration, and I urge your thoughtful consideration and your action on each of these reports.

UTILITIES COMMISSION

The fourth report of the Reorganization Commission deals with the Utilities Commission. Based upon careful study and an expression of views by members of the Utilities Commission, it is recommended that the membership of this body be reduced from five to three commissioners, and that compensation and retirement benefits be improved. I endorse this proposal, and add this observation of my own. I think it will be in the interest of the state for the General Assembly to provide that the compensation and retirement benefits for the members of the Utilities Commission be equivalent to those of Superior Court judges, and this should be done irrespective of your action on the proposal to reduce the members from five to three.

I am informed that the Utilities Commission will, of its own accord, suggest for your consideration some minor and technical changes in the present statutes, and they will recommend that you authorize a study during the next biennium of the entire utilities law to the end that it can be revised and brought up-to-date.

STATE LEGISLATIVE BUILDING

Another report of the Reorganization Commission deals with a new legislative building. I will not attempt at this time to review the reasons supporting this suggestion. These are capably set forth in the fifth report filed by the Reorganization Commission, and I think are generally understood. We all agree that our present Capitol building should be carefully preserved.

North Carolina, her expanding economy, and the business of her legislature have all grown enormously since the time 118 years ago that this building was first occupied, but the facilities provided for our General Assembly are almost exactly the same as they were in 1840. I believe a separate and suitable structure should be erected close by the Capitol Square. Specific recommendations will be given you next Monday.

STATE BOARD OF ALCOHOLIC CONTROL

The eighth report of the Reorganization Commission considers the State Board of Alcoholic Control. This board has from its establishment consisted of a chairman and two associate members, with the chairman serving as full-time official.

The Reorganization Commission concludes that the chief administrative officer of this board should not be the chairman but a full-time director chosen by the board. This would permit a clear delineation between the policy-making, rule-making, and adjudicatory functions, which should remain in the board, and the administrative function which the board would delegate to its director.

I heartily endorse this recommendation and urge its adoption.

The recommendation of the Reorganization Commission contemplates that the State Board of Alcoholic Control will consist of three part-time policy members, with a full-time director as the chief administrative officer of the board. The present members of this board inform me that in their judgment the affairs of this sensitive agency would be better conducted and the public interest better served, with a five-member policy board. As is well known, it is not always possible to have all members of a part-time board present at every meeting, because of illness, unavoidable conflict in schedules or other good cause, and this is more serious with a three man board!

I join with the ABC Board in recommending that you enact legislation providing for a five-member policy board, with a full-time director as its chief administrative officer.

The position of director or administrator of this agency should be more nearly a career job, as we need to keep a high level of professional and impersonal law enforcement in the affairs of the State Board of Alcoholic Control.

Apparently, the failure of the General Assembly, session after session, to authorize a state-wide referendum on the liquor question indicates that the elected representatives of the people feel that no change should be made in our control system.

If this is the case, we should do everything possible to see that the State Board of Alcoholic Control does in fact effectively control the entire liquor traffic as required by law. The legislative branch, as well as the executive, has the responsibility to insure by the enactment of proper laws that we have a board of control which is active and fearless, with officers and employees of the board who are intelligent, energetic, and fearless, and that no favoritism or privilege is allowed anyone or any group.

In short, I suggest that there should be strict and impartial enforcement of all laws affecting liquor, wine, and beer. If this is not done, we should do away with the system entirely.

TAX LAW STUDY

The 1957 General Assembly directed the continuance of a study of our tax laws which was begun in 1955. The report now before you for consideration deals mainly with the property tax, the only major area of taxation which was not covered by the previous study.

The Tax Study Commission concluded that several aspects of our property tax administration are in great need of improvement.

For example, it was found that ratios of assessed value to the actual market value of real estate vary considerably from county to county and vary widely between parcels of real estate located within the same county. In one instance, tax assessment of property varied from an unbelievable 4 per cent to 129 per cent of current market value, within the same county.

It was also found that different types of property were often assessed at different percentages of market value within a given county. For example, real estate might be assessed at 40 per cent of market value, automobiles at 6 per cent of market value, and retail inventories at 50 per cent of cost.

The commission gave special attention to the very questionable practice of property tax exemption, finding a growing tendency for counties or small groups of counties to secure local acts to exempt particular types of property within those counties. This of course leads to very undesirable tax competition between counties. Furthermore, these sorts of tax exemptions appear to be in direct conflict with the state constitution.

Under present general law, it is required that our counties revalue real estate every four years. By special and local acts the General Assembly in the past has frequently authorized postponement of real property reassessment. It appears that *no county* revalues real property as frequently as every four years, and some counties have not had a general revaluation of real property for tax purposes in *more than twenty years.*

Certainly, there is no greater fiscal obligation upon government than to insure that our tax laws are equitable and that unjust weight does not fall upon any individual taxpayer or upon any particular group of taxpayers.

The people of North Carolina want and should have equitable property tax laws, which are capable of being impartially administered.

Now is the time and the opportunity to remedy these matters which have been forcefully brought to our attention. I urge your consideration of and action on the recommendations submitted by the Tax Study Commission.

MUNICIPAL GOVERNMENT STUDY

In compliance with a mandate of the 1957 General Assembly, a commission consisting of six members of the House and three members of the Senate has given careful and intensive thought to the problems confronting municipal government in North Carolina. That commission has filed an outstanding report, comprehensive in its grasp of the problems confronting municipal governments and in its challenge to the state to plan wisely and well for our continued urban growth and the economic development of North Carolina.

On the basis of available evidence on population trends, the Municipal Government Commission has estimated that by 1980 an additional 1,500,000 people will be living in and around North Carolina cities and towns. Such a development will make North Carolina an urban state in the sense that more of our citizens will be living in urban areas than in rural. I am convinced, as I believe you will be, that we must have better cooperation on the part of the state, the cities, and the counties. We must give more emphasis to effective community planning, and we must insure that our municipal tax system is improved to the extent that it is both adequate and equitable for meeting future needs.

May I emphasize that all available evidence points conclusively to the fact that we shall experience a rapid and extensive urban growth in this state. It will be one of two kinds. It will either be a desirable and healthy growth, bringing to our citizens countless advantages; or, it will be an undesirable and unhealthy development which will imperil our future, compound our problems of municipal finance, and deface our countryside with an unsightly, unsanitary, slum-breeding conglomeration, as has happened to many other states.

With respect to financing municipal government, this report concludes that the present municipal tax system is essentially adequate and equitable for the foreseeable future, if the basic recommendations of the Tax Study Commission dealing with the property tax are put into effect.

Recommendations of the Municipal Government Commission, including the matter of extending city limits, will be placed before you for consideration and action.

OTHER SPECIAL STUDIES

Reports by other legislative study commissions which will be before you are those dealing with the selection of University Trustees, cancer control and care, nursing and boarding homes, map laws, and operations of motor boats.

CONSTITUTIONAL REVISION

Two of the most important reports come to you from the commission which has been studying revision of our state constitution and the Committee of the North Carolina Bar Association which has been studying the operation and administration of our courts.

Each of these reports is very significant and each contains the careful findings and recommendations of able and devoted citizens. With your permission, I shall omit at this time discussion of the recommendations for court improvement and the general revision of our state constitution, and make these the subject of a special message to the General Assembly at a later date.

CONCLUSION

My remarks today have encompassed a far-reaching legislative program which is designed to improve many governmental services, and to accelerate the continued growth and progress of our economy. Some may think it is too ambitious a program for a governor who is dealing with his last session of the General Assembly, but I want you to know that my approach to this legislative program is based entirely upon my desire to do the best I can for North Carolina and its people in the time I have left as governor. It is my hope that this program, if it meets your approval, will make a permanent contribution to the progress of our state in the years ahead.

In my travels outside the state and nation, I have often had people ask me: "Why do North Carolinians love their state so much?" I have never been able to give an adequate answer, except to acknowledge the fact that this love *does* exist and that it is a strong motivating force underlying all the things that have been accomplished in North Carolina during the past half century.

We do have a wonderful state, blessed with many natural resources and with fine, honest, hard-working people. Our General Assembly is always a good and representative cross-section of our population, and has served well the people of our state. We all recognize that the year 1959 will be a year of great legislative decisions, and I welcome the careful consideration, the wisdom, and the experience which you will bring to bear on the many problems and challenges confronting us. There is unlimited opportunity ahead for North Carolina if we act wisely, vigorously, and with a full realization of the needs of our people.

Let us all work together for what we consider best for North Carolina, receiving our reward through the personal joy and happiness in serving our fellow citizens who have given us this opportunity to represent them in the operation of their state government. There can be no greater reward! I shall eagerly look forward to working with you.

Thank you and God bless you!

BUDGET MESSAGE TO THE GENERAL ASSEMBLY

February 9, 1959

[Four days after the delivery of his biennial message the Governor again appeared before the General Assembly to outline his budget recommendations and observations for the next biennium. The spoken portion of this message, which lasted about fifty minutes, was more fully explained in a mimeographed "Budget Report," which was distributed to all members of the General Assembly along with printed copies of four other budget documents. The budget, prepared by the Governor and the Advisory Budget Commission, called for the spending of $1,200,000,000, this being an increase of $50,500,000 in General Fund appropriations, during the next two years. A "windfall" in the form of a tax withholding plan and an estimated 6.3 per cent increase in tax revenues were expected to provide for the increased appropriations without resorting to any new taxes.]

Mr. President, Mr. Speaker, and Members of the General Assembly of North Carolina:

In my biennial message delivered to you last Thursday, many aspects of the affairs of our state were discussed. As stated in that message, the broad range of items considered prevented inclusion of our budget-revenue recommendations and observations for the next biennium.

Necessarily in dealing with such a tremendous subject as our budget we will have to speak tonight in a somewhat summary form. I am, however, attaching copies of the Budget Report of the Governor and Advisory Budget Commission to your copies of this message. The Budget Report more fully explains our recommendations, and I strongly urge that you read it carefully and give it your considered study.

I am also submitting herewith copies of all the budget documents. These are the "A" Budget, the "B" Budget, the Capital Improvements Budget, and the Budget Digest. These documents contain the specific appropriations recommended for each agency and institution. I am also submitting copies of the budget revenue and appropriation bills which will be introduced in due course.

I would like to express publicly to the members of the Advisory Budget Commission the sincere appreciation of the state and of myself for their outstanding service. They are: William Copeland of Murfreesboro, Kemp Doughton of Sparta, Joe Eagles of Wilson, Carl Venters of Jacksonville, William Womble of Winston-Salem, and Nelson Woodson of Salisbury. These distinguished citizens have served tirelessly and unselfishly, and have given greatly of their time and ability.

In preparing the recommended budget for the 1959-61 biennium the Advisory Budget Commission and I have given detailed, careful, and sympathetic consideration to the requests submitted by each of the state agencies and institutions. At the same time, we have been conscious of our duty of seeing, insofar as we are able, that the tax dollars of the people of North Carolina are spent only to the extent necessary to provide governmental services for which there is a clearly demonstrated need.

Let us now consider the appropriations which are recommended.

Total recommended expenditures for operations and for capital improvements, which total includes receipts, both from the federal government and collections from other sources, amount to $1,214,925,934.

This tremendous total may be broken down into major subheads as follows:

(1) $754,078,551 for operating expenses for *General Fund* agencies and institutions, with $192,880,662 to be realized from agency receipts (including federal funds) and $561,197,889 to be derived from tax and non-tax revenues and use of credit balance.

(2) $354,211,054 for operating expenses for *Highway Fund* agencies, with $57,139,132 to be realized from receipts (including federal funds) and $297,071,922 to come from highway taxes, fees, and use of credit balance.

(3) For *Capital Improvements,* the sum of $45,374,149, most of which we recommend be secured from the sale of bonds. Included in the total figure of $1,214,925,934 is the amount of $61,262,180 from other special funds such as Employment Security Commission, University Enterprises, Wildlife, Banking, etc.

While the amounts recommended are large, I assure you they are not nearly as large as the amounts which were requested. The total amount requested from the General Fund for operations of the General Fund agencies and institutions is $630,344,701, which is $119,695,809, or 23.4 per cent above estimated General Fund expenditures for the present biennium. To grant all of these requests would require $141,143,322 above the General Fund revenues we estimate will be realized during the present biennium, and would necessitate increasing the tax burden of all North Carolinians by a substantial amount—a result which all of us would like to avoid if at all possible.

Thus, as budget commissions and governors have probably done every biennium for many decades, we had to face the problem of analyzing these requests and determining as best we could which we felt are truly necessary and which, at least for the time being, can be omitted.

To help distinguish between the urgency of the multitudinous and highly varied requests we have been aided by the new form in which agency requests were prepared. As was explained during the legislative briefing sessions held in November, requests for funds necessary *to continue existing services and programs at present quality levels* are contained in what we call the *"A" Budget;* while the *"B" Budget* consists of funds *necessary to support expansions, improvements, and new programs.*

Saying that we were aided by this new method of presenting requests does not mean—as you will see from our recommendations—that we automatically approved everything requested for the continuation of present services, and then recommended such improvements, expansions, and new programs as we felt could be afforded within available funds. On the contrary, we reviewed with great care all requests made—those in the "A" Budget as well as those in the "B" Budget.

Of the combined "A" and "B" Budget requests for General Fund appropriations, we recommend $561,197,889, which is $50,548,997, or approximately 10 per cent above estimated General Fund expenditures for the present biennium. Of the recommended total $541,623,059 is for "A" Budget purposes and is $5,262,884 less than requested, while $19,574,830 is for "B" Budget purposes and is $63,883,928 less than requested.

Speaking of the "B" Budget recommendations—and it should be remembered that these are for expansions, improvements, and new programs—you may well feel on first impression that all such additional expenditures can be done without. However, after careful evaluation we have concluded that some of the requests contained in the "B" Budget are seriously needed, and we have accordingly recommended them to you.

We believe you will agree that a General Fund operating budget which provides for an increase of $50,548,997, or approximately 10 per cent referred to above, in General Fund expenditures for the present biennium is one which would appear to provide adequately for all necessary services. Indeed, some of you may feel that an appropriation increase of the size we recommend may well be beyond that required for necessary services. In any event, the recommended increase certainly requires a justifying explanation. Such an explanation I shall now try to give you by discussing briefly the major factors which are responsible for this substantial increase.

PUBLIC SCHOOLS

By far the greatest portion of the recommended budget is for public education. And this, in my opinon, is as it should be!

There will be an average of 21,000 additional school children enrolled each year of the next biennium. To employ the new teachers necessary to handle this growth in enrollment will require an increase of approximately $15,500,000 in the biennial appropriation for the nine months school term. This gives a total of approximately $311,500,000 for the biennium just to continue our public schools on the same basis as at present. We are not content, however, to provide merely for continuation. We are recommending certain additional appropriations in connection with the public schools.

Authorities in the field of education, including our State Board of Education, have for some time pointed to the low starting salaries of beginning public school teachers as one of the principal deterrents in attracting qualified people to enter the teaching profession. To help solve this problem, the State Board has recommended increases in starting salaries which would provide holders of "A" certificates a minimum starting salary of $3,100 as compared with the present $2,799. We agree with the board's recommendation as to increasing the salary of beginning teachers and have recommended appropriations to take care of this with comparable increases in the starting salaries of holders of Class "G", "B", and "C" certificates, and for vocational education teachers where applicable. We have not, however, recommended that all salaries above the starting salary be raised. Our suggestion as to how the State Board of Education can implement these proposals within the funds recommended are contained in the Budget Report to which I refer you.

Another recommendation of the State Board with which we agree and for which we recommend the necessary appropriations is that of paying the teachers (including those vocational education teachers to which it will be applicable) for the extra week of work which we are told many of them are already doing before the opening and after the closing of the regular 180 day term. We feel that if this extra pay for these extra days of preparation and for cleaning up last minute details will insure a full program of teaching for the entire 180 days, (and it certainly should) it will be well worth the biennial cost of $6,899,556. And I would like to add that if this recommendation is approved by you, I am sure our school administrators and teachers will see that the state gets what it is paying for. Certainly the students' education will be benefited by the elimination of what is reported in many instances to be a hesitant, part-time start at the beginning of the school year and the several days let-up toward the end of the year. I should also like to express our hope that the full 180 days term will be dedicated to teaching the fundamental knowledge which our children need and must have today and tomorrow. I am sure our school people will welcome the interest and cooperation of all parents and citizens in this matter.

In our recommendations for educational purposes we have also included funds for needed supervisory personnel in the Department of Public Instruction. We agree with the superintendent of public instruction that this extra supervisory service from the state level should materially improve the quality of the teaching program.

HIGHER EDUCATION

In the area of higher education our recommendations include approximately $40,000,000 for operating funds. This is an increase of $3,500,000, or approximately 10 per cent above estimated expenditures for the current biennium.

Included in the recommendations for higher education is an appropriation of $1,500,000 for allotment to the several institutions of higher learning for selective increases in faculty salaries. It will be recalled that funds appropriated by the 1957 General Assembly for salary changes of college personnel were made available to the presidents of the institutions to be distributed on a discretionary basis subject to the approval of the director of the budget. This was to encourage the awarding of pay raises on a merit basis. In most instances the presidents fully accepted this responsibility and have made good use of funds that were available. We recommend the same sort of provision, with the same approval required, be made for the next biennium.

It should be mentioned in connection with the proposed salary fund for college teaching personnel, that these college persons are not eligible for the regular merit salary increments which are provided for state employees generally. Furthermore, with respect to some of the institutions, we have declined to recommend additional college teachers to maintain what seems to us to be light student and teaching-hour loads. We feel that the work load of faculty personnel at comparable institutions should be more equal than at present, and that some increase of work load at certain of the institutions is necessary if the state is to be able to absorb the large increase in enrollment which is expected during the next several years.

INDUSTRIAL EDUCATION

Among our recommendations in the field of education we have also included provisions for expansion of the industrial training program authorized by the 1957 General Assembly. This program contemplated the establishment of highly flexible methods by which North Carolina workers could be trained for employment in industries which require special skills and which we hoped would be coming to our state in increasing numbers. The State Board of Education, assisted by a group of legislators, devoted a great deal of careful and fruitful study to the details of how such a program could be set up. The plan finally submitted by the board and approved by the Governor and Advisory Budget Commission is one which in our view gives North Carolina a good industrial training program. Pursuant to this plan seven industrial education centers have already been established in as many communities, and we are recommending appropriations for the operation of eleven more such centers.

May I also call your attention to the fact that the total appropriations recommended for public schools (including vocational education) and higher education, which total includes retirement contributions for employees and debt service on bonds issued for educational purposes, amount *to approximately $418,750,000, or 74.6 per cent of the entire General Fund recommended for the coming biennium.*

NATURAL RESOURCES AND INDUSTRIAL DEVELOPMENT

Another area of governmental activity in which we make certain recommendations of particular interest is that of natural resources and industrial development.

Appropriations of approximately $4,750,000 are recommended for operations of the Department of Conservation and Development which includes divisions of Forestry, Parks, Minerals, Water Resources, Advertising, Commerce and Industry, and others. The industrial development program is moving along well, and to take advantage of the success achieved we recommend increased amounts for advertising and distribution of promotional materials.

Speaking of industrial developments in our state, we recently announced some thrilling new plans concerning the Research Triangle area. In my thinking about the future of the Research Triangle I had up until recently considered the project as definitely a long-range one with its great potential being many years away, but very tangible and practical results are already making themselves known. Private donations exceeding $1,500,000 have now been secured from North Carolinians to finance operations of a Research Institute including $300,000 for construction of a building. We are recommending that the state contribute $200,000 as a non-recurring grant-in-aid to this project for the purchase of equipment to be used by the Research Institute. I feel that the state could make no better investment in the future of education and research than to make this modest grant—especially in view of the general financial support already gotten from private sources.

The Research Triangle Foundation is a non-profit, quasi-public institution. I know of no project in which I have had the privilege of participating of which I am more proud. Nor do I know of any other activity now going on which has more potential value—both from the standpoint of dollars and cents, and otherwise—for the proper development of our great state and the welfare of its people. It is my firm believe that in a relatively few years the benefits of the Research Triangle will be felt in every section of North Carolina and that its influence and prestige will be felt throughout the nation and the entire world.

Another of our recommendations I would like to mention in connection with the field of natural resources is one which would authorize a project to help stabilize and preserve our great Outer Banks.

Many of you may not be aware of the real seriousness of the situation along our coast, but if these protective outer banks are destroyed, our sounds are going to become part of the ocean and extensive coastal lands are going to be ruined with flooding salt water and wave damage. Furthermore, the scenic beauty of much of coastal North Carolina will be forever destroyed.

Effects of the hurricanes which have hit our coast during recent years, added to our own careless land practices in the area, have now brought us to a point that something must be done—and done quickly. We are, therefore, recommending appropriations of $200,000 for the necessary surveys, engineering studies, etc., in connection with our inlets, shorelines. dunes, etc., and $400,000 for the purchase of certain land by the state. State ownership of this land will make us eligible for financial assistance from the federal government in connection with our continuing effort to meet this tremendous problem. We strongly urge that you approve these appropriations.

STATE PERSONNEL MATTERS

A budget-appropriation problem which faces the Advisory Budget Commission, the governor, and the General Assembly almost every biennium is that having to do with salaries of state employees. This is, of course, a natural occurrence since our state government, like any other functioning organization, is made up primarily of people doing jobs. And like any other organization, the way these people do their jobs will determine whether our government will be good or bad, efficient or inefficient, successful or unsuccessful. It, therefore, is necessary that each governor and each General Assembly, representing the interest of the people whose government this is, make sure that the conditions of employment in state government are such as will attract and retain qualified employees and will encourage and permit them to perform their assigned tasks in a thoroughly competent manner. Salaries are, of course, a major factor in this area, although certainly not the only factor.

As pointed out in the Budget Report, we have given a great deal of attention and study to the question of salaries of state employees. I might add that we have also considered other conditions of state employment, including retirement benefits, paid vacations, paid sick leave, holidays, periodic salary range revisions, merit salary increases, etc.

As a result of our review of these matters we have concluded that the state of North Carolina, in general, treats its employees very well. With our combination of State Retirement and Social Security benefits, we have a very good retirement program. In fact, except for one shortcoming which I will mention later, we have a far better retirement program than most governmental units, and indeed better than many large private industries. Vacation and sick leave provisions are also generous—with an annual vacation of three calendar weeks, and two weeks per year sick leave. Sick leave is cumulative in an unlimited amount. In addition to the three weeks annual leave and two weeks sick leave, the state grants a minimum of nine holidays per year, and petty leave privileges which amount to fourteen working hours—or almost two working days pear year. Altogether the leave with pay provisions add up to about thirty-five days per year, or at five working days per week—seven calendar weeks.

Our study of salaries now being paid by the state revealed that, generally speaking, state salaries are reasonably competitive with comparable jobs in other governmental units and in private industry. We have noted that between September, 1956 and September, 1958, the average salary for state employees, excluding teachers and other public school employees, increased from $3,309 to $3,904, a jump of $505, or 17.98 per cent. This increase has been brought about by the general salary raise given by the 1957 General Assembly and the distribution of regular merit salary increments.

Although we have concluded that most state salaries are competitive at present rates, it is, of course, highly probable that during the next two years the salaries paid for some of the jobs in state government will need adjusting upward if we are to maintain capital improvements totalling $42,765,000, and we propose that our competitive position. To take care of this problem we recommend a biennial appropriation of $2,000,000 ($1,400,000 from the General Fund and $600,000 from the Highway Fund) to be used for this purpose in connection with jobs subject to the State Personnel Act. We propose that, during the next biennium, the Personnel Department, in cooperation with the heads of the agencies and institutions, make a continuing review of all such jobs, and subject to the approval of the director of the budget, make appropriate salary rate adjustments as needed.

I am sure you will be interested in knowing that for all employees, including teachers and college personnel, we have recommended in the total budget for the next biennium approximately $16,000,000 for salary adjustments in addition to the $2,000,000 just mentioned. This gives a total of approximately $18,000,000 to be used for this purpose. This total is made up of the $2,000,000 for salary adjustments of employees subject to the Personnel Act (including highway employees); $4,043,833 for regular merit salary increments also for employees subject to the Personnel Act; $1,525,000 for college professional personnel, including Agricultural Experiment Station personnel; $1,968,612 for increasing beginning teachers' salaries; $1,556,000 for automatic increments for school personnel; and $6,899,556 for the extra week's pay for teachers.

There are a few other situations in connection with employment conditions of state employees which I would like to recommend that you consider. Under present laws governing the Retirement System, the state, as the employer, matches an employee's contribution to the Retirement Fund until that employee reaches the age of sixty. After that point the state makes no further contribution. I recommend that these contributions continue until the employee reaches the age of sixty-five. I also recommend that you make $70 the minimum payment to retired employees who are now drawing either pensions or retirement benefits, as compared with the present minimum of $60. The administrators of the Retirement System inform me that both of these recommendations can be implemented without requiring any change in the contributions made by the state or by employees to the Retirement System. They advise this is possible because of the very sound actuarial practices followed by those responsible for the management and investment policies of the State Retirement System.

I would like to recommend that per diem allowances for state employees who must travel be raised from the present $8.00 to $9.00 for in-state travel, and from the present $11 to $12 for out-of-state travel. Per diem allowances have not been increased since 1953, and simply do not cover present day costs. I recommend also that when state employees are required to move their residence for the convenience of the state, that moving expenses be paid by the state. The cost of these proposals can, in my opinion, be absorbed in the amounts presently recommended in the budgets of the various agencies.

There has been some mention of the need in our state government for longevity pay. This grows out of the fact that many of the employees who have been with the state for long periods of time have reached the top of their salary range and are frozen at their present rate. I recommend that the General Assembly make provisions for a study of this problem during the next biennium and that those making this study prepare specific recommendations to be considered by the General Assembly at its next session.

As already stated, conditions of employment for state workers constitute, in my opinion, the key factor in maintaining an efficient state government. As said in my message last Thursday, we can all be proud of the loyal and efficient service rendered by the state employees generally, and I sincerely hope you will approve the recommendations made for the benefit of our state employees.

OTHER GOVERNMENTAL ACTIVITIES

The limitations of time forbid a discussion of our recommendations for each General Fund agency and institution of state government. However, we can make a quick run-down of the percentage increases provided in each governmental area. These several areas together include all General Fund agencies or institutions not already mentioned, and the size of these increases will demonstrate that all have been provided for in the recommended General Fund budget.

In the area of general government, which includes such agencies as the offices of the governor, the secretary of state, the auditor, the treasurer, and the Departments of Insurance, Administration, Revenue, Personnel, and Utilities Commission, courts, etc., we recommend an increase in operating appropriations which amounts to 7.3 per cent; in Public Welfare the recommended increase is 7.7 per cent; for the State Department of Agriculture the over-all increase, including General Fund and Agriculture Fund appropriations is 8.5 per cent; in the field of public safety and regulations, which includes the Department of Labor, Motor Vehicles, Civil Defense, etc., the recommended increase in General Fund appropriations is 8.5 per cent; for health and hospital agencies it is 9.8 per cent; and, for correctional schools the increase recommended is 21.6 per cent.

AGENCIES SUPPORTED BY HIGHWAY FUNDS

As you know, several of the agencies of the state are supported, either in whole or in part, out of highway funds, and the proportion of highway revenue appropriated to the Highway Department itself is steadily decreasing. Recommended appropriations from the Highway Fund to be used by the Highway Department during the next biennium amount to $235,166,685, which constitutes only a 1.1 per cent increase over Highway Fund money to be expended by the department during the present biennium. We are speaking now of state funds received from highway taxes and fees, and the figures just cited do not include federal appropriations which, unfortunately for our state, are going down compared to the last biennium.

Motor transportation generally, including both private and commercial transportation, is growing very fast in North Carolina. Ours is a large state, geographically speaking, and our state highway system includes 70,000 miles—the largest number of miles or roads of any state-maintained system in the nation. As we develop industrially, and as our communities and economy expand, the use of our highways will increase rapidly. This means that more and more money will be needed to take care of highway maintenance and construction if we are to have the modern highways demanded of a growing and progressive state.

While our maintenance costs are increasing and needs for new construction are becoming greater, the Highway Fund is being called upon to support larger and larger appropriations for agencies other than the Highway Department. For example, we recommend for the State Probation Commission an increase for the next biennium of $221,034, or 29.1 per cent over estimated expenditures by this agency for 1957-1959. We know from the state-wide standpoint this recommendation should be granted because, in addition to having worthwhile humanitarian results, it will help keep down the size of our prison population and the cost of these operations.

For the same reasons we recommend an increase of $172,186, or 31 per cent for the Paroles Commission. This agency is doing a good and necessary job, and I urge your support of this increase.

The Prison Department, although making excellent headway toward its own support must, nevertheless, rely on funds secured from the continued use of prisoners by the Highway Department. It is generally recognized that so far as highway matters are concerned, it would be more economical to use fewer prisoners and rely on modern machinery to get the job done. We cannot do this, however, because without the money received from the Highway Fund in payment for the labor of these prisoners, the source of support for prison operations would have to come from somewhere else. And, unless there is other worthwhile work in which prisoners could be engaged, it would be unwise, as a matter of prison policy to take these prisoners off highway work. In spite of the fact that prison enterprises are using more and more prisoners, we can use only a few hundred in industries and must still continue to assign 7,000 of them to the Highway Department at a cost of $5.00 per day per prisoner for a total cost of $17,570,000 for the biennium.

In the recommended budget we have not increased the number of prisoners to be assigned to the Highway Department but, of course, we have had to budget for an increased prison population.

Another large agency supported from highway revenues is the Department of Motor Vehicles, but this one is more directly connected with highway use. Highway Fund appropriations recommended for this department for the next biennium amount to approximately $17,225,000, which is an increase of 9 per cent over estimated expenditures for the present biennium. In this increase we have provided for twenty-five new patrolmen to help take care of traffic growth and new duties assigned patrolmen.

In summing up the matter of appropriations from the Highway Fund, it should be pointed out that we are recommending from highway funds for non-highway agencies (Probation, Paroles, and Prison) a total of $26,301,623, which includes the cost of Prison labor used on the highways. As already stated, approximately $17,500,000 is budgeted from highway revenues for the Department of Motor Vehicles. In addition we must provide approximately $29,750,000 to the highway bond debt service reserve and $14,000,000 to reserve for state aid to municipalities.

The appropriations just mentioned, combined with the fact that during the present biennium Highway expenditures included a surplus of some $8,250,000 from the 1955-57 biennium, are responsible for the relative smallness of the percentage increase in funds available to the Highway Department for the next biennium. This percentage increase, as already mentioned, is only 1.1 per cent even though state highway revenues as a whole are estimated to increase 7.4 per cent.

I would like to conclude the portion of this message dealing with Highway Fund appropriations by pointing out that at some point serious consideration should be given to the problem of ever-increasing amounts of highway revenues which, under our present laws, will be necessary to support activities other than the maintenance and construction of highways.

CAPITAL IMPROVEMENTS

For General Fund agencies and institutions we recommend capital improvements totalling $42,765,000, and we propose that this amount be raised by the issuance of bonds and reappropriation of the Revolving Fund which was set up in 1957. Of the total improvements recommended, slightly in excess of $25,000,000 is for education, and approximately $21,500,000 of this amount is for higher education.

During the past eighteen months the Board of Higher Education has made a thorough and detailed study of the building needs of the three branches of the University and the other state-supported institutions of higher learning. The study, which was carried on in cooperation with the institutions themselves, enabled the board to recommend a long-range program which would substantially take care of the building needs of all the institutions through the year 1970. The net cost of this program, as recommended by the board, would be in excess of $78,000,000. Actually, the cost would be approximately $90,000,000, but an estimated $12,000,000 would be returned in dormitory rentals.

In our opinion the board has, by this study, rendered an excellent service, and its members are to be commended for it. However, the Advisory Budget Commission and I concluded that the state cannot, at this time, provide for all the recommended projects.

Our capital improvement recommendations for the institutions of higher learning would take care of the expected large increase in college enrollment through 1963. Since it would probably be three or four years before projects provided by a bond issue could be completed, and since the heaviest period of expected increase in college enrollment will occur during the next four or five years, we feel very strongly that our recommendations constitute the minimum that the 1959 General Assembly should provide for capital improvements at our institutions of higher learning.

I would like to add to this my own recommendation that you dedicate any surplus revenues beyond your final revenue estimates which might come in during the 1959-61 biennium for the building of some of the other projects in the board's long-range program which we have not included in our minimum needs. This would be very helpful!

Included in our total recommendations for capital improvements are projects for hospitals (primarily mental institutions), costing approximately $8,000,000. These projects include a large expansion at Butner Training School and extensive renovations at Morganton and at the State Hospitals at Raleigh and Butner.

We have also included in our recommendations the sum of $4,500,000 for the planning and construction of a new legislative building. This project was originally recommended by the Commission on Reorganization of State Government which, during the past year, made a thorough study of the problem. The Reorganization Commission held a public hearing on the question, well publicized in advance, at which not one citizen or official raised any objection to this proposal, and indeed all who spoke favored it enthusiastically. The commission's report recommended the figure of $7,000,000 for this building, but, considering the Study Commission's recommendation in connection with other needed capital improvements, we recommend an appropriation for this purpose of not less than $4,500,000.

The Advisory Budget Commission and I, along with the Commission on Reorganization of State Government, feel that now is time to do something about this very serious problem which becomes more acute every year. It seems to me very short-sighted to continue requiring the members of the General Assembly, engaged in what is by far the most important business in the state, to work under the harassing conditions such as now exist and which are far worse than other states have to endure. It is my firm belief that if every citizen of North Carolina could come here and watch you try to do your work under these trying conditions, the overwhelming majority would say that in fairness to the public whose business you are carrying on, better facilities should be provided.

All of us strongly recommend that no change whatever be made in the present Capitol building or its grounds, but that it remain as a museum or monument to the greatness of North Carolina, its traditions and its history. I cannot express too strongly my sincere opinion that this recommendation for a legislative building should be approved.

The recommendation which we have included for land acquisition will put the state in a very good position so far as land needs are concerned and will give us space for further building needs for many years to come. We think the acquiring of this additional land will be a very wise move.

Time does not permit any discussion of the various other capital improvements projects recommended but, of course, each is set out in detail in the Capital Improvements Budget with which you will be working during your deliberations.

GENERAL FUND REVENUES

We would like to discuss how the appropriations which we have recommended are to be financed. As already mentioned, we are of the opinion that the Capital Improvements program should be financed by a reappropriation of the Revolving Fund and by the issuance of bonds. Appropriations for operating expenses will, however, have to come from revenues and through use of the available credit balance. It is estimated that the available General Fund credit balance at the end of the present biennium (June 30, 1959) will be $13,762,053 which, as you know, is far from the $63,000,000 credit balance appropriated by the 1957 General Assembly.

Several months ago I made a public statement to the effect that the General Assembly would probably have to levy new taxes this session in order to support necessary appropriations. That statement was made in view of economic conditions then prevailing, but fortunately our country has substantially recovered from the recession. I am happy to report that, on the basis of available economic data, it now appears that we are in for a period of favorable economic progress.

Naturally, no one can say with absolute accuracy what the future holds for our economy which is dependent on many, many factors over which most of us have no control—factors such as world markets, federal spending, defense needs, foreign relations, etc. But, under law, the Budget Commission and I are required to make revenue recommendations and a balanced budget! We have, therefore, with the advice and counsel of the commissioner of revenue and the director of tax research and others, felt justified in making General Fund revenue estimates for the 1959-61 biennium which contemplate a revenue increase of 6.3 per cent, or $30,745,947 over the $489,201,379 in General Fund revenues estimated for the present biennium.

This increase of $30,745,947 in General Fund revenues will provide a total of approximately $520,000,000 from General Fund revenues during the coming biennium. Our credit balance of approximately $13,750,000 added to the $520,000,000 in revenues, will give us a total of approximately $534,000,000 available for the next biennium's General Fund appropriations without making any change in our present tax laws. As already mentioned, however, the recommended General Fund appropriations are more than $561,000,000, which means that we will need an additional $27,500,000 to provide sufficient revenues to support the recommended appropriations.

It is our recommendation that the additional $27,500,000 be secured by the adoption of a withholding and "pay-as-you-go" plan in connection with the state income tax. This plan, together with the increased revenues we have just mentioned, will make new taxes unnecessary and we are delighted to so announce. Except for some minor administrative changes which will not appreciably affect total revenues, we do not recommend any other changes in our tax laws, nor do we recommend any increase in existing rates. There are few states in the Union that can say this.

An article in the January 12 issue of *Newsweek* had this to say, and I quote, "Throughout the nation hard-pressed states and local governments are getting ready to tap the public pocketbooks as probably never before." The article points out that taxes are to go up in about thirty-four states, including most of our southern neighbors. In California the deficit reported in the article is $285,000,000, and in New York it is $220,000,000. So, you can see why I am particularly pleased to announce that our budget recommendations will not call for any additional taxes other than the change in connection with the withholding provisions.

Our highway revenue estimates, arrived at in the same manner as General Fund estimates, will provide a biennial increase of 7.4 per cent, or approximately $18,500,000. In total amounts we estimate that state highway revenues, under existing taxes, for the

Governor Hodges and Buell G. Duncan, president of the Charlotte Chamber of Commerce at a dinner held on the occasion of the General Assembly's visit to Charlotte, March 4, 1959.

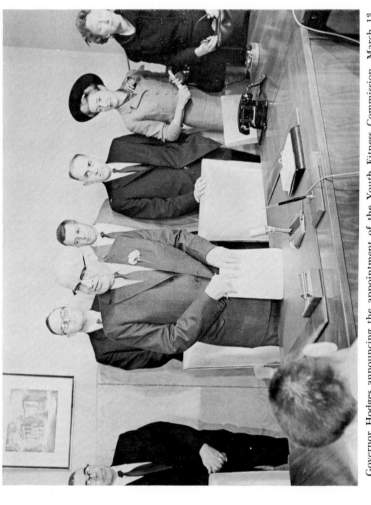

Governor Hodges announcing the appointment of the Youth Fitness Commission, March 13, 1959. *Left to right:* Dr. W. T. Anderson, A. Hartwell Campbell, Governor Hodges, Billy Jo Patton, R. Grady Wilmoth, Mrs. Dail Holderness, and Mrs. J. Spencer Love.

next biennium will be $265,834,000 as compared with $247,455,470 for the present biennium.

SCHOOL INCENTIVE FUND

There is an additional recommendation I would like to make in connection with the financing of our pubic schools. It is one which proposes to set up a State School Incentive Fund of $10,000,000 for each year to be matched by local communities in accordance with their ability to pay. It comes not from the Advisory Budget Commission but from the Commission on Public School Finance with my support and, in my opinion, it is one of the most important of all the recommendations I make to you. It does not transfer any load from the state. It simply adds more money—state and local—to help strengthen our schools.

It is estimated that $10,000,000, if made available by the state yearly, will bring forth an additional $6,500,000 yearly when matched by the communities according to the formula outlined in the School Finance Report. Because of the time which will be necessary to set up the matching formula and administrative machinery for this fund, I recommend that $10,000,000 be made available beginning in the second year of the biennium. It is my hope, of course, that the appropriation will be continued thereafter.

This total of $10,000,000 which I strongly recommend you make available is not figured in our revenue estimates, but for this particular important development for the future of our schools, I would like to see you make the necessary appropriations. If economic conditions should improve beyond the rates originally estimated by the Advisory Budget Commission and myself, it may be possible to secure the necessary funds for this appropriation by increasing our revenue estimates. This is something that you will want to consider in the coming months. If, however, in the days ahead, economic conditions should worsen or fail to continue their improvement, I will join you in recommending the levying of sufficient taxes to provide the needed amount.

I will not repeat here the reasons already given in my previous message as to why I think this incentive approach recommended by the distinguished Commission on Public School Finance should be adopted. It is backed by staunch friends of the public schools and I understand by the professional school people in general. It is my sincere conviction that those interested in the long-range good of our schools share my belief that unless some such approach is made in North Carolina our public schools will continue to lose standing and, as you know, they are already too close to the bottom in our nation in many financial respects.

When we add the proposed $10,000,000 to the amounts recommended for the higher minimum salaries and the pay for an extra week, and also include the $6,500,000 to come from local communities for matching the $10,000,000, it will mean that in the second year of the coming biennium there will be available to the counties to use for any items in their current expense school budgets an amount of money which, if they should choose to use entirely for teacher salary increases, could provide a percentage increase of 16.7 per cent over amounts being paid for teacher salaries during the present biennium. And even if we were to exclude from this total the amount required for the extra week's pay, which some may reasonably point out should not be considered an increase in salary, the percentage salary increase possible in the second year of the biennium over the present biennium would still be 13.9 per cent. Let me emphasize that the local units can spend the money for any item in their current expense school budget.

GOVERNOR'S SALARY

There is one additional recommendation we would like to make to you. At present the salary of the governor is $15,000 per year. It has not been increased since 1949, whereas, salaries, particularly those at the executive level in government and industry, have gone steadily and rapidly upward since that time. In fact, there are several positions in our state agencies or institutions which carry salaries larger than that paid the governor. In keeping with the dignity and prestige of the office and of the state, we recommend that, starting with the next governor, this salary be raised from $15,000 to $25,000 per year. I particularly want to emphasize that this increase is recommended to begin with the *next* governor, and is not to become effective during my own term of office.

Inasmuch as the term of the next governor will begin six months before the end of the next biennium, we have included in the proposed budget recommendations the sum of $5,000 to provide, as of January 1, 1961, for the increased salary for the six months period.

CONCLUSION

In concluding this message I should like to express my great faith in our state and my tremendous optimism about its future. North Carolina, in its traditional method of going neither too fast to the new nor staying too long with the old, is moving toward a brighter and better life for all of its people. It is my task and your task to see that not only is this progress made possible, but that it is actively encouraged. If our state is to continue its march into an enlightened future, our children must have good public schools, our colleges must be able to take care of those who can benefit from higher education, our streets and highways must be modern and up-to-date, and all our programs of development must be adequately financed. At the same time, we must make provision for our aged, for our sick, for our mentally ill, and for all others who, through no fault of their own, are unable to participate actively in the glorious progress which our state is making. Our strength is enough to carry them all if we do not stint. And we must not!

The budget figures and fiscal information presented tonight are very important and deserve your careful study and consideration. Let us remember, however, that these same figures represent more than a state balance sheet. They also represent a program by which we are able to meet genuine needs of our people. Wisely appropriated tax monies can readily be translated into needed services for all our citizens.

The Budget Commission and myself are well aware that the final decision on all these matters we have recommended is yours. We have done the best we could with a difficult task. We hope we have been of service to you in making careful analysis of the various programs. We think our recommendations adequately provide for the things we know our state believes in. We know that you will make some changes in what has been proposed and, in fact, we would not feel nearly so confident in the future of this state if we did not know that your collective wisdom would be brought to bear on all of these proposals before final decision is reached.

We are glad you are here. I want to work with you in every way possible for the good of our state.

I wish you Godspeed in your task.

Thank you.

SPECIAL MESSAGE TO THE GENERAL ASSEMBLY
March 12, 1959

[A fifteen-member constitutional study commission, authorized by the 1957 General Assembly, had recommended that a complete revision of the North Carolina state constitution be drafted and submitted to the General Assembly. Governor Hodges reviewed the commission's proposals and in general expressed agreement with them in this special message to the General Assembly. On the matter of court reform, however, he threw his weight behind the proposals of a committee of the State Bar Association which asked for a uniform court system administered by the Supreme Court in contrast to the recommendations of the Constitutional Study Commission which proposed to leave rule-making and administrative powers over the courts in the hands of the legislature. The Governor also: (1) urged the legislature to "look seriously" at the question of allowing a second term and giving the veto power to North Carolina governors, (2) reiterated his earlier stand for retaining the provision for a "general and uniform system of public schools" in the state constitution, and (3) repeated his previously announced support of the Tax Study Commission's recommendation of a constitutional amendment prohibiting the legislature from delegating authority to exempt property from taxation.]

Mr. President, Mr. Speaker, and Members of the General Assembly of North Carolina:

I thank you for your courtesy in permitting me to appear again before a joint session of the General Assembly. I am indeed grateful for this opportunity to present for your consideration my recommendations on the revision of the state constitution, including, of course, the article dealing with the administration of justice in North Carolina.

The distinguished fifteen-member Constitutional Study Commission, which was authorized by you in 1957, has completed its work after more than a year of very intensive study and its report has been submitted for your consideration. The members of this commission deserve our warm and sincere thanks for the good service they have rendered our state.

It was in the year 1776 that the Provincial Congress of North Carolina ratified our state's first constitution. Under the first document, the governor, Council of State, and judges were all elected by the General Assembly.

In 1835, several basic amendments to our constitution were submitted to a vote of the people and were approved. These provided for election of the governor by the people, and also made fundamental changes in legislative representation and reapportionment.

The year 1868 marks the next milestone in the historical development of our state constitution. Following the Civil War and while our state was still undergoing "active reconstruction" a completely revised constitution was approved by vote of the people. The 1868 constitution is basically the one which we have today, and which is the subject of our present study and consideration.

Since the adoption of the 1868 constitution, 158 proposed amendments have been submitted to a vote of the people, and 135 of them have been approved. It is not surprising, therefore, to find that this patchwork of amendments has resulted in considerable inconsistency and obscurity in language. In addition, some detailed provisions of our constitution are now obsolete.

The Constitutional Study Commission informs us that early in its deliberations it reached the decision that a complete revision of the constitution should be drafted and submitted to the General Assembly. This was done primarily for purposes of language clarification, and the suggested revision does not contemplate, by any means, a sweeping and wholesale revision of our basic form of government.

I have given very careful study to the report of the Constitutional Study Commission, and am in complete agreement that we need to revise our constitution, and I sincerely hope you will agree.

ARTICLE II, LEGISLATIVE DEPARTMENT

One of the most important problems to be considered in any revision of our constitution has to do with legislative apportionment. Our present constitutional provisions governing membership and apportionment for the House of Representatives and providing for 120 members date from the year 1835. Then, North Carolina had only sixty-five counties. Then, fifty-five House seats were available for allocation on the basis of population after allotting each county at least one representative, thereby giving an effective voice to the factor of population in that branch of our

General Assembly. Today, 124 years later, we have 100 counties in the state, with the same number of representatives and with the same allocation formula used in 1835. This means, after allocation of one representative per county, there remain only twenty seats to be apportioned among the larger counties on the basis of population.

Our Senate membership of fifty members also originated in 1835, but it was not until 1868 that the provision for our present system of districts, containing "equal proportions" of the state's population, was placed in our constitution. Therefore, at the present time the Senate, by reason of our constitutional provision, is intended to give effective representation to the factor of population; and by reason of the existence of 100 counties and the limited number of representatives to be apportioned thereto, our House, under the constitution, gives emphasis to representation on the basis of geographical units rather than population.

Neither Senate nor House representation has been reapportioned since 1941. Since then, the population of North Carolina has increased from approximately 3,500,000 to more than an estimated 4,600,000. And we are confronted with the undesirable situation in which, because of its failure to act, the General Assembly itself is subject to the charge that it has ignored a clear and plain requirement of the constitution.

There are many ways of reapportionment. I personally would not object to adding to the number of senators and/or representatives, but I am willing to leave that to you. I do want to say, with all emphasis possible, you should take action of some kind that will definitely and continually insure reapportionment when due. This is your duty!

ARTICLE III, EXECUTIVE DEPARTMENT

The Study Commission report properly provides for succession in the executive branch but does not discuss the constitutional provision prohibiting the governor from serving more than one consecutive term. Based on my own experience of working on a long-range state program, I think a governor should be allowed a second consecutive term if the people vote to return him to office. Under no conditions should such a change, if made, apply to me, but I hope you will look seriously at the second term and at the lack of veto power. It is somewhat difficult to understand why our state is the only one in the Union in which the governor lacks the veto power.

ARTICLE V, REVENUE, TAXATION, AND PUBLIC DEBT

The Constitutional Study Commission recommends revision of the language of Article V in accordance with the report of the Tax Study Commission. As I said in my biennial message:

There is no greater fiscal obligation upon government than to insure that our tax laws are equitable and that unjust weight does not fall upon any individual taxpayer nor upon any particular group of taxpayers.

This suggested revision for tax administration improvement is sound and should be adopted.

ARTICLE VII, EDUCATION

Our present constitution contains language to the effect that "the General Assembly . . . shall provide . . . for a general and uniform system of public schools." This language was placed in our state constitution in 1868 and through these many years has provided a sound and enduring beacon light for the people of North Carolina. It has meant that the people of our state were interested in education for the children of this state, throughout the length and breadth of the state. It has kept before us a high ideal, a worthy objective, and a practical guide. It has meant that the General Assembly would take appropriate action to promote and encourage education in all corners of the state, in all sections, and in all places. Historically, this constitutional provision has not been interpreted to mean that as a physical fact every locality in the state should have exactly the same public school facilities and exactly the same level of achievement. This has not been the case because historically the support and maintenance of our public schools began with the localities themselves. However, the mandate which has been constant on the General Assembly has been that educational opportunity and authority would, under law, be available to all localities and counties throughout the state.

The written report of the Constitutional Commission in its explanation of the suggested deletion of this requirement states that the phrase should be removed "as a possible source of conflict with the local option provisions" which were adopted in 1956.

Since the release of this report the attorney general has advised that there is no overriding legal reason for deleting the "general and uniform" provision. Based upon this view of the legal question, the chairman of the Constitutional Study Commission has also stated that he believes all or most of the individual members of the commission would prefer not to delete this language in the absence of compelling legal reason to do so. I have previously made public my own position on this matter, and simply reiterate that in my view the provision for "general and uniform system of public schools" should be retained in our constitution.

ARTICLE IV, JUDICIAL DEPARTMENT

In my opinion, the most important aspect of constitutional revision concerns the judicial branch of our government and the vital need for improvement in the administration of justice.

As you know, I am not a lawyer, but from the beginning of my service as governor of the state I have had a great interest in our courts and in all aspects of the administration of justice. As governor, I have constantly been impressed with the great importance of the judicial branch of our government. The operation of our courts, the actions of our judges, solicitors, and all other officers directly connected with our courts have a daily impact on the citizens of North Carolina, in every community of the state.

In speaking to the North Carolina Bar Association's annual convention at Asheville in 1955, I expressed to them my conviction that the lawyers of North Carolina should take the lead in making a thorough and objective study of our courts, and based upon their findings, then take the lead to show our state what should be done to improve the administration of justice in North Carolina.

The lawyers of this state, acting through their State Bar Association, accepted this challenge. By the time of the next annual meeting of the North Carolina Bar Association in 1956, we were fortunate in securing a sizeable grant in private foundation funds to carry forward this work.

Since 1955, we have had in North Carolina the most thorough study of our courts in the history of our state, and one of the most complete and thorough studies of the courts of any state that has been made at any time, anywhere in our nation. We are indeed grateful to the able and devoted chairman and to members of the Bar Association Court Committee for the public service they have rendered our state.

The fact that it was felt we should undertake a careful appraisal of the organization and administration of our courts did not mean then and still does not mean that we do not appreciate the good service which our lawyers, judges, and courts in general have rendered to North Carolina in the past and are continuing to render. It was simply recognized that we had, and still have, some serious shortcomings which ought to be corrected.

May I make this further observation on the background of the court study which was conducted by the committee of the North Carolina Bar Association. The leaders of our bar early came to the conclusion that any effective action to improve the administration of courts in our state must have the active interest and participation of lay citizens, who would work with the lawyers and the judges and other court officials. Accordingly, when the basic research studies were being completed and ready for consideration by the court study committee in 1957, the president of the North Carolina Bar Association appointed an equal number of laymen to work on the committee with the lawyer members.

From the time that this great project was undertaken in 1955, every effort was made to seek and obtain the assistance and advice of the bench and bar of this state, in first discovering the day-to-day working of the courts and ascertaining the problems which exist, and then in considering the various points of view as to how best to remedy the faults which were found to exist. I am told that every recommendation which was made by this committee in its final report is the result of suggestions made by some lawyer or some judge in North Carolina. In short, what has been put forward for our consideration is not something handed to us from another state or another country, but something evolved, considered, discussed, and presented by our own people. In turn, the court study committee has itself conducted its studies and its deliberations in full public view. Our people have had the opportunity to become acquainted with first the tentative and then the final conclusions of the committee, and have had the opportunity to consider and to discuss with their neighbors and fellow citizens that which has been considered and discussed by the committee itself.

What are some of the facts and some of the problems which have been brought to light during the course of this careful study of our courts?

First, looking generally at the total picture in our state, we see one Supreme Court, 100 Superior Courts, 256 recorder-type courts, 144 mayors' courts, and 940 justice of the peace courts. These all add up to a total of at least 1,441 courts at all levels and of all jurisdictions. Of greatest impact, however, in considering the total court picture is the fact that we cannot with complete accuracy say that we have a judicial "system." About the only thing that these 1,441 courts have in common is that each exercises some share of the judicial authority of the state.

Let us look at the financing of our 1,441 separate courts. For the state as a whole, we have learned that the counties spend on the courts approximately $700,000 more than they collect in fees and costs. We have learned that for the state as a whole, municipalities have operated their courts at an annual profit of almost $900,000. This means, unfortunately, that many of our municipal courts are operated as profit-making enterprises, in that costs and fees are arbitrarily set in excess of reasonably anticipated expenditures for the operation of these courts. In a recent year, the justice of the peace courts in North Carolina handled over 88,000 criminal cases, in which their fee was not collected unless the defendant was found guilty. There is but one characterization of this aspect of the justice of the peace court: as a system, this is not justice; this is a travesty of justice.

We know that, from the standpoint of organization, administration, and questionable financing, our greatest problems are found in the courts below the Superior Court level. We have able and outstanding Superior Court judges and for the most part we know that our courts at this level are conducted in a way to justify our praise and commendation. Yet, we must also recognize that there are some administrative and organizational problems at the Superior Court level. It is a fact, for example, that there is a growing backlog of cases awaiting trial in the Superior Courts. In the fiscal year 1957-58, the number of civil cases on the docket of fifty-two Superior Courts on which data was obtained increased by 1,866. Upon a detailed check of the records of forty-four Superior Courts, it was found that of a total of 12,276 civil cases then awaiting trial, 62 per cent had been pending more than one year, and 43 per cent had been pending more than two years. Of the 6,179 criminal cases pending in the 100 Superior Courts on January 1, 1957, approximately 20 per cent had been pending more than a year. In one solicitorial district in North Carolina, the number of criminal cases pending increased by 300 in the fiscal year 1957-58.

Much court time is lost, and delay in handling litigation is inevitable, under our present system of attempting to fix Superior Court terms by statute two or more years in advance. This condition is aggravated by the lack of systematic calendaring practices in many Superior Courts and by the frequent granting of continuances in civil cases. In 1957, 63 per cent of the civil and mixed terms in our Superior Courts used less than a full five-day week. In 1957-58, only 75 per cent of the scheduled days of civil court in the Superior Courts of North Carolina were actually used. Yet, the number of pending cases continues to increase.

A majority of our recorder-type courts now in active operation were established under one of the present dozen "general laws" which authorized establishment of these type courts. Yet, these courts in fact vary widely in every respect: in the manner of selection of judges, solicitors, and clerks; in civil and criminal jurisdiction; in procedures; in the fees and costs which are charged; and in the availability of jury trial. For a defendant who pleads guilty to a minor criminal charge, costs in these inferior courts vary from $7.00 in one court to $28 in another. Quite often, the fees charged in some of these courts have no relationship whatever to the actual cost of the case being tried.

In 1957, North Carolina had approximately 940 active justices of the peace courts, and 144 active mayors' courts of comparable jurisdiction. In twenty counties in our state, these were the only courts available below the Superior Court level. Unquestionably, many of these type courts are conducted in a dignified and efficient way, and perform a most useful public service in being available for the trial of petty civil and criminal cases. Yet, we know that in all too many instances the justice of the peace courts are operated primarily as bill-collecting agencies, exercising the power and dignity of the state of North Carolina for this purpose and doing this so well that some justices of the peace in this state earn incomes larger than the salary of a Superior Court judge. The almost complete lack of any reliable record-keeping and reporting by justices of the peace courts, the casual manner in which many of these courts conduct judicial proceedings, the existence of a system under which the presiding magistrate is paid in criminal cases only if he find the defendant guilty, all add up to an overwhelming indictment of the system. And the State Association of Justices of the Peace has made some recommendations for improvements.

We now come to the question of what should we do to eliminate those serious problems which we know exist in the administration of our courts.

These are objectives which have been pinpointed by the Bar Association Committee, and which merit our most careful consideration:

(1) Combine all North Carolina courts into one organization to bring uniformity and coordination to the administration of justice.

(2) Make the Chief Justice of the North Carolina Supreme Court the executive head of this state-wide court system, and by thus pinpointing administrative responsibility in the operation of our courts, enable the people of the state to get maximum results with minimum cost and loss of time to taxpayers and litigants.

(3) Add laymen to the Judicial Council, which is now composed of lawyers only, and make it both an advisory body to the executive head of the court system as well as a liaison agency between the courts and the people of the state.

(4) Give the Supreme Court the power to make the rules for the mechanics of operating the courts and for trying cases in them, and the responsibility for keeping these rules up to date.

(5) Provide for a uniform method of selecting judges and trial magistrates for the local courts, below the Superior Court level, throughout the entire state, to help insure unbiased and prompt judgment in all cases brought before such courts.

(6) Put the selection of citizens for jury service into the hands of sworn jury commissioners who will perform their duties under the supervision of the Superior Court judge, with the purpose of insuring that juries will always consist of responsible, capable, and conscientious citizens.

We can obtain these laudable objectives by appropriate revision of Article IV of our state constitution. As you know, sometime ago the Bar Association Court Study Committee released its recommendations, together with a suggested draft of the judiciary article of our constitution, and this has been widely distributed and publicized over the state. In addition, the Constitutional Study Commission has also given very careful consideration to the problem of our courts and also suggests for your consideration a revision of the judiciary article of our constitution.

I shall not take the time to compare these two suggested drafts in detail, but will state clearly my view on selection of judges. Neither the report of the Bar Association Committee nor the report of the Constitutional Study Commission recommends any change in the method of selecting the judges of the Supreme Courts, and as I have said before, I think we should continue to elect the judges for these courts.

As for judges of the district courts, I basically favor their election, but as some are now elected and some appointed, I would leave the precise method of selection to the General Assembly. I agree with both study groups that the justices of the peace (or trial magistrates or commissioners) should be appointed.

Both the Bar Association Committee and the Constitutional Study Commission reached the conclusion that we need a substantial revision in the judiciary article of the constitution. In evaluating the specific approaches we may take on court organization and administration, I would like to give special emphasis to one fact. The state of North Carolina has a continuing and inescapable obligation to everyone of her citizens—and indeed to every person who comes within her borders—to provide a system of courts, in every one of which justice may be had promptly, at reasonable cost to the parties.

This obligation, the state cannot avoid. Nor can we in good faith pass this duty on to the counties and municipalities and then criticize our counties and municipalities for administering *their* courts in the light of *their* local interests.

There may have been a time—and perhaps not too long ago, when our courts were largely a local concern—when a breakdown in the administration of justice in a given court affected very few people except those of the town or county in which the court was located. But certainly today, with our extensive business and commercial activities of state-wide and interstate character, with our highly mobile population, with the large number of visitors coming into and through the state, it is a matter of the most profound concern to the state as a whole when any single court fails to meet high standards of judicial administration.

If we are to meet this obligation of the state to provide for the just, uniform, and efficient administration of justice, we must view all of the courts as part of the single judicial system through which this obligation is met. At the same time, this system must be one in which the people of the state at the local level will continue to take a vital interest and in which they will have a share of responsibility for making it work properly.

There is no officer or agency of our state government with clear responsibility for continuously observing and examining our entire court system, for taking action to remedy administrative defects which are found, and doing so in the light of needs of the whole system of courts as well as the individual specific needs of a single court. If real improvement is to be made in the courts of North Carolina, this responsibility must be constitutionally vested somewhere. And there are only two agencies in which such responsibility can be appropriately vested, the Supreme Court of North Carolina or the General Assembly. Both are selected by the people. Both are responsible to the people. Both bodies now exercise vast powers which greatly affect the lives and property of all citizens. Both do so responsibly and ably. The people of North Carolina trust the General Assembly and the Supreme Court. The question which confronts us must, therefore, be answered not in terms of which of these branches of our government we would trust more or less, but which can carry out this responsibility of judicial administration most effectively.

Under our fundamental philosophy of the separation of powers, it would seem that the responsibility for *judicial administration* should be placed in the Supreme Court. The Supreme Court is almost continuously in session and it is intimately and solely concerned with the business of the courts. As our highest appellate court, and by the nature of its duties, the members of that court think in terms of the state-wide interest. It seems to me that the Supreme Court, with proper administrative help, on the basis of all practical measurements, is better fitted to carry out this task of court administration than is the General Assembly.

Without attempting to say precisely what item of detail should be written into the constitution, it is my opinion that we should vest the responsibility for administration of a unified court system in the Supreme Court of North Carolina. If the Supreme Court is to have responsibility for the effective administration of the court system, it must also have essential authority to carry out this responsibility.

I realize that vesting such authority and responsibility for judicial administration in our highest appellate court is open to the objection that when this is done by the constitution itself, the legislative branch is thereafter restricted, if through action or inaction by the judiciary, such an approach is ineffective, or found to be generally unacceptable to our people.

If this delegation of responsibility, without recourse except by amendment of the constitution, be deemed unwise, it is my recommendation that we vest this responsibility in the judiciary, subject to the constitutional provision that any authority with respect to judicial administration vested in the Supreme Court by this revision may be exercised by the General Assembly itself, by a three-fifths vote of the Senate and the House of Representatives, without a vote of the people.

Let me emphasize that under the recommendations submitted by the Bar Association Court Study Committee there are many subjects with respect to the judicial branch on which the General Assembly retains its present full control. The General Assembly would determine the number of Superior Court judges and solicitors, district court judges and solicitors, and justices of the peace (or trial commissioners or magistrates, whichever term is used), and would fix their compensation. The General Assembly would fix all court fees and costs, except those of the appellate court. The number and boundaries of the judicial and solicitorial districts would continue to be fixed by the General Assembly. The General Assembly would have over-all budgetary supervision of the courts, as it should, and would continue to possess adequate and effective authority to take all appropriate action with respect to basic policy matters in the operation of our courts.

There is one other important aspect of court administration which does not involve revision of the constitution. A few days ago, in response to your specific request at the 1957 Session, the Court Study Committee submitted to you a separate report on the position of Superior Court solicitors. That report recommends, among other things, that by statutory enactment Superior Court solicitors be made full-time officials.

Each of the twenty-one Superior Court solicitors throughout the state receives the same pay and allowances from the state, yet the amount of work they are called upon to do in prosecuting the criminal docket varies widely from one district to another. One solicitorial district contains two counties, another district contains ten. This number of days of criminal court which must be attended by the solicitor varied from sixty-eight days in one district to 214 in another, during the same year. The number of cases disposed of varied from 498 in one district to 1,666 in another district in the same year.

Aside from the disparity in work-load distribution among our Superior Court solicitors, which should be re-examined periodically, it seems to me that the time has come when our solicitors should devote full time to their public duties. Inevitably, there is a potential conflict of interest present when, if nothing else, the time and energy demands of a private law practice compete directly with the demand of public service.

I am sure you will want to give very careful consideration to the study and recommendations on the solicitors, and I urge that you take action to make them full-time officials and do whatever else necessary to make this important position more effective.

CONCLUSION

The revision of our state constitution confronts us with a serious and challenging task. This is a task demanding and deserving of our very best labors. It is a task which demands thorough consideration and thorough discussion. Decisions will not and should not be reached in haste or in such a way that valid and varied points of view are not appropriately considered. I have every confidence that this General Assembly will rise to this great task, and will revise our 1868 constitution in keeping with the times and to prepare for North Carolina's great future. I believe that the next few weeks will provide you ample time in which to consider these revisions and make your decisions on the constitution you will submit to a vote of the people. I believe that 1959 should, and will, take its place, along with 1776, 1835, and 1868, as a milestone in the constitutional history of North Carolina.

Thank you, and may God bless each of you as you continue your service for our state.

PROCLAMATIONS

PROCLAMATIONS

[The following seven proclamations and one writ of election have been selected from a larger number of such papers to illustrate this phase of the work of the Governor's office during the years 1959-1960.]

HARRY S. TRUMAN DAY

EXECUTIVE DEPARTMENT
RALEIGH

A PROCLAMATION BY THE GOVERNOR

May 5, 1959

Whereas, May 8, 1959, will mark the seventy-fifth anniversary of the birth of former President Harry S. Truman;

And whereas, Mr. Truman's many friends have chosen this date as an appropriate occasion on which to acknowledge his years of dedicated and distinguished service to the nation;

And whereas, the former President displayed uncommon qualities of leadership in guiding the destiny of this nation during one of the most crucial periods of its history;

And whereas, during this time, which witnessed the dawn of the atomic age, the end of World War II, the creation of the United Nations and the rise of the Communist threat throughout the world, Mr. Truman provided courageous and decisive leadership;

And whereas, his personal integrity and charm, his contagious optimism in all matters, his faith in the American people, and his courage in the face of great odds, have established him in our history as a great citizen;

And whereas, the people of the state of North Carolina have frequently demonstrated their admiration and support for this man as a public servant and as a private citizen:

Now, therefore, I, Luther H. Hodges, Governor of the State of North Carolina, do hereby proclaim May 8, 1959, as Harry S. Truman Day in North Carolina.

In witness whereof, I have hereunto set my hand and caused the Great Seal of the State of North Carolina to (Seal) be affixed hereto. Done at the city of Raleigh, the fifth day of May, in the year of our Lord one thousand nine hundred and fifty-nine.

Luther H. Hodges, *Governor*
Edward L. Rankin, Jr., *Private Secretary.*

THANKSGIVING DAY

EXECUTIVE DEPARTMENT
RALEIGH

A PROCLAMATION BY THE GOVERNOR
November 18, 1959

Whereas, a great and meaningful tradition was begun on a crisp, autumn day in 1621, when our dedicated and deeply religious Pilgrim Fathers celebrated their first harvest with a feast of brotherhood and thanksgiving;

And whereas, on that memorable occasion the courageous settlers expressed their gratitude to God for His guidance in their flight from religious and political oppression, and for His benevolence in sparing them to take up a new life of freedom and unprecedented opportunity;

And whereas, the citizens of this nation, appreciative of their great heritage, continue to perpetuate the humble faith of their forefathers by celebrating Thanksgiving Day as a national holiday;

And whereas, we continue to reap, as individuals and as a nation, a bountiful harvest of both material wealth and those less tangible blessings that are the products of honest devotion to spiritual values;

And whereas, we face, as our predecessors did, many grave and perplexing problems in a world torn by conflicting ideologies; and, in keeping with our religious heritage, we pray for calm and courageous leadership, for a keen understanding of the people and events that shape our destiny, for our deep and abiding faith in fundamental democratic principles to be preserved, for an increasingly devout demonstration of our dedication as a Christian nation;

And whereas, this season is traditionally a time for sharing the American abundance with those less fortunate than ourselves, thereby demonstrating this nation's inherent compassion and friendship, while at the same time paying homage to God for the many blessings He has bestowed upon:

Now, therefore, I, Luther H. Hodges, Governor of North Carolina, do hereby proclaim Thursday, November 26, a legal holiday in North Carolina and request that all the citizens of our state, with their families and friends, render sincere and heartfelt thanks to Almighty God for all His many benefits.

(Seal)   In witness whereof, I have hereunto set my hand and caused the Great Seal of the State of North Carolina to be affixed. Done at the city of Raleigh, this the eighteenth day of November, in the year of our Lord one thousand nine hundred and fifty-nine.

Luther H. Hodges, *Governor.*

Edward L. Rankin, Jr., *Private Secretary.*

BANK HOLIDAY

EXECUTIVE DEPARTMENT
RALEIGH

A PROCLAMATION BY THE GOVERNOR
December 4, 1959

Whereas, December 26, 1959, a state and national holiday, falls on Saturday;

And whereas, by general consent, many businesses will enjoy Saturday, December 26, 1959, as a holiday;

And whereas, a request has been made by the North Carolina Bankers Association that Saturday, December 26, 1959, be declared a banking holiday:

Now, therefore, I, Luther H. Hodges, Governor of the State of North Carolina, by and with the advice and consent of the

Council of State, under and by virtue of authority of Section 53-77 of the General Statutes of North Carolina, do hereby designate Saturday, December 26, 1959, as a banking holiday. During such period of holiday, all of the ordinary and usual operations and business of all banking corporations, state or national, in this state shall be suspended, and during such period no banking corporation shall pay out or receive deposits, make loans or discounts, transfer credits, or transact any other banking business whatsoever except such acts as are authorized by the aforesaid law.

Done at our capital city of Raleigh this fourth day (Seal) December, in the year of our Lord one thousand nine hundred and fifty-nine.

Luther H. Hodges, *Governor*
Edward L. Rankin, Jr., *Private Secretary.*

WRIT OF ELECTION

STATE OF NORTH CAROLINA
OFFICE OF THE GOVERNOR

June 7, 1960

To The Honorable Joseph M. Bryan, Chairman of the State Board of Elections, to the said State Board of Elections, to the several county boards of election of the counties of Buncombe, Cherokee, Clay, Graham, Haywood, Henderson, Jackson, Macon, Swain, and Transylvania, the counties comprising the Twelfth Congressional District, and to all officers and persons concerned, Greeting:

Whereas, the Honorable David M. Hall, representative from the Twelfth Congressional District in the Congress of the United States, has died, leaving a vacancy in said office for the unexpired term, the said death having occurred since the last general election and before the term to which he had been elected had expired:

Now, therefore, in compliance with Section 163-105 of the General Statutes of North Carolina, I, Luther H. Hodges, Governor of North Carolina, hereby issue this writ of election and order, require, and command that an election be held in the said Twelfth Congressional District, and in all the precincts thereof, on the twenty-fifth day of June, one thousand nine hundred and sixty, and at the time and places, and under the laws and regulations provided for such elections, wherein the qualified voters of the said Twelfth Congressional District may elect a Representative in Congress to fill the unexpired term of the said Honorable David M. Hall.

To that end you, and all officers and persons charged with any duty in the premises, are required to make such provision and take such measures as may be directed by law.

(Seal) Witness my hand and the Great Seal of the State of North Carolina, this seventh day of June, in the year of our Lord one thousand nine hundred and sixty.

Luther H. Hodges, *Governor.*

Thad Eure, *Secretary of State.*

HURRICANE DONNA

EXECUTIVE DEPARTMENT
RALEIGH

A PROCLAMATION BY THE GOVERNOR

September 14, 1960

Whereas, on Sunday and Monday, September 11 and 12, Hurricane Donna struck the coastal and eastern areas of our state with terrific force and fury, causing great damage and destruction resulting in major disaster conditions;

And whereas, hurricane force winds and above normal high tides caused great damage and destruction to homes, businesses, streets, farm land, crops and live stock, state and federal highways, public utilities and facilities;

And whereas, state and local agencies, including the Civil Defense organizations and the American Red Cross have been actively engaged in rendering assistance;

And whereas, all available state and local governmental funds are, or will be, committed to this purpose;

And whereas, many of the governing bodies of the stricken areas have requested that their areas be designated as a major disaster area;

And whereas, serious damage was suffered by many primary federal aid highways and emergency relief funds are needed for the immediate rehabilitation and repair of said highways under the provisions of Section 13-A, U. S. Code annotated;

And whereas, federal assistance will be needed for the relief of agricultural damage and losses:

Now, therefore, I, Luther H. Hodges, Governor of North Carolina, do hereby declare a state of emergency to exist in those areas in the state of North Carolina affected by Hurricane Donna on or during the aforesaid period, and I do hereby designate the same as major disaster areas.

Done at the city of Raleigh, this fourteenth day of (Seal)   September, in the year of our Lord one thousand nine hundred and sixty.

Luther H. Hodges, *Governor.*

Harold T. Makepeace, *Private Secretary.*

AMENDMENT TO PROCLAMATION OF

SEPTEMBER 14, 1960

Executive Department
Raleigh

A Proclamation by the Governor

October 20, 1960

Whereas, on the fourteenth day of September, 1960, I issued a proclamation as governor of the state of North Carolina declaring a state of emergency to exist in those areas in our state affected by Hurricane Donna during the period September 11 and 12, and I did designate by said proclamation the affected areas as major disaster areas;

And whereas, no positive mention was made of the "incessant and destructive rainfall" accompanying the high winds of Hurricane Donna;

And whereas, it now appears that certain federal agencies will be unable to make disaster loans in said affected areas unless it appears in said proclamation that "excessive rainfall" accompanied said storm bringing great damage to growing crops, lands, and properties;

And whereas, I do now by this document amend said proclamation by me dated September 14, 1960, so as to include the necessary language descriptive of the excessive rainfall:

Now, therefore, I, Luther H. Hodges, Governor of North Carolina, do hereby amend the proclamation by me made with respect to Hurricane Donna on September 14, 1960, as follows:

Amend paragraph 2 of said proclamation by inserting in line 1 after the word "winds", a comma and the following words "incessant and excessive rainfall commencing on the early morning of September 12 causing four to seven inches of rainfall in said area during the ensuing twenty-four hour period."

(Seal) Done at the city of Raleigh, this twentieth day of October, in the year of our Lord one thousand nine hundred and sixty.

Luther H. Hodges, *Governor.*
Harold T. Makepeace, *Private Secretary.*

PRESIDENTIAL ELECTORS

EXECUTIVE DEPARTMENT
RALEIGH

A PROCLAMATION BY THE GOVERNOR
November 30, 1960

Whereas, the State Board of Elections of the state of North Carolina has canvassed the returns of the votes cast for electors for President and Vice President of the United States at the General Elections held on November 8, 1960;

And whereas, said State Board of Elections has prepared and certified an abstract of same to the secretary of state of the state of North Carolina;

And whereas, said secretary of state has, under his hand and the seal of his office, certified to the undersigned governor of the state of North Carolina the names of as many persons receiving the highest number of votes for electors of President and Vice President of the United States as the state of North Carolina is entitled to in the Electoral College:

Now, therefore, I, Luther H. Hodges, Governor of the State of North Carolina, pursuant to the power and authority vested in me by the provisions contained in the General Statutes of North Carolina, Section 163-110, do hereby proclaim that the following persons have been duly elected as electors for President and Vice President of the United States:

ELECTORS AT LARGE

W. Frank Taylor   D. Hiden Ramsey

ELECTOR	CONGRESSIONAL DISTRICT
Edgar Gurganus	First
Olin Reed	Second
Dr. John D. Robinson, Sr.	Third
Daniel L. Bell	Fourth
E. T. Pullen, Jr.	Fifth
O. A. Kirkman	Sixth
R. M. Kermon	Seventh
Miss Edith Marsh	Eighth
Mrs. Stella Anderson	Ninth
Charles M. Walton	Tenth
John M. Akers	Eleventh
Robert R. Livingston	Twelfth

and each of the electors above named are hereby enjoined to attend a meeting at the Capitol in the city of Raleigh, North Carolina, at noon, on the nineteenth day of December, 1960, for the purpose of voting for the President and Vice President of the United States, as required by law.

Done at our capital city of Raleigh, this thirtieth day
(Seal) of November, in the year of our Lord one thousand
nine hundred and sixty, and in the one hundred and
eighty-fifth year of our American Independence.

Luther H. Hodges, *Governor.*

Harold T. Makepeace, *Private Secretary.*

INAUGURATION OF TERRY SANFORD

EXECUTIVE DEPARTMENT
RALEIGH

A PROCLAMATION BY THE GOVERNOR
December 30, 1960

Whereas, the constitution of North Carolina provides that the supreme executive power of the state shall be vested in a governor and stipulates that his term of office shall be for four years, commencing on the first of January next after his election by the qualified electors of the state and shall continue until his successor is elected and qualified;

And whereas, in the general election of November 8, 1960, the Honorable Terry Sanford was elected governor at the same time that other constitutional state officers were chosen, and the results of this election have been certified by legally prescribed authority;

And whereas, the Honorable Terry Sanford and other elected constitutional officers will take their oaths of office in a ceremony beginning at noon on January 5, 1961;

And whereas, the constitution has been amended to defer the beginning of the biennial session of the General Assembly from January to February, thus preventing the General Assembly from performing customary functions in connection with the inauguration of the governor and other constitutional state officers:

Now, therefore, I, Luther H. Hodges, Governor of the State of North Carolina, do hereby proclaim Wednesday and Thursday,

January 4 and 5, 1961, as the period for the festivities and ceremonies pertaining to the inauguration arranged by the Governor's
Inaugural Committee.

(Seal)　　Done at our capital city of Raleigh, this thirtieth day
of December, in the year of our Lord one thousand
nine hundred and sixty, and in the one hundred and
eighty-fifth year of our American Independence.

Luther H. Hodges, *Governor.*

Harold T. Makepeace, *Private Secretary.*

PUBLIC ADDRESSES

PUBLIC ADDRESSES

[During the years 1959-1960 Governor Hodges made 164 speeches of which more or less complete typescript copies are available, plus approximately fifty-five others which he is known to have made extemporaneously or from rough notes. Fifty-four of these speeches, considered to be among the more important ones, are here printed in their entirety; seventy are described in brief summaries appearing on pp. 493-541; and the remainder are listed by date and title only on pp. 545-551.]

ADDRESS AT A STATE HIGHWAY CONFERENCE

RALEIGH

January 21, 1959

[About 600 highway planners and builders attended this conference, which was arranged by the Department of Civil Engineering at North Carolina State College and the State Highway Commission for the purpose of (1) making available to all participating agencies the latest developments in highway engineering, (2) providing an opportunity for the exchange of ideas in this field of endeavor, and (3) promoting greater cooperation and understanding between the various agencies and organizations concerned with highway activities. In an address before a banquet session of the group at the Sir Walter Hotel, Governor Hodges reviewed the state's highway history up to and including the recently adopted point system of priorities to determine each county's share of secondary road money. Comparing highway matters to a three-legged stool with (1) engineering, (2) administration, and (3) public relations as underpinnings, he stressed the importance of each of these factors in planning and carrying forward an effective highway program.]

I would like to thank the State College Department of Civil Engineering and the College Extension Division, the State Highway Commission and the cooperating private organizations both for arranging this conference and for giving me an opportunity to speak to you here tonight. The fact that this conference is being held and the fact that you have come here from throughout the state to participate impress me that North Carolinians know and appreciate the value of a modern, up-to-date highway system. It is indicative of the fact that we in North Carolina realize that the responsibility for providing and maintaining a good modern highway system is not exclusively that of the State Highway Commission. We know that good highways are the product of cooperation — not only among highway officials, counties, municipalities, and the construction companies, but among all the people of the state.

This is why I am so pleased that this conference is being held. This is why I am excited about the prospect of what can be accomplished here. The Department of Civil Engineering at State College is to be commended for the manner in which it is conducting this conference, and considerable credit is due the Highway Commission, equipment distributors, general contractors, and the North Carolina League of Municipalities for their efforts in this important event. I would like to commend, on behalf of the people of this state, each individual who has had a part in planning and carrying out your program, for each of you has made a definite contribution to the future of North Carolina. I sincerely hope that this will be the first of many such conferences and that the opportunities for achievement inherent in an event such as this will be fully developed.

I think it is encouraging to have our contractors and equipment dealers sharing in the planning of this conference. Mr. W. F. Babcock, our fine director of highways, has told me of the splendid work and cooperation of these two groups during the past twelve months — especially their assistance in formulating a completely new set of construction specifications. These specifications are designed to insure that the Highway Department gets the best possible construction work on all projects and that the contractors can proceed with their work with the assurance that they are meeting required standards. We hope contractors and suppliers will give us constructive criticism because we want to do the best job possible.

We all recognize, of course, that highway progress in North Carolina would have been impossible without the loyal and dedicated work of the thousands of rank-and-file highway employees who help plan, improve, build, and maintain our public roads. North Carolina has been very fortunate with the high quality of its personnel down through the years. At this time of the year, we are especially conscious of the splendid work being done by the highway maintenance forces who must keep our roads open during bitter and changing winter weather. We have had many good letters from citizens praising our highway forces.

North Carolina State College, one of the nation's great land-grant colleges, has worked closely with the State Highway Commission in many recent projects, including the organizing of a program of "in service" training within the department. This program makes sense because it utilizes the manpower we already possess, and opens new opportunities for advancement to our long-time career employees. The college also helped train the instructors used to conduct this program.

I understand that State College also participated in a cooperative research program which tackled such problems as developing better all-weather secondary roads, minimizing the damage from "frost heave," etc. From all this activity has come greater interest in "graduate" courses in civil engineering at the college, and we all are delighted that more graduate students accepted positions with the department than ever before. We sincerely hope the number increases.

As I understand it, the purpose of this conference is threefold. Its first objective is to make available to all participating agencies the very latest information relating to current development in highway engineering and allied fields. Secondly, it is designed to provide an opportunity for the exchange of ideas among individuals in the same fields of endeavor. Finally, it is hoped that an event of this sort will promote greater cooperation and understanding between the various agencies and organizations directly concerned with highway activities. In other words, the primary aim of this conference is to make it easier for each of us, as individuals or as representatives of large organizations, to move ahead more efficiently toward the achievement of our common objective — a highway system from which the people of North Carolina will derive the maximum benefit, at the lowest cost, consistent with quality.

Certainly, this is an imposing and tremendously challenging objective. I have said many times before, and I would like to reiterate at this time, that there are few, if any, services provided by government which have a more profound impact upon virtually all phases of our individual and community life than that of highway development. And, I might add, that by the same token there is no area which demands more careful and experienced planning and genuine cooperation on the part of everyone involved. It has been my observation that highways are very personal to the majority of our people. Inevitably, it seems that every person judges a road in direct relation to the service it provides or fails to provide him as an individual. This is as it should be. It is the one factor that all of us, whether we be public officials or private citizens working in the public interest, must keep constantly in mind in all matters relating to our highway program. It is the individual citizen, whether he uses the highway for business or pleasure, who, in the final analysis, determines the quality of our highway system. It is not enough that he be "let in" on highway plans. Rather, it is essential that he be given a part in the formulation of those plans.

North Carolinians know the value of their highways. They think of them not merely as stretches of concrete or asphalt to be admired as engineering models, but as avenues that lead to a better way of life. To the average citizen of this state, highways mean education for his children, markets for his agricultural and industrial products, raw materials for his business or industry, and sales for his manufactured products. They are a means of social, religious, cultural, and economic contact — a means of getting to and from work, and a pathway of recreation and the great outdoors. Highways are not an end within themselves, but a means to an end.

Those of us who must daily concern ourselves with the growth and development of this state are perhaps more aware than others of the vital role that our highways play. We know that progress is closely related to highway development.

The people of North Carolina have every right to be proud of their highways, and those of you attending this conference have every right to be proud of the role that you have played in providing those highways. We have more than 70,000 miles of highways, reaching into every part of our state. Well over half of those miles are paved, providing convenient, comfortable access to homes, markets, churches, schools, shopping centers, and recreation areas. Our state is a closely knit community, bound together socially, economically, and culturally by a great network of highways that stand as a monument to the determination of our people to fulfill the destiny that is theirs.

I think it is good for us, occasionally, to look back on the road we have traveled. In so doing, we get a clearer perspective of where we have come and where we must go. This is a good practice to follow in any field of endeavor, but I think it is especially applicable here. Certainly, it reveals a dramatic, almost unbelievable, story of progress.

To the North Carolinian of a century ago it would have seemed just as fantastic for you to describe our present highway system as it would have been for you to talk of earth satellites, moon rockets, and nuclear powered submarines. At that point in our history, the plank road had come to be accepted as the ideal mode of over-land transportation—second only to the railroad. Then as now, North Carolinians recognized the value of good roads. Evidence of this is seen in the fact that between 1849 and 1860 North Carolina incorporated no less than eighty-one plank-road companies, with an authorized capital stock aggregate of $5,807,500. Much of this stock was never paid and many of the proposed roads were never constructed, but it is certainly significant that this interest was shown just fifteen years after the first plank road experiment was tried on the American continent.

These plank roads — or "farmers' railroad" as they were frequently called — were strictly commercial, built by private companies and operated as toll roads. In a speech before the Highway Employees Association last September, I discussed these plank roads in great detail. I did so for two reasons — to illustrate the importance of highways throughout the history of our state, and to emphasize the fact that it is nothing new for North Carolinians to occupy a position of leadership in this field. This latter fact was dramatically illustrated in 1854 when the famed "Appian Way," which ran from Fayetteville to Salem to Bethania, was completed. This road covered a distance of 129 miles and was the longest plank road ever built in the world.

Here then, in the decade from 1850 to 1860, North Carolina forged ahead of other states in the development of its highways. The effort was throttled by the outbreak of the Civil War, and it lay dormant through the tragic years of Reconstruction. But it was an effort that would not die, an effort that would emerge again in the dawn of the new century to grow into the vast, modern highway system that we know today. The effort that was initiated a century ago has today grown to maturity. And it has grown, not by accident, but by intent. It has grown because the people of this state will not conceive that anything is impossible if they are convinced it will benefit North Carolina. Nor can we overlook the fact that it has grown because the task of converting a dream into reality was entrusted to men and women who knew the true meaning of loyalty, dedication, and devotion to duty.

North Carolina owes a great debt of gratitude to these people, whether they be highway employees or the representatives or private enterprise engaged in highway work. Together you form perhaps the largest single-purpose group in the state, a fact that places a great responsibility on your shoulders. Individually and collectively you comprise a tremendous force for the advancement of our state. If in the years ahead North Carolina acquires the national stature that we fully expect to acquire, and if the people of this state come to enjoy the prosperity that is potentially theirs, those of you here in this room can glory in the knowledge that your contribution to this development has been one of primary significance.

The highway program in our state, and in all the states for that matter, has never faced a more serious and challenging future than is now the case with the giant interstate program getting under way and gaining momentum, and I am proud of what North Carolina has done on its interstate system. The action of the last Congress in providing additional emergency funds for this interstate program has focused even greater attention of the road building program in North Carolina and throughout the nation. Highway officials have been given the tools to complete the largest public works program in American history; and there is high hope that the excellent engineering standards of these future highways have put us on the right road and headed us in the right direction. I hope we will not have to slow down on account of money, although this poses a problem as you well know. As I see it, the eventual success of any highway program depends upon three things. In the matter of building and maintaining highways with public dollars, there can be no excuse for bad engineering and planning — no substitute for good businesslike administration and modern financial accounting. In like manner there is nothing more important than public understanding, for from such understanding is born support on the part of our people. Without this understanding even the most ambitious plans will be thwarted by confusion, suspicion, and outright opposition.

In this connection, highway matters may be likened to a three-legged stool with engineering, administration, and public relations as the underpinnings. With these as strong legs, a good highway program can be planned and carried forward effectively. If one is lacking, however, the other two are rendered ineffective in relation to the over-all program.

North Carolina is in a rather unique position with regard to highways in that we are one of only four states which assume final responsibility at the state level for primary as well as county roads. Our commission has the total responsibility for designing, building, improving, and maintaining the more than 70,000 miles of public roads and highways that I mentioned previously. In this respect our responsibility is larger than that of any other state in the nation. This fact represents both a challenge and a wonderful opportunity for service. The opportunity is the chance to provide all of our people in all areas of the state with fair, equal, and uniform treatment under a single highway administration. We are striving diligently at the present time to provide this kind of treatment under a highway reorganization program which has been in effect less than two years.

I am sure that all of you are familiar with the changes in procedures and policies that have come about as a result of this reorganization program. These changes were made, not necessarily because the old methods were wrong, but because in many instances new trends and new demands had made them outmoded, and it was felt that greater efficiency and greater public understanding could be affected by reorganization.

In the new organization considerable emphasis is being placed on long-range planning in which the opinions of many groups are considered before highways are either located or designed. In this connection, I would like to re-emphasize the point that the value of a highway can be determined only by a careful measure of its usefulness. The best thinking of a good many differing factions should go into any long-range highway program and, while construction engineers are very capable of dealing with the technical matters involved, I am not convinced that they are in a position to determine what is always best in terms of final highway use and highway value.

Too many engineers alone are apt to develop their thinking only in terms of what is economical or advisable from the engineer's viewpoint where, in reality, their scope should be much wider. Engineers and highway planners must temper their thinking to the extent that they consider what is good from all sides. They must never hesitate to consult with and give honest consideration to the opinions of recognized leaders in other fields.

Highway planning is a matter of considerable concern for both rural and urban sociologists whose business it is to consider how we live today and how we might live tomorrow. Our highway program must take into consideration the trends in agriculture as our farm population decreases and our cities and towns grow. The development of industrial and business land uses must also be considered and the potential for such development should be carefully studied. Highway planners must constantly ask themselves, "What will happen to adjacent land should the highway go here?" The procurement of raw materials and the sale of finished products, the availability of water power, the recreational and transportation potential of areas to be traversed by a highway—all of these things must be taken into careful consideration if the greatest benefit is to be derived from any highway building program.

In our own state there has been a rather significant trend among the farm families to seek employment in nearby factories, or processing plants, or industries on a part-time basis. This places our secondary roads program in a new light. No longer do our farmers go to the market once a week. In many areas of our state, previously rural areas are now becoming suburbs of adjacent industrial municipalities. Is this the trend for the future? Should such trends continue, they will certainly warrant even more careful scrutiny in planning for the highways of the future.

Left to right: Crawford H. Greenewalt, president of E. I. du Pont de Nemours and Company; Norman A. Cocke, president of the Duke Power Company; Governor Hodges; and Edwin Pate, president of the North Carolina Citizens Association at a meeting of the association, at which Greenewalt spoke, in Raleigh, March 25, 1959.

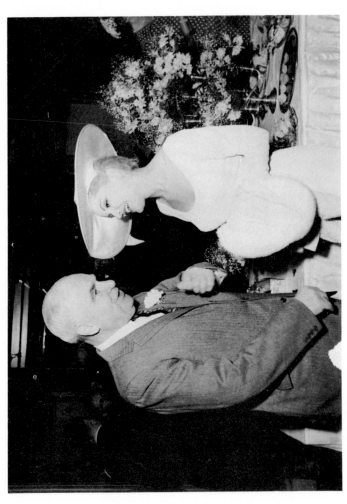

Governor Hodges with Debra Paget, Queen of the Wilmington Azalea Festival, April 3, 1959.

In an expanding long-range highway planning program here in our state, we are seeking the answers to these and many other questions for the sole purpose of rendering the greatest possible service to our four and one-half million people, and we want to do this in such a way that our people will understand and applaud what we are attempting to accomplish.

Surveys recently conducted show that it would require over $1,000,000,000 to bring our primary and secondary highways in North Carolina up to the level of service which we feel would be ideal. The fact that our limited budget will not permit the paving of every road which needs to be paved, or the widening or improvement of every facility which is now below par, points up very graphically *our public responsibility for placing highway dollars where they will accomplish the most good for the greatest number of people.* Under our new program one of the first steps was to survey the actual needs and to estimate the cost of filling these needs without regard to individuals or to prejudice or to influence. This study resulted in the planning more than a year ago of more than one-fourth of all the interstate projects in the state. A priority list was established and approved for designing and programming, as quickly as possible, those sections of interstate highways where the needs was shown to be the greatest.

The giant secondary road network of North Carolina, comprising almost six out of every seven miles of public highways, was completely surveyed for the purpose of determining which of those unpaved roads provided the greatest public service. In this connection, the commission designed secondary road needs in the broadest possible way and established paving priority lists in every county to be followed to the letter in providing hard-surfacing for those roads which needed it most. A point system was approved to be applied state-wide in assigning points to each unpaved road on the relative traffic use of the road, its land uses and its public service characteristics and uses. The points were added up and the road with the greatest number of points in each county will be paved first and so, in order, down the list without favoritism or partiality.

As most of you know, all secondary roads in the state are now being numbered and the department hopes to have this project completed by spring. This will greatly increase the speed and efficiency with which the highway people can deal with secondary road matters, and this should give our citizens on secondary roads greater pride in their roads.

Allocation of funds likewise was determined to each county on basis of its relative need in comparison with all the other counties in the state. I think it is indicative of the fairness of this procedure that not one county has complained about this method of allocation even though the actual amounts vary from just over $20,000 to more than half a million dollars. This was quite a change from the old system, and it provides evidence that the people of North Carolina, when given full information, will support any forward looking program so long as it is based on the equitable treatment of all concerned. Letters by the hundreds bear testimony that the average citizen likes what he sees.

This brings us very logically to the third phase of our new highway program. It has been my experience that, if you deal with people fairly and honestly, and if they know and understand the reasons behind your actions, they are both reasonable and understanding of what you are trying to do. Good public relations is essential to any public program. When we deal with highways, good public relations is absolutely essential.

I have long felt, and I believe the people of our state feel, that they should be given a voice in highway matters and that they should be afforded the opportunity of having full information concerning the policies and procedures of any government agency, which, in reality, exists for the sole purpose of serving them. Good public relations for the Highway Department is essentially this: (1) Do a good job, the best you know how, and (2) Tell the people your story, what you have done and what you plan to do. Good public relations requires an ability to get along with people, to give careful consideration to their opinions, to alter one's own thinking when other viewpoints have merit, and to endeavor to see that others understand your thinking even though they may not agree with it. Good public relations is a matter of give and take on a common ground of respect for the others' viewpoint. We consider this an important aspect of the new highway program.

Not only is the commission trying to provide more information to the general public through the various available new media, but it is working very diligently to consult with people more often before determining where its highways should go and how they should be built. Toward this end, meetings have been held within the past year in each of the 100 counties of our state. Such meetings give our highway officials an opportunity to meet with officials and other interested individuals at the local and county levels and, at the same time, give the local people an opportunity to get to know the individuals responsible for our highway programs. This type of relationship between the men who direct our highway program and the people at the local level cannot help but result in greater understanding and, consequently, more equitable and beneficial planning.

At this point I would like to stress the fact that, in the final analysis, the success or failure of a public relations program rests with those of you who work in the field. The men and women who represent the Highway Commission in the cities, towns, and the counties of North Carolina can accomplish more than anyone else in this important area through personal contact with the people you serve. News releases from Raleigh—important as they are — cannot replace your personal contacts and cannot do the entire job. This is a vitally important part of your job. You have a responsibility to know what is going on within the Highway Department so that you can interpret these activities with relation to their effect on your locality. To the average citizen, you are the Highway Department. As such, you have it within your power to create a favorable or unfavorable impression of the work being carried out by your department. If you are well informed, the impression will be a favorable one. If you are not well informed, the impression you create will be unfavorable and the effect can be far-reaching; courtesy and thoughtfulness on your part will help immensely. It is important, therefore, that each of you know the value of good public relations and that you keep this important facet of the highway program in mind at all times.

Let me conclude by pointing out that we have come a long way in the development of a truly outstanding highway system in North Carolina. I believe the tools with which to carry forward this program have been provided. I am equally confident that the ability and determination needed to use these tools effectively is inherent in the people charged with that responsibility.

The task before us now is to build on the foundation that has been provided. This applies not only to highways, but to every phase of economic development in our state. North Carolina is on the threshold of an era of great prosperity. There is much work yet to be done, many problems to overcome, many decisions to be made; but I have no doubt that you will meet the challenges of the future with the same confidence and dedication that you have exhibited in the past.

Let me again commend the sponsors of this conference and the individuals who have worked so hard to insure its success. You have made a real contribution to North Carolina.

ADDRESS AT MEETING OF THE BOARD OF CONSERVATION AND DEVELOPMENT

DURHAM
January 26, 1959

[Following the custom of holding its quarterly meetings at various places in the state, the Board of Conservation and Development met in Durham on this occasion. Addressing the group on the evening of January 26, Governor Hodges painted a bright picture of North Carolina's industrial future, citing figures to show that $253,000,000 had been invested in new and expanded industrial facilities during 1958. He referred to Durham as "a city that knows from past experience that nothing is impossible," and described the nearby Research Triangle as "a striking example of what North Carolina can do for itself." Continuing in this optimistic vein, he characterized the current growth of North Carolina's established industries and the location of new ones in the state as not only a reflection of economic progress, but also as evidence "that we are keeping pace with the fast-moving world in which we live."]

It is good to be in Durham for this quarterly meeting of the State Board of Conservation and Development. I know that I speak for the board when I say that we deeply appreciate your gracious hospitality and the obvious interest which you share with us in the proper conservation and development of all our resources. We are proud of all our board members and very proud to have two members from Durham—Charles Allen, outstanding banker, and H. C. Kennett, a leader in poultry processing.

It is invigorating to visit in Durham and to feel the confidence, the optimism, and the determination that is exhibited here by so many people. It is difficult to realize that less than 100 years ago this great community was known only as a rail stop, a convenient point of transfer for students and others en route to the State University at Chapel Hill. When you think about the progress that has been made here, it becomes obvious that there is a lesson to be learned from this city and its people. It is a lesson that teaches us what can be accomplished when a group of energetic people combine their talents and work industriously to take full advantage of every opportunity afforded them and, if need be, to create their own opportunities.

It is perhaps symbolic of the spirit of this community that it chose one of the darkest periods in our state's history to begin its almost unprecedented quest for prosperity. J. D. Cameron, in a sketch published in 1881, said of Durham, "It lingered in an undisturbed obscurity until the chance operations of the latter days of the (Civil) War gave it notoriety as the halting place of the victorious army of Sherman." Whatever else we may say of Sherman and his soldiers, it must be conceded that they appreciated good smoking tobacco—a quality for which the people of Durham and North Carolina have just cause to be thankful. When the federal troops arrived here in the last days of the war, they were quick to learn what the soldiers of the Confederacy had long known—that the smoking tobacco produced in J. R. Green's small factory here was the best to be found anywhere.

The soldiers ransacked the factory and helped themselves to such an extent that Green was temporarily out of business. He wasted little time, however, and in short order he had acquired a partner, W. T. Blackwell, and the factory was back in operation. Even more important was the fact that the soldiers, both northern and southern, were quick to spread the word about the quality of Green's tobacco. Competitors sought to capitalize on Green and Blackwell's fame by duplicating the latter's brand name, but this unfair practice was short lived. The Durham manufacturers countered by adopting the picture of a Durham Bull for their trademark. Almost over night, "Bull Durham Smoking Tobacco" was making North Carolina famous and insuring the future growth and development of this city.

Some indication of this community's sudden awakening can be seen in the fact that in 1868—three years after the end of the war—only one tobacco factory was in operation. Yet, by 1872, four years later, the city boasted twelve factories. In less than ten years from that date, Durham's factories were producing large quantities of tobacco for the world market, its warehouses were selling from ten to twelve million pounds of tobacco annually, and its population had risen from a few hundred to more than 3,600 people.

Today, Durham ranks fourth in population among the cities of our state. It is a city of greatly diversified interests, a city that knows from past experience that nothing is impossible. It is a city filled with people who tell you in complete confidence that, "We've come a long way in a short time but, brother, you ain't seen nothing yet." And, I might add, that this is the same kind of spirit that has spread throughout our state in recent years—a spirit that is largely responsible for North Carolina's ascendency to a position of leadership in many areas of regional and national significance.

I sincerely feel that the most important factor in this ascendency has been the willingness and the ability of the individual citizen to take the initiative in programs of mutual benefit within their community. No one is more aware of the necessity for this type of local enterprise than are the board members and the staff members of the Department of Conservation and Development here tonight. All of us who must operate at the state level, who must concern ourselves with all areas of the state and every facet of the state's economy, will be the first to acknowledge that all of our efforts would come to nought were it not for the active support and enthusiastic cooperation of the people at the local level.

An excellent example of this type of local initiative was the event staged here last October in the form of "Durham's Salute to Industry". At that time your Committee of One Hundred, led by such people as J. Fleming Wiley and Paul Wright, brought here to Durham and to North Carolina a group of this nation's leading industrialists and businessmen. *Business Week* magazine called the gathering "the jackpot of business brass." No effort was made to "put the pressure on" the guests. They were simply shown what Durham and our Research Triangle area had to offer in the way of business opportunities, and it was left for them to reach their own conclusions. Those of us who attended the event were tremendously pleased with the reaction, and I am confident that the efforts that went into the staging of "Durham's Salute to Industry" will in the final analysis seem insignificant when compared to the results obtained.

I think it goes without saying that many of these results will be tied closely to the growth and development of our Research Triangle. The possibilities inherent in the Triangle program are limitless, not only for the Durham-Raleigh-Chapel Hill area, but for the entire state of North Carolina. If there had ever been any reservations in anyone's mind regarding the benefits to be derived from this program, certainly those doubts were erased on January 9 with the dramatic announcement that $1,500,000 had been contributed by business and industry in North Carolina to develop further the Research Triangle as a center for industrial and governmental research. These funds, raised in a campaign headed by State Senator Archie K. Davis of Winston-Salem, will be used to (1) establish a Research Triangle Institute which will do research work on a contract basis for industry, business, and government, (2) house the Research Institute in a new building which will be started immediately in the 4,000-acre Research Park, located in the center of the Research Triangle area, and (3) to control the Research Triangle Park, which was assembled in 1957 and held privately by Karl Robbins of New York City, and which will now pass to the non-profit Research Triangle Foundation. The Park management, which will continue to be known as the Pinelands Corporation, is proceeding immediately with plans to develop the property as an industrial research campus where industrial concerns may buy sites for laboratories and associated production activities. This January 9 meeting and announcement gave North Carolina one of its finest days!

I am convinced that the events of recent days relative to the Research Triangle will be recorded as truly historic dates in the economic life of our state. I am equally certain that the self-sacrifice, dedication, and truly enlightened leadership that converted this dream into a reality, will not soon be forgotten by the people of this state. It would be impossible for me to recognize all of the individuals who have contributed to this project, but I think it is particularly appropriate on this occasion that we acknowledge the great debt of gratitude that is owed Durham's own Watts Hill, Sr., for the work he has done. Without the magnificent leadership and untiring service of such men as this, the Research Triangle might still be nothing more than another good idea, or a gleam in someone's eye!

Watts Hill was one of the first to comprehend the Triangle's great potential when the idea was first advanced five or more years ago. He played a leading role in raising initial operating funds in the Durham area and he gave enormously of his time in promotion work—traveling, entertaining visitors, and otherwise selling the Triangle idea. He gave financial aid to the Astra Corporation to enable this company to move into the Triangle. When Brandon Hodges died and illness made it necessary for Robert Hanes to limit his activities, Watts Hill readily accepted the leadership burden. In this capacity he was a key figure in the establishment of the Research Triangle Institute, an organization of which he now serves as chairman of the Board of Governors. He was also instrumental in helping raise money for the Research Triangle Foundation. At the present time he is actively participating in the physical planning of the Research Triangle Park. Certainly, this is an outstanding example of unselfish and dedicated service to the people of this state. Durham should be proud of this oustanding citizen. The state is!

One significant thing about the Research Triangle has been the fact that the project was initiated, promoted, and nurtured to maturity largely through the close and effective cooperation of many different groups—each with its own unique interests, yet each displaying an eagerness to cooperate with the others in the attainment of mutually beneficial goals. Here we have seen three leading communities and counties, three of the nation's leading institutions of higher learning, all local governments involved, all state agencies concerned, a large number of our state's most influential businesses and industries, and many generous and farsighted individuals—all merging their talents and resources to achieve something of incalculable value to our four and one-half million people. There has been nothing else like this in the

United States. Further cooperation—great vision in future planning will still be vital for our greatest success.

The Research Triangle as it stands today, with its tremendous potential just beginning to unfold, is also a striking example of what North Carolina can do for itself. Good citizens like Robert M. Hanes, Watts Hill, Archie Davis, Akers Moore, and many, many others readily volunteered to furnish the type of skilled and dedicated leadership which we couldn't have bought. This is the kind of wonderful spirit which is being shown across North Carolina in many different programs and projects, all designed to help make North Carolina a better, more beautiful, and more prosperous place in which to live, work, and play.

As you know, it has been my pleasure as governor to help organize some of these projects and also my pleasure to share in others by giving my active support and endorsement. It is my belief that a governor or any leader in state government should do everything possible to *stimulate* and *encourage* our people and our communities to accomplish and build great things for themselves, but let the people carry on when the ideas take hold. Good ideas and good programs are merely "seed corn" which should be planted properly and nourished with plenty of hard work, careful cultivation, and attention by the people who will make the harvest.

We have had a splendid response from individuals, organizations, and communities in working with many beneficial programs during the past four years. Such programs have had great appeal to our people because they challenge, they exact local initiative, and they show promise of direct results for local enterprise. For example, our Business Development Corporation, which was designed to stimulate business activity throughout our state has proved very successful. As of the first of this year, this organization had loaned $2,898,490 in venture capital to small businesses and had loan commitments totaling $5,676,465. Another example was our Small Industries Plan and the fruitful efforts, strongly implemented through Conservation and Development, to encourage the activities of regional or area development organizations. And, Conservation and Development has worked most cooperatively with our Department of Agriculture and our State College School of Agriculture. In each of these instances we have endeavored simply to point out the possibilities of industrial and business development, with local citizens and their organizations completing the job. The role of state government here, as I see it, is, first, to encourage home-grown enterprise and, secondly, to attract prospective industries to North Carolina. The final job of selling an industry on North Carolina is left primarily to the people *at the local level.*

May I repeat publicly what I often said, "Neither the state of North Carolina, nor the governor, nor the Department of Conservation and Development, can locate or establish an industry in a particular city or county." It's up to the industrial prospects to make their own decisions, which they do. It's up to the towns, cities, and counties to furnish the State Department of Conservation and Development or direct to the prospect the things they have to offer. And it's a long, hard, continuous job to attract and land a new industry. It may take months or years or it may come quickly.

All of you will be interested to know that nearly every mail brings to my desk an inquiry from a prospect for our state. This is new and exciting!

This philosophy of encouraging local leadership and enterprise was carried into the field of agriculture with the establishment of the Governor's Farm Advisory Committee. It was also the basis of our efforts to encourage and implement the rapid growth of food processing industry in North Carolina. Still another area in which we have endeavored to exploit the talents and energies of the private citizen has been in the field of education. In the last few years we have seen the establishment of our highly successful trade schools, which serve a multiple purpose—providing specialized technical training as conveniently as possible for those desiring it, providing a flexible curriculum designed to fit the student to the job available to him, and at the same time, providing prospective industries with an assurance that an ample supply of skilled labor can be provided. The state has approved seven of these industrial education centers and others are up for approval.

Our Citizens Committee for Better Schools has made a real contribution to this state in the time since its establishment, and it has done so in a field which holds the key to North Carolina's future. The same might be said for the thousands upon thousands of North Carolinians who have enthusiastically answered our oft-repeated challenge to build and support community and church-related colleges.

And there are many other programs in which the citizens of this state have shown real enthusiasm for working together for the benefit of all our people. Consider, if you will, the voluntary man-power that has gone into—and the good that has been de-rived from—the activities of the Travel Council, the campaigns to encourage forest fire prevention and proper woodland man-agement, the Keep North Carolina Beautiful (or Anti-litterbug) Campaign, the Traffic Safety Council, Hurricane Rehabilitation, the Court Improvement Study, our Nuclear Energy Committee, the Occupational Health Program, and many others. Your state government has had a hand in each of these volunteer programs, but the real work must be done by private citizens with the pa-tience, wisdom, and energy to make a contribution to the people of North Carolina.

I would like especially to commend the Department of Conser-vation and Development for the assistance it has given in these, as well as their regular, programs during the past year. This board has displayed exceptional qualities of leadership during a year in which North Carolina forged ahead on many fronts. Director Bill Saunders and his associates have worked tirelessly to make 1958 a banner year in this state's history. Close team work on the part of this board, Conservation and Development De-partment personnel, and many thousands of North Carolinians has resulted in solid progress during the year—progress that will leave its mark on this state for all times to come.

The effort to strengthen and diversify our industrial develop-ment program on a state-wide basis reached new heights during 1958 with $253,074,000 invested in new and expanded facilities. This record program was made possible by 423 new and expanded facilities which provided 21,757 new jobs with an annual payroll of $72,633,000. Percentage-wise, this was a 32.48 per cent increase in investments over 1957, a 34.06 per cent increase in jobs made available, and a 35.23 per cent increase in payrolls. Employment in North Carolina's accelerating industrial drive showed a 36.74 per cent increase, and payrolls reflected an increase of 63.54 per cent. Dollar-wise, this represents a gain of over $28,000,000 in payrolls.

Equally significant, to my way of thinking, is the fact that, in addition to providing new jobs and job opportunities, 1958's industrial development effort reflected a continuation of the trend toward industrial diversification.

As most of you know, figures recently released jointly by the Department of Conservation and Development and my office show that, of new plants established in 1958, metal working industries led all industrial categories with total investments of $67,155,000. Chemicals were second with an outlay of $63,087,000. Tobacco manufacturers were third with expenditure of $33, 605,000, and textiles were fourth with $30,014,000. Food and kindred products were fifth, and furniture and fixtures were sixth.

We are excited about the growth of all these industries in our state, not simply because they reflect economic progress, but because it shows that our established industries—tobacco, textiles, and furniture—are enjoying a normal, healthy growth while our newer industries—metal working, electronics, and chemicals—show that we are keeping pace with the fast-moving world in which we live. Another exciting development highlighted by the 1958 record is the progress made in our food processing industry. During 1958, that facet of the state's economy spent over $21,000,000 for sixty-three new and expanded facilities designed primarily to process, package, and market our agricultural products. This development during the past twelve months provided 2,346 new jobs and added $6,814,000 to the industry's payroll figures.

I would like to take this opportunity to commend H. C. Kennett for the wonderful contribution he has made to the food processing industry in this state—especially his work in the poultry producing and processing program of the Central Carolina Farmers Exchange. I understand that this program, which exploits every beneficial aspect of the poultry business, is now processing 100,000 broilers a week, and that plans are under way to increase this number in the near future. This project is making a very tangible contribution to the economy of this section and we are all indebted to Mr. Kennett and his associates for the time and effort they have devoted to the program.

The food processing picture is even more significant than statistics on capital outlay, job opportunities, and payrolls would indicate. A good example is the Swift and Company meat processing facility at Wilson, which represents a capital outlay of over $3,000,000, but which company officials indicate will contribute from $15,000,000 to $17,000,000 to the eastern North Carolina economy each year for such things as livestock, supplies, labor, etc. Another example is the Gerber Products Company which is in the process of establishing processing and marketing facilities in the Asheville area. Gerber officials estimate that they will buy 40,000 tons of fruits and vegetables in the western North Carolina area each year, which should mean between $2,500,000 and $3,000,000 annually for producers. And on Saturday I had the pleasure of talking to the North Carolina Meat Packers Association. You will be happy to know that we now have sixty meat packers and processers in North Carolina.

Nor can we overlook the tremendous progress that has been made during the past year in connection with forestry and forestry-related industries. We have just begun to realize the vast potential available to us in this field. In many ways, the forests of North Carolina hold as much promise for the future as do our electronics and chemical industries. We have a greater percentage of woodlands than any other state.

Another area in which important progress has been registered during the past year has been in the field of water resource management. Progress in this field cannot be expressed in terms of dollars and cents, but let me assure you that the economic future of this state is very closely related to our work in the water resources field. Our natural abundance of water in this state has, until recently, caused us to overlook an ever-increasing number of problems related to this resource. The Department of Conservation and Development, hampered by public indifference, is to be commended on the fact that it began work many years ago, collecting and analyzing information about our water resources. Had it not been for this foresighted action we might today be in a far more precarious position in this field.

When the need for more activity was realized, our legislature, in 1955, authorized the establishment of the State Board of Water Commissioners and assigned the board the responsibility of reappraising our entire water program and making recommendations with regard to future action. Since that time this board, headed by General James R. Townsend of Greensboro, has compiled and studied all available water resource information. It has also made a statewide study of industrial and municipal water use and conducted an inventory to determine the nature of our major water problems. The Department of Conservation and Development has cooperated closely in this program, as has the Institute of Government in Chapel Hill, and many other agencies, both state and federal. The work of this board was climaxed recently with the recommendation that a single water agency, combining the duties and responsibilities of all other state agencies working in this field, be established. The one agency excluded from this recommendation for the time being is the Stream Sanitation Committee. The Department of Conservation and Development has concurred in this recommendation, and it has been endorsed by the Committee on Reorganization of State Government.

This, of course, is only one of many vitally important issues facing our General Assembly. As you know the 1957 General Assembly authorized and directed me to appoint a total of ten study commissions or committees. This action was based on the recognition that there were several major problem areas at both state and local government levels to which the legislature itself should give more than the usual amount of attention. Accordingly, it was the desire of the legislature, as expressed in its various resolutions, to have responsible and able citizens first look at various problems involved, make extensive factual investigations, and then pinpoint specific recommendations which the legislature could consider when it convenes in about two weeks.

Study groups were named to deal with such matters as taxes, municipal government, school finance, the constitution, governmental reorganization, map laws, nursing and boarding homes, cancer, the University Trustees, and motor boat laws. Another equally important study, which has been under way for the past three years, has dealt with our court system. This study did not originate with our legislature, but the study committee has been asked to report to the 1959 General Assembly. I have said before and I would like to say again that a mere recital of the names of those on these study commissions which have been hard at work during the past year gives us a clear indication of the scope and importance of the many governmental problems with which we are faced. And let me add that the public spirited citizens who have served on these various committees and commissions have earned a deep debt of gratitude from the people of North Carolina.

I would like especially to call this board's attention to a recommendation from the Map Law Study Commission which suggests reactivation of the program for an "official survey base." An official survey base consists of a series of location monuments, or markers, placed throughout the state and identified in terms of longitude and latitude. As I understand it, a fully developed and adequate official survey base would be one which has one marker or monument approximately every square mile. This would place such a marker within one half mile of any point in the state. With such a series of markers, appropriately identified and placed throughout our state, land surveying, mapping and other such activities could then be made in terms of the official survey base markers. Such a program was first authorized by our legislature in 1939, but comparatively little work has been done to carry out the project. I have mentioned this program because it ties in closely with Conservation and Development Department activities and because I think the proposal merits your close attention.

I believe it is apparent to all of you that the days and months ahead will be crucial ones in the history of North Carolina. Great changes have taken place in North Carolina since the last session of the General Assembly. I am confident that these changes have been for the good and that this state has moved a step closer to the era of prosperity that will mean a better life for all our citizens. The task ahead of us is twofold. We must consolidate the gains that have been achieved and we must maintain the momentum that has brought us this far, and we must keep the people informed. The Department of Conservation and Development, because it has played a major role in our progress, shares a major portion of the responsibility for seeing that we do not slacken our efforts in the future. One of your greatest responsibilities will be to continue the program of encouraging and assisting the people of this state at the local level in their development activities.

North Carolina has more than 200 chambers of commerce, 104 industrial corporations, six area development groups and nine Committees of One Hundred or their equivalent. At least twenty of these organizations were "born" during 1958, many of them as a direct result of the activities of this department. I want to thank all of them for their help. They made the Philadelphia, Chicago, and New York trips pay off. They will help insure our state's future success. There is absolutely no limit to what can be accomplished by this tremendous force if the proper assistance and guidance is provided at the state level. This is an exciting challenge and it provides unlimited opportunities for this board and this department. If your past activities are any indication, then I feel confident in predicting that this challenge will be met and that the future well being of this state and its people will be insured.

Thank you!

ADDRESS AT JUNIOR CHAMBER OF COMMERCE DISTINGUISHED SERVICE AWARD DINNER

PLYMOUTH
January 28, 1959

[Representatives from several civic clubs attended this dinner meeting in the Fellowship Hall of the Christian Church at Plymouth. The Governor utilized the occasion to emphasize the importance of the tourist trade as an untapped reserve of great potential wealth for North Carolina, and also to reiterate his concern for stabilization of the Outer Banks.]

It is a genuine pleasure to be here in Plymouth this evening to participate in so gratifying a program, and I am glad we have several of our legislators present. The meeting here tonight

Governor Hodges with Porter M. Jarvis, president of Swift and Company (*left*) and Dallas Miller, manager of the Swift plant at Wilson, North Carolina (*right*), at Swift and Company Open House in Wilson, April 18, 1959.

The Governor, wearing the familiar carnation, poses for the camera in front of the State Capitol, June, 1959.

symbolizes the wonderful spirit of community service that typifies civic club activity in North Carolina. It would be impossible to appraise the debt that this state owes its civic club members for the many and varied services they render. This event tonight — the presentation of the Junior Chamber of Commerce Distinguished Award—is, to me, a thrilling occasion. For it not only recognizes an individual who has served his community well, but it recognizes the thing that this individual stands for — the responsibility of every citizen to give of his time and talent to the service of his neighbors.

There are those in every community who shun civic club membership on the pretext that they haven't the time or that they just aren't "joiners." In some instances, this reluctance is both justified and understandable, but is most cases these individuals simply haven't taken time to consider their responsibility to their community, their fellow citizens—and to themselves. It just hasn't occurred to them that there is more to being a good citizen than obeying laws and paying taxes. And, I might add, that they haven't discovered what they are missing in the way of personal satisfaction that comes from making a real contribution to one's own community.

I am especially pleased with the fact that the audience here this evening is composed of representatives from all your civic organizations. This indicates that you have that "something extra" in the way of community spirit that frequently means the difference between making progress and maintaining the status quo. What better way is there to insure progress than for community and civic leaders to sit down together, to discuss their mutual problems, analyze their opportunities, determine their objectives and formulate ways and means of attaining those objectives?

I dare not guess how many different interests are represented here at this dinner, but I believe it would be safe to assume that no significant area of interest has been overlooked. There are those of you here who represent small businesses and those of you who represent larger organizations. Some of you are solely interested in agriculture and its products, while others are primarily concerned with government, industry, and professional work. All of you have your own unique problems, your own special interests, and your own hopes and aspirations. Yet, each of you has taken time away from your business to participate in civic club activities. This is significant because it means that each of you realizes the importance of community responsibility. It means that you have acknowledged the fact that you, individually, will gain by your community's progress — that you, as a member of this community, this county, or this section of the state, will benefit, even if indirectly, from anything that benefits, your neighbor.

This is tremendously important because here in this room you have the talent, the resources, and the organization to achieve almost anything within the realm of your imagination. It is exciting just to stand here and contemplate the power for community and area development that can be wielded by the people here tonight. It is doubly exciting when you consider that this great potential is backed up by a regional heritage of initiative, know-how, and determination.

The challenge before you now is to determine the best means by which you can take full advantage of this reservoir of dedication and talent. Progress has already been made—significant progress — but I think you will agree with me that we have hardly begun to tap the great potential that is available to us in this section of North Carolina. If proof of this is needed, we have only to look at the per capita income figures for Washington and its adjoining counties. The figures do not reflect the vast natural and human resources that this region possesses.

Bearing in mind that the per capita income average for North Carolina counties is $1,317 and that we rank forty-fifth among the states, let us look for a moment at the figures for the counties in this area. Washington's per capita income stands at $1,132— the highest in this particular region and primarily because of your large industry. Beaufort has a per capita income of $974. Bertie has an income of $908. Hyde's income is $553. Martin stands at $1,127. And Tyrrell has a per capita income of $884. Only Martin and Washington rank above fiftieth place on the state's per capita income ladder, Washington being thirty-third in the state.

I have cited these figures, not to embarrass or condemn, but simply to emphasize the fact that there is much work to be done if the people of this section are to obtain the benefits inherent in the opportunities available to them. And while statistics— especially those relating to per capita income — do not always present an accurate picture of the conditions that exist within a county or an area of the state, they are, at least, indicative. Let me say at this point that the picture I have drawn is, by no, means, unique to the Washington-Albemarle area. Similar conditions exist in other sections of the state. As a matter of fact, only in the heavily industrialized portions of the Piedmont do we have difficulty finding a low income area. Ten of our 100 counties furnish 50 cent of our industrial payrolls. This is a condition that has caused me great concern during the more than four years that I have served as governor. And it is a condition that I have endeavored to rectify with all the means at my command. The success of these efforts cannot be determined overnight, but there is every reason to belive that we are moving in the right direction—that in the not too distant future the regional economic balance that we seek will become a wonderful reality. The Research Triangle and the various local organizations will help us achieve our goal.

I have confidence in the direction we are going because the raw materials we need to attain our goal already exist in great quantity. We have the natural tools with which to do the job, and we have the people with the ability and the determination. Here, in eastern North Carolina, the opportunities are practically limitless. The burden of the one-crop agricultural economy is gradually being lifted. Diversified farming is becoming the rule rather than the exception. Here in Washington County, for instance, farm income gains are being registered on such items as livestock, poultry and eggs, dairy products, and honey. In 1957, these products added more than $44,000 to farm incomes while staggering losses were being registered by tobacco, cotton, corn, peanuts, and other traditional crops. This clearly illustrates the disadvantage of an unbalanced agricultural program and, at the same time, demonstrates the wisdom of diversification.

One of the most exciting developments in North Carolina in the past few years—mainly because it holds such promise for areas such as yours — has been the growth of the food processing industry. During 1958, more than $21,000,000 was invested in this industry to build or expand sixty-three separate processing plants. This activity provided 2,346 new jobs for the people of this state and added $6,814,000 to our industrial payrolls. Earlier this week, in a speech before the Board of Conservation and Development, I stressed the fact that the food processing picture is even more significant than statistics on capital outlay, job opportunities, and payrolls would indicate. An example I cited was the new Swift and Company meat packing facility at Wilson. This plant represents a capital investment of over $3,000,000, but according to company officials, the new industry will contribute between $15,000,000 and $17,000,000 annually to the eastern North Carolina economy for such things as livestock, supplies, and labor. You will be interested in the fact that the manager of the Swift plant recently described the Coastal Plain section of our state as second to none in its capacity for producing livestock.

Still another area in which eastern North Carolina holds a great potential is forestry. Certainly, there can be little doubt about the bright future ahead for our state's forestry industry. Much has been accomplished in this field in recent years. We have come to recognize the value of this industry, and we have displayed a willingness to take whatever steps may be necessary to see that our people get the maximum benefit from this great resource.

At the present time, and for some years back, this state has held undisputed leadership among the southern states in several phases of forestry development — principally, education and research. These are vitally important and I think we should continue to place emphasis here. I mention this because other states are beginning to recognize the importance of these two factors, and it will be necessary for us to maintain our activity in this field if we are to retain leadership.

Almost 20,000,000 acres in North Carolina are covered by forests. This represents well over 60 per cent of the total land area. The value of forest products derived from these wooded lands exceeded $750,000,000 in the latest count — and Washington County holds a sizable share of this investment. These values are almost equally divided among lumber, paper products, plywood, pulp, and furniture. The value of pulp and paper products alone has increased roughly 800 per cent since 1939.

It is estimated by competent authorities that the demand for paper and similar wood products will double by 1975. There is every reason to believe that the production of these products in North Carolina will at least keep pace with the national demand and probably exceed it. In other words, every factor points to the rapidly growing importance of our forestry industry.

There is one other opportunity that you, as community and area leaders, must not overlook here in this part of the state. I refer to the opportunity you have to capitalize on the increasing emphasis that is being placed on the tourist trade in our coastal areas. This, without doubt, is one of North Carolina's virtually untapped reservoirs of wealth. The establishment of the National Seashore Park is providing a much needed impetus in that region and national interest is gradually coming to focus on the attractions that our coast has to offer. A good indication of future opportunities in this area can be seen in the fact that only recently the popular magazine, *Sports Illustrated,* devoted nine pages to a detailed description of the hunting and fishing facilities on our Outer Banks. This type of promotion will bring increasing numbers of visitors to this coastal region and you will be missing a fabulous opportunity if you do not take advantage of their presence.

Because of this great potential, it is more important than ever that we give immediate attention to the devastation that is being wrought on our Outer Banks by the ravages of storm and ocean. The Banks are literally being eaten away and it is quite possible that within the foreseeable future this historic, beautiful, and potentially rich portion of our state will be lost to the Atlantic Ocean. I do not have to tell you what such a loss would mean to these "mainland" coastal counties. Obviously, we cannot permit this to happen. We must find a solution to this problem, and we must find it as soon as possible.

This is not a coastal problem; it is a North Carolina problem. Every citizen of this state has a vital interest in the Outer Banks. I emphasized my conviction on this point by dealing in detail with this matter in a speech several months ago in Asheville. I do feel, however, that the primary concern is felt here in the East, and it is from this section that the leadership must come to prompt immediate action on this situation.

In conclusion, I would like to commend the people of this community and this county for the effort they are exerting to bring desirable industry to this section. I would especially like to commend the Jaycees for their cooperation with our Department of Conservation and Development in the preparation of the community data sheet, setting forth this community's vital statistics. This is the kind of effort that pays big dividends. Let me add, however, that you must guard against directing all your energies toward attracting outside industry. The opportunities available here in diversified farming, food processing, forestry, and small industries are limitless, and you are missing a good bet if you fail to capitalize on these opportunities yourselves.

Again, let me thank you for the opportunity of coming here and participating in this wonderful event. It is evident that you possess the community spirit and the intelligent leadership that, in the very near future, will bring to this community, this county, and this great section of our state an increasingly higher standard of living and a better way of life for your people.

Thank you!

ADDRESS AT THE EIGHTH ANNUAL CONVENTION OF THE NORTH CAROLINA WHOLESALERS ASSOCIATION, INCORPORATED

DURHAM
February 7, 1959

[This was the Governor's second address in Durham within less than two weeks, and was characterized by the same note of optimism and enthusiasm that prevailed in his speech before the Board of Conservation and Development meeting on January 26. For the wholesalers he reviewed North Carolina's progress in road building, education, agriculture, and industry, and in a broad projection of the state's industrial future, forecast developments which he expected to occur within the next twenty years. North Carolina, he said, "is moving rapidly toward its rendezvous with prosperity. . . . Our opportunities are unlimited; our resources abundant; our people energetic and determined. With these tools at our command, we cannot fail in our dream of building a more prosperous North Carolina."]

I would like to thank you for giving me the opportunity to participate briefly in the Eighth Annual Convention of the North Carolina Wholesalers Association. This is my second visit to Durham in less than two weeks, and I am pleased to say that on both occasions I have been given the privilege of addressing groups of North Carolinians who have a vital interest in the future development of our state. Twelve days ago I met with the Board of Conservation and Development and was thrilled by the enthusiasm and optimism with which that dedicated and energetic group viewed the future possibilities for economic development in North Carolina. Tonight, I am in Durham again—this time to meet with a group of our citizens who share our interest in economic development and who stand to benefit tremendously from the era of prosperity envisioned by our Conservation and Development officials.

I am keenly aware of the important position that the wholesaler holds in our business world and in our present and future development programs. Your influence is felt at every level of business activity. Without the wholesaler, much of the business operations in this state, or any other state for that matter, would grind to a halt in short order. Your merchandising knowledge is valuable to the producer, the retailer, and the consumer. As wholesalers, you can reflect consumer desires and trends and have considerable influence in determining the quality, quantity, and type of products that are produced and sold in our state. I had about thirty years experience in dealing with wholesalers throughout the country, and know some of your problems.

This is a great responsibility and one that I am sure you are well aware of. You must also be aware of the fact that as our state moves steadily forward in search of a better way of life for its people, this responsibility will increase in direct proportion to the progress made.

What kind of progress can we expect? What changes will take place within the next, five, ten, or twenty years? How will these changes effect the wholesaler? I know that I do not have to tell a group of North Carolina businessmen how difficult it is to predict, with any great degree of accuracy, conditions that will exist even two or three years in the future. When we attempt to look several decades ahead, the task becomes even more difficult and we greatly increase the possibility that our predictions will be too conservative with regard to some things in a dynamic state like North Carolina. I think it is important, however, that we try to look and plan as far ahead as possible; for only when we know what to expect can we forge the tools that will be needed to insure the future prosperity of our people.

Two items of tremendous concern to far-sighted businessmen are population and income trend. If North Carolina's present rate of population increase continues for the next two decades, it will be necessary for us to provide living accommodations, employment, and other necessities for approximately 1,500,000 more citizens, and most of them will go to our rapidly developing urban centers. A projection of the population increase over the past decade shows that we may expect our present population of 4,498,000 to rise to between 5,900,000 and 6,000,000 people. Even so, the North Carolinian of 1980 can expect to enjoy a standard of living considerably higher than that enjoyed today. On a basis of the average per capita income increase during the years from 1947 through 1957, the per capita income in 1980 could exceed $3,450. This, of course, represents a considerable increase over the $1,317 recorded on 1957. What does this mean to the wholesaler? Simply this — there will be 1,500,000 more consumers creating demands for the goods that he supplies, and the purchasing power available with which to secure those goods will have more than doubled.

It is also significant to note that our civilian labor force is expected to increase by more than 500,000 people in the next twenty years. Our experts, who base their predictions on past growth, estimate that the North Carolina labor force—which includes non-agricultural employment and employment in manufacturing — will rise from the present 1,850,000 people to at least 2,400,000 within the next fifteen to twenty years.

Highways hold great importance for the wholesaler in terms of both direct and indirect benefits. A good highway system means lower production costs on the materials you handle, lower costs when you acquire those materials, and additional savings when you distribute those materials to the retail market. Carry it a step further, this could mean lower prices to the consumer, resulting in more sales, a faster turn over, increased production, and greater profit all the way down the line. Our highway officials anticipate that by 1980 the interstate highway system will have been completed, with its 775 miles of completely controlled access facilities crisscrossing our state from north to south and east to west.

Spur roads, connecting with the interstate system, will be developed on a limited access basis and urban traffic will move through most cities on expressways or belt lines without any delay points. Our highway planners, are, at the present time, proceeding on the assumption that traffic growth will continue at normal rates and that the traffic on our highways will increase by at least 100 percent within the next fifteen to twenty years. To facilitate traffic flow throughout the state, especially in urban areas where the more complicated bottlenecks occur, the Highway Commission is working more and more with cities and towns on cooperative traffic studies, and it is believed that by 1980 master thoroughfare plans will have been developed for most of our strategically located municipalities; also legislation to be considered soon could aid municipalities in their highway problems.

These, of course, are just a few of the things that will affect the operation of your businesses in the years ahead. It is vitally important that you consider these fatcors because they not only form a basis for future business planning, but they also illustrate the reasons for our optimism about the future of North Carolina and its people.

Fortunately, we do not have to look to the decades ahead for evidence of the fact that North Carolina is moving rapidly toward its rendezvous with prosperity. That evidence is all around us today, beneficially affecting every remote facet of our economy. We are growing industrially. In the field of agriculture, the future looks brighter as we begin to face up to our changing farm problems.

Our mutual friend, Senator John Jordan, has indicated an interest in the farm problem, and I'm sure there is no serious disagreement between us on that—or any other basic matters. The

farm problem is very important, and I would like to say that I
have tried consistently for several years now to challenge our
farmers and farm leaders to realize —

1. That our farm economy is changing rapidly.
2. That the tobacco program is in serious danger and can
   affect our state's economy adversely.
3. That we should diversify our agriculture.
4. That we should establish many processing plants to use
   our farm products.
5. That we should find jobs for displaced farmers — realizing
   that all over America the percentage of farm workers is
   decreasing.

The response from farmers, farm leaders, and others has been
most encouraging, and North Carolina is moving ahead rapidly
in agricultural diversification and the establishment of more food
processing plants. The Governor's Farm Advisory Committee has
been most helpful in acting as a constructive forum for discussion and action on current farm problems.

The effort to strengthen and diversify our industrial development program on a state-wide basis, and give new jobs to farmers
and others, reached new heights during 1958 with $253,074,000
invested in new and expanded facilities. A total of 423 industrial
enterprises were either initiated or expanded during the past
year, providing 21,757 new jobs and adding $72,633,000 to our
annual payroll. As I said in my biennial message Thursday,
North Carolina has increased its investments by 32.5 per cent in
1958 while the national average was *down* 17.4 per cent.

Equally significant, to my way of thinking, is the fact that,
in addition to providing new jobs and job opportunities, 1958's
industrial development effort reflected a continuation of the trend
toward industrial diversification. This fact is clearly illustrated
by figures compiled recently by the Department of Conservation and Development and released several weeks ago from my
office. These figures show that of the new plants established in
North Carolina in 1958, metal working industries led all industrial categories with total investments of $67,155,000. Chemicals
were second with an outlay of $63,087,000. Tobacco manufac-
turers were third with expenditures of $33,605,000 and textiles

were fourth with $30,014,000. Food and kindred products were fifth, and furniture and fixtures were sixth.

We have every right to be excited about the growth of all these industries in our state, not simply because they reflect economic progress, but because it shows that our established industries — tobacco, textiles, and furniture — are enjoying a normal, healthy growth while our newer industries — metal working, electronics, and chemicals — show that we are keeping pace with the fast moving world in which we live.

Another exciting development, highlighted by the 1958 record, is the progress made in our food processing industry. During the past year, more than $21,000,000 was invested in sixty-three new and expanded facilities designed primarily to process, package, and market our agricultural products. This development alone accounted for 2,346 new jobs and added $6,814,000 to the industries' payroll figures. The truly significant aspect of the food processing picture is that we have only begun to develop the tremendous potential that is available to us in this field in North Carolina. There can be no question about the fact that these opportunities exist. Our job is to find them and develop them to the best advantage.

This is a responsibility that you as wholesalers must share. By actively participating in efforts designed to build our food processing industry, you make, not only a good investment for your own business, but an investment in the economic future of your state.

Many of the products that you supply to your retail outlets are produced in other states and shipped into North Carolina. The transportation of these goods increases their cost to you, reduces your margin of profit, necessitates higher retail prices, and restricts sales. Add also the fact that production profits go to out-of-state producers and it becomes perfectly apparent that we in North Carolina are missing a good bet.

Many of these products — especially food products which I know interest most of the members of this association—can be produced profitably right here in our own state. As a matter of fact, many are being produced at the present time — and there is every indication that our farmers are more than willing to ex-

pand their food production operations if they can be assured of
a suitable market. This is desirable for many reasons. Of particular importance to all of us is the fact that it will contribute the
much needed balance to our agricultural economy which I've
mentioned and, consequently, to the over-all economy of the
state. From the standpoint of the wholesaler, the increased production of marketable food products in our own state would reduce the initial cost of the products you handle and result in
greater profits for your businesses. It would also make it possible for you to work in closer contact with your suppliers and
thereby exercise greater control over the quality of the goods you
handle. It is easy to see how this would also work to the advantage
of the producer.

Let me add, too, that this cooperative approach applies, not
only to our growing food producing, processing, and marketing
industry, but to all our industries. You are primarily concerned
with your own businesses and with activities affecting those
businesses. This is as it should be. But it is especially important
that you not lose sight of the fact that as North Carolinians you
have a responsibility to the state as a whole. One of the principal
reasons for the gains registered in our development program in
recent years has been the emergence of a wonderful cooperative
spirit among all our business and industrial interests. In my
capacity as governor, I have endeavored to promote this spirit
and to coordinate the tremendous amount of energy it has
generated. I have been gratified with the results of these efforts.

I know that it isn't necessary for me to outline for a group
of North Carolina businessmen the many ways that you can contribute to the economic growth of our state. Most of you, I am
sure, are already engaged in development programs at the local,
county, and regional level. The work you have done in the past
— and are doing at the present time — is deserving of commendation. As a matter of fact, the existence of this association indicates
that you are aware of the importance of collective effort in the
pursuit of your individual goals. You know the value of working
together, and you know that only by working together can the
people of North Carolina realize their full potential.

I would like to urge that, in the weeks and months ahead,
each of you take an active interest in the affairs of our General

Assembly. Many issues to come before the legislature will affect you directly. Every issue to come before the legislature will affect you one way or the other. And, make no mistake about the fact that the support — or lack of it — given the members of the General Assembly by the members of this association and all our citizens, will vitally affect the effectiveness with which our representatives deal with the problems confronting them.

As I pointed out in my biennial message on Thursday, many of the problems and issues to come before the legislature will be recurring ones, as is the case with revenues and appropriations. Other important decisions will have to be made to compensate for the changes that have taken place in our economic and cultural life. I told the members of the General Assembly that our best efforts will be required merely to meet the challenges that are already apparent to us. This applies to every North Carolinian and not just to the members of the legislature.

As you know, the 1957 General Assembly authorized and directed me to appoint a total of ten study commissions or committees. This action was based on the knowledge that there were several major problem areas affecting both state and local government that merited special attention. Study groups were named to deal with such matters as taxes, municipal government, school finance, the constitution, governmental reorganization, map laws, nursing and boarding homes, cancer, the University Trustees, and motor boat regulations. Still another important study that has been under way for the past three years, which I hope you will look at, has dealt with our court system. With your help we can improve our court system. It is all too apparent that the months to come will be crucial ones in the history of our state. Great changes have taken place since the last session of the General Assembly. These changes, have, for the most part, been good changes — reflecting the beneficial transformation that is taking place.

As I tried to indicate to the General Assembly Thursday, our future, its economy and its "Better Living" are inseparably bound to education. We need and must have more and better schools and colleges, with programs that are practical and up-to-date and efficient. And, we should never forget the fundamentals, the liberal arts, as we develop a rounded program.

On Monday night I shall spell out some recommendations for support of schools and colleges, and I hope they have your backing. The fundamental of getting support from all levels of government is so sound and far-reaching that I believe it will be supported. Governor Aycock, nearly sixty years ago, said every child should be encouraged to "burgeon out" all that is within him; and I feel the same principle should be encouraged with counties and local communities where school support is concerned.

I have absolute faith in the direction in which we are moving, and I am confident that our efforts, if continued, will bring a better way of life to our people. The task ahead is twofold. We must consolidate the gains that have been achieved, and we must maintain the momentum that has brought us this far. I can assure you that your state government will continue to do everything within its power to assist local and regional groups in their development programs — and I am certain that we can count on organizations such as yours to contribute to this effort whenever and wherever the opportunity presents itself.

Let me at this point, mention a final item that I understand a few members of this association have raised some questions about. This is the proposal advanced by the small retailers and others, that the present system of sales taxes be replaced by a wholesale sales tax — primarily for the purpose of simplifying the compliance problem and facilitating administration of the tax laws. The advocates of this plan feel that these objectives would be achieved if the state's 70,000 retailers could pay their tax to the 7,000 wholesalers when they purchase merchandise—thereby reducing the number of firms the state would have to deal with to one-tenth the present number.

I have discussed this proposal with our Revenue Department officials, and it has been pointed out that there are a number of things that should be considered with regard to the plan. For example, if all consumer purchases in North Carolina were from local retail merchants who had purchased all of their goods from North Carolina wholesale establishments, the plan would be workable and desirable. Such is not the case, however. Many lines of merchandise are purchased from out-of-state jobbers, wholesalers, and manufacturers. Other items are purchased from both in-state and out-of state wholesalers. In view of these facts, it would be necessary—if the wholesale tax plan is to work properly—to levy a rather high rate wholesale tax and at the same time to levey a tax on retail merchants based on their purchases of goods for resale, with a tax credit against the purchase tax for the tax already paid to wholesalers. If such a levy were initiated, it would very likely be necessary to levy a one-time floor tax on the retailers, based on the amount of goods on hand.

From the standpoint of the retail merchant, such a change would have some immediate financial drawbacks, plus compliance problems at least as great as those presented by the present sales tax. Since the retail merchant would have to pay the tax when he purchased goods from the wholesaler, it would necessitate an immediate increase in the retailer's working capital requirements, and the retail merchants, on the whole, would lose the benefit of the present discount for prompt payment of sales tax obligations. It is estimated that this would amount to approximately $2,000,000 per year. There is also some question as to whether the auditing burden of the state would be lessened.

From the standpoint of the wholesale merchant, such a tax levy would impose considerable business hardship and at the same time create a difficult compliance problem. The greatest hardship on the wholesaler would be that such a tax would tend to encourage the purchase of merchandise by retailers from out-of-state sources, since those sources would be outside North Carolina's jurisdiction. This problem would be intensified by the fact that the wholesale tax levy at a rate high enough to produce the revenue that the retail sales tax now produces would be higher than the wholesaler's margin on many items now handled. The compliance problem would be difficult since it would probably be necessary for wholesalers to use stamps to place on invoices to retailers to indicate payment of the tax levy by the retailer.

From the standpoint of the public, the change would mean that since the retailer would have paid the tax when purchasing his goods, the tax levy would be included in the markup and the taxpayer would have no way of knowing how much tax he is paying. With the tax included in the markup, the amount of money paid by the public would be larger for the state to realize the same amount of revenue it realizes under the present system. Here again we would have an incentive for the public to go out-of-state to purchase desired goods.

I will not go into details on the administrative and compliance aspects of this proposal, except to express the view of our revenue officials that problems would be more numerous under the wholesale tax system.

In conclusion, let me re-state my conviction that there is no problem facing this state that cannot be overcome if we will continue to work together in the future as we have in the past. Our opportunities are unlimited; our resources abundant; our people, energetic and determined. With these tools at our command, we cannot fail in our dream of building a more prosperous North Carolina.

Thank you.

_____

ADDRESS AT A JOINT MEETING OF THE WADESBORO MERCHANTS ASSOCIATION AND CHAMBER OF COMMERCE

WADESBORO
February 20, 1959

[Following an excursion into Anson County history, the Governor made use of this occasion to defend the 1959-61 budget which had been presented to the General Assembly a short time previously. He advocated in particular the provision calling for an incentive plan whereby the state would offer approximately $10,000,000 a year to the counties for approximately $6,000,000 of matching funds to be used exclusively for increasing teachers' salaries. He also expressed confidence that the withholding "windfall" would enable North Carolina to balance its budget without resorting to new taxes, while "most of the states are making up deficits by increasing taxes." Concluding on a note of optimism that was typical of his speeches of this period, he declared himself " 'bullish' on North Carolina" and of the opinion that its economy "will continue to advance . . . and all of us can be happy about it."]

I am glad to be present at this meeting of the Chamber of Commerce and the Merchants Association here in Wadesboro. It is always a great pleasure for me to visit an area of this state that has stamped an indelible mark on our history, made signif-

Governor Hodges with Governor Robert E. Smylie of Idaho (*left*) and Governor LeRoy Collins of Florida (*right*) in Moscow during the American governors' visit to the U.S.S.R. in June, 1959.

Governor Hodges standing in Red Square, Moscow, during a visit to Russia with eight other American state governors during June and July, 1959.

icant contributions to our growth and development, and stands ready today to meet the challenges of the years ahead with confidence and determination. This description can be applied to many sections of North Carolina, but to none more appropriately than Anson County. Our history books attest to the richness of your heritage and to the significance of the contributions made here. Your presence this evening provides ample evidence of your enthusiasm and interest in the future.

The history of Anson County is also the history of Piedmont North Carolina — and it is a history that should be an everlasting source of pride and inspiration to those of you who are now charged with the responsibility of charting this region's course in the months and years that lie ahead.

Anson County was created in 1750 to provide political identity for the great numbers of Scotch-Irish, Germans, and Welsh that poured into this area from Virginia, Pennsylvania, and South Carolina during the preceding decade. Those who came from the North were driven largely by economic necessity, but they were, by no means, devoid of the pioneering spirit that was to stand them in good stead in this "back country" section of the colony. They came down the "Wagon Road," following the river valleys, and it was here that they found the freedom and the opportunities they sought.

Some writers have described these settlers — particularly the Scotch-Irish—as "clannish, contentious, and hard to get along with." Certainly, they were independent people, capable of making their own decisions and holding tenaciously to those decisions once made. The Scotch-Irishman had tremendous faith in himself — a characteristic that is amply illustrated by the words of one brief, to the point, prayer attributed to him, "Lord, grant that I may always be right, for Thou knowest that I am hard to turn." This trait became quite evident when, a short time later, he appeared on the state's political scene and initiated the movement that would eventually bring an end to the frequently high-handed domination of colonial government by the eastern counties.

Another universal characteristic among these early North Carolinians was their capacity for thrift. One historian has labeled the Scotch-Irishman as a man "who keeps the commandments of

God, and just about everything else he can get his hands on."

There can be little question, however, about the fact that the Scotch-Irish, German, and Welsh settlers made a tremendous contribution to the economic, spiritual, and cultural development of North Carolina. They were a hearty, industrious people and their influence is felt, not only here in Anson County, but in every section of our state today.

In the beginning, Anson County was tied to North Carolina only politically. Its trade routes ran north and south along the Catawba and Yadkin Rivers into South Carolina and, eventually, to Charleston. There was little to encourage commerce with the eastern counties. Serviceable roads were non-existent. Rivers simply didn't run in the right direction. And it is entirely probable that the attitude of the easterners toward their "back-woods" neighbors served to discourage east-west trade for a number of years.

Boundary disputes and other conflicts developed between the two Carolinas, however, with the result that the east and west factions in North Carolina were forced to, at least, acknowledge their political relationship. South Carolina placed heavy duties on goods imported from North Carolina. We retaliated by placing an even heavier duty on spirituous liquors brought into Anson County from South Carolina. We also enacted a law forbidding South Carolina cattle to range into North Carolina. A much more sensible step was taken in 1762 when the North Carolina lawmakers incorporated the town of Campellton at the head of navigation on the Cape Fear River. They did so with the expressed hope that "the trade of the counties of Anson and Rowan, which at present centers at Charleston, South Carolina, to the great prejudice of this Province, will be drawn to the said town."

This act acknowledged the importance of cooperation within the colony. It was only a beginning — and a meager one, at that— but it brought two great sections of this state closer together and sowed the seeds that would germinate during the decades that followed to produce the wonderful esprit de corps that characterizes the people of North Carolina today. Sectional differences would continue, for they were the natural product of geographical variety, religious differences, and differing types of social life grounded on differences in economy. Add also the political factors which became increasingly potent causes of sectional strife. Personal ambitions, family jealousies, and local rivalries also played a part.

All of the causes were interrelated. Geographical factors contributed to economic differences in agriculture, industry, and trade in the various regions. Economic differences created social distinctions. Racial and social factors were involved in religious rivalries. And, needless to say, all of these factors contributed to political controversies.

There was one other factor that drew the people of the east and west closer together — in spite of their differences on other matters. The people of both sections took common delight in making life as difficult as possible for the governor of the state. And they were especially quick to persist in this practice when they felt the governor was indulging himself at the expense of the taxpayers. I might add that, with respect to this latter item, perhaps things have changed very little in the past two centuries.

Governor Tryon had the dubious honor of being particularly adept at drawing the east and west closer together by means of over-indulgence. He came through this section in the summer of 1767 en route to the Indian lands to supervise the establishment of a boundary line "between the frontiers of North Carolina and the Cherokee Hunting Grounds." The settlers in this region readily agreed to the need for a boundary, but they openly expressed the view that it was not at all necessary for Governor Tryon to undertake the project personally. They became mildly irritated when the Governor marched through on his way to the west, accompanied by two regiments of militia, sixteen servants and assistants, some Indian helpers and only two surveyors. The westerners' irritation lost its mildness when it was learned that the expedition would cost roughly 1,490 pounds. The final blow came when they learned that the actual running of the line was not begun until Governor Tryon and his cavalcade had returned home. Spokesmen for the western counties roared that the Governor's expedition was a "pompous, ridiculous, unnecessary and wasteful expenditure" of public funds. A year later, the Piedmont settlers provided evidence that they had not forgotten the incident by presenting a signed petition to the legislature, condemning the Governor and other officials for their abuse of power.

Even in these modern, progressive days we still have east-west-Piedmont feelings where state government is concerned — but more and more we are getting together, and looking at common problems from a more state-wide viewpoint.

Here in Wadesboro and Anson County is ample evidence that you are interested in progress. It is evident here this evening in the fact that two organizations, representing a wide variety of interests, have met with but a single objective in mind — that of promoting the growth and development of your community and your county. Your enthusiasm indicates that you have that "something extra" in the way of community spirit that frequently means the difference between making progress and maintaining the status quo. What better way is there to insure progress than for community and civic leaders to sit down together, to discuss their mutual problems, analyze their opportunities, determine their objectives, and formulate ways and means of attaining those objectives?

The challenge before you now is to determine the best means by which you can take full advantage of your community resources and spirit. Let's look at the per capita income figures for your county. The figures do not reflect the vast natural and human resources that your community and your county possess. Bearing in mind that the per capita income average for North Carolina counties is $1,317 and that we rank forty-fifth among the states, what is your county's position? According to the latest statistics available, Anson County ranks seventy-third among our 100 counties with a per capita income of $774. Only one of your neighboring counties — Union — stands below you with a $763 per capita income and a ranking of seventy-fourth. Among your other adjoining counties, Stanly is ranked thirty-second in the state with an income of $1,154, Richmond stands thirty-sixth with $1,117, and Montgomery is rated fortieth with a per capita income of $1,091. Of the eleven counties that compose your Piedmont Area Development Association, only four are classified below fiftieth place in North Carolina. These are Lincoln, Cleveland, Union, and Anson. Six of the remaining counties rate among the top thirty counties of the state, four are among the top twenty, and two—Mecklenburg and Cabarrus—are classified among the top ten.

I have cited these figures not to embarrass or condemn, but simply to emphasize the fact that there is much work to be done if the people of this community and county are to obtain the benefits inherent in the opportunities available to them. And while statistics — especially those relating to per capita income — do not always present an accurate picture of the conditions that exist within a county or an area of the state, they are, at least indicative.

Let me say at this point that the picture I have drawn of the counties in this area is considerably brighter than the picture to be found in some other sections of North Carolina. You face a great challenge as you set to work in your efforts to move up the economic ladder. But, you can find some consolation in the knowledge that there are others who have even further to climb. I have visited many of these areas in the past year, however, and in almost every instance I was thrilled by the enthusiasm and confidence with which those people are facing up to the problems confronting them.

I would especially like to commend the people of Anson County for their foresight in the realm of forestry. It is an established fact that North Carolina's forests hold one of the major keys to our growth in the future. Much has been accomplished in this field in recent years. We have come to recognize the value of this industry and we have displayed a willingness to take whatever steps may be necessary to see that our people get the maximum benefit from this great resource. Almost 20,000,000 acres in North Carolina are covered by forests. This represents well over 60 per cent of the total land area. The value of forest products derived from the wooded land exceeded $750,000,000 in the last count. These values are almost equally divided among lumber, plywood, pulp and paper products, and furniture. The value of pulp and paper products alone has increased roughly 800 per cent in North Carolina since 1939.

Anson County apparently realized this potential several years ago and moved quickly to take advantage of the opportunities it offered. During the 1953-54 planting season, less than 200,000 pine seedlings were planted in Anson County. By 1955-56, the figure had risen to 752,000 seedlings. Agricultural losses and special promotional activities were largely responsible for the fact that in 1956-57 more than 2,840,000 seedlings were planted in this county. Last year the figure rose to 4,224,000 and our forestry officials estimate that during the 1958-59 season a minimum of 6,500,000 pine seedlings will be planted in Anson County soil.

Three years ago, when more than 1,000,000 seedlings arrived in this county on a single day, your county agent called the event "the dawning of a new day", for Anson County farmers. I believe that you will agree that events occurring since that date have proved him absolutely right. And, while it will be fifteen to twenty years before the whole benefit or the current activity is realized, it is comforting to know that this stable economic factor exists. At least four companies are in the market for your pulpwood, and there is every indication that the demand will continue to exceed the supply for many years to come.

This, of course, is only one facet of your economic development program. You have a responsibility to continue, or better still, increase, your activities designed to attract industries to this area. This is a long-range proposition, and you should not expect results overnight. Determination and perseverance are the prime fatcors in this type of activity. If you are easily discouraged, you cannot hope to succeed. I know, for instance, that many of you who worked diligently to bring the proposed $12,000,000 atomic reactor to Anson County have been disappointed at the delays encountered in this project. This is certainly understandable, but I see no cause for you to become discouraged. We fervently hope that the reactor will be constructed as soon as certain decisions are made in Washington, D. C. I do not see how we can question the sincerity of the reactor promoters on this matter. Nor do I see how we can doubt that, in this atomic age, the need for this reactor is growing.

I can see a great future here in Anson and adjoining counties, especially when the industrial reactor gets started. Of course, the testing reactor will employ hundreds, and satellite or supporting plants will develop nearby if we plan and work properly. If each man in this room, and others like you, determines to do his part to make this a bigger and greater community, you will not fail.

In nearby Rockingham, Richmond County, things are looking better. New industries are being announced, and a community that has had heavier blows than most places, is beginning to look up. I recall a visit in my office some months ago of determined city and county officials and community leaders from Richmond County, and they were determined to pull themselves up.

It makes all of us proud to know that North Carolina, although ranking low in the United States in per capita income standings, with its agricultural economy threatened, has determined to lift itself up and last year had its biggest year in history in new investments and in new and expanded industries. The total was over $225,000,000, and $75,000,000 in new payrolls, and much of this is in agricultural and food processing plants which help our farmers make the transition from a changing one-crop economy to a diversified agriculture-business economy.

We are happily diversifying our crops from tobacco to hogs and cattle, fruits and vegetables and we are constantly improving our farming methods.

It has been my extreme pleasure to work with other state people and many local chamber of commerce and industrial groups in telling the state's story to hundreds of prospects all over America. Our story is one of a state alive to its opportunities, with its towns and cities and counties planning for their future. It is a story of fiscal and financial responsibility, and government with a healthy attitude toward free enterprise and business development. It's a story of a state and its cities cleaning up its streets and highways, and spotlighting the litterbug. It's a state that believes in education and research, although its people may differ on how best to develop financially these necessary ingredients. It's a state that doesn't have give-a-way or gimmicks for newcomers, but expects all to be good citizens, individual or corporate.

We will continue our progress both in the state and Anson County so long as we put the state and/or the community first. I have a great desire to see the smaller counties grow and prosper, and if they develop and exercise leadership they will grow. Too many times, as I have said, smaller and poorer counties statistically, reach out for state aid when they would get further faster if they did things for themselves!

We will make even greater progress in the future if we join together and pass some needed legislation that will help make us a better state, and from which all of our 100 counties will benefit.

I am talking of improved courts and a better state constitution, sounder property tax laws, more far-reaching and sounder school financing which will help us close the ever-widening gap in teachers' salaries in North Carolina as compared to the U. S. A. May I take this opportunity to point out something about teachers' pay and school support which I recommended in my budget message, and which few of the papers have mentioned. I refer to the incentive plan which offers $10,000,000 a year of state money to the counties for approximately $6,000,000 of matching funds, which if used exclusively for teachers' salaries would provide a total raise of over 13 per cent. This is in addition to the week's extra pay recommended!

However, I am not greatly concerned, as I am sure the General Assembly will after full deliberation, make the best decisions possible for the state. This 1959 General Assembly is fortunate that it can balance its budget without raising its taxes, and at the same time add $50,000,000 in new appropriations or a full 10 per cent increase in appropriations for state services. Very few states can do this. On the contrary, most of the states are making up deficits or increasing taxes. I am proud of our state's position.

Let me give you some very interesting figures from our Budget Bureau which will illustrate two very important things in state finance which much of the public and many of the legislators do not understand.

GENERAL FUND APPROPRIATIONS FOR CURRENT OPERATIONS AND REVENUE ESTIMATES

Biennium	Appropriations	Revenue Estimates	Appropriations for Current Operating Expenditures in Excess of Estimated Revenues
1947-49	$206,148,563	$186,172,600	$19,975,963
1949-51	288,250,735	261,661,000	26,589,735
1951-53	358,413,120	343,081,038	15,332,082
1953-55	407,828,467	379,454,428	28,374,039
1955-57	427,648,895*	413,681,118	13,967,777
1957-59	518,632,693**	486,394,928	32,237,765

* NOTE: $19,000,000 added in new taxes
** NOTE: Does not include $2,000,000 paid to retire bond anticipation notes.

This means we are in good shape and our withholding tax "windfall" is not unusual.

I am "bullish" on North Carolina, and think our economy will continue to advance. We have a great future in North Carolina and all of us can be happy about it.

In closing, may I offer this advice. In all your efforts to develop your community and your county, let us not forget that all our planning — whether immediate or long-range — should be made in terms of the individual family and its standard of living. Whatever we do, whatever our source of economic productivity, we must always think in terms of human beings and their capabilities, their hopes, their dreams, and their desire to give their children the best that life has to offer. If we do this, we shall not fail in our efforts to raise the living standard of our people and make life far more meaningful and far more secure for all of our citizens. I would like to commend the Wadesboro Merchants Association and Chamber of Commerce for their efforts in the past and for the great promise that they hold for the future.

Thank you!

ADDRESS AT A CHAMBER OF COMMERCE BANQUET

MOORESVILLE

March 6, 1959

[Governor Hodges and local dignitaries honored publisher Tom Mc-Knight and the staff of his *Mooresville Tribune* at a dinner on the occasion of this paper's receiving the North Carolina Press Association's first prize for community service in 1958. John I. Anderson, president of the North Carolina Press Association, presented the award along with second and third prizes to the Goldsboro *News-Argus* and the *Charlotte News*, respectively. The Governor commended the prize-winners as well as the state's newspapers generally, commented briefly upon the history of Iredell County, and praised "the wonderful community-industry relationship" which he found in Mooresville in contrast with the industrial conflict which had developed in connection with a strike that was currently in progress at Henderson.]

I am indebted to the Mooresville Chamber of Commerce, the wonderful people of this community, and the North Carolina Press Association for the opportunity given me to come here to

this wide awake, progressive community for the purpose of participating in what I consider an exciting and extremely significant
occasion. Perhaps, more directly, my appreciation should be
directed to Tom McKnight and the staff of the *Mooresville
Tribune,* who, by their unstinting devotion to the highest principles of their profession, are directly responsible for our being
here. I am proud to have a small part in honoring my old friend
and college-mate, Tom McKnight.

This event is especially gratifying because it recognizes perhaps the most important function that an individual or corporate
citizen of a community can perform. I refer, of course, to sincere,
dedicated community service—the kind of service that is rendered
with selfless enthusiasm, motivated by a genuine desire to
contribute to the development and general well-being of the
community as a whole.

We are here this evening to recognize not just one individual
and the medium through which he has served his community, but
to recognize what this individual and his medium represents—
the responsibility of every citizen in every community to give
enthusiastically of his time and talents to the building of a progressively better way of life for every other citizen within his
realm of influence. Certainly, there can be no nobler purpose
in life for an individual or institution — especially an institution
such as a newspaper which, by its very nature, is uniquely
equipped to render such service.

I would like to commend publisher Tom McKnight and his
staff on their acceptance of this community responsibility, and for
the energetic manner in which the *Mooresville Tribune* has
sought to meet the many challenges that are inherent in aggressive,
responsible civic leadership. To the people of Mooresville and
Iredell County, I would like to say that the honor that comes to
this newspaper tonight is a great distinction. This honor represents journalistic achievement in its highest form. It is the greatest honor that can be bestowed upon a newspaper in this state by
the North Carolina Press Association. It is a recognition that carries an added element of distinction by virtue of the fact that
it is awarded by those best qualified to judge journalistic excellence, namely, the other newspapers of this state.

The principal criterion for this award is *service to the community,* and for this reason each of you who is associated with the *Tribune* can take great pride in your achievements. By the same token, the people of this community and this county can, and should, and I am sure *do* take pride in this newspaper.

I would also like to recognize and congratulate the staffs of the Goldsboro *News Argus* and the *Charlotte News* (two other good newspapers) which I understand placed second and third respectively in the state-wide competition for this coveted award. Every person connected with these newspapers merits the praise of the communities they have served, for they have made a contribution that will have a beneficial and lasting effect on the economic, cultural, and spiritual life of their reading communities.

To me, the presentation of annual community service awards to our outstanding newspapers by the members of their own profession represents far more than mere public recognition of professional accomplishments. To me it represents, not only acceptance of community responsibility by the majority of our North Carolina newspapers, but an open assertion that superior achievement in this field is a desirable and commendable objective.

I am sure this audience is well aware of the fact that a responsible, alert, and energetic newspaper is one of the greatest assets that any community can possess. There is practically no limit to the amount of good that can be accomplished by such a paper. It has frequently been said that a good newspaper will stand like a mirror before a community — reflecting its moods and character, its strong points and its shortcomings, its successes and its failures, its past, its present, and its hope for the future. Certainly, the good newspaper will reflect these things. But, if it is to be a real asset to the community, if it is to exploit fully its potential for community service, it must do more. Above all, it must lead and lead honestly. It must point the way in clear and unmistakable terms. It must praise when praise is warranted and, by the same token, it must condemn when condemnation is justified.

To be really effective, the newspaper must be so intimately a part of the community that it feels, not the delayed action of the pulse, but the life-giving warmth and strength of the heartbeat itself. It must be so much a part of the people that it not only shares their pain and sorrow, their joy and happiness, but naturally anticipates these emotions even before they are felt by the community. This task is not an easy one, for the newspaper, if it is to exercise true leadership, must also stand apart. It must maintain an objectivity which at times may not be compatible with the more subjective or more sensitive feelings of the people and the community it seeks to serve. It must be courageous, but not reckless. It must be responsive to the public will, but it must never sacrifice integrity as the price for popularity. It should not be antagonistic without justification, but it should have the strength to stand alone when it knows its cause is just.

North Carolinians can be justly proud of the fact that the great majority of their newspapers meet the qualifications that I have outlined. I have said on many occasions that our state is blessed with good newspapers as compared to many other states. The policies of our North Carolina papers are controlled, for the most part, by men and women who recognize the responsibility of their position and meet those responsibilities with integrity and understanding.

The people of this state owe a great debt of gratitude to these men and women for the very real contribution they have made to the development of our individual communities and our entire state in recent years. They have been a primary force in the all-important effort to educate our people as to our income situation, to the need for industry, and for diversification in both industry and agriculture. I do not minimize the role played by our chambers of commerce, merchants' associations and other development organizations, for without them, little progress would be made. Still, I am sure that these organizations will agree that their jobs would be considerably more difficult and their successes less frequent were it not for the existence of a cooperative press.

Here in Mooresville, you are fortunate in having both an active newspaper and an energetic chamber of commerce. Add the fact that these two forces are backed up by an equally energetic and ambitious citizenry and you discover the reasons for the atmosphere of well-being and confidence that prevails in this community. Of particular importance is the fact that this sense of well-being is maintained in an atmosphere devoid of complacency. This highly desirable condition—while enviable—

is by no means surprising to those who know the history of this region and the traditional character of its people.

Traveling across this bustling yet beautiful county today, it is difficult to imagine that little more than a century and a half ago Iredell County was the prairie land of North Carolina, a part of the vast, rolling plateau that formed this Piedmont region. Professor E. R. Rockwell of Davidson College has described the Iredell County of 150 years ago as "open and mostly clear of timber, so that the sight could reach a great distance. The undergrowth was kept down by the Indians burning it over so often. The bottoms were thick canebrakes and the hills and plains were covered with a natural growth of wild peavines, which furnished abundant pasture for stock of all kinds.

"Buffaloes, bulls, bears, deer, panthers, etc., roamed through all the land, furnishing provisions for the early settlers as well as the savages. There are traditions connected with many spots where the ancestors of the present residents saw immense herds of buffalo."

These early settlers, who came from Pennsylvania around 1750, were Ulster and Highland Scots. There were, for the most part, simple, frugal, and enduring people, proud of their traditions, possessed of great faith in themselves and intensely religious. They settled first in the area west of present-day Statesville, and a short time later, in the areas further south. Others who came to settle in this promising region were the Scotch-Irish who came from the North, and the English, who migrated in a body from Montgomery County, Maryland. Cultural differences and other factors created animosities between these various racial groups—animosities that make it practically impossible to generalize about the character of the people who settled here. Certain conditions, however, created common interests and led to cooperative action. The ever-present threat of attack from hostile Indians and other perils related to frontier life formed a basis for effective, if not altogether enthusiastic, relationships. Of necessity, they were subsistence farmers, cultivating corn, oats, barley, and relatively small quantities of tobacco. Surplus tobacco was packed in large barrels and rolled to markets at Lynchburg and Richmond. Barley was used to make malt and corn was converted into whisky — one of the staples in this early day economy.

I think it is interesting to note that long before the American wild west came into its own, North Carolina's own brand of cowboy was riding the range right here in Iredell County. The broad plains and natural pastures were utilized by the pioneers to raise cattle in large numbers. The production of cattle far exceeded the needs of the settlers and since markets were limited in North Carolina, it was frequently necessary for the cattle men to drive their herds great distances. There are accounts on record of cattle drives originating here in Iredell County and terminating in such distant markets as Charleston and Philadelphia.

Two other important factors, held in comomn by the early residents of Iredell, were religious dedication and a traditional concern for the education of their young people. The first deed to land issued in this county went to a Presbyterian minister — a representative of the faith that would come to dominate the region. Next came the Methodists, then the Baptists, followed by other Protestant denominations. All found acceptance here in Iredell.

Some indication of the religious diversity can be seen in the fact that six denominations were represented at a revival meeting held in this county less than fifty years after its first settlers arrived. Fourteen Presbyterian ministers participated in this meeting, along with three Methodists, two Baptists, two Lutherans and one clergyman each from the Episcopal and Dutch Calvinist churches. Strange as it may seem, religious fervor and the distillery industry became dominant, if not entirely compatible, factors in the county's early days.

Even stranger is the fact that the churches, even those within a single denomination, differed widely in their views pertaining to spirituous beverages. One history relates that "Preachers chewed tobacco, smoked and frequently drank as hard as did the members of their congregations." It was not unusual according to this historian for ministers to conclude Sunday evening services and then "repair to a house where spirits were sold, and spend the evening in drinking, and sometimes deal out such hard blows to each other" that on at least one occasion they were hauled into court and fined. This social relationship between the minister and his people was a holdover of the old custom of holding "church ales", a practice that flourished in the British Isles in the time of King James I. The custom was abandoned in Britain and, eventually, in this country. Still a degree of tolerance remained in some quarters. One historical account points out that "Few ministers were criticized for taking a 'refreshment' within the privacy of their own homes 'to keep off the chills and fevers' . . . . but few congregations would tolerate a drinking parson."

Counteracting this comparatively liberal view were numerous highly effective ministers who opposed the use of spirits with such vehemence that life became unbearable for many in the county who could not or would not mend their ways. It is known that in the 1830's one congregation, composed largely of individuals whose livelihood depended largely upon the manufacture and sale of liquor, threatened to leave the county if their minister didn't relax his efforts to destroy their trade. Apparently the minister saw this as an excellent opportunity to rid the county of some undesirable residents. His condemnation of the liquor trade became even more persistent and within a year forty members of his congregation had loaded their belongings into wagons and headed west. Some moved as far away as Canada to escape the minister's wrath. Times have changed for the better!

This exodus, however, was only part of a trend that began at the dawn of the nineteenth century and continued for fifty years. During this period, Iredell participated in a large way in the mass departure of people from the Piedmont to the West. Many went west to claim land given them for service in the Revolutionary War. Others moved out when farming practices changed. The subsistence farmer felt the pressure of commercialized cotton growing and moved west to seek new opportunities. They moved on to Kentucky and Tennessee, then to Missouri and Illinois, and some even settled in Texas, Wyoming, Utah, and California. It is doubtful that they ever found a land more promising than the one they left behind. One writer has speculated that those who remained may have been less adventurous. But he didn't rule out the possibility that they simply had more stamina and stubbornness. To this conjecture I would like to add that it is even more probable that those who remained here in Iredell did so, not through lack of vision or ambition, but because of these qualities. They saw the great industrial and agricultural potential that existed here, the unlimited opportunities that the future held—and they wanted to contribute to and become a part of that future.

Iredell has come a long way since the days when her cowboys drove their cattle to market in Charleston and Philadelphia. Today, this county lays just claim to the title—"North Carolina's Number One Dairy County." Even more significant is the fact that this important industry is continuing to expand. In 1955, there were 9,200 cattle in the county. Today, the number exceeds 30,000. Some indication of the importance of this industry can be seen in the fact that in 1957, when gross farm income in the county registered a loss of $1,651,115, cattle and dairy products showed gains in excess of $580,000. All things considered, the agricultural picture is bright in Iredell County today. The trend is toward more cattle, fewer row crops, larger farms, more diversification, and a continuing interest in the development of even better farming practices.

All that has been said for Iredell's agriculture can be applied with even more enthusiasm to the county's industrial development. Commerce and industry have long been important factors in the area economy, but only in recent decades has it come to dominate the scene. This transition has been accomplished with a patience and ease that reflects great credit on the county and its people. There have been no great upheavals, no sudden acceleration, nothing to disrupt the orderly yet progressive development of this region. Foresight, confidence, determination, and planning have been the keys to this progress, and they have paid big dividends. Iredell ranks well up the per capita income ladder in North Carolina, and the position is justly deserved. I am very proud of Iredell and its progress.

No less can be said of Mooresville. Your progress in the past has been notable and, vastly more important, the opportunities available to you for future development are practically unlimited. Mooresville possesses all the qualities that a community needs to face the exciting years ahead with enthusiasm and confidence. Your mayor has been quoted as saying, "It is a joy to live in a community where there is such an atmosphere of responsibility." Your Chamber of Commerce manager has remarked that, "There aren't enough nights in the week for all the meetings they have here." What more can be said for the spirit of a community?

Governor Hodges examines a leaf of Soviet tobacco in the Armenian building at the Industrial and Agricultural Exposition in Moscow during the American state governors' visit to Russia in June and July, 1959.

Dr. Fred N. Briggs (*left*), dean of the University of California College of Agriculture at Davis, extends greetings to Governor Hodges and Voit Gilmore (*right*) during the Governor's visit to the West Coast in July, 1959, when he spent part of a day at Davis inspecting California's contributions to agricultural industry through engineering and food science.

Good living and continued prosperity thrive on this kind of spirit, and as long as you maintain this awareness of citizenship responsibility, you will go steadily forward.

I think it is particularly appropriate at this time to commend this community and its people for the wonderful community-industry relationship that exists here. We have seen this week what can happen to a community when this relationship ceases to exist. Such relationships are built on mutual trust and the acknowledgement of mutual responsibility. When this "partnership" is permitted to collapse, the result is disastrous and lasting. Scars from conflicts of this type do not heal quickly, sometimes never. The progress of many decades can be wiped out overnight —and with it goes the hopes and ambitions of many people. Let me urge you to do everything in your power to maintain the wholesome and mutually beneficial atmosphere that prevails here. It can be your community's greatest asset.

Let me conclude with a commendation to your Chamber of Commerce for the exceptionally fine job it has done since its organization in 1953. Working closely with your Development Association and the Mooresville Merchant's Association, you have exemplified the spirit of this community and its people. You have been aggressive and the evidences of your work are apparent. Your plans for cooperating with city officials in modernizing your business district are especially commendable. I understand that these plans call for redecorating many of your business houses, both inside and out, converting your Main Street into a mall, building several off-street parking lots, widening the streets in your business district, and making many other improvements. This is an ambitious undertaking and one that will require time to complete, but you will be repaid many times for your efforts.

It has been a great pleasure to visit with you on this wonderful occasion. Again, my congratulations to Tom McKnight and the staff of the *Mooresville Tribune,* and sincere best wishes in your continuing efforts to serve this community.

Thank you.

REMARKS AND INTRODUCTION OF CRAWFORD H.
GREENEWALT, PRESIDENT OF E. I. DUPONT DE
NEMOURS COMPANY AT A DINNER OF THE
NORTH CAROLINA CITIZENS ASSOCIATION

Raleigh
March 25, 1959

[During his six years in office, Governor Hodges was on the program
of four of the annual meetings of this group of businessmen interested
in keeping an eye on taxes and state spending. On this, as on previous
occasions, he took advantage of an opportunity to explain and defend the
biennial budget which was currently before the General Assembly.]

I am glad to attend this annual dinner sponsored by the North
Carolina Citizens Association, and to see so many friends from
across our state. I welcome the pleasant dual task assigned me
of making some comments about our state and of introducing our
distinguished speaker tonight.

First, may I make a few remarks addressed to each of you as
citizens. The name of your association indicates that you are
proud to be citizens of our state and nation, and I commend you
for your interest in the welfare of North Carolina and hope you
will always keep informed on the public issues which confront
our state. There are plenty of governmental issues, problems, and
opportunities to occupy your attention at this time. At least,
the members of the 1959 General Assembly, many of whom are
here, will verify that fact, I am sure.

It is natural that much of the debate and discussion in the
state and the General Assembly now swirls around the biennial
budget and the recommendations made by the Advisory Budget
Commission and the Governor. The Joint Appropriations Committee is now toward the end of its hearings and the parade of
requests for additional appropriations continues. By next week
when requests are all in, the extra amounts will probably add
up to $75,000,000—$100,000,000 more than now recommended.
This is all part of the executive budget system and tradition under
which the North Carolina General Assembly operates in determining the new budget. It should be remembered that through
the budget, and through it alone, we have the opportunity to

appraise and evaluate the services of our government and through the demoncratic processes to decide to curtail, expand, or amend the services which our government renders. So we as citizens should not become alarmed at the debate or sound and fury in the legislature, the press, or in public forums about the budget and its recommendations.

You will be interested to know that for the coming biennium, starting July 1, 1959, and ending June 30, 1961, the Advisory Budget Commission and the Governor have recommended $1,215,000,000 for state expenditures for all services. Of this total amount, less than $300,000,000 comes from federal funds and agency receipts (such as college tuitions, etc.). The recommended expenditures for general fund current operations for the biennium amounts to about $561,000,000.

We are recommending an increase in general fund expenditures for 1959-61 beyond the figures spent during the current biennium of more than $50,000,000 or approximately *10 per cent*. When we compare this with our sister state of South Carolina, where they are recommending 1.5 per cent increase, you can see that we have been generous even though some people for the moment do not think so.

The Advisory Budget Commission and I are proud to be able to recommend a balanced budget *without any new taxes* and there has been practically no increase in taxes for the last twelve years. We put in a $19,000,000 tax increase in 1955, but through improved economic conditions we created over a $60,000,000 surplus during the biennium. We were able in 1957 to reduce taxes in order to make equitable certain corporate taxes and this estimate of loss in tax revenue was beyond $14,000,000—the fact is we are going to lose less than half of that, and that makes us all happy.

To those who are suggesting that our recommendation for putting in withholding taxes, beginning next year is not sound, as it will mean postponing taxes that will have to be raised in the 1961-63 biennium, I would like to give them the following figures:

On the same revenue structure—in other words the same tax base—we appropriated in North Carolina for the general fund in

1947-49 about $200,000,000. The same revenue base now produces over $500,000,000 and in each biennium we have had a good cash balance which was used for the next biennium's operation needs.

I think that with North Carolina's economy growing as it is, soundly and strongly, we will continue to get these increases. Whether the increases satisfy everyone is doubtful, since no one, no group of people, no agency ever seems to get enough appropriations, or certainly never gets as much as they think they should get.

In the $50,000,000 increase we have proposed, more than half is for public schools, including $8,000,000 increase in income for all the teachers.

The total dollars recommended by the Governor and the Advisory Budget Commission for public schools alone for the 1959-61 biennium, including all items such as textbooks, bond retirement, etc., is $370,919,499.

North Carolina is paying 95 per cent of the total salaries for its public school teachers. Under this system of going to the General Assembly for practically all of the salary money for teachers the gap between what North Carolina pays on the average and the nation's average continues to widen. According to new figures just released, the *gap* has widened from $280 in 1950-51 to an estimated $1,005 in 1958-59 ($3,770 to $4,775).

Your incoming president, the able and distinguished Holt McPherson of High Point, is president of the North Carolina Citizens Committee for Better Schools. He now becomes your president of the "North Carolina Citizens Association for Better State Government" so to speak. The two jobs fall on broad shoulders and should complement each other.

I would like to issue a challenge to you and to make a prophecy. You members and friends of the North Carolina Citizens Association have most to gain or most to lose in the long run, depending on how good our public schools and teachers will be. You should have more than a passing interest and more than a property tax interest.

My challenge to each of you is to read and study the comprehensive and enlightening report called the North Carolina Public School Finance report. It will give you much valuable information on tax and property valuations and other important data as it explains the school incentive fund which I proposed to the General Assembly. In a few words, this report proposes that the state spend $10,000,000 each year beyond its regular support—matching about $6,000,000 a year from the counties on a voluntary basis. It states our conviction that the state should continue and enlarge its support of schools but urges further support from the local level.

My prophecy is that in not more than ten years we will be in worse shape than we are now comparatively if we do not adopt some such plan! Those who argue that it may mean more property taxes will find in the School Finance Study report that our property taxes take a smaller percentage than they did twenty-five years ago.

I would like to see the state continue its state-wide support of a nine-months, twelve grade system, plus adding a modest amount each biennium more or less in keeping with the cost of living rise and in addition put up a $10,000,000 yearly matching fund to challenge the counties. This program should have the support of the professional school people and the public.

The budget covers revenues and appropriations and is, of course, the largest single legislative matter to claim the attention of the legislators. However, there is also a large, constructive program which the General Assembly is working on with intelligence and determination. This program includes some new approaches to some old and pressing problems, but I have every faith that the members of the General Assembly will grasp the facts involved and will, in general, vote for what is best for the state's welfare.

During every session of the General Assembly there are always some who delight in speculating on "how the lines are forming . . . who are the anti-administration leaders, etc." and a few who appear to delight in controversy and confusion. From my own experience, I am impressed with the patriotism of our legislators and find that they love their state as much as anyone else—and frequently more than most of the legislative critics. I have found that they generally vote as they believe, and when the chips are down on a big issue will not be side-tracked by personal considerations or feelings.

This General Assembly, I hope, will pass laws which will improve our courts and revise our 1868 constitution so that both will fit a great and growing state. They will pass laws, I hope, which will improve our property tax situation in the various counties. Our legislators will do many other things which the state needs to have done, and they will do it in a fine and patriotic manner. This is a wonderful state with tremendous possibilities, and we will not be hobbled by selfish or petty motives or acts. Discord—whether actual or fancied—may make newspaper headlines, but solid achievements by individuals, groups, and communities deserve our attention much more.

The headlines and front pages, for example, have heralded the unhappy story of the bitter and dangerous Henderson strike. Yet we all know that this strike and the violence resulting is *not* typical of labor-management relations or modern industrial operations in North Carolina. It became necessary for me as governor to send more than 100 highway patrolmen into Vance County to assist local law enforcement officers in maintaining law and order after local people requested help. We are still at work trying to help settle the strike. It's a tough problem.

Now here are some significant figures to remember. They have to do with our industrial growth. We secured last year for this state—when I say "we" I mean the hundred or more development associations, chambers of commerce, state government departments, etc.—over $253,000,000 in new and expanded industry, 22,000 new jobs for displaced farm workers and others. During 1958 North Carolina's industrial development increased by 32.5 per cent over 1957 while the nation as a whole was suffering a loss of over 17 per cent. In other words we did 5 per cent better than the national average.

Figures on our agricultural income have just been disclosed. In 1958 we did more than $1,000,000,000 and this is most encouraging. Not only did we add to the value of our chief product— tobacco—but we have diversified all along the farm front. We became second in the nation in the number of chickens or broilers raised. It is now upwards of 150,000,000 a year.

One of the finest things on the horizon in North Carolina, especially as we look to our future, is the new interest in research and the establishment of a Research Triangle. I want to take this opportunity of thanking many of you in the audience for the part you played, not only in leadership, but in actual donations to the $1,500,000 that has been raised in getting the Research Institute started. This institute announced yesterday an award from the Atomic Energy Commission which is both sizeable and significant. This is only the beginning. Many awards and contracts will come to the state and to the Research Triangle. Experiences wherever research institutes have started reveal that they grow and grow bigger and better if they are well handled. This one, in my opinion, is in good hands. May I say to you businessmen there is nothing more fundamental, more far-reaching, and more promising than the Research Triangle and what it can mean to all business, industry, and government in North Carolina. Please understand that when I say industry I, of course, include agriculture as it is now one of the larger and more important parts of our great industrial growth. Many of the more dramatic things that have developed from research have been in agriculture, including what North Carolinians proudly claim in their "atomic peanut."

For our speaker tonight we have the head of one of the most dramatic research organizations in the world—the du Pont Company. This company and its management are a shining example to all the rest of us. In their first major research location back in 1924, they had fifty technical people. They now have more than 1,000 at this one location. They have moved in research from an expenditure of $1,000,000 per year to $70,000,000 per year, and during the period of the last thirty-five years of their life they have spent over $600,000,000 on research. Their ratio of spending approximately $3.00 for plant and equipment for every $1.00 spent in research means that they spent over $1,800,000,000 in new plants and equipment. Most of the things they are making now neither they nor anyone else knew about in the middle 1920's. I would like to say now that we in North Carolina are very proud of their various expansions into North Carolina, including the large and successful dacron plant in Kinston and the new and dramatic silicon manufacturing facility in Transylvania County near Brevard. We appreciate their confidence in us and hope it will be sustained and developed.

In our distinguished speaker this evening, we have an unusual man. He joined the du Pont Company in 1922, immediately after receiving a chemical engineering degree from the Massachusetts Institute of Technology. For two years he worked as control chemist in the heavy chemicals laboratory in the Philadelphia Works of the Paint, Lacquer and Heavy Chemicals Department. He has then moved to Wilmington, Delaware, where he was assigned to experimental work.

During this period he was active in the development of nylon, being primarily concerned with the transfer of the fiber synthesis from the laboratory to the pilot plant stage.

He was elected director of the du Pont Company in January, 1942, and in June of that year was made chemical director of the Grasselli Chemicals Department. The demand of the company's war production program took him out of industrial research in 1943, and he was made technical director in the Explosives Department, working directly with the atomic energy program. He was responsible for maintaining liaison between du Pont and the University of Chicago, translating the university's nuclear research developments into practical application. After completing this work in 1945, he moved steadily upward in the organization, and on May 31, 1946, he was elected vice-president and a member of the executive committee. He became vice-chairman of the committee in 1947 and held that post until his election to the presidency of the company in 1948.

May I now speak briefly of Mr. Greenewalt's philosophy rather than about Mr. Greenewalt himself. He is an "uncommon man," who, by the way, has written a book on this very subject, "The Uncommon Man." It is not about himself, but about the modern executive in a modern corporate organization. Mr. Greenewalt discusses the new role of the executive in a growing corporation, and in a time when many young college graduates and too many of our people in general seem to seek only security and conformity, Mr. Greenewalt asks for the opposite. He wants his managers and executives in general to be daring and original, yet at the same time be able to work as a hard-hitting team.

Mr. Greenewalt indicates that a successful executive works hard for more than himself alone, or for a greater salary and more personal recognition. Given intellectual freedom of action, he will produce for the good of the company or organization.

After Mr. Greenewalt had discussed in his book the various virtues and attributes of a modern-day executive, he finally says in effect that it is not salesmanship nor financial wizardry or productive shrewdness that makes a real executive, but "human understanding, human sympathy." He adds: "Men's qualifications to reach high positions are not based so much on their technical competence or job know-how, as on what kind of people they are. Contrary to accepted thought, a good manager manages quite as much with his heart as with his head; quite as much with instinct and intuition as with precise formulas."

We are fortunate indeed to have a man with broad human sympathies and understanding, as well as a great sense of humor, to talk to us tonight. I proudly present to this distinguished audience Crawford H. Greenewalt, president of E. I. du Pont de Nemours and Company.

Thank you!

ADDRESS AT TRYON PALACE COMMISSION DINNER

New Bern

April 9, 1959

[This address climaxed a two-day celebration marking the official opening of the restored Tryon Palace at New Bern and was the second of two speeches made by Governor Hodges in connection with that event. On the preceding day, he had addressed a luncheon honoring members of the Senate and House of Representatives who had held a brief session in the palace, harking back to the time when the building served as a meeting place for the General Assembly. The Tryon Palace Commission had guided the work of restoring the eighteenth century structure, which was expected to rival Colonial Williamsburg as a tourist attraction.]

One hundred and ninety years ago, a western North Carolina farmer, incensed at the idea of spending public funds for the construction of a "palace" for the governor's use in New Bern, protested that "Not one man in twenty of the four most populous counties (in North Carolina) will ever see this famous house when built . . . ." The protest may have been perfectly valid almost two centuries ago, but I think it has been dramatically evident here in the past few days that the estimate has been reversed and it is very unlikely that one citizen in twenty will miss the opportunity to see "this famous house" in the months and years ahead.

My experiences here in New Bern during the past two days have been both exciting and tremendously gratifying. We have seen the final realization of a dream that has stirred the imagination of North Carolinians for many years. We have seen the revival of a proud chapter in the history of our state—a revival that adds greatly to our knowledge of the past and our appreciation of the wonderful heritage that the people of this state possess.

Those who are responsible for the restoration of Tryon Palace merit the praise of every citizen of North Carolina. They—and I most certainly include the dedicated members of this commission—have given this state a great treasure, the value of which cannot be expressed in terms of the money involved or the economic benefits that will naturally accrue. The benefits to be derived will be so numerous and varied that any effort to appraise them will very likely prove inadequate. Suffice it to say that these benefits will more than compensate for the effort and expense involved in making them available.

It would be a simple matter for me to devote the time allotted this evening to a commendation of the many individuals and groups that have contributed to the success of this undertaking. In fact, it would not be difficult to devote the entire time to the praise of Mr. and Mrs. J. E. Latham and Mr. and Mrs. John A. Kellenberger, without whom Tryon Palace restored might still be a little more than a dream. Their patriotism and generosity are deeply appreciated by a most grateful state. Certainly, this historic site will stand in the years ahead as a testimonial to their generosity and their love of North Carolina. I knew Mr. and Mrs. Latham personally and admired them greatly. I feel even closer to Mr. and Mrs. John Kellenberger. We owe much also to Miss Gertrude Carraway, her staff, and the many volunteers for their work in this restoration.

Achievements of this kind, however, are not the work of men and women who seek or desire public recognition for their services. Far greater incentive than this is needed to draw forth the determination and dedication required of those who provide the leadership for projects such as this. Our state, our nation, and the world owes a great debt of gratitude to such people.

As I pointed out yesterday in my talk here in New Bern before the members of the General Assembly, North Carolina has not matched her sister states in the preservation of her historic landmarks and in the promotion of those she has preserved. It is for this reason that it is now especially exciting to see the growing interest among people in all parts of the state in this type of program. I said yesterday—and I would like to restate my conviction this evening—that this upsurge of interest in the past indicates a growing awareness of the rich heritage that is ours, a realization that pride in this heritage is justified and, even more important, a new-found determination on the part of our people to preserve it as an inspiration to our future generations. North Carolinians possess a fabulous history, and it is not only our privilege, but our duty and responsibility to perpetuate it in the minds of our people.

Our Department of Archives and History and our volunteer lay groups who have formed historical and preservation societies deserve credit for their emphases. And we are appreciative of the several General Assemblies of the state which have helped not only in the Tryon Palace restoration but many other undertakings of lesser magnitude. The meeting yesterday of the 1959 General Assembly in regular session in our first state capitol was significant and helpful.

Our North Carolina history is especially important because it contributes to the "esprit de corps" that exists in our state today. It is the foundation of our way of life—a way of life that is unique in its simplicity, yet deeply profound in its meaning—born of confidence and humility, and nurtured by the knowledge that deeds and not words are the measure of true achievement. We have only to look for a moment at our heritage to find ample reason for our pride and ample justification for our efforts at preservation and restoration.

Prior to the arrival of the first explorers along our coast, the 52,000 square miles that formed what is now North Carolina was inhabited by between 30,000 and 35,000 Indians. There are known to have been at least twenty-nine tribes, though only five were historically significant. These were the Hatteras, with whom the early settlers had their first contact; the Chowanoc, who were the first to show hostility toward the settlers; the Tuscarora, largest and most warlike of the eastern tribes; and the Catawbas and Cherokees, who left their imprint on the Piedmont and mountain sections of the state. Today, only the Cherokees retain a vestige of tribal unity and tradition, but the poignant story of this tribe is told today in the outdoor drama, "Unto These Hills."

These were the inhabitants of the land when it was first visited in 1524 by Giovanni da Verrazzano, a Florentine navigator in the service of France. He explored our coast and certain inland areas and later wrote reports that pictured our land as a veritable paradise. The French, however, were too involved with other things at the time and made no attempt at colonization. Two years later, in 1526, a Spanish expedition attempted a settlement on the coast, but found Verrazzano's "Paradise" to be somewhat less than hospitable. They abandoned the settlement when disease and starvation took a heavy toll.

Almost two decades later, in 1540, the great Hernando de Soto led an expedition north from Florida and penetrated the mountains in the southwestern corner of the state. From North Carolina, he turned west on the trek that led to the discovery of the Mississippi River. Other Spanish expeditions came in 1561, 1566, and 1567, but none succeeded in planting a permanent colony . . .

Finally, in 1584, an English expedition, commissioned by Sir Walter Raleigh and led by Philip Amadas and Arthur Barlow, came to the North Carolina coast in search of a suitable site for a settlement. This expedition spent several months on the island of Roanoke and then returned to England carrying two Indians—Wanchese and Manteo—and an enthusiastic report about the site they had found. In less than a year's time, the first English colony had been transported to America and settled on North Carolina's Roanoke Island. A year later the group gave up and returned to England, but another came in 1587 to take its place. Two historic events occurred in the months that followed. The Indian chief Manteo was baptised in the Christian faith, and a child, Virginia Dare, was born.

Here, at the dawn of this state's recorded history, was an indication of the role North Carolina was destined to play in the more than three and one-half centuries that have followed. The Roanoke Island colony was doomed to vanish into oblivion in less than three years, but its existence had not been in vain. It had provided North Carolina with a rich tradition and a pioneering spirit that had remained with us to this day. North Carolina had become the site of the first English colony in the New World. It had witnessed the first Protestant baptism in America. And it had been the home of the first English child to be born on the new continent. All of these great historical events are immortalized in Paul Green's moving outdoor drama—"The Lost Colony"— which is performed during the summer months on the site of the original settlement just up the coast from New Bern.

In the decades that followed, North Carolina was settled—not from the sea—but by small groups that migrated into the area from other colonies that had settled to the north and south. They came slowly at first, then in growing numbers, and they filled our Coastal Plains, our rolling Piedmont and our mountains with industrious and dedicated people. There were Anglo-Saxons, Scotch-Irish, Swiss, and Germans. They were hard-working and fiercely independent. They were proud of their new land and jealous of their freedom. They were, for the most part, simple men and women, but they possessed the qualities that gave us the great heritage that we bear so proudly today.

New Bern was one of the settlements established almost two and one-half centuries ago by these early North Carolinians—and while it was not one of the first settlements, it was certainly one of the most significant. This town was founded in 1710 by German Palatines, along with a few Swiss and English. Some indication of the character and determination of these people can be seen in the hardships they overcame in order to reach and hold this bit of land. The first group of settlers left England in January, 1710, and roughly one-half of them died during the thirteen weeks required to reach their destination—the Virginia coast. As they entered the James River, a French privateer pounced on one of the two vessels and robbed the settlers of all their posessions. Still determined to reach this area, the survivors marched overland, gathering supplies from other settlers as they went. When they arrived here they found themselves in a wilderness during a hot and unhealthy season and without food or shelter. It became necessary for them to sell almost all their remaining possessions to neighboring inhabitants in order to live.

Baron Von Graffenried, one of the principal instigators of the colony, arrived here in New Bern on September 10, 1710, with 100 Swiss settlers. He described conditions as wretched, with "sickness, want, and desperation having reached their climax." In the year that followed he managed to revive the colony and in September, 1711, he wrote that "a happy state of things" existed. The happiness was short-lived, for later the same month, the Tuscarora Indians swept down on New Bern, slaughtered 130 of its inhabitants—men, women, and children—and all but erased the colony from the face of the earth.

Many of its people died, but the spirit that brought them to this land did not. During the next decade the town was gradually rebuilt, and in 1723 it was formally incorporated. New Bern was on its way to becoming the most important town in North Carolina. Its colonial growth was, of course, climaxed with its designation as the first fixed capital of the state—and with the simultaneous construction of the fabulous building that would never lose the name given it by those who opposed its erection—Tryon's "Palace".

It was during this century that North Carolinians converted their traditional love of liberty into a united effort that would bring them complete independence. We are all proud of the fact that our forefathers led in this fight. It was on April 12, 1776—more than a month before any of the other colonies acted—that North Carolina's delegation to the Continental Congress received instructions to vote for freedom from England. This audacious act was set forth in the document we know as the Halifax Resolves—and the date on which the act was perpetrated is displayed on our state flag.

The same spirit of independent thought and action prompted North Carolina to seek no counsel but its own when the time came to subscribe to the provisions of the United States Constitution. In fact, we refused to sign until the Bill of Rights was written in the document, and even then we were the last of the thirteen colonies to forsake complete independence.

At the time of the Civil War there was wide-spread sentiment in the state to remain with the Union—even after our sister states had joined the Confederacy. As a matter of fact, it is not at all improbable that we would have held to this position had not President Lincoln and his advisors misinterpreted our independent nature and demanded that we take up arms against our neighbors.

Once the die was cast, North Carolina devoted its total energy to the "Cause," though the records show that the state was just as reluctant about surrendering the rights of its citizens to the Confederacy as it had been earlier with the Union. In the final analysis, North Carolina contributed 125,000 men to the southern army, a number larger than its voting population—and suffered one-fourth of all the South's casualties. These North Carolinians added another proud chapter to our history by being "First at Bethel, Farthest at Gettysburg and Chickamauga, and Last at Appomattox."

I have touched only a few of the highlights in the dramatic story of our people and their past. There is much more, of course, for there are many details that I have omitted. I could tell of the three Presidents and other great leaders that our state has given the nation. I could relate the great store of fact and fiction surrounding the exploits of the fabled pirates who buried their treasures in the great sand dunes along our Outer Banks. And I could tell you of the brothers who came to those same dunes half a century ago to experiment with a machine they called an airplane—an experiment, incidentally, that gave our state another first as the "birthplace of aviation."

Yes, we in North Carolina have every right to be proud of the people and the events that have given us a great tradition. And it is right and proper that we should do everything in our power to perpetuate this tradition. We have a responsibility as citizens and as parents to insure that future generations of North Carolinians hold the same pride in their past that we hold today. There is no better way of insuring this pride than by preserving, as we have here in Tryon Palace, the physical evidences of our heritage.

The people of New Bern have done a wonderful job of preserving their history—and they have, at the same time, created a tourist attraction that rivals any this state has to offer. There is, of course, more that can and should be done here, and I sincerely hope that the event we celebrate today will spur further efforts to carry on with this program. Actually, this achievement should provide the incentive for even more interest and activity in the years ahead. There is no reason at all why New Bern cannot grow to rival Williamsburg as the epitome of colonial restoration. Certainly, the raw material is here. I hope we can have continued state and local interest, and also other great benefactors like Mrs. Latham.

In conclusion, let me say that other North Carolina communities can profit by the example that has been set here in New Bern. Few of our communities are as well-endowed historically as New Bern, but almost every city has some historical project that can be developed if there is interest and determination. As I have pointed out, North Carolina boasts a history that is filled with exciting events and significant accomplishments. We have only to dedicate ourselves to reviving the evidences of these historic milestones and our efforts will be richly rewarded.

May I again express to each of you our appreciation for the contribution you have made to this event. It is a contribution that will not soon be forgotten in North Carolina.

Thank you!

ADDRESS AT SWIFT AND COMPANY PLANT DEDICATION

WILSON

April 18, 1959

[The Governor had made an address of welcome at ceremonies of breaking ground for this major meat packing plant on February 20, 1958. Now completed as the newest and one of the largest of Swift's plants, it represented a significant economic development in eastern North Carolina. Following the Governor's address, which was delivered at the Wilson Country Club, he and Swift President Porter M. Jarvis were honor guests at an open house program at the new plant.]

It is a most gratifying experience to return here to Wilson today to see the progress that has been made since my visit about a year ago to participate in the ground-breaking ceremonies for this significant new industry. It is also my distinct pleasure on this occasion to extend a very warm welcome to President Jarvis, Vice-President Fletchall, and the other Swift and Company officials who are here to share in the excitement of this event with us. I know that I speak, not only for the people of this community and this county, but for all the people of our state when I say that we are glad you are here, that we are proud of this new industry, and that we will do everything within our power to insure its success. May I commend the state, county, and city officials, business and civic leaders for their assistance and cooperation in bringing to the state this magnificent plant. It was truly a cooperative movement.

And I would like again to praise Wilson for its forward-looking program of putting its house in order to attract industry, businesses, and individual citizens. Other cities in the state would do well to look at what you have accomplished and what you plan for the future.

Last February I joined other state and local officials in welcoming Swift and Company to this community, and I recall stating that there was cause for rejoicing in the fact that the world's largest meat packing company had selected Wilson and eastern North Carolina as the site for its newest, most modern beef and pork processing plant. On that occasion we were looking to the future, anticipating the benefits that were certain to be derived from the establishment of this important facility. Today, the dream has become a reality and, while we must continue to look to the future for the realization of all the benefits that can accrue from this industry, we can now move forward confident in the knowledge that great progress has been made. The foundation for significant economic advancement has been laid. The job now is to build on that foundation—to insure that no facet of this opportunity is overlooked, to make absolutely certain that both the company and the people who stand to benefit from its presence here, take maximum advantage of the opportunity that is now available.

Swift and Company did not come to Wilson by chance. It came because it is convinced beyond any doubt that there exists here the proper combination of factors needed for a successful business operation. One of the most important of these factors is the demonstrated willingness of the people in this region to shoulder a reasonable share of the responsibility for meeting the requirements that an industry of this type imposes. The responsibility for the decision to locate here belongs to the company. The responsibility for insuring its success belongs to everyone—not just the livestock producers and others who will benefit directly from this operation, but all the people of this community, this county, and this great eastern section of our state.

I have said many times that economic development is a cooperative venture, requiring the sincere, purposeful action and support of every person even remotely concerned. This support is even more important in an undertaking of this type than would be the case with an industry that is largely self-sufficient, that draws little more than its labor force from the area in which it is located. Here you have an industry that must draw not only its manpower but also its raw material from this immediate area if it is to function at top efficiency. This is a tremendously important factor because it greatly increases the contribution that this industry can make to the regional economy. It not only provides employment for many of our people, but at the same time it provides an excellent market for our livestock that is being produced in increasing numbers throughout eastern North Carolina. It is evident, therefore, that the benefits you receive from this Swift plant will grow in direct proportion to the speed and effectiveness with which you meet its livestock requirements.

Of particular significance to me is the fact that this plant is ideally suited to the pattern of economic deevlopment that has been established here in the eastern portion of our state. Here we have a full-fledged, completely modern facility that not only complements, but encourages, the program of agricultural diversification that has been under way in this area for some time. Let me add that it is important—especially here in the east—that this trend toward a more balanced economy continues. I do not have to remind you of the serious condition that developed in this and the other predominantly agricultural counties in 1957 when the ever-present threat that is inherent in a one-crop economy became a reality. In that one year, agricultural losses in Wilson and its six adjoining counties amounted to more than $38,000,000. The loss in Wilson alone was estimated at approximately $4,000,000.

During this same period—and this underlines the importance of this new industry—these same seven counties—Edgecombe, Greene, Johnston, Nash, Pitt, Wayne and Wilson—boosted their income from livestock sales by $2,768,000. This, of course, did not—and will not in the near future—compensate for heavy tobacco crop losses, but it clearly points the way to an alleviation of this threat. Tobacco is, and will remain for many years to come, the backbone of this state's economy, but we have learned the hard way that it is both desirable and necessary that we have other sources of income to depend upon when the tobacco crop has a bad year. Sound industrial growth—especially in food processing—offers one good answer to this economic problem in eastern North Carolina.

North Carolina is a new frontier for the meat producing and processing industry, and this area will play a major role in the development of that frontier. A survey has indicated that forty-one counties in eastern North Carolina can expect to feel the economic influence of this plant when it is in full operation. This area represents 42 per cent of our total farm population, 80 per cent of the sows and gilts kept for breeding, 34 per cent of the corn acreage in the state. These factors give some idea of the livestock production potential that exists here.

Our people have already begun to develop this potential as shown by the fact that the value of hogs sold in North Carolina in 1958 was $65,814,275—an increase of almost $15,500,000 over the figure for 1957. Equally dramatic was the rise in cattle sales— from $30,548,303 in 1957 to $43,764,834 in 1958. Total livestock and livestock product sales for the two-year period climbed from $262,190,719 to $331,099,315—an increase of almost $70,000,000, or 26 per cent increase. This figure includes poultry and dairy products, as well as cattle and hogs, but individually or combined they serve to illustrate the tremendous amount of interest that has been stimulated in the field of livestock production and marketing in North Carolina in the last few years.

This is an encouraging picture—made even more exciting by the fact that this new Swift and Company plant has become a part of the picture—helping the people of this state meet the challenge of the future, and, at the same time, presenting a challenge in itself. This plant began operations on January 21 this year, and by the end of that month the company had purchased from North Carolina producers and slaughtered 2,872 hogs. In February the plant processed 17,000 hogs. During March, more than 12,200 were slaughtered—bringing the total to roughly 32,000 in less than three months of operation. During the same period, approximately 3,300 cattle were purchased and processed, along with 600 to 700 calves. These figures would certainly seem to indicate that the industry will live up to its estimate that it will contribute from $15,000,000 to $17,000,000 to the area economy annually in its purchases.

This, very definitely, is a challenge to the livestock producers in this area. As a matter of fact, it should present a challenge to many individuals who are not currently engaged in livestock production. The market is here and it should certainly be developed. It should be supplied with quality beef and pork in sufficient quantity to meet its maximum requirements. And it should be supplied with this livestock on a year-around business-like basis. A plant of this type does not operate seasonally. It must operate at full capacity at all times if it is to operate profitably—and if it is to make its maximum contribution to the community and the area it serves.

It is my understanding that the company has already found it necessary to purchase some cattle from our neighboring states in order to meet its needs. This works to the disadvantage of both the company and the North Carolina producer. It means inconvenience and increased costs for the company, and it means that the purchase price of the livestock has gone into the economy of another state. This is a situation that we can and must remedy—and it is certainly to our advantage to do so as quickly as possible. Our grass is greener in our state, so let's take advantage of it. Give the cows and hogs a chance to "grow up" in North Carolina.

Let me assure the Swift and Company officials present here today, that the people of eastern North Carolina are wonderful people who appreciate what you have done in coming here. They can and will produce the livestock that this plant requires. Dallas Miller has pointed out that this section of our state can produce corn and other feeds just as well as any area in the Midwest, in fact, far better than some; and he has, in a number of speeches that have been called to my attention, expressed the conviction that eastern North Carolina has the human and natural resources that will enable it to compete with any place in the country in livestock production. He has also remarked that "if the North Carolina farmer would raise his own grain, raise his own livestock, and then feed the grain to his livestock over a period of years, he'd never go broke." I whole-heartedly agree with this view, but I would like to carry it a step further. I would predict that if the North Carolina farmer will follow Mr. Miller's advice, our Tar Heel farmers not only will not go broke, but will find economic opportunities available that were never before imagined.

Our people in this state are rapidly getting a state-wide point of view by seeing our over-all problems and doing the things necessary to correct these problems. We are seeing that farm diversification is necessary, that encouraging local industry, especially the processing of farm products, is most helpful. Further, we are becoming less provincial in putting one segment of the economy against another. We all realize the importance of our great farming interests, but at the same time we are cooperating in bringing in industry to furnish jobs to those who need them. There is plenty of room in North Carolina for growth and expansion in agriculture and industry.

In conclusion, I would like to commend the officials of this company for the genuine interest they have shown in North Carolina and its people. Your enthusiasm about what we are trying to accomplish in this state and your desire to be a part of the wonderful future that we envision for our people has been very real and very sincere. We know that you have a great deal to give North Carolina and we believe that we can contribute in like manner to your company. Working together, we can derive much that will be of mutual benefit.

May I say again that we are glad Swift and Company has come to Wilson. We are proud of this new industry and we pledge our full cooperation to insure its success.

Thank you.

REMARKS ACCEPTING A PORTRAIT OF FORMER GOVERNOR J. MELVILLE BROUGHTON

RALEIGH

April 23, 1959

[The two houses of the legislature in joint session, along with the Council of State, the Supreme Court, members of the Broughton family, and an overflow crowd in the galleries, assembled for this occasion in the Hall of the House of Representatives. Associate Justice Emory B. Denny eulogized Governor Broughton in an address presenting the portrait, which Governor Hodges accepted on behalf of the state of North Carolina. The portrait, painted by Joseph Wallace King of Winston-Salem, was unveiled by Harriet W. Broughton and J. Melville Broughton III, grandchildren of the former governor.]

Thank you very much for the privilege of participating with you this evening in a tribute to an outstanding governor, a great North Carolinian and, above all, a truly dedicated man. I am here tonight to accept, on behalf of the people of this state, a gift that will be highly treasured by present and future generations of North Carolinians.

We are honored and pleased to have the members of Governor Broughton's family with us on this occasion, and we are deeply indebted to them for the wonderful gift they have presented this state.

North Carolina was extremely fortunate in having the leadership and wise counsel of Melville Broughton during one of the most crucial periods in our history. His record during the early months of his administration in 1941 indicates that he saw clearly the inevitability of this nation's involvement in World War II. We will stand eternally indebted to his foresightedness, for he not only directed the resources of this state to meet the challenge of the war years, but worked untiringly to insure our emergence from the war on a sound economic, cultural, and spiritual basis. He labored under the most trying circumstances. His efforts on behalf of education, good health, stable government, and other vital domestic programs were constantly hampered by wartime restrictions. Yet, great progress was made in all these fields.

Governor Broughton campaigned unceasingly to bring more and better education to the young people of North Carolina. As a state senator in 1927 and 1929, he led the unsuccessful fight to increase school terms from six to eight months. His efforts were not wasted, however, and the eight-month term was approved by a later legislature. When he became governor, he recommended a further extension to nine months and the addition of a twelfth grade. Both recommendations were approved.

Other outstanding achievements during his administration included the establishment of the Teachers' and State Employees' Retirement System, the establishment of state aid to public libraries, the reorganization of state hospitals and correctional institutions under consolidated boards, and the inauguration of a movement for a broad medical care and hospital program.

Governor Broughton and his administration set the stage for much of the progress that we are making today in North Carolina. Furthermore, his legacy of dedicated public service is being carried on by members of his family who are continuing to serve North Carolina with the same unselfish devotion. Most of you are familiar, I am sure, with the contribution Mrs. Broughton has made as a distinguished member of the Tryon Palace and the State Prison Commissions, and with the service rendered by Melville Broughton, Jr., as chairman of the State Highway Commission.

In conclusion, may I express to Mrs. Broughton and the members of her family the very warm and sincere appreciation of the people of North Carolina for the gift presented this evening. You have given us far more than a portrait of a beloved governor and United States Senator. You have given us a visible reminder of a great North Carolinian who will live for all time in the hearts and minds of the people he served.

I consider it a great honor to accept, on behalf of the state of North Carolina, this portrait of Governor J. Melville Broughton. It will be a cherished memorial, forever occupying a position of honor in our state, just as the words and deeds of the man it represents will forever occupy a position of honor in our history.

ADDRESS AT THE COMMISSIONING OF CHAMPION PAPER AND FIBRE COMPANY'S NO. 20 MACHINE

CANTON
May 1, 1959

[The Champion Paper and Fibre Company had installed and was now commissioning a new paper-making machine which would provide 225 new jobs for North Carolina industry. Such events were always popular with Governor Hodges, as they indicated progress in his efforts to secure more employment and a higher per capita income for the state. On this occasion, as at Mooresville on March 6 (see pp. 123-131), he referred indirectly to the Henderson strike in complimenting Haywood County as a place where "harmony and friendliness reign" and "where there is industrial peace instead of dissensions."]

I would like to thank the people of Haywood County and officials of the Champion Paper and Fibre Company for inviting me here today to take part in this truly significant ceremony. This is a big event in the lives of both a county and a company that have long-standing reputations for doing things in a big way. That this reputation has been maintained in recent years is clearly evident, not only in the achievement we are recognizing here in Canton today, but in the atmosphere of confidence and general well-being that prevails throughout the county.

The people of Haywood are to be congratulated on the present state of affairs in this county. Here we find a combination of human and natural resources being properly devoleped to produce a healthy, balanced economy which, in turn, will mean a better and increasingly more prosperous way of life for the people of the county.

According to the best estimates, the first white settlers found their way into this section of North Carolina around the year 1785. Unlike the settlers in other regions, who stayed for brief periods of time and then moved on to the West, the pioneers who came to Haywood planted their roots firmly in the rich soil of these beautiful hills and valleys. Evidence of this can be seen in the fact that the names brought to this county by many of its first citizens are still prevalent in the population today. These early settlers seemed to feel that once they arrived here there was little need of looking further—that they had found the promised land.

This view was apparently shared by large numbers of people, for less than twenty-five years after the first settlers arrived, there were enough permanent residents in the area to warrant it designation as a county. The act creating the county was passed by the General Assembly on December 23, 1808.

Formed from what was then part of Buncombe County, Haywood spread out over more than 3,000 square miles of western North Carolina. In the years that followed, Haywood gave up much of its land area to the formation of other counties, but it clung tenaciously to its unique character and wonderful traditions.

Haywood is a county that today combines the rustic and casual life with the ultra-modern and fast-moving. Its people believe in progress, but not progress at any price. They know that the future holds great promise for those who have the courage and ability to take advantage of its opportunities. But, they also know that the past and the present hold much that is good and well worth preserving. It has been said that Haywood County folks like to hear the wail of a hound dog over the whine of their machinery; that they will tune up a tractor or a guitar with equal agility and enthusiasm. This is as it should be, for it gives purpose to progress. It shows that the people here know not only how to earn a living but how to live as well.

I think it is well for us to pause occasionally to get our bearings —to make sure that we have not lost our direction. We can build larger factories to house larger machines to produce a variety of products in greater abundance, but if we lose sight of why we do these things, then we have achieved little. Unless we keep in mind at all times that the ultimate aim of all our efforts is to bring greater happiness and a richer, more purposeful life to all our people, we will fail the trust that has been put in us.

It is perfectly evident that you have not lost sight of this aim here in Haywood County, and I am happy to say that the same is true in general of the state of North Carolina. This is one of the big reasons for the progress we have enjoyed in this state in recent years, and it is one of the main reasons for my confidence and enthusiasm about the future.

The occasion that brings us here today more than justifies this confidence in the ability of this state and its people to grow and develop and prosper in the years ahead. Where else but in North Carolina would the governor be able to visit the leading beef cattle producing county in his state and stand on the highest-priced farmland in the South for the purpose of commissioning the largest fine paper machine in the world. Add the fact that within the same county you find one of the state's largest rubber factories, one of its largest shoe factories, one of its largest dairy industries, its second largest Burley tobacco crop, one of its largest vacation and recreation areas, a flourishing hatching-egg business, a huge hydro-electric power plant—and it becomes fairly obvious why North Carolina is proud of Haywood County and why Haywood County should be proud of itself. If more evidence of this county's worth is needed, I might add that it is politically enlightened, having frequently and overwhelmingly demonstrated its allegiance to the Democratic party.

It is good to get away from Raleigh and its politically-charged atmosphere. It's good to be here in the mountains with people who are not divided in their purpose but also are united in a common cause and who have great loyalties to each other.

It's good to be here in a plant that pays among the highest wages in the county, and not have to listen to discussions as to whether seventy-five cents an hour is too much wage for people. It's good to be here where there is industrial peace instead of dissensions, where management fulfills its corporate, community, and public relationships—where a company recognizes its obligations to deal fairly and openly with everyone. It's good to pay respects to Mr. Reuben Robertson, Sr., one of the greatest men I've ever known and to his son, Reuben, Jr., who is a public spirited, able industrialist of the highest type.

I am happy to come to a place where peace and harmony and friendliness reigns, and where the future looks brighter even than the present.

Even with an impressive list of superlatives to its credit, Haywood County has ample reason to take pride in the Number 20 machine we are dedicating here today. This is far more than just another piece of machinery. It is the product of almost a decade of dreaming and careful planning on the part of a great company. It is a work of art, fashioned by talented men who had one great thing in common—faith. This machine would not exist today were it not for the fact that the men who had a hand in its construction had faith in themselves, faith in this company, faith in this county and this state and, above all, faith in the future.

Champion's management people were beginning to visualize a new, ultra-modern paper machine as far back as 1951. They had confidence then that the state and national economies would continue to grow and that the company, along with the paper industry in general, would share in that growth. The company realized that its own growth in a highly competitive industry would depend, to a large degree, on how well it met the present and future needs of its employees, its customers, and its shareholders. It wisely decided that additional production facilities would provide part of the answer.

Planners and machine designers, basing their work on extensive studies, began work in 1953. In 1956, the board of directors, after reviewing the design plans and considering other pertinent factors, authorized the necessary expenditure—providing for the machine to be financed in part from a large-scale debenture issue and in part from plowed back earnings. Construction on buildings to house the machine was begun in 1957, and the first actual assembly work on the machine itself began in June of last year. On February 17 of this year, the final adjustments were made in the equipment, the switch was thrown, and Number 20 was placed in operation. I understand that salable paper was produced twenty-four hours after the first test run was begun—proof of the value of good planning and good engineering. This was certainly a credit to the company and to the men and women who contributed to this great effort.

The impact of this machine has undoubtedly already made itself felt. Depending on the grade of paper being produced, Number 20 is capable of adding 200 to 300 tons of paper per day to the mill's production. This raises the Carolina division's overall paper and paperboard capacity output to about 980 tons daily. Of particular interest to farmers and other landowners in Haywood and other western North Carolina counties is the fact that pulpwood consumption will be increased by 350 to 400 cords per day. I am told that approximately 2,150 cords are now used daily and that roughly 90 per cent of this wood is sold to the company by owners of small wood lots in the surrounding counties. For this pulpwood, the company pays out more than $11,000,000 annually. This figure will very likely increase as the full capacity of this new machine is reached. It offers both a challenge and an opportunity to the pulpwood producers of this area to get ready money, and by proper forestry practices to insure income for the years ahead.

Equally significant is the fact that the operation of Number 20 has made available new jobs for 225 people—which, when added to the more than 3,000 already employed by Champion, gives some indication of the importance of this industry in Haywood County and in North Carolina. This additional employment will raise the company's annual payroll by roughly $1,000,-000, bringing the yearly total to $18,000,000.

I think it is also noteworthy, and of great interest to transportation people, that shipment of the new tonnage to customers is expected to raise the division's annual freight bill to a total of about $10,000,000.

The concentration of Number 20's operations on its specialties of bond, tablet, and mimeograph papers will also increase the efficiency of the company's other machines since they will be able to concentrate on other types of paper and time will not be lost in changing grades on machines. This greater efficiency, plus the new tonnage, will make it possible for Champion to produce another 90,000 to 100,000 tons a year and give the company an annual output of about 700,000 tons of paper and paperboard. This new productive capacity will certainly underscore Champion's place in an indsutry in which it is already counted as one of the largest manufacturers of fine printing paper. Customers, shareholders, and employees will all benefit from this greater efficiency and productivity. So also will this community, this county, and this state.

May I conclude by saying that North Carolina is proud of Champion and its people. We are proud of your management, proud of your work force, proud of your initiative and enterprise, and proud of the fact that North Carolinians have again had the opportunity to prove, through the achievements of this company, that they can achieve any goal they choose to reach.

Thank you.

ADDRESS AT DEDICATION OF THE ARCHIE ELLEDGE SEWAGE TREATMENT PLANT

WINSTON-SALEM

May 1, 1959

[This address, made on the grounds of a new sewage treatment plant in Winston-Salem, was the second of three speeches made by Governor Hodges within the space of five hours of the same day. At two in the afternoon he had spoken at ceremonies of the Champion Paper and Fibre Company at Canton, nearly 200 miles to the west (see pp. 154-159), and at six in the evening he would address a dinner meeting at the Forsyth Country Club in connection with the Northwest Day Executives' Tour (see p. 496).]

Mayor Kurfees, other distinguished guests:

I greatly appreciate the opportunity you have given me to join you here today in the dedication of this magnificent new plant. The existence of this facility in Winston-Salem is far more than an indication of this city's determination to meet its responsibilities to its own citizens and its neighbors. It is dramatic evidence of faith in the future on the part of your people, foresightedness on the part of your civic leadership, and real dedication to progress on the part of the city itself.

There may be those who have difficulty comparing a sewage treatment plant with those forms of civic progress that perhaps provide more immediate and more tangible evidence of their contribution to the economic growth of a community.

This plant is an indication of this community's long-range development program. It shows planning on the part of the community. The municipal body that fails or is reluctant to put its house in order cannot expect to draw a very enthusiastic reponse from potential investors. The municipality that will not invest in itself is certainly being presumptuous to expect others to do so. By the same token, the municipality that has faith in its own future, and is willing to back that faith with action, can find confidence, in the knowledge that its dedication to progress will not go unrewarded.

I have said many times that the economic development program that counts luck as an important ingredient is doomed to failure from the beginning. It is not by chance that one community is chosen and another ignored. Not infrequently, you hear the classic complaint that a particular community or a particular section of the state is being favored by some one or some thing in a position to influence the placement of industries or open the door to other business opportunities. This, of course, is not true—it is usually a community itself that lands an industry or expands old ones as you have done so well here in Winston-Salem and Forsyth.

Those of you here who have devoted your time and effort to the development of your city, your county, or your region; those of you who know from experience the complexities of economic progress, will surely agree with me when I say, with complete conviction, that neither luck nor favoritism merit consideration when formulating a sound economic development program. There are no free rides on the road to prosperity. For this reason, the city or county or state that is seriously endeavoring to move ahead economically or otherwise must demonstrate its willingness to carry its fair share of the load.

Winston-Salem has long demonstrated this highly desirable trait. The combined civic club—chamber of commerce meeting that I attended here last September was a fine example of community spirit being transformed into a powerful force for community betterment. I recall that on that occasion I discussed the significance of civic and business leaders getting together to combine their tremendous energy and talent and to work toward mutually beneficial objectives. I pointed out at that time that such a display of municipal unity was both constructive and inspirational. It provided concrete evidence of the fact that Winston-Salem and its people know the real meaning of community responsibility. It showed that you have here the proper blend of individual initiative and group cooperation.

This spirit is no less evident in Winston-Salem today. The dedication of this new sewage treatment plant clearly demonstrates your continuing determination to move forward as a community — to keep step with the rapid strides that our state is taking toward a better way of life for our people. I feel that it also illustrates the importance of individual leadership and preseverance in community affairs. This plant has not been named for Archie Elledge simply to honor an outstanding public servant. Certainly, the honor in intended—and well deserved—but I prefer to think that this plant has been named for a man who, with uncommon foresight, saw a need and unhesitatingly shouldered the burden of responsible leadership required to meet the need.

Almost a decade ago, Archie Elledge realized that the continuing growth and development of this city was being threatened by the lack of adequate sewage treatment facilities. It would have been a simple matter for him to point out this need and leave its solution to others, but such was not the case. He campaigned actively, first, to gain the necessary backing of municipal and business leaders, and then, to convince the public. When he had accomplished these two objectives, he assumed the responsibility of seeing the program through. His record as chairman and, at the present time, a member of the Public Works Committee of the Board of Aldermen has been a model of dedicated public service.

I am told that Elledge was most active and influential in the successful effort to gain public approval for the issuance of $6,500,000 in sewer improvement bonds in 1954. I can only echo the sentiment expressed by your Board of Aldermen last October when it passed the resolution naming this plant: . . . "the part taken by Archie Elledge in the accomplishment of this notable project deserves to be recognized and to be remembered by the citizens of Winston-Salem." I commend Mr. Elledge on his vision, his leadership ability, and his dedication to public service.

May I also commend the two state agencies that contributed

to this project—the State Board of Health and the State Stream Sanitation Committee. Both have shown an active interest in this undertaking from the beginning. It was in 1950 that the Stream Sanitation Committee staff joined city engineers for the purpose of investigating, to a limited degree, the various water borne industrial wastes being discharged either to streams within the city or the sanitary sewage system of the city, and to conduct pilot plant studies to determine the effectiveness of the high rate trickling filter sewage treatment process on sewage and industrial waste then being received at the existing treatment plant. This cooperative effort proved to be of considerable value in later investigations conducted relative to the overall improvement program.

I understand that this new plant is the largest of its type, in terms of capacity, in North Carolina, and that it is the most modern that can be designed. Our stream sanitation officials tell me that this plant provides complete treatment for all of the sewage and industrial waste in and adjacent to the city. When you consider the plight of some of our municipalities, it must be a tremendous source of pride to the people of Winston-Salem to know that your community owns a plant that will treat 18,000,000 gallons of sewage and industrial waste daily, eliminating at least 90 per cent of the pollution. And I am quite sure that it will be a great consolation to city officials to know that a high percentage of complaints will also be elmininated.

I cannot stress too strongly the importance of other communities, large and small, throughout our state following the example that has been set here in Winston-Salem. You have not only increased your capacity for treating industrial waste, but you have laid the lines and made other improvements in your entire system which will enable you to accommodate a growing and expanding community. And you have greatly increased the quantity of water that is available for use in the Winston-Salem area. Achievements of this nature do not go unnoticed. I cannot, of course, say that the events of this day will alone insure this city's future prosperity, but I have no hesitancy about saying that the beneficial effects of this achievement will be helpful and will be felt for many decades to come.

Steady progress is being made throughout North Carolina in

improving the overall quality of our water resources, which are so vital to the progress of our state. During the past year the Division of Water Pollution Control, serving as administrative agent for the Stream Sanitation Committee, concentrated on expediting basic stream studies preparatory to assigning classifications to the waters of the state, and in administering the state's responsibilities in establishing an effective stream pollution prevention and abatement program.

The stream study program has been directed toward obtaining useful, up-to-date data on water use, sources of pollution, and existing water quality. During 1958 this work resulted in the completion of pollution surveys in the Hiwassee, Little River, and Tar River basins, representing an area equivalent to 13.46 per cent of the state. Classifications were assigned to the waters of the French Broad basin and three public hearings were held in the Cape Fear basin for the purpose of presenting classification proposals to the public. This brought the number of river basins studied to twelve (88.7 per cent of the state) and the number of basins classified to six (56 per cent of the state). The division also conducted sixteen special plant studies, considered essential in providing up-to-date and dependable data relating to the volume and characteristics of sewage and waste being discharged in our streams.

The program of the Pollution Control Section of the division has, during the past twelve months, been concerned primarily with the development and execution of comprehensive pollution abatement plans in classified river basins, the encouragement of voluntary abatement projects, and the administration of the program of federal grants, under Public Law 660, for the construction of municipal sewage treatment works. These federal funds have stimulated municipal pollution abatement efforts throughout the state. Allocations during the past year totaled $1,260,950, and I think it speaks well for our communities that many more applications were received than could be supported by available funds.

These activities indicate that the people of North Carolina are becoming more and more aware of the importance of pollution abatement on a state-wide basis. This is a good thing for it shows we are laying a solid foundation for future progress.

The city of Winston-Salem, its people and its leaders, are to be congratulated on the foresight they have shown. Here is striking evidence of your willingness to carry your share of the load. You have shown that here is a community that believes in itself, has faith in its future and the future of this state, and has the determination to make that future a prosperous one.

Thank you.

REMARKS ACCEPTING A PORTRAIT OF FORMER GOVERNOR W. KERR SCOTT

RALEIGH
May 7, 1959

[A joint session of the General Assembly, together with the family and a large concourse of the friends of W. Kerr Scott, packed the Hall of the House of Representatives for this event. House Speaker Addison Hewlett introduced Terry Sanford, a former Scott lieutenant and a future governor of North Carolina, who made the principal address, eulogizing Governor Scott, after which the Scott portrait was accepted by Governor Hodges on behalf of the state of North Carolina. The portrait, done by Howard Chandler Christy, was unveiled by Elizabeth White Lowdermilk of Cayuga Falls, Ohio, a granddaughter of former Governor Scott.]

I consider it a privilege to join you here this evening in paying tribute to a man who, during almost forty years of public service, gave unstintingly of his time, his great energy, and his unique talents to the building of a better way of life for the people he loved—the people of North Carolina. It is, indeed, an honor to represent the people of this state on this special occasion, for few men in the history of North Carolina could match Kerr Scott in the deep, personal affection accorded him by the people he sought to serve.

We are especially pleased to have with us this evening the members of Governor Scott's family, several of whom have traveled a considerable distance in order to be present for this significant event in their lives and in the life of our state. We are deeply indebted to each of them for their wonderful gift.

In the decades ahead, North Carolina's history will record

the many achievements of the Scott administration, undiminished in importance. They are engraved on the face of our land in many forms and they will not soon be forgotton by our people. The roads he helped pave, the schools he helped to build, the medical programs he established or expanded, the principles of government he lived by—all stand as solid evidence of his dedication and ability.

In his term as governor, Kerr Scott directed the addition of almost 15,000 miles of paving to the state highway system—mainly secondary or farm to market roads. Permanent improvements, costing more than $331,000,000, were made at state-supported institutions of higher learning and at the various state operated medical and health institutions during his four years in office.

At Governor Scott's insistence, an annual appropriation of $550,000 was established for use in a much needed public school health program. Realizing that the expansion of the state's port facilities was essential to the state's future development, he supported efforts that led to an appropriation of $7,500,000 for ports at Wilmington and Morehead.

Many words have been used to describe the man we honor here this evening. To some he was stubborn, stern, tenacious, uncompromising. To others he was understanding, gentle, practical, and even sentimental. I perfer to think that he possessed a degree of all these qualities, for there are times when each is needed—times when gentleness and understanding produce results, and other times when a man must stand his ground—alone if necessary—to get the job done. Faith in one's self and courage to fight for one's convictions are essential qualities of leadership. Kerr Scott, most certainly, possessed those qualities.

It has also been said of this man that he was unpredictable. Perhaps, in some ways, he was. He was a man who kept his own counsel, who had a wonderful sense of timing and a flair for the dramatic. His actions carried impact, and there were undoubtedly those who had difficulty anticipating the method he would use to attain his goals. But, if he was unpredictable, it was only in the methods he used and not in the goals he sought. From the first day he entered public life—as a county agent in 1920—he was guided by a driving ambition and desire to make North Carolina a better place in which to live. In his decades of devoted service—as a farm agent, as master of the State Grange, as commissioner of agriculture, as governor and as United States Senator —he never once lost sight of this objective.

North Carolina is today, and will remain, a better place in which to live because of the contributions made by this great citizen and dedicated public servant—W. Kerr Scott.

May I conclude by expressing to Mrs. Scott and the members of her family the very sincere and heartfelt appreciation of the people of this state for the wonderful gift you have presented this evening. It is a great honor for me to accept this portrait of Governor Scott on behalf of the state of North Carolina. It will be displayed with great pride and I am certain that it will serve in the years ahead as an inspiration to all who love this state and its people.

Thank you!

REMARKS AT PHILLIPS PETROLEUM
COMPANY AWARD DINNER

RALEIGH
May 9, 1959

[The occasion of these remarks was a dinner at the Sir Walter Hotel honoring the Raleigh division of the Phillips Petroleum Company, which was receiving the K. S. Adams Award for the greatest percentage gain in products sales during the past year in competition with sixteen other sales divisions of the Phillips Company throughout the nation. About 300 Phillips people from North Carolina, South Carolina, and Virginia were present at the dinner. N. W. O'Haver, division manager for the Carolinas and Virginia, received the award, which was presented by Stanley Learned, chairman of the executive committee and assistant to the president of the Phillips Petroleum Company. The Governor took advantage of the occasion to advocate the establishment of an oil refinery on the coast of North Carolina.]

I am honored that you have given me the privilege of sharing with the Phillips Petroleum Company and its people an event that holds great significance for the company and especially, in this instance, for the Raleigh division. Mrs. Hodges and I deeply regret that we will not be able to meet your board chairman, Mr. K. S. Adams and Mrs. Adams. We certainly wish for Mr. Adams a complete recovery from his sudden illness. However, we have enjoyed getting to know Mr. Stanley Learned, Mr. Ted Lyons, and your other company officials and their wives. We extend to all of them a most cordial and friendly welcome to North Carolina.

I would also like to congratulate the officers and personnel of the Raleigh division on the honor they are receiving this evening. I understand that seventeen sales divisions, covering thirty-six states, compete annually for this coveted award. It is honor enough to win the K. S. Adams Award at any time, but when the newest of the seventeen divisions is selected the first year it enters the competition, then the honor acquires even greater significance. Every person in the division should be proud of this achievement. I know my long-time personal friend, Senator Clarence Stone, one of your distributors, is "bustin' with pride."

I have watched with considerable interest, the growth of this Raleigh division since the company entered this regional market in 1954. I have seen pipeline terminals established at Greensboro and Charlotte, and a water terminal located at Wilmington—investments costing approximately $1,500,000. Capital expenditures and commitments of service station construction are in excess of $3,000,000. The staff operating out of the Raleigh office has increased to 125 people with an annual payroll of $750,000.

I am not surprised by this progress because, when Phillips established the Raleigh division, you invested wisely in one of the fastest-growing and most progressive areas of the nation. This division covers North Carolina, South Carolina, Virginia, and fringe areas of Georgia, Tennessee, and Kentucky. You will not find a comparable area in the country that possesses as great a potential for economic development as this. The future belongs to the South. If your company has been *impressed* by this division's initial growth, then I confidently predict that you will be *astonished* by what the future holds.

I do not have to remind this audience that industrial development and prosperity in the oil industry are closely related, but

I would call your attention to the fact that North Carolina's industrial growth in recent years has been phenomenal. During 1958, our efforts to strengthen and diversify our industrial economy resulted in investments in new and expanded industries amounting to $253,074,000. A total of 21,757 new jobs were created for our people and annual payrolls increased by $72,633,000. At a time when industrial growth throughout the nation was dropping more than 17 per cent below the previous year's total, North Carolina was gaining 32.5 per cent. In other words, we did 50 per cent better than the national average.

I was delighted to read in your recent report to your stockholders that your company took the recent general recession in its stride. And I was particularly pleased to note that you attributed much of your success to "the stabilizing effects of broad diversification." I note that your program of diversification and the results you obtained from this program very closely parallels the program of agricultural and industrial diversification that we have been advocating in this state for many years. And we have been getting results. For instance, of all the new industrial plants established in North Carolina in 1958, the largest investment—$67,155,000—was in metal working. Chemical plants—with an outlay of $63,087,000—was second. Then came tobacco manufacturing with capital investments totaling $33,605,000 and textiles with $30,014,000. Go back a few years and you will find that the two leaders—metal working and chemicals—were hardly worth a mention in our industrial surveys.

Another exciting development in 1958 was the progress made in our food processing industry. More than $21,000,000 was invested last year in sixty-three separate facilities designed primarily to process, package, and market our agricultural products. More than 2,300 new jobs were created in this one industry, boosting the income of our people by more than $6,814,000. And greater things are yet to come. Swift and Company has just established a multi-million dollar meat packing plant in Wilson, forty-seven miles to the east; Gerber is investing millions in a processing and marketing facility at Asheville, 250 miles to the west; and the

Ball Brothers Company is building a huge glass container manufacturing plant, also at Asheville.

The point I am making is that North Carolina—because it
possesses all the essential qualities needed to insure continued
growth and development—is a sound investment for your company.
I think the occasion that brought you here this evening is striking
proof of this fact. This may be the first, but it will not be the
last award that this division will receive. It is inevitable that this
area of the nation assumes a greater share of the industrial leadership that for too many years has been concentrated in other areas.
Markets for all products are expanding, and industry will continue to expand to meet the need.

I hope you will not feel that I am taking advantage of this occasion when I suggest that there are unlimited opportunities here
for continued expansion of your own company's operations.
North Carolina, for instance, would be an excellent location for
the establishment of a refinery. Our deep water ports are ideally
situated to handle imports of crude oil from South America or
the Middle East. A refinery located near one of these ports could
economically process and distribute your products to meet rapidly
growing demands throughout this growing region.

I am confident that such an operation would be practical and
profitable. One of the main reasons for my confidence, not just in
this operation, but in all economic activity affecting North Carolina, is the people. I know the people of this state, and I know
that they are determined to build a progressively better life for
themselves and those who will come after them. They are productive, are conscientious in their work—and I can give you the names
of a hundred industrialists in the state, old and new, who will
attest to this fact. These men have confidence in themselves and
faith in their ability to achieve whatever goal they seek. They
know the potential here, and they have demonstrated their burning desire to convert this potential into reality. I think it is evident that they are succeeding—and I glory in their success.

In conclusion, may I again express our pride in the honor that
has come to the Raleigh division and, at the same time, our pride
in having so many distinguished visitors in our state. And, if I
may presume to speak for the Raleigh division, I would like to

say with complete confidence, that it would be a real pleasure to have Mr. Adams come to North Carolina next year to visit the Raleigh division and attend the groundbreaking ceremony of a new refinery on our coast.

Thank you!

***

STATEMENT ON EDUCATIONAL TELEVISION FACILITIES BEFORE THE COMMITTEE ON INTERSTATE AND FOREIGN COMMERCE

WASHINGTON, D. C.
May 13, 1959

[This statement was read for Governor Hodges by Earl Wynn, Professor of Radio, Television, and Motion Pictures and Director of the Communications Center at the University of North Carolina in Chapel Hill. The Governor had remained in Raleigh to make a television appearance in favor of the school incentive fund legislation which he had recommended to the General Assembly (see pp. 997-998).]

I deeply appreciate this opportunity to submit a statement at these public hearings on proposed federal legislation which would expedite the utilization of educational television facilities. My responsibilities in connection with the meeting of the General Assembly of North Carolina prevent my making this statement in person.

I have been governor of North Carolina since November 7, 1954. WUNC-TV has been telecasting since January 8, 1955. As you will note, the lengths of our service to North Carolina almost precisely correspond. However, neither WUNC-TV nor I began our educational and public service careers on those dates. The planning for WUNC-TV took many years. I served as lieutenant governor of North Carolina during most of the planning period and was serving in that office when the late William B. Umstead, then governor of North Carolina, died in office. It was during his governorship and my lieutenant governorship that the University of North Carolina decided to enter the field of educational television and began to plan toward that end. It was Governor Umstead who appointed the North Carolina Radio and Television Commission in February of 1953 to assist the University of North Carolina in charting the course for educational television in our state.

I have been actively interested in educational television in North Carolina since its beginnings in our state and during the period of my most active participation in the affairs of our state.

I am pleased to speak in favor of educational television, and in support of federal aid to erect new educational television facilities.

Let me quote an editorial from the *Greensboro Daily News,* Greensboro, North Carolina, an outstanding newspaper, dated Monday, April 27, 1959:

> Senate approval of a bill to provide federal aid for educational TV is not only recognition of but high compliment to the pioneering work done by station WUNC-TV in North Carolina.
>
> Since its start in 1955, the University of North Carolina station, with studios at the Greensboro, Raleigh, and Chapel Hill units of the Consolidated University, has gradually evolved a program of increasing impact upon the cultural and educational life and goals of the state.
>
> While practically all of WUNC-TV's program now falls under the broad term of educational, we are thinking of two partciular facets, one fitting into the public school classroom and the other offering a number of courses in adult education. While many take these courses for credit, the *Daily News* is confident that numerous listeners also tune in on them for personal educational, cultural, and informational benefit. In either instance, they are of inestimable value in a better informed and stimulated citizenry. It is not merely possible but probable that TV's role will become even more important and effective in the education of the future. Enough has already been accomplished to show educational TV's worth and to convince the Senate of its service and its potentialities.
>
> Those who do not utilize the opportunities offered by WUNC-TV are indeed missing something. The program is broad and varied enough to offer something which should appeal to just about everybody. For instance, we have found panel discussions, with sharp clashes of views, on current events and developments and a series of lectures on Russian history especially interesting and informative. The U.S.S.R., with whom this country is trying to live, is more understandable on the basis of background given in the series at point.
>
> Educational TV, as exemplified by what is happening in North Carolina, has a definite role, is accomplishing much and is here not merely to stay but to expand. It is well for the Congress to recognize these facts and to aid a program which contributes to an enlightened citizenry

when increasing complexities darken issues which must be decided at the polls.

Greensboro is located near the center of our state, and at the Woman's College of the Consolidated University of North Carolina in Greensboro is located one of the three studios of WUNC-TV. This editorial, only one of many I could quote, is typical of the great interest being shown by our people in the coverage area of WUNC-TV.

Let me now quote from a typical, unsolicited letter, from outside of the coverage area of WUNC-TV (and there are also many of these):

> Montreat, N. C.
> Box 47
> October 30, 1958
>
> Altogether—I am hoping and wondering, as to the possibilities for extending the coverage of WUNC to Western North Carolina. We don't like to be envious of the areas nearer Chapel Hill, but we are residents of the state, even over here in Western N. C.—and it would be a wonderfully fine thing if we could take advantage of some of the really fine programs, which we see listed in the TV Guide, as originating in WUNC-TV.
>
> I am sure you have this in mind, but will appreciate some word from you as to progress along this line. It would seem that in spite of the economy talk which is always present in the legislature, and rightly so, it would be difficult to find any purpose which would be more commendable than to extend the facilities of the educational institutions of the state—to all of the state.
>
> This is bound to come—I trust that it may be soon.
>
> Sincerely yours,
> John P. Williams

We recognize that all North Carolinians are entitled to the educational television service now available to those who live in the central part of our state, approximately two-thirds of our 4,500,000 citizens.

I shall not attempt to list or even summarize the vast amount of programming which WUNC-TV has originated in the field of government and related public issues. It has worked hard and effectively to keep the people of North Carolina informed about their state, their government, and the nation in which we live. WUNC-TV has contributed much to the welfare of North Carolina, and I hope that it will be able to continue serving our people for many years to come.

While the state of North Carolina has provided most of the funds for the operation of WUNC-TV since July, 1955, it cannot provide the necessary capital funds to erect new and additional educational television facilities which would assure making available this valuable service to all the people of North Carolina. The passage of a proposed educational television legislation now before this committee would be most beneficial in extending this valuable network of education and information across North Carolina.

ADDRESS AT DEDICATION OF THE ELLIOTT DUNCAN ELEMENTARY SCHOOL

MAYODAN
May 30, 1959

[The Governor was in his home county on this occasion to dedicate a school named after the retiring principal who had spent twenty-seven years in the town's school system.]

It is always a pleasure to visit again in my own Rockingham County and to see again many old friends. This event is an eloquent expression of a community's respect and admiration for a friend of mine and a man who richly deserves every token of appreciation that you can bestow upon him. Certainly, he has earned this recognition—both as an educator and as a citizen.

Elliott Duncan's life is a story of a man's courage, determination, and faith in himself. It is also a story of unselfish dedication to the cause of good public education and to the service of his friends and neighbors. The man that we have gathered here to honor today first came to Mayodan and Rockingham County in 1907, an orphan at the age of thirteen. For several years he worked in the local textile mills, but his desire for a better education prompted him to give up his job and enter Saint Pauls School in Beaufort. Graduating in 1914, he immediately entered the University of North Carolina where he received has bachelor's degree in 1918. Returning to Mayodan in that year, he became principal of the local school. Except for a six-year period in the early 20's, when he served as principal at Walnut Cove and at his former school in Beaufort, he has been here ever since.

It would be presumptuous of me to attempt to tell this audience of the contribution that Elliott Duncan has made to this community during the past thirty-three years. This community today bears ample evidence of these contributions. They are seen, not only in the educational life of this town, but in the civic, religious, and cultural life as well. A clergyman in his church has written that "he works not for credit or honor, but out of a deep devotion and loyalty to his fellowman." A former student has written "he has always been completely selfless in his concern for his students, and he has given freely of a wealth of love and understanding to them." A member of his faculty has told of the good he has done in the community, of his "humble spirit" and the example of Christian living he has set for the children under his care. Sentiments of this type are not expressed lightly and without considerable reason. I am sure that the citizens of this community join with me when I say that we are proud to have Elliott Duncan as a friend.

May I also say that I am proud of this community and this county, for the event that you have arranged here today is far more than a mere tribute to a deserving and truly outstanding man. It is also resounding evidence of your continued interest in your schools, and in the education of your young people. In this enthusiastic recognition of the contribution that Elliott Duncan has made to your community and its people, there is a good indication of the high value you place on education itself. It is also dramatic evidence of the fact that North Carolina has traveled far in a relatively short time in this tremendously important field.

I think it is well for us to look, occasionally, at the road we have traveled in education in order to gain a perspective of where we are at the present time and where we are going in the future. Our history shows that in Colonial days little success was accorded the effort to promote interest in education. Schooling was simply not for the masses. Education was for "gentlemen" and those of the professional classes. These members of the elite received elementary training in church schools, but had to leave the state for their higher education. It was not until after the Revolution that it became apparent that the success of democratic government would depend largely on educated leaders and educated people.

The North Carolina Constitution of 1776 acknowledged this when it provided "that a school or schools shall be established by the Legislature for the convenient instruction of youth . . . ." This provision resulted in the establishment, not of public schools, put private academies. More than 200 such academies were chartered between 1777 and 1830, but they were, for the most part, poorly supported and poorly run. They contributed little to the advancement of education in North Carolina.

Much of the responsibility for this poor state of affairs fell upon the General Assembly, but it was a responsibility shared by the citizens of the day who, generally, were indifferent to the need or value of educating their young people.

Some progress was made in the years leading to the Civil War, and for this progress the state is indebted to its religious institutions. The people came gradually to demand better educational facilities, especially in the field of higher education—and the churches responded. Such schools as Wake Forest, Davidson, and Duke stand today in evidence of this response. Some credit, however, does go to the state, for, finally, during this pre-Civil War period, the first public school law was enacted by the legislature.

This law recommended the division of the state into 1,250 districts, estimating an average school population for each district of 108 children between the ages of eight and fifteen; the establishment of normal schools; and the holding of an election in each county to vote on the issue of "schools" or "no schools." It is also significant that during this period the seeds were sown for the establishment of many small schools that have, down through the years, contributed so much to North Carolina.

During and following the Civil War, little progress was made. Unsettled conditions, Reconstruction, and economic hardship were just a few of the factors that accounted for this tragic lack of advancement. These problems continued to plague us even into the twentieth century, and it has taken considerable courage, determination, and sacrifice to overcome them. But, overcome them we have, and I feel certain that the men who fought for better education in North Carolina a century ago would be extremely pleased with conditions in their state today. They would also be pleased that, in spite of the progress made, we are more enthusiastic today than ever about education. There is no vestige of complacency in our attitude. On the contrary, North Carolinians are well aware that education is an integral factor in building a better, more prosperous life for all. We all recognize that our young people are our citizens of the future, and our educational efforts are directed to help them develop their full potential as educated, alert men and women.

More than 100 years ago, Daniel Webster wrote, "If we work upon marble, it will perish; if on brass, time will efface it; if we rear temples, they will crumble into dust; but if we work upon immortal minds, and imbue them with principles, with the just fear of God and love of our fellow-men, we engrave on those tablets something that will brighten to all eternity."

This is a fact that we have long recognized in North Carolina. It is the philosophy that we have followed—and it has made us strong. If we continue to follow it, as we most certainly shall, it will give us the strength needed to face the challenging years ahead.

Again, it has been a most pleasant and gratifying experience to join you here today in this program of recognition for an outstanding citizen of this community and the state of North Carolina. We are indebted to Elliott Duncan for the service he has rendered, and I am sure that you join me in wishing for him the very best of everything in the future.

Thank you.

ADDRESS AT THE 184TH ANNIVERSARY OF THE CORPS OF ENGINEERS, U. S. ARMY

Wilmington
June 16, 1959

[This address, which was used to bid farewell to Colonel H. C. Rowland who was being transferred from his Wilmington assignment, was read for Governor Hodges by Edward L. Rankin, Jr., his private secretary. The Governor was too busy with legislative matters coming up during the last days of the 1959 General Assembly to get away from his office in Raleigh at this time.]

It is a pleasure to join with Colonel Rowland, members of his staff, and friends of the Corps of Engineers, U. S. Army, in ceremonies marking the 184th anniversary of the founding of the corps. Its brilliant record, in peace and war, certainly justifies its proud but modest motto.

I should like to take this opportunity to pay a well-deserved tribute to Colonel Rowland, a talented and hard-working Army engineer who has made a remarkable record of dedicated service during his tour of duty in this district. We know him to be a true friend of North Carolina who has responded freely and effectively to our requests for help and advice on so many occasions. It was my pleasure to have him with me during visits to the coast during and after our destructive hurricanes, and I found him to be a valued and trusted adviser on so many of the serious coastal problems facing our state. We shall miss him greatly, but wish him Godspeed and continued success in his new assignment.

The story of the corps opens with the Revolution. The colonists had few professional engineers. Colonel Richard Gridley, soon to be appointed chief engineer of the "Grand Army," was a self-trained, practical engineer.

Wars, even in those days, could not be won without professional engineers. General Washington sought aid from France, then a great engineering center. Louis XVI secretly sent four highly-trained, professional engineers from France to assist Washington. They were to report to Washington at Philadelphia but landed at New River, North Carolina, in June 1777. Engineers from other European countries also voluntarily joined the Americans. Around these men, Washington built his army's engineering capability which played a major role in winning independence. Both the Corps of Engineers and the American engineering profession sprang from that beginning.

In 1802, Congress provided for a complete reorganization of the army which included the establishment of a separate Corps of Engineers as a military academy with headquarters at West Point, New York. Thus, in the beginning the Corps of Engineers and the United States Military Academy were one and the same. The corps, for many years, was the only means of educating and training engineers in the United States. The corps continued to operate West Point until the Civil War period. Our early civilian engineering schools came out of this source.

Spurred by the War of 1812, the corps recognized the critical need for roads, waterways, and harbors to move troops and supplies and to develop the economic expansion necessary to sustain military strength. While the construction of such improvements at that time was a state, local, or private responsibility, the Army Engineers were constantly called upon for engineering assistance as the army was the only source of available engineering talent.

Accordingly, the corps began the survey of coastal streams and harbors; the location of routes for roads, railroads, and canals connecting the seaboard with the interior; built one of the earliest steamboats to explore the Ohio, Mississippi, and Missouri Rivers; recommended improvement of these rivers and the connection of the Mississippi by canal with Lake Michigan; opened up harbors for steamships on the Great Lakes; and performed many other tasks essential to the internal growth of our young nation.

Army Engineers also led the way in exploring the great West. They sent exploring and surveying parties across the Great Plains. They crossed the Rockies. They went down the great Columbia River to its mouth on the Pacific. Long, Fremont, Bonneville, and many others, were army engineer pathfinders through the wilderness to the far Northwest.

Then came the War with Mexico. Our national territory was pushed to the Pacific in the Southwest, to include California. The part played by army engineer officers was impressive. The roll call of engineers in the Mexican War reads like a roster of famous

Photo by Hugh Morton

Governor Hodges reporting on his trip to Russia at the National Governors' Conference in San Juan, Puerto Rico, August 3, 1959.

Roy Thompson of the *Winston-Salem Journal* (*left*), Governor Hodges, and Miles H. Wolff, executive editor of the *Greensboro Daily News* (*right*), at North Carolina Conference of News and Feature Writers, Chapel Hill, September 5, 1959.

Union and Confederate Generals—Totten (chief engineer), Lee, McClellan, Johnston, Meade, Beauregard, Pope, Halleck, Fremont. To these add Grant, Jackson, and Sherman, of the other arms, for they, too, were qualified engineers as graduates of the Military Academy.

Following the Mexican War, army engineers spearheaded the first western transcontinental railroads. Routes for the first four great systems were surveyed during the 1850's. It is an ironical fact that the first reconnaissances for the lines of the Union Pacific —which played such an important part in holding the West in the Union—were made under direction of West Point graduate Jefferson Davis, United States Secretary of War.

In 1861, the Corps of Engineers prepared the initial plan for curbing floods of the Mississippi. Important progress in the development of hydraulic engineering, useful in bringing other large rivers under control, was first developed during this period.

When the War Between the States began, there were ninety-three engineer officers in the United States Army. Fifteen resigned and joined the Confederate Army. Seventy-seven remained in the Union service. Only one did not serve in the war. Fifty-five of these ninety-three officers became generals. During this titanic struggle, great armies were moved over vast stretches of terrain. Military engineers were indispensable to the commanders on both sides.

When peace came again, engineer officers had their great opportunity in the new peacetime work of the corps. The Civil Works Program, begun in 1824 by the passage of the first Rivers and Harbors Act, was revived to benefit all sections of the reunited nation. Floods along the lower Mississippi were recognized as a growing menace. The corps took over the task of building a continuous levee system, still one of the greatest engineering accomplishments of all times.

The Corps of Engineers has contributed much to the construction of Washington, our nation's capital. The city was originally planned by Major Pierre L'Enfant, one of the brilliant young French engineers who joined the corps during the Revolution. Among the many structures the corps has built, completed, or improved are the great dome of the United States Capitol, the

Washington Monument, the Lincoln Memorial, Key and Memorial bridges, the Library of Congress, the State Department building, the Pentagon, Walter Reed Army Medical Center, and the Washington National Airport. The corps constructed and still operates the Washington Aquaduct.

The most monumental and significant peacetime undertaking of the Corps of Engineers was the construction of the Panama Canal. After two private companies had failed to complete the canal (approximately $300,000,000 had been expended), a treaty was negotiated with the newly created Republic of Panama resulting in acquisition of the canal zone. President Theodore Roosevelt selected an army engineer, Colonel George Washington Goethals, as chief engineer of the canal project. Goethals, with help from Colonel W. C. Gorgas, Medical Department, U. S. Army, and others, was successful in the completion and opening of the canal for traffic in 1914.

The expansion of the corps between 1916 and 1918 was a startling story. From 256 officers in 1916, officer personnel of the corps grew to 11,175 in 1918 and from 2,200 enlisted men to 285,000 for the same period. In World War I, the corps was assigned its first great military-construction task. The construction of ports, supply bases, railroads, roads, bridges, power and water utilities, hospitals, and other means of supporting an expeditionary force of 2,000,000 men fighting almost 4,000 miles from home, was a new and challenging experience.

The period between the two World Wars brought a revolutionary change in the Civil Works Program, particularly in the development of the nation's water resources. Congress in 1936 passed the Flood Control Act. That act authorized the corps to carry out broad, comprehensive surveys, embracing power, navigation, flood control, irrigation, and other water uses, for each of the nation's major river basins. This was a big step toward public and private water conservation and development within the framework of sound river basin planning.

Congress on December 1, 1941, authorized the transfer of the construction division from the construction quartermaster to the Corps of Engineers. The engineers were charged with camp, barracks, and other military construction. Many of the ordnance and war industry plants created with federal funds were built by the engineers or by private contractors under the corps' supervision and control.

The strategic Alcan Highway, built during the second World War by the corps in record-breaking time, is an engineering achievement in the same class as the construction of the Panama Canal and the flood-control measures undertaken by the corps in the Mississippi Valley.

World War II has often been called an "engineer's war" as, in the past, the army engineers were cast in the role of the advance element of combat. Engineer troops were responsible for establishing, under fire, forty-four of sixty-one major beach-heads. They were the first to hit the Normandy beachhead. They cleared the mine fields, assisted in the reduction of fortifications, and bulldozed roads into the interior. Their construction skill kept the mechanized army moving forward.

Probably the most far-reaching engineering service the army engineers were called upon to provide during World War II was the assignment to staff the Manhattan Engineer District, which produced the first atomic bomb.

When the fighting in World War II ended, the corps moved quickly into the current large and comprehensive water resource conservation and development programs. Projects such as the great dams on the Missouri, the Columbia, and other rivers were quickly gotten underway. These were followed by projects such as the recanalization of the Ohio, the construction of the St. Lawrence Seaway, the modernization of the Great Lakes navigation system, and many other similar projects.

When it appeared the Korean campaign was to be the prelude to global warfare, the engineers' feat of building great air bases simultaneously in the Polar Artic wastes and on the African deserts was a major influence in deterring the aggressors.

Today the Army Corps of Engineers is the largest and most highly diversified engineering organization in the world. It is capable of carrying out expeditiously and successfully any mission that may be assigned to it.

Its peacetime mission is dual: military-construction and civil works functions.

Briefly stated, its military-construction mission is to build facilities of every kind, in any part of the world, required by the army, most of the facilities required by the air force, and various facilities for the navy, the Atomic Energy Commission, and other federal agencies.

This mission is carried out primarily through the employment, under contract, of American engineering and construction concerns.

Should war break out, the army engineers will have a parallel responsibility for combat engineering. This is engineering in direct support of, or as an actual part of, battle operations. Typical examples are the destruction of enemy-placed obstacles, overcoming natural obstacles, the construction of fortifications, placement of mines, and other engineering works required by friendly forces.

Both assignments—construction and combat engineering—draw upon the resourceful and experienced military-civil construction organization-in-being, the Army's Corps of Engineers. This organization's intimate knowledge of the capacity and capabilities of the construction industry enables it to draw in turn upon the total construction and engineering resources of the American people.

The Corps of Engineers, under its Civil Works Program, is responsible for the development and conservation of the nation's water resources. This program is a major contributing factor to the continued growth and stability of agriculture and industry. It is accomplished through increased flood protection measures, low-cost water transportation, improved navigation channels and harbors, hydro-electric power, abatement of stream pollution, and the provision of storage for water for industrial, municipal, and other uses. The program also includes construction of great dams, navigation locks, and harbor facilities; the maintenance of navigation channels; construction and relocation of bridges, highways, and railroads; carrying out vast levee-building and revetment programs; control of river channels; and the design and construction of such special purpose structures as the Sunny Point Army Terminal.

In addition to its construction tasks, the Corps of Engineers has a statutory flood-fighting responsibility, as a means of assuring the effective functioning of flood-control works during an emergency. This responsibility includes rescue work, the strengthening, raising, extending, or other modification of flood-control structures, and the repair, restoration, or maintenance of flood-control works threatened or destroyed. Nationwide stand-by organizations, including access to civilian construction organizations and the support of other branches of the military services, are maintained and may be utilized during flood and other emergencies.

Although it is proper to discuss briefly the history and mission of the corps as we celebrate the 184th anniversary of its founding, we are naturally more concerned with the work undertaken by the district offices, our most direct contact with the corps. Six engineer district offices, Charleston, Huntington, Nashville, Norfolk, Savannah, and Wilmington, have some degree of responsibility for the civil works programs within the state of North Carolina. However, the greater responsibility for these programs, as well as all military-construction projects, rests with the Wilmington district. Let us look briefly at some of the work accomplished by that district.

In 1829, the Baltimore district office of the Corps of Engineers assumed responsibility for all navigational work in the state of North Carolina. It was at that time the federal government began improving the Cape Fear River. Wilmington, in those years, was the only import-export city in the state. Fayetteville, 120 miles inland on the Cape Fear River, was the hub of a great trading area. Flat-bottomed boats brought farm products from Fayetteville to Wilmington for trans-shipment to the outside world and carried back manufactured items from New England and foreign lands.

The Wilmington district office was established in 1885. It was quite natural that the Wilmington district office gave top priority to improving navigation in the Cape Fear River, then about eight feet deep at Wilmington and a scant ten feet on the ocean bar channel. Keeping pace with an ever growing commerce, the river's channel to the sea was straightened and deepened in successive steps from the original eight feet to today's depth of thirty-four feet. A study is now being conducted to determine if further channel improvement is warranted.

Beginning in 1912, three locks and dams were constructed on the Cape Fear between Wilmington and Fayetteville to provide a channel eight feet deep. Commerce on this route now approximates 450,000 tons annually.

Originally, the Cape Fear River had three outlets to the sea—two at its mouth at Fort Caswell and a third, New Inlet, some ten miles upstream across the narrow peninsula formed by the river and ocean. New Inlet was closed with a rock dam in 1876-81 to reduce shoaling and to restrict the channel width in the immediate area. Subsequently, the two bar channels at Fort Caswell were merged into one to provide and maintain a deeper channel.

In the 1930's with the dredging of a harbor and approach channel thirty feet deep, a second deep-water port came into service at Morehead City. Prior to this work, water depth there averaged about ten feet.

Another major civil works project constructed by the district, also in the 1930's, was the dredging of the 308-mile North Carolina section of the Atlantic Intracoastal Waterway. The district maintains and operates five bridges over the waterway at Coinjock, Fairfield, Wilkerson Creek, and Core Creek. Other bridges on the waterway are North Carolina obligations.

In all of the district's civil works activities, the construction and maintenance of waterway projects along the state's famed Outer Banks continues to present a formidable challenge. Oregon and Ocracoke Inlets, two major connecting links between the sea and sound, are constantly shifting, as unpredictable today as they were in Black Beard's time.

Extensive hurricane rehabilitation work, including stream clearance and the closure of Long Beach Inlet, has been undertaken by the corps for the Federal Civil Defense Administration. Approximately 470 miles of stream channels will be cleared at an estimated cost of $400,000. Closing of Long Beach Inlet, a major engineering feat, was accomplished at a cost of approximately $165,000. Several beach erosion studies, in cooperation with the state of North Carolina and local communities, are also underway.

Major military installations completed or constructed in entirety by the district during World War II included Fort Bragg,

Camp Butner, Camp Davis, Raleigh-Durham Air Force Base, Greensboro Reserve Training Center, Camp Mackall, Pope Field, Seymour Johnson Air Force Base, Bluethenthal Air Force Base, and Winston-Salem Air Force Base, at a total cost of over $100,000,000.

In addition, the Wilmington District designed and constructed airfields at New Bern, Manteo, and Beaufort for the Civil Aeronautics Administration.

Army and air force construction obligations from the onset of the Korean War in 1950 to the present time cover a wide and diversified range of activities. Some projects, the expansion of Fort Bragg and Pope Air Force Base, for example, followed in large part conventional military-construction patterns. Numerous other projects, however, were new departures and presented challenges not found in the hurry and bustle of World War II days.

Among the "first-run" projects was the Sunny Point Army Terminal on the Cape Fear River almost in sight of the District Office in Wilmington. "Sunny Point," as the terminal is popularly known now, was designed and constructed for the specific purpose of handling ammunition. First of this type and purpose ever built, it embodies every known safety device for the protection of personnel and property. Total cost of the project was approximately $23,000,000.

Among other major construction projects were three hospitals: the 500-bed Veterans Administration Hospital at Durham, with ten floors, at a cost of $7,000,000; the 500-bed General Hospital at Fort Bragg, nine stories, at a cost of $8,000,000; and the fifty-bed single story structure at Seymour Johnson Air Force Base at Goldsboro, at a cost of $1,700,000.

The hospital at Seymour Johnson Air Force Base represented only a segment of a vast reactivation program of the field which had lain idle and left to deteriorate since World War II. Total cost of restoring and modernizing the base was approximately $30,000,000.

Construction at Fort Bragg includes a permanent troop housing development, 1,500 Capehart Family Housing units, an air base for helicopters and light planes, and a communication system. Total cost was approximately $65,000,000.

At nearby Pope Air Force Base, the runway was extended, a hangar, dormitories, and numerous supporting facilities were constructed at a cost of some $10,000,000.

At Charlotte, the old World War II Quartermaster Depot was rehabilitated and modified for production of the NIKE guided missile. The cost was approximately $10,000,000. A similar center at Burlington was constructed at a cost of approximately $3,500,000.

Cost of construction of Army and Air Force Reserve Training Centers in the state was approximately $1,300,000.

The current fiscal year military-construction program totals approximately $16,000,000 and the civil works program $3,600,000—a total of nearly $20,000,000.

The military construction and civil works programs mean a great deal to the economy and welfare of the state of North Carolina. Civil works programs should and must be expanded. This may be accomplished provided local officials, who usually initiate civil works projects, state officials, and personnel of the U. S. Army engineer district offices cooperate in the development of the project.

Civil works projects, generally speaking, are usually of primary concern to local communities rather than to the state as a whole. However, the state should assume its share of responsibility for civil works projects that are not solely local in character.

This administration has recognized and assumed that responsibility. The General Assembly has created a Department of Water Resources that is responsible for the coordination of the state water resource activities. These activities will include practically all projects falling within the civil works program. The General Assembly has also authorized the expenditure of funds not to exceed $150,000 during the biennium commencing July 1, 1959, and ending June 30, 1961, for the purpose of supplementing those funds provided by the federal government under the provisions of Public Law 520, 71st Congress, as amended; Public Law 71, 84th Congress; Public Law 826, 84th Congress; and by local political sub-divisions of the state for the construction of shore protective works within the state. However, such expenditures shall not be allocated or made until it is found that the local political subdivisions interested therein shall have provided two-thirds of the non-federal share of the cost of any given project and shall not in any case exceed one-third of the non-federal share of the cost of such projects. The General Assembly has also provided $600,000 for the acquisition of that area of the Outer Banks extending from Ocracoke Inlet to Cape Lookout and for a co-operative state-federal engineering study to determine the protective measures that should be constructed to rehabilitate and perserve that section of the Outer Banks.

State officials have cooperated with officials of local communities, with the U. S. Army engineer district offices, and with members of the North Carolina Congressional Delegation in the preparation and presentation of economic justification for such civil works projects as the Wilkesboro Reservoir; Wilmington Harbor, including improvement to the channel to the ocean bar near Southport; Beaufort Harbor; Morehead City Harbor; Rollinson Channel; Pantego and Cucklers' Creek; Dismal Swamp Canal; Manteo (Shallowbag) Bay; Stumpy Point Bay; and many other similar projects. State officials are also cooperating with officials of local communities and the U. S. Army district engineer offices in studies concerned with methods to minimize damage to the coastal areas caused by hurricanes; stablization and deepening of Ocracoke, Drum, Bogue, Masonboro, and Lockwood Folly Inlets; Cape Fear and Neuse River basins studies; and many other civil works program studies.

I am confident the Civil Works program will be expanded as the Congress, state and local officials are becoming more and more aware of the need to control, utilize, and conserve the nation's water resources, one of the state's greatest assets. District offices are in key positions to further this work. Without their complete cooperation the program will lag. Colonel Rowland, as well as Colonel Stuart of the Charleston district, has shown great understanding of our problems and has worked diligently to assist the state in solving them. I do not mean to imply that other district engineer officers have not been cooperative and understanding; they have, but insofar as North Carolina is concerned, the greatest responsibility for the Civil Works Program rests first with the Wilmington district and, next, with the Charleston district.

This would be a happier occasion if we were welcoming Colonel Rowland to North Carolina rather than saying good-by. His current tour of duty is rapidly approaching its end.

We will miss Colonel Rowland when he leaves. He has my best wishes, as well as those of all our citizens who have worked with him, for a happy and long life and for continued success in his work.

I deeply appreciate the spirit all of you have shown and your cooperation. The advice and counsel of this Wilmington office, always given upon request, has been of great help to me and to other state and local officials. The work that all of you have accomplished, as members of the corps, and the plans you have made for future Civil Works projects, has been and will be of untold value to our state.

ADDRESS AT THE LOS ANGELES TOWN HALL

Los Angeles, California
July 21, 1959

[Governor Hodges arrived in Los Angeles from Copenhagen, Denmark, on July 20, after a three-weeks tour of Soviet Russia with eight other governors, and spent the rest of the week on the West Coast. Addressing the Town Hall, a large civic group in Los Angeles, on the subject "A Businessman Governor Looks at the Business of Government," he cited his own experience as this type of governor in North Carolina and described the progress made in the state under his administration. Following the speech, which was made at a luncheon in one of the Los Angeles hotels, he toured the nearby Space Technology Laboratory with General James H. Doolittle.]

It is a distinct honor for me to meet with the members of this nationally-known civic organization, and to have this opportunity to talk briefly about the business of government. As the leading nation in the free world, we must always remember that our very existence depends upon how effectively we operate our political parties and our various levels of government.

As business and professional people, I hope you find my viewpoint as a businessman governor interesting. I shall seek to learn more about this exciting city of Los Angeles, your great golden

state of California, and the remarkable expansion and growth
here on the West Coast. Representing the people of North Carolina, I want to extend the warmest greetings and best wishes
from our great state.

I have just flown directly to southern California across the
North Pole from Copenhagen. It was my privilege to be one of
nine American governors who just completed a twenty-one day
tour of Soviet Russia. So I also bring you greetings from your
Russian neighbors just across the top of the world. And they are
your neighbors, (geographically speaking, at least)—as well as
ours—whether we like it or not, in this dazzling age of jet planes,
missiles, and space travel.

Great emphasis in recent years has been placed on a better understanding of the people in other lands. In an effort to reach
through and below the layers of governmental bureaucracy here
and abroad, there has been great stress laid upon the importance
of people-to-people visitations, etc. Our trip to Russia was part
of this direct approach to learn more about Russia and to tell the
Russians, where possible, more about America, especially about
her individual states and our form of government. While such
trips are definitely worthwhile, I am also convinced that we should
expand this people-to-people sharing of information right here at
home in America. We have much to learn of each other in our
own country. As a matter of fact, we must understand each other
as human beings first before we will have much success in understanding our regional and national problems.

We must realize that New England is not just Harvard College with its suburbs; that California has something other than
sun-kissed oranges; that the whole West is not a desert whose
citizens are seeking pork barrel money for building higher and
bigger dams; that every person in Texas does not own an oil
well; that the Middle West does have something other than corn
and pigs; and that the South now not only wears shoes, but makes
them as well.

In North Carolina there is a growing awareness of the importance of getting better acquainted with other sections, and many
far-ranging tours are being made by state and local groups by
plane and bus. More than 130 Tar Heels last month flew to

California in charter aircraft to take a first-hand look at your agriculture and food processing. They returned home much impressed with what they saw, and—more important—with a better understanding of California, its people and its problems. They also witnessed how California is taking the cotton growing business away from the South, despite serious natural barriers here. It was a sobering experience for our farmers to see Californians use former desert land, now irrigated, to produce three to four bales of cotton per acre. The North Carolina yield is less than half this per acre.

In 1952, after more than thirty years in textile manufacturing and selling, and following several assignments with the federal government in Washington and overseas, I decided to become a candidate for lieutenant governor in North Carolina. This decision was not easily reached because I had not been actively engaged in state-wide political campaigns in North Carolina, although I had been an active Democrat, voter, and civic-minded citizen. For many years as an active member of a civic club, I had recognized the basic fact that our political parties and our various levels of government would never rise above the type of men and women who operated the parties and the governmental organizations. I have always been greatly impressed with the vital necessity for each citizen to participate as actively as possible in politics and government. Actually, the two cannot be separated because if you want to accomplish something in government you soon find that you must work through a political party to get results. Politics has been defined as the science of government. Whether this is true or not, we should never forget that political parties and political leaders direct and operate our federal, state, and local governments. It is through political parties that the people express their will at the polls, whether selecting a constable or a President.

As a retired businessman, perhaps my approach to political campaigning and political office was a little unusual in North Carolina—or elsewhere. I was fortunate in having enough financial security so that I did not have to have the job. Furthermore, I approached my campaign as objectively, honestly and with the same vigor as I did in my business and in my business and industrial obligations. This meant speaking out frankly and on all subjects, and making no promises to any one other than that I would devote my energies and my efforts to building a better North Carolina for all our people. In any event, I was fortunate enough to be elected as lieutenant governor, served in this capacity for approximately two years when the governor of North Carolina died suddenly and thereby catapulted me into the governor's chair. I later won my own four-year term by election.

You do not have to be a keen observer of politics and government to note that campaign promises and campaign platforms are a great deal easier to formulate than they are to carry out. After I had been elected lieutenant governor, and later after I was governor, *Business Week* magazine interviewed me on the difference of being a businessman and a politician. I told the writer that there did not need to be any differences except that a politician (including a governor) could not move ahead just by giving orders—he had to "sell" himself, his ideas, and his program.

In this connection, I might say that too many businessmen and industrialists who make great successes in their businesses are "flops" in politics and government. Why is this? Probably because too many of these new public servants try to give orders, get terribly impatient with government bureaucrats (many of whom are honest, hard working, and dedicated people), and fail to practice good public relations.

If business men would study and learn politics and government as they do their own business problems, if they would practice their best employee relations, if they would realize that government is our biggest business, and if they would use their usual direct, straightforward approach and not try to appear as "big shots", then they would do much better and would achieve success rather than failure.

The business of government should be everybody's business. We badly need greater participation in politics by all our people—especially our business and professional men. Those of us who respond to the call for public service must realize that we will get criticism, some of it unfair, but we must be able to take it on the chin and move ahead toward our objectives. Any public official who tries to accomplish anything will be criticized. It's all in a day's work. We must operate in the public view as reported, interpreted, and photographed by the press, radio, and television. All of this calls for good public relations, and sometimes it is tough going, but the job must be done. I invite you to join in.

As a businessman governor, without promises having been made, I set out to do everything I could to improve the economic status of our state. I approached the problem as I would approach a business problem. It was difficult for me to believe that North Carolina was actually forty-fourth in per capita income among the forty-eight states, so I had the University of North Carolina statisticians double-check this fact, and they proved that we were just as bad off as the statistical tables said we were. Although North Carolina ranks as the South's number one industrial state, we are confronted with some tremendous economic problems, not to mention a swiftly-moving economic transition. North Carolina has the nation's largest farm population. In the nation as a whole, the number of people engaged in farming is about 12 to 13 per cent. In North Carolina it is near 30 per cent. Also, we have the second largest number of farms of any state. So it is easy to see that our economy is out of balance from the standpoint of the number of people we have on the farms, and something had to be done to provide new opportunities for the increasing number of farm people who would have to leave farming to seek a livelihood in other pursuits.

To complicate the matter further, North Carolina is the world's greatest producer of flue cured tobacco and this means, of course, that it is the major cash crop. Tobacco growing has its serious problems also; markets can be uncertain, and a sudden drop in tobacco income has very severe effects upon our state's total economy. The direct impact of this one major crop on our state is graphically revealed by what happened in 1957. The decrease in tobacco farm income alone during 1957, over the previous year, amounted to $137,313,000, or a drop of 27.1 per cent. This serious drop was due to several factors, including acreage reductions and adverse weather conditions. As a result of this single farm income loss, and in spite of a record year of industrial growth, North

Carolina's per capita income dropped from forty-fourth to forty-fifth in the nation.

While North Carolina leads the South in industrial production, this industrial growth has been built primarily on three giant natural resources—cotton, tobacco, and forests—which translate into textiles, tobacco processing, and furniture manufacturing. These primary industries have contributed a great deal to the industrial development of the state, but they are traditionally low skill, low pay industries.

My program to help answer these problems included heavy emphasis on industrialization, a better distribution of industry in the state (50 per cent of the present industry can be found in ten of our 100 counties), encouragement of local communities to organize their own industries to process natural resources, more food processing, agricultural diversification, better forestry utilization, and the organization of a research committee to do something about the remarkable educational resources available in the close proximity of the University of North Carolina, Duke University, and North Carolina State College.

To stimulate interest and to encourage greater participation by local communities in any phase of this program, I averaged 200 speeches a year—often doing three a day in three different communities—and was gratified to see the warm response from local leaders—whether business, professional, civic, or agricultural. I quickly found out that people will respond to objective, energetic leadership. We encouraged the formation of local and regional development organizations which could develop their own programs for their own cities, counties, and areas—whether the primary needs seemed to be agricultural, industrial, educational, etc. To provide long-term venture capital for small local industries, I helped raise $1,000,000 in stock to establish the North Carolina Business Development Corporation. During the past three years, this private institution has approved seventy-eight loans totaling more than $7,000,000, which includes $644,980 participation by banks in several of the individual loans. Loans have been made to many types of businesses and industry across the state, some newly created and others long established, but each loan has resulted in the expansion of production and an increase in employment. More than 10,000 jobs have been created or maintained by these loans, and this is what really counts because we are striving mightily to provide jobs, pay checks, and economic opportunity for our people.

North Carolina's industrial growth in recent years has been phenomenal. We have succeeded in shattering our own development records each year since 1956, while running far ahead of the regional and national expansion averages. In 1958, while the nation—suffering the effects of a serious recession, invested 17.4 per cent *less* in new and expanded industrial facilities, North Carolina registered an *increase* of 32.5 per cent. During this one year, more than $253,000,000 was invested in 423 new plants and expansions, providing 21,757 new jobs and increasing our industrial payroll by $72,633,000.

During the period, 1956-1958, investments in 1,037 new and established industries in North Carolina totaled $592,319,500. New jobs were created for 53,897 people—many of whom were displaced farm workers—and payrolls were boosted by $170,753,900.

All of my early problems, however, did not turn out to be economic. Scarcely six months before I became governor, the United States Supreme Court handed down its first decision on school integration. This was a problem of such magnitude that it completely overshadowed everything else until some reasonable answer could be found. To give you some idea of the complexity involved, in North Carolina our Negro population varies from .3 of 1 per cent in one of our 100 counties up to 67 percent in another one of our counties. So, obviously, the race problem varies among our 100 counties as it can and does vary among the states of the nation. As a result, our approach in North Carolina to the school integration problem has been one of placing the basic responsibility for the operation of our public schools upon local school boards who are closest to the schools, the people, and the districts served. So far, our North Carolina approach of moderation has operated satisfactorily; several of our cities have voluntarily accepted Negro applicants to white schools although the vast majority of the Negro children are voluntarily attending their own public schools.

Mrs. Hodges, Governor Hodges, and Mrs. Lewis R. Holding at a Sunday evening buffet during the Southern Governors' Conference at Asheville, October 11, 1959.

Group of participants in the Southern Governors' Conference at Asheville on a visit to Mount Mitchell, October 13, 1959. Seated *(left to right)*: John M. Patterson, Alabama; J. Caleb Boggs, Delaware; J. Lindsay Almond, Virginia; James P. Coleman, Mississippi; Governor Hodges. Standing *(left to right)*: Ernest F. Hollings, South Carolina; Orval E. Faubus, Arkansas; Cecil H. Underwood, West Virginia; J. Millard Tawes, Maryland.

It is my honest conviction that if the truth were really known concerning the basic attitudes and feeling of the average person in those states outside the South, with respect to racial relations, we would find that it is not a great deal different from that of the southern citizen. Any difference is largely explained by the differences in the degree of the problem and the historic background—or lack of it—of the different sections of our nation.

I do think that the attitude of the average person throughout this country is changing on this volatile question. Attitudes are changing, not only about the school segregation problem, but about other things on which the United States Supreme Court has recently ruled, especially those affecting so-called individual rights. I think that there is a deepening concern on the part of the average man, whether from the North or the South, from the East or West, whether Republican, Democrat, or so-called Independent. There is a genuine concern about where we are going. He is concerned that in our seeming desire to protect individual liberties we are often throwing individual responsibility to the wind.

Naturally we all have our own points of view on questions such as racial equality and the responsibility of individuals in relation to their government. As I see it, the southern point of view means the preservation of the initiative and personality of the individual, of the local governmental unit, and of the state. This point of view carries with it a reverence for our forefathers and for the principles which inspired them. It includes a deep and abiding sense of patriotism for state and nation. It means that we do not hastily take up fancy new theories and that we do not like undue concentration of a governmental power nor an exaggerated influence of minority pressure groups.

The southern point of view means a certain kind of conservatism, born of caution and suffering—a conservatism based upon respect for those things and practices of the past which time has proved good and worthy—a conservatism based upon a realistic appraisal of the hard facts of life as they exist at the present.

We as southerners know that we are not perfect and we know that we can improve. As an indivisible part of these United States, we shall continue to make our earnest and sincere contributions to the welfare of our beloved nation. The South is a region of unlimited potential.

When we urge and support the fundamental principle of regional responsibility and freedom, of state responsibility and freedom, of local responsibility and freedom, and of individual responsibility and freedom, we are promoting and protecting the interests of the individual citizen in California, Massachusetts, Texas, and Minnesota and each and everyone of our many other great states just as we are attempting to hold inviolate for ourselves the freedoms that are dear to us.

It is not, in my humble opinion, in the national interest for minority groups, of whatever race, color or belief, to be used as political pawns by either or both of our major political parties. Of course, every civilized nation has a legitimate and proper concern for the protection of the rights of individuals. Certainly, there can be such a thing as tyranny by majority rule. But what we are faced with today is, in my opinion, exactly the reverse. It is high time more of our political leaders came out for the "majority" in this country instead of persisting in an unsightly scramble to appease "minorities" as a means of gaining political advantage.

What we need in both of our major political parties and in all sections of this nation is love and concern for our country first with political expediency or advantage placed last.

In my travels outside my state and nation, I have often had people ask me: "Why do North Carolinians love their state so much?" I have never been able to give an adequate answer, except to acknowledge the fact that this love *does* exist and that it is a strong motivating force underlying all the things that have been accomplished in North Carolina during the past half century.

I know that Californians also love their state with the same unselfish affection that moves people to work together for the common good of all. As Americans, we should unite as one people in supporting and working for what is best for our nation and the unchanging principles for which it stands. This can be accomplished by emphasizing our strong common heritage as a democratic, freedom-loving people. In other words, let us accentuate the many basic things that unite us as Americans. We must not allow anyone to exploit the few differences, whether on a state or regional basis, that may divide us.

The United States, operating through our federal government, cannot provide the world leadership thrust upon our nation unless our citizens generally understand and are willing to meet the challenge of these difficult times. This challenge also requires the best leadership available at every level of govenment and at every level of our political parties.

It is often said that everybody's business is nobody's business. Government today, whether in the town council, county board of commissioners, state legislature, governor's office, White House, or the Congress, is *everybody's* business which must be tended by *everybody*. As business, professional, and civic leaders, you share heavily in the responsibility to provide the enlightened, capable, and unselfish leadership needed in politics and government today. I know that you will do your part.

COMMENTS ON THE WORK OF THE 1959 GENERAL ASSEMBLY

On State-wide Radio and Television Network

August 13, 1959

[These comments occupied approximately fifteen minutes of a thirty-minute program originating on television from Station WTVD in Durham, and on radio from Station WPTF in Raleigh. The remainder of the half hour was used by the Governor to answer questions about his trip to Russia. The Governor's Russian trip, which began on June 21, and a subsequent vacation on the West Coast, were in part responsible for delaying this address until nearly two months after the adjournment of the General Assembly on June 20.]

You will recall that last February I recommended to the General Assembly a far-reaching legislative program, and most of these recommendations were approved by the General Assembly.

THE STATE BUDGET

The greatest single item to confront any legislature is the state budget. The 1959 General Assembly, so far as budget matters are concerned, was progressive. For the 1959-61 biennium, the two-year period just begun, General Fund appropriations made by the legislature for current operations amount to $582,325,723, an increase of approximately 14 per cent over General Fund expenditures for operations during the past biennium. Highway Fund appropriations amount to $271,141,761, which is an increase of approximately 5 per cent. When we add federal funds and all other receipts which go to support our state government, the total state budget for the coming biennium amounts to $1,264,252,531. This includes funds for schools, higher education, highways, agriculture, etc.

As you know, by far the greatest portion of our state budget is for public schools and our institutions of higher learning. For the public schools alone, the 1959 General Assembly appropriated for the two-year period ahead $377,000,000, an increase of $37,000,000 over the preceding budget.

As usual, there was great discussion and some disagreement on some school matters and on teacher pay. In addition, keen interest was shown in how North Carolina stands in its teaching and educational methods. Several study commissions were authorized to study our schools. This is good and I hope the public will get aroused at local and state levels to the point where we will demand the best schools and be willing to pay for them. We are losing ground because we have refused until now to look at our school problems realistically.

The General Assembly provided very liberally for our institutions of higher education. A total of $45,500,000 was appropriated for the two-year period for all our institutions of higher learning, compared with $36,000,000 appropriated the last biennium. This is an increase of approximately 25 per cent in appropriations for the University and state-supported colleges.

We are proud of our university and other state-supported colleges. The assembly provided liberally for salary improvements and gave the institutions great flexibility in salary administration.

For public welfare, the total amount appropriated from state funds comes to about $21,000,000, an increase of 17 per cent over the preceding budget period expenditures. This increase in welfare funds will provide for the expected increase in case loads under the various assistance programs and—I wish to emphasize this—a continuation of the average monthly payments for the various programs at rates not less than those applying during 1958-59.

The General Assembly, following the administration's recommendation provided liberal increases in the budget for our correctional schools and for probation and parole programs—all of which are most important.

For the state's building needs, the General Assembly authorized appropriations of about $49,000,000, most of which will be obtained by the issuance of bonds. A bond election has been set for Tuesday, October 27th, which will allow the voters of the state to vote on issuing $34,400,000 in general bonds, the proceeds of which will be used to erect new facilities at our institutions of higher education, to provide needed health and hospital facilities, including a new training school in western North Carolina for mentally-defective children. During the coming weeks, we will have more to say about this bond issue and its importance to the state.

An increase in salaries was provided for state employees and teachers, including an additional 5 per cent contingency raise for teachers. We were also able to provide definite improvements in our retirement system. The state will now match contributions for each eligible employee's retirement account up to age sixty-five, instead of age sixty. The minimum monthly retirement pay was raised from $60 to $70 for all members of the Teachers' and State Employees' Retirement System having as much as twenty years of creditable service. Benefits for those members who retired prior to July 1, 1959 were increased by 15 per cent.

Last January I decided, with the advice of the Advisory Budget Commission, not to recommend additional taxes to the 1959 General Assembly because we determined that a good state budget could be worked out for this coming period, with increases for practically every state function, and this could be done without imposing new taxes upon the citizens of North Carolina. This was done and I believe the great majority of our citizens are happy that our state did not raise tax rates.

A key point in our budget recommendations to the General Assembly was the adoption of a withholding plan for income tax payments. The withholding plan which was proposed and was adopted will do two things. First, it will provide—through the so-called windfall—a sufficient additional sum which will enable us to have, without extra taxes, additional millions for education, welfare, and health expenditures; and second, the withholding of income tax payments on a weekly or monthly basis will enable us to have a more efficient administration of our present tax laws, including the collection of taxes from some groups which are now not taxed. I am convinced that the withholding plan, which will begin in January, 1960, will be a welcomed convenience for the average citizen in North Carolina who pays state income taxes. I have talked to many people and I know that many will prefer that a small amount be set aside from their weekly or monthly pay checks to take care of their state income tax rather than be confronted with the necessity of one large payment in April of each year. It is estimated that the average amount to be withheld each week would be seventy-five cents to $1.00 per individual taxpayer.

We in North Carolina believe in sound state finances. For the next two years we have been able to provide a record budget of expenditures for public services without an increase in tax rates and without levying new taxes. Many states have not been this fortunate. With the continued improvement in the nation's economy and North Carolina's growth, and the resulting impact on our tax revenues, there is every possibility that our overall state financial situation will be good in 1961 when we again work out a two-year state budget.

THE MINIMUM WAGE LAW

A very important proposal which I recommended to the General Assembly was a minimum wage of at least seventy-five cents an hour. As I said in making this recommendation to the General Assembly, "It is enough to say that employers can afford it, em-

ployees deserve it, and the state's economic progress demands it."
This law will become effective January 1, 1960, and it will mean
improved wages for some 55,000 workers. It is estimated that the
average earnings of this group will be increased by $300 per year
for each worker, creating new purchasing power in this group
amounting to $16,500,000 a year. North Carolina is the only state
in the South which has a minimum wage law.

POLIO VACCINATION

Another legislative development of widespread interest to all
of us concerns our continuing battle against the dread disease of
polio. We were convinced that our nation had had sufficient experience in the use of polio vaccine to establish beyond question
its great value. We have long had state laws requiring vaccination
against such contagious diseases as diphtheria, smallpox, and so on.
Some of us thought the same should apply to vaccination against
polio. The General Assembly was also convinced of this need and
enacted into the law the requirement that all children before attending our public schools should have immunization against
polio. May I remind you that this disease can strike without
warning. Health officials throughout the nation have become
greatly concerned this summer because of the increased number
of polio cases, many resulting in death. We have had a serious
increase in polio in several of our counties in recent weeks, and
I hope each of you will take the necessary precautions for protecting your family.

EMPLOYMENT SECURITY BENEFITS

You will recall the economic slump which affected much of
our nation during 1958. In many parts of the country, unemployment was very acute. It was above the average in many places in
North Carolina, and many of our citizens had exhausted unemployment benefits, which under our law were authorized for
a period of twenty-six consecutive weeks. I recommended to the
General Assembly that our statutes be amended to authorize an
extension of eight weeks for which benefits could be paid during
unemployment emergencies. This was passed, and it means that

North Carolina's unemployment benefits are among the best in the nation.

LAWS AFFECTING PRISON SYSTEM ADMINISTRATION

The 1959 General Assembly approved two proposals of particular interest and importance in the administration of our prison system. One of these was the so-called state use law, or a law which in effect required state departments, institutions, and agencies supported directly by state funds to utilize prison industry products when feasible. As explained to the General Assembly, we are confronted with a steady increase in prison population and in the public interest we should take appropriate action to provide constructive employment for as many prisoners as possible. This is not only desirable from the standpoint of giving the prisoners something to do and in many instances affording prisoners some prospect of rehabilitation, but this is also important in terms of the financial burden on the state. Our prison-work release law, passed by the 1957 General Assembly, was amended to make it more workable and already greater use is being made of it.

REORGANIZATION OF STATE AGENCIES

Most of the recommendations on the Commission on Reorganization of State Government were approved by the 1959 General Assembly. The laws were amended to create an Interstate Cooperation Commission, to take the place of two separate agencies previously operating in this area. Laws providing for two turnpike authorities and a state planning board were repealed because they were no longer needed. The laws were amended to clarify responsibility for a records management program, and to improve our management of state-owned lands. Procedures were clarified for appointments of acting state officials in the event of physical or mental incapacity of the officeholder, and an important recommendation for the establishment of a State Department of Water Resources was approved. In the latter instance, the responsibility for water resources had been scattered among three or four different agencies. These duties were brought together under one agency, and I am confident that North Carolina will, under the new State Board of Water Resources, do a much better job in the years ahead in this most important area.

Another outstanding legislative decision was the provision for a new legislative building. For a great many years, our General Assembly has been seriously hampered in the official discharge of its duties because of crowded conditions and inadequate committee facilities. Although the present Capitol will be left untouched, the state will erect a separate and suitable structure near the present Capitol, which will provide an adequate hall for our Senate and House of Representatives, as well as committee rooms and other facilities for the members of the General Assembly.

During the recent session of the General Assembly, there was considerable talk about our highway organization, and a bill was introduced to return the Highway Commission to the old set-up of fourteen commissioners, which could have taken us back to the situation we had prior to 1957 when individual commissioners exercised the chief authority in connection with rural or secondary roads in each of their respective divisions.

I believe that the people of this state prefer and will demand that the vast amount of money which we spend on our highways be spent according to established need, on the basis of standards which we all can see and understand rather than on the basis of decisions reached by a single individual—too often in response to politicial influence rather than need. That is what I am talking about when I talk about a state-wide policy in administering highway funds, and I am convinced that a great majority of our citizens and taxpayers agree with this principle.

ELECTION LAWS

The 1959 legislature enacted several amendments to our election laws which were worthwhile. However, I must express my personal disappointment that the General Assembly did not see fit to do away with the civilian absentee ballot and to provide for use of voting machines.

ADMINISTRATION OF PROPERTY TAX LAWS

I am especially pleased that the General Assembly adopted statutes approving the important recommendations of the Tax Study Commission to enable us to have improved administration in the property tax field. One measure requires uniform assessment of property for tax purposes and another requires periodic and systematic revaluation of property. We should thank the General Assembly for recognizing the problems in this area and for taking appropriate action to insure that our property tax laws are equitable and that unjust weight does not fall upon any individual taxpayer nor upon any particular group of taxpayers.

MUNICIPAL GOVERNMENT LAWS

Other important recommendations approved by the General Assembly grew out of studies concerning municipal government. Although the representatives from some counties saw fit to adopt amendments excluding application to specific counties, basic laws were enacted to authorize counties to meet the increasing problems in zoning and regulation of the use of land and to regulate the subdivision of land in areas outside municipalities.

A new law affecting cities and counties allows them to provide extra funds for law enforcement personnel. This law grew out of the Henderson strike situation which pointed up the need for cities and counties to assume more effective law enforcement responsibility.

HIGHWAY SAFETY LAWS

Certain measures were proposed during the General Assembly session which would have had the effect of weakening our highway safety laws. These were defeated. A law was enacted to set up a point system for determining when the Department of Motor Vehicles could suspend the driver's license of those who are convicted of several violations of the motor vehicle laws. This certainly is very desirable legislation and was especially needed to take the place of the habitual violator section of our motor vehicle law which had been held invalid by our courts.

As a further aid to highway safety, sufficient funds were appropriated to add twenty-five additional highway patrolmen.

CONSTITUTIONAL REVISION

I think that unquestionably the greatest disappointment of the 1959 General Assembly to the people all over North Carolina was the failure to approve revision of the constitution, including the improvement of our courts.

It does no good to blame individuals or groups for this failure. I joined House and Senate leaders in urging that the legislation be withdrawn in the closing days of the General Assembly because we felt that good legislation was being emasculated.

I am confident that the work which has gone before will yet bear fruit. The issue of constitutional revision and effective improvement in our courts is very much alive, and I believe and I hope that this matter will be considered again by either a special or regular session of the General Assembly, and I urge the public to continue its great interest.

CONCLUSION

In closing may I say that the 1959 General Assembly was a hard-working group, and the people of North Carolina can be proud of what it accomplished. I would like to add my word of thanks to the officers and members for their devoted service.

My travels in recent months have made me more appreciative of the good government which we have enjoyed here in North Carolina. North Carolina stands high in the nation and in the world as a state with stable, progressive government. We must always strive to maintain and improve this reputation and tradition if our state is to meet successfully the many challenges ahead.

ADDRESS AT INDUSTRY APPRECIATION DAY

LAURINBURG

August 20, 1959

[North Carolina's first clock factory and the newest of the state's wide variety of industries was being opened on this occasion at Laurinburg, where a plant had been located by the Ingraham Company, one of the nation's oldest and best known makers of clocks, watches, and timing devices, with main offices and factory at Bristol, Connecticut. The dedicatory exercises also took the form of a "salute" to all of Laurinburg's and Scotland County's forty other industries and to local and state leaders, business and political, who had made the founding and growth of these industries possible. Governor Hodges, fresh from his tour of Soviet Russia and a sampling of that country's industries, took the occasion to point up sharply the difference between what he saw in Russia and what he saw exemplified at Laurinburg. A sizeable crowd gathered in front of the three-acre Ingraham plant for the speaking, which was followed by a ribbon-cutting by the Governor and an open house at the plant during the rest of the afternoon and evening.]

I would like to thank the people of Laurinburg and Scotland County, those persons responsible for this Industry Appreciation Day, and officials of the Ingraham Company for inviting me here today for this significant event.

It is also a pleasure to witness additional evidence of this state's continued economic growth and development. Our people are working hard to raise their standard of living and to provide a better life for all. This event is a striking contrast to what I have seen recently during my tour of the Soviet Union along with eight other American governors. The sharp contrast between the Soviet and American economies is a matter of great concern and interest for all of us—and the world. The contrast is between one society in which the hopes and aspirations of the people are subservient to those of the state, and another society—our own—in which the state is the servant of the people, and in which free men and women work together voluntarily for the spiritual, cultural, and economic advancement of all.

I do not imply that the Soviet people are in any way submissive or lacking in enthusiasm for their way of life. It was my observation while visiting throughout their country that they are, for the most part, dedicated, hard-working people who have an immense pride in the progress they have made and who have confidence in their form of government—a system with which you and I disagree.

We must not continue to be misled into thinking that the Soviet people are in any large measure dissatisfied with communism or with the leaders, who, in one way or another, control their lives from the cradle to the grave. To be sure, there are some who object to the subordination of individual freedoms, who recognize the evils of international communism, but their voices are stilled by the masses of Soviet people who know only that their living standard has been raised, that illiteracy has been all but erased from their land, that their lives—controlled as they may be—have, for the first time in the memory of most, been given the security of food and shelter and retirement.

The threat to world peace that emanates from the Soviet Union has its origin, not with the masses of people, but with the Soviet leaders who are clever, unscrupulous, ambitious, diplomatically arrogant, and frighteningly confident of their ability to dominate world affairs by fair means or foul. I am convinced also that much of the tension that exists is the product of misinformation and a lack of basic understanding on the part of all concerned.

My contacts with the Soviet people convinced me that they are just as sincere in their desire for peace as are the people of our country. I might add that they are equally sincere in the belief that *we*, not they, are the major threat to the peace of the world. They believe this because they have been misled, because it suits the purpose of their leaders to misrepresent the United States and its people to the people of their country. Most of this misrepresentation has been, and continues to be, intentional, but much of it is also the result of misunderstanding. There is little we can do at present to counteract, within the Soviet Union, the falsifications perpetrated by the Red leaders, but there is much that can and must be done to correct misunderstanding—both among the leaders and the people. We can do this without compromising our principles or our position of leadership in the Free World. This is the reason many of us have been urging a greater exchange of peoples between our nations.

This was also the purpose of the visit which I have recently completed in the company of eight other governors. We went to Russia to tell the people of that country as much as possible about our way of life and our sincere desire for peace—and also to learn as much as possible about their way of life. I am convinced that we accomplished some good, that we made a dent, small though it may have been, in the great void of misunderstanding that exists. If we did this, then our trip was more than justified.

Perhaps these references to the international struggle for men's minds are not entirely appropriate to this particular occasion, but I know you are interested in peace, and I cannot help comparing this event and this gathering with comparable meetings I had with people in the Soviet Union only a few weeks ago. Strange as it may seem, there is a similarity to be found in the warmth and hospitality of the people and in the enthusiasm for the future that exists in both countries. There is one great difference, however, that causes me to thank God for this country and this state and for the wonderful privilege of citizenship that makes me a part of this event here today in Laurinburg and Scotland County. The difference lies in the fact that we have gathered here to celebrate a triumph of cooperative voluntary effort to promote individual and regional prosperity through the exercise of free enterprise prerogatives. In the Soviet Union, the price for such progress is the subjugation of the individual to the will of the state. The incentive is not produced by a voluntary desire for personal or community progress, but by a cleverly disguised "produce or else" philosophy handed down by Kremlin leaders. Their people do not admit this—do not even realize it in most instances—but they have little freedom of choice as we know it.

Perhaps this will explain why I am especially pleased to be with you today and to join you in this display of appreciation for the contribution that your industries, both old and new, have made and are continuing to make to the growth and development of this region. It is not surprising that the people of this community and county have chosen to make this public statement of pride in the progress that has been made here. The people of this section have a tradition of pride and a history of accomplishment that justifies that pride. As far back as the early part of the eighteenth century, when the first Scotch Highlanders moved inland from the Carolina coast to settle in the upper reaches of the Cape Fear Valley, they displayed their pride in this region by erecting signs in the coastal areas which read, "The best land lies 100 miles west of here." The story is told that, because of the signs, only those who could read came to Scotland County—a fact that, if true, might account for this county's outstanding history of dedication to the cause of good education.

In any event, the area was settled by sturdy men and women who had faith in themselves and their ability to build a new and better way of life here on this fertile land. They were followed by others who were no less enthusiastic about the opportunities afforded them here. These were the English and lowland Scots, the Welsh, who found their way here along the Pee Dee River, and still later the Scotch-Irish from Ulster, Each group found cause for pride in their new land. Each benefitted from the bounty that the land yielded. And each contributed to the progress that has been made during the more than two centuries that have elapsed since the first literate Scotsman painted his sign and planted it in the sands of the Carolina coast.

Evidence of the manner in which the progressive ways of these early settlers have persisted to the present time can be seen in the business-like, cooperative approach the citizens of this area have taken in recent years to the matter of industrial development. This is especially evident in the fact that you long ago adopted a "first things first" approach to the challenge and set about laying the groundwork that is needed to insure solid economic growth. Laurinburg has set an example for other communities to follow in creating an atmosphere that is conducive to steady progress.

The people of Laurinburg and their Scotland County neighbors have demonstrated time and time again that they know the value of advance planning and that they are more than willing to take the steps necessary to take full advantage of that planning. It is by no means surprising that you were selected by the Ingraham Company as the site for this superb new plant. You have shown in the past that you possess both the tangible and intangible qualities that hold promise of a successful industrial operation. I have said many times, in all parts of our state, that industrial sites are not chosen by instinct or by any set rules involving chance. They are chosen after careful scrutiny of cold hard facts derived from experience and study. Every phase of community life is considered in detail before the location experts make their recommendation. Nothing is overlooked. It may be interesting to some to know that one of the first requests made by the Ingraham Company when it began considering Laurinburg was for a picture of your main street.

Schools and churches have always played an important role in the life of this region, and you can be sure that the company took note of this fact. I have no doubt that consideration was given to the fact that the court house lawn here boasts a unique monument "erected by popular subscription to the memory of a private school master," for in erecting this unusual monument the people here erected a testimonial to their historic insistence on good education for their young people. Your successful effort to bring about the establishment of the new Consolidated Presbyterian College here would certainly indicate that this enthusiasm has not diminished. Your activities in the whole field of education reflect great credit on this community and county, and I wholeheartedly commend you on the success you have achieved. May I add a special commendation for Scotland County's Negro citizens for the support they have given the very fine Laurinburg Institute and for initiative they displayed in the establishment of a library. Both of these institutions deserve the continued support of all the people in the county and, judging from your past history, I feel certain that this support will be given.

The foresightedness and cooperative spirit that you have displayed in the development of your educational facilities is also manifested in other phases of community life. Your outstanding determination to provide adequate hospital accommodations for your people is evidence of this fact. The Scotland County Memorial Hospital, with its accompanying nurses' home, is a monument to your dedication and your generosity. Much the same can be said with regard to the manner in which you have carried out your public housing project. Certainly, it is to your credit that you are the smallest community in North Carolina to sponsor a project of this type, designed to replace sub-standard housing with

Photo by Aurilla Goodnight Studio

The Governor in a characteristic role—speaking at Alexander County Industry Appreciation Day at Taylorsville, October 16, 1959.

Governor Hodges, Edward L. Rankin, Jr. (*center*), and John Harden (*right*) inspecting the statue of Sir Walter Raleigh in London during the European Industry Hunt, November 2, 1959.

clean, modern units that complement rather than detract from your town.

Still another factor—one that has become tremendously important in promoting economic growth in recent years—is the ability of a community to provide recreational facilities and activities for its citizens, young and old. You have done an exceptionally good job in this respect. Few communities of this size can boast such a well-rounded program, but this is to be expected from a community that in four months time raised $40,000 in private subscriptions for the construction of a public swimming pool.

These are but a few of the things that make Laurinburg an outstanding community and Scotland an outstanding county. Many of your achievements were recognized a few years ago when you were chosen one of the ten top cities in the United States by the National Municipal League and *Look* Magazine. There is little I can add to that distinction except to commend you on the very obvious fact that you have not rested on your laurels. The people here have maintained their enthusiasm for progress and in so doing you have insured a prosperous future for this region.

This new industrial plant is symbolic of that future and it is for this reason that it is a genuine pleasure for me to extend a very warm and sincere welcome to the Ingraham Company as it joins our industrial family. I know that the relationship between this community and this company will be a very pleasant and mutually beneficial one. I am sure this new industry will get along well with already established industries here of which we are proud. Much has been said in North Carolina in recent years about the kind of industries we want in our state—industries that are forward-looking and enthusiastic about being a part of the wonderful future that we envision for North Carolina and its people. The company that we welcome here today is such an industry. This company has much to offer the citizens of this area— just as the citizens here have much to offer the company. I have no doubt that the combination will result in a most successful operation.

May I conclude by again commending the people of Laurinburg and Scotland County on the progress that has been made here and on the cooperative spirit that is largely responsible for that progress. It is my sincere hope that other communities throughout our state will follow the example you have set. For when the spirit exhibited here becomes universal in North Carolina (and it's becoming evident in many places) then the better way of life we seek for all our people will have become a reality.

Thank you.

ADDRESS AT A BANQUET HONORING DR. A. G. DAWSON, NEW EXECUTIVE SECRETARY OF THE NORTH CAROLINA EDUCATION ASSOCIATION

SOUTHERN PINES
September 4, 1959

[Governor Hodges had often disagreed with the policies of the North Carolina Education Association. In this hard-hitting speech, he reiterated his stand for more local support of public education and assailed the view "on the part of some people that the state must do everything and that communities should not be concerned with their public school finances, especially teacher pay." This attitude he characterized as "a false philosophy which is digging the grave of educational backwardness" for North Carolina. The address was heard by about 500 persons who assembled in the Southern Pines High School Auditorium. On account of the hot September night, the Governor removed his coat and spoke in his shirt sleeves.]

It is a pleasure to be here in Southern Pines tonight on this occasion being held in honor of Dr. A. C. Dawson who, as we all know, is assuming the position of executive secretary of the North Carolina Education Association. I would like to offer my congratulations, both of Dr. Dawson and to the association. It is good that a man of vision and courage as well as wide and practical experience in matters of public education has been chosen for this position. And it is good that all of you friends and neighbors of Dr. Dawson have gotten together here tonight to demonstrate your confidence in him.

I have always felt that a man in public life—and the executive secretary of the NCEA is in public life—should, above all, have the backing of his home folks. Obviously, Dr. Dawson has this backing, and this means a lot. The fact that he came here in 1937 from Atlantic Christian College and stayed twenty-two years is good evidence that you liked him. Southern Pines has done well under Dr. Dawson's leadership, and your community achievement philosophy of education will help the state as your own man goes to higher and broader duties.

Dr. Dawson, you are assuming your new duties at a time when conditions are such that you and the NCEA wil have an almost singular opportunity to make great and lasting contributions to the common good through your activities in the field of education. At the same time, the challenges and responsibilities which face you and the association at this time are so great that to a lesser man the prospect might be almost fearsome.

And why do we say that present conditions offer an almost singular opportunity for contribution in the field of public education?

First, it appears that the general public is perhaps more "education-conscious" than at any time in the memory of most of us. This condition may be attributable in a large measure to the challenge presented by the Russians when they blasted Sputnik I into the heavens. I like to think, however, that this newly demonstrated public interest grows out of something even more basic; namely, the determination of the American people to pass on to their children something better than the parents experienced. I am convinced that this admirable characteristic of our people exists and has existed ever since the founding of our country. It may take a dramatic incident, such as a Sputnik and the emergence of Russian scientific developments, to bring this basic determination to the top of our thinking, but it is always there and ready to be used by those who know how to use it.

It is also of great importance that the concern of the public in education matters is not limited solely to the promotion of improved scientific and technical education. There is a growing realization on the part of the general public that the true extent of the progress of mankind will depend on our knowledge of each other. There is more and more understanding that if we do not learn to develop our relations with each other in peace—and here I mean our relations as between ourselves as individuals, as between our own communities, and as between ourselves and other nations—all of the advanced scientific and technical knowledge we acquire will but finally serve to destroy us all.

A few weeks ago Under Secretary of State, C. Douglas Dillon, was quoted as having said, "If we are to stay the course, there must be much greater and deeper knowledge of world events among our citizenry. Unfortunately, such widespread knowledge of world affairs is lacking in our country today." In a speech made at Chapel Hill a few years ago, Adlai Stevenson called upon a group of educational enthusiasts to develop broad education among our people in order that they could participate intelligently in the great decisions which are upon us. Governor Stevenson described these decisions as "so crucial that no man nor group of men can be safely entrusted with them, decisions that must be made by a collective wisdom that has to be infinitely greater than any of its individual parts, a wisdom that rises above its source."

The kind of education that must be developed to meet needs such as these just mentioned is to be found in the study of the humanities—the history and literature not only of our own country but of other countries and other civilizations, the study of languages, the study of social problems and economics—national and world-wide, etc. Thus, this better education our people are seeking is broad and all encompassing which means that the best efforts of all will be needed to do what has to be done.

There is also at this time a greater enthusiasm on the part of our state legislators as to the needs and problems of education. This may be merely a reflection of the basic interest of the people themselves but, whatever its source, it is there.

In the 1959 General Assembly there was deep concern on the part of the legislators as to the future course of public school education in North Carolina. It is true that some of them, as happens in every legislative session, were beating their political drums for more teacher pay without enough concern as to what the state and the children would get for the money! I gather from talking to old timers and from my own experience that there never has been so much concern as to where we are going in our public school work as there is now.

Out of this 1959 General Assembly came the following study commissions on the public school situation: the Commission for the Study of a Twelve-month's Use of Public School Buildings and Facilities for Public School Purposes; the Commission to Study the Public School Education of Exceptionally Talented Children; and the North Carolina Commission for the Study of Teacher Merit Pay and Implementation of the Revised Public School Curriculum.

In addition, there were several other commissions discussed, but not authorized. From the 1957 General Assembly had come the authorization of a study on public school finance. The study was made by some of the most devoted citizens of North Carolina and without exception friendly to and deeply interested in and concerned about education. After exhaustive study, much consultation, and preparation of some amazingly revealing figures, they made recommendations which, in my humble opinion, if they had been adopted, would have thrust North Carolina forward far better prepared to meet the challenge of the future so far as public support for public education is concerned. I refer, of course, to the school incentive fund whereby the state would have matched funds with localities which decided to enrich their curriculum, improve salaries, and to help their schools generally.

There has developed in North Carolina since the 1930's an almost rigid philosophy on the part of some people that the state must do everything and that communities should not be concerned with their public school finances, especially teacher pay. (There are many exceptions to this, of course, including Southern Pines.) This is a false philosophy which is digging the grave of educational backwardness for us.

Let me state one more time what I stated in my message to the legislature in February, 1959 regarding my attitude toward public school support:

North Carolina has in the past, considering our resources, made a good effort in support of our public schools. Notwithstanding our effort, however, we still rank near the bottom in per pupil expenditure for education, and our ranking in teachers' salaries continues to be comparatively low, although our national rank in teacher pay is substantially better (thirty-eighth) than our national income rank (forty-fourth).

I, for one, do *not* desire to see the state 'unload' the burden of public school financing on the counties. The report of the Committee on the Study of Public School Finance does *not* make any such recommendation.

We need to do more for public education in North Carolina, both in the total number of dollars we provide and in the comparative effort that we put forth. Our future economic growth and strength will depend on how well we do in our educational efforts at all levels.

I have no resentment toward the failure of the legislature or the county commissioners or others to support this program of local participation to a greater extent. In my own heart I feel that our approach is sound. I also believe that many, many superintendents and other members of the NCEA and of the school profession generally feel exactly as I do. Several of them have told me so privately, and I wish more had spoken out publicly.

We need more than the usual biennial campaign for an "X" per cent of teacher pay raise. At one time there was a discussion in the last General Assembly about authorizing an added number of millions of dollars for teachers beyond what the Advisory Budget Commission and I had recommended for direct raises. A group of *top* school people came one day to Raleigh to urge legislators to support the larger amount. I said to a superintendent who is a close friend of mine, "If this much energy and brain power were devoted to the long-range planning for the future quality and proper financing of North Carolina schools, nothing could stop us."

Until long-range, basic policy decisions are made, education will not *ever* receive "satisfactory" financial support from any General Assembly. It is not that the legislature is unwilling to do more for education, but rather it is not clear as to how it should proceed or *what* it should do. I have said publicly time and time again, and I say it one more time, that nobody has recommended enough of a raise for good teachers to suit me. We might differ on where it is to come from and how it is going to be paid, but I want to go on record that I do not think that for a good school system and good teachers we are paying any ways near enough. When our average North Carolina pay (the amount paid by the state) is exceeded by 40 to 50 per cent in a single Virginia city, then we are in bad shape. In this Virginia city, the state pays probably half of the teachers' salaries and the locality pays the balance, and the "balance" is pretty high and they get good teachers. Charlotte and a few other cities in North Carolina do the same thing, but such leaders are too few.

Many people in the state and many legislators interpret the word "uniform" to mean that education is the sole responsibility of the state, and they have the idea there should be no need for "supplements." If this philosophy is continued, it will continue to limit and blight our educational progress.

Another very proper interpretation of the word "uniform" is that it means the state should provide a good basic uniform program and that enriching the education opportunities should come from local supplementary taxes.

I think that one of our difficulties is that we have no long-range specific policy for the sound building of our public school system. I would like to point out to you and to the public that there are two dangers in connection with this.

One danger is that the legislature, not knowing which way to go, will not go at all, except on an irrational, forced political basis.

The second is—and this is what the school people must learn—that other agencies of the government are now demanding much more of the tax dollar, whereas before public schools were the main thing. I am referring to the tremendous millions that we are spending on mental hospitals, public welfare, and for correctional institutions, etc.

Our expenditures over a period of years will be enormous in all lines. Our expenditures for schools at the state level will be enormous, but as we raise more money, or taxes, or debts, the people will increasingly ask the question, "What are the schools doing with the money?" Are we broadening our courses so much in our schools that we are in danger of doing nothing well because we are trying to do everything, even if poorly?

The public and legislature alike are asking, "Are we getting the most from the dollar we are spending for education?" We are finding too often that the answer is "no." They are concerned with "quality" as well as "quantity," particularly as it affects teachers and curriculum and, therefore, ultimately the pupil.

I am convinced from my recent trip to the Soviet Union that we can learn some things from their educational system that would help up. I strongly oppose their overall political or educational system. It is contrary to my beliefs, but I believe that I am a better American citizen from having gone there. We do not violate our principles of democracy, of self-government, when we admit that the Soviet educational system requires more discipline of the children, requires an acquaintanceship and experience with manual labor, and that the Soviet is more serious-minded in handling the children in educational matters than we are. Their educational leaders make the decisions rather than leaving these decisions to immature children or unconcerned parents.

These comments are made with a desire to be constructive, and I am sure many teachers and other school people have some of the same concern about these basic questions.

I fully realize that some people throughout the state, including a few public school persons, have in the past made a point of charging me with being "against the teachers" or "against the schools." This is, of course, untrue! The charge has, ostensibly, come about because of the budget decisions I have made as governor. A governor has a great and trying responsibility of trying to work out a reasonably adequate budget for literally dozens of important state services, including education. I honestly think that regardless of the amount appropriated for public schools at the state level there would be some people who sincerely and conscientiously would feel that the amount appropriated was inadequate. By the same token, we would usually find others who would think the appropriation was too high. Just for the record, I will point out that since I have had the privilege of serving as governor, with some responsibility in budget matters, the state biennial appropriation for public schools has increased $93,661,638 or 40.46 per cent.

I am *not* against the teachers. I am *for* the children, and I am *for* the teachers who are for the children, and I am for paying the teachers more money, very much more than they are getting. But, I join with many others in saying I want to be sure that we are paying it soundly and that we are getting our money's worth, and I want to be sure that the public is aroused and that at all levels it accepts its responsibility in public school financing, curriculum study, and other things. I believe the record will show that I have tried to help and challenge public education, college and university education, both public and private; further, that I have appointed one of the strongest state school boards in history— men dedicated to doing the job for our 1,000,000 school children.

What does all this mean to the professional leaders in education? This stirring interest of the people in the field of education has revealed not only our basic determination that our youth be educated; it has also revealed—and has even developed—some degree of suspicion as to whether present educational programs and policies are doing the job. It has called forth inquiry as to whether professional organizations are interested only in cementing the status-quo at higher salaries, or whether they are in truth interested in producing an improved product in the form of better educated people. It has brought forth further penetrating questions concerning the use of the public education dollar which to my knowledge have not been answered. I would like to say that these are not new questions raised by the 1959 General Assembly. Let me repeat for you some questions, which were contained in a talk I made to the North Carolina Citizens Committee for Better Schools in January, 1957. I asked then and I ask now:

What is the future of the tremendous financing program for public school buildings?

How are we in North Carolina to build the ever-growing number of need classrooms?

Can we find money for these buildings, or must we do as some other places are doing and that is lease or rent these buildings?

Whose responsibility is it besides the state to help support schools, including current operations and teachers' salaries?

Why the nine months of twenty days each that make up our school year?

Why aren't teachers paid on a more practical, dignified, year-round basis, having in mind the child, his needs, the community, and its responsibility?

Why is it that we must keep on providing the same number (or more) classes and teachers in vocational agriculture when comparatively fewer and fewer are able to find profitable employment in farming? Why can't money spent for such unneeded classes be devoted to more needed purposes (such as classes in science and languages)?

Why can't we look hard and long at certification and make corrections as, and if, needed?

Why can't we do more things to attract young people into teaching, more things other than salary increases which all of us admit are needed?

Where is the interest in North Carolina in public schools at the local level, and has that interest been tapped for its full potential, and if not, why not?

Why has Duplin County, with limited resources, but with enlightened leadership of such men as Dallas Herring, been able to do such a magnificent job? The same thing could be said for other counties in the state.

Why is there lack of interest in some North Carolina communities?

Why are less than half of the administrative units in North Carolina levying some kind of supplementary tax to enrich and broaden the curriculum and school program in the community?

Why, on the other hand, are there some twenty or thirty towns within the counties (not special administrative units in themselves) that have been able to vote special supplements?

In those communities where supplements and support have not been given, is it because of the lack of confidence in the school people, or is it because of the lack of leadership on the part of the school people, or is it because of the lack of leadership on the part of citizens?

What are the objections on the part of professionals for testing teachers as to their fitness for teaching special subjects or teaching at all? I am not suggesting that those who don't rate very well be pushed out, I am simply saying that the principle ought to be recognized and we ought to know and use modern testing methods, to do the best we know how.

All the above questions were asked nearly three years ago, and now may I ask, why, during the 1957 and 1959 General Assemblies was resistance to merit pay raises for teachers so determined? What is the basis for the position that teachers cannot be distinguished on the basis of merit? What is so peculiar about public school teachers that they cannot be rated fairly on a merit basis, when administrators of our North Carolina University and colleges enthusiastically support the awarding of pay raises for college teachers on a merit basis? I know some of the problems which make this difficult, including political pressure at the local level, but I believe the public will back school leaders who try to do a conscientious job in this field. And I am glad our State Board of Education is studying this problem.

What are the real reasons why an approach along the lines of the incentive fund plan which I mentioned earlier received practically no support in the 1959 General Assembly? How is it that other states seem to find the incentive programs or other plans for school financing so satisfactory while North Carolina refuses even to try out such an approach? Why did state and local school officials, the State Board of Education and the NCEA keep quiet on such a vital issue as the incentive plan?

These are some of the questions that cry for an answer, Dr. Dawson. These are some of the questions that the professionals such as yourself and the members of the NCEA must help answer. These are some of the questions that must be answered before any real progress is going to be made in meeting the needs of our schools, including adequate teacher salaries—paid lobbyists, letter-writing campaigns, political threats and political promises to the contrary notwithstanding.

Please understand, Dr. Dawson, and all of you here, or any who may see these words elsewhere, my comments are not meant to be destructively critical; on the contrary, I want to help. I am a great believer in long-range planning. I believe in planning for the future in business, in government, in education and in all other activities. I am also a believer in planning for the long-range future of mankind itself, especially that portion of it within the borders of this state and nation. It is my firm conviction that any long-range plan for the future of the human race which fails to provide intelligent directions and programs for the improved education of its children is without substance and is in fact nothing more than a noise in the wind.

May I add a word of deep hope that candidates for North Carolina offices at all levels will think clearly on the subject of education and instead of just being for "education" that they will be for a long-range, detailed program of improved education, and a concern for real accomplishment by all our children. We need and must have high grade and courageous political leadership, and we need and must have the same kind of education leadership.

Now, having analyzed and criticized, I want to say I think we are improving all along and that there is a great future ahead of us, if we all do our part. I think there is going to be greater cooperation than ever among the various educational agencies, the State Board of Education, the Citizens Committee for Better Schools, the NCEA, parent-teacher associations, and other groups. I believe there is going to be a greater realization than ever before as to what will be needed in education and how we are going to pay for it. I believe that we will finally realize that we cannot do it much differently from the other states which may be moving forward more rapidly in education. I believe the time will come when county commissioners, landowners, and other leaders who have fought taxes at the level will look realistically and honestly at their total taxes in comparison with other states and will find that ours are low, and will find that their property taxes are low as compared to many years ago, considering the state's economy and its progress. I believe that if they and others will decide that they must have a modern educational system, effective and progressive, of which they can be proud, they will be disturbed with the tired old game of political football played with our schools for the last couple of decades. But I believe that it will take leadership at the local level, by legislators both present and future, by citizens such as are here tonight and such as exist in many places throughout this glorious state; and above all it will take a dedicated, courageous leadership on the part of the school profession that we have not yet seen.

We can be proud of North Carolina and the attitude and behavior of its wonderful citizens. Courage and wisdom have been shown in handling the very difficult school segregation problem. We have put our children and our schools *first* and our people have shown wisdom and understanding in the handling of these difficult situations and have done it at the local level.

Let us continue to put first things first, meeting the problems as they arise in our various localities. Let us continue to live and work together, paramounting the many things that unite us rather than the few things that could divide us. Let us say over and over again to each other that our schools must be kept open with pride and not be closed with bitterness!

And, may we challenge all our people in our cities and our counties to rise up in support of more and better schools so that our children now and in the future that lies ahead are able to complete with children of all states and all nations. You will, Dr. Dawson, have a part in making all this come about. You will help awaken and produce this kind of courageous and far-seeing leadership. Yours will be a thrilling experience. You have the ability, experience, and imagination to do a great job for a great cause. As evidenced by this dinner tonight, given by your home folks, in your honor, you will have the support to do the task. To all of their good wishes I would like to add my own, and say that all of us will follow your career with interest and a desire to help. I might add in closing that you will find your greatest support in the people of North Carolina, once you convince them you are on the right track. Our people have a history of dedication to the cause of public education. Our state is known throughout the nation for its willingness to sacrifice in the interest of its children. This traditional attitude you will find of inestimable value in your efforts. God bless you!

ADDRESS AT A NORTH CAROLINA NEWS AND FEATURE WRITERS CONFERENCE

CHAPEL HILL
September 5, 1959

[Speaking on his "Impressions of the Press" at this meeting in the Carolina Inn at Chapel Hill, Governor Hodges had both warm praise and some criticism of the state's newspapers and their editors and reporters. His criticisms were directed largely at certain reporters who, he claimed, use political news stories to exert their own influence in politics. In a question and answer period following the speech, the Governor disclaimed any plans for a future in politics, but left the gate open in case "lightning should strike" and bring him the Democratic party's nomination for vice-president.]

When Roy Thompson of the *Winston-Salem Journal* spoke to me about this engagement more than a year ago, I must admit that I was intrigued with the topic he suggested—"my impressions, critical or otherwise, of the press of North Carolina." As an elected public official for the past seven years, I have had close contact and daily working relationships (and most of it very pleasant) with much of the press in our state. During recent months, I have mentioned Roy's assignment to me to a number of people and found that the idea brought an immediate reaction—one way or the other. Some were horrified at the thought of any public official saying anything even vaguely critical of the press. Others eagerly responded: "Give 'em hell!"

One well-known minister in North Carolina immediately informed me, with tongue in cheek, that the King James Version of the Bible had two references in which people could not see Jesus, "because of the press." He cited Mark 2:4, where the four men brought the cripple to Jesus, and . . . "they could not come nigh unto him for the press . . ." My friend then pointed out that Luke 8:19 stated that "then came to him his mother and his brethren and could not come at him for the press." If it is any reasurance to you, the Revised Standard Version uses the word "crowd" instead of "press" in both verses.

So we see that any discussion of what's right—or wrong—with the press is a matter of vital interest among many people in North Carolina, and perhaps ranks along with politics, religion, and sex as another time-honored subject of partisan debate.

In any event, I hasten to point out before I start "swinging" that most of my impressions of the press in North Carolina are good. As I have said frequently in speeches within and without the state, North Carolina is extremely well blessed with newspapers—both in quality and quantity. I should like to emphasize that I am a layman with no professional training in journalism and certainly shall not attempt a technical discussion on newspaper operations. My observations are those of a public official and citizen with a deep interest in North Carolina and its welfare—as well as a deep interest in the newspapers of this state and the success with which they keep our people well informed. As governor, I find it is often my duty and opportunity to speak knowingly—if possible—to professional organizations about their respective fields. One of my greatest ventures resulted from an invitation from the North Carolina Bar Association to talk—as a layman—to our lawyers about our courts and the need for improvement there.

Perhaps some of you recall the special press conference which I held in December, 1954, shortly after taking office following the death of Governor Umstead. At that conference, I recognized the responsibility which you as newsmen have in dealing with that most perishable commodity—news. I also recognized your record of service to your communities, counties, and state throughout the years, and pledged that we in state government would make every effort to keep you informed to the best of our ability on the progress and problems of your government. This we have attempted to do.

I also sought your continued understanding and support in the problems which we all faced as citizens of North Carolina. May I say now that the vast majority of the newspapers in North Carolina—both daily and non-daily—have been generous in their understanding and coverage of what I have tried to do to help North Carolina and its people. For this generous and thoughtful support, I am deeply grateful.

In my many travels across North Carolina, I have been impressed so many times with the contributions being made by responsible, alert, and energetic newspapers. There is practically no limit to the amount of good that can be accomplished by such a newspaper. It has been frequently said that a good newspaper will stand like a mirror before a community—reflecting its moods and character, its strong points and its shortcomings, its successes and its failures, its past, its present, and its hopes for the future. Certainly, a good newspaper will reflect these things. But, if it is to be a real asset to the community, it must do more—much more. It must lead and lead honestly in encouraging worthwhile community growth and development. Some newspapers, like individuals, fall short here.

To be really effective, a local newspaper must be so intimately a part of a community or its circulation area that it feels, not the delayed action of the pulse, but the life-giving warmth and strength of the heart beat itself. It must be so much a part of the people that it not only shares their pains and sorrows, their joy and happiness, but naturally anticipates these emotions even before they are felt by the community. This task is not an easy one for the newspaper. If it is to exercise true leadership, it must also stand apart. It must maintain an objectivity, which at times may not be compatible with the more subjective or more sensitive feelings of the people in the community it seeks to serve. It must be courageous, but not reckless. It must be responsive to the public will, but it must never sacrifice integrity as the price for popularity.

North Carolinians can be justly proud of the fact that the great majority of their newspapers meet the qualifications I have just outlined. The policies of our North Carolina papers are controlled, for the most part, by honest men and women who recognize the responsibility of their position and who meet these responsibilities with integrity and understanding. Newspapers have been a primary force in recent years in efforts to educate North Carolinians concerning our economic problems, our per capita income situation, and the need for greater economic opportunity, more industry, and the need for diversification of both industry and agriculture.

Fortunately for North Carolina, "the press has done more than all things else to diffuse intelligence among the people and to acquaint the world with the character of our state and her natural resources." This was a statement made by a North Carolina editor at the ninth annual meeting of the North Carolina Press Association in Winston in 1881. He pointed with pride to the fact that the press had forced the passage of the charter of the Central Railroad, had fostered the University, the colleges, the public schools, and had always ranged itself on the side of learning, liberty, social order, and sound morals.

This editor also claimed that "there is more potency in the click of the type in the composing stick than in the click of the musket. The roar of the steam printing press is more powerful in the councils of the world than the roar of artillery." His fellow editors were urged to give and take with good humor in politics, not to lose their tempers and, above all, "let us be true to the welfare and glory of North Carolina."

I certainly agree that the printed word is a tool with almost unlimited power. Sometimes I wonder if newspaper people gen-

Governor Hodges with Hamburg Mayor Max Brauer (*left*) at a dinner given by the Governor for selected German officials and businessmen in Hamburg during the European Industry Mission, November 3, 1959.

Governor Hodges talking with the mayor of Amsterdam, G. Van Hall (*left*) during the European Industry Mission, November 4, 1959.

erally fully realize the terrific responsibility they have in dealing day in and day out in disseminating the printed word. Since Biblical days, mankind has been moved to great acts, misled into evil deeds, and inspired beyond description by the printed word.

Down through the centuries, people have come to accept the printed word as fact—with or without good reason. I shall never forget overhearing a man remark with excitement that he had just heard an important news bulletin on television and that he could hardly wait until morning to see if it was in the newspapers so he would know that it was true. He had heard the spoken word but he was not ready to believe it until he saw it in cold print. What a fearful responsibility you have in putting down the printed word!

Once printed, even the most dubious statement often has a way of acquiring new respectability. Anyone who has attempted to wrestle a correction or retraction from a stubborn editor can verify this fact. Back in the pre-1900's, when the free-wheeling, colorful, and often irresponsible newspapers of that day were having a grand time sandbagging their political foes, there was a classic example of such an effort to gain a retraction. The old *Greensboro Patriot* once laid into a political candidate by declaring that he "wasn't fit to carry guts to a hog." The outraged candidate immediately demanded a retraction and got it—to his dismay—as follows:

"In our last week's paper we animadverted to the fact that one Alfred M. Scales (later governor), brigadier general in the armies of the later Confederate States of America, has announced his candidacy for the Democratic nomination for Congress from this, the Imperial Fifth District of North Carolina, and asseverated in our opinion that aforementioned Scales wasn't fit to carry guts to a hog.

"Whereupon aforesaid Scales served notice upon us that we would either meet him on the field of honor or that on his next visit to Greensboro he would horsewhip us. After careful consideration, we have arrived at the conclusion that there is no man in the district better suited than Scales to carry guts to a hog."

The constitutional guarantee of a free press is acknowledgement that the people have the right to know what and how and why, and that they must have the opportunity to know in order to make wise decisions as citizens in a democracy. The press must remain free so that the people may have that opportunity—most often described as "the people's right to know." While there is no disagreement about the people's right to know, there are some who express serious doubt that the press is the *only* medium through which the people must be informed. This doubt is perhaps most often expressed where major newspapers have merged to such an extent that a newspaper monopoly exists in a city, county, or section of the state. We recognize such mergers usually result from economic necessity, but where there is lively competition among news media for the privilege of informing the people in a given area, there is usually little criticism of this nature.

It is a rather frustrating experience for a public official to work diligently in drafting what he considers to be a most important statement concerning his position or his program, and then to have this statement—no matter how brief or carefully written—turned inside out and upside down through the journalistic gymnastics of a young reporter who picked up the statement ten minutes before. From such experiences, a responsible public official will naturally wonder about the role of the press in informing the people on what they should know.

As newspaper readers, we tend to accept as truth the majority of the news items which we read in our daily newspapers because we have no personal knowledge of these events, and we assume that the reporters and editors responsible for the news stories do have some factual knowledge upon which to base their articles. Also, we know from experience that most of the news stories which we read in our newspapers *are* usually factual and true. Many of the differences of opinion between reader and reporter arise where the reader also has personal knowledge about what actually happened, and perhaps even has more knowledge about the event than the reporter who wrote the news story. This is especially true in the case of public officials who attend a meeting or a conference and have all the facts, and then read the newspaper accounts the next day about what transpired and what was accomplished or not accomplished. I am perfectly aware of the handicaps under which a reporter labors in getting all the facts and also aware that he may not have all the facts because they were not made available by the same public official who chose to be critical of the final story written.

All this leads us to the obvious conclusion that the good news reporter is above price. Our mutual friend, D. Hiden Ramsey of Asheville, said that without a good reporter "no truly good newspaper can be published. He must have an alert mind, fast energy, and ability to write clearly, the capacity to hear correctly and to report accurately what he has heard. He must have a high sense of professional honesty. He must be able to report correctly events and opinions which he loathes as well as the events and opinions which he approves. He is a newspaper's conscience out on the firing line. He provides or edits or chooses the news which is the very life and blood of any newspaper." May I observe parenthetically that from what I've heard very few newspapers pay enough money for that kind of a reporter.

I have had the privilege of knowing and associating with many qualified reporters, and I fully realize that the biased and prejudiced reporter who writes slanted copy is definitely the exception in North Carolina and throughout the nation. Yet the harm which results from the work of one dishonest or careless news reporter is difficult to calculate. It certainly reflects unfavorably upon all editors and reporters and upon the press in general. This type of reporter was apparently responsible for the distorted and actually untrue story which was first filed on the so-called Monroe "kissing case."

I understand that a New York newspaper actually "broke" the story in which it was stated—among other things—that under North Carolina law white offenders are treated as juveniles until they are twenty years old, but that a Negro boy can be treated as a delinquent only until he is sixteen. I shall not dwell on the details of this unhappy incident, except to say that this obvious lie was only part of a newspaper story which swiftly left our state to travel across our nation and around the world faster than our latest model Atlas missile. Before we at the state level had learned of the news story and its wild claims of injustice, and before we could nail down the actual facts, this story was creating resentment, bitterness, and misunderstanding against North Carolina and the South among peoples all over the world.

Despite the best efforts which we could make to state clearly the actual facts as they were, the truth could never catch up with the original falsehood. Weeks later after the full facts had been released to all news media, my office was still receiving protests from people in other parts of America and in other countries quoting current news stories or news broadcasts containing the original "big lie."

Every newsman has the basic responsibility to be accurate and to seek the truth. It is when he attempts to interpret his findings that objectivity—and the truth—sometimes suffer. Especially is it true when the reporter has strong personal feelings on the subject about which he is writing, or when he is harnessed by a firm policy or position taken by his editor or the publisher.

Perhaps in the realm of political writing, it is most difficult for the non-journalist to understand where basic responsibilities rest. I was told by one of your North Carolina newspaper writers recently that he felt that many reporters were like some politicians, always seeking advantage—in other words, that they used political news stories as a means of exerting their own influence in politics. This is not honest news reporting.

Let me give you one recent example. A well-known political writer in North Carolina, in a signed article, stated as a fact, without qualification, that Harold Makepeace, the director of our secondary roads, "recently made an informal survey to decide who the team (meaning the Hodges administration, I assume) should support in the 1960 gubernatorial primary. Interestingly enough, the name of Makepeace's erstwhile boss, Mel Broughton, came up high and Lieutenant Governor Luther Barnhardt bowed out because he didn't show up so well."

This story did not include the fact that Harold Makepeace had flatly denied earlier rumors that he had made any such survey, and that he had also denied vigorously that he had any part in the decision reached by Lieutenant Governor Barnhardt in not putting forth his name as a candidate for governor. I know Harold Makepeace, a respected friend, to be an honorable and honest man. I believe him when he stated publicly that he did not make any such political survey and had nothing whatsoever to do with the matter of the Lieutenant Governor's withdrawal. Yet this political writer apparently did *not* believe Mr. Makepeace, did *not* carry his denial and handled the entire matter as if the suvery *et al* were established facts.

In a later article this reporter qualified somewhat his earlier statements concerning this situation, and pointed out that Mr. Makepeace had denied making any such political survey. I realize that "politics" is a difficult term to define, and that it means different things to different people. Perhaps those of us in the public and political arena do take the matter of accuracy in political writing too seriously, but I am convinced that the average newspaper reader does not understand all these shadings and still tends to believe what he reads—whether it is the details of a train wreck or the opinions and speculations of a political writer—unless the writer is careful to clarify what is personal opinion and what can be based on facts.

While we are in the political arena, let's look at another example of journalistic assumption. A newsman for another major state daily wrote a summary of legislative activity in which he pointed out that Addison Hewlett was elected Speaker of the House "over Representative Carl Venters of Onslow, Governor Hodges' choice in the race." For such a misstatement of fact to pop up again in August many months after all my statements of neutrality in the speakership race gives me some pause. Many months before the 1959 General Assembly convened, I announced publicly and to each candidate for speaker that I would take no part in the speaker's race. It was stated at that time that I had a very high opinion of both candidates and that I thought that the House of Representatives was in a very fortunate position in having two good men from which to choose its speaker.

As the speaker's race warmed up prior to the General Assembly, I was again asked about my position on the race and I repeated again and again that I would have no part in the race and did *not* have a candidate. Furthermore, I was extremely careful not to interfere in any way with the active political activity and maneuvers going on among my legislative friends in the General Assembly, because I had many friends on both sides. Yet, news stories persisted in linking me with Mr. Venters and attempted to have me actively opposing Mr. Hewlett, who was eventually elected to the speaker's position. I was often urged by partisans on both sides to take part.

I will say once more for the record and to emphasize the discussion we are having here, that I never took the slightest part in this race—regardless of what any reporter or any politican says.

As most of you recall, the budget recommended by the Advisory Budget Commission and myself came under considerable editorial attack by some of the newspapers in the state. These editorial writers had every right to their opinions and certainly made use of this privilege.

Starting early in the session, I introduced some statistics at one of my press conferences which showed that the method of helping finance a biennial budget by using a projected state credit balance was nothing new. As a matter of fact, these figures clearly showed that each General Assembly for six previous sessions had actually made a practice of utilizing a large credit balance to balance the budget and to move the state's programs ahead.

Strangely enough, these facts and figures were not carried in any newspaper that I saw, although the information was furnished to the press time and time again through our regular press conferences. In all candor, it would appear to any reasonable person that the critics of our recommended budget had made up their minds on the matter and did not care to be confused with new facts and figures. In any event, it was late in the General Assembly before any mention of these basic figures was made in the press. Happily, we did not depend upon the press to reach the members of the General Assembly with this information but went directly to the legislators with mimeographed copies of our state's fiscal record, and a majority of these men saw and understood the significance and the precedent formed by this record. You had a real responsibility to see that the people had these facts which were incontrovertible.

In all this discussion about opinion versus facts, it might appear that our editorial writers would be least concerned with such problems since their purpose in life is to express opinion. Alas, this is not so. Since most opinions are usually based on what facts are at hand, the editorial writer must do the best he can to marshal his facts and information if he is going to make any impression with the conclusions reached. In view of the complexity of the many problems and issues which apparently must be debated, dissected, and reconstructed on our editorial pages, I think that our editorial writers do a remarkably good job. I have found many of their editorials very helpful to me. I am just grateful that I do not have the job of writing so profoundly each day on so many public issues.

About forty years ago I had the responsibility of getting out a plant newspaper once a week. Our editor took sick and I had the responsibility and the opportunity to write the editorials that week. I was horrified and pleased! I could hardly wait to see my words of wisdom in warm print (it's cold print when the other man writes it).

While I am passing out dubious bouquets, let us dwell for a moment on the headline writer. Recently, I made a state-wide telecast in which I devoted—at the request of the TV news directors—fifteen minutes to my recent trip to Russia and fifteen minutes on my reactions and comments on the work of the 1959 General Assembly. In the fifteen-minute comments on the General Assembly, I made a real effort to bend over backwards and not be critical of the General Assembly, except to mention in passing my disappointment that the legislature had failed to revise the constitution, including court reform. That one item was the only near criticism, yet here is the headline from one North Carolina newspaper covering this state-wide address: "Hodges Points Out Failure of General Assembly."

Sydney J. Harris, the columnist, recently gave the needle to news photographers about their habit of always urging their subjects to smile. Mr. Harris said that while he was attending a medical convention a news photographer posed several of the leading doctors around a chart they had been studying and then commanded them: "Now, let's all have a big smile on our faces!" The photo came out later in the papers with the medical men grinning delightedly at the chart which has the bold legend written above it: "Infant Mortality Rate in Illinois for 1958."

Dean Norval Neil Luxon of the School of Journalism here at

the University has said that the first responsibility of a journalist is to select the news for the reader. The process of selection determines the news that you and I may read each day in our newspaper. This choice naturally depends upon the individual making the decision on any given day, but normally follows policy decided by the publisher and the responsible editor. All of this leads to the delicate question of "balancing" the news of the day and the hour to provide the readers with a comprehensive, intelligent, and accurate summary of the most important news. Newspapers, of course, must sell their products to stay in business and to do this must include those news items which people are interested in. At the same time, the newspapers must also include those news items which they think people should know about. As one North Carolina journalist put it, "Finding the right pattern is one of the neatest tricks any newsman accomplishes."

Whatever this trick may prove to be, the fact remains that many people are seriously concerned over the lack of constructive news on the front pages of our newspapers as compared with the prominent—and often sensational—play given to the more sordid side of life. I know that this is an ancient problem in the newspaper business, but like death and taxes, it remains with you and your readers.

Henry Belk of Goldsboro, a towering giant in more than mere physical stature, attempted to describe that illusive thing called news. He said to the *heartless one*, news is rape, murder, suicide, shootings, tragedy, storms, battles, divorces, etc. To the *poet*, the news is moonlight and starlight and summer dawns, gentle breezes; the essential immortality of man, his courage, his indomitable soul; it is the wind and sand and surf, and friendship and fellowship and faith. To the *philosopher*, news is man's relation to man, man's learning what life means, the principles of truth and beauty, of ability to determine one's own place in life, of what makes courage, of what makes weakened souls, of the nature of war and peace and of the eternal and everlasting climb of man from his ape-like beginnings to an even higher plane.

Mr. Belk concludes by saying that to the *editor* news is all of these things and more. "It is a balance one against the other. It is the mirror of life, of the reflection of the little things which man gives himself to, his bornings and his dyings, his babies, his church, his clubs, his comings and his goings, and of his great loneliness and his need always for assurance. Of such is news."

Here lies a tremendous and exciting challenge for any news editor because I believe Mr. Belk is right. News consists of many things about mankind, and I do not believe that there is any journalistic formula which would day in and day out place the views of the "heartless one" over the poet, the philosopher, or that hardworking decent human being, the editor. May I as a reader-citizen observe that I think you'd be pleasantly surprised how much the public would enjoy more constructive articles— rather than so much emphasis on the sordid, the tragic, and the bad things that are happening in the world.

I cannot conclude this discussion without reminding you that the dramatic story of North Carolina today, its people, its problems, its growth, its vast potential, its new ideas, and its leadership in the South and the nation—all of these things have not been told completely by the press or by anyone else. The story is an unfolding one and should be told in its proper perspective and giving the unpleasant as well as the pleasant and encouraging. I am confident that the press of North Carolina can and will do the job, and the people will like it!

In closing, I would like to leave you with a few observations:

1. Community and area growth and development deserve and must have good newspapers with a responsibility beyond their first and foremost duties to inform the public on public affairs. They should also bring their influence and leadership to bear on the side of community and area improvement and the constant promotion of anything worthwhile that will help our people.

2. The Press of North Carolina cannot meet this challenge unless it has enough trained and skilled personnel. Only last month the head of the School of Journalism at Ohio State University stated that "the rising star of science has stolen the glamorous show from journalism, the traditional idol of so many of our young people." He advised editors to step up their competition with engineering, science, and medicine for the brightest young minds available. I know this is a familiar refrain for Dean Luxon who is working so hard to strengthen and expand the School of

Journalism here at the University. It is good to know that the newspapers of North Carolina strongly support this School of Journalism and have contributed so generously through the Journalism Foundation which now has funds in excess of $100,000.

3. Newspapers need to encourage a better understanding of their basic responsibilities and their part in the scheme of life Too long have newspaper editors assumed that their readers understood all about their operations and their problems. While urging everyone else to stress selling, newspapers have been too modest or careless about selling themselves. With good public relations goes an ability to accept criticism in good grace and to accept it in good spirit. All of us need this! Dr. Robert M. Hutchins, the former boy genius, recently charged that newspapers "are the only uncriticized institution in the country. You will not criticize one another, and any suggestion that anybody else might do so sets you to muttering about the First Amendment." The good, honest newspaper must protect and preserve its reputation and position by speaking out on what it stands for and what it is attempting to do in serving its readers and its area.

4. Our people must be kept well-informed by the press of North Carolina. The Honorable George Patton, a veteran Superior Court judge and former attorney general of North Carolina, once said: "Freedom of thought is the original freedom. It finds its best means of expression in an unfettered press. We are indeed an unfortunate people if we do not comprehend this simple truth.

"Freedom of the press is nothing more than the prerogative of writing and publishing what each citizen thinks and can utter with his tongue. The use of this prerogative is as proper as is it to think and speak. To oppress it is as unjust as it would be to bind the senses and tongues of all citizens."

Thank you for listening. The majority of the newspapers in North Carolina do a wonderful and vital job of keeping our people well informed. We are grateful for having such a responsible and alert press in a free society.

ADDRESS AT THE ANNUAL MEETING OF THE NATIONAL ASSOCIATION OF STATE AUDITORS, COMPTROLLERS, AND TREASURERS

PHILADELPHIA, PENNSYLVANIA
September 16, 1959

[Governor Hodges and eight other state governors made a three-weeks tour of Soviet Russia in late June and early July, 1959. Observations and impressions gathered on the tour formed the content of this address, the substance of which the Governor was to repeat on a number of later occasions. (See pp. 501-502, 503, 504, and 507 for summaries of similar addresses at Elon College, Rochester and New York City, New York, Asheville, and Goldsboro; and pp. 596-597 for an account of the Governor's experiences with the Russian news media.) Other accounts of the tour were contained in a series of letters written by Governor Hodges from Russia between June 24 and July 16, which appeared in the *Greensboro Daily News* on July 3, 10, 14, 17, 19, 22, 24, 26, and 28, 1959. These were later brought together and published in a 100-page booklet entitled *A Governor Sees the Soviet* (Printed as a public service by private contributions. 1959). Still another account, reproducing material contained in the above-mentioned speeches, was printed in the *North Carolina Clubwoman,* XXXVI (April, 1960), 1, 3-5, 10. The Governor declined to accept any pay for his letters to the *Greensboro Daily News,* but suggested that the fee be given to the Friends of the Library of the Woman's College of the University of North Carolina—which was done.]

I am honored to have this opportunity to meet with the members of this distinguished and influential organization on the occasion of your annual convention. Our mutual friend Henry Bridges who is our North Carolina state auditor has told me many times about your group and of his pride in this organization. Naturally we in North Carolina are proud of the esteem in which you hold Henry and of the honors you have given him! When Henry asked me to be with you tonight, I accepted readily although I can be here but a few hours.

As a person with some experience in both government and business, I certainly recognize that the members of this organization occupy some of the most important and responsible positions in state government. Too few people fully appreciate the vital services rendered by the members of this association. Yours is a responsible, complex, difficult, and, in many instances, thankless job—one that the average citizen does not understand and makes little effort to understand. As your job becomes more and more complex—as it does almost daily—there could develop a correspondingly greater void between you and the public served.

I am sure that all of you will agree with me that this would be most unfortunate and undesirable. Your work, as much as that of any other government official, can affect both directly and indirectly the present and future well-being of all our citizens. The fact that many people simple do not understand the nature of the service you render and the tremendous responsibility that you have for the smooth and stable operation of government is not altogether the fault of the auditor, the comptroller, or the treasurer, but it is a situation with which you might do well to concern yourselves, both as individual public officials and as an organization. You owe it to yourself, your individual states, and the people you serve to make the work you are doing better understood by the average citizen, whether he is a businessman or factory worker or farmer. There is no reason why the members of this association should not be just as public relations conscious as officials in any other branch of government.

In the years ahead, as the business of government continues to grow and becomes more and more complicated, we will need more public interest and greater understanding and cooperation than ever before. Greater demands are being made on governments today than at any other time in our history. This is true at all levels, local, state, and federal. These demands create problems that we must meet with great courage and no little ingenuity if we are to fulfill our responsibilities as government officials.

Cooperation from and understanding on the part of the average citizen will be absolutely essential if we are to get the job done. It is for this reason that I strongly recommend that you do everything in your power to create public interest in the work you are doing, and to make absolutely certain that no opportunity is missed to solicit public cooperation and facilitate public understanding whenever possible.

To accomplish this goal it is necessary to *communicate clearly* with the general public, with all government agencies with which you work, and with all news media, financial and trade publications, etc. This will require more than a speech now and then to a local civic club.

The average citizen is far more interested in all phases of government than you may think. In North Carolina we have made a determined effort in recent years by every proper means to encourage our people to work together as individuals, as towns, counties, and regions to meet our economic problems with courage, energy, and imagination This has meant at times "selling" North Carolina to our own people, but the increasing understanding and unity of purpose has brought a closer liaison between the people and their government officials. The program for economic development and growth that we have been promoting in our state is not billed as the governor's program or the government's program or the legislature's program. *It is the North Carolina program!* We have preached that in any effective plan for the advancement of our state, our state officials have their specific responsibilities, the people's representatives in the legislature have their responsibilities, and the people themselves have their responsibilities. Each group is ineffectve without the full cooperation of the others.

I think that the record we have compiled in North Carolina in recent years is ample evidence of the fact that the procedure we have followed is effective. Our industrial growth in recent years has been excellent! We have succeeded in shattering our own development records each year since 1956, while running far ahead of the regional and national expansion averages. In 1958, while the nation—suffering the effects of a recession—invested 17.4 per cent less in new and expanded industrial facilities, North Carolina registered an increase of 32.5 per cent. During this one year in North Carolina more than $253,000,000 was invested in 423 new plants and expansions, providing 21,757 new jobs and increasing our industrial payrolls by $72,633,00.

I have mentioned these facts and figures merely to illustrate what can be accomplished when government officials and the people they serve work together in harmony to attain specific aims and objectives. I mention it also as a means of stating my firm conviction that the responsibility for developing this harmony lies with the public official. A visiting state governor told me last month in Raleigh that he was pleasantly surprised at the spirit of cooperation that existed among our state officials and department heads. Each of you would do well to analyze your own particular situation and determine whether or not you are really doing your part in your state's cooperative endeavor!

However, my primary purpose here at your meeting is to outline for you some of the observations and impressions gathered during my recent tour of the Soviet Union. Less than two months ago, I returned to this country after having spent three and one-half weeks in the Soviet Union in the company of eight other American governors. So far as I know this was the first time an official group of state governors had paid a visit to a foreign country with a serious mission in mind. Our mission was to learn as much as possible about the economic and social philosophy of the Soviet Government, to meet the people of that vast country, and, wherever possible, to promote a better understanding of our own country and its peaceful intentions in world affairs.

May I say at the beginning that my experience left me more devoted to the American system of democratic government and personal freedom than ever before. I believe more strongly in the free enterprise system with its incentives, as opposed to the socialists' system which subjugates individual freedom and initiative. I do not like the basic philosophy of Soviet government, and I cannot condone the methods employed to support that philosophy. Still, if I am to be perfectly honest with you, I must concede that the Soviet Union is making great progress in a wide variety of fields. I must also concede that I was not fully prepared for many of the things I saw and learned during my visit.

It was a revelation to me to learn that the Soviet Union is actually composed of fifteen separate republics; that it has scores and scores of nationalities, many of whom are preserving their own traditions and history and languages; and that it has over 100 different languages and dialects within its borders. I learned a lot of geography. When I hear about the Uzbek Republic in the future, it will mean more to me, as will its capital, Tashkent. The fabled historical city of Samarcand, which lived 2,000 years ago and withered away with its mosques, I will now see alive, bustling, planning for the future and caring little for the past. And, I will see Alma Ata, the capital of the Kazak Republic, smack up against the Sinkiang Province of China with the snow-capped Himalayan Mountains looking down at us, to be approached as a comparatively new city in a rapidly developing region.

Before leaving for the Soviet Union, we asked their officials for approval of an itinerary. We asked to see certain officials in the various republics and at the federal level in Moscow. We asked to visit certain cities and places. In practically every instance the approval (characteristically given at the last moment) was accorded. We encountered little trouble and the hospitality was commendable. We traveled over 10,000 miles in the Soviet Union, visited five republics, saw the prime ministers and their cabinets at these various places, and saw any number of Soviet or national ministers, including Premier Khrushchev himself.

May I say that the people we met from Khrushchev down through the ministers were uniformly highly intelligent. They knew their subjects, they knew their work, they knew their history, and, of course, they knew the Communist party line. We spent many hours with these people, discussing every phase of social, economic, and political activity, and at the same time making ourselves available for questions about our individual states and our great nation. We welcomed questions and tried to answer them frankly. We found, and this is rather important, that the Soviet people knew much more about us and our systems of education, etc., than we knew about them and their methods.

We looked hard and carefully at the Soviet system and we came away with a frightening impression of what they are doing and, more important, what they can and probably will do in the future. Time will not permit, of course, our discussing all phases of the Soviet system and their lives. I would like to touch on two or three things, however. First of all, the people!

The man in the street of the Soviet Union is generally friendly to the United States and its people. The people have a misguided opinion of our government in that they have been taught by their leaders that we are warmongers intent on destroying the Soviet system. Yet, as individuals, they are not unlike us. We saw this in many cases. I carried with me throughout the trip many items representing or explaining the characteristics of my state—North

Carolina made cigarettes, post cards, pamphlets from our advertising agency and other such items. To the prime ministers in each of the republics we visited, I presented a one-page summary of activities in North Carolina relating to agriculture, education, welfare, etc. The smallest thing given to the people in the streets, whether it was a pencil or note book, or a single cigarette, was deeply appreciated. They crowded around us and talked freely. This was particularly true of students. When we made an unscheduled appearance at a wrestling match and it was announced that we were American governors, 2,000 Soviet citizens stood and cheered. This evidence of interest and friendship was repeated many times.

Contrary to what we may have been led to believe in the past, the Soviet people are in no way submissive or lacking in enthusiasm for their present way of life. It was my observation that they are, for the most part dedicated, hard-working people who have an immense pride in the progress they have made and who have confidence in their form of government. We must not continue to be misled into thinking that the Soviet people are, in any large measure, dissatisfied with Communism or with the leaders, who in one way or another, control their lives from the cradle to the grave.

To be sure, there are some who object to the subordination of individual freedom, who recognize the evils of international Communism, but their voices are stilled by the masses of Soviet people who know only that their living standard has been raised, that illiteracy has been all but erased from their land, that their lives—controlled as they may be—have, for the first time in the memory of most, been given the security of food and shelter and retirement. The average Soviet citizen is proud of what has been accomplished in the four decades since the Bolshevik Revolution. The reason for this pride is evident throughout the country. A good example is the city of Tashkent, capital of the Uzbek Republic, which had existed for hundreds of years with practically no progress. Ninety per cent of the people were illiterate, there were no public schools as we know them, and only one or two ancient colleges or universities for the privileged few. Prior to the revolution little advancement had been made in the development of industry, agriculture, transportation, and cer-

Left to right: Baxter C. Young, Jr. and Henry T. Link, both of Lexington; Governor Hodges; and H. Cloyd Philpott, also of Lexington and later lieutenant governor, at Keflavik, Iceland, en route home from the European Industry Mission, November 15, 1959.

Photo by Hugh Morton

Senator John F. Kennedy and Governor Hodges at a Democratic fund-raising dinner in Washington, D. C., January 23, 1960.

tainly not in education. Today there are thousands of public schools, thirty or more colleges and universities, and the standard of living has been raised immeasurably. These people are eating better than ever before, dressing better, watching their children receive an education that was never before available, and glorying in the promise of even greater things in the future. Is it not reasonable, then, that they should enthusiastically support the system of government responsible for this progress? And, since the Soviet citizen has never known complete freedom under the czars or later and cannot fully comprehend our dedication to individual human rights, he has no real basis for dissatisfaction with the control under which he lives.

The average Soviet citizen is perfectly content to live with a system of government which says, in effect, "If you are willing to give yourself to the state and work hard at the job assigned you by the state for the rest of your life, then the state will provide you with all the things needed to insure a reasonably comfortable existence." The state will take care of the baby in a nursery school while the mother is at work, and most mothers do work—a great many of them doing manual labor. From nursery school the child will move into state-owned and state-supported kindergartens. At the age of seven the child will enter the state run elementary school system. After the Soviet citizen has gone to work, he is guaranteed around 400 rubles a month, which according to their standard of four rubles to our $1.00 is roughly $100 a month. If he is a dedicated worker, he can make much more than this. A scientist, for example, will earn 6,000 rubles a month and in some cases will get bonuses in addition. At retirement age, the Russian worker is guaranteed a minimum of 400 rubles a month (everyone is limited to a maximum of 1200 rubles, regardless of standing or previous earnings). Throughout life the state protects him with a well-rounded and effective health and hospitalization program without any charge. Incidentally, 54 per cent of all doctors in the Soviet Union are women.

It was interesting to me to find that the Soviet people, from Premier Khrushchev down to the man on the street, are both proud and sensitive. They do not want other nations, particularly the United States, to look down their noses at them. They admire the United States and its achievements and they do not hesitate to emulate us when it serves their purposes. They want to catch up with us and pass us in all material things that reflect a nation's greatness, and they say so openly and with complete confidence that this objective will be achieved. Let me say, at this point, that it was disturbing to me to see the progress being made in the Soviet Union and to realize that they are advancing in industry and in other fields at a much faster *rate* than we are in this country. Their planned rate of national income over the next seven years is 7.5 per cent per year. The "G.N.P.", or gross national product is planned for 8.6 per cent increase per year. Their planned capital investment is in dollars per year $75,000,000,000 at the rate of four rubles to one dollar or over $30,000,000,000 per year at exchange of ten rubles to one dollar.

Much has been written and said in the past year or two about the quality of Soviet education. After studying the Soviet system and comparing it with the system that we have in this country, I must say that although I favor our democratic system which has given us so much progress, there are some things that we could learn from the Soviets. I mentioned before that at the age of seven the child is guaranteed the right and, at the same time compelled to go to school for eight years. But, from about the third grade on the child is given more and more actual physical work to do. He is taught the values and dignity of hard work and, especially, manual labor. He is oriented or counseled by Soviet teachers and leaders and is in effect attached to some industry in the community and is made to work during that period. His classes are serious and, for the most part, the student is genuinely appreciative of the opportunity for an education. He spends six days each week in school and little of that time is wasted.

After completing eight years of elementary work, he can move on to what is comparable to our high schools—provided he shows the aptitude and the interest and can meet other requirements. He continues to work part time while in high school and when he finishes, if he does, he may go directly into the industry or work he has been trained for, or if he has shown exceptional ability he will be permitted to enter a college or a university. Tests for entrance into a college are servere. He does not go to college because his parents went or because it is the thing to do or because he hasn't yet decided what he wants to do in life. The Soviet student generally knows by the time he is ready for college what he wants to do in life, and he approaches this phase of his education with a seriousness, and concentration that we see too infrequently in this country. The Soviet master plan for the future becomes evident at this point and we see that they have long ago determined the number of engineers they will need, the number of doctors, the number of lawyers, and the number of teachers of various kinds. We see also that the educational faculties have been tailored to accommodate, as near as possible, the precise number of students that will be required to carry out the state-controlled program in various fields.

I visited a public school, which was not unlike our older ones, and I also visited the fantastic University of Moscow. At the University there are 30,000 students with nearly 10,000 students housed and taught in a single twenty-six story building. I talked with the chancellor of the University in an effort to learn more about their system and educational procedures. The conclusion gathered from these talks was that the Russians are going about the business of education seriously and effectively.

We were particularly interested in their program for developing scientists and we found that, in one comparatively small, relatively backward republic, there were 1,800 scientists in the Academy of Science. There are the well paid people in Soviet education. A scientist will make 6,500 rubles a month and can increase this amount to 10,000 rubles by doing special work or being recognized for his achievements in some special field. This group of people is available to both universities and industries, and there is little doubt that they represent a powerful force in the Soviet Union. There must be 20,000 or 30,000 fully trained scientists at the present time. This was one of the disturbing revelations of my visit, for these are the people who can thrust the Soviet Union forward rapidly in the fields of education, science, research, and technology. This represents a very serious challenge to this nation and to the free world—a challenge that we must meet as quickly and effectively as possible.

It is a great tragedy that the Soviet people have been indoctrinated against worshiping God, against the church, and against religion in general. I visited a Soviet church and found that the congregation consisted mostly of old women with shawls around their heads. Very few children or young adults were present. Many other former churches, we found, have now been converted into museums. I think the Soviet government is completely wrong in discouraging religious activity in their country and I think the great masses of their people are wrong in submitting to and apparently condoning this action. They are missing the fine spiritual side of life which all of us as human beings need more and more each day.

The Communist party, of course, controls everything in the Soviet Union. There are only about six or seven million communists—about 3 per cent of the total population—but party members are strategically placed, enabling them to exercise prescribed control over every phase of Soviet life.

The Soviet political organization starting with the Presidium and through the Supreme Soviet (or Congress) down to the lowest level, has a grand total of 1,800,000 elected officials throughout the Union—of this entire group 38 per cent are women, 43 per cent are collective farmers, 19 per cent are workers. Interesting enough 55 per cent are non-party members, but we must keep in mind that even though there are only six to seven million members of the Communist party out of a population upwards of 200,000,000, there are enough party members to see that there is representation in the smallest factory, store, or any other kind of enterprise. They pretty much control and tell the government what to do.

This whole procedure and relationship between the party and the government is complicated and I do not claim to understand it all, although I have been very studious in trying to learn and have done a lot of listening.

The Communists do a lot of meeting and a lot of discussing and they create or force actions if necessary in political and economic affairs. Practically 99 per cent of the people vote, and although they vote for only one person and one party, the people have, according to explanation given to us by Mr. Georgadze, eliminated the other candidates in their local meetings and discussions. It is claimed these extra candidates are eliminated by vote at unofficial meetings before the election. Perhaps this might be called a Communist primary!

The Communists insist that by the use of long and repeated discussions on the qualifications of the people who are applying for elective office (and there could be from three to five for each office down the line) the best man is finally chosen. I will have to say this, that judging from the officials we have met at various levels, and that goes from the city up through the state and to the federal level and right into the Kremlin, the Communists certainly have picked some able people—far abler than many of us thought was possible.

We have not realized in this country the true significance of Stalin's death and Khrushchev's ascendancy to power. Much of the control and planning has been decentralized to give more responsibility to the people located at what would be comparable to our state and local level. We were told by Khrushchev and others that the political trials are over and that there are no political prisoners left in the Soviet Union.

It would appear that the Soviets are attempting to open up and get closer to other parts of the world. I do not know that the exchange of visits between President Eisenhower and Premier Khrushchev will accomplish a great deal of good, but when we consider the grim alternatives—the possibility of a devastating world war—then these efforts to promote international understanding and friendship appear reasonable and sensible as an honorable means at our command to combat the misunderstanding that exists between our nations.

I am convinced that the threat to world peace that emanates from the Soviet Union has its origin, not with the masses of people, but with the Soviet leaders who are extremely clever, ambitious, diplomatically arrogant, and frighteningly confident of their ability eventually to dominate world affairs. I am equally convinced that much of the tension that exists is the product of misinformation and a lack of basic understanding on the part of all concerned.

It is also my conviction that the Soviet people are just as sincere in their desire for peace as are the people of our country. I might add that they are equally sincere in the belief that we, not they, are the major threat to the peace of the world. They believe this because they have been misled, because it suits the purpose of their leaders to misrepresent the United States and its people to the people of their country. Most of this misrepresentation has been, and continues to be intentional, but much of it is also the result of misunderstanding. There is little we can do at present to counteract, within the Soviet Union these falsifications by the Red leaders, but there is much that can and must be done to correct this misunderstanding, among both the leaders and the people. We can do this without compromising our principles or our position of leadership in a free world.

This is the reason many of us have been urging a greater exchange of people between our nations. It is the reason that the eight other governors and I who visited the Soviet Union recommended to President Eisenhower that an invitation be extended to Premier Khrushchev to visit this country and to see for himself that we are neither a nation of warmongers nor a nation of downtrodden people. I do not believe that the exchange of visits between the President and Mr. Khrushchev will produce any world-shaking developments, but I am convinced that some good will be accomplished, that a dent will be made, small though it may be, in the great wall of misunderstanding that now separates our two great powers. This, in itself, would more than justify the exchange.

Let me say that I think I am a better citizen, both of this country and of the world, for having gone to the Soviet Union to see their system in operation. I feel that I have learned a great deal, and I hope that everyone in this country will see the wisdom of learning as much as possible about the nation that poses such a serious threat to our wonderful way of life. We have a responsibility as citizens of this country to be well informed about the Soviet, to learn something of the discipline they are instilling in their children, both in school and in work; to develop within ourselves a greater appreciation of the need for scientific teaching, for the study of languages, and for the careful preparation of the men and women who represent us in the foreign service.

I hope we will understand that we need to pay more attention to our professors and scientists and school teachers—seeing that they get the job done while at the same time seeing that they are adequately compensated, both in terms of money and in terms of respect, for their efforts. I hope we will think more carefully about our planning, both short range and long range. Certainly, we face a tremendous challenge, but it is a challenge that can and must be met; and in so doing, the average citizen will find as I have, that our great nation with its traditional dedication to the dignity of the human being remains far superior to any other system of government that man has yet devised.

May I conclude my remarks this evening with one final—and I think, important—observation. I am sure that we all agree that the international situation is serious and deserving of our constant consideration. Our every day life is vitally affected by international conditions, and we as public officials and citizens of a democracy have a responsibility to keep well informed on these matters and to act, whenever possible, to ease the tensions that exist.

It is tremendously important also, that we promote understanding among our own people in the United States. There are many factors—economic, social, and otherwise—that breed discord, disunity, and even hatred between people within our own borders. In almost every instance, these differences are the product of misinformation and lack of understanding.

I am convinced that the great emphasis we have placed on personal contacts and the exchange of information on a worldwide basis should also be applied right here at home. We have much to learn from and about each other in our own country. As a matter of fact, we must understand each other as human beings and as fellow Americans first before we will have much success in understanding our regional and national problems. Just last week the press carried a statement from a professor who said that the racial difficulties we are now having were "peanuts" to what we would probably experience all over America in 1975!

We must realize that New England is not just Harvard College and rock-bound coasts, that California and Florida have something other than sunkissed oranges and new hotels, that the West is not a desert whose citizens are seeking pork barrel money for building higher and bigger dams, that every person in Texas does not own an oil well, that the Middle West is more than tall corn and pigs, and that the South now not only wears shoes, but makes them as well.

We must learn each other regionally as you have done as individuals in your association. We sadly need tolerance and understanding on the part of all our people. It is not, in my humble opinion, in the national interest for minority groups, of whatever race, color, or belief, to be used as political pawns by either or both of our major political parties. Of course, every civilized nation has a legitimate and proper concern for the protection of the rights of individuals. Certainly, there can be such a thing as tyranny by majority rule. But what we are faced with today is, in my opinion, exactly the reverse. It is high time more of political leaders came out for the "majority" in this country instead of persisting in an unsightly scramble to appease "minorities" as a means of gaining political advantage.

What we need in both of our major political parties and in all sections of this nation is love and concern for our country first with political expediency or advantage placed last. Above all we need more leaders who can think in terms of what is best for all our people—more leaders who have the courage to speak, not for the North or South or East or West, but for the American people as a whole.

The members of this association are in an excellent position to promote this spirit of cooperation throughout the nation. I urge you to do so at every possible opportunity; for through such action you will be serving the best interests of the people who depend upon you for advice and intelligent leadership. I can think of no better way for you to fulfill the basic responsibility that is yours as a public official and as an American citizen interested in the growth and sound development of this great nation.

Thank you!

ADDRESS BEFORE THE ANNUAL MEETING OF THE NORTH CAROLINA STATE HIGHWAY EMPLOYEES ASSOCIATION

DURHAM

September 25, 1959

[This address, at 10:30 in the morning, was the first of four speeches made by Governor Hodges on the same day. At noon he addressed the fall meeting of the Customer Relations Council of the North Carolina Motor Carriers

Association at a luncheon in the Sedgefield Inn at Greensboro (see p. 502 for summary of this address), and in the late afternoon and early evening he spoke in turn at the dedication of a new sewage treatment plant in Fayetteville (see pp. 502-503 for summary) and to a combined meeting of the civic clubs of that city. The address at Durham was made to about 225 delegates attending a state highway and prison employees convention. Highway Director William F. Babcock and Highway Chairman J. Melville Broughton were also speakers at the Durham meeting.]

I am glad to be with you in Durham today and to see all of you again! You are the chosen representatives of more than 8,000 state highway employees who are engaged daily in providing our citizens with an important and vital service.

I could not approach these remarks honestly without pausing at the very outset to pay tribute to those who have made our highway system so outstanding. North Carolina has a national reputation for the quality of its road system. While this is due in part to the wisdom and vision and work of highway commissions past and present, it is largely because of the excellent work of our highway employees. Whether you are engaged in administration, engineering, or operating a road machine, it is your responsibility to build our streets and highways and then maintain them to a high standard. The job you are doing is reflecting great credit on you and our over-all Highway Department within the borders of our state and throughout the nation. It is quite impossible to measure accurately the contribution you have made and are making to the citizenry of North Carolina, but I do know that progress, in this age of the automobile and truck, is largely dependent on the extent and quality of our mobility. Progress, in all its aspects, moves on our streets and roads and highways. An adequate transportation system is needed for the advancement of farming, business, industry, education, as well as our social and cultural life. In the larger sense you are not dealing with stone or asphalt or concrete—you are building avenues for all forms of advancement.

I am well aware of the fact that your best efforts frequently bring forth complaints rather than commendation. This is the price of public service and all of us, in government service, perform our daily tasks in a goldfish bowl of public opinion where a job well done is usually taken for granted while a mistake by one employee—regardless how small—will be held up to public criticism. Highways have always been a controversial topic. You hear and read a great deal about them for the simple reason that they are highly important to all of us—important and even personal.

I never speak of our highway program in North Carolina without a sense of pride in the over-all efficiency and effectiveness of our highway employees' work. You are doing a commendable job on a difficult and hard to understand task and, though they may be slow to say so, I believe our four and one-half million people and our hundreds of thousands of visitors would agree with me.

Your highway commissioners, your director, and other leaders have a serious responsibility to provide you with the necessary policies and tools to carry on your work. I have great confidence in what they have been doing in recent months. A great deal of their effort has been directed at providing North Carolina with a good highway service based on fair and uniform treatment for all people. We are one state and one people and the roads which connect us, each with the other, are just as important in one area of the state as in another.

Laying aside divisional highway commissioner authority in 1957 did not imply criticism of individual commissioner activity or purpose. It simply assured a return to the precepts set down in the original Highway Commission statute passed in 1921— that highway commissioners should represent the road needs of all the state. The Highway Study Commission report in 1956 and the General Assembly in the year following simply said that a system which tends to divide our state or to set one area into competition with another is wrong. In my opinion the principle of uniformity in highway service cannot be successfully attacked. The people of North Carolina who support the highway system through taxation have every right to demand and to receive good, uniform service.

There have been isolated comments from some places to the effect that creation of a state-wide Highway Commission has removed the road program from the people. In this connection, I am not so much impressed with the criticism when the facts of the case do not support the criticism. The present Highway Commission has gathered information about road needs in every part of the state. In the summer of 1957, your own division and district engineers were asked to supply the commission with a listing of the most critical road needs. Every municipal government and every county governing board was asked to do the same thing. Your own personnel studied every mile of primary and secondary roads, noting deficiencies and costs to bring every road up to a uniform minimum level of service.

To get a still better grasp of this problem, your commission has toured the entire state holding public hearings to gauge personally the road needs and the opinions of our citizens. Your division personnel are holding public hearings regularly in all the counties of the state to explain the road program and to hear complaints from citizens.

I am not so much concerned with charges that politics would build three bridges in eastern North Carolina as I am concerned with the fact that the programming of the bridges will fulfill a need which the commissioners heard about at every hearing they held in the coastal section and which need has been discussed for years! If building the US 220 bypass around Asheboro, or planning much needed improvements to US route 70 and 74 in the west, or completion of an interstate highway between Durham and Greensboro—if these answers to well known and publicly documented road needs are politics, then I say let us have more of this kind of politics.

Our Highway Commission was given a highly important mandate from the General Assembly—to measure actual highway needs in all areas of the state and to develop consistent or uniform policies which would comply with needs in the order of their importance. In other words, I believe this mandate instructs the Highway Commission to get the most roads possible for every highway tax dollar available and to deal honestly and objectively with everyone—whether an individual city, town, or county. I have watched our commission rather carefully as it has sought to carry out this mandate, and I believe it is being done forthrightly and courageously.

While one or two county boards of commissioners have directed criticism at the commission, I am impressed by the fact that the State Association of County Commissioners and *many* county boards of commissioners have voted confidence in the present program as a fair and equitable basis for accomplishing road work, and have worked closely with the commission in the development of these policies. Unfortunately one criticism seems to get more attention than a dozen approvals.

Criticism should never be ignored or resented. It should be carefully analyzed for it can frequently bring improvement. By the same token, however, we should never allow isolated criticism to cloud over or diffuse our real purposes and goals—to provide the best possible road service for the most people, regardless of who they are or where they live.

I believe your present Highway Commission has given you a great many policies or tools with which to do your job better. For one thing, you are not tied down with an arbitrary allocation of funds based simply on the area, population, and mileage in your respective divisions. Such allocations are now made on the basis of need—proven long-range need. All highway projects are subjected to close analysis, based not only on what the need of today is but generally on what the need may be twenty or thirty years hence. On many projects this means that more money is being spent on particular projects to secure broad rights of way or to protect the highway investment with greater control of access, better location, or better design. Such advance planning accomplished in close cooperation with municipalities or counties or local people will go a long way toward elimination of patchwork on our roads. It will also prevent the all too common practice of costly re-building too soon after projects are opened to traffic. Building permanence into highways and constructing them on wider strips of land to allow for additional laning in the future makes good sense. It means that we will discard fewer highways in the future and it will prevent the costly job of tearing down homes and buildings along the road to get more highway room at a later date.

Our new policies on right of way acquisition make sense to me. Your director told me the other day that your right of way personnel acquired over 95 per cent of the land for one inter-state road at the appraised value and without going to court. You will never achieve perfection, of course, on the critical problem of right of way purchases for you are frequently dealing with an owner unwilling to sell. It is also true that some property owners frequently have distorted views on the value of their holdings. These things are natural and understandable. However, the real merit in your policy lies in the fact that outside appraisals are being obtained on all needed properties, and we are endeavoring to settle claims in close relation to the appraisals.

This is highly important, for huge amounts of public funds are involved—well over $1,000,000 of North Carolina tax money goes into right of way purchases per month. The state has no right to underpay one property owner who might be easy to deal with while satisfying the personal greed of another owner with a large overpayment. The right of way appraisal gives us a good base for negotiations and, if I were a juryman on a right of way case, I would be impressed with the fact that commission personnel had tried hard to establish carefully the true value of a holding before trying to negotiate settlement. It may take a long while to educate the public and the juries to the real merits of the appraisal system, but I feel that a good start has been made, and I hope the public will interest itself in what is being done.

Our methods of notifying persons whose property might be involved in future construction is paying big dividends. There was a time when the governor's office received a good many letters charging injustices or lack of proper notification. I am happy to tell you that the volume of this mail has been reduced considerably. At the same time that you have been working more closely with individuals on right of way cases, your attorneys have cut in half the number of unsettled claims, some of which dated back several years.

The press will continue to play up troublesome cases where property owners shout that they have been cheated. This, too, is only natural, for it seems that controversy invariably makes the headlines. So long as you are on sound ground with your offer, are treating people fairly, and can honestly stick by a decision, you should certainly do so, for I do not believe that the public wants a highway commission which would throw money around loosely simply to avoid criticism.

I had occasion recently to look into one right of way case on which the owner had written me a letter. After reviewing it carefully I was convinced the right of way representative had done a good job in his negotiations and had made a very reasonable offer. I am confident there are hundreds of other similar cases.

Before preparing this address, I reread the speeches which Director Babcock made before your convention in both 1957 and 1958. In both speeches, several goals were outlined. Looking back after two years, I was happy to see several of the goals reached.

Starting salaries and salary ranges in a good many instances have been raised to assure that the department can get and keep qualified personnel, and your salaries are now more in line with the highway organizations in other states.

Our maintenance employees have been classified and their work week shortened. An organizational chart has been completed showing every highway job, and the desirable complement of personnel needed to do the job effectively has been determined.

Although Mr. Broughton and Mr. Babcock will probably deal with it in detail, I am happy to see you get a uniform payday plan worked out with measures to assure that it can be started with a minimum of hardship on employees. While one newspaper reported considerable criticism of the plan, I was pleased to see representatives of your own association endorse it, as they had previously approved the idea.

You now have a uniform retirement plan which will enable you as individuals to plan ahead. It assures that as older people reach retirement age, new job opportunities for younger people open up. The retirement of one individual has a chain reaction down through the organization as employees move up the ladder to more responsible and more remunerative positions.

I'd like to refresh the memory of all state employees and the public on some recommendations I made last February to the General Assembly. I said:

With our combination of State Retirement and Social Security benefits, we have a very good retirement program. In fact, . . . we have a far better retirement program than most governmental units, and indeed better than many large private industries. Vacation and sick leave provisions are also generous—with an annual vacation of three calendar weeks, and two weeks per year sick leave. Sick leave is cumulative in an unlimited amount. In addition to the three weeks annual leave and two weeks sick leave, the state grants a minimum of nine holidays per year, and petty leave privileges which amount to fourteen working hours—or almost two working days per year. Altogether the leave with pay provisions add up to about thirty-five days per year, or at five working days per week—seven calendar weeks.

Our study of salaries now being paid by the state revealed that, generally speaking, state salaries are reasonably competitive with comparable jobs in other governmental units and in private industry. We have noted that between September, 1956, and September, 1958, the average salary for state employees, excluding teachers and other public school employees, increased from $3309 to $3904, a jump of $595, or 17.98 per cent. This increase has been brought about by the general salary raise given by the 1957 General Assembly and the distribution of regular merit salary increments.

Although we have concluded that most state salaries are competitive at present rates, it is, of course, highly probably that during the next two years the salaries paid for some of the jobs in state government will need adjusting upward if we are to maintain our competitive position. To take care of this problem, we recommend a biennial appropriation of $2,000,000 ($1,400,000 from the General Fund and $600,000 from the Highway Fund) to be used for this purpose in connection with jobs subject to the State Personnel Act. We propose that, during the next biennium, the Personnel Department, in cooperation with the heads of the agencies and institutions, make a continuing review of all such jobs, and subject to the approval of the director of the budget, make appropriate salary rate adjustments as needed.

I am sure you will be interested in knowing that for all employees, including teachers and college personnel, we have recommended in the total budget for the next biennium approximately $16,000,000 for salary adjustments in addition to the $2,000,000 just mentioned. This gives a total of approximately $18,000,000 to be used for this purpose. This total is made up of the $2,000,000 for salary adjustments of employees subject to the Personnel Act (including highway employees); $4,043,833 for regular merit salary increments also for employees subject to the Personnel Act; $1,525,000 for college professional personnel, including Agricultural Experiment Station personnel; $1,968,612 for increasing beginning teachers' salaries; $1,556,000 for automatic increments for school personnel; and $6,899,556 for the extra week's pay for teachers.

There are a few other situations in connection with employment conditions of state employees which I would like to recommend that you consider. Under present laws governing the retirement system, the state, as the employer, matches an employee's contribution to the Retirement Fund until that employee reaches the age of sixty. After that point the state makes no further contribution. I recommend that these contributions continue until the employee reaches the age of sixty-five. I also recommend that you make $70 the minimum payment to retired employees who are now drawing either pensions or retirement benefits, as compared with the present minimum of $60. The administrators of the retirement system inform me that both of these recommendations can be implemented without requiring any change in the contributions made by the state or by employees to the retirement system. They advise this is possible because of the very sound actuarial practices followed by those responsible for the management and investment policies of the state retirement system.

I would like to recommend that per diem allowances for state employees who must travel be raised from the present $8.00 to $9.00 for in-state travel, and from the present $11 to $12 for out-of-state travel. Per diem allowances have not been increased since 1953, and simply do not cover present day costs. I recommend also that when state employees are required to move their residence for the convenience of the state, that moving expenses be paid by the state. The cost of these proposals can, in my opinion, be absorbed in the amounts presently recommended in the budgets of the various agencies.

There has been some mention of the need in our state government for longevity pay. This grows out of the fact that many of the employees who have been with the state for long periods of time have reached the top of their salary range and are frozen at their present rate. I recommend that the General Assembly make provisions for a study of this problem during the next biennium and that those making this study prepare specific recommendations to be considered by the General Assembly at its next session.

As already stated, conditions of employment for state workers constitute, in my opinion, the key factor in maintaining an efficient state government. As said in my message last Thursday, we can all be proud of the loyal and efficient service rendered by the state employees generally, and I sincerely hope you will approve the recommendations made for the benefit of our state employees.

From my own personal experiences with reorganizations in business and government, I know that any changes—even improvements—cause personal irritation and for a short period a lowering of morale because of uncertainty. This may have been true in your case, but I hope this phase is over. May I appeal to you and through you to the thousands you represent, to pitch in and make this organization even more outstanding than it now is.

And if you have criticisms or problems, take them to your supervisors who will see that your complaints get prompt attention and consideration. I understand that the commission will originate soon new procedures to handle such internal matters.

Other progressive steps have been taken in our Highway Department. The electronic computer has been installed to handle routine engineering and accounting calculations and thus free engineering and accounting personnel for more productive work. I am told that use of the computer can save many thousands of dollars on a single highway design problem and has, indeed, saved well over its total annual cost in the first three months of operation. Thus it becomes an investment which will return

Left to right: Richard Thomas, A. C. Gilbert, Jr., Governor Hodges, and Gerald G. Hotchkiss at annual meeting of the Greater New Haven Chamber of Commerce, New Haven, Connecticut, January 28, 1960.

Governor Hodges speaking at the Harvard University Business School, January 29, 1960. Oscar D. Williams, Jr., of Raleigh is seated on the left.

large dividends in money savings, time savings, and in the development of more useful high ways.

Your commission has given you a department of photogrammetry to enable you to keep upwards of $300,000 annually within the state rather than see it go to out-of-state contracting firms. It will also allow you a much wider use of the more efficient aerial survey procedure on a great many more projects than before. In establishing the computer section and the photogrammetric department, North Carolina's Highway Commission joins the ranks of over forty other state highway departments which had established similar practices in recent years.

The value of such progressive steps cannot be measured intrinsically, however. The true value can only be measured in the final end product—the highway itself. A highway cannot begin to return the public investment until it is opened for traffic, and you have been making notable progress. You are maintaining a schedule on interstate work which has placed your commission and your state in a position of national leadership, and you are getting more credit for it than you perhaps realize.

Just the other day I read an article in a newspaper for another state. It read in part—"Our state is making good progress in its interstate program, but it will have to gallop to keep up with North Carolina." The writer then proceeded to point out that their state had only seven miles of these roads open while North Carolina had almost 150 miles. The year 1958 was a record contract year for us, and during the first six months of 1949 we are continuing the pace. Almost 1,500 miles of secondary roads have been hard surfaced while a similar mileage has been stabilized to minimum standards. In the past two years, more than 1,600 secondary road bridges have been reconstructed to provide better than the minimum level of bridge service.

In the same two-year period well over $150,000,000 has gone into road improvements and when a great many other states declared moratoriums on contract lettings because of exhausted funds, North Carolina continued with its lettings.

The last decade has seen a tremendous amount of highway progress in our state. Thousands of miles of secondary roads have been paved. Scores of cities have been bypassed and hundreds upon hundreds of miles of primary roads have been rebuilt or relocated. Massive bridge projects have been completed and the great interstate program has been well started.

Much progress has been made in other fields in this decade. There has been a steady and important shift of population away from the rural areas and into urban or suburban sections. Fewer and fewer farmers have produced more and more products. North Carolina's industrial progress has been outstanding and our economy is better balanced and far more stable. Cities and towns have almost doubled in population. Automobile registration ten years ago was under 1,000,000. Today it is well over 1,500,000. One of the parks in North Carolina has become the nation's most visited park attraction, and hundreds of thousands of visitors have made our tourist industry one of our most productive.

Each of these developments has had a marked influence on our need for better streets and highways, and the hundreds of millions of dollars which have been poured into the road program have never completely satisfied our needs.

The next ten years will bring an even greater strain on our transportation network. The trend toward urbanization will continue at an accelerated pace and will probably be 50 per cent urban and 50 per cent rural. Motor vehicle registration will surely top 2,000,000, and our population could easily grow to 5,000,000 or 6,000,000.

In the area of highway work during the next ten years, you will have practically finished the interstate system. You will have provided hundred of miles of four laning through rural areas and you will have built giant expressways around or through most of the urban areas. You will have spent hundreds of millions of dollars on road improvement projects and well over half a billion on highway maintenance; and this is assuming that revenues remain constant, while, actually, they will go up. In ten more years the bond issue for secondary roads will be retired and I strongly suspect that most every road in the state that has a traffic of fifty vehicles or more daily will have been hard surfaced.

The cities and towns of our state will have adopted, in concert with the state, major thoroughfare plans for the development of more efficient streets and highways and a good many of the jointly conceived improvements will have been completed. I would certainly hope that these streets and highways will be far safer to use than the ones we have built over the past decade or so, and that the death rate, even with more cars and people, will not run as high as it is now. I am confident this will be the case, for the advance planning which has been done during the past two years has pointed in that direction. We are now building more controlled or limited access facilities as a means of guaranteeing permanence of capacity and greater safety. More and more intersections are being grade separated, and we are gradually doing away with delay points and nuisances which slow the driver, confuse or irritate him, and cause traffic tie-ups and pile ups. We are cutting down grades and straightening out curves and increasing sight distances. I hope that the time will soon come when our planning will permit us to acquire rights of way years ahead of construction and then reserve it against the day when construction will be needed.

This will come, I am sure, as a result of your cooperative planning with cities and with the development of a state-wide master highway plan. Just this week I was told by one of the city officials in our state that his dealings with our highway director and his associates were most refreshing when compared to his experiences elsewhere. The designation of eighteen major routes as trunk line highways, a task which has already been completed, was the first step in the direction of a master highway plan, and the improvements which our Highway Commission has already approved on the trunk line system, amounting to over 115,000,000 of dollars, are long-range plans for the calculated needs of 1980.

I was pleased to see your Highway Commission establish its Long Range Planning Department, and I am pleased that the members of this department have been moving over the entire state in lending assistance to cities and towns, counties, highway associations, and the commission's own personnel. These men are the highway architects of the future, and the care and effort they are putting into road projects at their inception will result in the saving of millions and millions of dollars and the development of a more adequate and permanent transportation network.

The job ahead of you is tremendous for you must meet the challenge of unparalleled public demand for better and better and more and more roads. You will face strong support in your efforts from the majority of our people who understand something about the importance of good roads and the tremendous effort and time which must go into their planning and construction. From some you will face opposition—the fellow who didn't get his road paved or the fellow who, though he can't understand why you're building such a big road, will be the first to get on it and drive it after the ribbon cutting ceremony. There'll be the fellow who will scream that he was ushered off his property by the state without adequate compensation. There'll be the lady whose rose bush you accidentally cut down with your motor grader or the fellow who stopped the road project with his shotgun. Let's work as hard as we can to keep such things to a minimum!

In an agency so large, so complex, and so important as our Highway Department you cannot help making a mistake now and then, and it is your mistake which you'll read about in the next day's newspaper. It isn't because the press is unfriendly—it's simply because such human errors make news stories.

Somehow you'll get the work done and, knowing something about your past and present work, I suspect the job will be done right well, for you take justifiable pride in the quality of the work you turn out. The Highway Commission is trying very hard to give you a professionally sound type of organization in which you can advance according to your desires and potentials. Developing your technology is a joint responsibility for both you and the commission, and the research and planning and the new methods you are using have brought representatives of many other state highway departments into our state to study you and your techniques. Just a week or so ago I was requested by a large newspaper in the U. S. A. to give them a story of our state-wide highway program as they thought it worthy of national attention.

Several other states are reviewing the reorganization of our commission. They are extremely interested in seeing how a state-wide commission operates with commissioners handling only policy making decisions and leaving the actual work to a highly professional highway department. I frankly believe we are out ahead of other states with our open-handed methods of building roads on a strictly needs basis. We are out ahead of other states in our planning and in our accomplished road work and, in recent months, we have been catching up with some of the other states which were out ahead of us. If your commission continues its program of building first where the needs are greatest, continues to consult closely with our citizens through its state-wide tour of public hearings, continues to modernize its equipment and its administration, continues its program of adequate long-range planning and its cooperative work with cities and counties, continues to publicize its road decisions far in advance of construction, then I think we can continue to have a better highway program year by year—a program which is close to the people and which the vast majority of people will support.

As you continue to bring excellence to your work in taking highway plans and transforming them into good roads, continue to maintain our highways adequately, continue surveys of highway adequacy and inadequacy and report your findings to the commission, continue to turn out highway work at an unparalleled pace, then all of us have much to look forward to—for ours will be a highway system thoughtfully planned, well located and designed, and efficiently reconstructed to provide long and useful service for a growing and prosperous state.

I wish I might stay through your convention and visit with each of you personally, but my schedule will not allow this pleasure. May I bring to you my personal best wishes for an enjoyable and profitable convention and may I say that it is a privilege to work with you in helping to provide a measure of public service which our people richly deserve.

ADDRESS AT AN INDUSTRIAL EDUCATION MEETING

BURLINGTON
September 30, 1959

[Two hundred state officials and other guests were in Burlington to see the new Industrial Education Center which had just been erected at a cost of $1,000,000, and to hear the Governor's address which was made at a luncheon meeting at the Alamance Country Club. Financed jointly by local industry and the local, state, and federal governments, the North Carolina Industrial Education Program was designed to equip people with the technical skills needed to take full advantage of the opportunities afforded by a rapidly expanding industrial economy. Eighteen such centers were projected, of which the one at Burlington was the first to be completed. In addition to Governor Hodges, there were speeches on this occasion by W. Dallas Herring of Rose Hill, chairman of the State Board of Education, Charles F. Carroll, state superintendent of public instruction, and Charles W. McCrary of Asheboro, chairman of the State Board of Education's committee on terminal education.]

In recent years the people of North Carolina have demonstrated their faith in themselves and their enthusiasm for the future by endorsing and actively supporting a variety of programs designed to bolster this state's economy and raise its standard of living. Because of this faith, this enthusiasm, and this support, these programs have contributed immeasurably to the progress that has been made. We are gathered here today to discuss, to learn more about, and to tell the state about another such program—one that I consider equal in importance to any we have undertaken in North Carolina in recent years.

Each of you has been invited here, not simply because you have proven in the past that you are interested in this state's growth and development, but because it is felt that you, collectively and as individuals, can contribute materially to the success of this vital and, I think, absolutely essential program. It is significant that many phases of social and commercial activity in North Carolina are represented at this meeting. I would like, personally, to thank each of you for being here—members of the General Assembly, school people, officials of state, county, and local governments, industrialists, and others. And I would especially like to welcome Mr. John H. Williams, chief of the National Industrial Equipment Reserve, to our state and express our sincere appreciation for the interest he has shown and the help he has given to the industrial education program in North Carolina.

For a long time there has been a recognized need for an improved program of industrial and technical education in North Carolina. If the state is to continue to expand industrially, and even to hold its own in competition with other states, it is essential that workers be trained in the techniques and skills of modern industry. Engineers must have the support of trained technicians. At the same time, it is recognized that there are thousands of young people in North Carolina available to meet this need, but who are inadequately trained in technical skills to take advantage of this opportunity. With industry's growing demand for trained workers on one side and an ample reservior of potentially skilled workers on the other, it has become imperative—and essential to the state's economy—that some type of program be established to bridge the gap between the supply and demand.

These people are, in effect, being denied a part in the economic revolution that is taking place in North Carolina—simply because uo to now no adequate facilities have been made available to help them through this transition. All our efforts to develop a balanced economy and bring greater prosperity to the citizens of this state will have gone for naught if we fail in our responsibility to supply the means by which our people can adjust to the changes. I think it has been dramatically illustrated in the early stages of our industrial education program that the people of North Carolina are eager to make this adjustment, to develop the new talents needed to meet this challenge. Those of us here— as leaders in education, government, and industry—have a responsibility to see that the people are given this opportunity.

It is quite apparent that the people here in the Burlington area have risen to this challenge. The establishment of this industrial education center is indicative of this area's determination to equip its people with the technical skills needed to take full advantage of the unlimited opportunities that a rapidly expanding industrial economy affords.

The program that led to the establishment of their center was initiated in 1956 when the State Board of Education, after giving much thought to the matter, requested that the Advisory Budget Commission allocate $2,000,000 for the establishment of eighteen industrial education centers in various parts of the state—the actual sites to be chosen on a basis of need as indicated by detailed studies. The 1957 General Assembly did not approve this full amount but, instead, requested further study. It did, however, appropriate, with some restrictions, $500,000 for the expansion and strengthening of trade and industrial education in the state.

From July, 1957, to March, 1958, the Board of Education, with assistance from industrial advisory groups, made a careful study of industrial education as it related to the needs of our citizens and their employment opportunities. All interested local boards of education were requested to conduct a survey of the annual job opportunities in their occupational areas to determine the number of skilled workers and technicians needed. When valid need existed and local challenge funds were available, these boards were encouraged to request that their locality be considered for the location of an area school to be known as an industrial education center. On April 11, 1958—eighteen months ago—the Advisory Budget Commission authorized use of the funds then conditionally available for this purpose.

Civic, educational, and industrial leaders here in the Burlington-Alamance County area began investigating the possibilities of this program as early as January, 1957. An industrial survey was made which revealed that Burlington and Alamance County had the second largest number of industrial employees in the state. The results of this study, along with other pertinent data, were presented to the Burlington Board of Education and, later, to the Vocational Education Department of the State Department of Public Instruction. A bond issue in the amount of $6,500,000 was voted for school building construction here on September 27, 1958. Prior to voting on the bond issue, the Alamance County Board of Education had agreed to allocate $87,500 of its share of the bond issue for the industrial center building. The Burlington Board of Education agreed to appropriate $162,500 for the industrial center from its allotment. When this $250,000 proved inadequate, the Burlington Board of Education, apparently recognizing the long-range significance of this program, agreed to furnish the additional money needed.

With admirable faith in themselves, in what they were trying to achieve, and in the people of Burlington and Alamance County, the actual planning for this industrial center was started several months before the bond issue was decided. Burlington School Superintendent Dr. L. E. Spikes assumed much of the responsibility in the planning and construction phases of the industrial center building.

It would, of course, be impossible to single out for special commendation all the individuals and groups who have contributed to the establishment of this center. I do, however, want to express appreciation to the people of Western Electric and the other industrial organizations in this area for the tremendous amount of time and effort they have devoted to this undertaking.

You have done, and are continuing to do, a marvelous job, and in so doing you are making a valuable and lasting contribution to North Carolina. Dr. Spikes has said "we believe that our industrial school has the potential to offer trained and skilled labor for practically all future needs of industry in this area." Certainly, this is an exciting and highly gratifying prospect, and it should serve as a challenge to all other areas of North Carolina that hope to realize full benefit from their industrial development.

Some indication of what this program can mean to our state can be seen in the fact that almost 1,000 students are already enrolled here at the Burlington center where they receive instructions from twelve full-time and nineteen part-time teachers. Classes run from 7:00 a.m. to 10:30 p.m. with courses being offered in machine shop, auto mechanics, electronics, sheetmetal, welding, knitting machine fixing, industrial chemistry, and other related subjects. The curriculum is arranged to meet current and anticipated industrial needs in this area. Other courses can and will be added as the need arises.

As an example of the way in which courses are tailored to local needs, the Guilford County Industrial Education Center, which has an enrollment of 250 students, offers, in addition to a number of the courses taught here, instruction in plumbing and sanitation, basic and specialized technical drafting, upholstery and upholstery sewing and cutting. The center in Wilson offers training in refrigeration, diesel engines, and sewing machine mechanics. In Goldsboro, emphasis is being placed on electronics, blueprint reading, and drafting. Incidentally, school superintendents in Wilson and Goldsboro both reported tremendous interest in this program from the beginning in their areas. From Wilson came the report that some students are commuting as much as 90 to 100 miles to attend classes. Reports from Goldsboro show that the demand there has exceeded all expectations and that their program will be considerably expanded as soon as their new building is completed. The director of the Goldsboro center, Kenneth Marshall, tells us that he has never before in his life "seen such a craving for knowledge."

Considerable interest and enthusiasm is also shown by those industries which stand to benefit from this program. An indication of this interest can be seen in a statement made recently by a spokesman of the Western Electric Company. This said that "In our experience in the Burlington area over the past years, there has been a very limited supply of skilled tradesmen, technicians, and draftsmen available to us. We are hopeful that the training center will eventually supply part of our needs in these critical employment fields and thereby reduce our out-of-area recruiting activities as well as lessen the amount of in-plant training presently required."

Similar interest has been shown by officials of Burlington Industries and by representatives of the Kayser-Roth Hosiery Company. A spokesman for Kayser-Roth said recently that his company "expects to derive far-reaching benefits from the industrial education center. Training in looping, seamless machine fixing, industrial maintenance, machine shop, and supervision will not only help develop skills for people going into hosiery for the first time, but will enable present hosiery employees to qualify for higher-paying jobs."

Judging from these endorsements, I do not think there can be any doubt about the need for an expanded industrial education program in North Carolina. Nor do I think there can be any doubt about the tremendous contribution this program will make to the future economic development. We have seen what has been accomplished here in Burlington and what is being accomplished at several other locations in the state. We must now ask ourselves the questions, "Where do we go from here?" "What must now be done to devlop the full potential of this program?" To answer these questions, and to understand more completely its state-wide scope, let us look for a moment at the over-all program.

The plan for financing this state-wide program, as it has developed, has brought help from a number of sources. Under Public Law 883 of the 80th Congress, the Department of Defense was authorized to lend to non-profit institutions certain equipment stored for use in the event of a national emergency. Members of the State Board of Education made several trips to Washington to present our case. Because of defense industries in our area, and because of the type of educational program planned, the Secretary of Defense authorized the use of defense tools in our North Carolina program. We have been alloted $735,000 in material from this source, and there are prospects for more in the immediate future. This equipment is loaned to the state under terms of a five-year contract.

Members of the state board also visited Washington to explain the North Carolina program to representatives of the Field Administration Division of the Department of Health, Education and Welfare—the agency that administers the National Surplus Property Program. Through this, and a cooperative working relationship with our state agency for surplus property, we have received $632,000 in usable equipment during the past year, for which the handling cost to North Carolina was $36,000. North Carolina industries, as I have pointed out, demonstrated their interest in this program by donating $107,000 in new equipment and promising $53,000 in additional materials. This includes sizeable equipment donation from major equipment manufacturers. Knitting machine manufacturers have donated new machines. Auto and tractor builders have participated generously—and there have been many others.

Just as our industries recognized these donations as investments in their own future, so should our local and area people recognize their part in the program as a lasting investment in their future.

The standards of quality for these centers, relative to student admission and student progress, are different from vocational educational programs we have been accustomed to in the past. For vocational education, as we have known it, simply does not meet the technical needs of the people in our modern industrial society. Vocational education places emphasis largely on manual *know-how*. Industrial education, as we interpret it in this program, teaches know-how also, but the emphasis is placed on *know-why*. An up-to-date industrial education program also features specialized teaching and specific student admission requirements. These are not features usually associated with the traditional form of vocational education.

One of the most important functions of any educational program is to keep the method of instruction up to date. To achieve this in industrial education it is necessary to study traditional offerings and modify the instructional content, technical information, and teaching methods relative to these occupations, and commensurate with the needs of the industries to be served. For

example, an examination, made sometime ago, of the competencies
of mechanical draftsmen in the Burlington area indicated inade-
quacies in the past curriclum. What the study actually revealed
was that the day of the pure mechanical draftsman is almost over,
because machine and tool design now involve a better than
average knowledge of the principles of hydraulics. electronics,
and pneumatics. To compensate for this need, the program here at
Burlington was revamped. The present program meets the demand
for more technical knowledge, and all concerned are aware of
their responsibility to remain constantly responsive to changes in
industrial technology in this area.

Our State Board of Education has developed policies governing
these centers which we believe make for a flexible program to
meet both today's and tomorrow's needs. A cooperative testing
program with the Employment Security Commission has established the minimun standards for student admission. The entrance
requirements vary with each course, but always include the basic
competencies necessary for job success in the area for which
training is given. Electronics students, for instance, must make a
certain minimum aptitude score in addition to having completed
two years of high school mathematics.

The decision as to whether a course should be continued or
dropped from the curriculum is determined annually on the
basis of a valid occupational survey which shows the employment
opportunities existing in the area served. Changes in the curriculum can be made without great difficulty because (1) once the
full program is in operation, there wi'l be little red tape involved
in exchanging equipment between centers to coincide with area
needs, and (2) the buildings, as demonstrated here, will be constructed in such a way as to eliminate inside load-bearing walls,
a condition that facilitates alterations with little effort.

Another feature of this program is that qualified high school
students may take their industrial education courses at the center
while taking their basic education courses at their own high
schools. Also, facilities will be open up to fourteen hours each day
to serve adults during off-work hours or in pre-employment
courses. All teachers at the centers are engineers or technicians
who have worked in industry within the past five years and who
will receive industrial experience again within the next five years

under the plan of certification. Many of the teachers hold responsible jobs in industry and serve part time at the center. Fifteen of the nineteen part-time instructors here in Burlington, for instance, are Western Electric engineers. As a result, the teaching staff is constantly aware of changes in technology as they relate to job requirements. These instructors, incidentally, are paid on a matching fund basis by the state and federal governments. Salary schedules and certification standards are established by the State Board of Education, and teachers are employed for specific courses of instruction of definite duration.

Perhaps I should also point out for those of you not already familiar with the program that each center is under the immediate supervision of a director and is administered by the local superintendent of schools and board of education under a state-wide plan supervised by the State Department of Public Instruction. All regulations governing the operation of the center are established by the State Board of Education. Each school has an advisory board appointed by the superintendent of schools and approved by the local board of education. This advisory group is composed of individuals familiar with the industrial needs of their particular area.

There are many aspects of this program that generate interest and enthusiasm. Our present industries, as we have seen, are wholeheartedly behind this effort. Prospective industries have shown tremendous interest in what we are trying to accomplish. Government officials and educators at all levels have given their enthusiastic endorsement. Our own state legislators have shown great interest. Even more significant to me, the people of our state who are benefitting from this program are enthusiastic. Those of us who have promoted this program from the beginning have actually been surprised by the number of people seeking to take advantage of this program to develop greater proficiency in their present jobs or to develop skills that will equip them for more responsible positions.

This, I think, testifies to the kind of worker we have in North Carolina. The North Carolina worker has amazed new industries with his attitude and his productivity. Given the opportunity, he will, of his own accord, improve his own competency—benefitting both himself and his employer. There can be no doubt that we have a responsibility to provide him with the facilities he needs to make the most of his ambitions.

It is especially important that we realize that the need for these facilities—for this program—is a present need and not something that we can postpone until some vague future date. It is not unreasonable to assume that the future of our entire industrial development program may be determined by the speed with which we activate this program. Evidence of this can be seen in the fact that the demand for this type of training has thus far exceeded our efforts to provide facilities. Consider also that our industrial growth is accelerating and that the demand will become even greater as the full force of this acceleration is felt.

Only last week William P. Saunders, director of our Department of Conservation and Development, informed me that he would be unable to accompany us on our upcoming trip to Europe because he would be too busy working with industrial prospects that have already indicated a desire to come to North Carolina. As a matter of fact, he stated that there are, at the present time, more good industrial prospects considering this state than at any one time in our history. This bears out my long-standing conviction that there is no limit to North Carolina's development potential. And this conviction is supported by facts. Our progress, especially our industrial growth, has been phenomenal in recent years. Development records have been shattered each year since 1956 and we have run far ahead of regional and national expansion averages. In 1958, while the nation— suffering the effects of a serious recession—invested 17.4 per cent less in new and expanded industrial facilities, North Carolina registered an increase of 32.5 per cent. During this one year, more than $253,000,000 was invested in 423 new plants and expansions, providing 21,757 new jobs and increasing our industrial payroll by $72,633,000.

Scores of North Carolina communities are helping to continue this pace. We are all very enthusiastic about what we have accomplished and what we expect to accomplish in the future. We are planning to work harder than ever to achieve our goal of a much higher standard of living for the people of this state. This determination is the basic motivation for our trip to Europe—October 31 to November 15—where we will seek new industry for our state and new business for our ports.

This progress raises the question of our readiness to develop this potential—to derive the maximum benefit from the opportunities before us. Certainly, we will not receive full benefit if our people cannot supply the technical skills that these new industries require. On the other hand, if our people can provide these skills, then they will not only benefit from present demands, but they will also profit, directly or indirectly, from the new industries that will be attracted to North Carolina by this competency.

I firmly believe that the answer lies in the establishment of industrial education centers throughout our state. To date, centers, in varying stages of development, have been placed in operation here in Burlington and at six other locations—Goldsboro, Wilson, Leaksville, Durham, Guilford County, and Wilmington. Eleven other centers are planned for Asheville, Hickory, Fayetteville, Lexington, Winston-Salem, Gastonia, Sanford, Kinston, Charlotte, Asheboro, and Raleigh. In order to activate and equip these additional centers and provide needed support for the units already operating, the State Board of Education requested the sum of $1,491,000 for the current biennium. This amount was approved in full by the Advisory Budget Commission, but was made subject to a vote of the people in the bond election for capital improvements, scheduled for October 27. That will be the date on which the people of this state will have an opportunity to express themselves on this and a variety of other programs that are essential to the progress of North Carolina. A favorable vote will authorize the issuance of bonds amounting to $34,400,000. More than half of this amount—$18,891,000—will be used for much-needed capital improvements in our state educational institutions. Included in this figure is the $1,491,000 needed to move forward with our industrial education program.

The other major benefactor of a favorable vote in the bond election will be our state mental institutions, which will receive $12,053,000. Other programs listed on the bond election ballot are community colleges, $1,500,000; local hospital construction,

$500,000; the National Guard armory, $100,000; state training schools, $466,000; the State Blind Rehabilitation Center, $140,000; construction of state port facilities at Southport, $500,000; and historical sites' restoration, $250,000. Certainly, all of these programs are deserving of our support, for each contributes to the social, cultural, or economic progress of North Carolina.

If our state is to continue to develop, industrially or otherwise; if we are to seize the opportunities that are available to us today—and will be even more abundant in the years ahead—then we must have a favorable vote on October 27. I am confident that the vote will be favorable—resoundingly so. I am confident because I believe that the people of North Carolina want to keep moving ahead in all fields that reflect greatness on the part of a state and its citizens. And, finally, I am confident because I believe that each of you here today will meet the responsibility that is yours to work for approval of this bond issue. Thousands of North Carolinians depend upon you for advice and leadership. You can serve those people in no better way than to encourage their enthusiastic support of this effort to build a better North Carolina.

May I conclude by again commending the people here in Burlington and Alamance County on this wonderful achievement. I think those present from outside Alamance County can draw inspiration from what has been accomplished here—inspiration that will enable you to move ahead rapidly with similar programs in your own areas of the state. In so doing, you will be rendering an invaluable service to North Carolina and its people. My best wishes to all of you!

Thank you.

ADDRESS OF WELCOME AT A JOINT ANNUAL SESSION OF THE SOUTHEASTERN REGION OF THE AMERICAN ASSOCIATION ON MENTAL DEFICIENCY AND THE NORTH CAROLINA ASSOCIATION FOR RETARDED CHILDREN

RALEIGH
October 8, 1959

[Governor Hodges evinced a deep sympathy for the mentally ill and often expressed his concern for North Carolina's progress in dealing with this problem. On this occasion he was pleased to remark that during the past twenty-five years, North Carolina had risen from forty-seventh in the nation to among the twenty top states in its efforts on behalf of the mentally ill.]

It gives me a great deal of pleasure and satisfaction to welcome the membership of these two outstanding associations to our state capital for this significant and purposeful meeting. This event is especially gratifying to me in that it symbolizes a determination on the part of all the states represented to fulfill their traditional responsibility to *all* their people.

There is additional satisfaction to be derived from the knowledge that your efforts here during the next three days will contribute materially to the future economic and social well-being of this great southeastern region. In meeting the challenge posed by mental deficiency, you are investing in the future of our people, and it is an investment that will repay you many times in the years to come. It will repay you each time a child finds understanding and purpose in a life once dark with fear and confusion. It will repay you each time a new bit of knowledge is acquired, a new cause discovered, a new treatment perfected. And it will repay you each time it restores to a family and to society a well-adjusted citizen, capable of facing the future with confidence and faith in his or her own abilities.

The American Association on Mental Deficiency is the oldest organization concerned specifically with the problem of mental retardation in this country, with a history of achievement dating back to the establishment of a training school in Elywn, Pennsylvania, in 1876. Down through the years this association has grown in size and importance, until now its beneficial effects are felt, not only in this country but throughout the world. I understand that your stated objectives are "to promote human progress and the general welfare of the mentally subnormal and deficient persons by furthering the creation and dissemination of knowledge of mental deficiency, by facilitating cooperation among professional persons engaged in work in the field of mental deficiency and allied fields, and by encouraging the best standards of treatment of the mentally deficient." Certainly, these are noble objectives—objectives that reflect your deep concern and your enlightened approach to one of the most difficult health problems of our day. Each of you is to be commended for the contribution you have made toward the solution of this problem. You can take pride in what has been accomplished in the past and you can draw encouragement from past achievements to stimulate your enthusiasm for the job that lies ahead.

All of the states represented here—North Carolina, South Carolina, Kentucky, Mississippi, Tennessee, Alabama, Georgia, Florida, and Virginia—have come a long way in a relatively short time in the care and treatment of their mentally ill and mentally deficient. We are especially proud of our record here in North Carolina. Twenty-five years ago this state ranked forty-seventh in the nation in the quality of its mental institutions and in the care it afforded its patients. Today, we rank among the top twenty states in the general quality of our over-all mental health program and we are particularly proud of our activities on behalf of those who are mentally retarded. Our Caswell Training School for mentally retarded children at Kinston has been described by an official of the National Association for Retarded Children as the finest such facility in the country. The relatively new Murdoch School at Camp Butner has also been recognized as an outstanding school—a fact that, I feel, reflects great credit on our people and serves as a great source of satisfaction to those individuals and groups who provided the vision and the leadership to make this progress possible.

I understand that a tour of the Butner facility has been arranged for this Saturday, and I sincerely hope that most of you will take advantage of this opportunity to see what we are doing in North Carolina in this field.

We all realize that much has been done in recent years to meet the challenge posed by mental illness and mental retardation. We also realize that much more remains to be done—so much more, in fact, that we will not see an end to the need in our generation. Still, we can take justifiable pride in the fact that we have participated in the winning of many of the battles that will make it possible for a future generation to win the war on mental health problems. We feel that, in North Carolina, we are nearing victory in the battle of the waiting list that has plagued us since the first day our state acknowledged a share in the responsibility for the care and treatment of its mentally ill. Only recently, aided by new drugs that enable us to accelerate the treatment of mentally ill, we were able to abolish waiting lists for general mental patients at our hospitals. Completion of the training school for Negroes at Goldsboro in 1957 made it possible for us to reduce considerably the waiting list for mentally retarded Negro children. Completion of the Murdoch School gave us valuable additional facilities adequate to care for a major portion of the mentally retarded white children in the state. Unfortunately, since the completion of these facilities, the incidence of mental retardation continues and we still have between 700 and 800 children in need of training and treatment. North Carolinians will have an opportunity to meet this challenge on October 27 by giving their approval to the issuance of $12,053,000 in bonds to expand present treatment. This is one of nine separate issues to be voted on by the people on that date, and I am confident that the total issue of $34,400,000 will be approved by a substantial majority of the voters.

We should realize, of course, that providing adequate schools and hospitals is only a small part of the job. We could provide five times the present number of hospitals, dormitories, and classrooms and they would add up to absolutely nothing without the highly skilled and dedicated personnel that is required to staff them. We have by no means won this battle in North Carolina, but I do think we have been most fortunate in that the men and women who work in this field in our state are of the highest professional caliber. Most of the credit for the fact that we have moved ahead in this field must be attributed to those dedicated individuals. Theirs is a particularly arduous task. Their labors are long and, of necessity, painstaking. Their triumphs, though tremendously gratifying, are not easily won. They must grope for evasive solutions in a field of service where unknown quantities are a dominant factor, where historic precedent is of little value, where it is frequently necessary to make one's own way without benefit of previously tested procedures. For their sacrifices, their devotion, and their dramatic accomplishments, we owe these people a sincere and profound debt of gratitude.

In this connection, it is encouraging to note that our medical colleges, universities, and various organizations in both the medical and educational fields have shown a steadily mounting interest in the mental health picture in recent years. These groups are affiliating themselves closer and closer with the activities and aims of our hospitals and schools, and the association is proving mutually beneficial. Our training schools are providing professional trained services for both medical students and resident psychiatrists from our universities. Monthly workshops are being held for public health nurses and welfare workers. Orientation courses are made available for public school teachers. Students from our universities also benefit from periodic lectures and seminars.

It is to be hoped that this growing interest in mental health will result in the availability of more trained personnel to relieve the present burden and pave the way for even more efficient care and treatment of the mentally ill and mentally deficient in the future. Certainly, this field of endeavor offers a tremendous challenge to the young man or woman seeking a profession in which the opportunities for accomplishment are almost unlimited. And few other professions can rival this one in the opportunity it affords for service to one's fellowman.

Much of the responsibility for the future success of your efforts in this field rests with the people here today and with others throughout our region who are cognizant of the need. You are people closely associated with the problems that must be overcome. You have helped provide the leadership that has brought us this far. You know the bright promise that the future holds.

It is for you and others who join you in this effort to chart the course that our states will follow in the years to come.

May I suggest that in carrying your program forward you will find, as you undoubtedly have in the past, that a well-informed public is your most valuable ally. There still remains in the public mind today some vestige of the deplorable ignorance that surrounded the subject of mental illness in years past. Much of that ignorance has now been wiped away by social acceptance of the fact that no stigma should be attached to mental illness. Still, there is much mystery enveloping the subject. Terms like schizophrenia, involutional melancholia, senile dementia, and psychoneurosis are often not understood, of course. This lack of understanding fosters suspicion and fear, and because one doesn't comprehend the problem he is reluctant to involve himself in the quest for its solution. We in North Carolina have found that our newspapers, our radio and television stations, and our other avenues of mass communication are most cooperative in efforts of this type. Tell your story to the press, periodicals, radio, and television. Show them what has been done in the past, what is being done at present, and what can and must be done in the future. There is no way for them to know unless you tell them. You will find great support for the work you are doing, and for the great service you are performing.

Our experience has demonstrated clearly that the general public is interested in the work being carried on in our hospitals and training schools. The job before you now is to stimulate this interest to such an extent that it materializes in the form of active support.

I should like to conclude with the observation that there is ample reason for optimism among those of you who are intimately concerned with mental health. The progress to date has been dramatic. The outlook for the future is exciting. New drugs, new treatment procedures, new facilities, and a growing knowledge of your subject hold great promise for the years to come. The opportunity for accomplishment is tremendous. You are limited only by the amount of effort and enthusiasm you are willing to devote to the task. I urge each of you to continue your dedicated leadership in this field. In so doing, you will make it possible for today's dream to become tomorrow's reality. And you will have richly earned the lasting gratitude of the people you serve.

May I again welcome each of you here and wish for you a most productive and successful meeting.

Thank you!

REMARKS ON "ONE OF MY MOST DIFFICULT PROB-
LEMS AS GOVERNOR" AT THE SOUTHERN
GOVERNORS' CONFERENCE

ASHEVILLE
October 12, 1959

[Each governor attending this meeting was assigned five minutes to describe one of the most difficult problems which he had encountered during
his term of office. Governor Hodges appropriately cited the pressure-packed
Henderson cotton mill strike which extended over a period of several months
during the spring and summer of 1959.]

Mr. Chairman and Fellow Governors:
I suspect that most of you have experienced right much apprehension, as I have, in approaching the assignment of discussing
in *five minutes* one of the most difficult problems you have faced
as governor. Perhaps we all might save ourselves some trouble if
we simply acknowledged that *this* five-minute assignment is itself
about the most difficult problem we have attempted to solve as
governors, and let the record stand on that.

Seriously, I have given a great deal of thought to this part of our
program and have looked forward very much to hearing from
each of you.

First, of course, I had to identify in my own mind "one of the
most difficult problems" I have faced since I became governor of
North Carolina nearly five years ago. By what criteria should I
pick and choose out of the multitude of matters which constantly
rain on the desk of the governor, with a sing-song impact, all playing a little tune entitled, "the buck stops here." Here, the problem is to be dealt with—solved if possible, but in any event, dealt
with!

I decided I would identify the problem, for purposes of this discussion, by considering what matter definitely involved a major public issue or issues, was widely recognized as such, and to me as governor presented over some period of time an extreme challenge to find some sort of solution.

Thus measured, certainly one of my most difficult problems was dealing with the well-publicized labor dispute which occurred at Henderson, in Vance County, North Carolina. Most of you recall, I am sure, seeing newspaper accounts last spring which told of the breakdown in law and order, the use of state highway patrolmen, and later, the unhappy story of my having to order out National Guard troops to put down the civil disorder at Henderson.

I cannot begin here even to outline the complete factual developments in the Henderson strike. I can only mention a few of the highlights.

(1) Both the union and the company involved were adamant and stubborn. They showed little progress in their own bargaining sessions.

(2) An avalanche of advice came to me from newspaper editors and others to the effect that I personally should intervene in the negotiations because I, somehow, could bring about a contract settlement.

(3) A great deal of criticism was directed against me from throughout the state for assigning highway patrolmen to assist in maintaining law and order. Many people advised me publicly and privately simply "to close the mills," until the dispute was settled. *At the same time,* I received an equal amount or more of criticism because I had not already ordered out hundreds of Guard troops, put the whole county under martial law, and incidentally put a large number of people in jail to insure maintenance of law and order.

(4) I did personally intervene in the negotiations by having representatives of both sides come to the Executive Mansion, and over a period of several days I personally went over tedious details of the entire contract, trying to persuade, reason, and bluster the parties to agree. I almost, but not quite, got the parties to a settlement.

(5) Finally, in a last minute desperate effort to restore peace and prevent further actions reflecting on the whole state, I went to Henderson and in a dramatic night session the parties did *verbally* agree. The settlement was announced to the world. I left Henderson that night last April hearing cheers from North Carolina citizens who believed their long bitter strike ended. The church bells were ringing. Two days latter, the bitter shock came. Instead of two-thirds of the jobs being open to returning strikers, as many understood to be the case, less than a third were available and the union officials refused to sign the written contract.

(6) Following this abortive settlement, I again had to order state highway patrolmen back to assist local officials in keeping law and order.

(7) As the days and weeks continued to go by, it became more and more evident that the union and the company would not reach any settlement.

(8) Eventually, I had to do what was completely repugnant to me, what I had continually hoped to avoid: call out National Guard troops to put down violence and disorder.

(9) During all this time I was faced with the fact that local law-enforcement officials—particularly at the county level which had the primary responsibilty—were very inadequate to the task and refused to assume their full responsibility for law and order.

(10) During all these months, in which I had to devote hours practically every day to the Henderson problem, our legislature was in regular session.

The Henderson story began, calmly enough, in November, 1958, when Local 578 and 584 of the Textile Workers Union of America went out on strike at the Harriet and Henderson Cotton Mills. The story ended, so far as a crisis in my office was concerned, on August 9, 1959, when I ordered the withdrawal of remaining Guard troops and for the first time in months the situation was left solely to local governing authorities, because the Guard restored order, and the violence was stopped.

From these comments, I believe you can understand why I describe the Henderson strike situation as one of my most difficult problems.

ADDRESS AT THE FALL MEETING OF THE BOARD OF CONSERVATION AND DEVELOPMENT WITH CHARLOTTE CIVIC LEADERS

CHARLOTTE

October 26, 1959

[This meeting occurred a few days before Governor Hodges was scheduled to leave with a group of North Carolina businessmen on an industry-hunting tour of Europe and on the day before the state was to vote on a $34,000,000 bond issue for capital improvements at hospitals, educational institutions, port utilities, and the like. The Governor presided over the first session of the meeting held in the morning at the modernistic Charlotte Public Library and addressed the group at a luncheon at noon in the Terrace Room of the Barringer Hotel. With his usual enthusiasm for North Carolina's industrial future, he outlined plans for the forthcoming European trip and argued for an affirmative vote in the next day's bond election.]

I am very happy indeed to be able to visit here in Charlotte with the other members of the Board of Conservation and Development. We are quite excited about the progress the state is making and particularly excited about what is happening in Charlotte and Mecklenburg County and the territory surrounding this growing section.

You have been very kind to have us here to provide our board members with an opportunity to see what is going on in this area. I feel that the board has shown wisdom in scheduling its quarterly meetings in various parts of the state as a means of showing its interest in all sections of North Carolina as well as creating interest on the part of the various cities and counties in what the board is trying to do in its many divisions. Because of the dramatic progress that is being made in industrial development, some may be inclined to think that the Commerce and Industry Division of the department is the only one that is active and contributing to this state's economic growth. This is most certainly not the case. Each division has its own area of responsibility, and each is making its own unique contribution to the welfare of our people. It is the combination of these contributions that produces results.

Our Ports Authority, for instance, has been quite busy, and these activities have resulted in expanding business. Ports Director D. Leon Williams informs us that the outlook is encouraging for the "two fastest growing ocean terminals in the South Atlantic." Import tonnages increased by approximately 32 per cent for the first six months of 1959 over the same period of 1958. Export tonnage increased by around 6 per cent during the same period. Money being spent at the state docks in Wilmington will add another 1,000 feet of wharf with forty six foot apron and will enable five rather than three 500-foot vessels to be berthed. When completed in November, the Wilmington terminal will be 2,510 feet long, and will have another 120,000 square foot transit shed. Also to be built is a new 100,000-square foot warehouse.

For the Morehead City terminals, construction of a new 80,000-square foot warehouse will begin this month. A new 90,000-square foot warehouse was completed in August. The fifth grain storage tank has also recently been completed at Morehead, and grain exports have steadily increased since its completion by the Carolina Grain Corporation, which leases the facilities from the Ports Authority.

During the last twelve months, nine new regularly scheduled steam ship services have added the two terminals to their ports of call. The latest of these are the American Export Lines and the Black Diamond Lines. Service by American Export Lines opens an entirely new trade route for the two North Carolina ports, as the route includes about 100 major ports in the Mediterranean area. Black Diamond Lines add new services to the Continent. Incidentally, one of the primary reasons for our oncoming trip to Europe is to promote new business for these ports—and we have every reason to believe these efforts will be successful. I will have more to say about this trip in a few minutes.

Another division of the Department of Conservation and Development which contributes tremendously to state-wide progress is the Advertising Division. Inquiries about North Carolina are coming in at the highest rate in our history. This division handled 35,217 inquiries during the current quarter, an increase of 19 per cent over the same period last year.

The Commercial Fisheries Division of the department has worked diligently during the past year to promote North Carolina's important fishing industry. Partly as a result of these efforts, the production of all species of shellfish shows an increase during this quarter, as compared to the same period in 1958. The oyster season opened October 1 and there is every indication that we will have a good year.

The department's Division of Community Planning is currently providing planning service to eighteen municipalities throughout the state. Approxmately twelve additional communities and one county have indicated an interest in receiving planning services from the division when new federal planning grants become available.

This board is tremendously interested in the most advantageous development of North Carolina's great forest resources, and the Division of Forestry is doing an excellent job of protecting this interest. A recent inventory at the state nurseries shows that there will be between 95,000,000 and 100,000,000 seedlings for distribution during the next planting season, and division personnel has already started its promotional campaign to urge the planting of these seedlings.

The Mineral Resources Division has continued its work on mapping the geology of the Albemarle quadrangle and on the study of the limestones of the Piedmont and mountain sections of the state. This division has also given aid on the drilling of two oil wells, one in Bladen County and one in Pender County.

In our state parks, administered by the Parks Division of the department, attendance dropped very slightly between January and September of this year—a fact that can be attributed to unusually bad weather during the peak summer season. Even so, camping activities increased by approximately 21 per cent.

All of these divisions deserve commendation for their activities and the conscientious manner in which their responsibilities are being met. All contributed to the progress that has been made and is continuing to be made in North Carolina.

There were some very exciting figures announced by Mr. Saunders this morning. When told that 1958, a recession year, brought into this state more than a quarter billion dollars worth of business, one was inclined to feel that this was most unusual and could not be duplicated. According to the director's report this morning, the nine months of 1959 are better than the first nine months of 1958. This report showed that the total investment for new plants and expansions thus far in 1959 was $171,689,000 as against $167,110,000 for the same period last year. The number of new plants and expansions increased from 324 last year to 395 this year. Especially important is the fact that the increase in investments was accompanied by a comparable rise in employment and in payrolls. In 1958 the number of employees added for the first nine months was 15,094. This year the figure is 25,723—an amazing increase of 70 per cent. Net payrolls in North Carolina for the first nine months of 1958 amounted to $47,758,000. This year that all-important figure is a dramatic $85,785,000.

This kind of success shows the greatest cooperation on the part of the various communities. counties, the more than 200 industrial development organizations, chambers of commerce, and other groups. Never have I seen such cooperation and never have I been so pleased at the great spirit that prevails among the counties, cities, and the state, and between the state departments and the governor's office. The Revenue Department, the Labor Department, the Department of Agriculture, the colleges, and others are just as interested in securing new industry, new agricultural business, processing plants, etc., as any of the rest of us. It pays off. It can't be bought. It must be earned. I have nothing but praise for all those who have helped and who are continuing to help. And, may I add that, judging from the results, there are very few North Carolinians who do not fall into this category.

Sometimes overlooked is the Business Development Corporation which was formed some several years ago and which many of you in this room from Charlotte helped to form. You recall citizens of the state bought stock to the amount of one million dollars. Banks, insurance companies, building and loan associations, and others joined in to furnish capital. You will be glad to know that, as of last Thursday, as reported to the press, the corporation had approved loans of more than $10,000,000, of which about one-half has already been advanced. Jobs have been provided for more than 12,000 people as a result of these loans. That is equal to a half year's work of a tremendous industry-getting on the part of Conservation and Development.

Exciting news continues to come in about the Research Triangle. Greater interest than ever before in planning on the part of the three counties and cities involved is moving along. A great future is envisioned by this kind of cooperation. The great Chemstrand Corporation has completed its plans for a large laboratory in the Triangle and construction will begin immediately. The Research Institute is moving along rapidly and is getting new contracts and commitments.

As many of you know, a North Carolina trade and industrial mission will leave for Europe next Saturday, October 31. Sixty North Carolina business and industrial leaders are joining me in a two-week trip to Europe. The purpose of our mission is to develop stronger trade with Europe through North Carolina state ports and to seek added industrial devlopment of North Carolina plants by European-based industry. In addition, we hope to work out arrangements with European contracted franchise agreements and attract assembly or re-packaging operations to the state.

Since commerce and industry always thrives best on a two-way street, members of the North Carolina delegation will be seeking to discover avenues of interest and sources of materials in Europe that are desirable in their present business. Of equal importance, contracts will also be reviewed with shippers and others with whom trade and industrial connections are also well established.

This is the approach we will use: luncheons and other events will be held to allow members of the North Carolina group to meet principals in these types of operations—electric and electronic manufacturing and assembly, chemical and industrial research and development, metalworking manufacturing, automobile assembly, servicing and distribution type firms, light industrial possibilities such as close-tolerance die-casting for use in other manufacturing, any type assembly or re-packaging for distribution in the eastern half of the United States, and franchise arrangements to allow manufacturing and sale of patent items by present or new industrial plants in North Carolina. Such plants might be supervised by technical and scientific talent of foreign countries with native industrial employment resources.

The party of sixty men plus our staff of four will leave the Raleigh-Durham Airport next Saturday afternoon on a chartered

Eastern Airliner. At 8:00 that evening we will take a Pan American Jet and arrive in London, England, at 7:30 Sunday morning. From London we travel in three groups. For my own group which will cover all cities the schedule reads like this: A London luncheon on Monday. A visit to Hamburg with Ports Authority people on Tuesday. A luncheon in Amsterdam on Wednesday. Guest of the Farm Bureau Federal Officials in Rotterdam on Wednesday evening. A Stuttgart luncheon on Thursday. A side trip to Frankfurt, Germany, on Friday. The party will move to Munich on Saturday—where among other things we will visit with the staff of Radio Free Europe and make a report. We will observe Sunday as a day of rest. On Monday we have a luncheon for the top industrial leaders in the area. Tuesday we go to Zurich, Switzerland. On Wednesday a luncheon for Swiss business and industrial leaders. On Thursday we will go to Paris to address the American Club of Paris at a noon session and have our dinner with French business and industrial leaders on Thursday evening. Friday will be spent in making calls in the area, and talk with people who have already expressed an interest in opportunities available in North Carolina. Saturday morning, November 14, we take another Jet plane for New York and North Carolina. There will be many special events, group meetings, dinners, etc.—all strictly business.

During the course of our two weeks in Europe, the North Carolina story will be told in all the cities just enumerated for you. The trip has been scheduled to allow ample time for follow-up visits with prospects by members of the group before they move on to the next stop.

I am sure you will be interested to know that our U. S. Departments of State and Commerce, as well as our contacts in England and Europe, are enthusiastic about North Carolina's approach. They tell us it is unique and a shining example of the free enterprise approach so badly needed in other areas of the world. Even the press, both domestic and foreign, have shown unusual interest—particularly since members of the party with the exception of four staff members are paying their own way. As further evidence of their faith in North Carolina, a large number of North Carolina businessmen and firms are generously sponsoring luncheons abroad. Two of our sponsors come from the

Charlotte area—the Southern Bell Telephone Company to be ably represented by your own Mack Wasson, and J. A. Jones Construction Company with Edwin L. Jones, Jr., as its representative.

You will also be interested to know that two devoted North Carolinians who had plans to be in Europe coincidentally with our visit are making arrangements to join the party on the Continent and add their voices to those of the original party.

It is equally significant to us that over one hundred men representing all facets of North Carolina's economy asked to be included on the trip. For obvious reasons it was impossible to accept all these generous offers. Our party is composed of representatives of all sizes of financial institutions, utilities, the building, services and trade group, manufacturing, and distribution.

The trip is being sponsored by members of the Board of Conservation and Development and the North Carolina State Ports Authority.

We are confident that members of the party will find their efforts in behalf of their fellow citizens one of the most rewarding experience of their lives.

The state is moving forward and needs to move forward on all fronts. We cannot move faster than we can afford to move, but we should try to afford more. We must get greater incomes so that we may have more and better education, better welfare grants for those who are in real need, and better opportunities for our people, hospitals, mental institutions, correctional schools, and other phases of life in North Carolina.

Our newest state agency, the Department of Water Resources, if off to a good start. But, in the months and years ahead, it will need the support and assistance of many other agencies and of the people of North Carolina, if this state is to meet its water needs and solve the many complex problems that exist in this field. Immediate measures are being taken, of course, but we should remember that many of our problems have been a long time accumulating and it will take some time to seek out equitable solutions.

I think it is particularly important that you of the Conservation and Development Board be reminded of the support and assistance that the new Department of Water Resources will require. After all, you gave up a part of your own department to the formation of this new agency—one entire division, the responsibilities of another, and some personnel from a third. Twice your board went on record in the early days of water reorganization planning as favoring the idea of centralizing the state's water resource responsibility and management. Thus, you had a big part in setting up the new department. I trust you will be equally as interested and diligent in offering the organization encouragement and assistance in maintaining the momentum it has generated.

As we work together for a better, more prosperous North Carolina, let's remember that we will get a chance tomorrow to vote on a $34,000,000 state-wide bond issue covering various items that are tremendously important to this state's continued progress. There are nine issues, the larger ones being for mental institutions and for education. These are:

1. State Educational Institutions—$18,891,000
2. State Mental Institutions—$12,053,000
3. Community Colleges—$1,500,000
4. Local Hospitals and Health Centers—$500,000
5. State Armory—$100,000
6. State Training Schools—$166,000
7. Rehabilitation Center for the Blind—$140,000
8. Port Facilities at Southport—$500,000
9. Historic Sites—$250,000

May I take a moment here to clear up two points of misunderstanding that appear to have developed in some areas with regard to this state bond issue. Some people seem to have the impression that approval of this bond election will increase ad valorem or property taxes. Let me assure that such is not the case. This is a state-wide election called by the 1959 General Assembly, and provision for repayment of the bonds has been made in our budget. There will also not be any increase in state taxes since the bonds will be retired in the usual manner from General Fund revenues.

I want to ask each board member, when our meeting is concluded tomorrow, to be sure to go home and vote and urge others to do so. I want to ask each person in this room to call two or three people between now and tomorrow and get them to vote. And, of course, be sure that nothing interferes with your own voting. We are moving forward in this state and we must continue to do so. This is just one way that you can help. It should be considered both a responsibility and a privilege.

Thank you.

ADDRESS IN CONNECTION WITH THE NORTH CAROLINA TRADE AND INDUSTRY MISSION TO ENGLAND

LONDON, ENGLAND
November 2, 1959

[Early in November, 1959, Governor Hodges led a party of some sixty-odd North Carolina industrialists, businessmen, and developmental officials on a fourteen-day tour of five European countries seeking business contacts and expounding the commercial opportunities of North Carolina. The party visited eight cities, in each of which the Governor made the same speech entitled "The North Carolina Story of Economic Opportunity." The first of these, here printed, was made to about 180 top figures in British industry and business at a luncheon at Grosvenor House in London. (See pp. 507-510 for accounts of the other seven speeches.) Lord Rootes, head of the British Dollar Export Council, told the Governor that his presentation of North Carolina's case "does not fall on deaf ears."]

It is a great pleasure for me to return to England and to Europe where I have visited often and where I lived and worked for the Economic Cooperation Administration of the United States Government some years ago in West Germany. In this job, as chief of the Industry Section, I worked closely with British counterparts. There are even more personal ties—one of my two daughters married a Britisher from Surrey, and they are now living in East Pakistan where he works with Burma Oil Company. Two of their children—twin girls—are now in boarding school here in England and will spend their Christmas holidays in North Carolina.

It is a special privilege and treat for me to come here as governor of North Carolina, U.S.A., leading a large delegation of our outstanding citizens who have paid their own way here to tell the North Carolina story of growth and opportunity to our European friends.

The purpose of this industrial, trade, and shipping mission is:

(1)   To develop stronger trade with Europe through North Carolina state ports, and to express our appreciation to those companies and organizations with whom our ports now do business, and

(2)   To seek added industrial development for North Carolina through European-financed plants, through European-controlled franchise agreements, and through assembly type or re-packing operations in our state, and

(3)   To create a better understanding and good will between our nations.

This good will mission is co-sponsored by our North Carolina State Board of Conservation and Development, which is responsible for a multitude of state activities such as industrial development, forestry, minerals, parks, fisheries, etc. and the North Carolina State Ports Authority, which is responsible for the operation of our two state-owned and state-financed deep water ports. Under this joint sponsorship, our group of business, industrial, and professional people have come to Europe in behalf of North Carolina, its people and its future.

We in North Carolina are well aware of our many ties with the British Isles through history, ancestry, culture, etc. The first English settlements in America were made in North Carolina in 1585-87, and the first child of English parentage was born there. She was Virginia Dare, who disappeared with the famous "Lost Colony" of Roanoke Island. Our capital city, Raleigh, was named after your famous Sir Walter Raleigh, who, among other things, is credited with introducing tobacco into England.

To prove Sir Walter's insight into the value and importance of tobacco in our state, North Carolina today grows 40 per cent of all tobacco grown in the United States, produces 64 per cent of all flue-cured (or cigarette) tobacco, has 73 per cent of all tobacco redrying plants, and manufactures 58 per cent of all tobacco products manufactured in the United States. We in North Carolina are also well aware of the great leadership which Great Britain has consistently shown for centuries in manufacturing and trade. Our North Carolina state ports, for example, are used by British firms to export into the U.S.A. such articles as chemicals, automobiles, staple fibers, chinaware, steel products, and of course—Scotch whisky. In return, you import from us such articles as tobacco, wheat, corn, soybeans, lumber, and frozen poultry. Like the people in Europe, and in all parts of the world, we in North Carolina seek economic advancement and economic opportunity. North Carolina, one of the leading southern states in the United States, has made great progress during the past half century, and we are grateful for this progress and this growth. However, we do have economic problems and during the past five years my primary aim as governor has been to raise the per capita income of our people through every worthwhile economic endeavor, such as industrial development, agricultural diversification, food processing, improved forestry, etc. We have stressed in our state the importance of public schools, higher education, and research as the basic foundation for all constructive programs —whatever they may be.

My efforts have received tremendous support and assistance from the people of North Carolina, our communities, our counties, and individual citizens who were willing to join in and help organize local or regional development groups designed to stimulate and encourage more industries, better farming, greater and more beautiful communities, etc. Since I became governor, more than 200 of our communities have formed these development organizations.

The most dramatic progress which we have made involves industrial growth. Since 1956, we have shattered our own industrial development records each year, while running far ahead of regional and national expansion averages. In 1958, while the nation—suffering the effects of an economic recession—invested 17.4 per cent *less* in new and expanded industrial facilities, North Carolina registered an *increase* of 32.5 per cent. During this one year, more than $253,000,000 were invested in 423 new plants and expansions, providing 21,757 new jobs and increasing our industrial payroll by $72,633,000.

Industrial development has continued to increase during the first nine months of 1959. Total investment for new plants for this period was $171,689,000 as against $167,110,000 for the same period in 1958. The number of new plants and expansions increased to 395 vs. 324. We were especially pleased at the exciting increase in number of new jobs created—25,723 as compared to

15,094, giving the state a *70 per cent* increase. When one is struggling to bring more income to more people in the state, it is easy to appreciate the significance of this increase.

What about the state of North Carolina? It is a great state with the modest motto of "To Be Rather Than To Seem" which reflects the basic simplicity of a people who are working together with great success in developing and expanding our economy. During my thirty-one years in textile manufacturing and selling in a nationally known concern, I had many good products to promote. Yet, nothing I sold touches North Carolina as a "product," containing so many desirable factors such as good people, diversified geography, excellent location, favorable climate, etc.

History—First, there appeared in our state the Indians, followed by early sixteenth century Spaniards under DeSoto, and then the Florentine Navigator Verrazzano explored the coast for France in about 1524. In 1585, Sir Walter Raleigh's colonists landed on Roanoke Island to plant the first English colony in America, and here the first child of English parentage was born in America. A special governmental commission is now planning observance of the 400th aniversary of the settlement of Roanoke Island in North Carolina—twenty years before the settlement of Jamestown, Virginia and more than thirty years prior to the founding of the Plymouth, Massachusetts, colony.

Location—As one of thirteen original colonies, North Carolina is located on the South Atlantic shore of the United States and has an area of 52,712 square miles—slightly larger than England. We are well located in the South, a great region which contains 32 per cent of the nation's land area, 33 per cent of the population, 36 per cent of the transportation, 33 per cent of foreign trade, 30 per cent of utility operations, 20 per cent of the banks, 26 per cent of the life insurance, 23 per cent of payrolls, 33 per cent of the cash farm incomes, 24 per cent of the nation s food, 39 per cent of the chemicals, 35 per cent of the oil-coal products, 52 per cent of textiles, 88 per cent of tobacco, 31 per cent of lumber, 21 per cent of apparel, 23 per cent of pulp-paper, 22 per cent of stone-clay-glass, and 28 per cent of furniture. Half of the 180,000,000 population of the United States lives within a 500-mile radius of North Carolina.

Population—North Carolina has approximately 4,500,000 people, divided roughly into one-third urban, one-third rural on farm, and one-third living in rural areas but non-farm. There is abundance of good labor—honest, hard-working people with a deep rooted spirit of independence, and with an agricultural background unafraid of a real day's work. Their productivity is unexcelled. We have 160,000 good people available for industrial work.

Transportation—Seventy thousand miles of public highways, with 36,000 being hard-surfaced. This is the largest state maintained road system in the United States. Excellent progress is being made on the 775 miles of the new interstate system for our state which will represent an investment of more than $350,000,000. We have twenty-six railroads, 635 motor carriers (including more long-line interstate carriers than any other state), two modern deep-water ports, and six airlines.

Climate—Since our geography ranges from sea level to 6,684 feet, we offer not only seasonal variety but variety within seasons. The annual mean temperautre is 59 degrees, ranging from an average of 42 degrees in winter to a high of 75 degrees mean in summer. With its long growing seasons and rich farm land, North Carolina has been a leading agricultural state since early colonial days. The new DuPont silicon plant was located in the western North Carolina mountain area after a nation-wide search because engineers found there the purest possible air. DuPont purchased a 10,000 acre plot for this new facility.

Water—There are many great rivers, huge reservoirs, and countless lakes and ponds. Under the surface there is a tremendous, practically untapped volume of water. Rainfall averages around forty-eight inches annually, and water experts tell us that there is sufficient water to meet all needs for the foreseeable future.

Taxes—Sound economic growth would be virtually impossible without sound and effective government at all levels. North Carolina has had a very stable and progressive state government for the past half century. The State Revenue Act was enacted in 1939, and no corporate tax increases have been required since that date. There have been several reductions, including major revision of the allocation formula for multi-state industries by the 1957 General Assembly which reduced such corporate taxes. We seek only new industries and businesses which are willing to pay their fair share of the tax burden. We believe that two words—*equitable* and *fair*—must be the guide for modern tax administration.

Education—North Carolina is an education-minded state. We believe that a good education is the birthright of every citizen. Our state-wide school system has over 1,000,000 school children of which 250,000 are Negro. We have over 30,000 teachers, including 9,000 Negro teachers whose average earnings exceed those of the white teachers. We have sixty-three senior and junior institutions of higher learning.

Most of you have heard a great deal, of course, about school integration problems in the South. This is a difficult problem in North Carolina, but we have worked diligently to bring about a reasonable solution. To give you some idea of the complexity involved, in North Carolina our Negro population varies from .03 per cent in one of our 100 counties up to 67 per cent in another one of our counties. So, obviously, the race problem varies among our 100 counties just as it varies among the fifty states of our nation. As a result, our approach in North Carolina to the school integration problem has been one of placing the basic responsibility for the operation of our public schools upon local school boards who are closest to the schools, the people, and the districts served. So far, our North Carolina approach of moderation has operated satisfactorily; several of our cities have voluntarily accepted Negro applicants to white schools although the vast majority of the Negro children are voluntarily attending their own public schools. Racial problems, prejudices, and discrimination based on race, creed, politics, etc., are not confined to the southern region of the United States nor indeed to the United States. All of these problems are world-wide and need the attention and understanding of people everywhere.

Of special interest to industrial leaders is our new sytem of regional schools known as "Industrial Education Centers." Under a program sponsored by the State Board of Education, the state will furnish equipment and pay the cost of instruction to selected high school youngsters and adults in training for skilled trade and technician areas. Eighteen of these regional centers have already been approved, and more than $2,000,000 in new buildings have been let to contract. It is estimated that these schools will provide new educational opportunities for approximately 8,000 students.

North Carolina's principal industries are textiles, tobacco processing, furniture, food processing, metal working, lumber and wood products, and chemicals. Since 1939, our industrial plants have doubled in number while the value of the goods they produce has climbed from $1,421,000,000 to $6,737,000,000. We are the nation's largest manufacturer of textile, tobacco, and household furniture products. Our textile industry, alone, employs half of the 481,000 industrial workers in the state, and the value of their annual production is placed at $830,000,000.

North Carolina is widely known for its sound and progressive government which has served our citizens well during the past half century. Through strong executive leadership and outstanding patriotic, devoted service of the members of our General Assembly during the years, our state government has kept step with the times and the needs of our people. We have been described as a conservative-progressive state operating squarely in the middle of the fiscal road. A balanced budget is, of course, the cornerstone of our financial policy. We are conservative in that we are unwilling to make spending commitments until we feel the expenditure is really justified, and until we know just where the money is to come from. We are progressive in that we are continually planning for the future, gearing our policies to the changing spirit of the times and the needs of our people.

Since the turn of the century, we have not hesitated to invest in schools, and roads, and port terminals, and health centers, and hospitals, and in institutions of higher learning. We have not forgotten the unfortunate and handicapped in all the rush of material progress. There has been vast improvement in our institutions for mental care, for example. In short, we sincerely believe that we have human, as well as material assets, which are entirely worthy of conservation and development.

There is a tremendous interest in our state in the cultural side of life. As just one example, we are very proud of our North Carolina Museum of Art, one of the South's newest and finest museums, located near our State Capitol in Raleigh. We were the first state in America to set aside public funds to purchase an art collection for its people. This collection now contains many of the great English, French, American, Flemish, Dutch, Italian, Spanish, German, and modern masterpieces, which actually trace the whole history of painting in our western civilization.

These are only some of the factors to be considered by any industrial prospect looking toward North Carolina. There are many others, of course. We all recognize that the *attitude* of the people in a community toward industry is most important. This attitude is reflected in how they have treated the industry they have, what facilities have been provided for housing, shopping facilities, health, education, recreation, etc., what they say in their local newspapers and how local government treats industrial taxpayers. While these are all factors over which state government has little, if any, control, we in North Carolina are tremendously aware of the importance of community attitude and have found the same awareness in hundreds of our fine communities across the state.

The "secret weapon" we have in North Carolina is our people. Their friendly attitude and their productivity have been commented on most favorably. For example, a spokesman for the General Electric Company, which has four large plants in North Carolina, explained why his company came to North Carolina, by citing "Opportunities for growth, the favorable business climate, a plentiful and cooperative labor supply, availability of utilities and transportation, combined with an ideal climate and living and recreational facilities."

J. A. Babcock, manager of the Westinghouse meter plant at Raleigh, said, in a published article last year, that "We have been especially pleased with the type of people who have sought employment at Westinghouse . . . The spirit of cooperation in the community and among our employees has convinced us that Raleigh and North Carolina were the right choice for Westinghouse."

From the manager of the huge DuPont facility in Kinston comes the statement: "One of the strongest factors leading to the DuPont decision to locate . . . in Kinston was the people—the people of Kinston and North Carolina."

We like industries that are research minded. Our state is research minded. As evidence of this fact, we have in North Carolina a great new project known as the Research Triangle. This

Governor Hodges with United States Senator Samuel J. Ervin, Jr., at the Jefferson-Jackson Day Dinner in Raleigh, February 6, 1960.

Photo by Jules Schick

Governor Hodges receiving a good citizenship award from the Philadelphia-Continental Chapter, Sons of the American Revolution, February 20, 1960. Charles R. Hansell (*left*), president of the chapter is making the presentation.

triangle embraces the territory in which are located the University of North Carolina in Chapel Hill, Duke University in Durham, and North Carolina State College in Raleigh. From a point in the center of this triangle it is no more than fifteen miles to the campus of any one of these three excellent institutions· The University at Chapel Hill and Duke University are two of the thirty-seven institutions which comprise the top ranking Association of American Universities, and North Carolina State College is recognized as one of the nation's major technical institutions, having, among other things, its own privately financed atomic reactor. In these three institutions there are approximately 2,000 faculty members and some 18,000 students. The combined library resources comprise 2,500,000 volumes. All scientific periodicals are available and there is an excellent inter-library loan system already at work among these three libraries so that any needed reference work from any one of the libraries can be placed at the researchers' disposal almost immediately.

Plans are being completed for a modern research institute which will do contract research in many basic fields. The giant Chemstrand Corporation, a national chemical producer, has announced the plans for locating its regional research laboratories in the Research Triangle. On October 28, 1959, it was my pleasure to announce that the Camille and Henry Dreyfus Foundation in New York City has made available a grant of $2,500,000 for the establishment of an international center of polymer chemistry at our new Research Triangle Institute. The new research center will be operated as a memorial laboratory in memory of Dr. Camille Dreyfus, a Swiss-born scientist who pioneered in the field of man-made fibers and who was once head of the great Celanese Corporation.

We have many hopes and aspirations in North Carolina. I firmly believe that we have the resources, the people, the energies, the courage, and the vision to make North Carolina one of the nation's leading states—a state well balanced between industry and agriculture, offering the kind of uncrowded living which we all seek in this age of congestion. We have only about one-tenth of the population that you have in Great Britain, and our area is almost equal in square miles.

We welcome your interest in North Carolina and hope that in

the near future you may have an opportunity to visit our beautiful state. We hope you will at this meeting and during our stay here get to know some of our group who represent industry, banking, and business of all kinds. We share a common interest in economic progress and peaceful cooperation and understanding among our great nations. Let us all work together as citizens of the free world, to gain a better, clearer understanding of each other and of our common interests and common goals. For all our group, I thank you most sincerely for the great honor and privilege you are giving us in being with you!

ADDRESS AT A RALEIGH CHAMBER OF COMMERCE BANKERS MEETING

RALEIGH
December 15, 1959

[Governor Hodges, "as a temporary citizen of Raleigh," welcomed three new banks that had recently begun operations in that city: the American Commercial Bank, Branch Banking and Trust Company, and the Scottish Bank. In addition, he urged the bankers to back North Carolina programs, such as the Business Development Corporation, the industrial education centers, and other activities of a similar nature.]

I am honored to have this opportunity to meet with a distinguished group of North Carolinians who, by virtue of their business interests and their positions of leadership and trust in the community, share my dedication to the growth and development of this great state. The Raleigh Chamber of Commerce is to be commended on its wisdom and foresightedness in arranging a meeting of this type, for it is an indication of the chamber's awareness of the important role that the banker plays in community affairs.

Certainly, no single group in the community has a greater stake in local, regional, or state-wide economic progress than the banker. And no group has greater reason, or is in a better position, to make a material contribution to that progress. It is entirely proper that both the banker and the community or area he serves acknowledge this fact, for it forms a basis for understanding and cooperation that can be a powerful and extremely effective force for economic development.

You are fortunate here in Raleigh—as are our citizens throughout North Carolina—to have men in the banking profession who recognize and accept local and regional responsibility, men who acknowledge their strategic position in the campaign being waged to bring greater abundance and a higher standard of living to all our people. It is never easy to occupy such a responsible position, but it can be tremendously gratifying. This is especially true when you consider that the greater your responsibility, the greater your opportunity for service.

The citizens of the Raleigh area have been doubly blessed in this respect. They are blessed not only by the quality of the banking services available to them, but by the quantity as well. In recent weeks Raleigh has been referred to as "the banking center of the South." This is, of course, due in part of the recent establishment in this community of three of North Carolina's larger banks. The impact of the added services of banks such as American Commercial of Charlotte, Branch Banking and Trust of Wilson, and the Scottish Bank of Lumberton is tremendous in itself—especially when you consider that Wachovia, First Citizens, and Security National were already well established in the business and community life of Raleigh. When we add the fact that the strong Mechanics and Farmers Bank of Durham serves the banking needs of many of this community's Negro citizens, then we find that there may be ample justification for Raleigh's growing reputation as a banking center.

In terms of combined resources, the banks represented in Raleigh have a massive total of nearly one and one-half billion dollars—$1,458,000,000 to be exact. Taking this total combined resources figure at face value, Raleigh can, with some rationalization, claim that its bank resources are the largest of any single community between Baltimore and Atlanta—with Atlanta only $35,500,000 (or roughly 2.5 per cent) ahead.

This comparison may not be entirely fair to some communities in Georgia and Virginia, where branch banking does not exist and great banking systems such as ours have not developed. Still, both Virginia and Georgia do have what amounts to holding companies.

So, perhaps our claims are not exaggerated. In any event, the important thing is that tremendous banking resources are available in this area and can be used to meet the opportunities and challenges that the future most certainly holds.

And, while it is both exciting and comforting to know that these great resources are available to us and will undoubtedly contribute to our progress, we should not lose sight of the fact that size in itself does not necessarily insure efficiency or service to the community. Actually, there is some substance to the contention that the bigger the bank—or any other business, for that matter—the greater the risk it runs of losing its personal relationship with the community and the people it has an obligation to serve. This could be particularly true with large system banks. Unless unusual care is exerted, it would be an easy matter for a bank with its main office in one city to lose sight of some of its community responsibilities to a city 150 miles away.

Fortunately, the six major banks represented in Raleigh give every evidence of understanding this problem. They have, from all indications, taken great care to urge their officers and employees to be a part of the spirit and life of the various communities they serve. This, I know to be true to the banks that have long been established here, and I am certain it is true with regard to the three newest banks.

So, as a temporary resident of the city of Raleigh, I am personally very delighted to see such a strong, impressive banking picture here. Raleigh, very definitely, is on the move, and it is—or certainly should be—gratifying to local citizens to know that their banks are ready, willing, and able to cooperate in every possible way to carry the community forward along the road to prosperity in the months and years ahead. This is a good thing, for there is much to be done.

We face many challenges, not only in this area, but throughout North Carolina—challenges that would have staggered the imagination of our leadership just a few years ago. The atomic age, the jet age, the age of space exploration did not just happen. We have reached our present stage of scientific development because men with fertile minds were willing to think in terms of dramatic and far-reaching potentialities. It is important, therefore, that those of us who are interested in economic, business, and industrial progress ask ourselves from time to time if we are keeping pace with developments in other fields. We use the word "vision" so frequently that it sometime sounds hackneyed, but I think it is important that we ask ourselves, do we really have it? Have we really used it? And the world "unselfish"; do we really try to put it into practice? And, are we foresighted enough, are we adequately equipped intellectually, emotionally, and psychologically to meet the complex challenges that the future poses? These are questions we must answer now, for the answers will indicate the degree to which we are prepared to take advantage of the limitless opportunities that the years ahead will unfold. Tomorrow will be too late. Tomorrow we will have lost the initiative. And in the highly competitive field of economic progress, once the initiative is lost, the incentive and enthusiasm we now possess will deteriorate—and we will have missed the greatest chance a people ever had to attain a superior economic status.

Across our state bankers have participated actively and, in many instances, taken the lead in the development of economic opportunities. The banks of this state have every right to feel proud of the fine contribution they have made. And I am certain that your future contribution will be even more significant. Most certainly, the opportunity will be there. I do not, of course, mean to imply that yours is, or should ever become, a benevolent position. You have as much to gain as anyone from the economic development of this state, and when you contribute to this development, you are making an investment that will repay you many times over. It is not necessary for me to tell this audience that the prosperity of your bank is a pretty accurate reflection of the prosperity of the community and the people you serve. You can find no better way to serve the best interests of your bank than to endeavor at all times to serve the best interests of your community and your state. You should become a part of the community or regional or state team, for experience has shown us that teamwork is the key to success is this complex business of economic progress. Teamwork is important because we are openly competing with communities in other states who also know and fully exploit the value of close cooperation. And banks are, not infrequently, leading the team in these other areas.

A good example is the Meadow Brook National Bank of Nassau

County on Long Island. In a recent article, appearing in the
American Banker, the chairman of the board of that bank stated
that,

> Toward the end of meeting our community responsibility, the Meadow
> Brook National Bank has developed a team approach for attracting
> and locating new industry on Long Island. In addition to providing
> local employment, the other motivating factors behind this program are:
> The desire to do our part in building the over-all economy of the area;
> new industries in a community means business for everyone. Plants must
> be built, supplies must be bought, maintenance services such as fuel oil,
> electricians, and plumbers must be contracted for.
>
> The first step in this team approach to attracting and locating industry
> is the development of prospects. All available means of advertising, such
> as ads in industrial journals, business newspapers, industrial directories,
> radio and displays in trade shows are used to develop prospects. One of
> our best sources of prospects are our thirty-eight offices throughout
> Nassau County. Banks are recognized as the centers of business informa-
> tion in each community and very frequently industrial prospects will
> visit the bank to seek out accurate information as to competent realtors,
> builders, and suppliers. Our contact officers are trained to recognize and
> evaluate good prospects. Once a prospect has been qualified, a conference
> is arranged.
>
> This meeting will generally consist of the prospect and members of
> his staff and bank personnel representing the mortgage department,
> commercial loan department, personnel department, public relations
> department, and business development department. It is the purpose
> of these conferences to discuss the needs and desires of the prospect.
>
> We explore such areas as what the move will do to the working capital
> structure of the firm; what will be his short-term financial requirements
> now and in the future; does he need a building loan and permanent
> mortgage or term monies to purchase new equipment.
>
> In addition to the multitude of financial questions asked and discussed,
> the other aspects of location, such as community attitudes, wage rates,
> availability of labor, trucking rates, sewage disposal, electric and gas
> availability are covered. Frequently, many of these questions can be
> answered to the prospect's satisfaction; those that cannot are investigated
> and reported to the prospect.
>
> Upon the conclusion of a satisfactory conference, our team approach to
> industrial development then carries the prospect and members of the
> bank staff into the field to look at sites or existing buildings. . . .
>
> Once the prospect has selected the site we continue to work closely
> with him. One major area is the hiring of personnel. A list of the re-
> quired office skills is turned over to our personnel department, who
> help in finding secretaries and clerks.
>
> Frequently office space, telephones, and secretarial help is made avail-
> able if the prospect wants to interview while the plant is being con-
> structed.

I have hit only the high spots in the report on this one bank's cooperative approach to industrial development and community responsibility, but I think it will serve to illustrate what a bank can do if it is sufficiently dedicated, and, at the same time, give you some indication of the kind of competiton we face in other parts of the U. S. A. Make no mistake about the fact that we are playing in the big league, and we are going to have to play big league ball if we expect to stay in the running.

We in North Carolina have the tools that will enable us to maintain our present momentum of progress if they are properly used. We have the people, the resources, the know-how, and the determination. All of these things have been put to good use in recent years and the results have been gratifying. The truth of this is evident in your own profession. It is evident in the fact that as of October 6, 1959, the date of the last report issued by our commissioner of banks, the total resources of North Carolina banks amounted to $3,027,291,868—an increase of $198,621,500,432 over the September 24 figure for the previous year. It is evident, I think, in the trend toward fewer small, limited-service banks and more large banks with the personnel and resources needed to meet the complex financial requirements of a rapidly expanding economy.

Beginning around the first of 1955 through December of this year the trend to bank mergers has been much greater than ever before. During this period there were twenty-five mergers, while only one new bank was established. Branches established amounted to 101. The net decrease in the number of banks since December 31, 1954 is approximately 13.4 per cent. The net increase in branches was 28.4 per cent. At present there are 154 state-chartered banks in North Carolina, operating 356 branches. Of this number, four are members of the Federal Reserve System, one is an uninsured institution, and the remaining 149 are insured by the Federal Deposit Insurance Corporation.

This vast network of financial institutions, very naturally, places a sizeable responsibility on the state government, which is charged with the task of insuring the people of the state that their banks are reputable and safe. It is a responsibility that cannot be taken lightly, and it is to the credit of our established banks that they are most cooperative in facilitating the execution of this vital function.

Our state examination policy is to make joint examinations with examiners from the Federal Reserve Bank of Richmond where the state member banks are concerned, to make joint examinations with the FDIC examiners where state-insured non-member banks are concerned, and to examine independently the one bank that is neither insured nor a member of the Federal Reserve System. One examination is made of each of these banks at least once a year, as required by law, and in instances where closer supervision is necessary, re-examinations are made. During the course of an examination, there is an emphasis given the need to increase capital and valuation reserves, to hire and train competent replacement personnel on every level, and we vigorously emphasize the need for an effective internal audit program and the use of certified public accountants.

I want you to know that your state government is well aware of its responsibility to provide and maintain an efficient and effective state bank examination program. The governor's office, the State Personnel Department and the Banking Commission have worked closely in the past, and are continuing to cooperate in an effort to make absolutely certain that our bank examiners are the best available for this vital job. Banks in the last few years have, for the most part, started paying better salaries to their employees. The state has endeavored to keep pace and, at the same time, prevent "raids" on its examining personnel, by making salary adjustments among its examiners whenever feasible. I am sure that you will agree with me that it is in the best interest of the banks of this state and the people they serve that we have experienced, capable people in these important positions.

With reference to the state's responsibility in the financial picture, you will also be interested in knowing that since 1949, the state has invested that part of the treasurer's cash balance that is not immediately needed to pay obligations in certificates of deposit of North Carolina banks, and/or U. S. Treasury obligations. By law, as you know, the rate charged banks must be not less than the going rate on short-term U. S. Treasury obligations. Due to the limitations on the rate that banks may pay, the state has not been permitted to invest in certificates of deposit at all times. The total amount of revenue derived from interest on investments from 1949 through June 30 of this year amounts to $29,694,170.82.

Certainly, the state's role in banking is an essential one, for it is absolutely necessary that we have strong, reliable, resourceful banks if we are going to develop our great potential in the years to come.

One impressive indication that this potential is being developed effectively even now can be seen in the fact that a higher percentage of new business incorporations were registered in North Carolina during the first ten months of this year than in any of the other states in the South Atlantic region. North Carolina registered a 65.3 per cent increase over the same ten-month period for 1958. Our nearest rival was Georgia, with a 50.9 per cent increase, followed by South Carolina, with an increase of 45.2 per cent. Trailing far behind North Carolina were Maryland, Delaware, Virginia, West Virginia, and Florida.

In January of this year there were 292 corporate filings in North Carolina, as compared with 173 in January of 1958—an increase of 68.7 per cent. In February there were 212 filings as compared with 106 in 1958—an increase of 100 per cent. In March there were 301 filings, a 118.8 per cent increase over the 138 recorded in 1958. In April the increase was 163.7 per cent—335 filings as compared to 127 for the same month in the previous year. And increases have been registered in each of the remaining months through the time of the last report in October. A total of 2,553 filings have been recorded in 1959, as compared with 1,544 for the same period in 1958.

One of the factors contributing to this business growth has undoubtedly been the successful operation of the Business Development Corporation of North Carolina, an agency established in 1956 for the specific purpose of promoting business activity throughout the state. May I thank you bankers throughout the state for your help in making this a great success. This corporation began active operations on April 1, 1956, and since that time has approved a total of ninety-six loans totaling approximately $10,600,000, including participation by banks in several of the individual loans. In its first nine months of operation the Corporation made twenty-five loans totaling $1,800,000. In 1957, a total of twenty-two loans was made in the amount of $1,700,000. In 1958, loans amounting to $2,300,000 were allotted to nineteen applicants. And thus far in 1959, thirty loans have been made, totaling $4,800,000.

Of these loans, forty-six amounting to $3,800,000 have been fully disbursed and at least an additional eighteen loans, totaling about $4,000,000 are expected to be disbursed from present commitments over the next several months as construction and expansion of plant facilities are completed.

It will be of interest to you to know that, at the present time, 146 financial institutions in North Carolina are members of the Business Development Corporation, making available to the Corporaton approximately $5,000,000. These include ninety-four banks, pledging $2,700,000; twelve life insurance companies, pledging $1,100,000; and forty building and loan associations, pledging $1,200,000.

There are 104 banks in the state that are not members of the corporation. The majority of these are relatively small institutions, but if all of them would join it would make available an additional $700,000, which would be very useful to the corporation in its program of promoting business expansion. Also, there are fourteen life insurance companies that do not hold membership. Most of these are new or small companies, but if they would all participate in this program, they could contribute an additional $200,000. Especially significant is the fact that there are 108 state-chartered building and loan associations in North Carolina that are not affiliated with the corporation. It is estimated that around $1,600,000 could be made available by these institutions who stand to benefit so much from the work of the corporation.

May I point out that within recent months thirty-one of the banks and insurance companies that became members of the Business Development Corporation in 1956 on the basis of their capital and surplus as of December 31, 1955, have re-applied for membership so as to give the corporation benefit of larger loans based upon increases in their capital and surplus accounts as of December 31, 1958. I would express the hope that the other banks and insurance companies will do likewise!

There are many reasons why every financial institution in North Carolina should participate in this program. I will not list these advantages since, I am sure, most of them are obvious. I would, however, like to cite one fact that stands out above all others in connection with this undertaking. Loans made by the Business Development Corporation since its establishment in 1956 have provided direct employment for more than 13,000 North Carolinians, and indirect benefits have affected more than 78,000 citizens in our state. Certainly, this is sufficient cause to warrant 100 per cent membership in this corporation by our financial institutions. It should not even be necessary for me to point out that the institutions themselves derive considerable benefits from this increased business activity and increased personal income.

There is one other tremendously important activity now transpiring in this state that I would like to solicit your interest in—one that holds the promise of contributing enormously to our industrial development and to the security and general well-being of our people. I refer to the establishment of industrial education centers at strategic locations throughout North Carolina. The state now has seven such centers in operation, with eleven more in the planning stage—a noteworthy accomplishment when you consider that the program was initiated only eighteen months ago.

Most of you, I feel certain, are familiar with the great need for such a program in this state. I would, however, like to call your attention to statements made a few weeks ago in Charlotte by Dr. Joseph T. Nerden, chief of the Bureau of Technical Institutes for the state of Connecticut—the state which, incidentally, has the highest per capita income in the nation.

Dr. Nerden told his Charlotte audience that, "The success of industry in your area will ultimately depend on the skilled labor supply you have to offer, and you won't have it without adequate technical schools.

"If industry can train people it doesn't need you. But industry doesn't have time to train tool-makers and electronic technicians, for example. That takes four or five years, and that's where a state can help industry: in pre-education.

"For every engineer produced today, there are two technicians needed. And engineers are working as technicians simply because there are not sufficient technicians available."

Dr. Nerden said "Industry has made our schools and schools can make industry." He points out that in Connecticut twice as much—$700 to $350—is spent per student in vocational school as compared to public school. "But trade schools," he said, "should not be dumping grounds for slow students. Good average students—we take only one of four applicants in Connecticut—are needed."

The state is doing everything within its power to push this program forward, for we believe very definitely that this training activity is of primary importance if we are to continue to grow industrially and if our people are to realize their maximum potential. But, here again, active support of these schools must come from the people at the local level, and the communities are responding. I would like to urge you to learn more about this vital program and lend your support whenever possible.

May I conclude by again thanking you for the privilege of meeting with you and discussing some of the problems and opportunities that we face as citizens of a dynamic and growing state. I have absolute faith in the direction in whch we are moving, and I am confident that our efforts will bring an increasingly more abundant life to our people. The task before us is twofold. We must consolidate the gains that have been achieved, and we must maintain the momentum that has brought us this far. I can assure you that your state government will continue to do everything it possibly can to achieve these aims.

It is my firm conviction that the people of North Carolina can overcome any problem or meet any challenge if we continue to work together and emphasize the positive approach to our problems rather than the negative. Our opportunities are unlimited, our resources abundant, our people energetic and determined. With these tools at our command we cannot fail in our dream of building a more prosperous North Carolina.

Thank you!

ADDRESS AT A MEETING OF THE EASTERN
NORTH CAROLINA TRAFFIC CLUB

RALEIGH
January 14, 1960

[The Eastern North Carolina Traffic Club is an organization of representatives of steamship lines, railroads, and trucking companies operating in the eastern part of the state. More than 300 delegates, including a number of key officials in the transportation industry, were present to hear the Governor address this meeting, which was said to have been the largest in the twenty-three year history of the club.]

It is always a wonderful experience to meet with a group of North Carolinians who have come together voluntarily—and I believe, in this case, eagerly—to exchange idea and to further develop the atmosphere of cooperation that has meant so much to the state in the past, and will, undoubtedly, mean even more in the months and years ahead. It is for this reason that I consider it a very distinct privilege to meet with you, and I would like to say that I feel each of you should be commended on the interest you are showing in the future of North Carolina through your membership in this organization and through your presence here this evening.

I know that the great majority of you represent business interests that stand to benefit directly from any contribution this organization makes toward the economic progress of North Carolina. But, I think it is equally evident that the progress that benefits your business is the progress that, in almost every instance, benefits the whole of North Carolina. Individually and collectively in the transportation field you occupy positions of importance and great responsibility in the economic life of this dynamic state. We are all working for the same thing—a better, more prosperous North Carolina—and we have all had sufficient experience in transportation and in other fields of endeavor to realize that our goal for North Carolina can best be achieved through intelligent, foresighted cooperation.

I would like to talk tonight especially about our state ports. This interest in ports is not a new interest in North Carolina. Actually, it is one of our oldest. The development of this state's ports has been a matter of major concern throughout our history. Even in colonial times there were loud and persistent complaints about the commercial dependence of eastern North Carolina upon Virginia ports. Later, when port facilities were developed in South Carolina, it changed our situation only in that we were commercially dependent upon two states instead of one. One hundred and forty years ago, Archibald D. Murphey, one of the most vocal advocates of internal improvements in the history of this state, wrote that,

Heretofore the production of the northern parts of the state have been sent to the markets of Virginia; and the trade of the Broad River, the Catawba and Pee Dee, have gone to South Carolina. Thus it has happened that we have shipped from our own ports not more than one-third of our agricultural products; and even a considerable portion of our staves, lumber, and naval stores, have been sent to other ports. This unfortunate division of our trade produces many bad effects.

It makes us appear a poor state in the Union.

It leaves us without markets at home: and thus we lose the profits upon our commerce. The annual loss of commercial profits sustained by North Carolina by not having markets of her own, is estimated at more than half a million dollars.

Our trade being scattered and most of it sent to the neighboring states, we have no large commercial city: and our whole population is devoid of that animating pride, which a large city and an extensive concentrated commerce contribute to inspire.

Four decades later, on the eve of the Civil War, the situation had changed little. One writer, Hinton Rowan Helper, became so upset by North Carolina's lack of progress in port development that he published a detailed study in which he drew an analogy between the ports of Boston, Massachusetts, and Beaufort, North Carolina. The analogy was illogical and showed clearly that abolitionist Helper considered slavery the basic cause for our inability to develop our ports, but it does serve to illustrate the continuing interest in port development·

Helper wrote that,

Massachusetts and North Carolina each have a harbor, Boston and Beaufort, which harbors, with the states that back them, are, by nature, possessed of about equal capacities and advantages for commercial and manufacturing enterprise. Boston has grown to be the second commercial city in the Union; her ships, freighted with the useful and unique inventions and manufacturers of her ingenious artisans and mechanics, glide triumphfully through the winds and over the waves of every ocean.

How is it with Beaufort, in North Carolina, whose harbor is said to be the safest and most commodious anywhere to be found on the Atlantic Coast south of the harbor of New York, and but little inferior to that? Has anybody ever heard of her? Upon what distant or benighted shore have our merchants and mariners ever hoisted our national ensign, or spread the arts of civilization and peaceful industry? . . .

Even as late as 1924, efforts were still being made—unsuccessfully, I might add—to interest the people of this state in the development of our ports and inland waterways. Governor Cameron Morrison, in his message to the General Assembly on August 7, 1924, made an eloquent plea for state support in promoting the expansion of facilities in our port cities. The General Assembly, apparently reluctant to take the responsibility for upsetting the state's tradtional "do nothing" policy toward port development, submitted the governor's proposal to a vote of the people. In the referendum, the "Ports Bill" was defeated, but the margin of defeat was a narrow one, indicating that our people had, at least, begun to think seriously about this important phase of economic progress.

Part of our problem in recent years has been an unhappy relationship between our two port cities which complicated the work of the previous Ports Authorities. Let us hope this situation is completely cleared up.

Fortunately, in very recent years, cooperation or lack of bitterness has prevailed with the result that concrete progress has been made toward the development of the potential of our deep water ports. The state is proud of the role that it has played in this development, but members of this organization and many other individuals throughout the state have helped in developing cooperation and are due credit for much of the progress that has been made.

This spirit of cooperation, which is just as important in the development of our ports as in any other phase of our development program, has never been more apparent or more effective than during the recent North Carolina Trade and Industry Mission to Europe. This was a superb example of what a state can do in its efforts to utilize the services of its citizens telling the story of economic opportunity to business and industrial leaders elsewhere. Ths trip was a natural culmination of earlier good-will missions made to New York, Chicago, and Philadelphia in the interest of industrial development and agricultural promotion.

It was my pleasure to lead a party of sixty-eight business and industrial leaders on the two weeks' trip to Western Europe— covering 11,000 miles, ten cities, and six countries. The impact of this trip in Europe was amazing and we were overwhelmed by the warm and friendly reception which our mission received. And, the interest shown, not only here in North Carolina but throughout the nation, was truly remarkable. Let me add that there is every indication that the benefits derived from the trip will be even more significant than we had expected. While the purpose of the trip was to obtain long-range benefits for our two ports and for industrial development, we are confident that there will be many immediate benefits also.

The results of this trip could have a most favorable effect on the economic progress of North Carolina—with the initial impact being felt in the ports areas and gradually spreading out across the state. This should be of particular interest to this audience, since it is fairly evident that one of the primary beneficiaries of this increased business activity will be our transportation industry. We will get foreign as well as domestic traffic for our ports and we should be prepared to handle it.

Most of you, I am sure, are familiar with those aspects of ports developments that directly affect the business interest you represent. I think we can all benefit, however, from the acquisition of a more comprehensive understanding of the whole ports operation. Such an understanding will better enable you to derive maximum benefit from the ports for the businesses you represent while, at the same time, equip you to work more effectively in promoting the general improvement of our ports facilities.

A study of the progress made by our state ports at Wilmington and Morehead City since their dedication in 1952, shows that tonnage figures have increased from 527,538 in 1952 to 731,936 in 1949—an increase of 71.2 per cent.

Actually, the progress has been more significant than these figures indicate. For instance, the increase in total tonnage handled at the Morehead City port during the past seven years is a little less than 11 per cent. This is a deceptive figure and one that failed to reflect the true picture of the real progress that has been made, especially in the categories of general cargo handled for export and import. To arrive at the true picture, we should take into account the fact that the liquid cargos, which are petroleum for Esso Standard and asphalt for Asphalt Trumbell Company, plus the military cargos, comprise by far the greater part of all tonnage handled through Morehead City. We should also consider the fact that since 1953, there has been a considerable decrease in the amount of liquid cargo handled at this port. This reduction was caused by the construction of a terminal on the Cape Fear River at Fayetteville, and the transfer to that facility of part of the liquid cargo business formerly handled at Morehead City. The Fayetteville terminal was completed in 1954 and since that time liquid cargo tonnage at Morehead City has dropped from 404,505 to 280,639. Another factor, which largely discredits the total tonnage figure as an indication of progress or lack of it at the Morehead City terminal, is the large but eratic and unpredictable amount of military cargo handled. In 1957, for instance, military cargo amounted to 93,203 tons. In 1958, when Marines from Camp Lejeune and Cherry Point embarked for Lebanon, the military cargo figure rose to more than 133,500 tons. In 1959, military activity at the port was at a minimum and the cargo figure dropped to 69,571 tons.

Neither of these factors, which, to a large extent, control the percentage increases and decreases at our state port facilities, provide a true indication of the flow of foreign trade and commerce exported and imported. This is not to say that this business is not revenue producing, or is not an important part of our operation at Morehead City, or that it does not play an important part in our over-all revenue structure. However, these commodities are domestically controlled, and while they are included in the total tonnages moving across our docks, they do not reflect the gross of the ports from a general cargo view point. The dramatic increase in general cargo handled can be illustrated by the fact that in 1953 Morehead City exported only 3,131 tons or approximately 6,262 hogsheads of tobacco, while in 1959 the exports amounted to 57,224 tons, or approximately 114,448 hogsheads of tobacco. This represents a percentage increase since 1953 of 1,727 per cent. In addition, there is presently in storage at Morehead City 11,243 tons of tobacco for export.

It should be noticed, at this point, that during the year 1958 the combined North Carolina ports exported slightly in excess of 25 per cent of all flue-cured tobacco exported from the United States. It should further be noticed that the total tonnage of tobacco exported through both Morehead City and Wilmington last year amounted to 73,826 tons. And, while U. S. figures are available for only ten months of 1959, it is estimated that North Carolina's exports will represent more than 33.3 per cent of all flue-cured tobacco exported from the United States during 1959. It is, of course, impossible for us to show the results of savings in dollars and cents to the exporters of tobacco, but it can be concluded that such savings are of a substantial nature. Otherwise, the flow of tobacco through our ports would not have increased as it has in recent years. I would like to add the personal conviction that this would not have been possible had it not been for the tremendous cooperation which we have received from our good friends in the tobacco exporting industry, as well as our good friends with the various steamship lines.

If further evidence of the development of the Morehead City facility is needed, it can be found in the fact that exports of liquid cargos, notably fish oil and glycol, increased 44.7 per cent in the last year and 768 per cent since 1953. The Ports Authority has been particularly active in soliciting and obtaining cargos in this category and they are certainly to be commended on their efforts.

At the same time, dry cargo imports through this terminal, not including the military, increased 264 per cent in 1959.

Another step toward progress in connection with general cargo was the establishment of the Carolina Grain Company in Morehead City in 1958. In its first year of operation, it exported 8,303 tons of grain, and this figure increased to approximately 21,000 tons in 1959. This produced a movement by rail of 252 cars and involved the use of 1,094 trucks. Present plans call for enlarging present grain facilities at this port, and this should result in a considerable increase of export grains in the future.

In addition to the rail and motor carriers transporting grains, there were 3,146 trucks operating in and out of Morehead City in

1959 as compared with 1,997 in 1958—an increase of 57.5 per cent. There were also 907 rail cars in operation in the area in 1959 as compared with 849 in 1958. All of this activity is further indication of the growth of foreign trade and commerce in the form of general commodities. The really significant factor is that while we had 8,000 tons less in petroleum and 64,000 less tons in military cargo in 1959, the general cargo tonnage was up 32,356 tons. Also significant is the fact that the port handled 220 ships in 1959 as against 204 in the previous year.

At the port in Wilmington, the conditions are somewhat different, largely because there are no captive industries located on state port property and cargos moving across the state docks at Wilmington are those of a dry general cargo nature. When considering Wilmington, we must keep in mind that there are many privately owned petroleum facilities, several bulk fertlizer facilities, and one of a general cargo dock which dock, of course, influenced the operation of the state ports. Still, the growth of the state docks at Wilmington has been very substantial and continuous since the facility was opened 1952. Imports have increased from 22,408 tons in 1952 to 131,283 tons in 1959· Exports have grown from 1,090 tons in 1952 to 152,773 tons in 1959. This represents a total increase in business of over 1,100 per cent.

Perhaps the simplest indication of the increase in activity at the state docks in Wilmington is the increase in the number of ships that have called at the ports to receive and discharge cargo. This number has risen from sixteen in 1952 to 254 in 1959. I think I can safely say that the increase would have been even more significant if we had had the facilities to accommodate a larger number of ships.

As a result of the rapid growth at Wilmington during 1959, it became impossible to handle all of the export-import traffic confined to the state docks. This resulted in the transfer of several ships and considerable tonnage to other berthing facilities at Wilmington. Let me add, at this point, that the state ports do not exist for the purpose of competing for business with privately owned terminals. The state ports exist because it was determined a number of years ago that additional facilities would be needed to implement this state's progress in the economic field. Our sole purpose is to bring more foreign trade and commercial activity to

North Carolina and to develop our ports to the point that they can accommodate this new business in an efficient and profitable manner. It may surprise some of you to learn, because of congested conditions at our ports, it has been necessary for us to decline a number of cargos, with the result that this traffic, and the profit that could have been derived from it, went to other ports in other states. And, I might add that I am of the opinion that if the economic trend involved in trade and commerce remains at its present level—and indications are that it will continue for a long period of time—the additional facilities which are being constructed and will be completed in the next few months, will be as congested at the end of this year as our present facilities are now. The state is, therefore, confronted with an obvious challenge to expand our port facilities to meet whatever demand is placed upon them, if private capital cannot do it. Certainly, it is to our advantage that it be done, for we benefit not only from the operation of the terminals themselves but from the increased business activity that will result throughout the state.

In an effort to meet what it considers its responsibility in this field, the state has, since 1949, invested $11,817,400 in the development of our port facilities. An initial appropriation of $7,500,000 in 1949, under the Scott administration, was used for the construction of the docks, erection of the necessary buildings, and the purchase of essential equipment. In 1957, the General Assembly appropriated an additional $3,390,000 to provide additional, much-needed docks, a transit shed, and warehouses at both Wilmington and Morehead City. In 1959, the third appropriation—this one amounting to $917,400—was made. This is being used to meet the demand for more warehouse space, railroads and roads, permanent improvements to existing transit sheds, repairs to the fender system on the docks, the construction of a garage, and the purchase of mechanized equipment. An additional $1,073,713 has been spent from the operating fund, bringing the total state investment in dock facilities to $12,891,113. This is still small compared to our neighbors, but I believe we are on the way, and I hope the next administration and the next General Assembly will authorize additional capital expenditures.

Not the least of those who stand to benefit from this investment and from the state's effort to establish and maintain adequate port facilities are our transportation companies, many of whom are represented here this evening. If you have any doubts about the benefits your companies receive from import-export activities, you have only to look at the record for the past several years. Since 1955, the number of motor carriers receiving or discharging cargo at the state docks at Wilmington has increased from 1,924, to 5,204. This represents an increase in business activity for you of more than 170 per cent in the past five years.

At the same time, the number of railroad cars receiving or discharging cargo at the docks has increased 52.1 per cent—from 2,888 in 1955 to 4,392 in 1959.

These figures represent far more than a mere tabulation of cold statistics; they represent new jobs, higher income, and a more abundant life for the people of North Carolina. And this, after all, is the motivating force behind all our efforts. Each of you has a responsibility to yourself, to the businesses you represent, and to the state of North Carolina to promote actively the development of our North Carolina ports. If more facilities are needed, then they should be provided. If more money is needed, then it should be forthcoming. We have a tremendous opportunity to contribute something of great and lasting value to our state and it is an opportunity that we cannot afford to miss.

I feel very strongly that our ports can play a significant role in bringing a better way of life to our people. I hope that your state government will continue to do whatever is necessary to meet this challenge and to make absolutely certain that the people of this state benefit in every way possible from this very important activity. I am confident that we can count on the members of this group to contribute to this effort whenever and wherever the opportunity presents itself·

Thank you.

ADDRESS AT THE HARVARD LAW SCHOOL FORUM

CAMBRIDGE, MASSACHUSETTS
January 29, 1960

[This was the last of four addresses made by Governor Hodges during a three-day visit to New York and New England. The other speeches were made respectively before the Greater New Haven (Connecticut) Chamber of

Commerce on January 27, before the Association of Cotton Textile Merchants of New York City on January 28, and at the Harvard Business School on the afternoon of January 29. (See pp. 516-517 for accounts of these speeches.) The address before the Law School Forum on "Public School Integration" was a review and defense of North Carolina's approach to the segregation problem and was similar in many respects to a number of speeches made by the Governor of this subject in 1955 and 1956 when the Supreme Court decisions of May 17, 1954, and May 31, 1955, were a pressing public issue in North Carolina.]

Mr. Moderator, Fellow Panel Members, Ladies and Gentlemen:
For the past three years or more, I have had relatively little public comment to make on the public school integration-segregation matter. During this time, this matter has not been a pressing public issue in North Carolina. This is true, not because North Carolina has not had the problem or has necessarily solved the problem for all time, but because beginning in 1955 and continuing through a special legislative session in 1956, basic guide rules for meeting specific problems as they arose were laid out, and within these channels we have been able to make our way as a state with a minimum of internal dissension or public discord.

But before I tell you in more detail exactly what North Carolina has done in response to the 1954 Supreme Court decision, let me make some preliminary remarks concerning that decision and refer also to the very strong reactions of millions of people most directly affected by that decision.

What I have to say to you tonight is said by one who is not a lawyer. Of necessity, I have during the last several year years given a great deal of study of legal issues. I believe I have had the benefit of good legal analysis and advice concerning the public school matter. But I am not prepared for nor shall I attempt a learned analysis of constitutional rules, theories, assumptions, or what-have-you in connection with the school segregation cases as decided by the highest court in our land. I will leave that function to persons more qualified, of whom there are many among the able and distinguished professors on the faculty of the Harvard Law School. Many of them, I feel sure, could easily prepare a convincing, plausible legal brief on either or *both* sides of the school decision. And probably all such briefs would earn from the dean of your Law School an "A" for quality, quantity, and number of footnotes. Now my limited lay experience with a legal brief is that to be a *brief*, it must not brief be, but extensively it must proclaim and *lengthy* is its honest name.

Since I am speaking to you on a subject in which law is involved but am not speaking to you as a lawyer or one learned in the law, let me attempt to state forthrightly my special concern and experience which, as I have persuaded myself, is my reason for being here tonight to participate in the Harvard Law School Forum. That is, as governor and chief executive of one of the states of the Union vitally affected by the 1954 decision, I was confronted with an immediate, overwhelming crisis threatening our state's entire system of public schools and the maintenance of law and order itself. And I had an immediate *executive* responsibility to do whatever could be done to lead and assist North Carolina in meeting that situation in a responsible and effective manner if at all possible. I could not enjoy the simple privilege of theorizing, philosophizing, analyzing, or criticizing; nor could I simply sit back and enjoy what seems to me the relatively easy task of writing a judicial opinion in calm, cloistered, judicial chambers, protected from the turbulent stormy assaults which do seem to haunt the *executive* ramparts.

Thus, I was faced with reality and not theory. My task was not to argue the law but to try to help the 4,500,000 people of North Carolina live with what the Supreme Court had decided was the law of the land.

The decision of the Supreme Court in the school segregation cases was announced May 17,1954. At that time, I was lieutenant governor of North Carolina, ex officio a member of the State Board of Education, and serving as elected chairman of that board. Due to the untimely death of Governor William B. Umstead, on November 9, 1954, I, as lieutenant governor, succeeded to the office of governor and (with an interim election in my own right) have been privileged to serve as governor of North Carolina since that time. I mention those dates merely to establish my official responsibility in connection with developments following May 17, 1954.

I do not wish to take a great deal of time to dwell on the differences of opinion among competent lawyers and scholars concerning the 1954 decision of the Supreme Court. Nor do I wish to take a great deal of time stating certain facts having to do with tradition, community mores, and strongly-held convictions with respect to maintaining separate public schools for different races. However, I do want to say enough on both of these matters to make the point that the governor of North Carolina did indeed face a very critical, overwhelming problem brought about by the 1954 change in the interpretation of the Federal Constitution.

First, I am sure that all of you will agree with me, regardless of your personal opinion concerning either the correctness or the desirability of the 1954 decision, that the decision did in fact precipitate a considerable legal debate throughout the country. Furthermore, this legal debate did not simply divide along regional lines, with all the *affirmatives* located North of the Mason-Dixon line and all the *negatives* located south of that same imaginary line.

It is accepted history that the Fourteenth Amendment to the Federal Constitution was adopted in the aftermath of the War Between the States. And the Congress which debated and approved the language of the Fourteenth Amendment for submission to the vote of the states also enacted federal statutes providing for operation of separate schools within the District of Columbia. It is also a matter of history that through the decades immediately following the adoption of the Fourteenth Amendment no less than twenty-five states, at one time or the other, had statutes either authorizing or requiring separate schools for the races. The states either permitting or requiring such practices were not by any means limited to those which we now group together and refer to as "Southern States." For example, at various times there were California, Delaware, Illinois, Indiana, Kansas, Missouri, Nevada, New Jersey, New York, Ohio, and Pennsylvania, all outside the southern or border state category. It is also a matter of historic fact that in various cases decided before 1900, as well as after 1900, the United States Supreme Court gave express approval to what is called the "separate but equal" rule.

Whatever the niceties of constitutional interpretation involved in the decision of those cases which came before our highest court before 1900, many states and local governments did proceed to establish and operate racially separate schools; and the Supreme Court did not, until very recent times, indicate that the rule of "separate but equal" might be in jeopardy so far as judicial interpretation was concerned.

It is thus clear that the 1954 decision amounted to a drastic change of the judicial mind, or a complete reversal of long-established interpretation by the Supreme Court.

This fact in and of itself did, in my opinion, make the problem vastly more difficult for the governor of a state which had chosen to maintain separate public schools for the races.

To state this particular thought in other words, if the United State Supreme Court had never decided, prior to 1954, any case involving the constitutionality of separate public facilities or the "separate but equal" rule, and then in 1954 for the first time did decide the question—and reach the same conclusion we have today —I believe that the reaction of millions of citizens towards the Court would have been vastly different from what the reaction in fact, was, and I further cannot help but believe that such reaction would not have involved the degree of condemnation of the Court that did occur.

I asked a lawyer acquaintance of mine to summarize as briefly and clearly as he could what he conceived to be reasonable, plausible, legal points which could be raised with respect to the 1954 Supreme Court decision, even though we accept the decision as an authoritative declaration of the law.

That lawyer gave to me the following points, which, as he expressed it, could be analyzed and developed into a competent and respectable legal commentary.

(1) The Court had previously decided the basic legal question and in this lawyer's opinion did not adequately consider and dispose of the judicial rule that a constitutional decision once established is not overruled unless the Court can say that it was wrong in its original decision and that its original decision should have been the other way at the time the original decision was rendered.

(2) Second, this lawyer feels that the 1954 decision is somewhat vulnerable in that the decision seems to have placed unusually great emphasis on certain textbook material dealing with sociology and psychology, and he takes the view that the Court might well have remanded the cases to a trial court to take additional evidence on sociology and psychology to be sure that it had the benefit of any and all of the many experts in those fields,

before reaching such an important decision which apparently was placed primarily on those grounds.

(3) Third, and of considerable importance in the mind of my lawyer friend, he pointed out that the Fourteenth Amendment itself contains the express language that "the Congress shall have power to enforce, by appropriate legislation, the provisions of this article." Thus, he suggested, the Supreme Court could have declined to make a direct ruling in the 1954 decision and the Court could have called to the attention of Congress that the Congress might by enactment of federal statutes give a new meaning to the Fourteenth Amendment, suggesting that the "separate but equal" rule must stand as the interpretation of the Court unless Congress saw fit to exercise express *statutory* authority given to the Congress by the language of the Fourteenth Amendment itself.

(4) Fourth, there are the very fundamental questions of judicial policy summed up by the term "judicial self-restraint." That is, although the Court may have the judicial authority to decide the constitutional question before it, it declines to do so on the grounds the question is one best settled by "political impacts" within the executive and legislative branches of the government.

I have mentioned these points to you as an illustration of the discussion and debate invoked by the 1954 decision.

I am sure that none of you will yield to the temptation, if indeed you are even tempted, of disdainfully dismissing all the legal discussion about the Supreme Court decision as merely reflecting a regional bias. I am sure we all recognize that serious questions of legal correctness have been raised, by serious and able lawyers and by distinguished citizens who had no regional axe to grind. That what I have just said is true is illustrated by a statement made by a distinguished judge in discussing the role of the Supreme Court in deciding cases under the Fourteenth Amendment, and I quote:

" . . . I do not know what the doctrine is as to the scope of these clauses; I cannot frame any definition that will explain when the Court will assume the role of a third legislative chamber and when it will limit its authority to keeping Congress and the states within their accredited authority."

And let me give you this further statement made by the same judge who seems to me to be saying that the Supreme Court should not assume to sit in moral judgment on either state or federal legislation, and I quote:

"For myself it would be most irksome to be ruled by a bevy of Platonic guardians, even if I knew how to choose them, which I assuredly do not. If they were in charge, I should miss the stimulus of living in a society where I have, at least theoretically, some part in the direction of public affairs."

I am sure that many of you have recognized that I have just quoted from the lectures of Judge Learned Hand, who graduated from the Harvard Law School in 1896, and who served for more than forty years on the federal bench, first as a federal district judge and then Judge of the Court of Appeals. He is acclaimed as one of America's very great judges. And the quotations I gave you come from Judge Hand's lectures which he delivered here in 1958, which have been published in a volume entitled *The Bill of Rights.*

May I remind you again that my purpose in mentioning the great legal controversy concerning the 1954 decision is to make the point that the mere fact such debate and controversy has occurred has of itself made the task of the state executive immensely more difficult.

I now move on to the non-legal factors present in North Carolina, and of course in other states, which combined in reaction to the 1954 decision to make the position of the state governor extremely difficult, and at times seemingly impossible. These are of course the factors of tradition, habit, personal beliefs, or depending on your point of view, personal prejudices. In short, these are the sum total of all the practical problems, social, economic, political, or otherwise, involved in the relationship of the white and the Negro races in this country, and indeed in many parts of the world.

The extensive state-suppported system of public education that we now have in North Carolina did not begin its great development until the turn of the present century. But before then and continuing until 1954, North Carolina had operated public schools in reliance on the "separate but equal" rule.

We all can call to mind at least some vague notion of the tremendous problem confronting the South during the Reconstruction era, and we all recognize as a matter of historic fact the tremendous difficulties confronting Negro citizens. Following the war, they were released from the legal status of slavery but, ill-equipped by education, training, or citizenship experience, they were not released into immediate assumption of the full responsibilities of citizenship. Therefore, we should not forget the background of extreme travail and difficulty through which Negro citizens had to come to citizenship responsibilities, and through which indeed our entire nation had to labor. Against this background, there developed in many states of the Union systems of public education under which Negro and white children attended separate schools.

There is one other very basic point which I think is extremely important and which, it seems to me, has often been overlooked in our discussion of the national difficulties in connection with this problem. That is, most of the states in the southern region, whether by necessity or by choice, have through the years depended upon a system of public rather than private schools to a far greater extent than states in the northeastern part of the nation. Generally speaking, there are relatively few private schools of the primary and secondary level in the southeastern part of the country. In these states there has been little of the separation of children into the private school on the one hand and the public school on other, on the basis of the economic status of the family. By and large, both rich and poor, well-to-do and less well-to-do families have sent their children to the public schools. This is still substantially the case.

Thus, we come to the 1950's at which time North Carolina had approximately 1,000,000 children in the public schools. Of this number, some 300,000 are Negro children. In addition, North Carolina employs a large number of Negro school teachers, principals, and professional personnel. In fact, we did, and I am informed still do, employ more Negro school personnel than the seven states of New York, Pennsylvania, Illinois, Ohio, Michigan, California, and Indiana all combined.

The percentage of Negro school children in North Carolina varies from less than 1 per cent in some counties to more than 72 per cent in another county. This variation in the population percentages undoubtedly suggests to you that any difficulties of a racial nature in the use of public facilities must be affected in some way by the population distribution in the particular community, as would also be true for states at large. As I will indicate to you shortly, we took this basic fact into account in deciding how North Carolina would attempt to solve the problems brought about by the 1954 Supreme Court decision.

You will recall that the 1954 decision did not present to the states the immediate impact of racial mixing in public schools. This was due to the fact that there was to be a second decision dealing with the implementation of the first. After further argument before the court, the so-called implementation decision in the school segregation cases was announced in May, 1955. This meant that from May, 1954, to May, 1955, there was a period of relative calm in most of the states, although I think it is only accurate to say that the nature of that calm was one of increasing anxiety.

In any event, North Carolina, as did other states, established formal committees of prominent citizens to give particular study to the problems involved. Such a committee had already been named by my predecessor, and I was fortunate in having the advice and counsel of that committee, as well as a later smaller committee appointed by me in 1955. The chairman of both of those committees was the Honorable Thomas Pearsall, a very distinguished and able citizen of our state, who had had a great deal of experience in the governmental, political, and educational life of the state and who was eminently qualified to serve in that capacity.

For my own part, from the time that I was suddenly called upon to assume the responsibilities of governor in November, 1954, and without knowing how North Carolina would meet the ever-darkening crisis, I set for myself two objectives:

1) To maintain, if possible, a system of public education for all the children of North Carolina; and

2) To maintain law and order.

I frankly confess to you today that there were many times during that period when it seemed that not only were the pillars of education about to fall, but also the pillars of stable and responsible government. I confess that at times during those days my faith was greater than my hope, and my faith was not always strong. There were times when it seemed almost that our state, our region, and indeed the whole nation, must suffer an orgy of great internal discord, and that we must pass through a period of neighbor against neighbor, citizen against citizen, state against state, and in truth a nation again divided against itself. I knew that somehow we must devise a road ahead which would be wide enough to accommodate us all without putting anyone in the ditch on either side.

By early 1955 our state legislature was in regular session, and the Advisory Committee on Education under the chairmanship of Mr. Pearsall was much concerned as to what recommendations, if any, should be placed before that session of the General Assembly. That committee in due time recommended to me, and I approved the recommendation and in turn recommended to the General Assembly, the repeal of all our statutes which then required that white and Negro children be assigned to separate schools. At the same time we recommended and the General Assembly enacted a pupil assignment law which placed in the local boards of education throughout the state full authority and responsibility for assignment of the pupils to the public schools in each respective local unit, in accordance with valid and reasonable standards. Our pupil assignment law is similar to those now adopted in other states, and the North Carolina statute was upheld sometime ago by the federal courts.

The repeal of statutes requiring separate schools for the races and adoption of a pupil assignment statute reflected a recognition on the part of our legislature that, given the 1954 Supreme Court decision, no good purpose could be served in trying to continue with laws on the books which the Court had already flatly ruled unconstitutional. The action of the legislature did not, I must say, reflect a desire on the part of the legislature or the general public to undertake racial mixing in the public schools. In fact, the strong general feeling then, as it is now, was that racial mixing in our public schools would be undesirable.

Even in the spring of 1955, it was evident that we would have to give further close study and attention to the problem, and I asked Mr. Pearsall and his committee to do this. The committee continued its work through 1955 and into the spring of 1956, at which time its reports were made to me and to the people of the state. In the meantime, in 1955 I suggested to the citizens of the state that it would be in the interest of our public schools and in the interest of maintaining peace throughout the state for all of our citizens to observe voluntary separation of the races in the public schools. In this connection, I would like to quote to you from a federal court decision announced in July, 1955. I believe that opinion was written by the late Judge John J. Parker, who was recognized as one of the nation's eminent federal jurists and who served for many years as chief judge of the Federal Court of Appeals for the Fourth Circuit. There is this language in that opinion:

> What it [the Court] has decided and all that it has decided is that a state may not deny to any person on account of race the right to attend any school that it maintains. This, under the decision of the Supreme Court, the state may not do directly or indirectly; but if the schools which it maintains are open to children of all races, no violation of the Constitution is involved even though the children of different races voluntarily attend different schools, as they attend different churches.
>
> Nothing in the Constitution or in the decision of the Supreme Court takes away from the people freedom to choose the schools they attend. The Constitution, in other words, does not require integration. It merely forbids discrimination.

As the year 1956 began, it was evident that the people throughout our state were increasingly concerned about the possible effects of the Supreme Court decision on public schools. There was not at that time any integration in North Carolina at the public school level, although some Negro students began attending the University of North Carolina in 1951.

Following the recommendations and report of the special advisory committee, I called the legislature into special session in July, 1956, and at that time recommended legislation which would provide what we came to call safety valves for the people.

My recommendation to the General Assembly called for an amendment to the state constitution which would (1) authorize tuition grants to be paid to the parents of any child assigned against the wishes of his parents to a school in which the races were mixed, such grants to be available for education in a private school chosen by the parents, if reassignment to a non-mixed public school could not be made; (2) authorize the people in any local community, by majority vote, to discontinue the operation of the public schools in that community if conditions developed which were unacceptable to the people in that community.

After full discussion and debate on these proposals, during which the entire General Assembly sat as a committee of the whole much of the time, the proposals were put to a vote in both Houses, and as I recall the proposal to amend the constitution was approved unanimously in the Senate of fifty members, and was passed in the House with only two dissenting votes out of a membership of 120. The vote of the people on adoption of the amendment to the state constitution was set for September 8, 1956, and in that election, in which a record number voted, more than 82 per cent of those voting approved the amendment to the state constitution which would provide for the safety valves I have described.

The mere statement of these facts does not, of course, give you the complete picture of the great discussion on the issues involved. On the one hand there were those who quite honestly felt that it would be a mistake to enact any law authorizing closing of schools, even by vote of the people.

There were many other citizens who were also opposed to the position I had taken, but for an entirely different reason. They, just as sincere and with just as great a regard for the state and what they deemed to be the public interest, believed that the proposals did not go nearly far enough and that far more drastic action should be taken to prevent absolutely any racial mixing of any degree whatsoever in any public school at any place at any time in North Carolina.

However, I believed that the people of North Carolina, regardless of their strong feelings and opposition to racial mixing in the public schools, would nevertheless be persuaded to see the reasonableness of the proposals which I was recommending. I believed that the people of the state would not take hasty and ill-considered action which could lead to the precipitate and unnecessary destruction of their public schools. I knew that the people of North Carolina had a deep and abiding respect for education and wanted their children to have every educational advantage possible.

I also believed that the people of the state were law-abiding citizens and they desired and would insist that whatever pro-

Governor Hodges, Holt McPherson, editor of the *High Point Enterprise* (*center*), and Willis H. Slane, Jr., president of the Hatteras Yacht Company of High Point (*right*), at the launching of a new fiber glass yacht at Morehead City, March 22, 1960.

Photo by Burnie Batchelor

Left to right: Harold Myrick, newly elected president of the North Carolina Citizens Association; Mrs. Myrick; David Rockefeller, speaker on the occasion; Mrs. Hodges; Governor Hodges, who introduced Rockefeller; Mrs. Holt McPherson; Holt McPherson, retiring president of the association, at the association's annual dinner in Raleigh, March 23, 1960.

blems might arise in this area should be resolved in a peaceful and orderly manner.

I had faith that these were indeed the true sentiments of our people, although I also knew that because of their own strong feelings in opposition to racial mixing in public schools it would be possible, if their leaders were of a different character, for our people to be persuaded to take an altogether different and tragic path.

May I summarize now the substance of the approach which North Carolina has taken. First, under our state law the local school boards have full and complete authority for assignment of pupils to the public schools, on the basis of reasonable administrative standards. There is nothing in the statutes which authorizes or requires that pupil assignments should be made in any respect on the basis of race. Second, our laws provide our citizens with a degree of choice on two levels. There is a choice available to the individual parent (and this choice is available to any and all races). If the parent objects to his child attending a school with a child of another race, the parent can ask the school board to reassign his child to another public school if one is available in which there is no racial mixing. If it is not possible for this to be done, the parent can if he so chooses withdraw his child from the public school, apply for an education expense grant equivalent to the per-student cost of educating his child in the public school, and enroll his child in a private school of his choice. This is the choice available to the individual parent in those situations where the community at large is willing to continue with whatever conditions prevail.

The other level of choice is to the community at large. If a situation develops which is unacceptable to the people as a whole in a school community and the people in that community prefer to have no public school rather than have schools in which there is racial mixing, the people have an opportunity of voting on the question of suspending the operation of their schools. A majority of those voting would determine the question. The statutes governing such elections are drawn to insure a convenient, full and free expression of sentiment, and if one decision is made today and then a short time later the people change their minds, a subsequent election can be called within a minimum of time. In short, there are no gimmicks and the election would not be so conducted or the ballot so worded as to favor one result or the other.

The North Carolina approach is in recognition of the simple and fundamental fact that to have public schools we must have public support of those schools.

As is generally known, since 1957 we have had some instances of children of both races attending the same public schools in North Carolina. All such assignments of Negro children to white schools have been made by action of local school boards, and in no instance that I recall was such an assignment by order of a court. In no instance has an election been called by citizens at the local level for the purpose of voting to close schools. Also, I understand that there has, up to the present time, been no case in which the parent has withdrawn his child from a public school and applied for a tuition grant on the grounds that he objected to his child attending school with a person of another race, although there have been reassignments to other public schools. This simply means that while our "maximum choice" legislation has been available, factual situations have not developed which have prompted citizens to avail themselves of the choices under state law, and no public school has been closed.

Nevertheless, I think it is very apparent to all thinking citizens in our state that the mere presence of these laws on our statute books has been of incalculable value in maintaining a generally calm and orderly approach to the problem by insuring to the citizens of our state that they would not be confronted with situations from which there was no reasonable and orderly alternative approach.

It is my hope that these comments on the problems which confronted our state as a result of the 1954 Supreme Court decision and the approach worked out by our state to meet those problems will give you a better understanding and appreciation of the attitude of the people of North Carolina.

I have said many times before that in my opinion the racial problem in America is not just a regional problem. It is a national problem. I have also said that the racial problem is not limited to the United States. It is in fact a world-wide problem.

It is only natural that at this time and perhaps increasingly during the months ahead there will be discussion and argument concerning what the federal government ought to do, should not do, or what laws Congress should pass or should not pass with regard to the racial problem in public education.

I am sure you can understand that I would hope that at least no action would be taken on the national level which would adversely affect the delicate balance we seem to have achieved in our own state, which is permitting us to meet the individual problems as they arise and, as we hope, work out our solutions over a period of time.

I know that such an opinion is not likely to be sanctioned by the vigorous partisans on this issue. I know that there are probably those who feel that the full power of the national government should be brought down upon the heads of what they would describe as backward and unruly states. I can only hope that such an attitude, if it does exist, is not in fact representative of our national spirit. Rather, I hope that the true spirit of America on this problem will be that exhibited by one who said:

> . . . that a society so riven that the spirit of moderation is gone, no court can save; that a society where that spirit flourishes, no court need save; that in a society which evades its responsibility by thrusting upon the courts the nurture of that spirit, that spirit in the end will perish. What is the spirit of moderation. It is the temper which does not press a partisan advantage to its bitter end, which can understand and will respect the other side, which feels a unity between all citizens—real and not the fictitious product of propaganda—which recognizes their common fate and their common aspirations—in a word, which has faith in the sacredness of the individual. If you ask me how such a temper and such a faith are bred and fostered, I cannot answer. They are the last flowers of civilization, delicate and easily overrun by the weeds of our sinful human nature; we may even now be witnessing their uprooting and disappearance until in the progress of the ages their seeds can once more find some friendly soil.

I have just taken the liberty to quote again from your own Judge Learned Hand (*The Spirit of Liberty*, p. 181.)

I close with this thought. We must always keep before us the great promise of America, which is the promise of freedom under responsible and democratic government—and I mean freedom for all citizens irrespective of race, religion, or creed. While our day-to-day progress toward more perfect realization of these ideals may seem to falter, and while all of us at one time or the other despair of doing good works, the spirit of America must always remain alive in our hearts.

I have pride in the America of the past; I have confidence in the America of today; I rejoice in my hopes for the America of the future which will, I know, be a more perfect Union—one nation, indivisible, with liberty and justice for all.

ADDRESS AT THE ANNUAL MEETING OF THE WILKES CHAMBER OF COMMERCE

NORTH WILKESBORO
February 1, 1960

[A projected dam on the Yadkin River was designed for flood control in Wilkes County and as a water supply for the growing city of Winston-Salem. These two areas were scheduled to vote early in March, 1960, on the question of issuing $600,000 in bonds by each of the participating areas to help construct the dam and pay for the water storage features of the project. Governor Hodges resorted to one of his favorite speeches, "The North Carolina Water Story," to urge a favorable vote in the forthcoming bond election.]

I have looked forward for a long time to visiting in this community and this county with a group of North Carolinians, who, I believe, will, within the next few years, realize the benefits to be derived from perseverance, confidence, faith, and dedication to progress. I have followed with great interest the effort you have made to move forward in recent years and, while you have encountered perhaps more than your share of disappointments and frustrations, I confidently believe that your future success will more than compensate you for the sacrifices you have made.

You have a rich tradition that dates back more than 200 years and is filled with those events that give people strength of character and form the basis for a cooperative spirit that is not only important, but absolutely necessary to progress. The first settlers came to Wilkes County in the 1750's and in less than twenty years the area has grown sufficiently in population to warrant its designation as a county. And a real county it was. Early records indicate that at one time the western boundary of Wilkes County was the Mississippi River. The town of Wilkesboro was established in 1788 and claims the distinction of having a post office before Raleigh. By the time of the Civil War the population of Wilkes County exceeded 12,000, and some indication of the kind of people who settled here can be seen in the fact that only one county in North Carolina—Mecklenburg—gave more soldiers to the Confederacy than did Wilkes.

This county took a major step forward in 1891 when the Southern Railway built a spur track into the county. The story is told that Wilkes was called upon to help finance this work and a bond campaign was waged with patriotic speeches and even a brass band imported from Winston-Salem. This railroad headed in the direction of Wilkesboro, but stopped on the north side of the river. One story is that there was not enough money left to build a bridge across the stream, but there were many Wilkesboro residents at the time who simply felt that the depot had been stolen. In any event, the town of North Wilkesboro rose at the spot where the rail line halted and, in short order, became the leading commercial center of the northwestern part of the state.

Lumber was a major industry in Wilkes County half a century ago—and it still holds a great potential—but I think it is significant that as early as 1910 the people in this region were practicing diversified farming on a major scale. Wheat, corn, rye, and buckwheat were just a few of the products being produced on the farms. Apples were not only being grown in large quantities but were being canned and dried for export, along with vegetables, herbs, poultry and dairy products. By 1944 you were producing more apples than any other county in the state. And I think it is significant that yours is one of the few counties that commercially produces all three types of tobacco—flue-cured, burley, and aromatic. At the same time, your livestock industry has grown tremendously and you have become a leading poultry producing county. You have also shown great ingenuity in using the by-products of this agricultural activity. I understand that your poultry industry provides a fertilizer that has, in many instances, revolutionized crop yields throughout the county. And I have been told that there is some validity to the claim that the county's surplus corn production is put to profitable use. As a matter of fact, I have been informed that if the profits from this latter industry could be figured in, the per capita income for Wilkes County would rival that of Forsyth or Mecklenburg.

In all seriousness, I would like to say that I am convinced that the per capita income here in Wilkes County can be raised considerably simply by pursuing more vigorously the course you are now following of farm and industry diversifications. Your per capita income, based on a projection of figures obtained several years ago, is $808—a figure that ranks you seventy-fifth in the state. Among your nine surrounding counties, you stand fourth, exceeded only by Surry, with a per capita income of $1,472; Iredell, with an income of $1,272; and Caldwell, with an income of $1,118. Ranked below you are Alexander, $792; Alleghany, $763; Watauga, $669; Yadkin, $627; and Ashe, $622. These figures certainly are not a true indication of the potential that is obviously present here in Wilkes County and throughout all the counties of northwestern North Carolina. To me, they represent little more than a challenge to you to continue and even expand on your efforts to exploit your opportunities. You have definite responsibility to continue your efforts to develop to a maximum degree your agricultural diversification. At the same time, you must redouble your efforts to bring more industry into this region—industry that will provide more jobs, higher income, and a more abundant life for your people.

One of the prerequisites for a great industrial development is an abundant supply of water for industrial use. Without water, your efforts to grow industrially can produce only limited results. With water, there is no limit to the progress that you can make. I commend this chamber of commerce and the people of this community and this county on the fact that they realized this many years ago and have worked untiringly to the present day to lay this basic foundation for progress.

The effort to bring about the construction of reservoir on the Yadkin River began in earnest more than two decades ago. It has been the primary project of this chamber since its organization in 1946, and I have no reservation about giving you great credit for the part you have played in bringing this project to what appears to be a successful conclusion. There have been many different plans advanced for controlling floods in the Yadkin valley—from a series of about three or four dams on the main branch of the Yadkin, to two dams, to a large hydro-electric type installation, to a series of small dams on the tributaries of the Yadkin, to the present plan for a single dam located about 4.3 miles west of the Wilkesboros. Through the years, your efforts have been hampered by opposition on a Congressional and on a local level, a lack of real interest, and more recently, the federal law, passed in 1958, which required local participation in projects of this type. In seeking to overcome this obstacle you found that legislation at the state level would be required to enable you to participate in such an undertaking. Among other things, you found that before federal appropriations could be made to initiate construction on the dam, arrangements would have to be made for local participation, which in turn required state legislation. I am glad that I had the privilege of working with you in overcoming some of these legislative hurdles, and I was delighted recently when, in spite of two presidential vetoes by Mr. Eisenhower, the money was made available to begin construction. We owe thanks to our Senators and Congressmen from North Carolina for their help.

It was determined by the Corps of Engineers that approximately $1,000,000 in local funds would be necessary to construct the dam, and I understand that a referendum will be held early in March in Wilkes County and at Winston-Salem to provide this money and to pay for the cost of the water storage feature of the dam. The referendum will, I believe, call for the issuance of $600,000 in bonds by each of the participating parties. I would like to urge that the people of the areas affected vote their whole-hearted support of this undertaking. It will be one of the best investments you can make in your own future. It will be an investment that will repay you many times. Each of you here must assume some responsibility to see that your bond issue is approved.

This cooperative approach between a county and a large city is made possible by the fact that Winston-Salem is primarily interested in a dependable water supply for the future and Wilkes County, which has an abundant supply, is interested primarily in flood control. With both flood control and storage features, the dam will serve both interests.

Certainly, the economy of this region will benefit from this dam. The control of floods, for example, will make available many ideal industrial sites for development. This is particularly important when you consider that almost all the good industrial sites in this area—particularly those accessible to railroads—are either wholly or partially in the flood plain. I understand also that the lake to be formed by this reservoir, while not large by comparison with some others, will be one of the most attractive in the Southeast. Such a lake will provide this area with a badly needed recreational area at a time when water sports, fishing, etc., are becoming increasingly popular. The Corps of Engineers has estimated that approximately 1,000,000 people live within a seventy-five mile radius of the reservoir site. With such an attraction close by, there is every reason to believe that tourist activity will increase noticeably in this region.

These, of course, are just a few of the more obvious benefits that will be derived from construction of the Wilkesboro Reservoir. Whether or not these benefits are to be realized will be determined by the voters in the up-coming referendum. I am confident that the vote will be a favorable one but on a matter as important as this, there must be no complacency. Each of you, as I have said, has a responsibility to work actively to insure the success of the bond issue.

Let me add that there is more at stake here than just the Wilkesboro dam. The people of this area are, in effect, pioneering in an undertaking that can have a far-reaching effect throughout North Carolina. Similar projects are planned for other areas of the state, and in all probability the actions of the people here will set a pattern for other flood-control structures to be constructed in the future. The storage feature in this dam may well serve as a break-through in the state's effort to derive maximum benefit from its water resources. It has long been established that North Carolina has more than enough water to meet all its present and anticipated needs. But we have not always had the water when we needed it. Storage is the obvious answer. It may well be that the people of Wilkes County and Winston-Salem may show the way to a greater economic prosperity for North Carolina.

Because of the importance of water in all our plans for the future of North Carolina, the state is doing everything possible to insure the wise and equitable use of this important resource. Evidence of this was seen in the action of the 1959 General Assembly establishing the State Department of Water Resources. Here, under one roof, we have centralized the responsibility formerly scattered among several agencies for the conservation and beneficial use of our lakes and streams.

The Department of Water Resources combines the duties and responsibilities which were formerly assigned to two divisions of the Department of Conservation and Development—the Division of Water Resources, Inlets, and Coastal Waterways, and the Division of Mineral Resources; to the Division of Water Pollution Control of the State Board of Health; and to the North Carolina Board of Water Commissioners. The new agency provides this state, for the first time in its history, with the machinery for a coordinated effort to develop a comprehensive water program. I like to think of this action as typical of the North Carolina way of doing things. It is a pioneering venture among the states of the nation, in that only a few states have taken such a step.

Yet, we did not rush into this step simply for the sake of pioneering. We acted only after a long, hard look at the situation and only after the proper ground work for the proposal had been laid. All interests concerned were consulted before the matter was taken to the General Assembly, and all were requested to express their views during their deliberations. The result was a measure that the state's water-using interest and its water agencies stood solidly behind. Because of the coopeartive attitude of all who had a hand in this undertaking, I feel confident that our state has taken a significant step in the right direction in the management of its water resources, and that the new department, with the support it deserves, will provide us with a clearly defined water program which will serve the best interest of the entire state.

My own confidence in the soundness of the reorganization has been justified by the manner in which those now in charge of our water resource activities have moved ahead with their task. The Board of Water Resources, under the able leadership of General James R. Townsend of Greensboro, lost no time in transferring plans for the department from paper to reality. The board was appointed on August 21, 1959; it met on August 28 and selected a director, Colonel Harry E. Brown, whom I consider an excellent choice; and the department was in operation on September 1—a going concern created of parts and pieces from four separate agencies or divisions which had had some share in the scattered responsibilities in the field of water resources.

The board brings into the service of the state a broad, strong background of varied experience in the complex water field. Serving with General Townsend are P. D. Davis of Durham, a consulting engineer with long experience in the water needs and problems of municipalities; Ben R. Lewis of Goldsboro, who has served ably on the Neuse River Watershed Authority; Dan K. Moore of Canton, a former Superior Court judge and a recognized authority on water law; C. H. Pruden, Jr., of Windsor, who has had experience in beach erosion and other water problems affecting our coastal areas; S. Vernon Stevens, Jr., of Broadway, a soil conservation district supervisor; and Glenn M. Tucker of Carolina Beach, experienced in hurricane rehabilitation work and waterways development.

The new department has two divisions—a Divisions of Navigable Waterways and a Division of Water Pollution Control. The Division of Navigable Waterways is responsible for initiating, planning, and executing immediate and long-range programs for the improvement of rivers, harbors, and inland ports, and for flood-control and related civil works projects. It is also responsible for cooperating with federal agencies in planning and developing navigation, flood-control, beach erosion prevention, and shore-protection projects.

This is a field in which North Carolina has lagged for years. For example, the current Public Works appropriation for civil functions totals $786,772,448, while funds for North Carolina amount to only $4,059,141. A primary reason for the lag has been the fact that nowhere did the state assign a clear-cut responsibility for assisting local interests with the complex, extended procedures required to obtain federal assistance. Just how difficult this process can be is no secret to you who have worked so long and so hard on the Wilkesboro Reservior project. Now, with the responsibility at the state level clearly assigned and in experienced hands, I am confident that North Carolina will make the best of future opportunities.

To meet the other requirement of the law establishing the Department of Water Resources, the Division of Stream Sanitation and Hydrology was established. It consists of the former Division of Water Pollution Control of the State Board of Health, and the former Division of Water Resources, Inlets, and Coastal Waterways of the Department of Conservation and Development. This division acts as administrative agent for the State Stream Sanitation Committee, the policy-making body for the state-wide antipollution program. It also administers the cooperative state-federal geological survey surface-water study and the state irrigation permit law, functions formerly assigned to the Department of Conservation and Development.

The Department of Water Resources Act also gave the board authority to establish other divisions. Under this authority a Division of Ground Water was established so that action in the entire wide range of water resource responsibility and management could be initiated. I shall not dwell on the significance of this step, except to point out that (1) approximately 70 per cent of the people of this state depend on wells as a source of water supply and more than half our municipalities get water from underground, and (2) our ground water supply, geologists tell us, is far greater than the total of all our surface sources combined.

It is, therefore, imperative that we learn all we can about the underground supply of water, because a lack of detailed knowledge has prevented the best development and utilization of this vast resource in the past. It is the intention of the new department to rectify this deficiency as rapidly as possible. The Ground Water Division is assigned the responsibility of planning, organizing, and directing a statewide program of ground water development and conservation, including comprehensive geological and quality studies of ground water, its existence, available quantity, and its quality. The division will work directly with officials of federal, state, and local government agencies, farm organizations, industries, and their consulting engineers relative to ground water problems.

Let me emphasize at this point that the department looks to its Ground Water Division to furnish direct assistance to municipalities, industries, agriculture, and others who are faced with, or anticipate, ground water problems. It is expected to arrange for any ground water studies that may be required. Already it has begun providing consultative services.

Because of your interest in water resource development in this area—and because you recognize its state-wide significance—I think you will be interested in the status of current programs in which the department is actively participating.

The Division of Navigable Waterways is furnishing liaison assistance in connection with several civil-works projects of the Corps of Engineers that are scheduled for this fiscal year. One of these is, of course, your own project here on the Yadkin River. It was most welcome news to me when Congress included in the current appropriation an initial construction fund of $910,000 for the project. I was also delighted to learn recently that the engineers have made plans to begin acquiring land—plans that will be instigated as soon as a favorable vote is registered in the upcoming referendum.

Another project of general interest is the proposed joint state-federal engineering study to determine the best methods to rehabilitate and preserve that portion of the Outer Banks extending from Ocracoke Inlet to Cape Lookout. Through the efforts of the Department of Water Resources, this study is expected to begin during this fiscal year. The cost, an estimated $130,000, will be shared equally by the state and federal governments. Other studies in this area, expected to cost approximately $65,000, will be made under the provision of existing federal statutes and will be wholly financed by the federal government. The latter studies will be of great value in the planning of shore protective works.

Another project is the deepening of the Morehead City Harbor to thirty-five feet. Approximately $600,000 has been appropriated by Congress for this work.

Others are continuing studies of the Cape Fear River Basin, the Neuse River Basin, and the Pantego and Cucklers Creek project.

Another duty the department performs, through its Division of Navigable Waterways, was given to it by another important piece of water legislation adopted by the 1959 General Assembly. This law is the enabling legislation to permit North Carolinians to obtain the benefits of the provisions of Public Law 566, Eighty-Third Congress, known as the small watershed protection program. It is administered by the Soil Conservation Service, U. S. Department of Agriculture.

In adopting the enabling act, the General Assembly assigned the Water Resources Department the responsibility of reviewing all watershed work plans submitted by small watershed improvement districts.

North Carolina has made amazing progress in this program, which farm and water experts consider to be of far-reaching significance in our efforts to manage and develop our water resources.

In North Carolina, forty-two applications for small watershed projects, involving flood control, drainage, or a combination of the two features, have been submitted. The area involved in the needed protection is 2,225,000 acres.

Twenty-six of these projects have received priority recommendations; seventeen have been approved for planning; and eleven are in operation.

I am informed that North Carolina ranks third in the nation in the number of projects in operation, preceded only by Texas with twenty and Georgia with twelve. It is pleasing to know that interest in the program is continually increasing from one end of the state to the other.

Cooperative ground-water studies, which the Department of Conservation and Development, through its Division of Mineral Resources, entered upon with U. S. Geological Survey, now are the responsibility of the Department of Water Resources.

The studies are being conducted in three areas. They consist of reconnaissance geological and hydrological studies in eleven counties, one group of which includes Wilkes County, along with Ashe, Alleghany, Surry, and Yadkin.

Similar studies for five other areas, covering twenty counties, have been completed, and the results are scheduled for publication during this year.

In addition to the cooperative studies, the department is conducting a joint study with the U. S. Geological Survey to determine if an adequate supply of potable ground water is available in the vicinity of Ocracoke Village.

North Carolina's statewide anti-pollution program is in the hands of the department's Division of Stream Sanitation and Hydrology. This work is of great significance to all of us because of the rapidly growing requirements of individuals, municipalities, agriculture, industry, wildlife, and recreation interests for clean water.

One of the most promising ways through which we may have all the clean water we will need is to make the water unsable over and over again. When one of us makes use of it, he can pass it along downstream, after proper treatment, in such condition that it can serve the next man, and so on.

I should like to take this opportunity at this point to congratulate the Division of Stream Sanitation and Hydrology for its part in the recently settled Roanoke River Controversy. The division and the State Stream Sanitation Committee, in common with other groups, was concerned over the harmful effects on downstream water quality which they felt would result from the operation of a proposed hydroelectric project. The result of the protracted negotiations serves as a crystal-clear demonstration of North Carolina's determination that the interests of all water users shall be considered and protected in the development and use of our water resources.

The program has made excellent progress during the approximately eight years it has been in operation. Studies have been completed in fourteen of the state's sixteen major river basins; the area covered comprises 98 per cent of the total area of the state. "Best usage" classifications, on which the efforts for pollution control and abatement are based, have been assigned to the waters of seven river basins comprising 66 per cent of the state. It is anticipated that all the streams of the state will have been classified by the end of 1962.

During the period 134 waste treatment projects, costing approximately $42,000,000, have been either completed or placed under construction; twelve additional projects, estimated to cost $12,000,000, have been approved for construction. Active planning is currently underway in connection with some seventy-five other projects throughout the state; applications for federal grants under the federal water pollution control act have been filed by eighty-two municipalities, and forty-seven of these have been approved for grants totaling $3,751,000, covering projects costing $25,000,000. There are thirty-four applications requesting grants totaling $4,365,526, covering projects having a total estimated cost of $25,000,000, awaiting grant funds.

Please note that the bulk of the money spent, or to be spent, comes from local sources—from municipalities and industries. The program exemplifies in a fine way the fact that North Carolinians, given an understanding of their needs and responsibilities, and the methods by which they can meet them, are willing to reach into their pockets to finance sound, demonstrated needs for progress.

And it will take a continued great effort on the part of everyone to keep pace in the anti-pollution program. Oddly, one of the best ways to measure a people's progress is the amount and complexity of the wastes they dump into their streams. Let me tell you that North Carolina, growing rapidly in population and modern industry, is counting on its streams to carry a tremendous load of wastes.

The Division of Stream Sanitation and Hydrology estimates that it will take $200,000,000 in the next ten years to preserve our streams as valuable assets and to prevent their becoming open sewers, unfit for any other use.

The division also tells me, however, that almost without exception our people and industries are willing to do the job.

The division also is responsible for the surface-water studies conducted cooperatively by the state and the U. S. Geological Survey. Approximately 135 permanent gauging stations keep continuous records of stream flow, and partial records are kept at more than 200 additional sites. A state-wide concentrated study of low flows is in progress as an aid to the development of municipal and industrial supplies and waste treatment. In the water-quality program, daily samples are collected for chemical and physical analyses from fourteen sampling stations. Samples for these purposes are also collected from approximately 400 miscellaneous sampling stations. In addition, a study of the degree to which salt-water intrusion is affecting our coastal streams is being conducted.

There, briefly and in highlight form, is the North Carolina water story today—where we stand, where we should go and where we intend to go.

Our newest state agency, the Department of Water Resources, is off to a good start. But in the months and years ahead, it will need the support and assistance of many other agencies, and of the people, if North Carolina is to meet its water needs and solve its problems. Immediate measures are being taken, of course, but we should remember that many of our problems have been a long time accumulating and it will take time to work them out.

Let me emphasize, as I have many times before, that the job we need to cannot be done entirely in Raleigh, nor by those of us in the government service in Raleigh alone. Local leadership and local initiative, with the state providing assistance and basic information, must play a major part if we North Carolinians are to make the most of our water resources.

I am sure that you and the other people of the Upper Yadkin Valley know and understand this principle, because you have lived and worked by it in your efforts to make the Wilkesboro Reservoir a reality.

A particular point of interest in your project is the fact that you are striking out into a new field—you are doing some pioneering of your own.

With the Wilkesboro Reservoir you are seeking not only the benefit of flood control, but also the benefit of drought control, by making the reservoir capacity large enough to store water in time of plenty to be available for improving the river flow in the dry season. You are setting an example that other Tar Heels in other river basins will do well to follow.

The potential is tremendous. Flood control will open up excellent space, now subject to flooding, for industrial development and other uses. The improved river flow will mean more certain water supplies for future needs. It will lessen the problem of pollution abatement. The reservoir will contribute to fish and wildlife conservation and increase recreation opportunities for you and visitors who will come to your area in larger numbers.

As much as you have done, one more challenge remains—providing the funds to pay for the drought-control feature of the project. I understand that plans for referenda in the area on the question are in the making.

Far from being discouraged by the continued effort you are called upon to make, I hope you will look on this not as an impossible obstacle, but rather as an opportunity to demonstrate, again, your faith in your future. I trust you will retain the strength of vision you showed in accepting the challenge at the start.

For spending of this sort is an investment in the future—an investment which, I am sure I hardly need say, will mean immense returns.

You have an unparalleled opportunity to do something for your area—to realize the promise of the great resource of water you have; to insure progress and growth for everyone who is fortunate enough to live in the Upper Yadkin Valley.

It is also an opportunity for you to blaze a trail in water-resource development in North Carolina; to set an example of seizing the opportunity for progress for which much of the rest of North Carolina can thank you in days to come.

Thank you for the privilege of being with you!

ADDRESS AT THE EIGHTH ANNUAL REGIONAL CONFERENCE OF THE ALABAMA COUNCIL, NATIONAL MANAGEMENT ASSOCIATION CLUBS

BIRMINGHAM, ALABAMA
March 12, 1960

[Governor Hodges was a frequent speaker on what industry expects, or has a right to expect, from government. On this occasion he reversed the question and spoke on what government expects of industry. Portions of the address were drawn from other speeches made by the Governor along this line. Dan A. Kimball, former Secretary of the Navy, and Robert F. Kennedy, a future Attorney General of the United States, shared the platform with Governor Hodges on this occasion.]

It is a wonderful experience to have the opportunity of participating in an event such as this—an event that clearly demonstrates the enthusiasm for the future and confident attitude toward continued progress throughout our great southern region. The Alabama Council of National Management Association Clubs is certainly to be commended on this conference, which in the past eight years has made a significant contribution to the economic well-being of this state and its people.

Three and one-half decades ago the National Management Association—known at that time as the National Association of

Foremen—was founded. It was founded on the unselfish principle that cooperation—the sharing of accumulated knowledge and ideas by management personnel—would greatly benefit not only the individual companies involved, but the individual states and the nation as well. That this principle was a sound one is evident in the fact that the association now boasts more than 72,000 members—joined together by mutual interests and a mutual desire to make a contribution to economic progress. If more evidence is needed to prove the value of such a program, that evidence is certainly apparent here in Birmingham this afternoon. It is demonstrated by the fact that you have taken time away from your businesses to attend this conference. And, it is apparent in the fact that you have chosen for your theme the all-important and ever-present need for a better and stronger working relationship between government and industry.

Because of my experience in both industry and government, this is a subject that holds great interest for me, and I am indebted to the sponsors of this conference for the privilege to taking part in this event. Might I add that my pleasure at being here is heightened by the opportunity to appear on the program with the former Secretary of the Navy, Mr. Kimball, and Mr. Robert Kennedy—two outstanding Americans whose presence adds stature to any gathering.

I have been asked to talk with you this afternoon on what government expects of industry. The answer can be very simple or it can be amazingly complicated. I could tell you that government expects industry to cooperate in its plans for building a better way of life for the people of a community, a state, or the nation. But this would seem to imply that the responsibility for initiating such plans rest exclusively with government—and this, most certainly, is not the case. Or, I could discuss with you the detailed mechanics of the industry-government relationship, but this, I fear, would take us too far from the spirit of the relationship, which is vitally important. I would prefer, therefore, to discuss the cooperative spirit, which is absolutely essential to an effective relationship, and the practical application of that spirit, which produces concrete and mutually beneficial results.

First, I believe it is important that we acknowledge the obvious fact that industry is no different from any other segment of the economy—commerce, or education, for example—in that it is only one segment of the economy. Industry is only one element, an essential element like any other, but nevertheless, only one element of its own society, of its own government. As such, what the industrial element of society expects of itself is what is expected of industry by government.

In other words, its own society expects of any of its elements that it be a good neighbor—that it accept and exercise social responsibility. This is trite, to be sure, but, I think we must all agree, it is fundamental. Government expects industry to be nothing more and nothing less than a good neighbor, but that's a lot!

And being a good neighbor is not only what society or government expects of each of its elements and is not only what industry as a group expects of itself, but also—and this is most practical—is what each individual unit of industry expects or should expect of itself. If an industry can live honestly and openly with itself, it can live honestly and openly in its society. This is why we in North Carolina have, during recent years of phenomenal industrial growth, stated openly and often that we do not want just any industry. In New York, Chicago, Philadelphia and, more recently, in Europe, I have, with the full support of our people, told groups of potential industrial investors that North Carolina wants only those industries that are prepared to meet fully their responsibilities as corporate citizens. This stand has been applauded by our established industries, and it has brought many reputable companies into our industrial family.

Being a good neighbor has many aspects—aspects of not doing things having adverse effects and aspects of doing things having beneficial effects. All aspects are exceedingly important.

The physical appearance aspects of being a good neighbor—neatness, attractiveness, good plant design—are apparent to each of you and their principles need not be discussed in detail. I will, however, mention one detailed application of these principles which seems both significant and interesting to me—the development and use of good neighbor performance standards in industrial zoning.

It is easy to say that an industry should be a good neighbor, speaking in physical effect terms, to adjoining properties. It is very encouraging to learn that industry actually has taken the lead in helping to develop standards that will accomplish this aim. The National Industrial Zoning Committee, composed to a major degree of representatives of industrial groups, has, in the last several years, been the motivating force in developing concepts of sound industrial zoning.

These concepts came to my attention most recently in Wake County, North Carolina, where our capital city of Raleigh is located. Here, in a county historically rural but now being subjected to the forces of suburbanization, local industrial leaders and local government officials have cooperated in the development of zoning performance standards for industry, standards that spell out in advance the standards of construction and operation under which any new industry will be expected to operate, standards that insure profitable conditions of operation to industry and sound measures of protection to adjoining properties whether industrial, commercial, residential, or whatever.

These standards are important in themselves and it is important that industry is willing and, in many instances, eager to accept them. The significant point now, however, is that local industrial developers and local governmental leaders were willing and able to cooperate in the development of the standards. This is good corporate citizenship. This is what government expects of industry.

We, in North Carolina, have been fortunate to have in our leadership Mr. Pearson Stewart, a highly capable and dedicated professional planner, who has helped us get started properly. We hope to accomplish much in our future planning activities.

May I note, parenthetically, that we in the state government in North Carolina took the initiative a few years ago in modernizing our state's tax structure to give industry more equitable treatment. Our old allocation formula was comparatively harsh and drastic and had placed us in a position of having to tax unfairly businesses which operate in more than one state. Industry was clearly paying a disproportionately high share of the taxes. We put this proposition to our legislature, which is rural dominated, and tax revision passed by an overwhelming vote—placing North Carolina on a competitive footing with other states while benefiting existing industry with a reduction in corporate taxes. We estimated our corporate tax reduction would cut our revenues

$14,000,000 but we did it because it was right. Government expects certain things of industry, to be sure, but government must never forget its own responsibility.

One aspect of being a good neighbor that should be of particullar concern to all of us—in both industry and government—is the effect of industrialization on our environment. Industrialization is essentially an urban influence. Even if a plant is located in a completely rural area, its effects are to a certain extent urban. Even if only one plant is in a given rural area and all its workers commute from homes way back in the countryside, even so, the problem of traffic concentration occurs and is part of the urban problem. Groups of industries in particular areas increase the urban influences of industry and increase the urban problems.

These urban problems need not be problems; they can just as well be opportunities. However, the urban effects of industrialization can be problems with disastrous results very easily. These results need not materialize if all of us, industry as well as government, take the initiative in planning ahead to insure that the problems are opportunities in disguise.

Provision must be made for proper zoning, proper subdivision control, proper reservation of public open spaces, proper local governmental foresight to insure that there is capital budgeting for local governmental capital needs. Provisions must be made to prevent scattered urban development without utilities, without coherence, without good design, from preventing appropriate development of the countryside. This is a comparatively new problem for us here in the South where industrialization on a grand scale has developed only in recent years. Fortunately, we are in a position to benefit from the experiences of others in this situation, and we have recognized the problem early enough to do something about it.

Essentially, these tasks are the responsibility of local government. These are the responsibilities of the entire community, not just one segment of society. But while industry is but one segment of society, it is a part of the whole and has its responsibility to act.

I submit that industry, being to a degree responsible for causing urbanization, has a responsibility to help guide urbanization. This is a responsibility which industry cannot carry out by itself. It can, however, with its prestige, encourage local governments to act, to do things, to adopt required ordinances, to provide open space. I realize full well that industry does not want, and should not be able to dictate actions to local governments. However, industry is a part of the community and as such has a responsibility to speak up.

We all realize that appropriate guidance of the tremendous forces of urbanization that are ahead of us will result in a great asset for industry itself. An attractive community in which to live and play is a sound community in which to have an industry. We all know that there is financial stability in being in an urban environment that is soundly managed and is a good place in which to live.

To my way of thinking, being a good neighbor very definitely includes the concept of growth. We expect our neighbor's children not only to be good neighbors and not trample our daffodils, but also to grow up and, if appropriate, to marry our children. Similarly with industry. We in government very definitely and strongly expect industry to do what it should do in normal processes of industrial life—grow, expand, and use available resources.

We expect industry, of course, to utilize the appropriate facilities and resources local to it—labor, natural resources, land, water, power. We expect industry to be an integral part of the economy. This is only natural. In addition, however, we expect industry to add to the local economy through the normal processes of being aggressively competitive within the appropriate industry. We expect industry, by this process, to add to the local economy, to raise it no matter at how high a level it my be. We expect industry to marry our daughter.

Specifically, industry should at all times demonstrate its good corporate citizenship by treating its workers fairly, by paying fair wages, and by endeavoring to develop leadership capability and fairness among foremen and other supervisors. In this way you inculcate the spirit of free enterprise, not only in the workers themselves, but in all who come into contact with your operation. Most of you, I am sure, are also aware of the fact that fair treatment of workers is good business. And, government expects the industrial neighbor to do everything possible to develop a successful and profitable business. This is not only to insure a sound economy and to provide government at all levels with the maximum tax resources needed to provide services for its citizens, but to strengthen the free enterprise system which is part and parcel of the success of America. Every industry in this country has a sacred responsibility to make the free enterprise system work. Each successful industrial establishment adds strength to the nation.

We must realize that our nation is engaged in a life or death struggle and that each of us will have a hand in determining the final outcome of that struggle.

Make no mistake about the fact that our industry faces a very real threat in the form of competition from the Soviet Union and other nations in world trade. In the company of eight other American governors, I made an extensive tour of the Soviet this past summer and it was all too apparent that the Communists are fashioning an economic weapon of awesome proportions to use against us. And, I have no doubt that they will use it viciously and efficiently in an effort to prove their contention that free enterprise cannot compete, cannot survive in the face of socialist productivity. This is a great challenge to both industry and government in every community of every state in this nation—a challenge that imposes on both these elements of our society tremendous responsibilities—a challenge that can only be met by closer cooperation between industry and government than we have ever known before. Certainly, it is a challenge that should draw us closer together. It not only should; it must. This is a matter in which we have no choice.

This is why government expects industry to be willing to grow and develop, to work closer with government at all levels and to make the most beneficial use of all available local resources. I am proud of the progress we have made in North Carolina toward the achievement of this objective. North Carolina industry has accepted the proposition that science is a key element in today's industrialization. I do not cite this as an unusual proposition but as one that has been firmly accepted in my own state.

The development of the resources of science is something that cannot possibly be done by sitting still. The very nature of science means that it must be constantly moving ahead. To promote this development, to increase the resource of science, North Carolina industry in large part has sponsored the Research Triangle of North Carolina, an effort dedicated to the proposition that a center of science is one prime requirement for the further growth and economic health of industry in North Carolina, both present and future. It is a prime example of industry-government cooperation.

The support of the Research Triangle by industry—contributions by industry and business of over $1,500,000 to the Triangle Foundation—is, I submit, an excellent example of industry wanting to grow and develop by the appropriate use of local facilities through its own efforts. North Carolina industry looks on the Research Triangle as one additional way it can grow, improve, compete, change as appropriate through the development of a major center of research to provide the resource of science for industry.

We believe that the development of an industrial research center will be speeded by catalytic action—or that the inevitable can be hastened. The catalytic action has taken the form of the establishment by North Carolinians of the Research Triangle Foundation. It is a superb example of local action to use local opportunities and resources, of willingness to use one's own resources—time, effort, money—in working toward a desired and mutually beneficial goal.

It was with a view of securing the cooperation of the various groups and individuals—the three universities (University of North Carolina, State College and Duke University), the three cities, the three counties, and a wide assortment of public and private groups—and of undertaking an active program of development that the private, non-profit Research Triangle Committee was formed in 1955. The late Robert M. Hanes of Winston-Salem was elected president of the committee. In 1959 the committee was expanded from twelve to twenty-five members, and its name changed to the Research Triangle Foundation of North Carolina.

The foundation is a non-profit organization whose purpose is to encourage the development and use of the research resources of the Triangle area. The foundation works within the bounds and desires of the three educational institutions. It was this group, composed of business, industrial, and educational leaders that raised the $1,500,000 in private funds to support the Research Park and the Research Triangle Institute—a corporation organized for the purpose of establishing and operating facilities for research in the physical, biological, medical, mathematical, agricultural, economic, and engineering sciences, and the contracting for the conduct of investigation and research in such sciences.

The institute will be somewhat similar to the Southern Research Institute here in Birmingham and the Southwestern Research Institute at San Antonio, Texas. It is building upon existing research strengths in the three universities and, while a separate organization, its policies are in large part determined by the three institutions so that research activities can be complementary, rather than competitive.

Established in January of last year, the institute to date has operating sections in statistics, operational science, and the industrial use of radioisotopes. In addition, it has received a $2,500,000 grant from the Dreyfus Foundation which grant will enable the institute to build and develop a world center of polymer research.

The foundation has a wholly owned subsidiary, the Research Triangle Park, a 4,600 acre campus in the center of the Triangle area, for the location of industrial and governmental research facilities which already has several research outfits.

The park is being developed in accordance with accepted principles of controlled and planned development. The site has been planned, prior to development. Utilities are being installed and roads constructed. Provisions are in force for continuing management. Restrictions and zoning providing for performance standards to insure good neighbor type of occupancy are in effect.

The foundation officials, park officials, and local government leaders in the Triangle area realize that the urban effects of the park will be far reaching. Partly to guide urban development immediately outside the park and partly to help themselves solve all the other urban problems that the park will create, the three cities and three counties involved have joined in the establishment of a planning commission. This commission, established by the General

Assembly, has the responsibility of recommending action to the component local governments. It is not a form of metropolitan government; it is, in effect, a local recognition of the need for governmental action and a willingness to accept that responsibility. In addition, Triangle legislators joined with others from all parts of North Carolina last spring to give our cities greatly improved annexation and planning powers to control the forthcoming urbanization.

These are some of the immediate tangible results of the Research Triangle effort—results of North Carolina's industry-government cooperation in insuring the most beneficial use of local facilities and resources.

We believe that the development of this additional and outstanding research center is in keeping with what government expects of industry, and I might add that in North Carolina the fact that we have the Research Triangle helps in the size and quality of our industrial expansion.

Another responsibility that industry and government share is that of leadership. Industrial leaders must, if the maximum benefits are to be obtained from this relationship, take a larger part in government. As individuals, you must not be hesitant about seeking public office—especially in the area in which your plant is located. You can make a real contribution to your community by serving on its governing bodies and you will, at the same time, find that in serving the community you better serve your own interest. You will also find, as I have, that it can be a most gratifying experience.

May I conclude by saying that government expects industry to be actively interested in all government-sponsored programs designed to promote the general welfare. These programs need not affect your operation directly—as would be the case in a water resources or stream sanitation program—to merit your active interest and participation. As a good neighbor, as a good corporate citizen you have a very definite obligation to contribute whatever you can.

It has been a real pleasure to meet with you here today, and I would like to express my sincere appreciation for your kind attention. The future is unlimited for our great nation if we are willing to work together for what is best and right for the majority of our people. We can and will build better communities, better states, and a better nation if we will base our action on the fundamental principles which guided our forefathers in the establishment of this country. We face a great challenge, but it is a challenge that can and must be answered. If we will but meet our responsibilities as individuals and as members of a free society, we have nothing to fear.

Thank you.

ADDRESS AT A LUNCHEON MEETING PRIOR TO THE DEDICATION OF THE UNIVERSITY OF NORTH CAROLINA COMPUTATION CENTER

CHAPEL HILL
March 30, 1960

[Representatives of the state government, the Consolidated University, the United States Bureau of the Census, the National Science Foundation, and the Sperry Rand Corporation were in Chapel Hill on this occasion to dedicate a $2,400,000 Univac computor, which had just been installed at the University of North Carolina and was scheduled to be used, along with similar instruments in Illinois and Washington, to compute statistics gathered in the 1960 Census. Governor Hodges traced an eight-year chain of events which resulted in the University's establishment of the new Computation Center and stressed the significance of the facility in relation to other research activities in the state, notably the North Carolina Research Triangle.]

I would like to thank President Friday for his very kind remarks and for the invitation to join you here today for an event that must certainly be regarded as a milestone in the history of this university and this state. I would like very much to think that my contribution to the establishment of this center has been as significant as President Friday intimates, but I would prefer that the full credit go to those far more deserving than I; namely, those dedicated individuals in the University, in the federal government, and in private industry who have worked so diligently for almost a decade to bring about the realization of this dream.

We are honored to have with us today many of the principal

officers of the three fine organizations which have joined with the University and the state in making this computation center a reality. On behalf of all the people of this state, it is a pleasure to welcome Dr. Robert W. Burgess and his associates from the Bureau of the Census, Dr. Allen T. Waterman and other representatives of the National Science Foundation, and Vice President J. W. Schnackel and his very distinguished delegation from the Remington Rand Corporation. I want all of you to know that we are genuinely grateful for the part you have each played in the establishment of this wonderful facility here on our University campus. The close coperation between all parties involved has been gratifying and I am certain that this center will long stand as a striking example of what can be accomplished in the public interest when dedicated men work together to achieve a mutually beneficial objective. We like to feel that this is the North Carolina way.

The story behind the Computation Center reaches back over eight years. It has its beginning during the administration of former University President Gordon Gray, at which time the initial conference was held—inspired by a memorandum written by Dr. William M. Whyburn, then head of the Mathematics Department, to Chancellor House. I am told that Dr. Whyburn's decision to investigate the possibility of obtaining an electronic computer was prompted by his inability to get budgetary approval of a request for a desk calculator. If this be the case, then I want to congratulate the doctor on the greatest comeback in the history of mankind. I might also suggest that he be turned down more often in his initial budget requests in the future if he is to produce such results.

During the intervening years there have been many conferences on the University campuses, here, in Raleigh and in Greensboro, meetings with the executives of Remington Rand, discussions with the senior officials of the National Science Foundation and the Bureau of the Census, appearances before Congressional delegations, discussions with state officials and agencies—all leading to this eventful day and these ceremonies to dedicate a Computation Center that ranks with the finest in the nation. In the conferences early in 1952 with Chancellor House, President Gray, and Dr. Whyburn, it was agreed that the faculty of our institutions should be canvassed to determine the nature and extent of our needs for computer services. In the spring of that year the first effort was made to obtain a logistics computer, but the lead proved unfruitful. During the interval between 1952 and 1955, a number of developments occurred to keep the flame of hope alive, but very little of a tangible nature was achieved. Early in 1955, the Bureau of the Census expressed an interest in cooperating with the University in efforts to secure a large computer. Several faculty conferences were held, resulting in a cooperative effort among our campuses to obtain a large scale computation center.

In December, 1956, the administrative officials of the University met with officials of Remington Rand in New York City for further discussions. Following this meeting, there were many conferences with Remington representatives and officials of the Bureau of the Census. On July 16, 1957, company and bureau officials met with representatives from the University, the Research Triangle, and state government. A proposal for a modern computation center was outlined. The type of installation proposed, together with accessories assembled for work that would be done by the Census Bureau, was priced at $2,400,000.

Remington Rand indicated a generous 50 per cent discount for an educational installation. Since it had been determined that we would seek a machine that would duplicate the equipment provided for the Bureau of the Census, the bureau indicated its willingness to contract in advance for services on the machine. The value of this advance service commitment was estimated in the range of $600,000 to $750,000. A proposal had been filed by the University with the National Science Foundation in the fall of 1956 requesting financial assistance on this project, including $500,000 toward the provision of this installation. This request was included in the appropriations request submitted by the foundation to Congress. Initially, Congress eliminated all requests made by the foundation, but later some appropriations were allowed and the $500,000 was made available to the University.

With resources available to purchase the equipment it became necessary to seek additional funds from the state to house this installation. University officials appeared before the Advisory Budget

Commission and the Department of Administration to explain the great potentialities held by the Computation Center for the University and the Research Triangle. Needless to say, the funds were made available to provide facilities for the adequate and proper housing of the center. Thus, on September 1, 1959, the Computation Center began operation. In this center, the University has one of the finest research facilities in the United States. Its director, Dr. John W. Carr, is recognized as a national and international authority in this field. Already, in the short time he has been here, he has brought to this campus some of the most distinguished scientists in the world for conferences and discussions on the rapidly advancing frontier of electronic computation. I make this point to illustrate our pleasure in having Dr. Carr with us to direct the development of this facility to its maximum potential, and to make it perfectly clear to all of you who have invested so heavily in this undertaking that we in North Carolina intend to move toward the development of that potential with utmost dispatch.

Frequently, after so long a struggle, the final realization of an elusive goal is anticlimatic. Let me assure you that such is not the case in this instance. It is not the case because the achievements we celebrate today are not the end, but the beginning. In eight years we have done little more than lay the ground work. Now, we must get on with the job. We must face up the challenging responsibility that this center imposes upon each of us—the responsibility of capitalizing on what has been accomplished. We are here today to dedicate, not a machine but an opportunity—an opportunity to move ahead faster, to dream bigger dreams, to become more efficient in pursuit of the one basic objective we all share—that of preserving our free way of life and making that life more abundant for ourselves, for our families, our friends and neighbors, and the generation of Americans that will follow us.

Some will probably think that I am being presumptuous when I draw an analogy between this facility and the preservation of our national freedom. Nevertheless, I believe the analogy to be a valid one. The free enterprise system, the basis of our freedom, is being seriously challenged today by extremely clever forces dedicated to our destruction. Believe me, it is a very real threat to our existence, one that must not, cannot be taken lightly if we are to survive.

As educators, industrialists, and individuals directly concerned with national security, most of you are, I am sure, aware of this threat. Most of you must also be aware of the obvious fact that our most effective weapon in combating this threat is efficiency— efficiency in education, efficiency in the conduct of our government at all levels, and efficiency in business and industry. In the past we have been content with the knowledge that we were the most efficient nation in the world—and, until recently, this contentment was perhaps justified. Now, things have changed. It has been dramatically proven to us that we can no longer afford the luxury of complacency. Our efficiency has been effectively challenged. We are, at the present moment, fighting an economic war—and make no mistake about the fact that the issue is in doubt. We could lose. We could lose everything—our national dignity, our freedom, our nation itself—without a bullet being fired, without a drop of blood being shed.

The greatest weapon we possess in this economic war is our traditional efficiency. It must now be mobilized as never before. Our educational sytem, our industry, our government must be brought to a peak of efficiency that will enable it to withstand the forces that are being set against this nation. Fortunately, we can accomplish this objective without sacrificing our dream of a more prosperous America in the years ahead. The efficiency that can keep us free can also work for the betterment of our people. That this is possible is evident in the occasion that has brought us here today. We are here to dedicate a symbol of efficiency—a product of our free enterprise system, established through the cooperative effort of educators, industrialists, and government representatives, designed and planned to benefit education, industry, and government. If we are to preserve our economic system we must all (managers, labor, educational institutions) join hands to make it productive, make it work!

I am, of course, particularly concerned with what this installation will mean to the University and the state of North Carolina. Certainly, the possibilities are enormous. The contribution that this center will make to the Research Triangle alone is so great that it actually defies appraisal. We have already seen tremendous interest shown in the center by officials of the research facilities that have come into the Triangle, or have shown interest in locating there. They are eager to take advantage of the potential that is here, and we have a responsibility to see that their requirements are met.

This type of cooperative relationship will work to the advantage of all concerned. It will benefit the researchers themselves by making their operations more efficient and less costly. It will benefit the University by providing experience for computer personnel, by providing needed income for expanded programs, and by insuring a work load commensurate with the capacity of this installation to perform. It will benefit the people of this state by attracting new industries and new research facilities to this area to take advantage of the center. And, it will focus attention on North Carolina and enhance our established reputation as a progressive state. May I say to all of you from without the state that this university will furnish the leadership and the spirit to make all these things come true!

I understand that even with the fantastic amount of work that will be done here by the Bureau of the Census it is not expected that the maximum capacity of this center will be reached for a number of years. This fact in itself is indicative of the tremendous opportunities opened to us by this facility. Might I also say at this point that we are proud of the part it will be our privilege to play in the Census Bureau's activities in the years to come. The computer system here, along with similar installations at the Armour Research Foundation of the Illinois Institute of Technology and at the Bureau headquarters in Washington will have the distinction of processing a major portion of the data collected during the 1960 census. This will reduce most significantly the time lag between the collection of census information and its publication. It is estimated that some information in previous censuses that have not been available for three or four years will now be ready for distribution by the end of this year. When we consider the vital importance of census information and the advantage of having that information at the earliest possible date, we have ample reason to be proud of the work that will be done in this center. This is a good example of the efficiency I men-

Governor Hodges receiving a distinguished salesman award from Micou Brown, president of the Raleigh Sales Executives Club, in Raleigh, April 5, 1960.

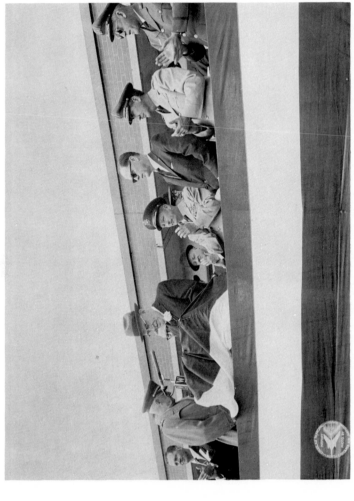

Left to right: Virgil Evans, Adjutant General Capus Waynick, Congressman Charles R. Jonas, Governor Hodges, State Senator J. Spencer Bell, Colonel William J. Payne, Mayor James S. Smith, Colonel Hook, and Colonel Battison at dedication of Air National Guard Operations and Training Building in Charlotte, April 10, 1960.

tioned earlier—the efficiency that will keep this nation strong and free.

This computation center is a symbol of progress—progress of the type that we in North Carolina have been greatly concerned with in recent years. We have dedicated many monuments to that progress—new schools, new manufacturing plants, super highways, housing developments, greater efficiency in government, unique cultural attractions, expanded recreational facilities, et cetera. These are all very tangible and very important evidences of the fact that we are moving ahead as a state. It may be that many of our people, accustomed to the more tangible evidences of advancement will have some difficulty in comprehending the full significance of the event we celebrate here today. For those who have reservations about the importance of this day, let me offer the assurance that this computation center has the potential for producing benefits comparable, if not exceeding, those of the more conventional manifestations of progress. I am convinced that this computation center will, at least indirectly make a tremendous contribution to the economy of our state. It will produce, in time, new factories, new jobs, new opportunities and, above all, new knowledge that will enable us to take greater advantage of our vast reservoir of human and natural resources.

May I conclude by saying again that I am honored to have been is a position to make a small contribution to this undertaking, for I am sincere in the belief that this will be remembered as a day of great significance in the history of our state. It has been a privilege to work with officials of the Bureau of the Census, the National Science Foundation, and the Remington Rand Corporation. I know that President Friday and his colleagues within the University, along with officials of the Research Triangle, genuinely concur with me in this sentiment. We are not unaware of the responsibility you have vested in us in making it possible for us to have this computation center here in Chapel Hill. Let me assure you that your faith is well-founded. We in North Carolina shall do everything in our power to justify your confidence in us and to insure that maximum use is made of this facility to build a better state, a better, more secure nation, and a better way of life for our people.

Thank you!

ADDRESS AT GROUND-BREAKING CEREMONIES
FOR WILMINGTON COLLEGE

WILMINGTON COLLEGE CAMPUS
April 1, 1960

[Wilmington College was the outgrowth of one of a number of emergency institutions sponsored by the North Carolina College Conference and the State Department of Public Instruction to provide first-year instruction for returning veterans of World War II. Subsequently taken over by the city of Wilmington and made into a two-year college, the institution was breaking ground at this time for a new building to house its expanding activities. The occasion afforded an opportunity for Governor Hodges to elaborate and repeat a number of views which he held in regard to the place of community colleges in the state's program of higher education. Following the ceremonies, which occurred at eleven o'clock in the morning, the Governor flew across the state to address a dinner meeting of the Princeton Club of Western North Carolina at Asheville that evening.]

I can think of no more enjoyable and meaningful task than the one that confronts us here today. It has been my privilege in recent years to join citizens throughout our state in many events that indicate our progress as a people. We have ceremoniously broken ground for great new industries, new highways, scientific research facilities, hospitals, and many other large and small undertakings that dramatically illustrate North Carolina's surge toward a higher economic and cultural status in the nation and throughout the world. It has been a tremendous thrill to participate in these events, and I do not wish to minimize their significance, but I feel very strongly that this occasion today, symbolically at least, has a potential value far greater than that of a new industry or one of the other more tangible evidences of progress.

New developments in industry or agriculture or some other facet of the economy show that we are becoming more adept at developing and driving maximum benefit from our vast natural resources. The continual expansion of our educational facilities shows that we are moving forward in the development of our far more valuable human resources—and this, of course, is the important thing. To concentrate our energies on the development of our natural resources without giving as much or more attention to our human resources would be foolish and unrealistic, and wouldn't be in keeping with the spirit of North Carolina.

The challenge we face today has been imposed upon this generation of North Carolinians by unprecedented technological and scientific advances which threaten to overwhelm our intellectual capacities and to outrun our educational facilities. It is our responsibility at all levels to see that these facilities are made available. Fortunately you in Wilmington and New Hanover County have done something about it and are doing more. I heartily congratulate you!

Our State Department of Public Instruction recently published the results of a study made to determine what happens to our young people after graduation from high school. The answer was not encouraging. Last year 42,954 boys and girls graduated from our public schools. Only 14,420 or 33.5 per cent enrolled in college. Of this total 11,785 enrolled in senior colleges and 2,635 entered junior colleges. One North Carolina editor has surmised that the only consolation we can find in these figures is that the percentage of those going to college remained constant despite the fact that the number of graduates increased. Less than one-tenth of the young people who did not enter college chose to equip themselves for careers by attending trade schools, and less than 5 per cent entered the military service. This means that well over half of our young people last year terminated their education on the high school steps. This is disturbing in itself, but even more tragic—and certainly indicative of the challenge we face—is the fact that included among those who did not enter college were 25 per cent of the students who had distinguished themselves scholastically in high school.

All of you here will, I am sure, agree with me that this is a situation that must be remedied immediately. It is a travesty on North Carolina's great reputation as an education-minded state. It shows a lack of challenge to the students and a lack of real concern on the part of many parents.

This is not a totally new problem but it is one that has acquired new significance in recent years. A quarter-century ago we were not faced with the demand for maximum intellectual ability that we are faced with today. Our society was not confronted with the need to seek quick solutions to so many varied and complex problems nor were the problems of the past so full of tension and difficulty as now. In past decades there was not the sense of urgency that prevails in all our important activities today. A few of our people may have been concerned about the future, but mostly we lived from day to day. Education was a personal or family matter with little or no relationship to the over-all picture of economic and social progress in the state or world affairs. We chose the opportunities we would exploit largely on a basis of personal or collective convenience, and let the others go by the way. In the year 1960 we cannot afford the luxury of this kind of complacency. We must make the best of every opportunity, and to do so we must develop our intellectual potential to the limit. We must mobilize all our resources to meet this responsibility. We must do the job ourselves, as individuals, without waiting for someone else to take the initiative. The stakes are too high for us to gamble. We must set ourselves a goal, as you have done here in Wilmington, and when that goal is achieved, we must set another and another and another.

Education must become more than a word in North Carolina. It must become a vital part of our everday activities. I do not have to tell you that our thinking with regard to education is in a state of flux. Our nation has been shocked by thoughts that our educational system is not reaching goals which are both necessary and desirable. It has been shocked by rising unit costs in education and by the obvious fact that enrollments are increasing as fast as unit costs have risen. And in face of these concerns we now are beginning to suspect that there is a deficit in learning among our young men and women which, as reflected in the supply of teachers, will impede progress no matter how much money is made available by taxpayers, philanthropists, parents, and students.

This is a time for disciplined thinking about education. The rah-rah stage has been overplayed. The great English orator and statesman Edmund Burke said, two centuries ago, that "Education is the cheap defense of nations." His words were never truer than they are today.

The people of North Carolina are ready to move toward greater opportunity for their boys and girls and young men and women. But North Carolina is not yet a "rich" state. It is absolutely

necessary that every dollar for education be wisely spent and
that dollars for education actually be spent for education. We
should not kid ourselves by thinking that educational progress
can be made simply by throwing more dollars into the hopper, as
important as that may be. As I said at my press conference last
week in announcing private money grants for curriculum study,
the people will furnish the money at all levels if they get really
interested.

Years ago, there were ten-year public schools and four-year colleges. We then moved to eleven-year schools and four-year colleges;
and more recently to twelve-year schools and four-year colleges.
Sixteen years is a long time in the cherished years of youth.
But add to this the additional years required by the learned
professions. Then ask the question, "Have we not, by blind adherence to graded systems, given too much weight to progression
by age groups, rather than by talents and achievement?" Have we
not placed too much emphasis upon "going to college" and upon
"getting a degree" at the expense of dedication to learning? Have
we not, as suggested recently by the president of Grinnell College
in Iowa, tended to construct dormitories which are like "near-re-
plicas of a new Hilton Hotel?" Have we not assumed that luxury
is necessary for the educational process and by this assumption
tended to price education out of the market so far as taxpayers
and many parents and students are concerned? Have we not, to
some degree, forgotten why we establish educational institutions?

More and more the forward planners in education are realizing
that we have stretched out our education too far. Last week the
head of Columbia University said, "Four years is too long for a
college education," and beginning next year, Northwestern University will cut two years off the time needed for a degree in
medicine.

In the midst of all these questions, these doubts, these accomplishments, and this wrestling with educational problems of great
importance, the state has seen fit to give a vote of confidence to
community colleges and I am proud to have had a part in its beginning and in its further development. North Carolina does not
want these colleges to become thirteenth and fourteenth grades
in another stretch-out of the time required for its youth to obtain
an education. This would be a serious mistake in my humble

opinion. Nor does it expect these colleges to blossom forth as growing replicas of existing four-year colleges. Perhaps some of the community colleges may in time become degree-granting institutions. But that time is not at hand, and I would hope that all such institutions will bear in mind the following statement from the Board of Higher Education (a board which, by the way, has demonstrated its belief in the necessity for institutions of this type.)

"Any future movement of an institution from the community college level to the four-year level should be preceded by an unmistakable attainment of institutional stature in instructional effort in the fundamental liberal arts and sciences at the freshman and sophomore level, and by an unmistakable demand from a significant number of highly qualified students for the advanced studies which are involved in this step."

This is a realistic approach, based on the knowledge that the present demand is for freshman and sophomore courses. A study by the board shows more than twice the demand at the so-called "general college" level than at the level comparable to junior and senior instruction. The study also reveals that the peak load is now, and will probably continue for a long time at the freshman and sophomore level. And, of course, you know that the heavy "drop-out" of students at the universities and colleges occurs in the first two years.

So here, at Wilmington College, you have the opportunity to provide, at comparatively low cost to all concerned, just as effective instruction as can be found anywhere. And, as you move forward in pursuit of this goal, I hope you will bear in mind that the stretchout system of our extended grade and high school is beginning to feel pressure as some high schools improve the quality of their work. If further evidence is needed to convince you that you here are meeting a wide-spread and growing need, let me quote from an article that appeared recently in the *Wall Street Journal*. The article, datelined Palo Alto, California, reads,

On a sunny afternoon here, ten students file into a spacious laboratory-classroom at modern Cubberly High School and begin a two-hour chemical analysis. They are determining the acidity of a dye called methyl red.

In another part of the high school, teacher Bernard Tanner's class of thirty-three senior English students analyzes the symbolism of E. M. Forster's novel, 'A Passage to India.' Not far away, Mrs. Elena Baran and a class of twenty-five teenagers converse in Russian.

Not many years ago such scholarly activity would have been found only on a college campus. But not any more. Cubberly High is one of a steadily growing list of secondary schools bringing college-level courses to high school classrooms.

Already the curricula in Ivy League colleges are beginning to feel the effects of high selectivity of students, and the improvement in the level and quality of work done in the high schools from which these colleges draw students. In some of these colleges, freshmen are entering with educational attainments which tend to eliminate the necessity for freshman courses as previously established, and college faculties are beginning to revise their thinking about curricula.

There are two ways of looking at this. The old-time thinking may lead us to the conclusion that this is bad, because some high schools are doing work which heretofore has been done in college— and doing it within the twelve-year pre-college stretch. On the other hand, we might look at this as did the Board of Higher Education in its 1959 biennial report:

> A large portion of the subject matter in courses which are required of freshmen and sophomores in college might just as well have been covered in academic high schools had the courses been available, the equipment and libraries at hand, and the will to study strong.
>
> This points up the possibility of a startling elevation of the level of education of tens of thousands of young men and women in North Carolina who cannot afford the time and money required for these courses in college . . . .
>
> In the years ahead, a simple choice will be continuously before the people of North Carolina: Shall the colleges teach subjects for which the high schools can progressively assume responsibility or shall these courses be taught in academic high schools?

I can foresee a possibility that in time the developments in your fine New Hanover High School will preclude the necessity of Wilmington College's teaching college algebra and trigonometry, and justify the admission of freshmen directly into calculus. I can even see the possibility that in two years of college work Wilmington College may in time be able to provide levels as advanced as now exist in four-year colleges, thus leaving to the four-year colleges the prerogative of appreciably raising their academic standards which happily they are beginning to do. May I at this moment point out a significant development. I am informed that the community colleges (including Wilmington) have set up entrance tests similar to those in effect at the University of North Carolina. May I raise the question as to whether or not East Carolina, West Carolina, and all the other state-supported colleges are planning to do the same. This system, if practiced by colleges, public and private, would do much to raise the standards of learning in our high schools. I do not think there is any real question about the ability of our young people to absorb additional knowledge at the lower levels. The question is whether or not we are prepared to take the steps necessary to facilitate this change in our educational practices. This will mean better high schools, larger consolidated ones with a challenging curriculum and with liberal financial support at all levels.

I believe that the ceremony that has brought us here today is an indication that we are prepared to go against tradition if it means greater educational opportunities for our young people and greater benefit for our state. You who have faith in the community college concept have a wonderful opportunity during this period of educational self-analysis to make a real contribution to the future of North Carolina, and I sincerely hope you make the best of it.

Thus, far, I have devoted my attention to the academic or university aspects of your curriculum. But you have also a structural commitment to train technicians, at the college level, and to other terminal vocational programs. In the community colleges in several of the more populous states these courses account for the major emphasis and for the greatest enrollment. The community college is uniquely fitted to do a superb job in this important area. Students can take such courses without leaving home and giving up their jobs in the community.

It is my hope and belief that Wilmington College will continue to think in terms of high quality performance as an instrument for education, rather than pursue the aim of institutional glorification. You have a wonderful reputation for personal and community service. The laurels will continue to be bestowed and progress will continue to be made as long as the purposes of Wilmington College are considered to be the reasons for its development.

There can be little doubt about the fact that North Carolina's three community colleges have made a distinct contribution to the progress of the state since their establishment. The Asheville-Biltmore College, which had its origin in 1927, the Charlotte and Wilmington Colleges, which began as "College Centers" in 1946-47, and the two Negro units, Williston and Carver, which were added in 1949, have brought educational opportunity to many North Carolinians who might otherwise have been denied. Today, with a combined enrollment of 1,836, that contribution is even more significant.

The General Assembly of 1955, which was my first Assembly as governor, appropriated the first funds to provide financial aid from the state level to the community colleges. The initial contribution for the 1955-57 biennium, described as "limited encouragement," amounted to $11,652 each for the Wilmington, Asheville, and Charlotte units and $4,664 for Carver College. Prior to 1957, the state made no demands of the existing colleges which were operating under the administrative surveillance of the respective local school boards. However, the General Assembly had created in 1955 a North Carolina Board of Higher Education "to plan a system of higher education for the state," and it was this board, in 1957, that recommended that a program of *increased* aid to community colleges be provided in the budget for 1957-59 and subsequent biennia.

During the course of discussion of this proposal, it was decided to provide appropriation support for current expense of the institutions at a rate of three dollars per student quarter hour of instruction delivered to North Carolina students in state-approved college-level courses. However, it was decided also to adopt a Community College Act to provide a basis for corporate organization of the institutions under local public ownership with their own boards of trustees separate from public school systems and with a share of state influence in the selection of governing boards. Local public school boards, county commissioners, and city councils participated in the selection of trustees. The manner in which the institutions qualify and receive state grants is specified by law. Separate grants are provided on a matching basis for capital improvements. Showing the state's continuing interest in community colleges, the 1959 General Assembly increased the reimbursement rate per student quarter hour to $3.25 in consideration of the schools' need to maintain their own administrative costs which had formerly been merged into the work of the local superintendent of schools. State reimbursement grants to the colleges increased from $39,620 in 1955-57 to $296,419 in 1957-59. The estimate for the current biennium is $445,293. For capital improvements both the 1957 and 1959 General Assembly approved matching grants amounting to $1,500,000.

These figures represent a rather sizable contribution on the part of the state to the community colleges, but I can think of few more worthwhile investments that the state could make. Certainly, it is an indication of the value that the state places on the community college program. And may I add it is the best dollar investment in a college education so far the state is concerned and although the several communities like Wilmington which have community colleges spend some of their own money, it is the best money they can spend. Think, ladies and gentlemen, of the effect on the hundreds of homes whose parents see their boys and girls day by day getting college training at home and helping to keep the family together. It is fundamentally good. Nothing is really appreciated unless we personally take part in it and help support it.

Much of the credit for this community college development goes, of course, to the Board of Higher Education, and I would like to take this opportunity to commend publicly this outstanding group of North Carolinians for the contribution they are making to the future of this state. The board is headed by Mr. L. P. McLendon of Greensboro, and its membership includes Mr. Charles H. Reynolds of Spindale, Mrs. T. R. Easterling of Rocky Mount, Mr. N. Elton Aydlett of Elizabeth City, Mr. Oliver C. Carmichael of Biltmore, Mr. W. Dallas Herring of Rose Hill, Mr. W. J. Kennedy, Jr., of Durham, Mr. Robert Lassiter, Jr., of Charlotte, and Mr. D. Hiden Ramsey of Asheville—all of whom have given generously of their time and effort to promote the cause of higher education in North Carolina.

Little, however, could have been accomplished without the enthusiastic support and dedicated leadership of the people in the communities who know the importance of this program. You have seen an opportunity to make a significant and lasting contribution to the future well-being of the young people who depend upon you for guidance, and you are making the best of that opportunity. The new buildings that will rise to house Wilmington College will be a testimonial to your willingness to accept the responsibility that is yours. They will also stand as a monument to your courage and your faith in the future of this community and this great state. You have done a magnificent job, and I again congratulate you!

Thank you.

ADDRESS AT REGION SIX, BOY SCOUTS OF AMERICA ANNUAL BANQUET

ATLANTA, GEORGIA
April 26, 1960

[Long interested in Boy Scout work, and already the recipient of many awards for Scouting activities, Governor Hodges on this occasion was one of three outstanding leaders awarded the highest honor an adult can attain in Scouting, the Silver Antelope Award. The banquet at which the Governor made this speech was an event of the annual convention of the Boy Scouts Region Six, which includes North Carolina, South Carolina, Georgia, and Florida. At the beginning of the speech a slight slip of the tongue during a joke turned into a barb aimed at the Republican party. "President Nixon," Governor Hodges began; "Uh . . . I mean Vice President Nixon. Friends, THAT will NEVER happen."]

I would like to express my genuine appreciation to each of you for the privilege of being here this evening, and for the very great honor you have bestowed upon me. The distinction of being asked to address this particular audience is, in itself, a singular honor. To be further recognized by such an audience for service to Scouting makes this easily one of the most gratifying moments of my life. This is an experience that I shall never forget, and an honor that I shall endeavor, to the best of my ability, to merit in my future activities. Please believe that my humility is genuine. St. Augustine once said, many centuries ago, that "the sufficiency of my merit is to know that my merit is not sufficient." I share that sentiment here this evening.

My personal humility, however, does not lessen the pride I have in my association with the Boy Scout organization in general and Region Six in particular. This pride is based on the conviction that the future of our nation, of our whole way of life, revolves around the mental, moral, and physical fitness of our young people, and the knowledge that no organization contributes more to the establishment and maintenance of a high degree of fitness than the Boy Scouts of America.

More than half a century has passed since that famous day in 1910 when a small boy with a wide-brim hat and short pants stepped out of a London fog and volunteered his services to the Chicago Publisher, William D. Boyce. The youngster's name has been lost to history, but his deed will never be forgotten. It was perhaps the most significant single act of courtesy performed in this century—a striking example of the potential consequences and beneficial effects of an isolated good deed. This one simple act, had such an impact on the American visitor that he returned to this country, gathered about him such dedicated men as Dan Beard, Ernest Seton, William Randolph Hearst, and James E. West, shared with them his ideas and enthusiasm, and launched one of the greatest youth programs the world has ever known.

From the beginning, the Scouting program captured the imagination of the American boy, drew him into closer association with his wonderful pioneer heritage, channeled his amazing energy into beneficial pursuits, and added new strength, both immediate and potential, to our national character. Boy Scouts rendered valuable service in the Ohio Valley floods of 1913, the Mississippi floods of the early 20's, the Texas City disaster in 1947, and in many other lesser known disasters of the past fifty years. In World War I, they sold $2000,000,000 worth of Liberty Bonds and Stamps, located 20,000,000 board feet of black walnut, needed for rifle stocks, and contributed in innumerable other ways to the war effort. During World War II, the ability of Boy Scouts to get the job done was recognized by President Roosevelt, who called upon them no less than sixty-nine times to perform some needed service in the national interest.

These are tangible contributions that Scouting has made to the growth and development of the nation and to the preservation of its security and high ideals. It is a contribution that has been felt at all levels of social activity, in a hundred large cities and thousands of small communities, in our churches and in our homes—wherever there has been an opportunity for service, the Scouts have been ready. Equally important, however, is the contribution that Scouting has made to the individual boy—the more than 33,000,000 young Americans who, because of the happy, constructive years spent in Scouting, know what Dan Beard meant when he said, "I had rather be an American boy than President of the United States or almost anything else."

Certainly, no youngster who has ever once sworn allegiance to the Scout Oath and Law can ever divest himself of the challenge this pledge imposes. Here in Scouting the young boy, frequently for the first time, is confronted with the basic concept of citizenship responsibility—concepts that, properly presented and enthusiastically accepted, will benefit both the individual and the society in which he lives. And, what more can we ask of our future business, civic, and governmental leaders than that they be trustworthy, loyal, helpful, friendly, courteous, kind, obedient, cheerful, thrifty, brave, clean, and reverent. Can we ask that they do more than pledge, on their honor, to do their best, to do their duty, to their God and their country? I say that there are no nobler ideals, and no more effective organization for promoting those ideals than the Boy Scouts of America.

For this reason, it is especially gratifying to know that we here in the Southeast have what I consider to be the most outstanding regional Scouting program in the country. This conviction is supported by the fact that you have again been named recipient of the Lorillard Spencer Trophy for the greatest accomplishment in the advancement of Scouting among the twelve regions of America during 1959. To win this recognition once is a great honor, but to have won it eight times in the nineteen years that it has been awarded is an amazing achievement—and one that certainly reflects tremendous credit on the adult leaders in this region.

I think we can be extremely proud of the fact that here in Region Six, we have almost 250,000 boys enrolled in the Scouting program. At the beginning of this year we had 99,388 boys in 3,424 Cub Scout Packs, 127,409 boys in 5,626 Scout Troops, and 22,669 boys in 1,734 Explorer Units. This represents a tremendous amount of Scouting activity and, at the same time, imposes a tremendous responsibility on the regional leadership. Charged with this responsibility are 95,453 volunteer Scouters and 243 professionals. It would be impossible for me to express, in so many words, the admiration I have for the these dedicated men and women who know what Scouting can mean to a boy, and give freely of their time and efforts to make the Scouting program work.

Four basic ingredients are needed for a successful Scouting program. The boy, of course, is the most essential ingredient. He has within him all the inquisitiveness, the desire, the multiplicity of interests, the natural ability, and the unbounded enthusiasm that form the springboard for all Scouting activities. Next we need the program itself—the carefully thought-out details of organization and incentive, designed to take maximum advantage of the boy's natural inclinations. Next we need support and acceptance by the community. We need more and more people who realize that it takes money to run a program of this type and, at the same time, people who know that a contribution to the Scouting program may very well be the soundest and most productive investment they will ever make. And finally we need competent, dedicated adult leadership—men and women who are willing to devote, not just a little, but a great deal of time to do this work. Scouting is not—even for the volunteer leader—a one-day-a-week proposition. The den mother or scoutmaster or explorer advisor who enters Scouting with the idea that the demand on his or her time will be limited to one or two hours on one afternoon or evening each week is in for a rude awakening. The good Scout leader cannot approach his responsibility casually. He must be a superb organizer, a gifted psychologist, an expert in all matters from bee-keeping to bird houses, a parent away from home and, above all, a diplomat. Not everyone can be a good Scout leader. As a matter of fact, the really good ones are fairly rare.

This is why I feel very strongly that capable leadership is the key to a successful Scouting program, whether it be at the council, district, or regional level. The volunteer leader is the person who has made Scouting the great thing that it is—the person who puts more into Scouting than any other.

We are extremely fortunate here in Region Six to have what I consider to be the most dedicated and capable adult leadership in the country. We have a tradition of this kind of leadership, and it is evident in the success of the Scouting program here. I would like to commend each of you present at this meeting, and through you, every leader in the region on the excellent job you have done in the past, the excellent job you are now doing, and the excellent job you will undoubtedly continue to do in the future. You are making a very real contribution to the mental, moral, and physical development of our young men and, in so doing, you are contributing immeasurably to the future economic, social, and cultural stability of the region you serve.

It is good to know that this great beneficial force is being exerted, not only in our own area but throughout the nation. It is good to know because we face an increasingly serious challenge in dealing with our young people. Much criticism has been leveled in recent years at the younger generation in America. It has been said that they have lost their enthusiasm for adventure, that their collective sense of values has become distorted, that they have become obsessed with a desire for security at any cost, that they are moraly corrupt, physically inadequate, and mentally unresponsive. I do not say that all these charges are groundless, but I do say that they are no more or no less applicable to the present younger generation than they have been to generations in the past. The same things, with some variations, were said about my generation and the one before that.

I think that the criticism we hear today is prompted by the fact that we are more concerned than ever before. If we seem more anxious for the young people to "measure up" today than at any time in our history, it is because we know that the stakes are much higher today than at any time in the past. It is because we are con-

378 Papers of Luther H. Hodges

vinced, and with good reason, that the future of this nation may
very well depend upon the ability of today's young citizens to meet
challenges of far greater significance than we have been called
upon to face in our lifetime. If we are overly critical, if we
demand too much, if we appear a little desperate in our efforts to
prepare today's youngsters for what the future holds, it is because
we are, perhaps, more interested in young people today than we
have ever been before. Criticism of youth in past decades has been
more in the form of commentary, involving very little real concern. Today, it is an expression of serious interest, based on a
knowledge of the opportunities that will be available to these
youngsters in the near future, and also an awareness of the challenges they will be called upon to face.

Scouting is preparing our young men to face up to the responsibilities they will inherit and, at the same time, it is teaching
them that they have responsibilities even now that must be met.
They are learning that citizenship is not something to be acquired
at the age of sixteen or eighteen or twenty-one—that the basic
privileges and the basic responsibilities of citizenship are acquired
at a much earlier age.

I wish we could channel the enthusiasm and dedication of you
Scout leaders into the field of politics and government. What a
joy it would be if our school board members, our councilmen, our
legislators, and our governors could serve so willingly and unselfishly and so honestly in government and politics as you do in
Scouting. This could change the face of the whole country,
especially in the South where our tensions and our problems are
rising!

We hear a great deal today about juvenile delinquency, and I
would be the last to deny that it is an extremely serious problem.
It is one of the distasteful facts of life that we must face squarely
if we are really concerned with the future of this country. It
is especially important that those of us who work closely with
young people concern ourselves with this problem, for we are in the
most advantageous position to seek workable solutions. And the
first step is to admit openly and frankly that the situation is bad
and getting worse.

In recent testimony before a Congressional subcommittee,

F.B.I. Director J. Edgar Hoover said, "We are witnessing one of the terrifying consequences of public apathy in the surge of youthful lawlessness across the nation. The problem of young people involved in criminal activity is tragic. And the increasing frequency of youth crimes is compounded by an increasing savagery in their commission. Both of these factors—increase in incidence and increase in savagery—hold ominous portents for the future."

Hoover further testified that

> On the basis of reports from 1,586 cities covering all types of arrests, we know that of the 2,340,004 persons arrested in these cities in 1958, slightly over 12 per cent were under the age of eighteen. Almost 20 per cent were under twenty-five years of age.
> In 1958 the arrests of juveniles under the age of eighteen increased 8.1 per cent over the previous year, while the arrests of adults rose only 1.8 per cent.
> Although youths under eighteen represent only 12.1 per cent of all persons arrested, they were the subjects of 64.1 per cent of the arrests for auto theft, 49.9 per cent of those for burglary and 48.5 per cent of those for larceny. This same age group accounted for 30.9 per cent of those arrested for receiving or possessing stolen property and 22.8 per cent of those arrested for robbery.
> An estimated 800,000 young Americans under the age of eighteen were arrested during the calendar year 1958. This is 3.4 per cent of the children in the ten to seventeen age group and it indicates that one out of every twenty-nine young people in that age group was arrested in 1958.
> Since 1952, the population group aged ten-seventeen has increased 28.8 per cent. Juvenile arrests in the same period and for the same group have risen 67.7 per cent. At this rate of increase, by 1965 we can anticipate approximately 1,109,000 juveniles will be arrested annually.

All this at a time when the fitness of our youth is of prime importance to the security of the nation.

These facts represent a tremendous challenge to the Scouting program. I cannot help but ask myself how many of these youngsters might have been saved, or might yet be saved, by exposure to Scouting. How many of them might have remembered at just the right moment that a Scout is trustworthy, that he has sworn to uphold not only his own honor but the honor of Scouting? I think the number might be considerable. That is why we must pledge ourselves to meet this challenge and meet it aggressively. We have to do more than open the door to Scouting. We must go out and

and invite the boy in. We must openly declare war on the evil forces in our society that breed corruption and dishonor among the young and impressionable segment of our population. These forces are at work in every community in our land and it is there that the decisive battles must be fought. And this is a battle that we cannot afford to lose. Our opponent is a deadly cancer eating at the source of this nation's vitality and strength—and we will need all the strength we can muster to preserve our national integrity in the years before us.

We cannot, for a moment, overlook the fact that we are, as individuals and as a nation, involved in a very serious competition with the Communist world—a competition that tests our national fiber on a day-to-day basis. Our traditional superiority is being effectively challenged in many fields—in athletics, in education, in industrial and agricultural production, and particularly in science. One of the reasons, if not the primary reason, that the Soviets have made such dramatic progress in recent years is that their young people are deadly serious in almost all their activities. If he is an athlete, his one ambition is to become good enough to enter international competition and "beat the Americans." If he is an engineering student, he wants to learn his trade with such proficiency that some day he can build something bigger and better than the Americans have. Education to him is a great privilege. He attends classes and studies, not to "get through" school, but to learn everything he possibly can, to develop his mental faculties to the maximum degree, to prepare himself to contribute to his nation's sworn objective of overtaking the United States in every field of human endeavor.

And the frightening thing about all this is that the young Russian is absolutely convinced that this objective will be realized —and in the not too distant future. He has great confidence in his own ability and he is convinced of our complacency. He is convinced that we have become obsessed with our so-called "good life" and could not meet his challenge even if we wanted to. He has, I think, grossly underestimated the American people, and especially the young people of this nation, but, at the same time, he poses a challenge that we cannot afford to disregard. The threat is real, and we are not a nation of people that can be satisfied with second place.

I do not mean that we should inject Scouting directly into this international conflict, but I do feel that we should do everything within our power to expand this program with the aim of creating a powerful, patriotic, dedicated young citizenry capable of warding off the attack being made on our morality here at home and our national security abroad. As I have pointed out before, we will need the generous and enthusiastic support of all the American people if Scouting is to grow to its full potential, if it is to exert the influence it is capable of exerting on the young people of the nation. I have been associated with this program for a good many years and I know something of the value received for each dollar invested. I can only say that I would like to know of some business investment that I could make that would guarantee such returns.

I know, for instance, that the total budget for the twelve local Boy Scout Councils in North Carolina is $777,677. This would appear to be a rather sizeable figure but actually it is insignificant when matched against the cost of juvenile crime prevention in the state. In the last year alone we appropriated almost twice that amount—$1,258,654—just for the operation of our five training schools for youthful offenders. And this does not include the original and continuing capital expenditures for buildings and other facilities at these schools. According to our commissioner of correction, the state of North Carolina spent $1,165 on each of 1,080 young boys and girls in our correctional institutions in 1958-59. I wonder how many of these young people might have been spared this stigma if a fraction of this investment had been spent to insure their participation in the Scouting program. And, while it is incidental to the salvaging of these young lives, I wonder how much more economical it is to support Scouting than to support a system of correction and training institutions. So you see, we are on solid ground in more ways than one when we campaign for more support and greater public interest in the Scouting program. Certainly, the general public has an obligation to share, with you, the responsibility for building this great program.

May I conclude by saying that this has been a delightful experi-

ence to meet with dedicated, purposeful, and enthusiastic people
and to share with them a firm belief in a worthwhile cause. Scouting is just such a cause, and its potential worth excities the imagination. In the final analysis, the decision will rest largely with you
as to whether Scouting meets the challenge that it faces. It will
require courage and sacrifice and unfailing patience. It will require continued faith in Scouting itself and in your ability and
determination to take full advantage of the opportunity for service that is yours. You have demonstrated in the past that you can
measure up to these requirements and I am confident that you
will be no less zealous in your future activities. It will not be easy,
but it will be eminently rewarding. For what greater reward can
one ask than the knowledge that you have made a significant and
lasting contribution to the well-being of your community, your
state, and your nation.

Thank you for having me here and giving me the opportunity
to talk to you!

ADDRESS AT THE BRAND NAMES FOUNDATION
DINNER HONORING THE BRAND NAME
RETAILERS-OF-THE-YEAR

New York City
May 6, 1960

[As a veteran of more than thirty years of selling in the textile business,
Governor Hodges considered himself as something of an expert in salesmanship. "Selling North Carolina" was the theme of this address, in which he
described some of his experiences and procedures in shifting from a career
of selling merchandise to that of "selling a state." One hundred and thirty-
seven Retailers-of-the-Year, including two from North Carolina, were honored by the Brand Names Foundation at a dinner held on this occasion at
the Waldorf-Astoria Hotel in New York.]

It is a distinct honor to have the privilege of meeting here this
evening with members and guests of the Brand Names Foundation—an organization that has made, and continues to make, a
unique and far-reaching contribution to the economic stability of
this nation. I am especially pleased to have the opportunity of

being with you on this particular occasion when you come together to honor individual business organizations—large and small—who have, within the past year, distinguished themselves in an outstanding manner. May I offer my congratulations to each of the 137 winners, with a special commendation for the two North Carolina firms (Sterling Jewelers of Fayetteville and Greer Hardware Company of Salisbury) that have been recognized here this evening. To be singled out as a "finalist" in this competition is a distinction within itself. To be selected as a winner is, of course, an even greater honor—one that carries with it tremendous prestige. It marks you as truly outstanding and establishes you as a leader, as an example for others to emulate—not just in your community or state or province, but throughout your nation, and not just in your particular retail category but in the all-embracing world of business.

And with this recognition you acquire new responsibility. As Retailer-of-the-Year you become far more than just another good business. You become, in the eyes of your contemporaries, the best. You become a symbol of all that is basic and sound and good in the American free enterprise system. And therein lies your responsibility. You become the showcase of that system, a spotlighted example of its inherent strength. You have, through diligent effort, ingenuity, courage, and determination, won this distinction. Now you must work even harder to maintain not only your own reputation but the reputation of the great economic system you represent. To perpetuate high standards of excellence, especially in a complex economy such as ours, is not easy. But the reward is certainly worth the effort. For the reward is our free way of life—the privilege of living in a free society and raising our children in a free and independent atmosphere where the concept of fair play prevails and a man's aspirations are limited only by his determination and his ability to produce. This is our America!

Make no mistake about the fact that you, the retailers, are the bulwark of economy. More than thirty years' experience in manufacturing and selling taught me never to minimize the importance of the man who stands between the producer and the consumer. He is the man who makes the wheels of industry turn. He is the man who makes the sale that counts. We can produce the most fabulous commodity in the world and advertise it to the limit through every available media, but unless the Main Street merchant is prepared to go a little beyond just making the commodity available, then we have wasted considerable effort. The item will sell, probably, but will it sell well enough on its own merit to justify the production investment? Probably not—unless the man behind the counter in your community and mine does his part and does it well. Without the hometown merchant who has what it takes to carry his share of the free enterprise load, there isn't much point in building a better mousetrap or anything else.

Don't misunderstand me. I do not for a moment underestimate the importance of the manufacturer, the distributor, and the advertising man. I've worked with all of them. Each is vitally important. As a matter of fact, each is absolutely essential to the smooth functioning of our economic machinery. But if there is one cog in the machine that is most important to the operation, it is the retailer. I suppose the average manufacturer likes to think that his product is good enough to sell itself. At least, this is a point he likes to make when discussing terms with his advertising agency. By the same token, the Madison Avenue boys like to think they can sell any product—good or bad—if they really set their minds to the task. Too often, I think, we all forget that neither is going to set the world on fire without the cooperation of the retail merchant, the man who makes the personal contact with the buying customer.

Most of you are probably familiar with the current television commercial that pictures the store manager as a misguided soul who, because of very poor judgment, neglected to fill his counters and storeroom with a particular product. He is berated and bludgeoned by housewives and, I believe, by the sponsor's representative until he finally sees the error of his ways and stocks up on the hot item. The insatiable demand continues and everyone is happy: the manufacturer, because his product is obviously superior; the advertising agency, because superior or not, they sold it; the store manager, because he didn't have to do a thing but sit back and count his money; and the customers, of course, because they got the quality product they expected by purchasing a brand name item. It's an effective commercial, but I'm afraid the "innocent by-stander" role assigned the retailer doesn't picture him in his true light. I've had the personal experience many times of shopping for a "brand name" when the retail clerk was surly or disinterested to the point the sale was never made. Yes, the retailer has a real, continuing, job of training.

I feel the Brand Names Foundation is to be highly commended on this annual awards dinner. It gives us all an opportunity to show that we do appreciate the retailer's considerable contribution to the economy. And, even more important, it shows the great teamwork that goes into making our economy the strong and vital force that it is, and our standard of living the highest the world has ever known. This is a good opportunity for us to remind ourselves that we are a team, that we each contribute and we each gain when progress is made, and that we all suffer when any member of the team falls down on the job. Each segment of the business economy faces two challenges—the individual challenge that calls for each retailer, each manufacturer, each distributor to maintain a high standard of quality in the product he makes and the service he renders; and the collective challenge that calls for unity and cooperation in the attainment of mutually beneficial objectives. Only when we meet these challenges with enthusiasm and courage do we take full advantage of the opportunities that are available to us. The system under which we operate demands that these challenges be met. It demands that in all things—in production and marketing, especially—we keep one criterion, one requirement foremost in our thoughts. That requirement is quality. For quality, as you very well know, breeds confidence, and confidence is essential to the establishment of a good name.

It was for this purpose—to promote quality—that this organization was founded in 1943. It is a noble purpose, and each of you can be justly proud of what has been accomplished in the past and what is being accomplished today by the Brand Names Foundation. A good name is vitally important, regardless of the product you are trying to sell. I learned this early in my business career with Marshall Field and Company, and the conviction grew when I became governor of the state of North Carolina. There is little difference in selling a piece of merchandise and in selling a

state—if you have confidence in the product. I have been exceptionally fortunate in having a good product to sell in both instances. The only real difference has been that in the case of
North Carolina it has been necessary, at times, to sell the product
to its owners, to convince the people of the state that they had a
product of superior quality and that properly marketed it would
herald the beginning of an era of unprecedented prosperity for
our state.

We approached the task of selling North Carolina in an objective and businesslike manner. We set about determining the
quality of the basic product, what we could do to improve it, and
just how we should go about the job of selling. We found that
basically the product was sound, that we were rich in human and
natural resources, that revolutionary changes in agriculture were
creating a labor surplus that could be quickly trained in manufacturing skills. We found that in agriculture the trend was away
from dangerous total dependence on traditional cash crops and in
the direction of diversification—a trend that would bring better
balance to the overall economy. Another asset was a traditionally
sound government and a long-standing reputation for integrity in
fiscal matters and and a good business climate. Still another asset
was geography—a temperate climate, abundant water, close
proximity to the nation's major markets, a superb transportation
system, unmatched variety in recreational and vacation facilities,
and a terrain that stretches from the picturesque Atlantic Coast to
the highest and most beautiful mountains east of the Mississippi
River. All things considered, we felt that we had a product that
should sell.

To make the product even more acceptable, we inaugurated a
comprehensive improvement program designed to (1) encourage
and facilitate more diversification in agriculture, (2) encourage
the expansion of existing industries, and (3) attract new industries.
To promote these activities we traveled about the state extensively,
traveling 60,000 to 70,000 miles a year, averaging over 100
speeches annually, urging the people, individually and collectively,
to work together, to invest in their own future, to take full
advantage of the opportunities that exist, and to make their own
opportunities whenever and wherever possible. The response has

been amazing. More than 200 local and area development corporations have been established to promote economic progress in their particular areas and to work for greater prosperity throughout the state. The activities of these groups are coordinated by our Department of Conservation and Development, which gives advice when it is needed and provides services that the local groups cannot reasonably be expected to provide.

The state has also played a significant role in other programs that benefit directly or indirectly the effort put forth at the local or regional level. We took the lead, for instance in raising several million dollars for the establishment of a Business Development Corporation, a private agency designed specifically to provide long-term venture capital for small local industries. Another program in which I have participated enthusiastically has been the development of the Research Triangle—an industrial research complex that has been established in a triangle formed by three great educational institutions—The University of North Carolina, Duke University, and North Carolina State College. This research complex is a non-profit foundation. The Research Triangle holds very definite promise of developing into one of the really great industrial research centers of the world. Already several firms have located their research facilities there and research activities are humming.

After determining that our product was ready for the market, we concerned ourselves with the best means of selling it to the customer—be he the casual tourist or the potential industrial investor. We knew our product would sell, but we also knew that it would not sell itself. We knew that we were entering an extremely competitive field with the other forty-nine States and that we would have to go out and "lay it on the line" if we expected results. We decided against the "hard sell" technique on the premise that (1) it isn't necessary when you have a quality product to sell, (2) it wouldn't be appreciated by or effective with the American industrialist who doesn't have a reputation for being easily sold, and (3) we didn't want the kind of industry in North Carolina that wasn't genuinely convinced and enthusiastic about the advantages of being there.

We chose the approach of advertising in leading popular and

trade publications, and personal contact. Our advertising simply
described the advantages of expanding in North Carolina and invited inquires. But our personal contact procedure was, as is
usually the case, the most effective. We felt that what we were
doing in our state would be of genuine interest to businessmen in
some of the leading industrial areas of the nation. We decided to
go to them and simply tell what we call the "North Carolina
Story."

This has involved considerable travel and considerable sacrifices on the part of many our our leading citizens, but the results
have been most beneficial to the state and extremely gratifying to
those who have participated. We came first to New York in 1957,
then traveled to Chicago in the spring of 1958, then to Philadelphia early in 1959, and finally, in the fall of 1959, to Europe,
where we visited eleven cities in six countries in a strenuous two-
week period.

On each of these trips I was accompanied by from fifty to 100
North Carolinians—each of them paying his own expenses and
each of them pledged to promote, not his own communities or his
own special interests, but our main product, North Carolina. We
made these trips, not with hat in hand and head bowed, but with
confidence and enthusiasm, armed with the unqualified conviction
that we had much to offer the industrial investor who might be
expanding or seeking new markets. We expressed a special interest
in plants that were contemplating expansions, plants that, because
of crowded conditions in their present locations or need to be
closer to their developing markets, have no choice but to look
elsewhere for plant locations. And we, of course, suggested that
North Carolina, located within 500 miles of 90,000,000 people
or half the population of the United States, would be ideally
suited to their needs.

On each of these trips we made ourselves available for talks
with any businessman who expressed immediate interest, and we
followed up the visits with personal contacts in the weeks following. As a matter of fact we have now established a permanent
representative here in New York and have a "follow-up" delegation currently in Europe—with, I might add, very encouraging
results.

This, then, is the way we in North Carolina sell our "brand name" product. And I do not believe there can be any question about the fact that we are getting the job done. We have shattered our own industrial development records each year since 1956, and there is every indication that a new mark will be set in 1960. Last year, we recorded 571 new or expanded industries—an increase of 35 per cent over the previous year. This growth represented a capital investment of more than $223,500,000, new jobs for 36,331 people, and new payrolls amounting to $118,268,000. In 1958 when the nation invested 17.4 per cent *less* in manufacturing establishments, we gained 32.5 per cent. The Department of Commerce reports that 1954-58 manufacturing employment figures for the USA showed a 1 per cent loss and North Carolina had a 7 per cent gain.

I do not think I am stretching the point when I draw an analogy between what we have done in North Carolina and what you are doing here in this fine organization. We are both interested in maintaining the quality of our product, in advertising it effectively, and in selling it with confidence to a satisfied customer. This is a noble ambition for both of us because, in both instances, we are endeavoring to raise the standard of living and add new strength to our free way of life. And, in so doing, we are adding new fiber to the free enterprise system, which I consider to be the basis of our national freedom.

It is very important for retailers, businessmen, and citizens generally not to take the American system of free enterprise for granted, as it is being seriously challenged right now by extremely clever forces that are dedicated to overcoming us. I visited the Soviet Union several weeks last year with eight other governors and I feel more strongly than ever that we must re-dedicate ourselves to our economic and social system and make it work, if we are to survive.

As businessmen and as citizens directly concerned with national security, most of you are, I am sure, aware of this threat. Most of you must also be aware of the obvious fact that our most effective weapon in combating this threat is a healthy, growing economy. In the past we have been content with the knowledge that our economic system was the most efficient, the most reliable in the world. We are still ahead, but we shouldn't take anything for granted! Until recently, there may have been some justification for such complacency. Things are changing. The free enterprise system is being challenged. We are, at the present moment, fighting an economic war—and make no mistake about the fact that the issue can become serious in the not too distant future. We could lose. We could lose everything—our national dignity, our freedom, our nation itself—without a bullet being fired, without a drop of blood being shed.

The greatest weapon we possess in this economic struggle is our down-to-earth, business know-how. It must be mobilized now as never before. It must be brought to a peak of efficiency that will enable it to withstand the forces that are being set against this nation. Fortunately, we can accomplish this objective without sacrificing our dream of greater prosperity and a higher standard of living in the years ahead. The know-how that can keep us free can also work for the betterment of our people. We can face the challenge from abroad and the opportunities here at home at the same time. We have only to apply ourselves, to use the tools at our command, to weather the storm and reach new heights.

Here again, it is simply a matter of maintaining the quality of the product and selling it with confidence. We here, in the United States and Canada, have the greatest product that mankind has ever known—freedom, founded on individual enterprise. It is the one product that should sell itself, but, unfortunately, the world is not a free market. So we must compete, and we must do so with great vigor and determination. It is not a competition we can enter into half-heartedly, nor is it a contest with clearly defined rules and regulations. It is a dog fight to determine whether or not our product is as durable as we claim.

I am confident that we will win, but I am in no way complacent. The forces that seek to destroy our way of life are cunning, dedicated, and certain of victory. We must fight back with greater cunning and greater dedication if we are to deny them that victory. We are each involved in this fight, for each of us can influence the economic stability of the nation. Each of us can contribute by conducting our day-to-day affairs in accordance with the high standards established by this organization to which I am speaking tonight. We can bolster the nation's integrity—its good name—by maintaining our own integrity at all levels of business activity.

This is the substance of your responsibility as businessmen and citizens in a free society.

There are two other things we must do if we are to preserve America—this great product of ours with the wonderful brand name of Uncle Sam!

First, we must see that we are not controlled or dominated by bigness or minorities—neither big business nor big labor. Big business has learned better how to behave; big labor, especially the Hoffa kind, has yet to learn, it seems. Neither must we be controlled nor dominated by minorities which appeal to many of our politicians' worse side rather than their better side.

Above all, we must promote understanding among our own people in the United States. There are many factors—economic, social, and otherwise—that breed discord, disunity, and even hatred between people within their own borders. In almost every instance, these differences are the product of misinformation and lack of understanding.

I am convinced that the great emphasis we have placed on personal contacts and the exchange of information on a world-wide basis should also be applied right here at home. We have much to learn from and about each other in our own country. As a matter of fact, we must understand each other as human beings and as fellow Americans first before we will have much success in understanding our regional and national problems. Just recently the press carried a statement from a professor who said that the racial difficulties we are now having were "peanuts" to what we would probably experience all over America in 1975! We must realize that New York is not just Broadway and Madison Avenue, that California and Florida have something other than sunkissed oranges and new hotels, that the West is not a desert whose citizens are seeking pork barrel money for building higher and bigger dams, that the East is not just Harvard and rock-bound coast, that every person in Texas does not own an oil well, that the Middle West is more than tall corn and pigs, and that the South now not only wears shoes, but makes them as well.

We must learn each other regionally as you have done as individuals in this organization. We sadly need tolerance and understanding on the part of all our people. It is not, in my humble opinion, in the national interest for minority groups, of whatever race, color, or belief, to be used as political pawns by either or both of our major political parties. Of course, every civilized nation has a legitimate and proper concern for the protection of the rights of individuals. Certainly, there can be such a thing as tyranny by majority rule. But what we are faced with today, is, in my opinion, exactly the reverse. It is high time more of our political leaders came out for the "majority" in this country instead of persisting in an unsightly scramble to appease "minorities" as a means of gaining political advantage.

What we need in both of our major political parties and in all sections of this nation is love and concern for our country first, with political expediency or advantage placed last. Above all, we need more leaders who can think in terms of what is best for all our people—more leaders who have the courage to speak, not for the North or South or East or West, but for the American people as a whole.

The members of this foundation are in an excellent position to promote this spirit of cooperation. I urge you to do so at every possible opportunity; for through such action, you will be serving the best interests of the people who depend upon you for advice and intelligent leadership. I can think of no better way for you to fulfill the basic responsibility that is yours as an American citizen interested in the growth and sound development of this great nation.

May I conclude by expressing again my pleasure at having the honor and privilege of meeting with you this evening. The future is unlimited for our great nation if we are willing to work together for what is best and right for the majority of our people. We can and will build the better way of life we all envision if we look to the future with the same courage and faith that guided our forefathers to this continent centuries ago. This is the challenge we face. It is a challenge that must be answered.

Thank you.

ADDRESS AT JUNIOR ACHIEVEMENT
OF CHARLOTTE DINNER

CHARLOTTE

May 7, 1960

[Junior Achievement companies are groups of high school students who organize and conduct small business enterprises under the guidance of volunteer advisers from sponsoring firms. Each company is composed of from ten to fifteen "achievers" who work over a period of nine months and deliberately cease operations in May of each year, often with a banquet at which citations are made and prizes distributed, as was done on this occasion in Charlotte. The Governor interjected a political note into his address by expressing the hope that in choosing between candidates for office in North Carolina this year, "we won't elect people who will carry the state backward, but choose people who will carry it forward." Although he mentioned no names, this statement was generally considered to be aimed against I. Beverly Lake, who was running for the Democratic nomination for governor on a pro-segregationist platform. Following his address to the Junior Achievers, the Governor attended and spoke briefly at a convention of the Toastmasters, of which organization he had just been made an honorary member, but stated that he was "so busy telling the North Carolina story that he would have to skip out"—for Kansas City and St. Louis.]

For the past five and one-half years, it has been my great privilege to serve as governor of a state that has clearly and dramatically demonstrated a great economic potential—a state that has shown that it possesses, in abundance, the human and natural resources needed to insure a prosperous future and a higher standard of living for all its people.

We are living in an era that has demanded much of our people, We have had to learn new skills, both in business and in government. It has been necessary for us to change our way of doing things in many instances and, not infrequently, we have been required to change our way of thinking about matters affecting our state as a whole. These have been challenging years, but they have also been exciting and very gratifying years. It has been challenging because, as a people, North Carolinians have never before been called upon to rise to such heights of cooperative endeavor. Never before have we been faced with so many opportunities calling for unity of thought and action on the part of our entire citizenry. And, it has been gratifying because individually and collectively we have risen to this challenge, recognized the opportunities available to us, and worked together unselfishly to take full advantage of those opportunities.

We have made great progress in recent years, but this is only the beginning. The determination, the cooperative spirit, the confidence, and the ability to get the job done that we have acquired must, in the years ahead, become not a basis for complacency, but a source of inspiration. We must prepare ourselves to build on the foundation that has been established. We must welcome new changes, economic and social, that test our newly acquired ability to react intelligently and with unity of purpose. We must learn to think big and to act big, to become more polished, more knowledgeable, in dealing with economic matters that affect the future of our state and its pepole. But, at the same time, we must retain our enthusiasn and the youthful spirit of adventure that has been so much a part of our economic progress in the past, and remains one of our strongest attributes today.

This is why it is such a wonderful experience to come here to Charlotte this evening to participate in this Junior Achievement Program. I can think of no activity involving the young people of our state that has greater potential value, both for the state and for the individual, than the activity that has brought us together on this occasion. Yours is a program that looks to the future, that recognizes the fact that North Carolina is on the move, that recognizes the importance of having a nucleus of energetic, business-minded young men capable of taking up where others leave off and moving on to even greater achievements.

Junior Achievement is a comparatively new program. Only in the past ten or twelve years has the significance of what you are doing captured the imagination of the American businessman. Ten years ago, less than 1,000 Junior Achievement companies were in operation throughout the nation. Today, I understand, there are more than 4,200 in operation and that interest in this program is the highest ever, both among the young people who take part and the business and civic organizations that provide sponsorship. I have been aware of this program for sometime, and have on various occasions had the privilege of endorsing it as one of the most outstanding training activities in the country, but I was not aware of its full scope until just recently. I was surprised to learn that approximately 70,000 young Americans

Governor Hodges speaking at the Annual Salute to Industry Banquet sponsored by the Bank of Virginia, Richmond, Virginia, April 27, 1960.

Dedication of the North Carolina Credit Union League's new office building at Greensboro, April 29, 1960. *Left to right*: B. L. Webster, managing director of the League; Luther C. Hodges, nephew of the Governor and president of the League; Gaines Kelley, former president; Governor Hodges; Rev. Claud B. Bowen, pastor of the First Baptist Church of Greensboro.

devoted more than 6,000,000 man hours to Junior Achievement enterprises in 1959.

Certainly, it is a great tribute to these young people that they have voluntarily and with considerable enthusiasm involved themselves in this type of activity. It shows, I think, that we have little need to fear that American business will, in the years ahead, fall into incompetent and disinterested hands. Even more important, I believe, is the fact that this interest on the part of our young boys and girls reveals the basic strength of the American free enterprise system. It shows that the youth of this nation have not lost the competitive urge, and that they regard the fascinating world of business as an arena in which they can test their natural abilities and acquired talents.

One writer has described Junior Achievement as "one of the most significant developments in practical education today." Another has said that the program gives youngsters a "glimpse of the soaring spirit of free enterprise." Certainly, there is ample evidence that both these statements are true. Complex problems of production, sales, and accounting can be encounterd just as readily in a $100 corporation as in a $1,000,000 corporation. In both instances, the solution of those problems require ingenuity, confidence, and business integrity.

I particularly like the story of the Junior Achievement Company in Detroit that showed real spirit in converting an apparent disaster into a triumph. This company, manufacturing ceramic spoon holders, lost its entire stock of raw materials and all its stockholder's capital when someone forgot to turn the heat off in the baking kiln one week end. Six of the eleven junior executives of the company admitted defeat and resigned. The other five, armed with only sketches of the item they intended to produce, conducted a door-to-door campaign, explained their bankruptcy, and solicited advance orders and advance payment for each item. With the money they received from these orders, they purchased more raw material, fired up their kiln, and went back into operation. When the company finally liquidated, the hard working young executives jubilantly paid back the seventy-five stockholders their initial investment of $96, plus a 10 per cent dividend. I cannot help but wonder how many adult corporations would have carried on under these conditions with the same tenacity and determination to fulfill their obligation to their stockholders. The five youngsters who stuck it out and pulled their company through a disastrous situation learned a very valuable lesson—one that no teacher, no textbook, and no classroom exercise could have taught.

They learned that, in the American free enterprise system, a set-back need not mean failure, that one of the great things about our way of doing business is that a man is never really down until he loses faith in himself, that as long as he has confidence in himself, in his ability to come back, he will usually find someone to share that confidence. This is one of the basic strengths of our system—one of the things that makes the system work and makes our nation great.

Even in the Junior Achievement companies that do fail—and I understand this is less than 25 per cent—there is an important lesson to be learned—perhaps, the *most* important. And that is that the free enterprise system challenges the individual to excel. It rewards initiative, hard work, and excellence. It condemns mediocrity. It provides an incentive to produce a better product or provide a better service. It guarantees nothing except the opportunity to compete. And this is the most significant factor in American business—significant because each individual, each company, each corporation is competing to provide the American people with a higher standard of living—and, in so doing, to strengthen the national economy. I said this same thing last night in New York City to 1500 businessmen from all fifty states.

If it is to survive, a corporation must have profits. If it is to have profits, it must provide a quality product at reasonable cost. If it provides such a product, it challenges its competitors to produce an even better product. It is a never-ending cycle that has given this nation the highest standard of living in the world.

There are those who say that this system is doomed to eventual failure and that we as a people and as a nation will fail with it. There are forces at work in the world today that are dedicated to the destruction of this system, and I would urge each of you to familiarize yourselves with this threat, which, I can assure you, is very real. But, at the same time, I would urge you not to lose confidence in the free enterprise principle. It has been threatened before, and each time it has emerged triumphant and risen to new heights. It has survived because of two basic factors that the doubters cannot seem to comprehend— (1) that the system itself is the greatest that mankind has ever devised, and (2) that its great strength lies in human nature, in the natural inclination of every human being to exercise free will, to improve his own lot and, above all, to chart his own destiny. I do not say that the system is perfect, but I do say, with complete conviction, that it is the nearest to perfection that man has ever come.

We, here in North Carolina, have seen free enterprise at work in recent years and it has been a fascinating thing to behold. It has been thrilling to watch great new industries sink their roots in North Carolina soil and then reach out in all directions to spread their beneficial effects throughout the economy—effects that take the form of new jobs, new payrolls, and new opportunities for our people. It has also been thrilling to see our old, established industries and business firms quickly adapt to new ideas, new procedures, new challenges; to watch them face up to the changing times with resolution, courage, and confidence. We have seen our people lose the timidity and over-cautious restraint that in times past has held us back. And we have seen them acquire in its stead a new spirit of enterprise, a sort of calculated audacity that has swept aside old toboos and opened the doors to progress.

Certainly, there is much yet to be done before we even begin to approach our maximum potential in industrial development, but there is ample cause for pride in what has been accomplished. If there are any who doubt that we have entered a new era, they have only to look at the facts. From 1954 through 1959, captal investments in 1,937 new and expanded manufacturing plants in North Carolina amounted to $1,037,000,000. This activity created approximately 109,000 new jobs and added almost $341,000,000 to our annual payroll.

Equally exciting have been the changes taking place in our agriculture. These changes have not been as obvious or as dramatic as the changes that have occurred in other facets of the economy, but they have been significant nevertheless. Our farm people are still beset by many complex and difficult problems—problems that are making it necessary for many of them to leave the land and seek their livelihood in industry and business. For those who would have preferred to remain on the farm, this is a perplexing and unfortunate development, but, at the same time, it is an inevitable result of the rapidly changing economic picture. It involves many factors over which we have very little or no control —mechanization, acreage allotments, crop quotas, consumer demands, etc. It is a situation that simply exists and must be faced realistically. It is not a situation that we can blame anyone or anything for. But, it is a situation that we can do, and are doing, something about.

We are moving away from our traditional dependence on the major cash crops and toward a more diversified agricultural economy. This will give us a better economic balance throughout the state, which, in turn, will strengthen the position of both the farmer and the average urban citizen. And we are, through industrial development, creating jobs for the people that agriculture can no longer support. I think we sometimes forget that North Carolina has the largest rural population in the country and that it is certainly reasonable to expect that a portion of this population will be affected by the trend toward industrialization in the South and throughout other parts of the nation. The important thing to realize is that the effect can be a beneficial one.

The free enterprise system works in farming as it does in other phases of the economy. The farmer has to have profits and to get those profits he has to produce for the markets. Our farm people know this and they are adapting to the changing times. Food processing is big business in North Carolina today, and it is getting bigger with each passing day. We are producing more livestock, more poultry, and more food crops than ever before in our history and, as has always been the case with our North Carolina farmers, they are proving once again that, given half a chance, they can out-farm anyone else in the world. Make no mistake about the fact that the Tar Heel farmer is emerging as a most significant force in the economic progress of this state.

I mention the agriculture situation here because to become good businessmen and women you must learn to look at the composite economic picture. You must learn early and well that all elements of the economy must move forward if real progress is to be made.

Let me urge each of you to continue your interest in business and economic affairs. Prepare yourselves for the dynamic future that faces you here in North Carolina. There was a time when our young people felt it necessary to leave home to seek their fortune. This is no longer the case. The opportunities are here today and they will be even more abundant in the years that lie ahead. The experience that you have gained through the Junior Achievement program will enable you to take advantage of these opportunities. It will benefit you and it will benefit your state. Make no mistake about the fact that North Carolina is counting heavily on each of you to use your talent to help capitalize on the work that is being done at the present time. You have it within your power to make the dreams of the present generation of business and government leaders come true. That dream is a more prosperous North Carolina and a higher income and a higher standard of living for North Carolina citizens. It will take courage and confidence and determination, but it can be done. And the young people here this evening are the people that can do it.

May I conclude by commending the many business firms in this area that have contributed time and effort and money to the Junior Achievement program. I will not say that you have done so unselfishly, for I think that would be a disservice to the program itself. You have given your support because you recognize what Junior Achievement can mean to the economic progress of your community, your state, and your nation—and because you have great faith in the ability of these young North Carolinians to measure up to the challenges that will confront them in the years ahead. But regardless of your motive, you are making a real contribution to the cause of free enterprise which is the lifeblood of our free society. You are performing a great service and I know that I speak for all the people of North Carolina when I say that we are indebted to you for this service you are rendering.

Thank you!

ADDRESS AT FORMAL DEDICATION OF THE BRANDON
P. HODGES WOOD PRODUCTS LABORATORY AT
NORTH CAROLINA STATE COLLEGE

RALEIGH
May 25, 1960

[Brandon P. Hodges of Asheville, not related to Luther H. Hodges, died
in December, 1957, after resigning as state treasurer to work with the
Champion Paper and Fibre Company at Canton, North Carolina. This building, erected on the campus of North Carolina State College and named in
his honor, was designed to serve the School of Forestry of that institution as
a laboratory for testing the strength and other qualities relating to wood
from which furniture and other wood products are made. State Treasurer
Edwin M. Gill responded on behalf of Mrs. Brandon Hodges to the Governor's dedicatory talk. Brandon P. Hodges, Jr., and his sister Sarah Jane were
present at the exercises, along with William C. Friday, president of the
Consolidated University of North Carolina, and William D. Carmichael,
Jr., vice-president and financial officer of the Consolidated University.]

It is a great pleasure to be here this afternoon to participate
in an event that honors the memory of a dear friend, and one
that holds great significance in the life of an industry that oc-
cupies an historic and tremendously important place in the
economic life of our state. The great forestry-related industries
that have meant so much to us in the past and hold so much promise for the future have been a source of strength and stability
in the progress of North Carolina and the South for more than
three-quarters of a century. It is especially gratifying to come here
today to join with you in the dedication of a structure that
symbolizes the enthusiasm for the future that is evident and
certainly justified in your industry today.

My pleasure in being given an opportunity to take part in this
dedication is greatly enhanced by the fact that we are paying
a well-deserved tribute to a great North Carolinian—Brandon P.
Hodges—a man who, throughout his life, held to the conviction
that dedicated public service is both a privilege and a responsibility, a man who regarded good citizenship as a personal challenge, and who met that challenge with courage and integrity.

The man to whom we so appropriately dedicate this memorial
today was educated in the public schools of Asheville, at the

University of North Carolina, and at Wake Forest College. A member of the North Carolina Bar, he early distinguished himself as judge pro tem of the Asheville Police Court and as county attorney, In the latter capacity he rendered signal service in the refinancing of Buncombe County's obligations during the depression. His obvious ability and dedication brought him to the North Carolina State Senate in 1943 and 1945, where he quickly assumed a position of leadership, serving as chairman of the Appropriations Committee and later as chairman of the Advisory Budget Commission. During the administration of Governor Gregg Cherry, he served the governor in the important post of legislative counsel.

On November 2, 1948, Brandon Hodges was elected treasurer of North Carolina, a post he held for five years. During this period he performed his important duties with exceptional ability, not only maintaining but enhancing North Carolina's long-standing and very valuable reputation for stability in fiscal affairs. At the same time he served on many important commissions and was chairman of the Board of Trustees of Western Carolina Teachers College in 1947-48. This state will forever be indebted to this man for the service he rendered as chairman of the Tax Study Commission which, during the years immediately following World War II, laid the ground work for much of the progress that North Carolina has enjoyed in the past decade.

Brandon Hodges was a person of comparatively rare intellectual ability, gifted with both the practical and technical knowledge needed to master the complex problems of public finance. Yet, he was capable at all times of maintaining balance and perspective. He thought of his job always in terms of the people he had pledged to serve. Taxation or a balanced budget were never regarded as detached or isolated matters, but as matters intricately involved in the hopes and dreams and ambitions of people. He was a practical businessman, a man of strong conviction and persuasiveness, but, above all—and this is the thing we remember him for—he was a humanitarian. Those who knew him most intimately knew this to be the guiding force in his life—that every action must be taken, not on the basis of precedent or expediency, but on the basis of what is best for the human being who will be affected by that action.

In the resolution passed by the Senate, shortly after the tragic and untimely death of Brandon Hodges in December of 1957, he was described as a "statesman whose mind was characterized by breadth of vision." And, in words uniquely appropriate to this particular occasion, the resolution stated, "It can be truly said of him that his view of the forest was not lost in an examination of the trees, and that he could rise above heated disputes to take a lofty look at the scene of debate or conflict. After others had expressed sharply differing views, it was good to hear his dispassionate, calm summing up of the problem, and his tactful suggestions for a solution. He was a man who led others through the warmth of his personality and through the moral suasion of his voice. His mind was of great capacity, his integrity complete, his vision unobstructed by prejudice. He saw the state as a whole, and, above all, believed that industry, agriculture, and every other phase of our life were made significant and meaningful through the beneficent influence of education."

The resolution concluded that "North Carolina will miss the wisdom and the foresight of Brandon Hodges, and those of us who knew him so well feel deeply the loss of a loyal, lovable, and dependable friend."

If one word had to be found with which to describe best the character of Brandon Hodges, I think that word would be "vision," for he was, indeed, a man of foresight and vision. And, it is because of this that I feel no more appropriate memorial could be dedicated to the man than this laboratory. He was a man who looked to the future, recognized its great potential, and directed his great energy to the realization of that potential. He eagerly embraced the regional concept in his thoughts and in his action. He looked not to the West or East but at all the southern states, and he saw this area moving forward, not by communities or counties or states, but as one powerful, coordinated force pulling together toward greater prosperity and the more abundant life.

Brandon Hodges envisioned this laboratory facility as a practical step in that direction. In the many-faceted forestry and wood products industry he saw, I feel certain, the opportunity for moving forward as a state. And he saw in this laboratory the catalyst for that forward progress. From here will come both the personnel and the ideas that will continually stimulate and challenge your industry. From here will come the tangible and intangible seedlings that will, day to day, breathe new strength and vitality into your activities—breeding benefits that will be felt directly or indirectly by every citizen within the range of this facility's influence.

It would be presumptuous of me to attempt to tell this audience what the years ahead hold for the forestry-related industries of this region. Most of you are closely associated with the industry—as educators, producers, manufacturers, etc.—and as such you are far more familiar than I with the details of the exciting progress that has been made in the recent past in this field. You must also know that there is little reason to doubt that the next few years will make many of the achievements of the past seem insignificant by comparison. All the evidence points to the fact that the next decade will bring a quality of maturity or sophistication to the industry that, here in our area, could mean comparatively great prosperity.

The forest products industry is regarded nationally as one of the most dynamic markets in the economy today. A recent economic study by one of the nation's leading manufatcuring companies concluded that, "Over the past years this industry has undergone a radical change, from logger and cutter of timber to a manufacturer utilizing the resources of the entire tree as a highly versatile raw material. From the basic log, the industry now derives building blocks of sawdust, chips, and thin sheets of wood which it then reconstitutes as pulp, paper board, plywood, and hardboard." Significantly, these new products have made possible new departures in architecture, furniture design, basic construction, and other fields—which, in turn, create a greater demand for the basic products thereby contributing to increased activity throughout the entire industry.

This is significant when viewed nationally, but it is even more signficant when viewed here in North Carolina or in the South. This state stands fifth in the nation in lumber production, first in the manufacture of wood furniture, and first in hardwood veneer and plywood. Twenty per cent of the state's industrial labor force is employed in the wood products industry. Every county in North Carolina contains forest land. Seventy of the 100 counties are over half forest; seventeen are more than three-fourths forest. The proportion of forest land ranges from as much as 91 per cent in Swain County in the west to as little as 25 per cent in Dare County on the coast. In all, there are more than 20,000,000 acres of forest land—and more than 19,000,000 acres of this are in the category of commercial forests in varying stages of productivity. And most of this land is owned by small farmers who are only beginning to realize the value of their holdings. When we consider that there are approximately 268,000 of these small land owners in North Carolina, it is not difficult to imagine why we consider the trend to expansion and diversification in the wood products industry as significant. We welcome the potential expansion of any facet of our economy, but we get especially excited when it promises to benefit so many of our people.

Wood-using industries are established in every county of this state. They provide year-around jobs for approximately 90,000 persons. Salaries and wages paid by these industries amount to about $300,000,000, annually. The goods they produce each year are now valued at approximately $1,000,000,000.

North Carolina's furniture industry today is a major factor in the economy. In the number of employees and salaries and wages paid, it stands second only to textiles. The 400 furniture factories provide year-around employment for 35,000 persons. Their annual income is around $103,000,000.

Today there are ten primary pulp and paper mills in North Carolina and thirty-three converting mills. In all there are sixty-seven pulp, paper, and paper products establishments in the state, employing 12,000 persons and with an annual payroll of $38,880,000. Through their manufacturing processes the mills add $91,424,000 to the value of their raw material. They spend $7,000,000 a year for new facilities and for maintenance of existing ones, and the goods produced by these mills are valued at more than $195,000,000 annually.

There are around 3,300 sawmills in North Carolina, providing full-time jobs for about 40,000 workers, with wages amounting to nearly $65,000,000 a year. Products of these mills are valued at $265,000,000 annually.

We also have, in North Carolina, sixty-three veneer plants, eight cooperage mills, nine tannin extract plants, five excelsior plants, twenty-five handle mills, twenty-three shuttle block mills and approximately fifteen miscellaneous wood-using plants. In other words, almost half (47 per cent) of all the manufacturing establishments in North Carolina are part of the wood products industry.

For our state I want to say thanks to all these owners and managers of the mills, plants, and factories of North Carolina connected with our forests and wood-related industries. The future of our forests and their production can be bright indeed.

I realize that there are many of you here who are probably familiar with most of the statistics I have cited. But I think they are pertinent to this occasion—because they give some indication of the importance of this laboratory. This facility has the responsibility of concerning itself with the future well-being of not just 90,000 citizens of this state who earn their livelihood in this industry, but, bearing in mind that this is a regional laboratory, many times that number throughout the South. And speaking of laboratories, we look forward to the establishment of the federal regional forestry laboratory here in our Research Triangle. We will welcome this facility and the whole state will cooperate in every way.

Clearly, there is a great challenge in our forest-related industries, but there is also a great opportunity. Timber demand is expected to be at least one-third greater by 1975 and 75 per cent greater by the end of this century. Paper and paperboard production, to cite just one item, will have to double within the next fifteen years to meet anticipated demands. This means that the opportunity for deriving tremendous economic benefit from this industry-wide increase in activity will depend largely upon our ability to develop new ideas, new practices, and new methods to keep pace with the demand. Much of the responsibility for meeting this challenge will rest in this research facility.

It is a challenge that must be met if we are to continue moving forward in this state and in this great southern region. If we proceed in the days ahead with the same courage and determination that has brought us to this point, then we have no need to fear the future. On the contrary, we have every reason to be enthusiastic, for we can move now with confidence in the knowledge that we are contributing significantly to the happiness and prosperity of our people.

COMMENCEMENT ADDRESS AT THE UNIVERSITY OF NORTH CAROLINA

CHAPEL HILL
June 6, 1960

[The commencement exercises, originally scheduled for Kenan Stadium, were moved on account of rain into the Woollen Gymnasium, where the Governor spoke to a much smaller crowd than would have assembled in the Stadium. An alumnus of the Class of 1919, he reminisced upon his career as a self-help student at the University and praised the institution for "opening spiritual and mental doors" to him as an individual as well as for the services and leadership which he said it was continuing to provide for the entire state of North Carolina.]

Mr. President, Mr. Chancellor, Distinguished Platform Guests, Members of the Faculty, Class of 1960, and Friends of the University:

I am deeply grateful for the high honor which has been extended to me in the invitation to speak on this occasion. To me, this is not *just another* university; it is my own University at Chapel Hill. This is my alma mater. And as one author has expressed it: this place is surely "the southern part of heaven."

It is of course an honor to be asked to speak at any school or college on the occasion of a commencement, but two such honors stand out in my mind. One is the honor which is mine today; the other is that time more than forty years ago when, as a senior here at Chapel Hill, I was asked to make the commencement talk at my own high school in Leaksville.

I shall not try this evening to *deliver* a commencement address. Rather. I want to chat with you informally and quite personally about some thoughts that come to my mind and heart.

I love North Carolina, and I love this University. To me they are of the same flesh and blood and spirit. This state and its people gave birth to this University and nurtured it through these 165 years since 1795. And during these years, the University has suffered along with our state the hardships and sorrow that have at various times beset our people; and this University has also been a sturdy, stable companion in times of joy and prosperity.

In the calm of this evening, I reflect back over the years and I am almost overwhelmed with a conviction of how much this University has done for me personally—so much more than I have ever been able to do for the University. It's true that I have been honored to have been given some authority with respect to University affairs. As chairman of its Board of Trustees I like to think that I have done at least a little in advancing the progress of the University. As governor of the state I like to think that I have been helpful in obtaining significant increases in financial support, and that I have been useful also in bringing about a sounder and stronger administrative relationship between the University and the state government. I am particularly glad that during recent years major offices within the University have been filled with excellent, outstanding, stalwart men—men upon whom this University and the state of North Carolina can depend.

But all of this seems small compared to that which was given to me by the University: namely, an opening of spiritual and mental doors for myself so that I could understand and meet the challenge of life as an individual.

I often think that the best way to find out where we are going and how we are going to get there is to look back to where we've been. I shall not try to go back to the beginning of this the oldest state university. That story has been recorded for all to read. But I would like to look back what to me is now just a few years.

I entered the University in September 1915—forty-five years ago—a short time in the history of this University and in the history of the state and the nation.

In 1915, parents generally were not interested in having their children go to college. It seemed to most parents to be a very difficult or impractical undertaking, for financial reasons—and anyway, did not seem to be necessary.

My own father said to me, "I can't send you. If you want to go, go ahead, but you will be entirely on your own."

The students of 1915 were not generally well prepared to go to college. Our public schools were struggling. This was particularly so in the small towns and poorer counties. For example, when I came here as a student in 1915, I was conditionally admitted because I had not had sufficient high school work on three subjects.

I arrived here in September 1915 with $62.50 which I had saved; and this amount plus my work during the summer months and part-time work while in school enabled me to graduate. I feel that my three years waiting on tables in Swain Hall (naturally called by the students, "Swine Hall") gave me an excellent basic education in the intricate and complex business of serving food. The tipping in those days was notoriously poor—in fact, there was none—otherwise, I might have been impressed with the financial inducements of the occupation, stayed with it, and worked my way up to be headwaiter at some respectable establishment. I still have memories of my "customers," ten medical students, their conversations, and their unforgettable odors from their laboratory work.

There were eighty-four of us in the graduating class of 1919, and some (including myself) had served in the Armed Forces for several months and had returned to graduate with our class. Compare the eighty-four in the class of 1919 with the 2,100 in the class of 1960!

When I was a student at Chapel Hill there were about 105 members of the faculty and a total student body of 1,369. Today, the number of faculty members in almost equal to the number of students in 1919 (more than a thousand), and today Chapel Hill has around 10,000 students in all schools and departments.

In 1919, the capital assets of the University at Chapel Hill totaled perhaps $1,700,000. Today, that figure is in the neighborhood of $70,000,000. In 1919, the annual operating budget of the University at Chapel Hill was $360,000; today, the annual operating budget is $23,000,000.

The 1919 financial figures concerning the University must strike us today as very, very low—but so were the income figures of our people.

The 1920 census showed the income for each person in North Carolina to average $357 a year. (The average for the nation then was $680). Parentheically, I might mention that our per capita income in North Carolina really went down during the early 30's to $187 a year which is probably less than some of you as students spend each month.

Now the United States has an average income per person of $2,057 against North Carolina's $1,384. North Carolina has moved up to two-thirds of the national average and I believe we can look forward confidently to equaling the national average by 1975.

Habits and customs have changed on this beautiful campus in the last forty years, just as they have changed throughout the state. I think that probably the revolutionary strides in transportation and communications have had the greatest impact on our daily habits.

Although I lived less than 100 miles from Chapel Hill, it took me from 7:00 in the morning until 6:00 at night to get from Leaksville to Chapel Hill. We came by rail and changed trains three times.

We practically never saw a newspaper except the few of us who might have gone to the Library. That, I must confess, was not a daily habit with many students.

We saw the Carolina-Virginia games from Gerrard Hall and made the runs and kicks by moving objects on a scoreboard according to information telegraphed from Richmond, Virginia.

Di and Phi Society halls were crowded with two to three hundred members each on Saturday nights. I wish they were crowded on any night in these times.

We have moved along since that time and have moved fast. Much of this movement I am sure represents substantial progress for our people. Some of the movement is probably just motion!

The state has progressed, but it has a long way to go, in spite of the fact that through much work on the part of many people there have been new investments in manufacturing establishments in this state in the last four years of over $1,000,000,000. Our per capita income still stays around forty-fifth in the nation of fifty states, primarily because of too great dependence upon an agricultural economy of mainly one crop. We have two and one-half times the national average of people living on our farms. This fact compounds our problems.

North Carolina is well and favorably known because of the way it has run its government, has handled its school and race issues, and the way it has moved forward progressively but with restraint and with a fine spirit of citizenship.

I have been asked scores of times and particularly in the last couple of years by national publications, "Why is North Carolina different?" I have answered my questioners by saying, "I am not sure that I know, but basically I believe that it is because of this University and the leadership and training it has given its students and its citizens for the last fifty to one hundred years." This University has projected itself and its services to every corner of the state and its leadership is unquestioned.

I could talk at length on this subject, but I think I will simply say that the state, the region, and the nation have been blessed by the dedication of the officials and faculty of this University through many years in spite of many difficulties. Its brilliant faculty, its dedicated officials, and its student body generally have had a deep and abiding sense of responsibility toward the state and its problems. This is a priceless ingredient which is paying off and will pay off in the years ahead.

This University, although big in size, still feels the same toward its students and the public as it did toward me and my fellow students and my public in 1919. This University and its leadership has not only a sense of responsibility toward its students and our people generally, but a warmth of interest is shown each individual student. This University is a simple institution, a warm and friendly institution. It does not put on airs and it does not want its students or graduates to put on airs.

Would I be pardoned if I make another personal reference? I was honored on another occasion by this University by being given an Honorary Doctor of Laws Degree, and Dr. Frank Graham, who was then president, told me personally that it was given to me because I had in my few years spent in New York City acted the same way that I had acted in Chapel Hill and my home town of Leaksville-Spray. This meant that I had joined the YMCA, the Rotary Club, had helped in community activities, etc. I had not made a big name for myself. I had not made a lot of money. I had not done anything outstanding. The University in its great spirit was giving an honor to one of its graduates who had tried to be an all-round good citizen!

I wonder if I could not suggest to you that most of you will not make a whole lot of money, will not make outstanding reputations. Most of you will do a good, normal job and will live good, clean, normal lives. May I add that is as it should be and may I challenge you to live a good life—one of service for your community, your state, and your nation.

Although you are getting degrees, you are not yet educated. None of us are. We never get to be. So, let's keep studying. Let's keep our intellectual curiosity. Let's endeavor to live happy, useful lives. I am sure that you do not want to have "security" alone. Anybody can have that. The Soviet youth has it. He has nothing to worry about except to be blindly loyal. You want opportunities, but beyond that you want challenges. And you will want to accept them with responsibility.

North Carolina in my estimation is still a land of great opportunity. In spite of its problems which it has had for many years, it is moving out into the light of progress. It is moving upward and onward! Job opportunities, service opportunities are many and are increasing in North Carolina. I hope that you find it possible to stay here—many of you. I hope you will continue to love this University and the state and that you will help them both in the years ahead.

ADDRESS AT A WESTERN NORTH CAROLINA INDUSTRIAL DEVELOPMENT CONFERENCE

Asheville
June 20, 1960

[Representatives from twenty-five western North Carolina counties attended this conference, which was one of four similar meetings held in various parts of the state by the State Board of Conservation and Development in an effort to stimulate interest in further industrial development in North Carolina. The Governor's address revealed his continued hope of improving the economy of North Carolina by attracting more industry to the state, especially the western section.]

Having spent the better portion of the past week in the great coastal region of our state, it is good to come now to the west, to remind myself of the great variety and beauty that ranges through North Carolina from the seashore to the mountains. It is a thrilling and wonderful experience to travel, as I have just done, over the broad expanse of this state and to marvel at the tremendous activity, the enthusiasm of the people, and the confidence in the future that is evident today and will be even more evident in the years ahead, if we handle our affairs properly.

In the east, in the Piedmont, and here in the west, things are on the move. Travel through the Coastal Plain today and you will see not only the rich green farm land yielding both new and traditional crops, but also new industries, new processing plants, and new business activity on all sides. Visit the bustling industrial Piedmont and you find not complacency, but a progressive spirit determined to continue building on the comparative solid foundation that has been established. And here in the west, we find people working together as never before, and trying (as this meeting today proves) to improve the situation in their several counties and this great western region.

This audience represents one-fourth of the counties in the state. Nearly three-quarters of a million North Carolinians are looking to you for the local and regional leadership that will enable them to take advantage of their opportunities, to move forward along sound lines, and eventually realize and enjoy the higher standard of living to which they are entitled.

This imposes upon each of you a sizeable responsibility. And it is a responsibility that extends beyond the confines of your own primary interest, your own community, or your own county. It is, first and foremost, a regional responsibility which by its very nature implies a state responsibility. You have made a good start toward meeting this responsibility through the establishment of area development associations. All but two of the counties represented at this meeting hold membership in these associations, and I am confident that each of them has derived material benefit from such cooperative efforts. Your Northwestern North Carolina, Western North Carolina, and Piedmont development organizations have certainly made contributions to the economic progress of this region and you are to be congratulated on the initiative and enthusiasm you have put into these undertakings. But, and I think most of you will agree with me on this, you have only begun to tap the vast resources available to you.

It is the purpose of this and the other three regional conferences that have been held across the state to encourage the continuation and expansion of your efforts and, as far as possible, to promote even greater cooperation—not just within your individual counties or development associations or region—but throughout all of North Carolina. No single community or county or section of this state has a monopoly on good ideas. Each of us can learn something from the other, and each has something to contribute. If this meeting serves no other purpose than to provide a forum for the exchange of ideas, then it will have been worthwhile.

I would like to commend the Commerce and Industry Division of our Department of Conservation and Development for its sponsorship of this event and on the initiative it has shown in arranging an informative and comprehensive program. We are particularly indebted to the speakers who have come here to share with us their considerable knowledge and experience in the industrial development field. Tom Dana of the General Electric Company in Hickory has discussed with you the very important subject of "Business Climate Appraisal" as it affects industrial development, and I can assure you his observations and suggestions are most pertinent. You have also heard Mr. R. D. Warwick of Statesville discuss what his community has done to attract industry. I believe that we must all agree the Statesville story is a good example of what one community can do when it decides to make the best of its opportunities, and I congratulate them for their accomplishments.

This afternoon you will hear Joseph Claud of the American Commercial Bank of Charlotte discuss the increasingly important matter of financing an industrial development program. Later, Edd Perdue, secretary-treasurer of Clarendue Metal Products, Incorporated, of Lenoir, will use his firm to illustrate the benefits to be gained by organizing and developing industry at the local level. All of these speakers are discussing subjects that must be studied and explored in detail in every community and county that approaches the subject of industrial development in a progressive, business-like way. I do not say that you should adopt all the suggestions or procedures outlined for you today, but I do say that you should give them careful consideration to see if they are applicable to your local or area situation.

Let me say at this time that I have not come here today simply to lend the prestige of the governor's office to this occasion. Nor have I come to talk to you in vague terms about the progress you have made, the problems you still face, or your hopes for the future. On the contrary, I have come here today to discuss facts and to be as practical and helpful as possible. I would like, therefore, to lay the groundwork for most of my remarks by looking individually at the twenty-five counties represented here in the light of their per capita income and population changes from 1950 to 1960.

The average per capita income for the counties represented here is a little over $1,000 ($1,003). Only two of your counties, Buncombe and Transylvania, have per capita income above the state average of $1,384. Fifteen of your counties have per capita income averages of less than $1,000. During the period of 1950 to 1960 sixteen of the counties represented at this meeting lost population. While the state was gaining 467,000 new citizens in the past ten years, this twenty-five-county area gained only 4,236. I cite these figures, not as criticism but because we have come here today to deal in facts, to recognize our problems, and to seek out reasonable, workable solutions. And I am sure you would not be here today if you did not agree that greater industrialization is the key to solving many of our difficulties. Look at the counties and their income, then look at their industries and the type of industry. Don't lose any of them, get some more.

Most of you are, I am sure, aware of the fact that economic progress doesn't just happen. Industries that are planning to move their operations or expand do not simply draw a name out of the hat and say, "This is it." The community or country or region that sits back and waits for lightning to strike is being extremely naive. Fortunately, we in North Carolina have come to realize that an industry locates where the cold, hard facts of good business practice dictate—and that is in an area that provides most of the basic essentials that are needed by that particular industry reasonably to insure a successful business operation. These essentials may differ somewhat with the individual industry, but the really basic requirements remain constant. One of the first prerequisities is, of course, an attractive community with clean streets and attractive buildings. Not infrequently, one of the first requests that an industry makes of a community in which it is considering an investment is for a picture of the main street. This has happened in North Carolina in the past and it will happen again in the future. It could very well happen to many of the communities represented here today. That is why it is important that you overlook no details in preparing your community for industrial development. Nothing is insignificant. Of course, it is not always easy to look at your own community objectively, but it is something you must do. You must ask yourself if your community measures up, if its busness district is modern and progressive, if its facilities for cultural, religious, educational, and recreational activities are adequate—and you must answer these questions frankly. You must not say that we are as good as some other community or that we have done everything that can be done. You will be fooling yourselves only.

If you find that your community is lacking in any respect, take it upon yourself to do something about it. Analyze your problems objectively, take the time needed to develop your plans intelligently, and then get on with the job.

Industry-community relationships are never so ideal that they cannot be improved. Cultural, educational, and recreational facilities are never so adequate that they cannot be expanded. A constant re-appraisal of all facets of the industry-community relationship is necessary if maximum benefit is to be derived at all times. Industry, itself, spurred on by mounting expenditures for research is an everchanging economic factor. Practices and procedures that were the ultimate in efficiency ten years ago have become out-dated. New equipment has revolutionized some industries overnight, confronting management with problems that could not even have been imagined a short time ago. Economic pressures brought on by domestic or foreign competition can vitally affect the operation of your local industry without your even being aware of it.

All of these things present a challenge to the people of the community to maintain close liaison with their present industries and to stand ready at all times to strengthen and encourage those industries in their constant battle with the changing times. This is one of the responsibilities you accept when you invite an industry to locate in your community, and it is certainly a responsibility you owe to the older established industries in your area.

I have no desire to duplicate what has been said or will be said by the other speakers on your program here today. For this reason, I will not go into detail on many items that constitute the so-called "good business climate." I would like to point out, however, that the final job of selling a community or county or region to a particular industry rests with the people at the local level. That is why this conference is so important. The state can do only so much. It can sell North Carolina, but it cannot sell a particular community or county. We can do and have done much to build North Carolina's reputation as a state in which a good business climate exists. Our success or failure in exploiting this reputation can be determined only by those of you who, in the final analysis, are called upon to lay goods on the line. If you are prepared to do so, then you reap the benefit of the total effort to sell North Carolina. If you are not prepared, then you let down not only the people of your own town and territory who depend upon you for leadership, but also the state that expects you to hold up your end of the bargain. Never forget that in the eyes of the industrial prospect your town represents not just an isolated community, but a state that has acquired, and must maintain, a reputation for unique business opportunity.

The prospect that comes to your town has been told that the great strength of North Carolina is its people, that they are cooperative, industrious, honest, progressive, and possessed of a pride that is justified by both historic tradition and the achievements of recent years. He has been assured that established industries in your area will testify to the cooperative spirit of your local government and the people of your community. He has been told that he can expect fair and equitable tax treatment and that his employees will be uniquely loyal and productive in return for fair wages and good treatment. He has been told that the various communities of North Carolina will make no unreasonable concession and that we, as a state, are simply not interested in the kind of industry that would require such concession. He has been told that your cities and counties will provide good public schools, housing, recreational and cultural facilities to insure the kind of community that produces a stable labor force.

These promises have been made to thousands of industrial prospects in this country and in Europe. They have been made in good faith, based on the conviction that the people of North Carolina are sufficiently dedicated to economic progress to continue living up to the excellent reputation they have built for themselves in recent years. It will require hard work, some sacrifice, and considerable determination to realize full advantage from our opportunities. I have never once, in the past five and one-half years, indicated to the people of this state that our ultimate goal, a higher standard of living, could be achieved with less than maximum effort. On the contrary, I have stated repeatedly, from one end of North Carolina to the other, that in the race for industrial development and economic stability, our state must run at top speed just to keep up.

The problem is even more difficult here in an area of our state that obviously faces the task of not keeping up, but catching up. And, while I do not offer this as consolation, I will point out that you are not alone in this respect. Other areas of the state, especially in the east, face a similar challenge. There is every indication that they are facing up to the challenge, just as you have been doing, and must continue to do, in this area. Your problem here, while perhaps magnified, is not unlike that faced by our state as a whole. Our economy is undergoing a rather violent upheaval. States that are traditionally dependent upon agriculture as the mainstay of their economy have, in the past decade, seen mechanization, acreage allotments, consumer requirements, foreign competition, and other factors knock the props from under the old concepts of economic stability. The ideal now is a balance between agricultural and non-agricultural employment. Simply stated, our rural areas can no longer support the large numbers of our people who formerly derived their income from farming. Unless we are to lose these valuable citizens permanently, we must, obviously provide them new types of agricultural jobs or new industrial jobs.

I do not imply that we should forget about farming and concentrate all our energies on industrial development. We must seek the desirable balance. In a newspaper article published several weeks ago, Professor Rupert B. Vance of the Sociology Department of the University of North Carolina pointed out that,

> The coming of new industry has not injured our agricultural economy. It has helped the farmer. Not only in new jobs for much of the displaced farm labor, but in the increased demands for products of the farm. When cities grow, new markets are created for farm products. Push and pull forces causing out-migration and in-migration have been due to the following factors.
>
> Out-migration: Farm unemployment due to mechanization, better seed, better fertilizers, counsel to farmers and resultant promotion of larger yields, so that ten farmers today can produce what it took thirty farmers to produce three decades ago; less need for manual laborers in cities; the mobile population because of World War II and the continuation of the draft in the Cold War.
>
> In-migration: New service industries in addition to manufacturing plants. Growth in distributing industries.

Five things that can be done to slow down the out-migration and speed up the in-migration, said Dr. Vance, are:

> 1. More education at all levels, in colleges and in the high schools, with emphasis on technical education, vocational training in technical high schools.
>
> 2. Diversification. We must get away from the one-crop industry just as the South got away from cotton.
>
> 3. Strive for industrialization, selectively.
>
> 4. Develop industries based on existing crops, such as vegetable crops, sea food, cucumbers, strawberries. Then when unemployment occurs on the farms at the same time crop yields show abundance, the unemployed can go into nearby food-processing.
>
> 5. Use of employment agencies, to fit round pegs into round holes. Both employers and employees could use employment agencies to better advantage, for jobs in this state and elsewhere.

Dr. Vance says an economy is better off when industry and agriculture are in between. He says,

> We have to face certain realities about both agriculture and industry, the climate and resources of our state and what we can do. North Carolina lacks two things that are essential to large-scale industrial development; these two things are: 1. Basic metals; coal, iron and steel. 2. Oil.

We have no Birmingham, and we don't have what Louisiana and Texas have.

To make up for these natural handicaps, North Carolina has had to exercise greater initiative in developing its resources, human and natural. We have done what New England did; New Englanders, lacking basic metals and oil, stressed new skills—watch-making, lock-making, electronics, metals, manufacture of high cost and larger profit products.

I think there is an even more striking example than New England to illustrate what can be accomplished, even under adverse conditions, when a people are dedicated to progress. I refer to the tiny country of Switzerland which is remarkably similar to our Appalachian area in many respects. Its terrain, its soil, its climate, its natural resources, and even its people—independent and industrious—closely resemble those of our Appalachian region.

But here, for all practical purposes, the similarity ends. While the small, land-locked Alpine country, which is extremely limited in natural resources, prospers, the Appalachian region of this and other Appalachian states fights for economic survival. While the Swiss gain steadily in population and readily accommodate a growing labor force, the Appalachians, as a whole, lose population and still cannot provide work for their people. In the past decade, while the nation was gaining 17 per cent, this region registered a decline due to the out-migration of more than 1,500,000 citizens. And according to a recent study by the Maryland Department of Economic Development, the people who left were mostly young men in their most productive years. This same study reveals that, even now, there are only 3,000,000 jobs available to accommodate a labor force of 3,500,000. And it is estimated that another half million jobs will be needed if labor force participation rates are to rise to the point required to raise regional income levels to the national average.

How do we account for the fact that the Swiss achieve so much more on so much less, For one thing, there is little waste. Almost 80 per cent of the land is classified as productive. On land similar to that in the counties represented here, the Swiss produce agricultural products valued at more than $600,000,000 annually. Dairying is the major agricultural industry, but they also grow large quantities of wheat, potatoes, sugar-beets, vegetables, and tobacco. *Most of these items are processed where they are grown for domestic consumption.* As a matter of fact, a vast amount of foodstuffs is imported, but much of it is processed within the country.

That Switzerland is a manufacturing country is evident in the fact that electric-power production exceeds 10,000,000,000 kilowatt-hours per year. Leading manufacturers, other than food, are clocks and watches, machinery, metalware, chemicals and dyes, textile knitted goods and embroidery. Their people are highly trained in basic education in technical and scientific subjects and in languages.

I think it is also significant that in Switzerland around 33 per cent of its people are employed in industry and handicrafts; whereas 64 per cent of the people in the Appalachian region are deriving a major portion of their income from the land. And while this represents 6 per cent of the nation's farm employment, the region produces only 3 per cent of the total value of farm products. Obviously, there is a great need here for a re-appraisal of the entire economic picture.

I think I should point out that the North Carolina portion of the Appalachian area is, in many ways, more fortunate than similar areas in some of the other Appalachian states involved—the coal mining sections of West Virginia, for example. The rather discouraging picture that can be applied, in a general way, to the entire Appalachian region, need not necessarily apply here in North Carolina. One reason is that we have a running start on most of the region in the development of the tourist trade. This is becoming an increasingly important factor in the economy of this region and our entire state. We registered a significant increase in income from the travel industry in the past season and there is every indication that new records will be set this year. Small industries, including handicrafts, food processing, etc., have great possibilities.

The most important factor, however, is the attitude of the people here in this western section of North Carolina. In the study I mentioned earlier pertaining to the Appalachian region, it was suggested that one of the major obstacles that would have to be overcome before the region could advance is the "psychological attitudes associated with prolonged economic difficulties." In other words, the people have become discouraged. I do not believe this has happened here in your area. I believe that the people here are well aware of their opportunities and that they have what it takes to make the best of those opportunities. This meeting today does not look to me like a gathering of crepe hangers.

Our entire state still has a long way to go before it begins to realize the benefits of its full potential, but I am convinced that we are on the right road.

We have, I believe, already fashioned the tools that will be needed to get the job done—and the major tool is industrial development. Another is diversification—both in agriculture and industry. Another is education. We must keep our schools open, and improve them steadily. Another is stable, honest government at both the local and state levels. And I hope each North Carolinian will make it his personal responsibility to take part in government and to vote at all elections—thereby helping maintain good government at all levels. And, finally, there is the spirit of cooperation shown here today which is most essential.

May I conclude by saying that while your primary concern at this time is the development of a better life through greater wealth in this region, you must not for a moment forget that to build a better Piedmont, or east or west, we must all work together to build a better North Carolina and not have jealousies or differences which divide us and retard our growth of education, better government, and higher standards of citizenship.

I would like to thank each of you for coming here today to participate in this conference and for giving me the opportunity to speak to you. I wish you every success in your efforts.

ADDRESS AT THE FOURTH SESSION OF THE
NATIONAL DEMOCRATIC CONVENTION

LOS ANGELES, CALIFORNIA
July 14, 1960

[As one of four governors from various parts of the nation invited to address the National Democratic Convention, Governor Hodges spoke for the South. He had at first supported Lyndon B. Johnson for the Presidential nomination, but now he urged all Democrats to "unite as patriotic Americans" under John F. Kennedy to give America the leadership it needs and "to restore faith in our nation and in the world in that concept of what America means to us and what it can mean to the world." Some observers suspected that the Governor had his eye on a cabinet or sub-cabinet post in the Kennedy administration, should the Democrats win in November. The speech was preceded by one of the most impressive demonstrations that occurred at the Convention. North Carolinians, aided by recruits from a score of other states, roared their approval of the man who had occupied the State House in Raleigh for six years.]

Mr. Chairman, Fellow Delegates, Fellow Americans, and Ladies and Gentlemen:

It is a high honor for me to be chosen as one of our governors to address this great convention and to represent the South in expressing our devotion to the Democratic party, as well as our hopes and plans for its victory this fall. It is good for our great national party to hear a grass-roots report from all regions of our nation.

May I say at the outset that the strength of our nation is dependent upon the combined strength of its various regions. We will not have maximum strength and stability without maximum understanding and cooperation between all regions and states. This strength is absolutely essential if we are to survive as a free nation and if we are to maintain our leadership in the family of nations.

During the past year I have made visits or speeches in various parts of the United States, including New England, New York, the South, the Midwest, and California. Along with eight other governors, I visited the Soviet Union for several weeks. This trip carried us into every major region of the Soviet Union where we talked at length with governmental officials high and low and with average citizens in the cities and on the farms.

Last fall I led a hard-working delegation of sixty-eight North Carolina businessmen on a flying visit to Western Europe to discuss trade and industry. We met and talked with over 1,500 European business and governmental leaders in frank discussions on mutual problems.

Ladies and gentlemen, wherever I went on these trips— whether to North, South, East, or West in America, whether to Soviet Russia or Western Europe—I was reminded how true it is that all people are basically the same. There are different customs, traditions, languages, and forms of government, yet I found that the average man and women possessed the same basic human desires and motivations—recognition as human beings, love and pride in their families, improvement in their living standards, a desire to be understood, and a very genuine desire for peace.

In our own country we in the various geographical areas are not very different from peoples of other nations. In truth, most Americans are descendants of peoples from other nations and we have inherited their customs, traditions, and characteristics. We are especially conscious of the contributions made by these different heritages during those early years when our forefathers worked to build our responsible and democratic government.

I have the privilege here today of representing the South, and to speak most briefly concerning its contributions, hopes, and desires.

It has been said that when two Southerners meet anywhere in the word they establish a contact of brotherhood, based on a shared past, however remote, born in the suffering of war, nurtured in the poverty of lean years, and cemented in the heat of criticism.

The southern point of view, in my mind, means the continued presence of a desirable and responsible independence and freedom—the kind of independence and freedom that make for growth in either an individual, a community, a state, or a nation. The southern point of view means the preservation of the initiative and personality of the individual, of the local governmental unit, and of the state. It carries with it a reverence for our fore-fathers and for the principles which inspired them. It includes, of course, a deep and abiding sense of patriotism for the United States of America.

In the South we have too often given the nation and the world an image which does not reflect truthfully this point of view. We may have been too careless or too proud to seek the understand-ing of others, and to tell the facts about our history, our tradi-tions, and our problems.

One of the chief problems of the South in recent years has to do with school segregation. Although the court has not ordered desegregation except where cases were before it, and its order would not apply unless a school board discriminated against an applicant because of race, the court decision has created great misunderstanding and problems.

In my own state we have not experienced great difficulties, but our problem differs from other states just as it varies with-in the 100 counties in North Carolina. Population ratios, local customs and, of course, local and state leadership intensify or moderate the problem. About every state and every nation is facing or will face problems or race and other relationship, and we should show tolerance, understanding, and—above all—patience.

There was no Marshall Plan for the defeated South, and re-covery was slow and painful. But for the past half century the South has worked hard to improve its economy and its standard of living. As late as 1938, the average income for the South was only one-half of the national average. Today it is three-fourths and by 1975 the South, for the first time since the Civil War, will equal the national average.

However, the outlook for the southern states is good and a recent official report from the U. S. Department of Commerce says that the value of manufactured products has more than doubled during the past fifteen years. More than 117,000 new firms have been established in this period, providing jobs for 1,400,000 people—a rise of 196 per cent. Manufacturing employ-ment is up 20 per cent as compared with a minus 1 per cent drop for the country. Electric energy produced is up 250 per cent versus 169 per cent for the nation as a whole. Retail sales show a 70 per cent jump versus 48 per cent, and world trade 138 per cent versus 111 per cent.

But enough statistics, just let me say to our fellow Americans and fellow Democrats that the South today is doing its share in the economic growth of our nation. My own state of North Carolina, for example, has for the last five years secured an average of over $200,000,000 a year in new manufacturing plants. This was achieved through the teamwork of state and local leaders and organizations, and without giving any tax concessions or gimmicks but entirely because we offered a good, healthy climate for growth and expansion.

The South believes in the Democratic party and has supported it in good years and bad, while many other areas *talked* Democratic but *voted* Republican. In 1952 and 1956 my own state gave more electoral votes to our Democratic national ticket than did any other state in the U.S.A. We believe in the Democratic party, what it stands for and what it will do for the average man of all races and creeds.

We have just nominated a great man for the presidency of the United States, and I confidently predict his election in November. Let's unite as patriotic Americans and loyal, hardworking Democrats to give America the Democratic leadership it needs to restore faith in our nation and in the world in that concept of what America means to us and what it can mean to the world.

There have been considerations that threatened to divide us, but I believe that we will emerge from this convention with a solid front, welded together in full realization that the considerations which unite us are more powerful, more fundamental, more important to the nation and to the free world.

Let's unite in a solid front with every region doing its part. Let's beat down the differences that exist among us. Let's keep our eyes firmly upon the important goals lying clearly before us. Let's win this election, not merely for the glory of the party but for the security of the future of our nation and of human liberty.

I close with this thought. We must always keep before us the great promise of America, which is the promise of freedom under responsible and democratic government, and I mean freedom for all citizens irrespective of race, religion, or creed. While our day-to-day progress toward more perfect realization of these ideals may seem to falter, and while all of us at one time or the other despair of doing great works, the spirit of America must always remain alive in our hearts.

I have pride in the America of the past; I have confidence in the America of today; I rejoice in my hopes for the America of the future which will, I know, be a more perfect Union—one nation, indivisible, with liberty and justice for all.

ADDRESS AT THE SEVENTH ANNUAL SOUTHEASTERN WORLD AFFAIRS CONFERENCE

BLUE RIDGE
July 23, 1960

[The American Freedom Association sponsors this annual convention which meets, usually for a period of three days, at the Blue Ridge Assembly near Black Mountain. As one of the featured speakers at the 1960 meeting, Governor Hodges expressed deep concern over the existing world situation and reiterated his belief that a strengthening of the American economy would be the most effective deterrent to the continuing spread of Communism in uncommitted areas around the world. At the close of the address, the Governor presented the Association's 1960 World Peace Award to Arthur Larson, director of the World Rule of Law Center at Duke University.]

It is with a genuine and urgent concern for the welfare of mankind and a very deep sense of appreciation for the noble aims and purposes of the American Freedom Association that I come here this evening to participate in this institute. I have not come to this meeting simply to lend the dignity of my office to a worthy occasion or to indicate my personal admiration and respect for the many distinguished North Carolinians who endorse and support this important program. Such considerations are, I think, insignificant when contrasted with the basic purpose of this assembly—namely, the strengthening and perpetuation of peace and freedom in our own land and throughout the world.

I have come here because I feel very strongly that it is the duty and responsibility of every citizen, especially at this most critical time in the recorded history of man, to involve himself wholeheartedly in the search for the answers that must be found if our nation, and the human race, for that matter, is to survive. There can be no doubt that man today possesses the means to destroy civilization as we know it.

Our own position in the international arena is not an enviable one. We did not seek free world leadership. We are not, by nature or tradition, people who care to involve ourselves very intimately in the affairs of other people and other nations. We have never sought, nor do we now seek, to impose our will on others. Still, because we emerged from World War II as the most powerful and most influential nation in the world, it was inevitable that we should inherit greater international responsibility. And as the Communist menace spread throughout the world, feeding on economic and social instability that is the natural aftermath of global conflict, it was inevitable that the United States should move to the forefront in defense of freedom and democratic ideals. Nations, like individuals, sometimes have little control over their destinies.

Certainly, there is much that we would do differently if we could relive the past two decades. We can benefit from the lessons learned in past experiences but we cannot rewrite history—even recent history—and we can find little real consolation in concerning ourselves unduly with what might have been. We must apply ourselves to the problems of today, and we must do so realistically and with great determination. We must accept the responsibility that has been dealt us by fate and by circumstance. We must pledge ourselves to measure up to the challenge that is ours as Americans and as human beings. And, finally, we must approach our task with full knowledge of the awesome fact that our time may be limited.

This is the conviction that has brought me here to your meeting this evening—a conviction that a reasonable approach can and must be found for world peace with honor, a conviction that widespread knowledge and understanding are prerequisites to international accord, and the conviction that the American

Freedom Association is making a significant contribution to such knowledge and understanding.

Your association is to be commended on the variety and thoroughness of its over-all program and its approach to carrying out that program. Your active interest in world law, indicated especially by your efforts to further the aims and objectives of the United Nations, is especially noteworthy. I have had the privilege in recent years of endorsing your High School World Peace Study and Speaking Program, and I consider this to be not only an effective means of attaining your immediate goals, but an effective means of preparing our young people for the complex responsibilities of world leadership they will inherit in the years to come.

It is apparent from a study of the stated purpose of your association that you are approaching the matter of securing a lasting world peace without delusions about the obstacles you must overcome. You have openly acknowledged the obvious fact that man can destroy himself now, today, by the simple act of pushing a button—that civilization itself hangs by a single thread that can be severed by one irresponsible act or one simple miscalculation. Even more indicative of your realistic approach is your acknowledgment of the fact that our freedom can be lost without a shot being fired. Your awareness of the economic struggle that is now being waged is gratifying to those of us who have for some time recognized this very real threat.

More and more Americans are beginning to realize that we can no longer take our free enterprise system for granted—that this system, which has been and remains the great strength of our nation, is being seriously challenged today by extremely clever forces that are dedicated to overcoming us. My visit to the Soviet Union last year convinced me that we must constantly re-dedicate ourselves to the preservation of our economic system if we are to survive. In the past we have been content with the knowledge that our system was the most efficient, the most reliable in the world. And, we are still ahead, but there is no longer any justification for complacency. Free enterprise is being challenged, and it is being challenged in a most effective and ruthless way.

There are many major issues facing the American voter in 1960. The only *real* world issue, I believe, is the preservation of world peace. All other considerations are secondary to this one over riding issue. But if we must be more detailed or more specific, then I would say that nothing is more important than strengthening the American economy. I do not have to tell this audience that this nation is the bulwark of the free world. If we falter for a moment, then the cause of freedom falters in every corner of the world. We are the one great deterrent to the continuing spread of Communism in uncommitted areas around the globe. In this capacity we carry a burden of responsibility that has never been equalled by another nation in history. And the only way we can meet this responsibility is to remain strong militarily and economically; and our Soviet opposition respects strength more than anything else. Even here the economy should be our first consideration; for unless we maintain a vigorous, growing economy, our ability to remain militarily strong and, at the same time, honor our economic and military commitments throughout the world will deteriorate.

Fortunately, we can accomplish this objective without sacrificing our dream of greater prosperity and a higher standard of living here at home in the years ahead. The burgeoning economy that can keep us free can also work for the betterment of our people. We can face the challenge from abroad and the opportunities here at home at the same time. We have only to apply ourselves, to use the tools at our command, and make the necessary sacrifices to weather the storm and reach new heights.

I am confident that America will measure up to its responsibilities, but I am in no way complacent. The forces that we must combat—the forces that seek to destroy our traditional way of life—are cunning, dedicated, and certain of victory. We must fight back with greater ability and greater dedication if we are to deny them that victory. We are each involved in this fight, for each of us can influence the economic stability of the nation. This is a thought that you should carry with you at all times, for it is basic to the concept of responsible citizenship in a free society.

It has not been my intention to imply that the cold war in which we are engaged at the present time must end in the eventual destruction of one of the opposing philosophies. In the first place, I do not believe that either system is so weak that it is likely to crumble under the pressures exerted by the other—at least, not in the lifetime of any of us here. Pressure will continue to be exerted by both sides, but there is evidence that the pressures will continue under close control. There is every indication, certainly there is hope, that the Communists will continue to pull their punches—so long as the free world remains strong. The Red leaders are ruthless and ambitious, yes—but they also know that a hot war at this time would be mutually destructive. This is why the Soviets, under the guise of "peaceful coexistence," have resorted to economic pressures, which they feel will topple this nation's economy, and the free world with it. And they are apparently convinced that they will succeed.

Our task then is obvious. We must maintain our military strength to deter armed aggression, and we must strive as never before to combat economic aggression. Once the Communists have been convinced that neither military nor economic pressures can prevail against us, we have won half the battle. Maybe "peaceful coexistence" can then become reality.

It is toward that day that many efforts, including those of your association, are directed. Whether we succeed eventually in actually establishing a world order in which all men and all nations can live side by side with integrity and hope will be determined largely by the action we take today. The seeds are being sown today that will produce tomorrow's success or failure. We will soon be in a national political campaign and the candidates of both major parties will talk of world peace as our greatest issue. We have cast our lot with the United Nations and whether we consider its past efforts successful or otherwise, the United Nations assuredly is the one international body that offers our greatest hope for an effective instrument for the future. I personally feel that the United Nations has achieved much in its relatively brief existence and that, given a reasonable period of world stability in which to work, it can, in fact, become the instrument for the establishment of a lasting world peace. I felt that when I served as a minor consultant at the San Francisco meeting in 1945, and I still feel it is the best vehicle of hope we have.

Effective world law, which is now being discussed more freely, will not come easy. To become effective, it will eventually require that all the nations of the world give up some of their presently asserted privilege of unilateral national action in international affairs—more so than any nation is now generally disposed to relinquish. Under present conditions, too few nations agree to this. First, there must be established throughout the world an atmosphere of respect and trust. And both of these qualities are byproducts of understanding—far greater understanding than man has ever acquired in the past. Man undoubtedly has the capacity for the degree of understanding that will be needed, but historic precedent does not reveal that he has ever approached this fulfillment. That is true in this country between our own regions. This is a sad commentary but a true one.

All over the world there is unrest among people as individuals and as nations, and we must, in dealing with these developments, be patient but firm, sympathetic but wise. Poor leadership, undue haste, and plain ignorance of the situations involved are more often than not the direct cause of explosive situations which threaten international peace and produce internal disorder within the nation concerned.

A great challenge confronts us—a challenge that could easily discourage us. But it is, at the same time, a challenge so vital to the future of our nation and the world that the idea of not accepting it is inconceivable. We are given no choice, for there is no alternative. We must learn to live in peace and understanding and we must respect law. We have only one course to follow as individuals and as a nation. We must courageously and confidently accept the challenge toward understanding, seek divine guidance in our deliberations, and move forward with complete faith in our eventual victory.

How does the American voter in the year 1960 fit into this dream of a lasting world peace? Quite possibly he is the key to the course the world will follow in the years ahead. He faces a tremendous responsibility—that of selecting the leadership that will guide the destiny of this nation and the free world through the next four extremely crucial and perhaps decisive years. I have no desire to inject political considerations into this particular discussion, but I would urge that this association encourage its membership, by every proper means, to give serious thought to the present condition of this nation's international relationships.

In concluding my remarks here this evening, it is a great personal pleasure to offer commendation to an outstanding man who has dedicated himself to pioneering in a relatively unique field—that of world law. He is, in effect, conducting a comprehensive search for world peace. In the process he is creating a better understanding of the problems we have been discussing here on this occasion. And in so doing he is making a most significant contribution to the eventual establishment of a world order in which men can look to the future with hope rather than apprehension. This man deserves great credit and our sincere thanks for his labor and his dedication.

I speak of Dr. Arthur Larson, distinguished director of the World Rule of Law Center at Duke University. In a comparatively brief time, Dr. Larson and his associates have proved the wisdom of initiating the program he directs. His activities have been instrumental in opening new avenues of thought and generating new causes for optimism about the years that stand before us. I consider it a privilege and a distinct honor, therefore, to present, on behalf of the membership of this association, the American Freedom Association Award to Dr. Arthur Larson.

ADDRESS AT A STATE-WIDE DEMOCRATIC MEETING

RALEIGH
August 9, 1960

[Twelve hundred cheering Democrats were on hand for this rally in the State Fair Arena at Raleigh. Governor Hodges set the tone of the meeting with a call for straight ticket voting and a slap at organized groups of intolerance. His pledge of unqualified support of Kennedy and Johnson brought hearty applause from the assembled crowd.]

My Fellow Democrats and Fellow North Carolinians:

In just a few minutes I shall have the pleasure of introducing and presenting to you the Democratic candidate for governor of North Carolina—who will be the next governor of this state. Before carrying out the pleasant task of introducing my successor, I am privileged to speak to you briefly, as one Democrat to another.

This is a great gathering of faithful, hard-working, loyal Democrats and I am proud to be a part of this group. Together, we, along with many thousands of other like-minded men and women, can do much for our party from this moment through November 8, and can continue serving it after a state and national victory this fall! Working together with a modern, practical, challenging organization, we will surprise ourselves as well as our competition as to how well we will do.

This is a "Democratic Year." The figures prove it. The Senate majority proves it (and yesterday it added still another Democrat, from North Dakota—the first time in history); the overwhelming House majority proves it; the thirty-five governors out of fifty states prove it; the preponderant majority of Democratic mayors in the chief U.S.A. cities prove it. The polls prove it—the man named Nixon admits it.

The country is crying for strong, active, pay-attention leadership! Our farmers are hoping and praying for leadership; our old people, our school people are looking for leadership and are looking to us Democrats! Our defenses—military and otherwise—and our standing in the world need "shoring up," need action, intelligent, forceful action. The man in the street and the factory, the woman in the home are disquieted, nervous, and long for a challenging leadership. Where will they turn? They can't get it unless and until they turn—to our party—the Democratic party.

What can we offer them? Plenty! No, the answer is not as easy as we have given it in the single word "plenty."

At this meeting here today we have part of the answer. Our North Carolina Democratic party organization—through regular, proper procedures—has elected a new state chairman and vice chairman. A few weeks ago, just before our Los Angeles convention, the delegates elected a new national committeeman and committeewoman. All of these four important officers were young people—good Democrats and winning Democrats.

At our national convention in Los Angeles, we nominated a young man as our presidential candidate—Jack Kennedy. He and his fellow workers, family, and friends were young people—active, loyal, hardworking, ingenious, and successful Democrats. Yes, we have young, vigorous leadership, with maturity of experience. There is an accent throughout the world on younger thinking people, and I hope many of us can qualify for this group. Our older people have not done too well at times, but many do have experience that may be helpful to our younger associates and I am sure there will be constant communication between the various segments of our party—as all are needed to insure success.

Although many Democrats attending the Los Angeles convention would have selected another presidential candidate, and in fact worked hard to do that, we did not succeed. Let me make it very plain today that we have no gripes about losing. We are not turning our backs on the party. We are not picking up our baseball and running home to sulk because we didn't get to be the pitcher. No, we will play on the Democratic team, whether out in the field, as short-stop, or as bat-boy, wherever we are most needed and wherever we can do the most good.

This is not blind party loyalty. We are fortunate to have a good team and good tickets—national and state! I believe that our national ticket will please a good majority of the voters of this nation. I believe that the national and state ticket will appeal to young people, old people, and all people. Let us not forget that there are several millions of men and women, particularly young men and women, in the fifty states who are not yet registered. Let us register them, and I am confident the overwhelming majority of them will vote for the Democratic candidates this fall.

I would like to commend the executive committee of the North Carolina Young Democratic Clubs for its forthright support of the Democratic party and the Democratic ticket for this fall.

Why do I say this? Simply because all of us, including our young people, our sons and daughters, our brothers and sisters are longing for a leadership that they can trust—that they feel is honest and courageous, that they feel is "looking way ahead" for this country. And because these same people want to see someone

Photo by *Hugh Morton*

Governor Hodges (*left*) and Hugh Morton (*right*) being interviewed by Wendy Barrie, WNTA-TV, during the North Carolina Industrial Mission to New York, May 16-18, 1960.

Photo by Hugh Morton

Governor Hodges speaking at a luncheon sponsored by the First Citizens Bank and Trust Company during the North Carolina Industrial Mission to New York City, May 18, 1960. Lewis R. Holding, president of the First Citizens Bank and Trust Company at the right.

in office who will restore our White House to a place of world leadership, restore our government to a hard-working dynamic agency of services, restore our lost prestige in the world and help bring some semblance of order to a careening, poorly-built poorly-supervised foreign relations policy and program.

We in the Democratic party have, as always, our problems, but we will overcome them in unity and hard work and in devotion to our country and our party. We have this time, at the national level the religious or church issue. If this issue were not present, I confidently believe our party would carry practically every state in the Union—if not all of them. Mr. Nixon, without the prejudice of the church issue, would probably suffer the greatest defeat in political history. As it is, he will get beat because, I believe, by this November the people of this country will vote for the best man regardless of his church affiliation.

I do not criticize or attempt to castigate an individual who in his own conscience feels that he must vote one way or the other. I do deplore write-ins and organized groups of intolerance and fear, whether of religion, race or otherwise.

We have a great national ticket, and I will support it. I accept at face value the statements made by our presidential candidate, Senator John Kennedy, as to his complete loyalty to our country and to the principle of separation of church and state which has been a guiding principle for this nation from its beginning, and which we should and shall always maintain. Furthermore, I believe that we in the South are well and ably represented on the national ticket by the greatest Senate majority leader in the history of this nation, the Honorable Lyndon Johnson.

Here in North Carolina there are those in this great assemblage today who, at the time of our two Democratic primaries, supported another candidate for governor. But again we followed usual procedures and today we meet with common interests— the good of North Carolina and the good of our Democratic party. This is wonderful; this bespeaks a great victory this fall.

Let's quit talking about the possibility of a Republican governor in North Carolina. There is no such possibility if we stick together and work hard—and we'll do both of these things. I don't have to criticize our North Carolina Republican friends personally to say the Democrats have proved for sixty years they can and do give good government, and the people are not going to take a chance on changing this.

Another reason we are not going to think seriously of a Republican governor is our own candidate—Terry Sanford. He has demonstrated he knows how to get nominated—he will demonstrate, with all of us helping, how to get elected. He is a good Democrat, is a good North Carolinian, and he will be a good governor.

For the good of North Carolina as well as the Democratic party, I pledge to Terry my every cooperation until the day of his inauguration as governor of this state and after that I will do whatever I can in service for my state and the Democratic party as a private citizen.

Ladies and gentlemen, fellow Democrats, fellow North Carolinians, I present to you the next governor of North Carolina— Terry Sanford.

ADDRESS AT THE SUMMER MEETING OF THE BOARD OF CONSERVATION AND DEVELOPMENT

NAGS HEAD
August 22, 1960

[Governor Hodges made it a point wherever possible to attend and speak before the quarterly meetings of the State Board of Conservation and Development, which were held at various places around the state. At this summer meeting in the Carolinian Hotel at Nags Head, he urged extensive development of the North Carolina coastal region, with emphasis on highways, bridges, ferries, and stabilization of the Outer Banks.]

I am happy to be here at Nags Head and in Dare County. There is great growth for the future in this territory. Let's get ready.

We need a convention hotel somewhere along the North Carolina coast. There are several lovely hotels like the Carolinian now, but they are not large enough to take care of a convention, and we have too many of our groups going out of state.

We also have too many people saying that other beaches are

cleaner and more attractive than our beaches in North Carolina. Let's change this.

It is highly pleasing to me and all other North Carolinians to note the many things that are being done to develop our whole North Carolina coast. One is the Chesapeake Bay Bridge-Tunnel, which will cause much North-South traffic to travel over U.S. Highway 17 and across much of the historic area we so proudly call "The Cradle of the Colony" in our potentially great Albemarle Sound section.

The estimated cost of this giant project, a private enterprise and for which tolls will be charged for its use, is $139,200,000 and the target date for its completion is January 1, 1964.

Opening of this bridge, which, traffic engineers estimate, will handle an average of 5,027 vehicles daily during its first full year of operation, should and will, in my opinion, mean much to the future development of this great Albemarle area in which Virginia Dare, the first English white child to be born in our America of today, was born and where so much has occurred since Sir Walter Raleigh's colonists first began their attempts at settlement on Roanoke Island in the late 1500's.

As to the Chesapeake Bay Bridge-Tunnel, a project which is most fascinating, it is interesting to know that traffic engineers employed by sponsors of this great feat of engineering say the fixed crossing will save one and one-half hours' driving time on Ocean Highway 17 from New York to Jacksonville, North Carolina. I repeat: LET'S GET READY for this great influx of travelers passing through the eastern section of our state. It will also mean much to U.S. 17 and other eastern North Carolina highways and towns.

Highly important to this wonderful coastal area in which so many people rest and relax is the construction by the state of the modern bridge across the Alligator River. This bridge, which should result in the increase of visitors to Dare County and other sections of the historic Albemarle Sound area, will cost approximately $2,800,000 and the expected date of its completion is in mid-1962.

This bridge will take its place with the Croatan Sound or Umstead Bridge, which was opened in 1957 and cost $2,750,000.

The Oregon Inlet bridge, now in the planning stage and on

which our State Highway Department says much remains to be done, will cost approximately $3,000,000 when completed. Hydographic studies are now being made regarding the ultimate location of this bridge.

These bridges are toll-free, and will make accessible areas that have been difficult and time-consuming to reach in the past. When all are completed and opened to the increased flow of traffic expected to result from their construction, the state will have invested approximately $8,500,000 and I consider it a very good investment in the efforts so many of our fine people are making to develop this historic section to its greatest potential. Again I say: LET'S GET READY and show our visitors to this section what advantages and opportunities it has for those desiring to make worthwhile investments in projects for future operation.

The Taylor brothers, born and raised in the Sealevel section of Carteret County, and who have gone on to fame and fortune in the world of business, are now operating a private ferry from Atlantic to Ocracoke. Tolls are charged for passengers and cars. They want the state to take this ferry over, as they began this service not as a money maker, but to help the people in their old home territory and at the same time cause more people to visit our famed Outer Banks and the Cape Hatteras National Seashore without having to travel so far.

Incidentally, the Taylor brothers have done much to help develop their old home section of our fascinating coastland. They have spent more than $2,000,000 of their own money to build a modern hospital at Sealevel to help care for the sick in that section; they have modernized what is now known as the Morehead Biltmore Hotel near Morehead City; and they continue to show an abiding interest in the region of their birth. Although all four now live outside North Carolina, they have not forgotten their old home area; and for what they have done to help develop the section over which they roamed as boys, the state of North Carolina owes them a big vote of thanks.

The time has come when the state should take a hard look at its ferry operations. It will need new and expensive boats if it is to consider the ferry run from Ocracoke to Atlantic or Cedar Island. Pamlico Sound needs dredging. This will be expensive.

But if Pamlico Sound is NOT dredged, boats will have trouble with their navigation.

The Hatteras to Ocracoke ferry is still on a temporary landing basis on Ocracoke Island.

A ferry at Southport is being urged on the state. Operation there will face tough navigation and may be expensive.

The state should consider whether or not all these ferries should be considered as combined operations and run privately at low fares for local people and lower fares for out-of-state people than are now being charged by the Taylor brothers with state subsidies being used where needed.

Following our custom of doing things when you can afford it and with highway revenues running dangerously low, it may be many years before we can carry out a program of expanded ferry operations. Meanwhile, we are holding up progress on opening an all-seashore highway or a combination of highways and bridges.

The whole area along our coast from Virginia to South Carolina needs developing, *with everybody helping.* This means local governments, individuals, and general popular opinion to help bring about this development. A full study should be made of what is needed and how it can be handled, and the various seashore organizations and other groups should cooperate to the limit.

The National Seashore Park, now operated by the federal government on lands furnished by the state of North Carolina, is a God-send to the region and over the next fifty years will be a wonderful magnet for tourists from all over eastern America. It has great potential.

The marlin fishing at Hatteras, with the Hatteras Marlin Club having put on an international tournament, is most attractive and has resulted in wide and favorable publicity for the great fishing areas we are now so near as we meet here on fabled Nags Head. The winner of the marlin tournament—namely, Puerto Rico with their Captain Esteban A. Bird, made a statement at the end of the tournament last June that Hatteras was the greatest marlin fishing ground in the world. It was a statement from a veteran and widely known fisherman that should mean much in causing other fishermen to visit this area.

There is also good marlin fishing off Oregon Inlet and Morehead City, but it takes longer to get to the marlin waters. And marlins caught are not wasted, either. I am glad that Captain Ottis Purifoy of Morehead City is seeking to develop a smoked fish for the state, and one of the species of fish he has been using is the marlin. It is a good product—I have tried it.

The whole Outer Banks furnish a great attraction, but they need attention. A large portion of the Outer Banks, particularly Ocracoke Island and the area extending from Ocracoke Inlet to Beaufort Inlet, is slowly being eaten away by erosion. Man-made destruction of the original trees, the destruction of sand dunes, the destruction of vegetation by livestock running at large, and the effects of hurricanes and severe storms have been the principal causes of this condition.

This is a matter of state-wide concern, as the Outer Banks are one of our most important assets. The principal reasons are:

1. This barrier reef has, in the past, provided a large degree of protection to the mainland from damage as a result of tidal action caused by hurricanes and severe storms. Formerly, this reef was covered with trees and other vegetation which, along with immense dunes created by wind action, made the Outer Banks a natural breakwater.

2. They are a major element in the state's vast tourist industry.

3. They protect the important Pamlico Sound commercial and sport fishery.

At my request, the 1957 General Assembly enacted legislation prohibiting grazing and the destruction of dunes and vegetation. That legislation was essential as the first step in saving that area. Livestock are still grazing on Shackleford Banks, but I am informed that this practice will be stopped in the next few weeks.

The rehabilitation of approximately seventy-six miles of the Outer Banks—extending from Whalebone Junction to Ocracoke Inlet—is the responsibility of the National Park Service, which handles the Seashore National Park. That agency is taking action to restore and rehabilitate the area under its control.

The next area southward, extending from Ocracoke Inlet to Beaufort Inlet, has deteriorated in some places to an alarming degree. It is the responsibilty of the state to take the lead in efforts to restore and preserve this portion of the Outer Banks although the land is under private ownership. The task will be time consuming and costly, and the state will need the complete cooperation of the federal government, local political subdivisions, and individuals.

Recognizing the state's responsibility, I asked the National Beach Erosion Board, in the fall of 1957, to prepare plans and specifications for an experimental study of dune rebuilding by the use of sand fences in the area extending from Ocracoke Inlet to Cape Lookout, and particularly in that area extending northeastward from Drum Inlet where the destruction was almost complete.

The 1959 General Assembly, at my request, appropriated $200,000 for engineering studies to determine the best methods to restore and rehabilitate the area between Ocracoke Inlet and Cape Lookout.

I, therefore, requested the U. S. Army Corps of Engineers to join with the state in such an engineering study of the above area. This request was approved on December 29, 1959. This will cost $130,000, of which $65,000 is to be provided by the federal government and $65,000 by the state. It will be completed by December, 1961.

A large portion of the Outer Banks extending from Ocracoke Inlet to Cape Lookout has deteriorated to such an extent that is not advisable to await completion of the joint engineering study, and Congressional action that may result, before commencing remedial action.

It was determined that the best interest of the state would be served by the acquisition of the land, approximately 22,823 acres, as it was doubtful that federal funds for restoration would be made available so long as the land was privately owned. Therefore, I asked the 1959 session of the General Assembly also to make available $400,000 for land acquisition.

The process of acquiring the land has been started. Right-of-entry has been obtained for approximately fourteen miles extending northeasterward from Drum Inlet, which will permit the initiation of restoration measures.

I have directed the Department of Water Resources to begin construction of sand fences in this area, as recommended by the Beach Erosion Board. The work, to cost about $110,000, will be performed by the use of labor from our North Carolina Prison Department and will begin on October 1, 1960. Bids are being mailed today on 95,000 feet of sand fencing.

It is recognized that this is a short-range program. Establishment of a long-range program to provide for the rehabilitation of the Ocracoke-Cape Lookout area must await completion of the comprehensive joint engineering study now being conducted by the Corps of Engineers and the state, and the provision of both federal and state funds for construction of shore protective measures as may be recommended as a result of the study. In the meantime, however, this first fourteen miles as mentioned above will get us started on what may be one of the most important projects ever undertaken by the state.

I have dealt primarily here with the interest that various state and federal agencies have taken in just one section of our coast line. This should not be interpreted as indicating a lack of interest or a lack of activity in other areas along the coast. In the Carolina Beach area, for instance, the Corps of Engineers has just completed combined hurricane and beach erosion studies, covering the area of Carolina Beach and extending southward to Fort Fisher. Total cost of the study was $49,950, of which local interest contributed $2,050.

At Wrightsville Beach the Corps of Engineers is currently conducting combined hurricane and beach erosion studies at a cost of $22,800 in federal funds. The report on this study is expected at an early date. I might add that the General Assembly of 1959 authorized an appropriation of up to $150,000 from the Contingency and Emergency Fund to supplement any local and federal funds that may be appropriated for shore protective work.

In the Fort Macon-Atlantic Beach area, the Corps of Engineers and the Division of State Parks of this department are cooperating in a beach erosion study of the Fort Macon and Atlantic

Beach areas of Bogue Banks. This study, which will include the Fort Macon State Park, is being carried out at a cost of which the state's share is $10,000. This report is expected in the near future. The Division of State Parks has available $150,000 to supplement federal funds for rehabilitation in the Fort Macon State Park Area.

In Ocracoke Inlet a program for the improvement of the inlet for navigation was authorized by Congress in July, 1960. The estimated cost will be $4,623,000, and efforts are being made at this time to get an appropriation in the current civil works bill before Congress.

The harbor and channel at Morehead City are being deepened to thirty-five feet at a cost of $1,500,000 in federal funds. Congress appropriated $558,000 in the past fiscal year to initiate the project; the remaining $942,000 needed to complete this undertaking is included in the budget for the current fiscal year.

Still another far-reaching and important project is being undertaken in the Pantego and Cucklers Creek area. This project provides for improvement of 15.2 miles of channel and construction or reinforcement of three miles of dike for flood control and drainage. The cost will be $536,000 in federal funds, of which $63,000 has been appropriated. The remaining $473,000 is in the budget for the current fiscal year. Local cooperation which is required, has been assured.

Finally, a project in the Core Creek area of Craven County for flood control, drainage, and channel improvement is being carried forward. This project will cost approximately $285,000 in federal funds, which $3,000 has been appropriated to date. Residents of the area are in the process of establishing a drainage district in order to provide the required assurance of local cooperation.

We have dwelt on these things affecting our coast because they need attention. I want to say that progress is continuing in all divisions of the Department of Conservation and Development and all board members and others will be interested. Director William P. Saunders and his entire staff of the department are doing a good job for the people of North Carolina.

Charles Parker, head of the State Advertising Division, reports that of the more than two and one-half million pieces of informational literature sent out in response to inquiries about North Carolina during the past biennium, more than 752,000 pieces of such material were distributed during the first six months of 1960. The total number of inquiries reached 116,502, an increase of 1,256 over the corresponding period in 1959.

The report of William R. Henderson, head of the Division of Commerce and Industry, is really exciting as well as encouraging to all those who give so much of their time and money at local and state levels to secure more industries and thus boost the per capita income of our people.

Bill Henderson's report shows there were 288 new and expanded industries announced for the state during the first six months of this year. These new and expanded industries represent investments totaling $139,008,000, added payroll of $50,546,000 annually, and added employees of 16,619. During the first six months of 1959 there were 263 new and expanded plants announced in the state. They had investments of $106,016,000, or almost $33,000,000 under those for the comparable period in 1960. I am particularly delighted over these figures and to note the large number of local expansions. This is positive proof that industry is growing and expanding in North Carolina. Let's keep our industrial climate such that this will continue to be true. We must not—we cannot—afford to let up in our combined efforts to provide more industrial payrolls in North Carolina. Reasons why we cannot afford to slow down in our industrial development efforts are too well known to elaborate upon them here. It is good to know that our next governor, the Honorable Terry Sanford, has said there will be no slowing down during his administration of efforts at state and local levels to bring more industry into the state and to provide all possible assistance to existing industries, which for so long have been such a major part of the state's financial backbone.

Gehrmann Holland, state commissioner of fisheries and head of our Division of Commercial Fisheries, reports that the oyster season for 1959-60 was one of the best since 1947 in price, quality, and production. This is indeed good news and indicates our long-range program to rehabilitate our oyster industry is beginning to pay off. We should continue our oyster rehabilitation program. The shrimp crop is also good and it is encouraging to note that fine catches of jumbo-size shrimp are being reported. I am glad to hear that advances are being made in other phases of our commercial fisheries program—a program which means so much to all North Carolinians. I am especially glad to note the sharp increases made in our catches of hard blue crabs in recent years, and this important part of our seafood industry is scheduled to get widespread publicity as a result of North Carolina entry in the National Crab Derby at Crisfield, Maryland, September 3, when hard blue crabs from many of the Atlantic Seaboard states will race.

Our Division of Community Planning under the direction of Robert Barbour is doing a good job in helping communities of the state to plan for their future. Planning work for Conover, Elizabeth City, Henderson, Hickory, Newton, and Thomasville has already been completed. Establishment of an area office of the division in Salisbury will serve Salisbury, Spencer, Mount Holly, Mount Airy, and Mocksville. These communities are paying the cost of the staff manning this area office. Planning assistance is also being given numerous other communities of the state under this program which was authorized by the 1957 session of the General Assembly.

State Forester Fred Claridge, who heads the Division of Forestry, reports that all possible efforts are being made to protect the forests of our state against their two greatest enemies —fire and disease. It is good to hear that owners of great forest tracts in this and other counties are giving full assistance to our Division of Forestry in the suppression and prevention of forest fires. The commanding general and his staff at the great Marine Base at Camp Lejeune have been of great assistance in helping fight fires occurring in the great and almost inaccessible sections of our coastal areas. Our State Prisons Department has also been of great help when needed. We must continue to use all possible precautions to protect our valuable woodlands from fire and disease.

It is also good to know that requests for forest management assistance continue to be extremely high.

Dr. Jasper L. Stuckey, state geologist and head of our Division of Mineral Resources, has also made a splendid report to the board. Figures he has collected for 1959 in cooperation with the U. S. Bureau of Mines indicate that the mineral industry in North Carolina is in a healthy condition, with most commodities showing an increase in both tonnage and value over the year 1958. Major expansions in brick and tile, in solite production, and in other minerals this year are indeed bright spots in this field of our great natural resources.

I understand that more than 1,000,000 persons have visited and used the facilities of our eleven state parks during the first seven months of 1960. This is good news and is added proof that our people can find ideal recreational areas without having to go outside North Carolina. Thomas W. Morse, our state parks superintendent, and his aides continue their efforts to make our state-owned recreational area second to none, and I am pleased that so many of our people, as well as thousands from outside our state, find the kind of rest and relaxation that benefits them so much in the busy world in which we live today.

May I repeat that industry is moving ahead in North Carolina? As I have said before, the matter of commerce and industry operation is sometimes more dramatic because it brings in money for all and helps carry on all other services. However, all services are of equal importance.

I am happy to be able to accompany another splended group of North Carolinians into Chicago, October 5 and 6, to tell industrialists in that area about the many advantages and opportunities that await them by locating plants or branch operations in our state. Trips we have made to Chicago, New York, Philadelphia, and Western Europe during the past three years have been productive, and I strongly believe that the industrial seeds sown in these areas by the splendid groups of North Carolinians, who have helped strengthen the economy of their state, will be paying off more and more in the years to come.

North Carolina is doing extremely well, I am happy to report. Our recent credit balance of $42,500,000 is an indication of how

well the state is coming along. The bringing in of the new taxpayers by the Department of Conservation and Development
and local groups working hard throughout the state is paying
off, and will continue to do so.

Now there has been some discussion of separating the Commerce and Industry Division from the other Divisions of the
Department of Conservation and Development. I doubt that
this would be helpful or practical. Bill Saunders tells me that
the other department heads do NOT want it done. I gather
that none of the board members feel that it should be done,
but that the present set-up is more economical and more productive. I agree that Commerce and Industry should remain
where it is.

Great credit is due the various local and regional organizations for the good work they are doing to help provide more
industrial payrolls in the state. They are understanding better
than ever their part and not looking entirely to the state for
help.

This state has just started its growth, and I urge all of you
to give it all you have. Push industrialization, agricultural diversification, food processing, tree farming, parks and recreation,
good fiscal planning, education (public schools and colleges).

Incidentally, the recent decision of the State Board of Education in recommending that high school graduates have a minimum of eighteen units for graduation from North Carolina
high schools instead of sixteen is most helpful, and I hope that
the superintendent of public instruction and all school superintendents will see that this is put in as fast as practical. Testing
in all state-owned colleges before admission of students is now
recommended and should be most helpful.

We are moving forward. The Research Triangle has great
possibilities. Chemstrand and the Research Triangle Institute
buildings are now near completion, and the Dreyfus Polymer
Laboratory will be under way in the next few weeks. It is also
expected that the U.S. Forest Service Regional Laboratory will
soon be under construction. Let's all get behind the program
of the state.

It is most exhilarating to be in the land where Virginia Dare first saw the light of day, and it is most fitting that we continue to commemorate her tragic mysterious disappearance along with her parents and others from historic Fort Raleigh where, indeed, the white race had its beginning in the America all of us love so much.

In conclusion, I would like to urge that all of us sing or talk about *The Old North State* every day, saying, "Carolina, Carolina, Heaven's Blessings Attend Her."

REMARKS AT THE ANNUAL CONVENTION OF THE NATIONAL ASSOCIATION OF LIFE UNDERWRITERS

WASHINGTON, D. C.
September 13, 1960

[Following the adjournment of the 1960 National Democratic Convention, Governor Hodges was asked to assume the position of honorary chairman of a Committee of Business and Professional Men and Women for the Kennedy-Johnson Ticket. In this capacity, he made a number of political speeches during September and October, 1960, of which the following is typical.]

Thank you very much for having me here this evening and for the privilege of representing the Democratic party before the membership of an organization that is vitally concerned with the future of this great nation. I can think of no more receptive forum for a discussion of the Democratic party, its principles, and its traditional dedication to progress, than before a group of people who, by the nature of their professional interest, are pledged to the service of society, to promoting, day by day, the health, happiness, and security of the American people.

I am familiar with your association, with its aims and purposes, its commendable "Code of Ethics," and its unceasing desire to benefit the average citizen by raising and maintaining high professional standards for the life underwriter. We have more than 2,200 members of this organization in North Carolina, working through forty-two local associations, and they have, as individuals and as a group, made a significant contribution to the growth and development of our state down through the years. We are proud of such men as Bill Andrews of Greensboro, your past president, and Ed Hicklin of Burlington, a past national trustee. These men bring credit to your association and your profession.

I would particularly like to commend this organization for its very frank interest, and its active participation, in affairs of government. This is not only your right, but your responsibility. As a large and influential nation-wide association, yours is a two-fold responsibility. You have the basic responsibility to maintain an interest in government, while, at the same time, you must continually guard against wielding any official influence in behalf of special interests that may conflict, directly or indirectly, with the more basic interests of the nation and the American people.

You have demonstrated your willingness to approach major issues with an open mind, to weigh the evidence on its merit and to make your decisions on a basis of what is best for the greatest number. It is for this reason that I consider it a privilege to come before this particular audience to speak, with sincerity and great personal conviction, on behalf of the Democratic party.

I might tell you that my work and training from 1919 to 1950 was in the textile industry—with the responsibility at one time of a score or more plants throughout the U.S.A. and other parts of the world. I know what five-cent-a-pound tobacco means from a tenant farmer father, and I know what eight cents an hour wage means. I know something of what it means to be the general manager of a sales and production operation of over $50,000,000 a year.

Through all these years I have felt that the best thing for a government to do was to raise the level of income of all its people. This means distributing wealth from the bottom up, but doesn't mean taking from one to give to the other. It does mean that workers, blue and white collar, should be given their share as the surest way of developing a strong and wealthy country. We have done well along these lines in this country, and I want us to continue it. I think the record will show that the Democratic party understands and helps the average man and woman more than the Republicans do.

I am happy to say that through this whole period, I have tried to work as a citizen interested in politics and political parties. And, I have worked under the assumption that I could do more good as a conservative businessman by staying in the party and helping rather than thumbing my nose at the party and its platform and with other conservatives risk the dangers of driving the party into the arms of extremists.

I think we will all agree that as individuals and as a nation we face today perhaps the most critical period in our history. We are confronted, both at home and abroad, by difficult problems that tax our comprehension and put to the test the basic concepts upon which our free society and our democratic government are based. For the first time since this nation won its independence, almost two centuries ago, serious questions are being raised about our national purpose, about our ability, as a people, to respond with courage and confidence, to the challenge posed by an ideology that draws its strength from deception and the ruthless exploitation of human dignity. For the first time in our history, the American ideal has lost favor in the eyes of great numbers of the world's population. There have been times in the past when we were not liked because we stood strong and resolute by our principles, but, at least, we were respected. Today, even the respect is vanishing in many areas of the world. There can be no question about the fact that American prestige has suffered some damaging blows in recent years. We have been placed in the position of having to defend our principles and our actions at every turn. In the great struggle for men's minds, we have lost the initiative—and there are many who believe we have lost our incentive, our will to win. And the really significant thing is that many Americans have begun to wonder as to where we are drifting!

In the very real economic and ideological war in which we are engaged with world communism, we have been on the defensive so long that it has become routine to wonder where they will hit us next. In the beginning, we tried to rationalize or treat as insignificant the Soviet advances in industry and

Governor Hodges with Arthur Godfrey during the North Carolina Industrial
Mission to New York, May 18, 1960.

Photo by Central Studios, Atlantic City, New Jersey

John H. Bolton, Jr., vice-president, Whitin Machine works (*left*) and William K. Child, president, American Textile Machinery Association (*right*), look on as Governor Hodges cuts the electronic beam which signaled start of operation, simultaneously, of 400 textile machines on display at the American Textile Machinery Exhibition in Atlantic City, May 22, 1960.

science. We told ourselves that while their satellites were larger, ours were better, or that the rapid expansion of their economy was not really important because it's easy to take big strides when you start with nothing. I spent some time in the Soviet Union last year and I'm greatly disturbed. We are fooling no one but yourselves when we "pooh pooh" what the Soviets are doing. Or, to put it more accurately, our national leadership is fooling no one but the American people. Today, after almost eight years of Republican leadership, we find that not only have the people of the world lost faith in us, but we have begun to lose faith in ourselves.

The American people have been so thoroughly conditioned to the fact that we are being beaten to the punch, that the punch doesn't hurt anymore when it lands. A day or two after we successfully recover our first tiny satellite from space, the Soviets orbit and recover a mammoth capsule carrying living creatures—and we accept this matter-of-factly. This is dangerous thinking.

Under the present administration, the Amercian people have been led to *accept* conditions in both domestic and world affairs that are not compatible with either our great heritage or our present capabilities, and if one criticizes, they yell "you are downgrading America." No one is downgrading America, as many of us still think the U.S.A. is the greatest of all, but we are not complacent—we are sincerely worried. If any of you know personally some of our military leaders, especially those who have left the Service in despair, talk to them personally and you'll be shocked at what they tell you. The Republican party has not kept faith with the American people. We are living in an era that demands much of us, and we need the kind of dynamic national leadership that can respond to these demands, a kind of leadership that is not living in the past and is not just taking it easy.

Our one great need today is for leaders that can summon up the determination, the spirit, the confidence, and the ability to get the job done that we have acquired during nearly 200 years of struggle and achievement. We need leaders that are not afraid of change, that will test and sharpen our ability to react intelligently and with unity of purpose to the challenges of this age in which we live. We need leaders that are not content with maintaining the status quo, for to stand still in this age is to fall far behind. We need men of vision who can look upon new frontiers with confidence, men who can rekindle the flame of enthusiasm and the youthful spirit of adventure that is uniquely traditional with our people and has been so much a part of our national character in the past, and remains one of our strongest attributes today. The Democratic party offers the nation this kind of leadership.

Listen to Jack Kennedy in his acceptance speech at Los Angeles.

> But I think the American people expect more from us than cries of indignation and attack. The times are too grave, the challenge too urgent, and the stakes too high—to permit the customary passions of political debate. We are not here to curse the darkness, but to light the candle that can guide us through that darkness to a safe and sane future. As Winston Churchill said on taking office some twenty years ago: if we open a quarrel between the present and the past, we shall be in danger of losing the future.
>
> Today our concern must be with that future. For the world is changing. The old era is ending. The old ways will not do.
>
> Woodrow Wilson's New Freedom promised our nation a new political and economic framework. Franklin Roosevelt's New Deal promised security and succor to those in need. But the New Frontier of which I speak is not a set of promises—it is a set of challenges. It sums up not what I intend to *offer* the American people, but what I intend to *ask* of them. It appeals to their pride, not to their pocketbook—it holds out the promise of more sacrifice instead of more security.
>
> But I tell you the New Frontier is here, whether we seek it or not. Beyond that frontier are the uncharted areas of science and space, unsolved problems of peace and war, unconquered pockets of ignorance and prejudice, unanswered questions of poverty and surplus. It would be easier to shrink back from that frontier, to look to the safe mediocrity of the past, to be lulled by good intentions and high rhetoric—and those who prefer that course should not cast their votes for me, regardless of party.
>
> But I believe the times demand invention, innovation, imagination, decision. I am asking each of you to be new pioneers on that New Frontier. My call is to the young in heart, regardless of age—to the stout in spirit, regardless of party—to all who respond to the Scriptural call: 'Be strong and of a good courage; be not afraid, neither be thou dismayed.'
>
> For courage—not complacency—is our need today—leadership—not salesmanship.

Those are words for a future—words of courage.

In Senator John Kennedy, we have, in my humble opinion, one of the greatest young men that has ever offered himself for public service. The fact that he has not come up the hard way from an economic point of view is more to his credit because he has worked diligently in public service, which is not true of many of us who came up the hard way but have held on to everything we had and have done little for those around us. Jack Kennedy deserves all the credit in the world for the kind of service he has rendered his state and the nation, both in times of war and in times of peace. He has courage. He has imagination. He has an understanding, and as we face some of the situations in the future, including those of the Congo and of Cuba, for examples, we need the kind of courage and constant attention that a president must have if he is to make a contribution. Have you read Jack Kennedy's book, *Profiles in Courage?* Read it. It is stimulating, challenging, and satisfying and shows the kind of thinking he does. Have you read what Senator Kennedy said about the church and his oath of office? I mention this because if it were not for the religious issue in North Carolina and other parts of the nation, candidate Nixon would suffer the greatest defeat in modern political history. He would be annihilated.

Senator Kennedy said in his acceptance speech, and I quote:

> I am fully aware of the fact that the Democratic party, by nominating someone of my faith, has taken on what many regard as a new and hazardous risk—new, at least, since 1928. But I look at it this way: the Democratic party has once again placed its confidence in the American people, and in their ability to render a free, fair judgment. And you have, at the same time, placed your confidence in me, and in my ability to render a free, fair judgment—to uphold the Constitution and my oath of office—and to reject any kind of religious pressure or obligation that might directly or indirectly interfere with my conduct of the presidency in the national interest. My record of fourteen years supporting public education—supporting completion separation of church and state—and resisting pressure from any source on any issue should be clear by now to everyone.
>
> I hope that no American, considering the really critical issues facing this country, will waste his franchise by voting either for me or against me solely on account of my religious affiliation. It is not relevant, I want to stress, what some other political or religious leader may have said on this subject. It is not relevant what abuses may have existed in other countries or in other times. It is not relevant what pressures,

if any, might conceivably be brought to bear on me. I am telling you
now what you are entitled to know: that my decisions on every public
policy will be my own—as an American, a Democrat and a free man.

I accept at face value what he said. I believe he is an honest,
straightforward Christian gentleman and he is the same man who
took the oath of allegiance as an officer of the United States Navy
and risked his life in its service. He took the oath of allegiance
when he became a Representative in the United States Congress
and when he became a Senator of the United States. Do you
really think this great country which in our early days became
a beacon light of freedom because of its emphasis on religious
freedom will seriously ask whether a president is to be a Jew,
a Quaker, or a Catholic? God forbid!

In Senators John Kennedy and Lyndon Johnson, and in the
basic philosophy of the Democratic party, there is faith in the
American system of democratic government, private competitive
enterprise, and individual initiative—a combination that made
this country great. Here there is faith in the American economic
system—faith that is greatly needed today, after seven and one-half
years of leadership by a political party that has shown little
evidence of faith in either the economic system or the American
people.

I want to quote you two extracts from the Democratic Party
Platform which the opposition never mentions.

Free competitive enterprise is the most creative and productive form
of economic order that the world has seen. We Democrats believe that
our economy can and must grow at an average rate of 5 per cent annually.

We will create an economy in which small business can take root,
grow, and flourish. As the first step in speeding economic growth, our
Democratic President will put an end to the present high interest, tight
money policy.

This nation cannot, at this critical time in its history and
in the history of the world, condone national leadership that is
less than courageous—leadership that has expressed concern about
whether we can afford as much as 8 per cent of our gross national
product to insure our security. We cannot endure the kind of
administration that prefers retrenchment to progress, an admini-

stration that, in effect, adopts the belief that we cannot afford progress.

We have here tonight, representing the Republican party, the Secretary of Commerce, the Honorable Frederick H. Mueller. He is the head of the Business and Industrial Department of our government. He knows what I'm talking about. He knows it takes leadership, imagination, and courage to build this country. May I tell you something of the North Carolina program of growth and development for the last decade. While the U.S.A. was losing 0.6 per cent in manufacturing employment, North Carolina went ahead 22 per cent. We have secured in new business and industry over this period over a quarter billion dollars a year. We raised no taxes but reduced corporate taxes. This development was under a Democratic administration—but the state had leadership, imagination, and courage, and it believes in the future.

On the other hand, during the period from 1953 through 1959 (under the Republicans) a period characterized by booms, stagnation, and recession—our annual average rate of economic growth has been only 2.4 per cent—about half the minimum rate needed and much less than other nations. This has resulted in the loss of millions of years of employment opportunity, involving a loss of about $200,000,000,000 in potential production. At the same time we have forfeited, at existing rates, about $65,000,000,000 in public revenues.

These are tragic facts and figures, but the most tragic thing about them is that they need not have happened. As a matter of fact, they could not have happened under competent national leadership—leadership that, as a matter of policy, sought to expand rather than depress the American economy. And you would have sold more life insurance to add to the protection and savings of our people.

I think it is good that the people of the United States are showing greater interest in political affairs today than they have ever shown before. It is good that the people acknowledge, through their interest, the problems and challenges that confront us. They are justified in looking upon the November election as perhaps the most important in our history. Because of this, I would encourage each of your here—and all Americans—to give much pray-

erful consideration to the decision you must make. Do not vote
as a Northerner or Southerner or Easterner of Westerner, or as a
Protestant, Jew, or Catholic. Do not be influenced by petty special
interests or personal considerations. The issues at stake are far
too important. Make your decision as an American citizen who
is concerned, above all else, for the future of the country. I think
you will find that the Democratic party offers the kind of leadership that can inspire confidence in the years ahead.

Thank you.

TWO-MINUTE INTRODUCTION OF
SENATOR JOHN F. KENNEDY

Raleigh
September 17, 1960

[Senator Kennedy was in Raleigh for a speech at the end of a two-day
barnstorming tour of North Carolina. Governor Hodges introduced the
Senator to a crowd of about 10,000 in Reynolds Coliseum on the North
Carolina State College campus.]

My fellow citizens:

It is my privilege to present to you a man I am confident will be
the next President of the United States.

My faith in this prediction is based partly on realization of the
crisis that our country faces. In criticial periods in the past competent leaders have arisen to see us safely through. I think we are
facing one of those periods. It seems to me that it has never before been so vitally important as it is now that we have a man
greatly devoted to truth and principle and dedicated to serve
his country.

Our Democratic candidate for President has faced in complete
frankness every question that has been raised in this campaign
as to his qualifications for the Presidency and has been discussing the issues with deep understanding of what these issues
mean. In order to insure his victory in North Carolina and the
nation in November, we need to do nothing more than to make
clear to the voters of this country the quality of his leadership

for this country, his concern for its welfare, and his vision about its danger and its destiny.

We will need greatness in the White House in the years just ahead of us if the United States and the Free World are to survive and grow stronger. Believing in the ability of our own people in North Carolina to sense greatness in leadership and to discriminate intelligently among those who offer themselves for high place, I feel confident that North Carolina will help to elect this great American in November!

With characteristic candor and force, our candidate has faced the so-called religious issue which is being ignobly employed to confuse and prejudice the people. North Carolina's state song was written by a great Catholic citizen 120 years ago. The native state of William Gaston should not need to be told that the measure of a man does not depend upon what church he belongs to, but on the quality of his heart and mind.

I proudly present a gallant soldier, a profound student of lofty statesmanship, and a statesman himself to this audience of my fellow North Carolinians who are well-qualified to sense the strength and devotion behind the simply spoken words of Senator John F. Kennedy.

I present to you the next President of the United States.

REMARKS AT THE DEDICATION OF THE SCHOOL OF JOURNALISM BUILDING AT THE UNIVERSITY OF NORTH CAROLINA

CHAPEL HILL
October 21, 1960

[Following the construction of a new building to house the School of Pharmacy at the University of North Carolina, Howell Hall, formerly occupied by that school, was renovated and turned over to the School of Journalism. Governor Hodges and Gordon Gray, former president of the University of North Carolina, William D. Snider, associate editor of the *Greensboro Daily News*, Ashley B. Futrell, president of the North Carolina Press Association, Holt McPherson, president of the Journalism Foundation, Mark Etheridge, publisher of the *Louisville Courier-Journal*, and Clifton Daniel, assistant managing editor of the *New York Times*, all shared the platform on the occasion of the School of Journalism's moving into its new quarters.]

I am honored to have the opportunity to participate in this program which holds great significance for this University, for our state and, I believe, for the nation. We live today in a world in which a free press in an exception rather than the rule. We live today in a world in which more than half the nations and a far greater proportion of the people know only what their rulers want them to know. Thus, the dedication of a building to house a great school of journalism on the campus of a great and free university carries a meaning far beyond the tangible brick and mortar of a building. We must on this occasion, not only dedicate a building but re-dedicate our lives, our convictions, our talents to the principle of freedom—freedom nourished and sustained by intelligent and *informed* citizens.

A recent factual report in one of the national news magazines shows, starkly, clearly, that the trend in many areas of the world is toward more press censorship. Today, we have more—not less press censorship than at the close of World War II. In the Communist countries today, control of the press is absolute. In the Middle East, each country censors local newspapers, and many maintain black lists of foreign newsmen who have shown a tendency to be criticial. In Africa, with the possible exception of Nigeria, press controls appears to pop up as rapidly as new governments. In the non-Communist areas of Asia, only Japan, Hong Kong, Malaya, and the Philippines have no restrictions on press and radio. Only in Latin America has the trend generally been away from censorship, excepting Cuba. In Cuba, Castro has stifled all press criticism, imprisoned editors who oppose him, and smashed the presses of newspapers that dared question his dictatorial policies. Of the world's 140 independent countries and important dependencies, we are told that only forty-four can boast a free press. In the remaining ninety-six, government control is either complete or restrictive to the point that it infringes upon basic human freedoms. I think it is significant that the countries which have been most vehement in their criticism of the United States and its Free World allies are themselves the most sensitive to criticism.

For these reasons it is good to take part in a ceremony that represents, not only an expression of our dedication to freedom of the press, but more important, we have here tangible expression of our determination to strengthen this freedom. And, certainly, there can be no more appropriate place for this activity than here on the campus of the University of North Carolina. This great institution, which opened its doors 165 years ago, has, throughout its distinguished history, championed the cause of liberal thought and action. This University has faced many hardships. Its very existence has been severely challenged on several occasions. But it has triumphed over every threat—and it has done so without sacrificing or compromising a single noble principle. This reflects great credit on the University itself, and on the people who have believed in it and fought for it through the years, but, even more, it reflects credit on the people of North Carolina who have supported this institution because they have known what the University means to the state.

Certainly the University has justified this faith on the part of our people. Its contribution to the social, economic, and cultural well-being of our state has been incalculable. And it has made this contribution, not on a basis of academic mediocrity or minimum standards of proficiency, but on the basis of academic excellence. This University holds the distinction of being one of the thirty-nine on the North American continent to belong to the American Association of Universities—"The Top Union." A nearby sister institution, Duke University, also has this honor.

Many have asked, "Why is the University of North Carolina outstanding? Why is it unique?" And they have found that there is no all-encompassing answer. That is because the University is many things to many people. That is as it should be. But if we must have an answer, I would suggest that the University is outstanding because it is a leader. It has exercised leadership in the unceasing fight for higher standards of education throughout North Carolina, and its influence has been felt in every corner of the state.

The University was one of the leaders, among public universities of the nation, in requiring tests for admission to the freshman class—a practice long advocated by the State Board of Higher Education. North Carolina can be proud of the fact that all but three of its public institutions of higher education have announced that they will require the Scholastic Aptitude Test for all applicants for admission to freshman classes in the fall of 1961. That this will be a tremendous asset to education in North Carolina is indicated by the fact that much improvement has already been noted in freshman classes entering the University under the testing program. Another indication of leadership in this field is the long-standing requirement that candidates for admission to the University Graduate School pass the Graduate Record Examination.

The University School of Education is still another indication of this institution's leadership in this vital area. Housed in a new $1,000,000 addition to Peabody Hall, this School of Education is widely recognized for its high standards. This high quality level has, to some degree, reduced quantitative output, but this is in keeping with the University's reputation for excellence, and is to be commended. This also reflects credit on the University administration and faculty; for these are the men and women who day by-day maintain, by their independent thought and action, that reputation for excellence.

There can be litle doubt that much of the greatness that permeates the character of this University grows from the wide variety of instruction offered here. Some insight into this variety can be seen in the fact that masters degrees are offered in forty-two fields, along with top flight professional training in the Schools of Education, Law, Medicine, Nursing, Dentistry, Social Work, Public Health, Library Science, Pharmacy, Business Administration and *Journalism*. The University has one of the widest ranges of Ph.D. programs in the nation. This coveted degree is awarded in twenty-seven fields, and most of you are aware, I am sure, that a Ph.D. from the University of North Carolina carries unusual prestige.

It should be a source of great pride to all of us here that the School of Journalism has, in its comparatively brief history,

:aught the spirit of this University, placing emphasis upon a
blending of solid liberal education with the more technical aspects of preparation for this important profession.

I think it would be most appropriate on this occasion to pay
tribute to the man who, for many years, was the personification
of this sound approach to journalistic training. I refer, of course,
to the late Oscar J. Coffin—"O. J." to his close friends and devoted
readers—"Skipper" to his students and thousands of others
throughout North Carolina who loved and respected him.
Skipper did not believe in "ivory tower" journalism, but he
was a firm advocate of liberal education. The mechanics of
newspapering were important, but so were economics, literature, political science, and the social sciences—especially North
Carolina history. He held that there were two books the writer
must master before he could call himself a good newspaperman—
the dictionary and the King James Version of the Bible. Skipper
Coffin dearly loved this state and its people and he knew what
good newspapers could mean to our future. He was a tolerant
and understanding person, but the one thing he could not
abide was irresponsible journalism. He was absolutely right,
and ours is a better state today for the lasting contribution he
made to this school and the newspaper profession.

Gone are the days when we can afford to produce journalists
who are mere technicians, brokers, as it were, in newspaper glam-
our and sensation, drawing their inspiration, not from ethics,
but from the circulation department. There are some glaring
exceptions to this lovely state of affairs, but I dare say those responsible did not graduate from this excellent School of
Journalism at Chapel Hill.

The day of completely responsible journalism—or writers
who study and think before they write—is nearer at hand, and
I am happy to know that our School of Journalism is in the
vanguard. Newspapers today do not only reflect public opinion;
they have the great power to influence public opinion. And this
kind of power, without self-discipline and devoid of careful and
good judgment, can be socially, culturally, and economically
destructive. We still have too much journalistic irresponsibility

in the nation (in various media), but North Carolina rates better than most others.

A great deterrent to the unprincipled use of this power of the press is a disciplined, informed, and dedicated writer—a writer who weighs his words in the balance of reason, and who has the courage and the integrity necessary to report all the facts, not just those which lend credence to personal prejudices.

It is to this end, to the development of responsible journalists, that this great building is being dedicated today. This is a high purpose, one which holds great meaning for the future of our state, and it is most gratifying to know that the foundation has already been laid for the perpetuation of this ethical training. Both your administrative and government officials readily acknowledge the importance of the work that will be carried on here, and I can assure you that you will have the full cooperation of the state which has a definite responsibility for the support of professional education. Its support, however, will come with greater enthusiasm if the professional schools emphasize quality and high principles.

I will be the first to concede that this University and some of our other educational institutions have not always received the full measure of support they deserved—but I do not think this has been the case in recent years. The University has expanded primarily because of the support it has received from the state of North Carolina. In just the six years I have been governor, the increase has been marked. In 1954 the enrollment here was around 7,140 and the faculty numbered slightly less than 800. Today the enrollment exceeds 10,150 and faculty membership has risen to 1,128. It is estimated that by 1962-63 the total enrollment will exceed 11,300.

To aid in this real and anticipated growth, the state has invested heavily in the University. In 1947, the total value of land, buildings, furnishings and equipment on this campus was placed at roughly $15,000,000. In 1959, the estimate is more than $65,500,000. Even allowing for increase in values due to inflation, these figures indicate the great physical expansion which has taken place on this campus.

Certainly, if this new journalism building is any indication

of the way the money has been spent, then the people of North
Carolina have received a bountiful return on their investment.
A marvelous job has been done here, and I would like to commend the architect and builders, as well as Dean Luxon and
his staff on their fine work. This school will be a credit to the
University and to the state of North Carolina, and I'm glad to
have a part in the dedication of this building.

May history record, through the future great accomplishments
of this school, that there was also a *re-dedication* here today to
the great principles of freedom and responsibility of the press.

SPEECH AS HONORARY NATIONAL CHAIRMAN OF THE COMMITTEE OF BUSINESS AND PROFESSIONAL MEN AND WOMEN FOR THE KENNEDY-JOHNSON TICKET

PHILADELPHIA, PENNSYLVANIA
October 24, 1960

[This speech, or variations of it, was made by Governor Hodges in the
interest of the Kennedy-Johnson ticket to business and professional groups,
in addition to the group at Philadelphia, at Chicago on September 19; at
Wilmington, Delaware, and Charlottesville, Virginia, on October 24; at
Wichita Falls and Dallas, Texas, on October 27; at Danville and Chatham,
Virginia, on October 31; and possibly at one or two other places.]

It is good to have a chance to talk with you about the
Kennedy-Johnson ticket because I believe that if you analyze
the situation frankly, you will agree that the Democratic party
and the Kennedy-Johnson ticket are best for the country, best
for you and your business or profession.

I have been honored to be asked to act as national chairman
of this organization of Business and Professional Men and
Women for Kennedy-Johnson. When Senator Kennedy asked
me if I would take the national honorary chairmanship, I said,
"I would like to see you and talk with you first." When I saw him,
I said, "Jack, many of my friends in business and professions and

industry feel that you are too radical; that you lean too much to
labor and that you will take the country down a socialistic road. I
want to be able to say to them as I ask for their support for you
and Senator Johnson that you are willing to listen to those of
us who call ourselves 'conservatives' after you are elected as well
as before you are elected. I want to know that you feel as I
believe you feel that we must have a sound government and
that you will run it on a sound basis." Senator Kennedy said
without hesitation, "You may speak to your friends with complete candor along the lines you mentioned. I will not only
talk with them about any ideas they have, but I want you
to know I am not a radical and that I will work for a balanced
budget, except in case of a national emergency, and you need
not have any concern about my soundness. I am glad to have
labor support," he said, "but I also want the support of management and business. I want to be President of all the people, not
just special groups."

I accepted the high honor accorded me and I say to you today
that there is no hesitation on my part to speak out publicly and
proudly for the Democratic ticket, which I feel sure is going to
be elected and which I think will mean much to this great
country of ours and to the leadership of the free world.

The Democratic party is a party of a dynamic, vigorous quality.
It moves forward and stimulates the economy. It serves the
people. Our two Democratic candidates have had great experience in originating legislation and seeing that its gets through
the Congress. They have given courageous leadership. Those
are qualities that will be needed in the White House and the
administration in the years ahead. Senator Kennedy, for example, introduced and personally got through Congress legislation
putting into effect many of the Hoover Commission recommendations affecting our economy and government reorganization.
This was *the* major revision in the nation's budget and accounting system in over twenty years.

For ten years Senator Lyndon Johnson has guided the Senate
Preparedness Sub-committee, giving us better defenses and saving
the taxpayers over $3,000,000,000. He is a master at handling
people and situations and he's a great patriot!

Part of the trouble in my state of North Carolina and elsewhere is that some people seem to feel it has become fashionable to vote Republican, as the Republican party seems to be associated with money and with society. This, in spite of the fact that the Democratic party has given this country such stalwart leaders as Woodrow Wilson, Franklin D. Roosevelt, Harry Truman, and now offers Jack Kennedy. Over against that, we have had, for example, Harding, Coolidge, Hoover, Landon as candidates, and now as a candidate, Mr. Nixon.

Speaking of being fashionable to vote Republican, I had an experience a few weeks ago in a southern city when someone asked me if I would come by the bank and speak to the chairman of the board, who was "quite a guy" they said. I asked for his background and they said he was from the southern part of the state, that he was originally a Baptist and a Democrat—now he was an Episcopalian and a Republican.

I am basically conservative, but I am for the party that helps people as a whole. This is not socialism, but sound and fair government. In the six years or more that I have been governor of North Carolina, I have had one leading objective and that is to raise the per capita income of the people and to raise their standard of living. We have worked night and day to get industry into the state so that we might have jobs for people who are losing their jobs on the farms. By getting the people jobs we are able to help them raise their standard of living. In the last five years our state has secured over $1,000,000,000 of new manufacturing investment.

I recall in the 1930's when the NRA was being formed that some of my southern mill-owner friends, who vote the state Democratic ticket and the national Republican ticket, and many of our Republican friends from New England fought against a thirty-cents an hour minimum wage and a forty-hour week. They said, in my presence, that if these things were done they would have to go out of business and the country would be ruined.

Republicans have said the same kind of thing since that time, and particularly in Congress. The Republicans have too often voted against legislation that helped the people as a whole. They voted against Social Security, minimum wages, rural electrification, aid to education, medical care. I challenge the Republicans to point to anything that they have originated which was basically for the people as a whole.

Let's analyze for a moment what the Republicans are talking about in this campaign as to why you should vote on their side.

They speak of experience, for example. Their experience includes:

Fiscal. In the 1952 campaign the Republican candidates, Eisenhower and Nixon, said that they would balance the budget, they would reduce federal spending, they would cut down the number of government employees, and they would save the country from these reckless Democrats.

What is the result of their great experience? Since World War II, we have had seven years in which the Democratic party was in charge of the executive branch of government and seven years in which the Republican party was in control. Including the staggering cost of the Korean War, the Democratic administration under President Truman, run up a deficit of $5,700,000,000 in seven years.

Under the Republican administration, President Eisenhower has run up a deficit of $19,000,000,000. When these figures are mentioned, the Republicans say they were deficits because of the Democratic Congress. As Lyndon Johnson says, let's look at the facts. Since 1954, when the Democrats took control of Congress, a total of $12,500,000,000 has been cut from the budget sent to the Congress by the Republican administration. So the deficit would have been $31,500,000,000 except for the cuts by Democrats. You will find very few people in the country who will believe this figure, or realize that it is true. They simply aren't willing to look at it.

When the Republicans took over in Washington in 1953 there were 67,000 employees in the Department of Agriculture. That number has now jumped to 98,000—an increase of nearly 50 per cent. The administrative cost of the farm price support operations has increased from $34,000,000 to $364,000,000 a year, or 970 per cent.

In 1952, when I was making campaign speeches for the Democratic party, I said that Mr. Eisenhower would be the "spend-ingest President" in all history and that he did not know the value of a dollar. Let's look at the record.

He has increased the national debt two or three times since he came into office. He has run the highest deficits in the history of the nation.

In the seven years, plus, of Republican administration under Eisenhower they have collected in taxes from the American people $480,000,000,000.

Against this, note that for the period from 1934 to 1953, including all the cost of World War II and the Korean War, the total expenditure under Roosevelt and Truman was $479,000,000,000.

In the 150 years from 1793 to 1943, the total expenditure was only about $150,000,000,000.

If the Republicans were to continue in office and spend for the next two years at the rate they have spent for the last seven, this one administration in less than ten years would have spent more than all Presidents of the United States from George Washington through Truman.

I ask you, "Are they *fiscal* experts?"

Social Welfare. What have they done in health, education, welfare, etc.? They have generally followed the lines of the Democratic-sponsored legislation of many years before, but they have not originated anything. Look at their voting record of opposition.

Foreign Affairs. How has their experience turned out in foreign affairs? I do not feel competent to discuss intricate details of foreign policy, but there is hardly a man, woman or child on the street that doesn't feel that something must be done. The present administration has failed miserably in keeping the proper stature and image of America throughout the world. Witness South America and the Nixon trip! Witness the summit meeting at Geneva and the projected one at Paris. Witness the U 2 incidents which brought us to a low, low point of American prestige. Nobody had ever caught us lying before. Witness Cuba, a disgraceful situation. Witness the Japanese riots, again disgraceful. Witness Red China and note that on Saturday, October 8, for the first time the United States (sponsoring a resolution of keeping Red China out of the United Nations) failed to get a majority of the votes of the ninety-nine members of the United Nations. This shows our waning influence with other nations.

Basically, gentlemen, those of you who are in business and in professions know what it means "to keep the store." May I say to you with all respect that proper attention has not been given in domestic or foreign affairs to "keeping the store" in the last several years. If it had not been for a constructive Congress and a basically strong America, we would have a worse state of affairs today.

The Republicans say they have built a better platform. Mr. Nixon had his own platform to suit what he thought would get him the most votes because he was one of the old-line Republican regulars. After Nixon had the mid-night tryst with Rockefeller, he made a 180 degree turn. Senator Johnson asked the question, "If Rockefeller could do that with a national platform in one sitting in the Waldorf-Astoria, what could Krushchev or someone do with Nixon if they really put the heat on?" I think it's an understatement to say that Mr. Nixon is an opportunist.

What do they say they have against Senator Kennedy? Well, first of all, his religion. But, Senator Kennedy has fully answered that in very complete detail, He stands foursquare for the Constitutional principle of separation of church and state. He's against federal aid to parochial schools—but, Vice President candidate Lodge a few days ago came out flatly for such federal aid! These are just a few pertinent facts.

They say Senator Kennedy wants to repeal or amend the Taft-Hartley Act and do away with the right to work law in the several states that have it. Well, the truth of the matter is that the provision of doing away with the right to work law has been in the platform for the last twelve years. It was not originated by Senator Kennedy.

They raise the question about the secondary boycott or situs picketing. They point out that Senator Kennedy introduced the bill which they say would be so bad. The background of this bill, Senate Bill 2643, was introduced by Senator Kennedy in the fall of '59 to repeal the secondary boycott provision of the Taft-Hartley law, to clear up certain misunderstandings. President Eisenhower's message of January 23, 1958, likewise recommended that the "secondary boycott provisions" of the Labor Act be amended to clear the matter up. The President also recommended the same thing in 1959. So, again the Republicans are using false propaganda against Senator Kennedy.

They claim that Senator Kennedy is too close to labor. Well, I am glad he is for good honest labor as against Hoffa and Bridges, who I understand are for Nixon.

They say Senator Kennedy is for socialized medicine. I know Senator Kennedy is for medical care for the aged. So am I. And so are you. It happens that Republican Governor Rockefeller, before the National Governors' Conference in Montana this summer, successfully sponsored a resolution through a meeting of governors (both Democratic and Republican) favoring the Social Security approach to medical care rather than the expenditure of $600,000,000 a year from the treasury, which is what Nixon is supporting.

May I say again that we are going to win this election, and in winning it we are going to bring to the leadership of this country a dynamic Democratic team—a team with a philosophy of service to the people.

Let me quote Senator Kennedy from the *Congressional Record* of January 18, 1960:

"Beneath today's surface gloss of peace and prosperity are increasingly dangerous, unsolved, long-postponed problems. The challenging revolutionary '60's will demand that the President place himself in the very thick of the fight, that he care passionately about the fate of the people he leads, that he be willing to serve them at the risk of incurring their momentary displeasure."

Gentlemen, this is from a man who has vision and great courage. He has captured the imagination of the people and will as President lead this country to new heights of leadership in the dangerous days ahead.

I hope you will join me in supporting the Democratic ticket of Kennedy-Johnson.

REMARKS AT THE DEDICATION OF THE
JOSEPH PALMER KNAPP BUILDING,
INSTITUTE OF GOVERNMENT,
UNIVERSITY OF NORTH
CAROLINA

CHAPEL HILL
November 30, 1960

[The Institute of Government at the University of North Carolina had its origin in 1923 in the mind of Albert Coates. then a professor in the University's Law School and director of the Institute until his retirement thirty-nine years later. Taken over by the University in the 1940's, the Institute continued to operate in a building opposite the Campus on East Franklin Street until Joseph Palmer Knapp, a New York millionaire living a part of each year in Currituck County, became interested and left in his will $500,000 to be used for the erection of a new building on condition that the state would match this sum with an equal amount. Governor Hodges was one of the speakers at the dedication of the handsome and commodious new building into which the Institute had already moved.]

Today, I am honored to have a part in this very significant and happy occasion.

We have come to dedicate this attractive, useful edifice of brick and mortar. Perhaps more important is that we commemorate here today a great achievement represented by more than thirty years of devoted public service by the man and his associates who constitute a flesh and blood edifice which is known far and wide as the Institute of Government. It is that flesh and blood edifice—the Institute of Government—which gives life and spirit to the brick and mortar building.

I have known Albert Coates forty-five years. I have admired and respected him forty-five years. He was an honored upper classman when I entered the University at Chapel Hill! He is a native North Carolinian, through and through—son of Johnston County soil, son of the University, and a native son who has never been shackled by local or state provincialism. The only boundaries to his far-ranging vision and creative spirit in the field of his work have been the unending reaches of the horizon itself. Albert Coates reached forth in the days of his youth to get the best of classroom training that was offered in this nation. Years ago, when he returned from that place called Harvard, his manner of speech, his accent, hadn't been damaged one bit. It was still solid authentic North Carolinian Tar Heel, to the core. But his thoughts, his vision, his imagination, his determined courage—then as now—were all of an unusual and unique quality measured by the best standards anywhere.

Albert Coates caught hold of a vision more than thirty years ago and he has never let it go. He dreamed, and by his own unceasing back-breaking efforts, his dreams were formed into substance. They were given life. We see a part of the culminating substance of that dream here in this lovely and useful building. We can also see a realization of that dream in 100 counties of this state, in every courthouse, in every city hall, in the General Assembly, in every state government office in Raleigh—in every place where there are public officials. All of these officials are better public officials because of the work and labors of the Institute of Government. Because of the Coates' dream come true, the administration of public affairs in North Carolina—at all levels—has been lifted up to standards of excellence second to none in the nation.

The dream of Albert Coates has not been contained within the physical borders of North Carolina. That dream has spilled over generously and extended its tangible influence far beyond the borders of our own state. Men have come from other places to study and learn from what has been done here. They have returned to their respective states, full of the ideas and inspiration that they saw produce such good results in North Carolina. Other states have raised up their own Institutes of Government, patterned after the one in Chapel Hill, and adapted to their own governmental climate and soil.

No higher tribute can be paid to the dream of mortal man than to be able to say the dream came into being and it stood the test of being. Upon becoming reality, it was seen as worthy, deserving of an enduring existence. Such is the tribute which we can and should justly pay to the dream of Albert Coates, and to his work and that of his able associates who down through the years have given new dimensions to the University of North Carolina in its service to the state.

I recently read an issue of the *University News Letter* which was published July 6, 1932, containing an article entitled, "The Task of Popular Government," written by Albert Coates. In that article was outlined a program and purposes of the Institute of Government—a blueprint of action which we have seen unfold before our eyes during these past decades. I want to quote some brief portions of that article written twenty-eight and one-half years ago by Albert Coates:

> Public officers are not born with the knowledge of the powers and duties of the offices to which they are elected . . . their private occupations and professions do not teach them the powers and duties of public officials. The uncertainties of political life do not offer them incentives to study the responsibilities of a public office before they seek it. The democracy which clothed them with the public trust does not provide them with training to fit them to discharge it.
>
> They go into office to learn by mistakes . . . in the school of hard knocks which sometimes knock harder on the public than on the public officer. The learning they acquire in this rough, ready and expensive fashion too often goes out of office with them at the end of their official terms . . . .
>
> If governmental administration is to improve within the limits of elective offices and short terms of office, we must find ways and means (1) of bringing to each governmental officer the methods, practices, and techniques rising out of the initiative and resourcefulness of other officers in similar offices in this and other states; (2) of collecting our steadily accumulating governmental experience and transmitting it to successive generations of governmental officers, enabling them to start nearer where their predecessors left off than where they began; (3) of eliminating the lost time and lost motion which now accompany the rotation of officers; (4) of creating a governmental tradition and morale compelling in its encouragement and inspiration to public officers to leave the public service better than they found it.

Over a period of thirty years some 40,000 city, county, state, and federal officials have come to schools of the Institute of Government. Last year alone more than 7,500 officials came here from the city halls, courthouses, county offices, state departments, and federal agencies operating in North Carolina, for schools and conferences running from three days to twelve weeks. And I am informed that many requests during the past year to use the facilities of this building simply could not be granted because the demand was greater than the supply. In addition to the teaching and training program of the Institute of Government conducted here in Chapel Hill, there are additional thousands of officials and citizens who go to schools with the Institute through the medium of various publications and periodicals published by the Institute, as well as those who attend regional conferences or study sessions held at various places throughout the state.

The Institute of Government has through these years since 1932 met the needs and the goals which were recognized then, perhaps even above and beyond the hopes which Albert Coates permitted himself during those years long ago. The job has been done, and it has been done well. I don't mean to say the job is finished. It can never be. Yesterday's and today's work, no matter how well done, cannot suffice for the work which must be done tomorrow and on all future tomorrows.

We are here today to dedicate a building, a dedication which would not be possible except for the life and spirit of Joseph Palmer Knapp. Mr. Knapp was a distinguished publisher, a distinguished American. Though not native born to North Carolina, this state became a second home for him, a home which we may believe ranked first in his heart. The story of Joseph Palmer Knapp has been told by Professor Coates in the dedication program, a story which includes his remarkable and unselfish interest in Currituck County and the great services which he rendered to the people of that area. Surely this building which serves so well as an important facility in lifting up the standards of governmental administration in North Carolina is a fitting memorial to a man who did so much over a period of years in lifting up the standards of living and in making a better life for the people in Currituck County and surrounding area. This building would not have been possible, we would not be here today, had it not been for the life of Joseph Palmer Knapp, which led him to establish the foundation bearing his name—to carry on after his death in those ways of service which he demonstrated during his lifetime.

We have come here to dedicate a building, dedication which again would not have been possible but for the life and spirit of Margaret Rutledge Knapp, the widow of Joseph Palmer Knapp. She knew of her husband's interest in the Institute of Government at Chapel Hill, and following his death she saw the means by which her husband's interest could be enduringly expressed and she saw an opportunity for a distinct public service, through the Joseph Palmer Knapp Foundation. She and her associates as directors of that foundation made known their decision in December, 1952 to give a half million dollars on a million dollar building for the Institute of Government. Legislative action, to match the Knapp Foundation grant with a like sum from the people of North Carolina, was taken by the 1953 General Assembly. In terms of its great contribution to North Carolina, the people of this state through the General Assembly could have properly taken upon themselves the entire burden for providing a suitable and needed building for the Institute of Government. Such would have been justified. I think it is perhaps a better reflection of the true spirit and purposes of the Institute of Government that this building was not financed in whole by public funds. Rather, the building was provided, I am happy to say, through the joint effort of private citizens and the state government in a cooperative endeavor which represents the true and guiding spirit of the Institute of Government, to make of our government in this state more nearly a government of the people, by the people, and for the people.

Let me quote again from the article written by Albert Coates in 1932:

Men in public office are more than common jobbers, or salaried employees. They represent more than the people who elected them. They are part and parcel of a great tradition. They are the heirs of generation upon generation of men and women who have struggled through suffering and blood to hand down their governmental institutions to their children a little stronger than they found them. They are trusted with the liberties of the people . . . . In the name of popular government, this generation is called upon to turn its present flaming governmental interest into constructive channels and through a far-reaching program of training our governmental personnel, simplifying our governmental structure, and vivifying our governmental education, bring new knowledge, new strength and new courage to officials in the cities, the counties, and the state of North Carolina, as in these trying times they strive to justify the faith of the people who clothed them with the public trust of public office.

To the trustees of the Joseph Palmer Knapp Foundation whose wise and far-sighted generosity led them to an expression of faith in the Institute of Government, the University of North Carolina, and our state itself, we express our heartfelt appreciation on this occasion. I wish we had more Joseph Knapps!

To the North Carolina General Assembly of 1953 and to my predecessor Governor William B. Umstead whose leadership brought forth an expression of faith in terms of a matching grant of public funds which made this building possible, let us on this occasion express our deep and abiding appreciation.

To the University of North Carolina which, though with some initial travail and skepticism, did nevertheless at a critical time nurture and sustain the Institute of Government, and through these years has insulated it, protected it, supported it, and has given it a priceless status of academic standing, let us on this occasion express our sincere appreciation.

To the people of North Carolina, public officials past and present and lay citizens, whose response to the opportunity of learning has been the keystone of achievement by the Institute of Government, let us on this occasion express our deepest gratitude.

This state is known for its good government, and is favorably known by comparison with many states and other units of government. Our state must continue good government, it must challenge the best people to offer for office as a public service. Its government and its state's services must not be impaired or weakened by too much partisanship between parties or too much partisanship between factions of the dominant party. The state comes first, and that ideal has guided well the Institute through the years.

As governor of North Carolina, it is my privilege, on behalf of the people of this state, to accept this buiding which has been dedicated to useful enduring service for all our people. May there be a re-dedication, by public officials and citizens throughout North Carolina, to the articles of faith and promise which undergird the Institute of Government, which led to its creation and which has inspired it to great service—to the end that we shall hand on to those who follow us our governmental institutions, stronger and better than we found them.

ADDRESS AT THE SEVENTH ANNUAL MEETING OF THE GOVERNOR'S TRAFFIC SAFETY COUNCIL

Raleigh

December 6, 1960

[Governor Hodges had created the Traffic Safety Council by his first executive order issued as governor on November 30, 1954. (See Vol. I, pp. 58-60.) At this session, the last time he would meet with the Council as Governor, he argued, as on several other occasions, for reform in the inferior courts which handle traffic cases in North Carolina. About 500 persons, including Motor Vehicles Commissioner Edward Scheidt and Governor-elect Terry Sanford, were present to hear the Governor's address, which was made at a luncheon at the Sir Walter Hotel.]

I welcome each of you to this the seventh annual meeting of the Governor's Traffic Safety Council. I am especially grateful to all of you who are here as lay citizens rather than in some official capacity with state government. You and the private organizations you represent are giving your time—and in many instances your money—because of your sincere desire to help North Carolina cope with the never-ending problem of traffic accidents on the streets and highways of North Carolina.

As I am sure you can understand, this particular meeting is of special significance to me personally. It is the last time that I shall have the opportunity to meet with this council as governor of our state. Slightly more than six years ago—to be exact, six years and six days ago—I issued my first executive order as governor of the state. That was on November 30, 1954, when by Executive Order No. 1 there was established the organization to be known as the Governor's Traffic Safety Council, for the purpose of promoting traffic through our state.

The commissioner of motor vehicles serves as chairman of this council, and I am sure that Commissioner Scheidt joins me in expressing warm appreciation to the many organizations, groups, and individuals throughout North Carolina who have given invaluable assistance during the past six years in the cause of traffic safety.

May I at this time say that I am delighted inded that we have a very special guest with us on this occasion, the Honorable Terry Sanford, governor-elect of North Carolina. I am sure that the people of North Carolina can look forward to an able and outstanding administration under his leadership.

The first annual meeting of this council was held on December 3, 1954. Let's take a few minutes of this time to see what has happened in traffic safety in North Carolina during the past six years, to see where we stood in 1954 and where we are today.

As of the end of the calendar year 1954, slightly more than 1,600,000 motor vehicles were registered in North Carolina, and as of November 21, 1960, 1,885,000 motor vehicles were registered in this state.

In 1954, the number of drivers licensed in North Carolina was 1,779,000, and as of a few days ago it was 2,158,555.

During 1954, there were 40,449 automobile accidents in this state; during 1959, there were 57,234; and as of September 30, 1960, more than 42,000 had been recorded in North Carolina during 1960.

In 1954, North Carolina had 991 traffic deaths. In 1959, we had 1,1953 traffic fatalities, and for 1960, 1,058 people (as of November 28) have died as a result of automobile accidents in this state.

In 1954, there were 15,600 persons injured in traffic accidents in North Carolina, and in 1959, the number had risen to 24,802. On the basis of statistics available so far for 1960, the total number injured this year will certainly be as great or greater than the total number for last year.

In 1954, estimated property damage from automobile accidents in North Carolina totaled more than $7,900,000. In 1959, the estimated total property damage from automobile accidents in this state was $10,900,000. The total property damage from automobile accidents occurring during 1960 will be as great or greater than that for 1959.

If we merely compare the total number of accidents in 1959 with the total number in 1954, and the total number of traffic fatalities in 1959 with the total number in 1954, we might conclude that we have gone backward rather than forward. Actually, however, the trend in North Carolina during the past six years has not been as discouraging, by any means, as the mere recital of total figures might indicate. We must take into account the greater density of traffic, the larger number of motor vehicles on our highways and streets, and make a more meaningful comparison than we get in comparing total accidents or total fatalities. We are all familiar with the standard comparative statistic that is used throughout the nation in measuring traffic fatalities. The figure most often used is the number of traffic fatalities per 100,000,000 motor vehicle miles.

Using this method, North Carolina had 6.5 traffic fatalities per 100,000,000 motor vehicle miles in 1959, compared to 6.8 fatalities per 100,000,000 miles in 1954. While we have a slight percentage reduction, about the best that we can claim for ourselves is that we have pretty much managed to hold our statistical own during the past six years.

Yet, we also have to recognize that in the national picture North Carolina has little to brag about so far as our record of traffic fatalities is concerned. We do not have by any means the highest traffic fatality rate—based on vehicle mileage—of all the states in the country. Neither can we, unfortunately, claim to have one of the lower fatality rates. In fact, North Carolina is above the national average in traffic fatalities!

For the calendar year 1959, our traffic fatality rate of 6.5 deaths per 100,000,000 vehicle miles was higher than the rate in thirty-three other states. Only thirteen states had a traffic fatality rate higher than North Carolina's. But let me mention some items on the plus side which have occurred in North Carolina during recent years.

For example, the North Carolina State Highway Patrol has received the outstanding achievement award from the International Association of Chiefs of Police for the years 1956, 1957, 1958, and 1959. This is America's highest honor in the field of traffic-law enforcement, and this means that the North Carolina Highway Patrol has had an enforcement program during these years which is truly outstanding in the nation.

Another "plus item" in North Carolina's efforts in traffic safety: the Drivers' License Division of our Department of Motor Vehicles received the outstanding achievement award of the National Safety Council for the years 1955, 1956, 1957, 1958, and 1959.

I might add that during the past two years North Carolina has also achieved national recognition for its driver-education program, having been one of only seven states in the nation to qualify for a top award.

In one sense, it may seem to some people somewhat strange that during recent years North Carolina has achieved top national ranking in traffic enforcement by our State Highway Patrol, in the work of our Drivers' Licensing Division, in driver education, and in other aspects of a traffic safety program. Yet, we have barely held our own during the past six years so far as the rate of traffic fatalities is concerned. Perhaps it is enough to remind ourselves that the problem of traffic accidents is many-sided, and an intelligent and sensible attack on the problem requires a constant many-sided offense. However, I do want to take this opportunity to express my own opinion as to an important factor in the field of traffic safety, which factor in my view is probably the weakest link in our chain of effort to reduce the toll of traffic accidents in North Carolina.

I refer to the handling of traffic accidents in the courts of our state. By far, the vast majority of all traffic citations are handled and disposed of in courts inferior to our superior courts, and I am informed, most of the traffic violations are disposed of in a justice of the peace court.

During the past six years I have probably received more complaints and more criticism about the handling of traffic violations in our courts than about any other aspect of government in our state. Of course, many of the complaints which I received were not well-founded—and in all cases I asked the Department of Motor Vehicles to make a good investigation to determine what exactly was involved. However, in too many instances, I have received letters of complaint which had some justification. Let me mention briefly just a few letters which I have received during the past twelve months.

This is a letter from an out-of-state resident who says that he was stopped by a Highway Patrolman and charged with going sixty-seven miles per hour in a fifty-five per hour zone. He goes on to say that he thought he was traveling at a proper rate of speed, but nevertheless he does not complain about being stopped for speeding if he was speeding because he is 100 per cent behind speeding control. He says and I quote:

> The above incident, by itself, would not have bothered me too much, were it not for subsequent events in . . . . I was taken before a justice of the peace and was asked how I would plead. I asked if it would do me any good to plead 'not guilty' and was told, no; that if I did, the officer would be sworn in and it would have taken a little longer. The fine for speeding was $5.00, which I considered rather low for a highway speeding violation. The costs were $10.50. I had never heard of costs exceeding the fine by more than a factor of two when one was fined for speeding and no appeal was involved . . . . Where the costs exceed the fine by such a figure, I cannot help but think that such a practice of stopping helpless tourists is encouraged.

This is from another letter, describing the judicial proceeding involving a traffic violation:

> We went in and there were about six or eight men, including at least one patrolman, in the reception room. All of the men looked to be officers of the law of some kind. That is the impression they made on me. We were directed into another room where Justice _____ had his desk. He, too, was courteous, polite, and friendly. I told him what the patrolman said about the minimum cost. He said it would be $25. Thereupon he ushered us into another room where there was a secretary, who was typing, and she took the $25. We were then ushered into a fourth room where there was another secretary and a typewriter and some type of printing press. She quickly printed some kind of statement, and told the driver where to sign. She then fixed a little slip of paper and handed the driver after he had signed. From there we went back to the reception room, and nothing whatever was said about a receipt for the $25; I saw no evidence whatsoever of any warrant, and nothing was said to us whatsoever regarding the importance of obeying the state laws. Apparently everyone was glad to see us, and I feel sure had we gotten into a 'speedtrap' immediately afterward they would again have been very glad to see us. During the few minutes we were on the circuit through this court everybody seemed busy typing and answering telephone calls. I distinctly heard one of the men in the reception room speak of 'field day.' I have often seen offices of justices of the peace, but I have never seen one quite as elaborate as this one, and I was never before in one which appeared to be so interested in making money as this one appeared to be. My own feeling is that it was most unfair all the way through.

This is from another letter I have received within the past year from a person describing his experience with a traffic violation in a justice of the peace court, and I quote:

I saw stacks of large bills in the desk drawer, so many in fact that the girl had to press down on the money to get the desk drawer closed. She was frantically typing reports favoring the JP and the arresting officers, which were stamped with a rubber stamp. One of these reports was pushed in front of me with instructions to read only the rubber stamp part, which was over the other lettering on a legal size sheet of paper. I never did get a chance to even know what the written information was. I started to read the document and had very quick instructions to stop, with nasty-nice reminders of what could be done to me. I, like all of the rest, wanted to pay up and get away from there. I was given the privilege of being their guest. The JP offered to put me up in a nice comfortable jail until the judge took a notion to hold court, or I could pay now. The JP said he was here for the sake of helping out-of-state people by taking our money himself and relieving us of the time it would take the judge to hold regular court. We, of course, were anxious to get away.

This particular letter then goes on to say that the writer will do all he can to keep out of North Carolina and help others to keep away.

I have quoted from these letters for one purpose, and that is to throw some light on the condition of our judicial process and the handling of traffic violations. I think we might assume that in each of these cases the individual driver involved was properly arrested for a traffic violation. Let us assume that the person was exceeding the speed limit, did improperly pass another vehicle, or whatever was involved. Yet, I am sure it is just as plain and obvious to you as it is to me that the best work of the best traffic policeman or patrolman it is possible to have, can be completely undone if what follows is often a farce of a judicial proceeding.

I do not wish to be understood as saying or believing that all justice of the peace courts are operated improperly. I know there are some justice of the peace courts that are operated properly, efficiently, and with dignity. However, there are enough exceptions to give the entire system a wholesale indictment, and there are enough things wrong with our present system of inferior courts that regardless of the type of person who is serving as magistrate or judge, the system itself will often deprive that person of the sort of dignity and stature that ought to characterize any judicial proceeding.

You, of course, know that amendment of our constitution to achieve better court administration was before the 1959 legislative session. Due to an inability of the House to agree with the Senate on exactly what language should go in the constitution, the great project of court improvement, on which more than four years of hard work had been spent, resulted in a heartbreaking failure— so far as achieving effective legislative action in 1959.

As I pointed out in a special message to the General Assembly in March, 1959, many of our inferior courts are operated by localities with an eye to profits from excess costs and fees, to help support the local governmental budget. It has been found, and these figures reflect the situation two or three years ago—and the money involved is probably considerably higher right now—that municipalities operated their courts throughout the state at an annual profit of almost $900,000. It has been determined beyond dispute that in inferior courts in North Carolina today a defendant who pleads guilty to a minor criminal charge will incur costs which vary, depending on which court he is in, and which county or municipality, from $7.00 in one court to $28 in another on the same identical charge. And of course, in so many instances the fees charged in these courts have no relationship whatever to the actual cost of the case which is being tried. I think this is a shameful situation which the General Assembly of this state ought to correct.

In a recent year, justice of the peace courts in this state handled over 88,000 criminal cases, in which their fee was not collected unless the defendant was found guilty. I said then to the General Assembly that there is but one characterization of this aspect of the justice of the peace court, and that is: "As a system, this is not justice; this is a travesty of justice."

I don't want to give the impression that the total picture in North Carolina reveals too strict handling in our courts or that everyone is automatically found guilty of the violation for which he is charged. We also know of many examples of the opposite extreme. This is where an individual is brought into court, the traffic violation proved against him, and he is let off lightly with a slap on the wrist. In too many cases that same person promptly goes out, gets under the steering wheel of an automobile, and commits another traffic violation. We know that juries in North Carolina are quite often reluctant to convict a person of driving under the influence apparently because they reason that person would lose his driver's license. What explains this sort of noblesse oblige attitude, this sort of sportsman's code? I cannot help but believe that the other extreme which I have just described through the medium of the letters I have quoted, which everyone knows exists in many of our inferior courts, has contributed to the attitude of some juries which seem to refuse to convict regardless of the evidence against the defendant. Maybe they figure they ought to tip the scales the other way, to sort of even things up.

While we do not expect and should not demand perfection from the judicial department of government, any more than from the executive branch, we do have a great challenge to improve the administration of our courts in North Carolina, and there is a crying need for some effective and responsible legislation which will eliminate certain conditions we have too long tolerated.

I will not attempt here, any more than I attempted in my special message to the General Assembly, to say in detail exactly what legislation should be passed or what language should or should not be put in the constitution of the state on the subject of court improvement, but I feel strongly that legislation is needed and I hope that under Governor Terry Sanford's leadership, at least the state can make a good start in improving our inferior courts.

And I would like to say to those of you who are here, because of your interest in traffic safety, you have a definite stake in court improvement and you should let your representatives and senators in the General Assembly know of your interest and concern.

In closing, I would like to leave with you this thought on the over-all problem of traffic safety and traffic accidents. Perhaps we should use another word than accident—maybe we ought to use the term traffic *incident* rather than traffic accident. How really accidental is it when John Q. Citizen pushes his foot down on the accelerator and drives his automobile down the road at a speed of seventy or seventy-five miles per hour? Would you term his action in doing that, "accidental?"

How accidental is it when John Q. Citizen takes a drink, another drink, and perhaps still another, and then goes out and gets under the steering wheel of his car? Was the fact of his drinking accidental?

How about the situation of a driver who is in a hurry to get home, or to get to work, or to get wherever he is going, and he comes to an intersection and drives right on without stopping. Was this act of improper driving an accident?

Yet, according to all of the statistics, the three situations I have mentioned to you—that is, speeding, driving while under the influence, failure to yield the right-of-way—these are the major contributing factors to highway accidents and to traffic fatalities in North Carolina and throughout the nation.

It seems to me that we ought to recognize that the speeding was deliberate, not accidental; the drinking was deliberate and not accidental; the failure to yield the right-of-way was deliberate and not accidental. Of course, in none of these situations in which a collision occurred did the driver intend *that* to happen. Yet, his actions were such that any reasonable person would tell you he would almost certainly have a traffic "accident" and those actions were all deliberate.

Perhaps we ought to change our terminology in this field and speak of *deliberate* highway *incidents*—not accidents. It might help all of us and the general public to re-orient our own thinking concerning the use of the automobile—to think of its use less in terms of a sporting proposition, where every man is more or less entitled to his first taste of blood—to put it somewhat crudely.

Perhaps after all, the big problem in traffic safety is to persuade the "good people" in our state and country to accept and live up to their responsibility in the operation of motor vehicles. Generally, it is the good, decent, and responsible person who is caught speeding, a little bit under the influence while driving, or a little bit careless. And it is the same good, average, decent man or woman who serves on juries, who is either concerned or is not concerned about the operation of the courts or the general level of traffic law enforcement in his community and in his state. I believe that our real problem in the area of traffic *incidents*—and in so many other things—comes back to the fact that it's the ordinary, average, really decent person who makes the problem, who violates the laws himself, and who tolerates the violation by others. If it were only the "bad guys," a very small percentage of our population, then I doubt that we would have much of a problem because everyone would be agreed that the real bad guy should be taken care of properly and expeditiously—put in jail or in any event taken from behind the steering wheel of an automobile.

This means for those of us who have special responsibilities on public problems such as traffic accidents that the problem is never-ending and our efforts in enforcement and in improving our courts must be never-ending.

Again, my sincere appreciation for the interest that each of you has expressed in being here on this occasion and my thanks for your contribution to help North Carolina move along the broad front to a safer North Carolina.

REMARKS ACCEPTING A PORTRAIT OF FORMER GOVERNOR J. C. B. EHRINGHAUS

RALEIGH
December 16, 1960

[Acceptance of the Ehringhaus portrait completed a collection of the portraits of all governors of North Carolina elected during the twentieth century. Major Lennox Polk McLendon of Greensboro, Ehringhaus' campaign manager in the primary of 1932, made the presentation address, and Governor Hodges accepted for the state, while Chief Justice John Wallace Winborne, a fraternity brother of Ehringhaus at the University of North Carolina, presided. About 300 people attended the ceremony, which was held in the Hall of the House of Representatives in the State Capitol.]

It is an honor and a happy privilege to come here this evening to accept, on behalf of the people of North Carolina, this fine portrait of one of the truly outstanding men, and, certainly, one of the most courageous and dedicated public servants, in the history of our state. North Carolina has been uncommonly blessed throughout its history in its capacity to produce "men to match its mountains"—men of vision and strong conviction, men who possessed that most essential qualification for enlightened leadership—an independent spirit and the courage to stand, alone, if necessary, by what he knows is right. Such a man was Governor Ehringhaus.

The privilege of gathering here this evening to honor the memory of a man who has meant so much to this state and its people is, in itself, sufficient reason to make this a happy and memorable occasion. There is added significance, however, in the fact that North Carolina now possesses distinguished portraits of all the men who have occupied the governor's office since the turn of the century. Seven portraits have been persented to the state since Mrs. Hodges and I moved into the Executive Mansion six years ago. This collection of portaits is a credit to North Carolina and one in which every citizen can take pride. I know that I express the sentiments of all North Carolinians when I voice appreciation to the devoted families and friends of Governors Morrison, Gardner, Hoey, Broughton, Cherry, Scott and, now, Ehringhaus for their generosity in making available to our state the portraits of these outstanding men.

I think it is also a credit to our state that the General Assembly has accepted the responsibility for commissioning future portraits for this collection.

My great respect for Governor Ehringhaus, both as a human being and as a public servant, is not based on what I have been told or what I have read. I regard it as an honor to have known the man personally. I served on his Highway Commission and had occasion to deal with him directly. Among all the governors in North Carolina's history, Governor Ehringhaus is one of my personal favorites. He possessed a dynamic personality which reflected, as Major McLendon has so eloquently revealed, both his fearlessness and his compassion.

It is, at times, difficult for us today to comprehend fully the trying circumstances under which many of North Carolina's past governors have labored, but some knowledge of those circumstances is essential if we are genuinely to appreciate the achievements of these men. To cite just one example—insignificant, perhaps, but certainly indicative of the general economic conditions that prevailed in the late 1920's and early 1930's—Governors Ehringhaus and Gardner found it necessary to furnish their own silver and linen to meet minimum requirements for hospitality at the Executive Mansion. The expense was one the state evidently felt it could not afford to meet.

Those of us who have been privileged to serve the people of North Carolina in more recent years have been more fortunate. We have been able to concern ourselves, for the most part, with the broader picture, unencumbered by the necessity of dealing constantly with matters of a negative nature. We have been able to take the offensive on the economic front, not because we possessed greater competence, but because the groundwork has been laid by those totally dedicated men who preceded us in this office. The path was smoothed and our journey made easier by such men as Governor Ehringhaus—men who fearlessly blazed the trail, men who were of such stature that they rose above the depressing reality of their difficult times and unashamedly dreamed the dream of North Carolina's greatness.

We owe a great debt of gratitude to the man we honor this evening. But, fortunately, it is a debt that we can pay. We can continue to build on the foundation he laid, a fundation that counts fearless leadership, personal integrity, dedication to progress, and love of this state and its people as it cornerstones. This is the Ehringhaus legacy, and it has served us well.

Again, on behalf of the citizens of North Carolina, I want to thank the Ehringhaus family and their many friends throughout our state for their generosity in making this portrait available. It is a fitting tribute to a great man.

Thank you.

REMARKS BEFORE A STATE-WIDE RADIO-TELEVISION AUDIENCE

RALEIGH
December 29, 1960

[Governor Hodges reviewed his six-year administration and issued some challenges for the future in this seven-minute talk, which was followed by a twenty-minute documentary film. The film depicted various activities of the administration, stressing in particular the Hodges role as a "businessman governor" and his wide-ranging public relations efforts to increase the state's industrial base.]

It is with mixed feelings that I have come here this evening to take part in this brief, yet comprehensive, review of North Carolina's progress. I am happy that this state and its people continue to move forward, continue to reach out, with great collective energy and imagination, to build a better way of life. As the past twenty minutes have shown, many people have contributed to North Carolina's growth and development—and may I say that I am genuinely grateful for the privilege of serving with such people in the past six years.

These have been the most memorable years of my life—difficult and frustrating at times, yes—but memorable and tremendously gratifying. They have been gratifying because they have given me a privileged insight into the wonderful people of North Carolina.

North Carolina has made great progress—not by accident, but by plain hard work and dedication. We have moved forward through recent decades and various administrations, in the principal areas of activity affecting the health, happiness, and prosperity of all the people. We have maintained our traditional adherence to the religious or spiritual ideals that are the motivating force behind all real progress and achievement. We have forged ahead culturally, pioneering in many fields where the less dedicated and, in some instances, the less audacious, have held back to their own disadvantage. Economically, we have set the pace for the South and, in some fields, for the nation.

In the far-ranging effort to strengthen our economy, we have had the help of more than 200 area development organizations, chambers of commerce, etc., all working as a team to develop North Carolina. These groups, composed of businessmen, farmers, industrialists, city and county officials, and others, have, for the most part, given freely of their time and talent to build their communities and our state. They are working today to make our cities and rural areas more attractive to investors. They are helping develop our great travel and recreation industry. And they are, themselves, investing in new businesses, small local industries, industrial development corporations, and in other progressive ventures designed to boost both our industrial and agricultural economies.

These conscientious and responsible citizens are cooperating with our old, established, and much appreciated, industries—to-bacco, textiles, furniture, etc.—to insure that these industries keep pace with the rapidly changing times. They are, in effect, leaving no avenue unexplored, no opportunity unheeded, in their inspiring effort to create and maintain good business climate in North Carolina.

In the past half-decade, capital investments in 1,937 new and expanded manufacturing plants have amounted to $1,037,000,000. This activity has created approximately 109,000 new jobs and added almost $341,000,000 to the annual payroll. And the momentum is continuing. I am happy to announce tonight that, during 1960, more than $233,600,000 has been invested in over 500 new and expanded manufacturing facilities. A total of 31,500 new jobs have been created and about $100,000,000 has been added in new payrolls. All this means jobs and a better standard of living for our people.

There are, I am glad to say, several other industries in the offing, one or two of large size, which should announce early in 1961. This is natural as it takes months, sometimes years, to finalize decisions.

An important factor in our industrial progress has been the policy of aggressively going after new industry throughout the United States (New York, Chicago, Philadelphia, and other localities) as well as several nations in western Europe. These "selling" trips, as hundreds of North Carolinians—who made these trips at their own expense—will testify, have been singularly successful because we had the finest product in the world to sell—North Carolina and its people. And let me add that the real job of selling was done at the local level throughout the state, by local officials and by every citizen who has contributed in any way to the creation of a good business climate.

With the enthusiastic cooperation of state and local governments, modern industrial education centers are being established as you have seen on the screen, at strategic locations, thoughout North Carolina to provide technical training for workers seeking employment or advancement in our new and expanding industries. Regular classes are now being taught in thirteen centers across the state and five more are either under construction or in the planning stage. Our industrial education program ranks high with prospective industrialists.

Another exciting and significant indication of our progress has been the success of our Research Triangle—the industrial research complex located in the center of the triangle formed by the University of North Carolina, Duke University, and North Carolina State College. Our citizens are becoming more and more aware of this project's fabulous potential, and they can be justifiably proud of the part they have played in its creation.

Our research developments, our colleges, our folk dramas, our art museum, our symphony and grass roots opera, and other forms of culture and education—all are helping to build a stronger and more enjoyable state in which to live and work.

I believe that the Honorable Terry Sanford, our incoming governor, will contribute significantly to the state's progress— particularly, in the all-important field of public education. I feel that Mr. Sanford's administration will also render notable services to North Carolina in many other fields affecting the well-being of the people, and that the state will continue to move courageously forward.

May I close by thanking each of you from a heart full of gratitude for all the things you have done for me, for your assistance and cooperation, for your support in trying times, for your loyalty when it was most needed and for your confidence and well wishes. I am particularly indebted to the members of the General Assembly, the Council of State, the heads of our various state agencies, and all state employees for their wonderful cooperation during my administration. It has also been a pleasure to work with the representatives of North Carolina's fine newspapers and radio and television stations. They have contributed much to the progress our state has made.

It has been a joy to serve you for the past six years and I hope I can continue in some proper way to serve the state and its people as I take on additional duties in our nation's capital.

SUMMARIES OF PUBLIC ADDRESSES

REMARKS AT RESEARCH TRIANGLE LUNCHEON

Several hundred North Carolinians attended this luncheon at the Sir Walter Hotel at which it was disclosed that $1,500,000 had been raised to launch the initial operations of the Research Triangle Institute. In his remarks the Governor reviewed the developments that had taken place since the original Research Triangle Committee had begun to function only two years earlier, and expressed his conviction that "this progress will mean a considerable amount of urban growth in this area, and benefits will accrue to all parts of the state." Other speakers included George Herbert, whose appointment as director of the Research Triangle Institute was announced at the meeting, and Archie K. Davis of Winston-Salem, president of the Research Triangle Foundation.

ADDRESS AT THE FIFTH ANNUAL MEETING OF THE NORTH CAROLINA MEAT PACKERS ASSOCIATION

Governor Hodges assured independent meat packers that they should have no fear of competing with the large packing companies that have established or are establishing facilities in the state. "Efficient operation is no longer the private property of the large company," he said. "The independent can operate just efficiently and just as economically as does the company with a nation-wide operation. You have the advantage of being able to specialize, to adapt quickly to ever-changing consumer demands, and to compensate for quantity with quality." Both the large and small packers can flourish in North Carolina "because farmers in increasing numbers are turning to livestock production to bolster their cash income." These companion activities, he said, must continue to expand to promote the state's balanced economy.

ADDRESS AT ANNUAL CELEBRITY NIGHT DINNER SPONSORED BY SIDNEY J. STERN LODGE, B'NAI B'RITH

GREENSBORO
March 22, 1959

Emanuel J. Evans, mayor of Durham, was the recipient of an award for distinguished public service by a Jewish citizen of North Carolina, presented at a banquet meeting at the Starmount Forest Country Club. Governor Hodges spoke warmly of "Mutt" Evans; "I can say with complete confidence that as long as there are men of his stature to guide the destinies of our cities and towns, this state need have no fear of the future." The award, he continued, also "adds a new element of dignity to the ideal of public service", and "calls attention to the continuity of the contributions that our Jewish citizens have made to the development of North Carolina."

REMARKS AT RESEARCH TRIANGLE INSTITUTE LUNCHEON

RALEIGH
March 24, 1959

Less than three months after the meeting of January 9, 1959, at which the Governor announced the establishment of the Research Triangle Institute, state leaders, Triangle officials, and representatives of Duke University, the University of North Carolina, and North Carolina State College gathered again at the Sir Walter Hotel to celebrate the decision of the U. S. Atomic Energy Commission to locate a new isotope research laboratory in the Triangle area. "The event that has taken place here today opens the door on a great, new field of potential economic development and expansion in North Carolina," said the Governor. "This laboratory will explore in an area that is just in its infancy— the use of isotopes in industry. Not only will it serve industry, but it also will help to attract industry to North Carolina and the Southeast. It definitely will be of regional significance." Dr. Paul E. Aebersold, Director of the Office of Isotope Development, U. S. Atomic Energy Commission, was another luncheon speaker.

ADDRESS AT LUNCHEON HONORING THE NORTH CAROLINA GENERAL ASSEMBLY AT OFFICIAL OPENING OF THE TRYON PALACE RESTORATION

New Bern
April 8, 1959

In recognition of the importance of the formal opening of Tryon Palace, the General Assembly travelled to New Bern to participate in the ceremonies. At a luncheon at the Scottish Rite Temple, Governor Hodges addressed the group. He took the opportunity to pay tribute to Mr. and Mrs. J. E. Latham and Mr. and Mrs. John A. Kellenberger, to whom the "restored Tryon Palace stands as a testimonial to their uncommon qualities of devotion, patriotism and generosity." The members of the General Assembly were also commended for the assistance they had rendered the project since 1945, when the legislature first decided to appropriate state funds for the restoration program. In this speech the Governor emphasized the educational, the esthetic, and the economic benefits of historical sites, and the need for local groups and citizens to sponsor such restorations. State government, he said, "is understandably limited in the support it can give to projects of this type. This should not be interpreted, however, as an indication of indifference. State agencies—particularly our Department of Archives and History and the Department of Conservation and Development—are intensely interested in these activities—and they stand ready to cooperate as far as possible. It is right and proper, however, that the initiative should come from the local level." The following day the Governor spoke at a dinner meeting of the Tryon Palace Commission (pp. 139-146).

ADDRESS AT NORTHWEST DAY EXECUTIVES' TOUR

Winston-Salem
May 1, 1959

This address at the Forsyth Country Club was the Governor's third for the day; earlier he had participated in ceremonies of the Champion Paper and Fibre Company in Canton (pp. 154-159), and in the afternoon had joined local officials in the dedication of a new sewage treatment plant in Winston-Salem (pp. 159-164). Many out-of-state guests were present for this dinner meeting sponsored by the Northwest North Carolina Development Association. Governor Hodges had high praise for this organization through which eleven counties, representing 104 communities, were pooling resources to improve the regional economy. When the association was formed in 1954, only seventeen communities were actively represented, and he expressed his pleasure in the increased participation, as well as the notable gains the area had registered in recent years. "It is my belief," he said, "that the governor and state government, in this type of activity, should stimulate and encourage our communities and our people to do things for themselves. Good ideas and good programs are merely 'seed corn' which should be planted properly and nourished with plenty of hard work, careful cultivation, and attention by the people who will make the harvest."

ADDRESS AT ECUSTA PAPER DIVISION, OLIN MATHIESON CHEMICAL CORPORATION, OPEN HOUSE

Pisgah Forest
May 8, 1959

One week after participating in ceremonies marking the expansion of plant facilities of the Champion Paper and Fibre Company in Canton (see pp. 154-159), the Governor returned to the western section of North Carolina to help officials of the Olin

Mathieson Chemical Corporation dedicate the installation of new machinery at their Ecusta Paper and Film Divisions. Again he discussed the economic development of the area, stressing the fact that Transylvania County is second only to Buncombe among the neighboring counties in the matter of per capita income. This progress he attributed largely to the establishment of the paper manufacturing industry in 1939, and the more recent location of a Dupont silicon plant in Brevard. Further evidence of continuing economic growth was the Gerber Products Company processing and marketing facility in the Asheville area, which planned to buy 40,000 tons of fruits and vegetables in western North Carolina each year, and the decision of the Ball Brothers Company to build an adjacent plant to produce bottles and jars. "It is clearly evident," the Governor predicted, "that this community, this county, and all of western North Carolina will benefit greatly from the economic transformation that is today reshaping the destiny of our entire state."

TELEVISION ADDRESS IN SUPPORT OF SCHOOL INCENTIVE FUND LEGISLATION

RALEIGH
May 13, 1959

A school incentive fund had been recommended by the Governor and the Advisory Budget Commission as a means of encouraging more local support of education. The plan called for an annual appropriation of $10,000,000 in state funds to be distributed on a matching basis among such counties as would increase their school expenditures. Governor Hodges, a strong supporter of the plan, came to its defense in a television appearance on the night before it was scheduled to come up for a vote in the House Education Committee. In addition to his arguments in support of the measure, the Governor sought to answer recent criticisms of his budget recommendations for education generally and also took the professional educators, including the North Carolina Education Association, to task for failure to solve or unwillingness to face up to some of their own problems. The school incentive fund was opposed by the poorer counties, by farm groups, and by the State Association of County Commissioners, and was voted down by the House Education Committee on May 14, 1959.

ADDRESS AT MEETING OF THE ASSOCIATION OF LIFE INSURANCE COUNSEL

WHITE SULPHUR SPRINGS, WEST VIRGINIA
May 25, 1959

Economic development of the South, and particularly of North Carolina, was the topic of Governor Hodges' address to the seventy-eighth annual meeting of life insurance lawyers. He pointed out that life insurance ownership in the South has increased at a far greater rate than in any other section of the country in the past two decades, and that the flow of benefit payments to families in the South is considerably above the national average. Another product of life insurance that has proven beneficial to the region has been the supply of capital funds used to boost the economy; between 1929 and 1958, $20,000,000,000 in capital funds were poured into the South by life insurance companies to meet expanded business and industrial needs. "These were not just dollar blocks of intangible investments. They represented power plants, factories, farm machinery, schools, highways, home construction, new businesses, and all the other facets of a rapidly expanding economy. In other words, they represented a higher standard of living—a better way of life for our people."

Governor Hodges speaking at the 250th anniversary of the founding of New Bern, June 11, 1960. *Left to right:* Mrs. Eduard Freimuller; Governor Hodges; Robert L. Stallings, Jr., mayor of New Bern; Dr. Eduard Freimuller, mayor of Bern, Switzerland; Mrs. Hodges.

Left to right: Terry Sanford, John Clark, Governor Hodges, and Basil Whitener at the Democratic National Convention in Los Angeles, California, July, 1960.

ADDRESS AT THE SEVENTY-FIFTH ANNIVERSARY DINNER AND LADIES NIGHT OF THE WATAUGA CLUB

RALEIGH
May 26, 1959

The program of this meeting was devoted to discussions of different aspects of the history of North Carolina, and Governor Hodges presented an analysis of the state in 1884 (the year of the founding of the Watauga Club) and the "goals it first envisioned at the dawn of its industrial revolution." How these goals have been met, and exceeded, occupied the major portion of his address. In passing, he discussed the conservation of natural resources, economic development, diversification of agriculture, highways and traffic safety, prisons, and the Research Triangle.

ADDRESS AT ROTARY INTERNATIONAL DINNER

NEW YORK CITY
June 9, 1959

The Governor's Russian trip prevented him from attending this meeting, and his prepared paper was read by John Harden of Greensboro. He repeated portions of earlier speeches in which the main theme was the "Southern point of view" and dealt frankly with the problems facing North Carolina, and which confronted him soon after assuming the office of Governor, following the Supreme Court decision on school segregation in 1954. He appealed to his audience representing every state to seek greater understanding of the problems of areas other than their own—"to be Americans first and then New Englanders or Californians, or Southerners."

ADDRESS AT KEARFOTT PLANT DEDICATION

BLACK MOUNTAIN
June 19, 1959

General Robert L. Eichelberger of Biltmore Forest substituted for Governor Hodges on the occasion of this plant dedication in Buncombe County. The address prepared for the Governor followed the pattern he used frequently in welcoming new industry to the state. He spoke of the character and determination of the people of the area, their active development groups, and analyzed the factors that led General Precision Equipment Company, parent organization of Kearfott, to select this site for a plant location. He noted with pride the amazing growth of the electronics industry which, although practically non-existent in North Carolina before World War II, now included some fifty electrical machinery and products plants in the state, employing about 30,000 workers. Observing that "the potential in this field is unlimited," he expressed assurance that "the Department of Conservation and Development and other pertinent agencies will continue their efforts to promote the growth and development of your industry along lines that will be beneficial to all concerned."

REMARKS AT ALLEGHANY COUNTY CENTENNIAL CELEBRATION

SPARTA
August 17, 1959

A week-long celebration commemorating the one hundredth anniversary of the establishment of Alleghany County, formally a part of Ashe, began with ceremonies at the Sparta Ball Park. In his remarks, Governor Hodges paid high tribute to the Doughton family of Alleghany for their distinguished service to their county, their state, and the nation. The accomplishments of Rufus A. Doughton, a former lieutenant governor, Robert L.

Doughton, long time chairman of the Ways and Means Committee of the United States House of Representatives, and Kemp Doughton, currently a member of the General Assembly and a former Speaker of the North Carolina House of Representatives, were singled out for special mention. Most of the address was devoted to a review of the Governor's recent trip to Russia.

ADDRESS AT FALL MEETING OF THE REBEL CHAPTER, YOUNG PRESIDENTS ORGANIZATION

SAPPHIRE VALLEY
September 18, 1959

Youthful heads of corporations from eight southeastern states comprise the membership of this chapter, described by the Governor as an "energetic, influential, and thoroughly fascinating organization." Speaking on the topic of the businessman's role in government, he urged the executives to take an increasingly active part in political affairs. "Government, if it is to function properly," he said, "must be conducted on a business-like basis," and for this reason "young businessmen of proven ability have a responsibility to take an interest in government." He discussed his own decision to enter politics after more than thirty years in textile manufacturing and selling, and commented on the ways in which sound business knowledge has been utilized to carry out the development program of North Carolina.

ADDRESS AT CHAPEL PROGRAM FOR STUDENTS AND FACULTY OF ELON COLLEGE

ELON COLLEGE
September 21, 1959

In this address to an Elon College student-faculty convocation, Governor Hodges discussed his impressions of the Soviet Union, based on his three and a half weeks' tour of that country with eight other governors. He placed special emphasis on the need for a better trained foreign service and for more effective foreign language study of offset Russian superiority in these areas. Otherwise, except for some comments on the history of Elon College and a tribute to its President Emeritus Leon Edgar Smith, the address was mainly a repetition of one made by the Governor at Philadelphia on the preceding Wednesday, September 16 (see pp. 237-250).

ADDRESS AT THE FALL MEETING OF THE CUSTOMER RELATIONS COUNCIL, NORTH CAROLINA MOTOR CARRIERS ASSOCIATION

GREENSBORO
September 25, 1959

The economic development of North Carolina, one of the Governor's favorite topics, was the subject of his address on this occasion. In keeping with the nature of his audience, he emphasized the benefits that would accrue to the trucking industry with the growth of a more vigorous economy. As on various other occasions, he quoted statistics to prove that the state was "moving rapidly toward its rendezvous with prosperity."

TALK AT THE DEDICATION OF NEW SEWAGE TREATMENT PLANT

FAYETTEVILLE
September 25, 1959

The construction of a $2,250,000 sewage treatment plant, designed for a predicted population of 65,000 in 1970, will "certainly have a favorable effect on the industrial potential of this community," Governor Hodges told a Fayetteville audience. "This facility will advertise to the world that the people of Fayetteville are looking to the future and that they know the value of long-range planning. . . . The community that will not invest in itself is certainly presumptuous to expect others to do so." He also pointed out that the plant should effectively protect the Cape Fear River and Cross Creek from further pollution due to sewage and industrial waste originating in Fayetteville. On this subject, he expressed his delight that the last General Assembly had created the North Carolina Department of Water Resources, a "pioneering venture" that provides North Carolina with the machinery for a coordinated effort to develop a comprehensive water program.

ADDRESS TO AN INTER-CITY ROTARY DINNER

Rochester, New York
October 5, 1959

The major theme of this address was an analysis of the Governor's Russian tour and another plea to help break down the "wall of misunderstanding" by a greater exchange of people between the two great powers. His final, and most forceful, observation was the need to "promote understanding among our own people in the United States." This appeal appears often in the Governor's speeches outside the southern states, and on this occasion he scored the political expediency of factions in both major parties who use minority groups as political pawns. He also gave his fellow Rotarians "an orientation as to what a businessman-Rotarian is faced with when he goes into politics and gets to the Governor's office," and explained his policy of accepting only civic club speeches where the clubs of a city, county, or district meet together.

ADDRESS AT A MEETING OF THE MUNICIPAL
FORUM OF NEW YORK

NEW YORK CITY
October 7, 1959

Governor Hodges repeated to this group, meeting in the Lawyers Club, the observations he had made two days earlier in Rochester on his Russian trip and the need for understanding and tolerance between sections in the United States. Speaking more directly to the financial interests represented, he talked of North Carolina's sound fiscal condition, and the state's reputation for fiscal integrity. "It is particularly gratifying," he said, "to compare the business-like methods that we use in North Carolina with the policies of some states where finances have become a political football and fiscal affairs are administered under the handicap of antiquated laws."

ADDRESS AT THIRTY-EIGHTH ANNUAL CONVENTION
OF THE NORTH CAROLINA ASSOCIATION
OF REALTORS, INC.

ASHEVILLE
October 15, 1959

Observations on his Russian trip were again the major topic of the Governor's luncheon address at the Grove Park Inn, but he devoted some time to a discussion of matters of direct interest to the realtors. The real estate business, he said, reacts quickly to economic fluctuations and is in many ways a barometer of business stability. He cited the decision of the Dupont Corporation to locate a dacron plant in Kinston, and the resultant benefits to that area, particularly in terms of real estate activity, as an illustration of the impact of industrial development on a community. He commended the last General Assembly for adopting statutes to provide improved administration in the property tax field, and he encouraged the realtors to continue and expand their "Living is Finer in North Carolina" program.

ADDRESS AT EIGHTH ANNUAL LEGISLATIVE WORK CONFERENCE OF THE SOUTHERN REGIONAL EDUCATION BOARD

LOUISVILLE, KENTUCKY
October 16, 1959

Speaking to a workshop on higher education, Governor Hodges chose to discuss one of his favorite projects, the Research Triangle, as a "symbol of the new South—awakened, objective, strong, determined, resourceful, and above all, united in the desire to bring new prosperity and a more abundant life to her people." He considered the concepts that led to the eventual physical reality of the Triangle: that science is a key element in today's industrial development, and that an academic environment is a very profitable location for industrial research activity. The advantages of the proximity of the University of North Carolina, Duke University, and North Carolina State College and the specific resources each institution offered the industrial scientist were discussed in detail. He reviewed the organization of the Research Triangle Foundation and the Research Triangle Institute and the progress to date of these organizations.

ADDRESS AT ALEXANDER COUNTY INDUSTRY APPRECIATION DAY

TAYLORSVILLE
October 16, 1959

This event, similar to many others he had attended across the state, was described by Governor Hodges as "exciting and gratifying." It represented two significant developments: first, that the people of the area had come to appreciate the importance of industry's role in the development and maintenance of a stable economic structure; secondly, it indicated an awareness of the fact that county-wide unity and cooperative effort provide the key to future prosperity. He commended the citizens of Alexander

county for the "courageous" admission that they had lagged behind their neighbors in industrial growth. The enthusiasm and
determination, however, he had witnessed during his tour of the
county indicates "that you have that 'something extra' in the
way of community and county pride that usually means the
difference between moving ahead or simply maintaining the
status quo." One of the worst mistakes, he continued, that an area
can make in planning an industrial development program is to
overlook the potential for expansion in its old industries; this
expression of appreciation to Alexander county's established industries constitutes a forward-looking step.

ADDRESS AT DEDICATION OF PITTSBURGH PLATE GLASS COMPANY PLANT

Shelby
October 21, 1959

In February, 1958, Governor Hodges had attended ground-
breaking ceremonies for a new fiberglass plant of the Pittsburgh
Plate Glass Company. On this occasion he returned for the
dedication ceremonies held in Shelby's Presbyterian Church. The
Company's original plans had specified a plant employing approximately 850 people to man a maximum of sixteen furnaces. The
Governor was "thrilled to learn" that a recent decision would
expand the plant's furnaces to twenty-four, and that more than
1,200 workers would be needed. He discussed the far-reaching
effects the new plant would have on the region and its people
and quoted comments on North Carolina's favorable industrial
climate by spokesmen for several industries that had recently
located in the state.

ADDRESS AT REGIONAL CIVIC CLUB MEETING

Goldsboro
October 22, 1959

Members of six civic club organizations, representing eight eastern counties, gathered in Goldsboro to eat barbecue and hear Governor Hodges tell of his Russian trip during the previous summer. The Governor, however, first urged the group of representative community leaders to channel this spirit of cooperation into a regional development program. "The potential here is unlimited. All that is needed is progressive, forward-looking leadership—leadership of the type that is gathered here this evening." He challenged them to undertake a five-point program that included agricultural diversification, industrial expansion, improvement of water resources handling, support of the Research Triangle, and increased local school support. "Those of you here this evening, as leaders in our communities and counties, have a responsibility to make sure that eastern North Carolina takes full advantage of the opportunities that the years ahead will bring."

ADDRESS IN CONNECTION WITH A NORTH CAROLINA TRADE AND INDUSTRY MISSION TO THE NETHERLANDS

Amsterdam
November 4, 1959

Governor Hodges, accompanied by sixty-six North Carolina industrialists, businessmen and development officials, spent fourteen days in five European countries seeking business contacts and expounding the commercial opportunities of North Carolina. This marked a new departure in American-European trade relations, for it was the first time an individual state had sent a trade and industry mission abroad. Amsterdam was the second stop on the eight-city itinerary, and here the Governor delivered a luncheon address to a large group of industrialists and government officials. Except for the introduction, it was identical to his speech in London two days earlier (pp. 291-300). Following this meeting, the Governor and part of his entourage proceeded to Germany, but thirty remained behind to consolidate and expand trade-promotion contacts in Amsterdam, Rotterdam, The Hague, and Utrecht.

ADDRESS IN CONNECTION WITH A NORTH CAROLINA TRADE AND INDUSTRY MISSION TO GERMANY

STUTTGART
November 5, 1959

In Stuttgart's Liderhalle Governor Hodges, with thirty of his group, lunched and talked for four hours with 300 German businessmen representing commercial and industrial interests in southwestern Germany. The Governor's formal address was the same one delivered at each of the eight cities he visited, describing North Carolina's economic boom, the desire for improved trade relations with Europe, and the development of increased shipping through state ports. Accompanied by seven others, the Governor then made a short trip to Frankfort for another speech, joining a group that had preceded him there to make advance arrangements. The delegation reassembled in Munich for a quiet weekend of rest and sightseeing, with the only scheduled business being an address by the Governor over Radio Free Europe on Saturday, November 7.

ADDRESS IN CONNECTION WITH A NORTH CAROLINA TRADE AND INDUSTRY MISSION TO GERMANY

MUNICH
November 9, 1959

Governor Hodges was host at a morning reception for 250 Munich civic and business leaders, at which he delivered his customary address. The purposes of the visit by the sixty-seven man delegation were outlined: to develop stronger trade with Europe through North Carolina state ports, and to express appreciation to those organizations with whom the port are already doing business; to seek out added industrial development for North Carolina through European-financed plants, through European-controlled franchise agreements, and through assembly or re-packing type operations in the state; and to create a better understanding and good will between the nations.

ADDRESS IN CONNECTION WITH A NORTH CAROLINA TRADE AND INDUSTRY MISSION TO SWITZERLAND

Zurich
November 11, 1959

Leaving Germany, the Governor's party traveled to Switzerland, where Zurich was the base of operations. Again the Governor spoke at a luncheon attended by 135 Swiss industrialists and bankers. As in his other addresses on the eight-city tour, he referred to school integration problems in the South, and explained North Carolina's moderate approach. "Racial problems, prejudices, and discrimination based on race, creed, politics, etc., are not confined to the southern region of the United States nor indeed to the United States," he said. "All of these problems are world-wide and need the attention and understanding of people everywhere."

ADDRESS IN CONNECTION WITH A NORTH CAROLINA TRADE AND INDUSTRY MISSION TO FRANCE

PARIS
November 12, 1959

From Zurich, the trade mission moved on to Paris where the Governor addressed a large gathering of French business and industrial leaders at an evening meeting. Recalling previous visits to Paris and Europe, he described it as "a special privilege and treat for me to return as Governor of North Carolina, U.S.A., leading a large delegation of our outstanding citizens who have paid their own way here to tell the North Carolina story of growth and opportunity to our European friends." Only an overnight trip to Brussels, Belgium, remained to complete the scheduled tour. Then Governor Hodges returned to Paris to board a flight back to the United States on November 14.

ADDRESS AT ANNUAL AWARDS DAY, DUPLIN COUNTY COMMUNITY DEVELOPMENT PROGRAM

KENANSVILLE
November 24, 1959

"Duplin County has provided an answer to those in other sections of our state who question the wisdom of agricultural diversity and cling too tenaciously to traditional farming practices," the Governor remarked as he presented statistics that reflected the success of diversification in terms of farm income. Increased poultry and egg production were largely responsible for the county's gains in the past year. This interest in diversification, Governor Hodges insisted, should not be interpreted to mean that he minimized the importance of tobacco, which remains the backbone of the state's agricultural economy. In answer to critics who charged that the recent trade mission to

Europe was only for the benefit of manufacturing and shipping interests, he explained that "many, many hours were spent selling the virtues of North Carolina tobacco, and seeking expanded markets for tobacco. I have no doubt that the North Carolina farmer will benefit, both directly and indirectly, from the contacts made during this trip." He mentioned European complaints about American tobacco and its price, and the threat of Rhodesian production.

ADDRESS AT WINTER MEETING OF THE CAROLINAS-VIRGINIA PURCHASING AGENTS ASSOCIATION

PINEHURST
December 5, 1959

Speaking to the quarterly meeting of purchasing agents of various businesses, schools, and governmental units in North Carolina, South Carolina, and Virginia, Governor Hodges thanked the organization for its interest in helping develop local and state suppliers who can provide needed products at competitive prices. He insisted, however, that much more remained to be done to keep North Carolina money at home. A recent survey had shown that of a total of $1,437,000,000 spent annually by North Carolina's companies and industries, only $71,000,750 was disbursed within the state. "I would like to see this Association set up the necessary machinery to seek out these opportunities and make them known to the state agencies that are charged with the responsibility of promoting economic growth. Our North Carolina purchasing people have already helped along this line. Let us know where you think a profitable supply operation can be established and we will take it from there. The capital is readily available in North Carolina, in South Carolina, in Virginia, and in the South today to back any sound business proposition."

ADDRESS AT ANNUAL DINNER OF THE SMITHFIELD CHAMBER OF COMMERCE

SMITHFIELD
December 14, 1959

"In spite of a terrific schedule, I accepted this invitation to indicate my interest in what you have done in regional and community developments." In this opening remark, Governor Hodges expressed the theme of his address to a large group of Johnston county businessmen. He traced the development of Johnston county, pointing out two dates that marked turning points in its growth—1898, when a modern tobacco market was established in Smithfield, and 1955, when the first locally-supported development corporation was chartered. In the following years, other citizens have invested in two additional corporations, resulting in the establishment of thee factories offering a potential employment of 1,300 in the Smithfield-Selma area. "The thing that impresses me most about what you have accomplished here," he said, "is that you have seized the initiative yourselves, that you have recognized the opportunities available to you and set out, on your own, to do something about them." He cautioned the group, however, that some sections of eastern North Carolina are being hampered in their economic growth by "petty jealousies and a lack of cooperation", and he made a strong plea for extended regional cooperation.

ADDRESS ON TELEVISION STATION WRAL

RALEIGH
January 7, 1960

This thirty-minute address, delivered at eight o'clock in the evening, was similar and in some portions identical to the Governor's address before the Raleigh Chamber of Commerce Bankers Meeting on December 15, 1959. (See pp. 300-310). Again, he reviewed the progress of the state's industrial development program in 1959, and outlined his hopes for the new year. "We shall continue this work through 1960," he said; "and, although, I'll not be your Governor after 1960, I hope you as citizens will see that progress continues." Political observers attached some significance to the fact that the Governor mentioned the name of only one person in the address, that of State Treasurer Edwin Gill, a close associate and potential gubernatorial candidate. The reference to Gill occurred in connection with his recent announcement that North Carolina bonds had been awarded the highest quality rating by Moody's Investment Service. Governor Hodges described this as "one of the most dramatic, yet almost unnoticed by the man in the street, announcements made in many years . . . It's a favorable reflection on the soundness and stability of your state government and is a reputation not enjoyed by many other states."

ADDRESS AT MID-WINTER MEETING, REGION XIII ASSOCIATION OF JUNIOR LEAGUES OF AMERICA, INCORPORATED

RALEIGH
January 12, 1960

Citizenship and community responsibility was the topic of this address, which was prepared for delivery before a regional conference of Junior League officials representing the two Carolinas. The subject was a favorite one with the Governor and one that was for him "always a pleasure to discuss with a group of people who have a well-established reputation for community service." He urged the ladies to take an active role in government and in community development: "Government agencies have been inclined to take over education and welfare," he said; "primarily because we as citizens have abdicated many of our responsibilities, so these two still should get much of your attention and support." There is, he asserted, a definite place for the "woman's touch" in the associations that are working for industrial expansion and general economic development, as well as in the political party of the individual's choice. The Raleigh *News and Observer* of January 13, 1960, reported that the Governor threw aside his prepared speech and spoke extemporaneously to the group, encouraging them to "get into the economies of your community."

ADDRESS AT ANNUAL MEETING OF THE JACKSONVILLE CHAMBER OF COMMERCE

JACKSONVILLE, NORTH CAROLINA
January 15, 1960

Onslow county, the site of the Camp Lejeune Marine Corps installation, ranks second in per capita income among the 100 counties of the state, and far above that of the neighboring counties. "If you ever question the economic value of Camp Lejeune to this community and this county, I would suggest that you consider these facts in the light of your number two position in the state," the Governor advised, as he pointed out that the Marine facility can be considered one of the largest, if not the largest, industry in North Carolina. A warning against complacency over this enviable record of progress was the major theme of the Governor's remarks. "It is paradoxical," he said, "that even moderate success tends to dull the tools that were used in forging that success—usually long before the maximum potential has been realized and the need for those tools has been eliminated." Efforts to bring a major manufacturing industry into the area had not been too successful in the past, but he encouraged the Chamber of Commerce to continue its work in this direction, because you cannot afford to "Leave it to the Marines." The Governor then discussed the economic importance of the ports of Wilmington and Morehead City, and was sharply critical of the bickering between the two cities that has hindered development. "These ports," he asserted, "occupy far too significant a position in this state's future to be hampered in their development by petty jealousies, fostered by individuals who lack the vision and understanding that is so desperately needed in North

Photo by Hugh Morton

Terry Sanford, Governor Hodges, and Senator John F. Kennedy at the North Carolina caucus during the Democratic National Convention at Los Angeles, July, 1960.

Governor Hodges speaking at the Democratic National Convention in Los Angeles, California, July 14, 1960.

Carolina during this dynamic period of economic transition." He deplored the fact that it was impossible to capitalize on opportunities presented on the Trade Mission to Europe, because the port facilities were not sufficiently large or adequately equipped to handle the business. A thorough public relations program is essential, he said, and the General Assembly must be adequately educated on needs in this respect.

REMARKS AT A MEETING OF THE NORTH CAROLINA SOCIETY

Washington, D. C.
January 16, 1960

Following his address to the Jacksonville Chamber of Commerce on January 15, Governor Hodges, accompanied by his private secretary Harold Makepeace, and Hugh Morton, a member of the State Board of Conservation and Development, flew to the nation's capital where the Governor had two meetings scheduled for the next day. At noon he attended a luncheon at the Park-Sheraton Hotel with a group of honorary Tar Heels, and that night he spoke at the North Carolina Society's annual meeting honoring the state's Congressional delegation. Again he reviewed the progress enjoyed by North Carolina in 1959, including the notable achievements of the General Assembly. On the debit side, he noted that no action had been taken on court reform, constitutional revision, and reapportionment. "These issues," he was sorry to say, "are still very much with us, and I predict that a special session of the next General Assembly will face up to its responsibility and deal with these matters intelligently and in the best interest of the state."

REMARKS AT ANNUAL MEETING OF THE GREATER NEW HAVEN CHAMBER OF COMMERCE

NEW HAVEN, CONNECTICUT
January 27, 1960

Governor Hodges was invited to tell Connecticut businessmen about North Carolina's program of industrial promotion which, in effect, posed a threat to New England communities sadly viewing many of their industries moving south. He explained that the state was striving to improve its economic situation, not only by the establishment of new industries, but also by emphasis on the expansion of existing plants and by a greater diversification of agriculture. After describing his ambitious efforts to tell the "North Carolina story" to potential industrial investors in Europe and in other sections of the United States, he reassured his audience that "these trips are not raiding parties . . . It is an economic fact of life that many industries are moving, and there is no secret about the fact that many of them are moving south. Our position has been, in effect, 'If you are planning a move, and especially if you are planning a move south, we think you will be interested in what North Carolina has to offer'." He reiterated the theme that the state is not interested in the type of industry that demands special concessions and is unwilling to "carry its fair share of the load"; and in conclusion, made his often repeated plea for understanding at home as well as abroad.

REMARKS AT THE ASSOCIATION OF COTTON TEXTILE MERCHANTS OF NEW YORK

NEW YORK CITY
January 28, 1960

The economic plight of textiles, which he characterized as North Carolina's leading industry, in the face of increasing foreign competition and governmental policies that worked hardships on the cotton manufacturer, was carefully analyzed by

Governor Hodges in this address. He suggested that textile machinery manufacturers redouble their efforts in research and that cotton manufacturers keep up-to-date in machinery and methods. He urged a very much greater interest in research on the part of the mills. In addition, he said that the textile executives might well "stay a little closer to the Democratic Congressmen and less close to a Republican President than they had in the past . . . from the standpoint of getting more favorable action on foreign imports and raw cotton prices." On the basis of his experiences in the Soviet Union during the past summer, including a visit to a modern, well equipped textile mill, he predicted that in the next decade or so the United States, including the textile industry, would be faced with very tough competition from the Soviets.

REMARKS AT A WASHINGTON'S BIRTHDAY LUNCHEON SPONSORED BY THE PHILADELPHIA-CONTINENTAL CHAPTER, SONS OF THE AMERICAN REVOLUTION

PHILADELPHIA, PENNSYLVANIA
February 20, 1960

Governer Hodges was presented a Good Citizenship Award by a Philadelphia chapter of the Sons of the American Revolution at a luncheon in the Grand Ballroom of the Bellevue-Stratford Hotel. His speech of acceptance dealt largely with the subject of patriotism. Our country, he said, needs "men who are not afraid to stand openly and proudly proclaim their patriotism. I fear that too many of our citizens have, in recent years, come to regard open display of patriotism as passé and beneath their dignity. 'Flagwaving' has become a derisive term, hurled by would-be sophisticates who seem to feel that some stigma is or should be attached to a man's love of his country . . . Let's all re-dedicate ourselves to greater patriotism of the kind practiced by George Washington, and let's be glad for the opportunities that are ours today."

REMARKS AT AN EASTERN NORTH CAROLINA INDUSTRIAL DEVELOPMENT CONFERENCE

GOLDSBORO
March 31, 1960

Before attending this conference, Governor Hodges had participated in cornerstone laying ceremonies for a new plant of the Lori Manufacturing Company, which planned to employ between 200 and 300 people in the manufacture of women's wear in Goldsboro, and which had been financed by local citizens. This arrangement he characterized as a good example of cooperation at work. At the luncheon conference, which was sponsored by the Commerce and Industry Division of the State Department of Conservation and Development, and was attended by representatives from thirty-five eastern North Carolina counties, the Governor acknowledged that he had created some animosity by recent speeches in which he said that the eastern section of the state was lagging in its efforts to take full advantage of its resources. He explained that his statements were prompted not by a desire to criticize, but by a genuine and long standing interest in the section and a sincere desire to help. It was very gratifying to note, he said, a marked increase in activity and cooperative endeavor in the area in recent months.

ADDRESS AT ANNUAL CONVENTION OF THE NORTH CAROLINA FEDERATION OF WOMEN'S CLUBS

RALEIGH
April 7, 1960

Speaking to delegates of the North Carolina Federation of Women's Clubs, representing 18,000 members in 357 clubs across the state, the Governor praised the activities of that organization, which he described as being "dedicated to voluntary service in promoting the civic, educational, cultural, and social betterment of North Carolina and as possessing "the organization, the outstanding leadership, and the ability to achieve your goals." In a timely reference to the political situation and the forthcoming elections, he reviewed the accomplishments of his administration, "to illustrate the kind of things we must work at if we are to help our state," and made a strong appeal to his audience to support candidates for public office on all levels who are willing to take positive stands on issues. "Do not accept generalities or vague, carefully-worded promises . . . At this crucial time in our history, North Carolina cannot afford to take a chance on what a candidate might do if elected. We must be sure that he doesn't lead us to negativism or to a campaign of hate and disunion." Portions of the speech were a repetition of the Governor's remarks on patriotism made to the Sons of the American Revolution at Philadelphia on February 20 (see p. 517).

(see p. 517).

ADDRESS AT FIRST ANNUAL YOUTH FITNESS CONFERENCE

RALEIGH
April 9, 1960

Young people from all sections of North Carolina attended this conference co-sponsored by the newly-appointed Governor's Youth Fitness Commission and the First Citizens Bank and Trust Company. The commission, not an official state body, was chartered as a non-profit organization for the purpose of promoting and correlating existing programs directed toward the physical, mental, and moral development of North Carolina Youth. Financial assistance from the Richardson Foundation had enabled the commission to establish headquarters and employ Robert V. Cox of Chapel Hill as executive director. Speaking in State College's Student Union building, Governor Hodges talked of the importance of young people in the state and in the nation, and the place of physical fitness in any development program. On the state level, he expressed the opinion that "we can, if we are serious enough about it, make of North Carolina a modern Sparta as far as strength and capacity for rugged endurance are concerned." He hoped that the colleges could lessen their dependence on out-of-state talent for their competitive teams, and that the state could raise its standing from its low position in regard to the physical fitness of its draftees and enlistees. Portions of this speech were repeated by the Governor in his address to the Boy Scouts in Altanta on April 26, 1960 (see pp. 373-382).

ADDRESS AT DEDICATION OF A NORTH CAROLINA NATIONAL GUARD OPERATIONS AND TRAINING BUILDING

CHARLOTTE
April 10, 1960

Viewing the great complex of airplanes and runways surrounding the Air National Guard facility in Charlotte, Governor Hodges marveled at the "fantastic progress" that had been made in aeronautics since the flight of the Wright brothers in 1903. He expressed high praise for the development of the North Carolina Air National Guard unit. First recognized by the federal government in 1948, the entire unit was called into active duty during the Korean emergency in 1950 and served with distinction. More recently, it had relieved Army Guard units for two weeks on strike duty at Henderson. "On that occasion,," said the Governor, "you reacted well in an extremely difficult situation and we are indebted to you for that service." He noted that more than $21,000,000 had been invested in facilities and equipment for the Charlotte facility, but he explained that the program is one that provides important military protection to the nation at a considerable savings to the taxpayers. On the subject of air travel, the Governor made some interesting personal comments. "In the past three years," he said, "I have traveled more than 196,000 miles—and 140,000 of those miles have been in the air—42,000 with the National Guard. I have flown in every conceivable type of aircraft . . . I have touched down at some of the largest, most modern airports in the world, and I have gotten down somehow in what I honestly believed to be more than my share of cow pastures and corn fields. So, you see, I am a fully accredited citizen of this advanced air age." Later in the day the Governor made an appearance and spoke on a program sponsored by the R. Murphy Williams Memorial Fund in Greensboro.

ADDRESS AT BOARD OF CONSERVATION AND DEVELOPMENT MEETING

GREENSBORO
April 11, 1960

This talk was devoted entirely to a review of the history and the activities of the Department of Conservation and Development and its policy-making governing body, the Board of Conservation and Development. The Governor told of the creation of the department by the 1925 General Assembly, at the suggestion of Governor Angus W. McLean, and traced the major structural changes that had occurred within its organization since that time. Referring to the eighteen members of the board by name, he praised them for their "knowledge, their leadership ability, and their proven devotion to North Carolina." During the preceding week he had asked each of the seven division heads within the department to prepare an outline of his activities, his primary ambition for his division, and his suggestions for ways in which other board members might help him to achieve that ambition. The Governor used these fact-filled resumés to illustrate the scope of the department's operation and to give some indication of the responsibility resting on the shoulders of the members of the board. The division heads who had prepared the summaries were Charles J. Parker of the Division of State Advertising; William R. Henderson of the Commerce and Industry Division; Robert D. Barbour of the Division of Community Planning; Fred H. Claridge of the Division of Forestry; C. Gehrman Holland of the Commercial Fisheries Division; Dr. Jasper L. Stuckey of the Division of Mineral Resources; and Thomas N. Morse of the Division of State Parks.

ADDRESS AT THE NEW YORK UNIVERSITY SCHOOL OF LAW

NEW YORK CITY
April 20, 1960

The Governor had been invited to speak at a student-faculty convocation of the Law School of New York University on some important public question. After correspondence on the subject, it was agreed that he would discuss the racial problem in the public schools, with emphasis on his experience in North Carolina. He explained that for the past three years or more this problem "has not been a pressing issue in our state . . . not because North Carolina has not been confronted with the problem nor because North Carolina has necessarily solved the problem for all time," but because "beginning in 1955 and continuing through a special legislative session in 1956, basic rules for meeting specific problems in this area as they arose were laid out, and within this framework we have been able to make our way as a state with a minimum of internal dissension or public discord." The address was similar in many respects to the one which the Governor had delivered before the Harvard Law School earlier in the year (see pp. 319-334).

REMARKS AT A CIVIL DEFENSE BRIEFING SESSION, OPERATION ALERT 1960

RALEIGH
April 26, 1960

Speaking to Civil Defense workers assembled in Raleigh at state headquarters for a training exercise, Governor Hodges warned against the major enemies of a survival program—complacency, lethargy, and a false sense of security created by the occasional lessening of cold war tensions. He expressed hope that Operation Alert 1960 would indicate that the general public indifference to Civil Defense preparedness is disappearing. Another major point was his insistence that Civil Defense "cannot be separated from government because it is government. Civil Defense is the preparation for and the carrying out of emergency operations by established agencies of government, which have been trained to cope with disaster . . . The responsibility for the emergency services set forth in the North Carolina Survival Plan is assigned to the agency or department of state government best equipped to establish that service." Following this session, which was held at 10:30 in the morning, the Governor flew to Atlanta to address a regional meeting of the Boy Scouts of America (see pp. 373-382).

REMARKS AT A SALUTE TO INDUSTRY BANQUET SPONSORED BY THE BANK OF VIRGINIA

RICHMOND, VIRGINIA
April 27, 1960

The Virginia Electric and Power Company had been selected to receive this salute, which is made annually by the Bank of Virginia, and Governor Hodges was invited to deliver the major address because of the wide-spread interests of the company in North Carolina as well as in its home state. "We in North Carolina," he said, "feel that the Virginia Electric and Power Company is very much a part of the wonderful progress we have made in economic development in recent years, and we look forward to an even more extensive and productive relationship in the years ahead . . . North Carolina is deeply indebted to this company for the ambitious development program it has undertaken in the northeastern section of our state." Beginning in 1948, VEPCO had initiated a comprehensive plan designed to harness, within a period of twenty-five years, the power-generating potential of the Roanoke River. The construction of the Roanoke Rapids Dam and Reservoir, completed in 1955, was the first step in the program, and only recently had difficulties been ironed out to make possible the erection of another dam and power station at a point on the river between Halifax and Northampton counties. As on various other occasions, the Governor emphasized the importance of a cooperative approach to area and regional planning and cited this event as an example of the spirit of cooperation that is a significant part of the transformation that is taking place in the southern states.

ADDRESS AT THE DEDICATION OF THE NORTH CAROLINA CREDIT UNION LEAGUE BUILDING

GREENSBORO
April 29, 1960

North Carolina, by virtue of an enabling act passed by the General Assembly in 1915 and the establishment of the state's first credit union in Lowe's Grove that same year, had been the fourth state in the nation to embrace the credit union concept. In 1960 there were more than 250 such groups in the state with approximately 100,000 members and assets in excess of $35,000,000, but the dedication of this building marked the opening of the organization's first permanent home office. Governor Hodges outlined the history of the credit union movement, with particular reference to North Carolina, and expressed a belief that "the growth and development of the Credit Union League—symbolized by the building we dedicate here today—is indicative of the progress we are making in North Carolina in many fields. I think it illustrates also that we have not deviated from our primary objective—that of providing a better life, a more abundant life, for all our people. And, just as you—through reasonable, convenient loans—make it possible for individuals to take advantage of their mounting opportunities, the state works diligently to provide the same type service for its business and corporate citizens. For we know that only when our economy is vibrant and alive can our people move forward in their own individual endeavors."

ADDRESS AT A STATE-WIDE CONFERENCE
ON TEACHER EDUCATION

Raleigh

April 29, 1960

Governor Hodges viewed this conference, the first of its kind held in the state, as an important event in the growing movement to give neded emphasis to the factor of quality in public education. Reviewing the highlights in the development of public schools in North Carolina, he expressed pride in the fact that the state "has year-in and year-out met in a commendable way the *quantitative* challenge in education. Indeed, *in terms of ability to pay,* we stand fourth in the whole nation in what we pay for teachers salaries," but he was "afraid that we have, until recent years, tended to neglect that second very important facet of the educational challenge, namely, *quality!*" Speaking as an interested citizen, not as a professional educator, he analyzed the factors that comprise quality education. Of special interest to his audience were his comments on teacher certification and a discussion of the merits of "teaching methods, as distinct from scholarship training of the teacher." "I would not presume to pass specific judgment on this particular question," he said, "but I am sure this conference and other discussions will arrive at some sensible answer." He spoke with high praise of the Curriculum Study Committee under the direction of Dr. I. E. Ready, whose purpose was to bring about improvement of the curriculum of the public schools by encouraging widespread lay-professional study and by a careful evaluation at the state level.

REMARKS AT A GENERAL ELECTRIC
CORPORATION LUNCHEON

New York City

May 16, 1960

This address, made at a luncheon sponsored by the management of the four General Electric plants located in North Carolina and

Walker Martin, General Electric's North Carolina distributor, was the first of five speeches that Governor Hodges was to make to various groups while on an industry-hunting trip to the New York area during the second half of May, 1960. The theme of these addresses, which were similar to those he had made in Europe during the previous summer, was stated in his introductory remarks on this occasion: "We have here today a group of outstanding businessmen whom we would like to interest in our state—men who, we believe, will want to be a part of what is going on in North Carolina once they have been given the *facts*. And I stress the word 'facts' because the North Carolina Story requires no embellishments nor any gimmicks." The generosity of the General Electric representatives in providing the luncheon was, he said, "an example of the type of corporate citizenship that prevails in North Carolina, an indication of the cooperative spirit that is very much a part of everything we do in our state."

REMARKS AT POWER COMPANIES LUNCHEON

NEW YORK CITY
May 17, 1960

Governor Hodges again told the "North Carolina Story," extolling the investment potential of his state, to a group of New York industrialists, financiers, and utility executives assembled for a luncheon at the Biltmore Hotel. The hosts on this occasion were the Carolina Power and Light Company, the Duke Power Company, and the Carolina Division of the Virginia Electric and Power Company. "These companies," the Governor remarked, "have faced a great challenge in our state in recent years. Upon them has rested the responsibility of meeting the power needs of a dynamic, rapidly expanding economy—an economy in which both domestic and industrial demands have soared fantastically. It is to our credit that they have not only met these demands, but have demonstrated dramatically their own faith in the future of our region by expanding their power-generating capacities in anticipation of tremendous economic growth in the years just ahead." The main portion of the speech was a repetition of the Governor's remarks at the General Electric Corporation luncheon on the preceding day.

REMARKS AT A LUNCHEON FOR NEW YORK BUSINESS AND INDUSTRIAL LEADERS

New York City
May 18, 1960

The First Citizens Bank and Trust Company sponsored this third luncheon designed to give the Governor and his party an opportunity to make business contacts and tell of the economic opportunity offered by North Carolina. "It is our honest conviction," he said, "that our state has much to offer the industrial investor who may be expanding or seeking new markets. We are not here with idle promises or concessions. This is not the way we do business in North Carolina. Our proposal, which I believe respects the intelligence and integrity of this audience, involves nothing more or less than a mutually beneficial business relationship." Factors to which the Governor attached significance were: the Business Development Corporation, a private agency designed to assist small businesses with the financing of their operations; industrial education centers, established across the state to provide technically trained personnel for new and expanding industries; the Research Triangle, exemplifying the state's interest in industrial research; the expansion of the deep-water ports at Wilmington and Morehead City; and the attitude of the people of the state in meeting the challenge of economic progress. A reflection of this final factor, he explained, was the fact that 100 citizens had accompanied him to New York at their own expense to assist in the good-will mission.

ADDRESS AT TEN TOP PLANTS OF THE YEAR DINNER

NEW YORK CITY
May 18, 1960

After addressing three luncheons in as many days at the Biltmore Hotel, Governor Hodges spoke on this occasion at the University Club of New York City, where *Factory* Magazine was recognizing its selection of the nation's "Ten Top Plants of 1960." His speech, emphasizing the value of individual enterprise, echoed many of the remarks he had made in New York on May 6 at a dinner of the Brand Names Foundation honoring that organization's selection of the "Retailers-of-the-Year" (see pp. 382-392). Each audience represented a notable group of potential industrial investors, to whom he was delighted to repeat his inventory of advantages offered by North Carolina to new industrial neighbors. Speaking of the struggle to secure America's freedom, based on individual enterprise, he suggested the need to "see that we are not controlled or dominated by bigness or minorities—neither big business nor big labor. Big business has learned better how to behave; big labor, especially the Hoffa kind, has yet to learn it seems. Neither must we be controlled nor dominated by minorities which appeal to many of our politicians' worse side rather than their better side."

ADDRESS AT AMERICAN TEXTILE MACHINERY EXHIBITION

ATLANTIC CITY, NEW JERSEY
May 22, 1960

For the first time in the history of this event, the American Textile Machinery Association had invited firms from foreign countries to display new designs at its annual exhibition, the result being that twelve nations were represented among the more than 400 participating exhibitors. Commending the sponsors for their action in this respect, Governor Hodges observed that, "all of us, I am sure, will concede that no nation or group of nations possess a monopoly on new ideas and new ways of getting the job done. Each of us can learn from the other—and it is especially important, in these times of international tension and distrust, that we acknowledge this fact, that we recognize our interdependence, and that we accept as our prime motivation a common desire to pool our talents and our knowledge and to work together for the economic, social, and cultural advancement of all men, regardless of nationality." Referring to the rapid developments that have characterized the textile industry in recent years, he challenged the manufacturers of textile machinery to redouble their efforts to provide new and better equipment. Expanding research programs, he insisted, are essential to the well-being of the industry.

ADDRESS AT EAST CENTRAL INDUSTRIAL DEVELOPMENT CONFERENCE

RALEIGH
May 24, 1960

The Commerce and Industry Division of the Department of Conservation and Development had arranged this all-day conference for representatives of nineteen counties in the east central section of the state to assemble and discuss their industrial development programs. Governor Hodges told the group that, "After having spent a major portion of the past week in the New York area, telling the North Carolina story of economic opportunity to hundreds of prospective industrial investors, it is, I think, most appropriate that I should return home to a meeting of this type—a meeting that clearly and dramatically shows that I was, if anything, understating the case when I told the New York audiences that North Carolina is on the move." The Governor's address was delivered at a luncheon meeting at the Raleigh Y. M. C. A. Earlier in the day the group had heard from representatives of the General Electric Corporation and the Farmville (North Carolina) Economic Council. Afternoon speakers represented the Wilmington building industry and the Duke Power Company.

ADDRESS AT A MEETING OF THE COMMUNITY BUILDERS' COUNCIL OF THE URBAN LAND INSTITUTE

RALEIGH

May 27, 1960

The Research Triangle was the subject of this luncheon address, with emphasis on the orderly planning of the research park area. "The Research Triangle of North Carolina," said Governor Hodges, "is a conscious effort to develop the resources of science as part of its program for both the present and the future. In this effort, North Carolina is earnestly attempting to exercise planning combined with action in making the problems of urban growth become, not problems, but opportunities." The Governor explained that the park could not be developed as an isolated area; that it had to be planned with consideration being given to the needs and problems of the surrounding area and the three university towns on which its function was dependent. Specific examples of the necessary coordination, which he discussed in some detail, were the road system, the water supply, sewage treatment, building restrictions, land-use regulations, and urban development immediately outside the park area.

ADDRESS AT DEPARTMENT OF CONSERVATION AND DEVELOPMENT WEST CENTRAL INDUSTRIAL DEVELOPMENT CONFERENCE

SALISBURY

June 7, 1960

This conference, arranged by the Department of Conservation and Development and attended by representatives from the twenty-one counties comprising the west central section of the state, was similar in nature to a meeting held by the same department for representatives of the nineteen east central counties on May 24 in Raleigh, where the Governor had also spoken. His address at

Salisbury was similar to that delivered in Raleigh and to a later address that he would deliver in Asheville on June 20 (see pp. 529 and 411-421). By a careful analysis of the per capita income and population trends in each county, he showed that the Piedmont region was one of economic extremes. Other sections of the state, the Governor explained, have "for the most part, an economic uniformity that makes both the problems and the possible solutions more obvious . . . You are faced with unique problems." A recent newspaper article by Professor Rupert B. Vance of the Sociology Department of the University of North Carolina was quoted by the Governor in some detail. Professor Vance had advocated the development of a richer agricultural-industrial economy in the state and had argued that the coming of new industry has not injured the state's agricultural economy. Other speakers on this occasion were James A. Babcock, plant manager of the Westinghouse Electric Corporation at Raleigh, Thomas Willis, executive director of the Farmville Economic Council, William Livesay manager of the Apex branch of the Durham Bank and Trust Company, and Nisbett Rodgers, president of the Mid-State Tile Company of Lexington.

REMARKS AT THE FIFTY-THIRD ANNUAL
CONVENTION OF THE NORTH CAROLINA
ASSOCIATION OF COUNTY COMMISSIONERS,
THE NORTH CAROLINA ASSOCIATION OF
COUNTY ACCOUNTANTS, AND THE
ASSOCIATION OF ASSESSING OFFICERS
OF NORTH CAROLINA

MOREHEAD CITY
June 21, 1960

The Governor had been asked to speak to this large group of county officials on the county's role in industrial development. He expressed his pleasure at the selection of this topic because "it indicates to me that you are fully aware of the complex economic forces at work in our state today, changing, sometimes drastically, many of our traditional economic concepts, and challenging each of us to develop new ideas that will enable our people to take maximum advantage of their opportunities." Answering the charge that the state's efforts in industrial development had been directed toward assisting local communities, with little thought being given to county organizations, he explained that this resulted from the simple fact "that communities are, in most cases, better organized and equipped to carry on industrial development operations. This does not imply that county government is less important than municipal government in the development effort. I dare say that in many instances the county government plays, by far, the most important role, certainly the most 'traditional role.' It is simply that because of the cohesiveness of the municipal organization, it is usually more reasonable to let them carry the ball at the local level. The benefit to the county is, of course, just as great regardless of who 'lands' the new industry."

REMARKS AT A NORTH CAROLINA GOVERNOR'S CONFERENCE ON AGING

RALEIGH
July 27, 1960

This state conference, a prelude to the 1961 White House Conference on Aging, had been planned and organized by the fifteen members of the North Carolina Governor's Coordinating Committee on Aging, appointed in 1956. The committee had been charged with the responsibility of reviewing activities within the state to meet any special needs or problems of the increasing number of older citizens, evaluating these needs, and suggesting measures by which they might be met. The main feature of the Governor's remarks was an expression of his strong conviction that the older persons of the state do not present unusual or special public problems to the extent that "we should isolate this particular group from all other citizens, and set them apart from the main stream of our citizenship . . . I think it is important that all of us avoid the erroneous implication that the older ctizens of North Carolina present today overwhelming public problems which weigh heavily on the shoulders of all other citizens." He discussed briefly each of the major topics which the conference would consider in smaller study groups the following day: research and population, income maintenance and employment, health and medical care, social services, education, recreation, family and community relationships, religion, and personnel.

ADDRESS AT DEDICATION OF THE ROSE HILL POULTRY PROCESSING PLANT

ROSE HILL
August 5, 1960

The dedication of a new poultry processing plant in Rose Hill gave the Governor an opportunity to praise the leadership in Duplin County that had fostered that county's remarkable strides in agricultural diversification. Duplin, he said, "has no secret ingredient, other than an uncommon dedication to good planning and hard work, especially with poultry production. I am no expert in these matters, but I can't believe that the chickens themselves have a preference for Duplin county. I believe that the 17,000,000 broilers and more than 55,000,000 eggs produced in this county last year could have been produced in a dozen other counties right here in eastern North Carolina." He told how, beginning in 1954, the full impact of federal restrictions and adverse economic trends hit the eastern North Carolina tobacco farmer, confronting him with a heavy loss of cash crop income. The only salvation lay in finding new sources of income. "Finding this solution and helping to implement it," said the Governor, "has been the primary objective of my administration during the past five and one-half years." He reminded his audience that when poultry was first suggested as a possible new source of income many farmers had been more than a little skeptical, but the idea had gained real momentum in Duplin and its neighboring counties of Bladen, Sampson, Pender, and Wayne where dramatic progress had been made. The Governor also utilized this opportunity to put in a political plug for the Democratic party: "We hope and pray that a reasonable and right federal program will continue long enough for us to adjust; and our best chance to get this kind of federal farm program is to put a Democratic administration back in Washington!"

REMARKS AT A CONFERENCE ON THE SOUTHERN REGIONAL EDUCATION BOARD

RALEIGH
August 24, 1960

Representatives of North Carolina's institutions of higher education had been invited to attend this conference to learn more about the program and activities of the Southern Regional Education Board. Dr. Robert C. Anderson and several members of his staff were present to speak to the group. This was the first meeting of its type, although plans were being made to hold similar conferences in each of the other fifteen states which are members of the board. In his opening address, the Governor reviewed the creation and organization of SREB, a regional higher education agency supported by the sixteen states in the Southern Governors' Conference. He emphasized the importance of regional cooperation in higher education because "we can no longer tolerate the luxury and even the wastefulness of duplicating educational facilities within a state, or even within a region, where the need and the demand for a particular program is simply not large enough to justify the existence of more than one or two institutions or facilities. This applies especially to graduate and certain professional programs."

ADDRESS AT THE PI KAPPA ALPHA FRATERNITY NATIONAL CONVENTION

Miami Beach, Florida
August 29, 1960

Governor Hodges had a personal interest in this fraternity convention because his son, Luther Hodges, Jr., was a member of its University of North Carolina chapter. In addition there were six other college chapters in North Carolina, as well as active alumni associations in Charlotte, High Point, and Raleigh. In this address he commended the fraternity for its National Leadership School, just completed on the campus of Florida Southern College. The stated purpose of the school was to train undergraduate chapter officers in the efficient management of chapter affairs. But the Governor said he preferred "to think that the ultimate goal in this type of training program is the development of leadership qualities that extend far beyond the competent management of a chapter or even a national fraternal organization . . . I believe strongly . . . that your Leadership School and the knowledge it imparts to those who attend reaches deeply into our entire social order, strengthening the democratic concept of citizenship responsibility upon which our whole way of life is based." He challenged its young men to go beyond the exercise of their traditional duties as citizens by dedicating themselves to the active preservation of the free enterprise system, and reminded them of the responsibilities that must accompany true freedom. "You as young people have less prejudice than do many of us who are older, and we need you in these troublous days when religious prejudice, race hatred, and other viruses affect our body politic, but you must show restraint and tolerance, even toward intolerance."

TALK AT A JAYCEES RALLY

CHESTERFIELD, VIRGINIA
September 5, 1960

Governor Hodges and Secretary of Agriculture Ezra Taft Benson shared the stump for their respective parties and Presidential candidates at this Labor Day rally held at the Chesterfield County Fair. Secretary Benson spoke for Nixon as "a man of experience and proven ability." Governor Hodges departed from his prepared text, which was more or less identical to that of his speech in Washington on September 13 (see pp. 448-456). to charge that the overall record of the Republicans since the 1930's demonstrated that party's neglect of the workingman. Addressing himself to the state in which he was speaking he urged Virginia, "a mother of Presidents and a mother of much of the great government we have had in this country to get in the line of march with loyal Democrats who believe that we have a destiny to fulfill, a nation to build, and a world to help."

REMARKS AT THE SOUTHERN GOVERNORS' CONFERENCE ROUND TABLE ON INDUSTRIAL DEVELOPMENT

HOT SPRINGS, ARKANSAS
September 27, 1960

Participating in a round table discussion on industrial development, Governor Hodges called upon other southern governors to take a personal interest in strengthening their industrial development programs, but cautioned them against placing emphasis on industry at the expense of other services needed by their people. He reviewed the industrial progress enjoyed by the southern states in the past decade and singled out the electronics industry as illustrating the South's potential in the expanding fields requiring skilled personnel. The creation and maintenance of a favorable "business climate," he explained, was the most significant factor in the effort to derive maximum benefits from present opportunities. Vigorous objective leadership on the part of governors and other leaders is needed, he said, to help dispel the ignorance and misunderstanding that has resulted in an unfavorable "image" of the South in recent years.

REMARKS AT A LUNCHEON FOR CHICAGO BUSINESS AND INDUSTRIAL LEADERS

CHICAGO, ILLINOIS
October 5, 1960

In the spring of 1958 Governor Hodges had led a delegation of Tar Heel industry-seekers to Chicago to tell the North Carolina story of economic opportunity to midwestern industrialists. On this follow-up visit, he told this large group lunching at the Palmer House at the expense of the natural gas utilities companies of North Carolina, that "we are even more enthusiastic today than we were two years ago . . . This is why we have come back to Chicago—to let you know that business opportunities in North Carolina have multiplied rather than diminished, to extend to you, once, again, a very warm and sincere invitation to consider North Carolina when you plan expansions." The growth of the fifteen natural gas companies of North Carolina, he explained, provides a dramatic illustration of the state's rapid growth in recent years. There was no natural gas in North Carolina until 1951 when the Transcontinental Gas Pipe Line Corporation's main line from Texas to New York passed through the state; in the ensuing years service had been extended to more than 100 communities. He stressed as "particularly significant" the fact "that this is an industry that not only contributes to the economy by its own activities but, at the same time, has the added advantage of being able to attract other industries—especially glass and fiberglass industries that are primarily dependent upon gas as a fuel for processing. Ball Brothers, Laurens Glass, Celanese, and Pittsburgh Plate Glass are among those who have come to North Carolina since the advent of natural gas."

REMARKS AT A LUNCHEON FOR CHICAGO BUSINESS AND INDUSTRIAL LEADERS

CHICAGO, ILLINOIS
October 6, 1960

This luncheon, similar in most respects to the one held on the previous day to give the Governor and his party an opportunity to meet with business and industrial contacts in Chicago, was sponsored by the five independent telephone companies of North Carolina. These companies, the Governor said in his prepared address, have not only met the vital communication needs of a dynamic, rapidly expanding economy, but also "have demonstrated dramatically their own faith in the future of our region by continually expanding their services and modernizing their facilities in anticipation of the heavy burden that will be imposed upon the communications industry by economic growth in the years ahead." Among the advantages which North Carolina has to offer to the industrial investor he emphasized the availibility of a reliable labor force, the result of both a rapidly expanding population and the increasing number of people leaving the farm for other employment. "These people, especially those from the farm," he said, "are not misfits. They are intelligent, hard-working, God-fearing, highly-respected citizens who have been caught up in an economic upheaval. They have lost none of their admirable qualities, especially their traditional adherence to the concept of a day's work for a day's pay."

ADDRESS AT THE FALL MEETING OF THE BOARD OF CONSERVATION AND DEVELOPMENT

HICKORY
October 17, 1960

Meeting with the Board of Conservation and Development for the last time as its chairman, Governor Hodges took this opportunity to review the activities of the board during the six years he had been associated with it. He voiced the idea that his philosophy of government was based on "an effort to ward off the ever-present specter of complacency and, at the same time, encourage continuous improvement of new goals." Transforming this philosophy into reality had occasionally been interpreted as undue criticism, but he insisted that his criticisms had only been motivated by a desire to improve services and benefit the people of North Carolina. In his opinion, "a governor who, in six years of administration, finds nothing that warrents his criticism is simply not doing his job, but is trying to run a popularity contest." He concluded his address by reminding the board members that "there is much yet to be done," and warning them against satisfaction with the status quo which implies that there is no room for improvement. The new administration, he said, would "bring in new ideas to challenge your ingenuity and your spirit," and he pointed out certain basic areas of activity that he felt would require continued attention in the years ahead.

ADDRESS AT ANNUAL MEETING OF THE TRAVEL COUNCIL OF NORTH CAROLINA

SOUTHERN PINES
October 23, 1960

In the final months of his administration, Governor Hodges often found himself addressing for the last time in his official capacity organizations with which he had been closely associated. The Travel Council of North Carolina had been organized in 1955, and as governor he had appointed the organizational committee authorized to draw up its charter and by-laws. This five-man committee, composed of Robert L. Thompson, Richard S. Tufts, Marley M. Melvin, S. B. Jones and S. Gilmer Sparger, were the honored guests at this dinner meeting. The most significant portion of the Governor's speech was the presentation of recently compiled figures revealing that the travel industry had surpassed the furniture industry to become the third largest industry in North Carolina; only textile and tobacco manufacturing contributed more to the state's economy. The Governor spoke briefly on some of the noteworthy projects sponsored by the council and encouraged the members to continue to move forward. "There is no limit," he said, "to what you can accomplish. You have the greatest state in the nation to work with, and the success you achieve will be limited only by the effort and dedication you put into your activities."

REMARKS AT DEDICATION OF
FIELDCREST MILLS PLANT

SMITHFIELD
December 2, 1960

Governor Hodges had been closely associated with Fieldcrest Mills for many years, when it was a subsidiary of Marshall Field and Company, and he expressed high praise for the organization and its personnel—"a company that personifies corporate citizenship at its best." The original plants of the company were in Spray, and the Governor viewed this expansion into eastern North Carolina as significant recognition of the fact that the section possesses the essential requirements for successful business operations. "It is always a delightful experience to come into one of the great agricultural counties of our state to participate in the dedication of a handsome, new manufacturing facility, as this indicates progress in balancing agriculture with industry." This speech echoed the theme of a previous address by the Governor, made before the Smithfield Chamber of Commerce on December 14, 1959, in which he cited Smithfield and Johnston County "as an example of what can be achieved when people put aside their differences and work together for mutual progress." (See p. 512 for summary of the earlier address.)

ADDRESS AT DEDICATION OF THE CAPE HATTERAS NATIONAL SEASHORE VISITOR CENTER

KITTY HAWK
December 17, 1960

On the fifty-seventh anniversary of man's first powered flight, Governor Hodges and other federal and state officials gathered at Kill Devil Hills to participate in the dedication of a new information building. The region had been officially designated a National Seashore Recreation Area in 1958, under the direction of the National Park Service, and this building was one of many improvements being made in the area. The Governor expressed his hope that the Park Service might "jointly restore the 'Lost Colony' theatre—building a more commodious and more attractive center in the Fort Raleigh area." Conrad Wirth, Director of the National Park Service, spoke also at the ceremonies.

LIST OF OTHER SPEECHES
AND ADDRESSES

LIST OF OTHER SPEECHES AND ADDRESSES

[This list contains the speeches, addresses, and other talks made by Governor Hodges during 1959-1960 in addition to those printed or digested in the preceding sections of this volume. An asterisk following the date on which a speech was made indicates that no copy of this speech has been preserved among the Governor's Papers.]

January 22, 1959   REMARKS AT BRIEFING OF NATIONAL GUARD COMMANDERS, Raleigh

February 10, 1959 *   GREETINGS TO THE SIR WALTER CABINET, Raleigh

February 26, 1959 *   REMARKS BEFORE A JOINT MEETING OF THE TRAVEL COUNCIL OF NORTH CAROLINA AND THE KEEP NORTH CAROLINA BEAUTIFUL EXECUTIVE COMMITTEE, Raleigh

March 11, 1959   REMARKS AT HOSIERY PROMOTION SPONSORED BY THE NATIONAL ASSOCIATION OF HOSIERY MANUFACTURERS, New York City

March 23, 1959   INTRODUCTION OF PRESTON J. MOORE, NATIONAL COMMANDER OF THE AMERICAN LEGION BEFORE A JOINT SESSION OF THE NORTH CAROLINA GENERAL ASSEMBLY, Raleigh

March 28, 1959 *   REMARKS AT ANNUAL JEFFERSON-JACKSON DAY DINNER, Raleigh

April 14, 1959   REMARKS ON TELEVISION U. S. HISTORY CLASS, Raleigh

April 15, 1959   COMMENTS AT DEDICATION OF WRAL-TV ADMINISTRATION BUILDING, Raleigh

May 8, 1959   REMARKS AT DEDICATION OF NEW RECEIVING HOME OF THE CHILDREN'S HOME SOCIETY OF NORTH CAROLINA, INCORPORATED, Greensboro

June 16, 1959 *   REMARKS AT DEDICATION OF NEW STUDIO OF WECT-TV (Read by Edward L. Rankin, Jr.), Wilmington

July 28, 1959 *   ADDRESS BEFORE THE SAN FRANCISCO ROTARY CLUB, San Francisco, California

July 29, 1959 *   REMARKS BEFORE GENERAL ELECTRIC MANAGEMENT COURSE, Crotonville, New York

August 28, 1959   REMARKS TO THE NEW BOARD OF WATER RESOURCES, Raleigh

September 8, 1959 *   GREETINGS ON THE OPENING PROGRAM FOR THE 1959-60 IN-SCHOOL TELEVISION SERIES, State College Studio, WUNC-TV, Raleigh

September 8, 1959   ADDRESS OF WELCOME AT ANNUAL JOINT MEETING OF THE FARMERS CO-OPERATIVE EXCHANGE AND NORTH CAROLINA COTTON GROWERS COOPERATIVE ASSOCIATION, Raleigh

September 11, 1959   MESSAGE TO OFFICIALS AND FRIENDS OF CAMPBELL COLLEGE (tape recording)

September 21, 1959 *   SPEECH AT INTERCITY ROTARY LUNCHEON, Greensboro

September 21, 1959   ADDRESS AT MEETING OF THE NORTH CAROLINA CIVIL DEFENSE ASSOCIATION, Durham

September 22, 1959   ADDRESS OF WELCOME AT SOUTHEASTERN PLANT ENGINEERING AND MAINTENANCE SEMINAR AND SHOW (Read by Edward L. Rankin, Jr.), Raleigh

September 22, 1959   TESTIMONY ON BEHALF OF NORTH CAROLINA IN THE SOUTHERN TRANSCONTINENTAL SERVICE CASE, Washington, D. C.

September 25, 1959 *   ADDRESS BEFORE CIVIC CLUBS, Fayetteville

September 28, 1959   ADDRESS AT GROUND-BREAKING CEREMONIES FOR THE DUKE POWER COMPANY HYDROELECTRIC PLANT AT COWAN'S FORD, Charlotte

September 28, 1959 *   ADDRESS BEFORE CHARLOTTE EXECUTIVES CLUB, Charlotte

October 2, 1959   REMARKS AT STATE CONVENTION OF YOUNG DEMOCRATIC CLUBS, Asheville

December 11, 1959 *   REMARKS AT PUBLIC AFFAIRS PRO-
GRAM, ST. AUGUSTINE'S COLLEGE, Ra-
leigh

December 11, 1959 *   ACCEPTANCE OF PORTRAIT OF GOV-
ERNOR R. GREGG CHERRY, Raleigh

January 13, 1960   GEETINGS AT MEETING OF NORTH
CAROLINA ASSOCIATION OF SOIL CON-
SERVATION DISTRICTS, Raleigh

January 18, 1960 *   REMARKS INTRODUCING GEORGE V.
ALLEN AT ANNUAL INSTITUTE OF RE-
LIGION, Raleigh

January 29, 1960 *   SPEECH AT HARVARD BUSINESS
SCHOOL, Cambridge, Massachusetts

February 5, 1960   GREETINGS TO THE DISTRICT CON-
GRESS, NATIONAL FORENSIC LEAGUE,
Raleigh

February 6, 1960 *   REMARKS AT ANNUAL JEFFERSON-
JACKSON DAY DINNER, Raleigh

March 2, 1960 *   WELCOMING ADDRESS AT DINNER HON-
ORING OFFICIALS, SPORTS WRITERS,
AND GUESTS ATTENDING THE ATLAN-
TIC COAST CONFERENCE BASKETBALL
TOURNAMENT, Raleigh

March 8, 1960   REMARKS AT GROUND-BREAKING CERE-
MONIES FOR THE HANES BUILDING,
Research Triangle

March 14, 1960 *   ADDRESS TO JOINT MEETING OF MEN
OF THE BAPTIST, PRESBYTERIAN, AND
METHODIST CHURCHES, Raeford

March 15, 1960   REMARKS AT DURHAM MERCHANTS
ASSOCIATION DINNER, Durham

March 17, 1960 *   ADDRESS BEFORE THE MEMBERS COUN-
CIL, NEW ORLEANS AREA CHAMBER OF
COMMERCE, New Orleans

March 31, 1960 *   TALK AT CORNERSTONE LAYING AT
NEW PLANT OF GOLDSBORO INDUS-
TRIES, Goldsboro

April 1, 1960 *   ADDRESS AT DINNER MEETING OF THE
PRINCETON CLUB OF WESTERN NORTH
CAROLINA, Asheville

April 4, 1960   SPEECH AT RALEIGH SALES EXECUTIVE
CLUB, Raleigh

April 5, 1960 *   REMARKS IN PRESENTING PORTRAIT TO THE DIALECTIC LITERARY SOCIETY AT THE UNIVERSITY OF NORTH CAROLINA, Chapel Hill

April 10, 1960 *   SPEECH ON PROGRAM SPONSORED BY THE R. MURPHY WILLIAMS MEMORIAL FUND, Greensboro

April 12, 1960 *   SPEECH AT NATIONAL SPORTSCASTERS AND SPORTSWRITERS AWARDS PROGRAM, Salisbury

April 24, 1960 *   SPEECH AT DEDICATION OF NEW NATIONAL GUARD ARMORY, Siler City

April 28, 1960 *   WELCOMING ADDRESS AT THE MOCK DEMOCRATIC NATIONAL CONVENTION, Chapel Hill

April 28, 1960 *   SPEECH AT DINNER MEETING OF THE DURHAM DIVISION OF THE RESEARCH TRIANGLE FOUNDATION, Durham

May 2, 1960   REMARKS AT ANNUAL MEETING, ADJUTANTS GENERAL ASSOCIATION OF THE UNITED STATES, Asheville

May 7, 1960 *   REMARKS AT THE TOASTMASTERS CONVENTION, Charlotte

May 10, 1960 *   ADDRESS AT THE SEVENTIETH ANNUAL CONVENTION OF THE MISSOURI BANKERS ASSOCIATION, St. Louis, Missouri

May 13, 1960   REMARKS AT INAUGURAL CEREMONIES FOR LEO W. JENKINS, EAST CAROLINA COLLEGE, Greenville

May 13, 1960   SPEECH TO RADIO AND TV NEWS DIRECTORS ASSOCIATION OF THE CAROLINAS, Raleigh

May 29, 1960 *   GREETINGS AT THE NORTH CAROLINA STATE COLLEGE COMMENCEMENT, Raleigh

May 29, 1960 *   COMMENCEMENT ADDRESS AT LOUISBURG COLLEGE, Louisburg

May 30, 1960 *   COMMENCEMENT ADDRESS AT DAVIDSON COLLEGE, Davidson

June 5, 1960 *   ADDRESS AT MORAVIAN COLLEGE COMMENCEMENT, Bethlehem, Pennsylvania

June 6, 1960 *   GREETINGS AT THE DUKE UNIVERSITY
                           COMMENCEMENT, Durham

June 21, 1960 *   REMARKS AT DEDICATION OF TENNEY
                           ENGINEERING, INCORPORATED, PLANT,
                           Wilmington

July 26, 1960   REMARKS AT ANNUAL STATE 4-H CLUB
                           WEEK PROGRAM, Raleigh

August 11, 1960 *   REMARKS AT DEDICATION CEREMO-
                           NIES FOR APEX MANUFACTURING COM-
                           PANY, Apex

September 8, 1960 *   REMARKS AT SOUTHWIDE DEMOCRAT-
                           IC PARTY GATHERING, Atlanta, Georgia

September 9, 1960 *   WELCOME AND GREETINGS AT THE
                           DEBUTANTE BALL, Raleigh

September 19, 1960   SPEECH IN FAVOR OF THE NATIONAL
                           DEMOCRATIC TICKET, Chicago

September 22, 1960   REMARKS AT DEDICATION OF AERO-
                           TRON PLANT, Raleigh

September 30, 1960   REMARKS AT DEDICATION OF LIGGETT
                           & MYERS RESEARCH CENTER, Durham

October 4, 1960 *   REMARKS AT FIFTH DISTRICT DEMO-
                           CRATIC RALLY, Winston-Salem

October 7, 1960 *   ADDRESS AT DEDICATION OF AKERS
                           MOTOR LINES NEW TERMINAL, Char-
                           lotte

October 14, 1960 *   SPEECH AT ELEVENTH DISTRICT DEM-
                           OCRATIC FUND-RAISING DINNER, Gas-
                           tonia

October 24, 1960   SPEECH IN THE INTEREST OF THE KEN-
                           NEDY-JOHNSON TICKET, Wilmington,
                           Delaware

October 24, 1960   SPEECH IN THE INTEREST OF THE KEN-
                           NEDY-JOHNSON TICKET, Charlottesville,
                           Virginia

October 27, 1960   SPEECH AT BANQUET IN THE INTEREST
                           OF THE KENNEDY-JOHNSON TICKET,
                           Wichita Falls, Texas

October 27, 1960   SPEECH IN THE INTEREST OF THE
                           KENNEDY-JOHNSON TICKET, Dallas,
                           Texas

October 31, 1960	SPEECH IN THE INTEREST OF THE KENNEDY-JOHNSON TICKET, Danville, Virginia
October 31, 1960	SPEECH IN THE INTEREST OF THE KENNEDY-JOHNSON TICKET, Chatham, Virginia
November 1, 1960 *	ADDRESS AT A LUNCHEON MEETING OF THE WAKE COUNTY DEMOCRATIC WOMEN'S CLUB, Raleigh
November 3, 1960	REMARKS ON TELEVISION PROGRAM HONORING JOHN MOTLEY MOREHEAD, Chapel Hill
November 6, 1960 *	SPEECH AT THE FIRST CHURCH OF THE BRETHREN IN OBSERVANCE OF WORLD COMMUNITY DAY, Spray
November 8, 1960 *	ADDRESS BEFORE ROTARY CLUB, Leaksville
November 10, 1960 *	SPEECH AT FORTIETH ANNIVERSARY MEETING OF THE CAROLINA COOPERATIVE COUNCIL OF FIELDCREST MILLS, Leaksville-Spray
November 11, 1960	REMARKS AT CELEBRATION OF THE FIFTIETH ANNIVERSARY OF NORTH CAROLINA COLLEGE, Durham
November 30, 1960 *	SPEECH AT WAKE COUNTY DINNER OBSERVANCE OF INDUSTRY APPRECIATION WEEK, Raleigh
December 9, 1960	REMARKS AT MEETING OF THE NORTH CAROLINA SOCIETY, New York City
December 15, 1960	REMARKS AT DEDICATION OF CUYAHOGA PRODUCTS COMPANY PLANT, Charlotte
December 16, 1960	REMARKS AT DEDICATION CEREMONIES FOR THE HANES BUILDING, Research Triangle

GREETINGS, STATEMENTS,
AND ARTICLES FOR THE PRESS

GREETINGS, STATEMENTS, AND ARTICLES FOR THE PRESS

[As in previous volumes of this series, no effort has been made to include here all the greetings, statements, press releases, and public announcements that emanated from the governor's office during 1959-1960. Those here printed have been selected as being among the more important documents in this category and as being illustrative of this phase of the Governor's activity.]

A REPLY TO CANON L. JOHN COLLINS

[This letter had reference to the so-called "kissing case," in which two Negro boys, eight and ten years old, were committed to the Morrison Training School by a juvenile court judge in Monroe, allegedly for holding and kissing a young white girl. The incident was much publicized by a section of the tabloid press, particularly in London, and was the subject of more than fifty letters received by the Governor's office from England and Scotland, all, according to the Governor, "based on misinformation." A cablegram from Canon Collins, to which this letter was sent in reply, had been received in Raleigh on December 19, 1958, while Governor Hodges was in Florida on a vacation. His reply, dated January 2, was not released to the press until January 8, in order, said the Governor "to be courteous" to the Canon, "which he wasn't to me."]

January 2, 1959

Canon L. John Collins
St. Paul's Cathedral
London, England
Dear Sir:

Upon my return to the office a few days ago, I read your cable communication concerning the case of two young Negro boys of Monroe, North Carolina, who were recently committed to the Morrison Training School by order of the Juvenile Court of Union County, North Carolina.

Your communication did not contain any return address, and I am undertaking this reply on the basis of newspaper reports as to your address in London.

Ordinarily I do not undertake to correspond with individuals through the medium of the newspapers. I do so in this instance because of the prominence of your position and on the assumption that you may have an interest in considering a few facts in this case which I will endeavor to relate to you. At the same time, I cannot avoid the conclusion that you are perhaps somewhat more interested in the publicity occasioned by your communication (inasmuch as you released it to the press by the time it was received in my office) than you are in receiving information from responsible officials. This is sad in view of the world's need for leaders who want to achieve understanding rather than controversy.

I deeply regret that inaccurate information has been widely publicized on this case, apparently prompted by some rather irresponsible people on this side who are more interested in personal publicity than in the actual facts of the case.

For your information, enclosed is a copy of an official report on this matter which I have received from the juvenile court judge. I have absolutely no reason to doubt the integrity of this official.

These two young Negro boys were not sentenced to "life imprisonment," as seems to have been reported in several newspaper accounts. They were not even "convicted" of a criminal offense. Under North Carolina law, a juvenile is not convicted of a criminal offense but the court is authorized to commit the juvenile to a training school. This applies in all cases, regardless of race.

Also, under the laws and practices governing our training schools, a juvenile may be released to his family, at any time when in the judgment of the school officials the family is able and willing to give some guidance to the child, and the best interest of the child will be served by returning him to his family. Again, the same law and practice applies to all cases, whether white or Negro children are involved.

According to my information, which is documented by independent reports of welfare agencies, the home and family background of the two young Negro boys in question leaves a very great deal to be desired. At the time of the offense in question, both of these young boys *were on probation* with the juvenile court for previous offenses. Unbelievable as it may seem to you, the circumstances and surroundings at the Morrison Training School to which these young boys were committed are usually far superior and more conductive to good conduct than the homes from which those committed come. This is the case in practically every instance of a commitment to our training schools.

The superintendent and staff of the training school in question are Negro and are well qualified by experience and education for their positions. You are free to write to the superintendent of the Morrison Training School at Hoffman, North Carolina, for any further information you may desire.

If your future travels bring you to the United States, we would welcome an opportunity to have you visit North Carolina and see at firsthand what is actually going on in our state relating to juvenile offenses and racial relations in general.

Not too long ago I read many newspaper accounts of the racial riots in Notting Hill, London. These racial incidents far surpassed, in violence, anything that has ever occurred in North Carolina. However, I am not so presumptuous as to hold the officials of London nor the officials of any church responsible for those events. Neither am I so presumptuous as to judge all of England or indeed all of London on the basis of newspaper accounts concerning the race riots in Notting Hill.

Following some publicity which the NAACP got in the papers on New Year's Day, the state director of our training schools issued a statement of information. A copy of this statement is enclosed, as you might be interested in knowing something about these boys and their families.

If you have any further question or comment or need further information, I shall of course be pleased to hear from you.

For your information, I am releasing a copy of this reply to the newspaper services but not until you have had a chance to receive this letter!

Sincerely,
/s/ Luther H. Hodges

ON THE ADMISSION OF THE
STATE OF ALASKA

January 8, 1959

The admission of the state of Alaska as the forty-ninth state of the United States of America is an event of importance to every American. Alaska is the first state admitted to the Union since 1912.

Speaking for the people of North Carolina, I should like to welcome Alaska to the Union as our forty-ninth state and to send greetings and best wishes to all our fellow Americans in the state of Alaska.

With its vast expanse of scenic beauty, its great reservoir of natural resources, its energetic citizenry and its new and challenging frontier, there can be no doubt that Alaska will more than meet its new responsibilities and take a prominent place among the great states of this Union.

North Carolina is pleased, therefore, to welcome this new state to the Union and to wish for Alaska and its people a wonderful and prosperous future.

ON THE SETTLEMENT OF A CONTROVERSY BETWEEN THE STATE BOARD OF HIGHER EDUCATION AND THE EXECUTIVE COMMITTEE OF THE BOARD OF TRUSTEES OF THE UNIVERSITY OF NORTH CAROLINA

January 12, 1959

[The State Board of Higher Education, created by the 1955 General Assembly, had become involved in a long-standing dispute with the University of North Carolina Board of Trustees over the question of the so-called "higher board's" jurisdiction. The settlement to which the Governor was here referring had reduced the higher board's power over budgetary matters and changed its functions in other respects, leaving to the higher board the authority to "plan and promote" a coordinated system of higher education but allowing each institution to continue operating "under the direction of its own board of trustees."]

I am pleased that a full agreement has been reached between the State Board of Higher Education and the Executive Committee of the University Trustees with reference to certain questions that had been raised concerning the powers, duties, and relationships of the two organizations.

When the questions first arose more than a year ago, I told the Board of Higher Education and the Executive Committee of the Trustees that reasonable men should get together and find a reasonable solution to the problems involved. Both groups responded by appointing special committees which have worked diligently and effectively to settle all issues. They have now reached a settlement which makes sense and should prove to be of great value to the future of higher education in North Carolina.

This agreement represents the constructive suggestions of *both* groups, working together for the mutual benefit of higher education, the University, and the state of North Carolina. The two committees had the advantage of four years' cumulative experience since the Board of Higher Education was authorized by the 1955 General Assembly. It is understandable that some changes or amendments might be suggested following the first four years of operations by any new agency with such great responsibilities and new programs affecting so many different state institutions.

I commend the special committees and the boards they represented for a job well done. Everyone will benefit from their efforts.

In keeping with the request of the Board of Higher Education, I am calling a conference in Raleigh on January 27 with the presidents and board chairmen of all state-supported institutions of higher learning, including the community colleges, so that they may also consider the recommendations of the committees.

From the results of this January 27 meeting, and the report of the two committees, I will propose legislation to the 1959 session of the General Assembly which will improve our overall organization in state-supported higher education. Such legislation will enable the State Board of Higher Education, the Consolidated University and its trustees, and other state institutions of higher learning to move ahead with new vigor and a better understanding of the common goals which we must share in higher education if we successfully meet the many challenges of today and the future.

ON PROPOSED LEGISLATION TO REQUIRE LABELLING TOBACCO PRODUCTS WITH SKULL AND CROSSBONES IN SOUTH DAKOTA
WESTERN UNION TELEGRAM

January 28, 1959

Honorable Ralph Herseth
Governor of South Dakota
Pierre, South Dakota

Have been greatly disturbed at action of South Dakota Senate bill providing that tobacco or cigarettes sold in your state will carry crossbones and skulls printed on package, and statement "not recommended by state of South Dakota." Since North Carolina is the leading tobacco growing and manufacturing state, we must in self-defense protest Senate action, and would like to have wire from you saying that bill will not become law.

I am sure you agree that this proposed legislation is punitive in nature and unwise. I know that you would not want the General Assembly of North Carolina to pass a law requiring that any farm products originating from South Dakota and offered for sale in North Carolina must carry labels warning that, according to the United States Department of Agriculture, South Dakota soil has the highest content in the nation of selenium, a well known poison. Such labeling would, of course, reflect unfavorably upon South Dakota in the sale of all its farm products throughout the United States, and such label would have to carry something equal to your skull and crossbones. Please advise.

I am looking forward to meeting you at the coming National Governors' Conference and associating with you.

/s/ Luther H. Hodges
Governor of North Carolina

January 31, 1959

I am very pleased to learn that the House of Representatives in South Dakota today killed a proposed bill to place a skull and crossbones label on cigarettes and other tobacco products. Governor Herseth responded to my telegram of January 28 in a most friendly manner and made it clear that the proposed bill did not originate with his administration.

I hope this closes the matter and ends any further punitive legislation against tobacco.

We assure Governor Herseth and members of the South Dakota legislature that North Carolina looks forward to continued friendy relations between our two states.

ON THE HENDERSON STRIKE

February-May, 1959

[A textile strike at the Harriet-Henderson Cotton Mills at Henderson in Vance County began early in February, 1959, and continued, with much recrimination on the side of both management and labor, together with some violence and many threats of violence, for nearly four months. The incident gave Governor Hodges much concern, occupied a great amount of his time, and was later referred to by him as "One of My Most Difficult Problems as Governor" (see pp. 280-282). The following are selections from the various letters, telegrams, and press releases that issued from the Governor's office in connection with the strike.]

WESTERN UNION TELEGRAM

February 24, 1959

Mr. John D. Cooper, President
Harriet-Henderson Cotton Mills
Henderson, North Carolina
Mr. Luther Jackson, President
Local 584, TWUA, AFL-CIO
Henderson, North Carolina
Mr. Charles Ranes, President
Local 578, TWUA, AFL-CIO
Henderson, North Carolina

Reports of violence and destruction of property in connection with strike at the Harriet-Henderson Cotton Mills are matters of genuine concern to all our citizens, and reflect very unfavorably upon the town of Henderson, the county of Vance and the state of North Carolina. The rising tensions and the continuance of these acts of violence constitute a threat to the maintenance of law and order which cannot be condoned.

The police of Henderson and the sheriff of Vance County have the primary responsibility for maintaining law and order in Henderson and Vance County. At the request of local officials the State Highway Patrol and the State Bureau of Investigation have rendered assistance and will continue to give appropriate assistance to local law enforcement officers.

There is a direct and personal responsibility upon each of you and your associates to see that everything possible is done to prevent any further law violations. There is also a direct and personal responsibility upon each of you to make every effort to settle this strike so that peace may be restored in Vance County.

I would like to remind you that the mediation services of the State Department of Labor continue to be available to assist all parties in settling this strike.

Luther H. Hodges
Governor of North Carolina

March 21, 1959

On Saturday, February 14, the sheriff of Vance County and the Henderson chief of police requested this office to provide Highway Patrol assistance to local law enforcement officers who were attempting to preserve law and order in and around the Harriet-Henderson Cotton Mills in Henderson. They stated that the strike at the mills was "causing trouble and civil disorder" and stated further that local law enforcement officers could not cope with possible violence which could result from the opening of mill gates on Monday, February 16. In view of this appeal for assistance from local officials in Vance County, I authorized and directed the State Highway Patrol to move sufficient men into Henderson on Monday, February 16, to assist local law enforcement officers in the maintenance of law and order.

Despite the efforts of local and state law enforcement officers, there were continued acts of violence and disorders in Vance County and it was later necessary to send additional patrolmen until the state now has between 100 and 150 men on duty at the strike scene each day. Since February 16, there have been many

Photo by Howard Ballew

North Carolinians and others demonstrate for Governor Hodges, following his address on July 14, 1960, at the Democratic National Convention at Los Angeles. Harold E. Marlowe of Los Angeles, a nephew of Governor Hodges, and C. Watson Brame of North Wilkesboro are in the foreground.

Left to right: John D. Larkins, Terry Sanford, Malcolm B. Sewell, and Governor Hodges at a Democratic rally in the State Fair Arena at Raleigh, August 10, 1960.

acts of violence reported, including sixteen bombings, a number of workers' homes damaged by these blasts, one person seriously injured by gunfire, and hundreds of anonymous telephone calls making threats and intimidations against workers, mill officials, police officers, and municipal officials. A truck-trailer loaded with cotton waste was burned, a warehouse was extensively damaged by fire, and shots were fired into automobiles containing workers and others. Nails, broken glass, rocks and wood were piled on public highways; and at least one near riot occurred, in which twenty-six persons were arrested by the Highway Patrol before order was restored. There have been more than 150 arrests made including thirty-nine charges for assault with a deadly weapon, forty-one charges for malicious damage to property, forty-nine charges for violating a restraining order issued by Resident Superior Court Judge William Y. Bickett, and twenty-seven charges for inciting a riot.

During the past five weeks, I have devoted an increasing number of hours each day in an effort to assist city and county officials in preserving law and order, and in talking with federal-state mediators, state officials, the management, the union, and officials of Henderson and Vance County about the seriousness of this strike and the necessity for an early settlement. For the past two weeks, I have held almost daily conferences with the attorney general, the commissioner of motor vehicles, and other state department officials in an effort to keep informed on every development of the strike. Working as quietly as possible, I have made every effort to persuade the management and the union to effect a settlement which will enable the company and the workers to resume normal operations.

It should be remembered that when the state of North Carolina found it necessary to send state patrolmen into Henderson and Vance County to assist local law enforcement officers, at their request, in preserving law and order, then the state as a whole became vitally concerned with the strike at Henderson. I have made this point with management and the union in urging them to settle their differences and end the strike.

It is apparent from the report I have just received from the federal-state mediators that no progress was made at the conference today. So long as negotiations between the two parties offered a hope of settlement, I have refrained from intervening.

In view of the apparent stalemate between management and union, and the serious effort which this strike is having upon the city of Henderson, the county of Vance and the state of North Carolina, I have sent the following telegram to the mill management and to the union:

Mr. John D. Cooper, Jr., President
Harriet-Henderson Cotton Mills
Henderson, North Carolina
Mr. Boyd E. Payton
Carolinas Director
Textile Workers Union of America
    AFL-CIO
Henderson, North Carolina

Deeply concerned to learn from mediators that no progress was made at your conference today. In view of the increasing threat to law and order which is resulting from the strike, I must, with great reluctance, intervene personally into the negotiations between management and labor at the Harriet-Henderson Cotton Mills. During the past several weeks I have done everything humanly and reasonably possible as governor to persuade both parties to effect a settlement through your own negotiations and the assistance of state and federal mediators. It is imperative that you meet with me in my office at 10:30 a.m., Monday, March 23, to effect a settlement. The state of North Carolina expects the management, the union, and every person in Vance County to cooperate in the maintenance of law and order.

Luther H. Hodges
Governor of North Carolina

March 24, 1959

The parties are still negotiating. No agreement has been reached on major issues. Certain proposals made by each of the parties are being considered.

The next meeting is being planned at present for 11:00 A.M. Friday so that mill management may prepare for NLRB hearing which is scheduled for Winston-Salem on Thursday.

April 2, 1959

The people of North Carolina, and especially of course the citizens of Henderson and Vance County, are concerned about the unfortunate strike which is now in its twentieth week in that community.

The textile company and the union, which are involved in a labor dispute there, disagree about matters which are not originally or primarily a governmental affair. Out of their dispute, however, has grown a situation of lawlessness and violence, of danger to life and property, which is very definitely and preeminently a governmental affair, first local and then state and local.

I have tried to keep in close and continuous touch with the developments at Henderson. I have, moreover, over the last several weeks, exerted every effort and influence to bring about a settlement agreement between the company and the union in their dispute.

After weeks of fruitless negotiations between the mills and the union with four federal and state mediators present, the meetings were broken off on Saturday, March 21.

I then intervened in the dispute to see if the prestige and influence of the governor's office could help resolve their differences. Starting Monday, March 23, I have met several hours a day for six days with representatives from the mill and the union.

Progress has been made but no agreement has been reached as of Thursday, April 2. The differences between them are still serious and are of long-standing.

Each seems to believe sincerely that it is justified in standing upon the position which it has taken even though each party has given something in their negotiations. It is my earnest hope that in the interest of all concerned the company and the union will both see fit to make further concessions which may yet bring them into agreement.

The chief and major difference between the parties when I intervened was one of arbitration, which the mill had up to then refused to grant. We were able to persuade the company to offer the union a new arbitration clause which was admittedly a limited one. The union finally accepted the rather extensive arbitration sections with the exception of two paragraphs. The negotiations finally broke down over the issue of job rights of the workers now in the mills as compared to the strikers, and also the question of the check-off of union dues.

I pointed out to both of the parties in the strongest manner possible that each of them had a responsibility beyond the representation of their own sides of the contorversy. I said that the continuance of their disagreement would further harm the community, the county, and the state, and could ultimately destroy the union and the mill and cause 1,000 workers to lose their jobs permanently. Further, that the reputations of the community and the county could be irreparably damaged.

It is not within my authority, however, to force the hand of either the company or the union in this matter. I have no prerogative to compel the company and the union to enter into any agreement or contract which they are not both willing to sign.

On the other hand, it is my authority and my duty, as governor, working with local enforcement officers, to enforce the laws of North Carolina with respect to violence and and to maintain peace and order within this state. This authority and duty I intend to fulfill.

The textile company has the right to operate and to continue operating its mills—so long as it does so within the law. The union and the striking employees have a right to strike and to continue striking—so long as they do so within the law. Neither side has any right whatever to resort to violence, or otherwise take the law into their own hands.

In North Carolina whoever seeks to break a strike by violence must be restrained. In North Carolina whoever seeks to win a strike by violence must be restrained. Whoever throws dynamite at Henderson, or elsewhere within our state, must be stopped and prosecuted. Peace and order must be maintained.

I earnestly appeal to the strikers and to all citizens of the city of Henderson and Vance County to heed the thoughts which I have here tried to outline. Let us see to it that whatever is done in North Carolina—whether in labor controversies or in other matters—is done peaceably and not by lawlessness and violence.

April 16, 1959

I am shocked to hear that three of our state patrolmen were injured by violence on the picket line today at Henderson. While their injuries fortunately were not serious, such violence will not be tolerated and I earnestly hope that those responsible will be promptly prosecuted to the extent of the law.

The city, county, and state are indebted to the patrol for what it has accomplished in maintaining law and order under difficult conditions, and I commend these men for their courage and their restraint.

I again remind union leaders and union members and sympathizers that they have a great responsibility for any violence, and I urge that they assume proper leadership in maintaining law and order.

April 16, 1959

Mr. John D. Cooper, President
Harriet-Henderson Cotton Mills
Henderson, North Carolina
Dear Mr. Cooper:

I understand that you are planning to begin a second shift at your mills on Monday, April 20.

As you know, I made an intensive and prolonged effort to help both sides to settle existing differences so that everyone could return to work. I stepped out of the negotiations personally only after *both* parties made it quite plain to me that they were then unwilling to move from their positions. As governor, I do not have the legal right to compel the union or the company to agree to any particular contract.

It is my duty, however, to assist local officials of Henderson and Vance County in the maintenance of law and order and to prevent anyone from taking the law into their own hands. This I shall continue to do.

I recognize that your company has every legal right to operate one or more shifts if it can persuade people to work for you, and that any person (whether a member of the union or not) has a right to cross any picket line and work for your company. While your legal right appears to be clear and undisputed, it is also my duty to call to your attention that your decision to begin a second and third shift at your mill will definitely heighten existing tensions in Henderson and Vance County and may actually result in bloodshed in spite of the best efforts of law enforcement personnel. This is an unpleasant and harsh reality which you must face.

Sometimes a person is confronted with a citizenship responsibility which transcends any strict legal rights, and on such occasions it can only be hoped that the individual who holds the power of decision will somehow be able to reconcile his personal and private rights with those greater interests of the community at large.

It is still my sincere hope that your company and the union will resume negotiations and settle this strike promptly.

Sincerely,

/s/ Luther H. Hodges

April 22, 1959

The situation at Henderson remains very bad. Furthermore, great confusion exists in the mind of the public about developments since the agreement between the two parties was reached last Friday night in Henderson.

The contract agreed to on Friday has not yet been signed because the union committee and Mr. Payton, head of the union for North Carolina, strongly feel they have been misled by the mills in regard to the jobs open for the strikers for the second and third shifts. When the mill started the second shift Monday afternoon, April 20, only a dozen or so strikers had been given jobs, with the balance being workers hired on first shift, and, according to the mill, before the agreement was concluded on Friday.

In the conference with the mill and union, held today in my office, the mill announced that of the 920 jobs available in the two plants for three shifts each, they had filled 698 prior to the agreement on Friday, April 17, leaving 222 jobs now available for the old workers. Although the mill had not told anyone how many people they had hired, the estimates from union and other sources never ran more than 450 to 500. The revelation of the fact that they had hired 698 people was very surprising to me, and I think the mill should have been more frank in disclosing the approximate figure, since we were negotiating in the last hours primarily about the jobs that would be open for the strikers on the second and third shifts.

My patience and that of the public is about exhausted. I have earnestly tried, over many weeks, to help settle this strike and restore peace. I believe I have been objective, impartial, and fair to both sides. Unfortunately, this prolonged strike has required a disproportionate amount of my time and energy during a legislative season when otherwise I could devote my time, along with members of the General Assembly, to affairs of all the people of the state.

Some three weeks ago I stepped out of the negotiations because we had reached a deadlock, primarily because of the attitude of the union representatives. It is my earnest belief that except for this situation, we could have settled the contract at that time and saved 250 jobs for the strikers, plus a limited check-off of union dues. By the union's refusal to come to an agreement at that time, they have lost jobs and standing because of the undue violence they have condoned or promoted.

I must continue to speak out frankly, respresenting the state and all the people. In these recent negotiations, culminating in no agreement, the mill has intentionally or otherwise misled all of us, including myself, the federal mediator, Yates Heafner, and the state mediator, Mr. Don Cilley, as to the number of jobs open on the second and third shifts for the strikers. Actually no numbers were mentioned in our discussions, but the clear impression was given me and the mediators that a substantial part of all the jobs on second and third shifts would be held for returning workers.

I was deeply interested in getting the contract signed the night of the agreement. In the meeting I innocently raised the question when we would complete the job. One of the mediators spoke up and said he had been dealing with the parties over the years and he was sure that both sides understood perfectly all the details of the agreement and if the signing was postponed until Monday there would not be the slightest difficulty. The mill and the union, in the meeting, agreed with the mediator's remarks.

Mr. Payton, head of the union, and the workers in mass meeting approved the agreement as read, but the formality of signing was held off because of the failure of the mill on Monday to hire more than a handful of strikers and the suspicion that there were few jobs left for them.

The union leaders in their enthusiasm probably oversold and misinterpreted the agreement. Further, both sides showed poor spirit in their handling of matters the following Monday.

We have an intolerable situation continuing. There is bad feeling existing, much of it because of what was left unsaid by the mill last Friday evening and on one previous occasion; also, what has been said of an unfriendly nature by both parties. The state, in carrying out its obligation to maintain law and order, has been an innocent victim and had done more than its share in helping maintain law and order.

With reluctance and yet with definite feeling that I am doing the best for the community and the state, I have wired the mill as follows:

> As said to you in conference in my office Wednesday, am greatly disturbed about developments and the attitude on your part which has eliminated the signing of contract on which agreement was made last Friday. Your failure to disclose the fact that you had hired around 700 people and that this left few jobs for the second and third shifts, although our conference dealt mainly with the question of jobs for returning workers, has created an impossible situation and has embarrassed me and others.
>
> I still hope you can come to a complete agreement with the union but until matters are cleared up satisfactorily, I feel that you should hold off second and third shifts. Please wire.

The Union, many of its members and sympathizers, have been and are properly being condemned by the public generally for their acts of violence and their lack of responsibility as citizens. I am requesting union officers and leaders, their members and sympathizers to refrain from any and all acts of violence, and I express the hope that the whole power of our state and local governments, including the courts, be organized if not now so constituted, to a point that will guarantee sure and swift justice of violators of the law. I shall expect the union and its committee to give this office written assurance that there will be no violence or encouragement of violence on the part of the members of the union.

There is much at stake for the county and the state, and I stand ready to help in any further negotiations if either party or both parties think I can help.

WESTERN UNION TELEGRAM

April 23, 1959

Mr. John D. Cooper, Jr., President
Harriet-Henderson Cotton Mills
Henderson, North Carolina

I have your wire which I presume is refusal of my appeal. My request for you to defer operation of second and third shifts is not based on surrender to violence but on your personal responsibility for the present difficulty and your responsibility to the public as covered in my letter to you of April 16 before you started second shift. I am making this letter public today. I ask you do nothing directly or indirectly to cause or encourage violence. Am wiring union further today about preventing violence and their responsibility.

Luther H. Hodges
Governor of North Carolina

May 8, 1959

Since February 16 a special detachment of State Highway Patrolmen has been on duty in Henderson and Vance County to assist local law enforcement officers in the maintenance of law and order. The number of patrolmen on duty in Vance County has been as high as 150 or approximately one-fourth of the entire State Highway Patrol.

Conditions during the past week or more have improved to such an extent that the state can withdraw its special detachment of patrolmen. It is my understanding from the mayor of Henderson and the sheriff of Vance County that approximately fifty-five local law enforcement officers are available for duty in and around the Harriet-Henderson Cotton Mills. This should be an adequate number of officers to maintain law and order under existing conditions.

Therefore, the State Highway Patrolmen will be withdrawn from strike duty over the weekend so they can return to their regular duties on our highways where they are urgently needed. This matter has been discussed in detail today with Mayor Singleton and Sheriff Cottrell.

However, if there is any further violence requiring state assistance next Monday or thereafter, I shall immediately order National Guard units into Henderson and Vance County to act as law enforcement officers. I am thereby notifying Mr. Boyd E. Payton, regional director, TWUA, and both local union leaders of this action, and emphasizing to them that the state of North Carolina expects every person in Vance County, whether a striker on or off the picket line, or a worker going to work, to be law-abiding citizens.

I wish to emphasize that the full responsibility for whether or not the state has to use National Guard troops will rest with those people in Vance County who choose to break the law and cause violence. I have not and shall not recognize the right of any person to violate the law, to throw rocks and stones, to fire bullets, to explode dynamite, or any of the other acts or words of intimidation which have occurred in Henderson and Vance County.

The people of Henderson and Vance County have a right to be free from violence and lawless activity. The people of the entire state have a right to expect that law and order will prevail in Vance County. The union has a right to strike in a peaceful manner and union members have a right to refuse to work. The mills have a legal right to operate and persons, union members or not, have a right to work under conditions of peace and order. All of these rights must be protected.

It is my earnest hope that peace will prevail and the National Guard will not have to be sent to Vance County. I urge the union and management to do everything possible to cooperate with local law enforcement officers who are charged with the responsibility for maintenance of law and order.

DESIGNATING SCIENCE YOUTH DAY
IN NORTH CAROLINA

February 4, 1959

In order to recognize the many contributions made by Thomas Alva Edison to the scientific and economic development of this nation, and to stress the need for greater interest in science on the part of our young people, North Carolina will observe February 11, 1959—the 112th anniversary of Edison's birth—as "Science Youth Day."

The inventive genius of Thomas Edison has immeasurably advanced the frontiers of American science and the welfare of all mankind. His work created industries employing millions of people and, in so doing, he contributed greatly to the technology upon which this nation's pre-eminence largely rests.

Recent events have shown that this strong scientific position is being seriously challenged and in this age of limitless scientific horizon, our country's need for men like Edison has never been more urgent. It has also become apparent that the only effective approach to meeting this need for scientific manpower is the motivation of more young Americans toward careers in science, and the removal of artificial barriers to preparation for these fields.

In recognition of these facts I am glad to designate February 11, 1959, as Science Youth Day in North Carolina and to urge the people of this state and its schools, teachers, parents, industries, and civic organizations to encourage our young people to take advantage of the great opportunities in modern science and technology.

DESIGNATING FARM BROADCASTING DAY
IN NORTH CAROLINA

February 6, 1959

Well-deserved recognition will be accorded North Carolina's radio and television farm broadcasters with the observance of Farm Broadcasting Day on Saturday, February 7.

Radio and television farm broadcasters serve a vital function in this state and throughout the nation. Our farmers derive innumerable benefits from farm news programs, market reports, and up-to-the-minute weather broadcasts. In addition to this essential agricultural information, our radio and television stations contribute to rural family life by providdng entertainment and education that might not otherwise be available.

In acknowledgement of this contribution to our predominantly agricultural state, I am happy to designate Saturday, February 7, 1959, as Farm Broadcasting Day in North Carolina and urge all of our citizens to give recognition to the achievements of radio and television stations and to encourage the broadcasters in their efforts to serve the agricultural community in North Carolina.

DESIGNATING EYE BANK WEEK
IN NORTH CAROLINA

February 13, 1959

To provide a suitable occasion for calling public attention to one of the most significant medical advances in recent decades, Eye Bank Week will be observed in North Carolina during the period February 15-21.

Sponsored by The Eye Bank for Restoring Sight, Incorporated, a North Carolina organization, the event is designed to spotlight the purpose of the organization and, at the same time, focus attention on the priceless contribution it is making on behalf our our fellow citizens whose God-given faculty for sight has been lost or seriously impaired.

Many thousands of people have regained their sight by means of corneal transplantation, and the promise of sight is held out for many thousands more who avail themselves of eye bank-related medical techniques.

In recognition of the fact that the month of February marks the fifteenth anniversary of the beginning of this great work, I am pleased to designate the week of February 15-21, 1959, as Eye Bank Week in North Carolina and to urge that the people of this state use this opportunity to familiarize themselves with the eye bank program and investigate the role they can play in bringing the benefits of this program to their less fortunate neighbors.

DESIGNATING EASTER SEAL MONTH IN NORTH CAROLINA

February 16, 1959

In order to provide the people of this state with an opportunity to participate in an exceptionally beneficial and gratifying program of service to their less-fortunate fellow-citizens, North Carolina will observe the period from February 27 through March 29 as Easter Seal Month.

The North Carolina Society for Crippled Children and Adults, which annually sponsors this event, has, since its organization, made a valuable contribution to the rehabilitation of our handicapped citizens and is certainly deserving of the continued support of the people of this state.

During 1958, more than $100,000 was expended in providing for the needs of crippled children and adults in North Carolina. Services provided included care and treatment, education, aids and appliances, physical and speech therapy, camping, and research.

In recognition of the contribution made to the health and well-being of our handicapped citizens through the Easter Seal program, I am glad to designate the period from February 27 through March 29, 1959, as Easter Seal Month in North Carolina and to urge that all North Carolinians support this noteworthy program.

DESIGNATING CHILD EVANGELISM WEEK IN NORTH CAROLINA

February 16, 1959

North Carolinians are being asked to join with the citizens of other states throughout the nation in the observance of Child Evangelism Week during the period February 22 - March 1.

Sponsored by the National Child Evangelism Fellowship, Incorporated, this non-sectarian and interdenominational event is designed to mobilize spiritual forces to combat the increasingly serious problem of juvenile delinquency and to promote religious activity among our young people.

We have only to acknowledge that almost half of the major crimes committed in the United States during 1958 were perpetrated by persons under eighteen years of age, and it becomes alarmingly evident that every means must be employed to reverse this trend.

In recognition of the fact that religious training is one of the most effective deterrents to delinquency, I am glad to designate the week of February 22 - March 1, 1959, as Child Evangelism Week in North Carolina and to urge that all our citizens cooperate in the sponsorship of home Bible classes and other programs formulated to combat this growing social problem.

URGING PROMPTNESS BY STATE DEPARTMENTS, AGENCIES, AND INSTITUTIONS IN PRESENTING PROPOSED LEGISLATION TO THE GENERAL ASSEMBLY

February 17, 1959

MEMORANDUM

TO: Heads of State Departments, Agencies, and Institutions

FROM: Luther H. Hodges, Governor

Last September I forwarded to you a letter I had received from the chairman of the Commission on Reorganization of

State Government, which strongly urged that all state departments, agencies, and institutions have their recommended legislation prepared and ready for introduction "during the first week of the legislative session."

In my memorandum to you dated September 5, 1958, I expressed complete concurrence with this suggestion and urged your cooperation in having your suggested legislation ready at the beginning of the session.

The Lieutenant Governor and the Speaker have remarked to me that very little legislation suggested by heads of departments, agencies, and institutions has been introduced up to this time.

I urge that if your department or agency plans to suggest legislation for consideration at this session, and appropriate bills have not yet been presented, that you please have these ready for introduction in the very near future. Your prompt action will be of assistance to the members of the General Assembly in enabling them to schedule their work and give adequate consideration to all measures coming before them.

IN OPPOSITION TO A SUGGESTION THAT PROVISION FOR "A GENERAL AND UNIFORM SYSTEM OF PUBLIC SCHOOLS" BE DELETED FROM THE STATE CONSTITUTION

February 23, 1959

Since last week's press conference the report of the Constitutional Commission has been made public. With the exception of one item, I should like to reserve my own comment on the specific suggestions in that report until my later special message to the General Assembly. I would like to make my position clear with respect to the suggestion that the language "a general and uniform system of public schools" should be deleted from the constitution.

Last month it was brought to my attention that the Study Commission was considering this possibility, and I expressed at that time to the chairman of the commission my strong reservation about such deletion.

I wish to state that in my opinion we should definitely retain the present constitutional provision for "a general and uniform system of public schools," subject only to our present constitutional provision for local option whereby citizens at the local level can in a popular election make their choice with respect to the operation of the local public schools. The attorney general has informed me that there is no overriding legal reason why this provision should be deleted from the constitution.

ON THE DEATH OF ROBERT M. HANES

March 11, 1959

I am deeply distressed and saddened to hear of the death of Robert M. Hanes. North Carolina has lost one of its most valued and best loved citizens.

It was my privilege to know Bob Hanes intimately for many years and I was proud to call him my friend. He gave a friendship that ever wavered, and I shall sorely miss him.

We worked together in many civic and business endeavors, including our associations in Germany during 1950-51 when he was ECA mission chief there. In this responsible governmental position, he showed the same courage, the same initiative and the same interest in human beings as he had always shown here in North Carolina.

He was active in political affairs in North Carolina, but always placed his interest in good government above individual personalities or party demands.

Bob Hanes was a great person with a warm personality, a keen mind and a genuine concern for helping his community, his sttate, and his nation in any worthwhile undertaking.

He was always busy, always on the move, but never too busy to accept another public service project that needed to be done. He has left to us a great legacy in public service of high order.

Governor Hodges and Charles R. Browning, president of Aeronautical Electronics, Incorporated, at Aerotron dedication in Raleigh, September 22, 1960.

The Governor and Mrs. Hodges returning from a South American trip, November 29, 1960.

ON THE TWENTIETH ANNIVERSARY OF RADIO STATION WRAL

March 20, 1959

It is a pleasure to congratulate Radio Station WRAL, its management and staff, upon the completion of twenty years of service to the people of the Capital area.

This outstanding broadcasting facility has shown initiative, imagination, and a commendable dedication to the public interest in its programming activities. WRAL has an outstanding record of providing the listening public with good entertainment, education, news, and sports, and, in so doing, it has made a noteworthy contribution to the general well-being of the people in this section of North Carolina.

WRAL has been a pioneer in many phases of radio broadcasting. On September 6, 1946, it became the first station in this state, and one of the first in the South, to initiate FM operations. I understand that today it is the oldest and most powerful continuously operated FM outlet in the South.

I extend best wishes to the management of Station WRAL and wish for it continued success in the years ahead.

DESIGNATING LET'S ALL PLAY BALL WEEK IN NORTH CAROLINA

April 3, 1959

In acknowledgement of the role that the game of baseball has played, and continues to play, in providing recreation and entertainment for youngsters and sports-minded adults in North Carolina, this state will join other states throughout the nation in observing "Let's All Play Ball Week" during the period April 4-11.

This event, which comes on the eve of the 1959 season, is designed to promote greater interest in all phases of professional and amateur baseball, ranging from the major leagues down to the little league. The motto for the event will be "Let's All Play Ball—It's Fun To Be A Fan."

North Carolina has long been recognized as the producer of many of the finest players ever to enter professional baseball. Our colleges and high schools have produced many outstanding teams and individual performers. Thousands of our youngsters participate in the game each year and become better citizens for having played.

In recognition of the fact that baseball exerts a wholesome influence on those who play and those who watch the game, I am happy to designate the week of April 4-11, 1959, as Let's All Play Ball Week in North Carolina and urge that all our citizens, young and old, remember that "It's Fun To Be A Fan."

ON REVISED REVENUE ESTIMATES
FOR THE 1959-1961
BUDGET

May 4, 1959

The revenue news is good! Tax collections for April show a decided improvement over previous estimates but, more important, over-all economic conditions have continued to improve in the nation and in North Carolina since revenue estimates were made last fall and given to the General Assembly in early February when it convened. We have waited until April individual income collections were tabulated before making any revised revenue estimates for the balance of this fiscal year ending June 30, 1959 and the coming biennium ending June 30, 1961. We are giving the news at the earliest possible moment.

These figures and comments have been reviewed with the presiding officers and the Finance and Appropriations chairmen of both houses of the General Assembly.

The 1959 legislative estimate of collections for fiscal year ending June 30, 1959 was $247,089,614. Our Revenue Department states that if the present pattern of collections continues the old estimates will be exceeded by approximately $5,500,000 for a total sum of $252,516,000.

Under 1957 law the first $5,000,000 above the legislative estimate must be applied toward bond anticipation notes and any amount collected over the figure of $252,089,614 is to be applied toward a contingency pay increase of 1.09 per cent for public school salaries, not to exceed a total amount of $1,219,495. Although the Revenue Department estimates show there will probably be only $426,386 available for this contingency, it is my personal hope that the full sum will materialize.

Regarding the 1959-61 biennium we have still further good news. After consultations with the Revenue, Tax Research, Budget Bureau, and the legislative leaders previously mentioned, and after a schedule-by-schedule analysis, we now estimate for 1959-61 a further increase in collections of approximately $16,000,000, consisting of $14,000,000 in revenue receipts and $2,000,000 in non-tax receipts (primarily from higher interest income on state funds invested). This would make total estimated revenues of $535,947,326, a percentage increase of 8.3 per cent and providing approximately $47,000,000 above 1957 legislative estimates for the current biennium. It should be pointed out that the revenue estimates made last fall and contained in the recommended budget called for an increase of $30,500,000, or 6.3 per cent over 1957 legislative estimates for the current biennium, and that this percentage figure is substantially higher than most other states. The new estimates put us even further beyond these other states.

We realize, of course, that these revised estimates could be adversely affected by changes in monetary policies and other factors over which we have no control, but we are confident that our state will continue its present progress.

I am happy that we can count on approximately $16,000,000 more money for further appropriations and it is my sincere hope that the extra amount estimated to be available will be used for the most part for public schools, the University, and other institutions of higher learning in the state.

These extra appropriations cannot be made without the adoption of the withholding method of collecting taxes (unless the Assembly wishes to add new taxes) as $27,500,000 is included in the recommended budget from this procedure.

Now that these revised estimates are in, I join with our legislative leaders in expressing the hope that the General Assembly can come to conclusions as soon as possible on the important matters of finance and appropriations.

DESIGNATING COTTON WEEK IN NORTH CAROLINA

May 11, 1959

The tremendous importance of cotton in the economy of this state will be called to the public's attention during the week of May 18-23 when North Carolina joins in the observance of National Cotton Week.

Sponsored in this state by the North Carolina Cotton Promotion Association, Inc., this event is designed to acquaint the people of North Carolina with all facets of the cotton industry and to encourage the more wide-spread use of this industry's products.

It is important that we remember that cotton remains one of our leading cash field crops in North Carolina. The production of cotton contributed more than $48,000,000 to the state's farm income in 1958, an increase of almost $9,000,000 over the previous year. More than 600,000 North Carolinians owe a portion of their livelihood to the production and processing of cotton and cotton-seed products, and personal income from all phases of this great industry exceed $750,000,000 annually.

In recognition of the cotton industry's contribution to the welfare of our people and the economic stability of our state, I am pleased to designate the week of May 18-23, 1959, as Cotton Week in North Carolina and to urge that all citizens of this state take advantage of this occasion to familiarize themselves with the value of our cotton industry.

DESIGNATING LETTERS FROM AMERICA WEEK IN NORTH CAROLINA

May 12, 1959

In order to build and maintain stronger bonds of friendship with our international neighbors, North Carolina and the nation will observe Letters from America Week during the period May 17-23.

Sponsored by the American Council for Nationalities Service and endorsed by President Eisenhower, the event is designed to encourage millions of Americans to become spokesmen for the United States through letters to relatives and friends abroad. It is an established fact that personal messages from thoughtful private citizens carry an impact that no formal effort by our government can match.

Americans and their way of life are too frequently misrepresented and misunderstood abroad. It is both a pleasant privilege and a responsibility for citizens of this country to use every means available to them to counteract these false impressions. A personal, thoughtful letter is a highly effective weapon in the struggle for men's minds.

I am glad, therefore, to designate May 17-23, 1959, as Letters from America Week in North Carolina and to encourage all North Carolinians to make a personal contribution to international understanding by participating in this program.

DESIGNATING NATIONAL TRANSPORTATION WEEK IN NORTH CAROLINA

May 12, 1959

In recognition of the importance of all forms of transportation in the maintenance of our free enterprise society, North Carolina is joining the nation this week in the observance of National Transportation Week.

Transportation forms a vital and essential link in the commerce of the nation, and carriers by rail, motor, ship, and aircraft have developed a transportation system in this country that is far superior to that of any other nation in the world.

Today, at a time when fast, efficient transportation is essential to the security of this nation, it is more important than ever that all Americans recognize the role played by transportation in our daily lives.

In acknowledgement of the value of good transportation in maintaining the national economy and the general health, happiness, and well-being of our people, I am glad to designate the week of May 10-16, 1959, as National Transportation Week in North Carolina and urge that all our citizens join in this observance.

ON CIVIL DEFENSE PREPAREDNESS AND TRAINING

June 4, 1959

We are living today—as we have lived since shortly after the close of World War II—in a state of international tension and under continuous threat of possible enemy attack. Due to the constant threat of aggression, each year the Congress appropriates approximately $40,000,000,000 for military defense measures.

There seems to be no noticeable change in the avowed purpose of our adversaries that they will impose upon us and the entire world a Communistic enslavement and Communistic way of life.

We must continue to build and maintain our military strength. We must continue to build our homefront defenses and to maintain their strength by training our officials and our citizens in the art of survival under nuclear attack because we know that our enemy has the capability to launch such an attack.

It is my considered opinion as chief executive of this state, that the matter of civil defense preparedness and training is essential to preserve our state and our nation. Public officials at all levels of government, whether elected or appointed, have a civil defense responsibility to discharge. This is true because civil defense is nothing more than the operation of government in grave emergency in the manner than will permit the saving of the most lives and permit the least damage to property.

The people of North Carolina—like the citizens of other states—are looking to their chosen officials for leadership, guidance, and instruction to prepare for and carry them safely through any civil defense emergency.

It is not only important, it is essential, that every echelon of government, whether it be local or state, prepare now for its own continuity by providing for successors in depth for each public official. All essential records should be duplicated by microfilm or some other means if records of land titles and other individual personal rights are to be preserved. These duplicates should be stored in some safe place for use if the originals are destroyed. In these days of uncertainty as to what the future may hold, it is highly important that we put some of our eggs in another basket.

I urge each of you here to enter this annual training exercise with resolute and sincere purpose. The problems that are presented to you in the next two days could, at some future time, become most realistic, and our very survival might depend on how well you are prepared and trained to cope with the situation. Disaster operations cannot be carried out by untrained people, no matter how willing they may be to assist. The people of our state expect us, as their chosen leaders, to know what to do, how to do it, and when to do it. I urge that everyone be prepared and ready for any emergency.

ENDORSEMENT OF A BILL TO ESTABLISH AN ADVISORY COMMISSION ON INTERGOVERNMENTAL RELATIONS

June 16, 1959

I wish to express my endorsement of the bill introduced by Representative Fountain, HB-6904, and an identical measure introduced in the Senate (S-2026) by Senator Muskie and others. The fact that in both the House and Senate these bills have strong bipartisan backing is a clear indication of itself that the proposed legislation is designed to meet a widely recognized need.

Furthermore, these bills are the result of a unanimous report by the House Committee on Government Operations, based upon very extensive hearings on intergovernmental relations conducted by the House Subcommittee in various parts of the nation.

From the beginning of my service as governor of North Carolina, I have had many occasions to deal with vital questions affecting federal-state relations. It is my present privilege to serve as a member of the Joint Federal-State Action Committee (an unofficial group of state and federal officials), of which the United States Secretary of the Treasury and the Governor of Idaho are currently the co-chairmen. In my capacity as governor and in my capacity as a member of this Joint Federal-State Action Committee, I have become thoroughly convinced that there is a strong need for a continuing and officially recognized advisory agency to give concentrated attention to federal-state problems.

Special studies in this area such as were made by the Commission on Intergovernmental Relations are helpful and of course the special attention to the over-all problem which has been given by the Intergovernmental Relations Subcommittee of the House Committee on Government Operations has made a great contribution to our understanding in this area. But what is needed is a continuing advisory agency which can take up specific selected problems, work out specific solutions and provide adequate follow-up to see that proposed action on specific problems is given adequate consideration by the federal government and by the states.

I will not attempt to state in further detail the argument in support of these bills. Such detailed analysis I am sure has been put before you by others, and the "Declaration of the Purpose" contained in the bill itself furnishes both a good statement of objectives as well as a statement of reasons for the enactment of these bills.

I do not take issue with the proposed organization of the commission, the membership, or the statement of duties. While I know that such details may well be subject to differences of opinion in minor respects, I am sure that if this committee agrees on the desirability of such legislation and on the basic approach suggested, there will be little difficulty in reaching agreement on the specific details.

I would venture one suggestion which I understand has, as a practical matter, not been worked out as yet. The bills as introduced contemplate that all the expenses of the Advisory Commission on Intergovernmental Relations would be paid by the federal government. I personally would prefer some arrangement whereby all the states would join together to meet at least 50 per cent of the expenses of this advisory commission. If this were done, the contribution from each of the fifty states would certainly be comparatively small. This may be considered a rather minor item and some may say that it makes little difference which of our tax pockets the appropriations for the commission should come from, that we are all citizens of the nation as well as citizens of a state. That is certainly true, but I am thinking more in terms of state governments as such stepping forward in a strong and vigorous manner to consider on the merits the problems which continually arise in the area of intergovernmental relations, and to seek to reach sound and constructive solutions to those problems.

To the extent that our states face up to our obligations in this respect, then to that extent will we meet and find solutions to the many questions confronting us in the area of federal-state relations. And to the extent that we find such solutions, we are achieving a stronger union of strong states, which to my way of thinking all adds up to a strong and united nation.

The proposed legislation is meritorious and I hope that this committee will act favorably on it, and in turn that the Senate and House of Representatives will give their approval.

STATEMENT FOR SPECIAL EDITION ON
"THE NORTH CAROLINA STORY"
BY THE RALEIGH *NEWS*
AND OBSERVER

June 21, 1959

It is a pleasure to share in this Special Edition prepared by the *News and Observer* to tell the North Carolina Story. This Special Edition should result in a better understanding of North Carolina, its people, its resources, and its bright future. I want to add my word of thanks to this newspaper for such a public service.

Much has been written and said in recent years about the dramatic transformation that has become generally known as "The North Carolina Story." This "story" has been discussed frequently among ourselves and, whenever and wherever possible, we have discussed it proudly with others. The story has been told with enthusiasm and in great detail in New York, in Chicago, in Philadelphia, and in a hundred other places throughout the land.

The story has been one of growth and development; of solid, purposeful progress in many fields. It has involved agriculture, industry, education, government, health, welfare, the arts, and all other facets of economic, social, and cultural advancement affecting the daily lives of our people. It has already brought a wide variety of tangible and intangible benefits to the citizens of this great state, and it holds the promise of unimagined prosperity for the future.

The reasons for our optimism about the years ahead are many and varied. One of the foremost reasons is the knowledge that we are building on a sound foundation carefully constructed by others who went before us.

Another important reason for our optimism is the realization, on the part of present-day North Carolinians, that we have the resources, the know-how, and the cooperative spirit needed to maintain the momentum that has been generated in the past few years.

This is no manufactured expression of self-confidence. It is a statement of fact. The people of this state have clearly demonstrated, and are continuing to demonstrate their ability to work together toward common goals, to take full advantage of opportunities that arise, and to create their own opportunities whenever possible.

In the more than four and one half years that I have had an opportunity to participate actively in the development of "The North Carolina Story," it has been my privilege to work closely with many dedicated people in all walks of life who worked cheerfully and unselfishly to find the best means of converting North Carolina's human and natural advantages into material benefits for our people. This has been a tremendously gratifying experience to me, as I sincerely want to see my fellow citizens have more and better jobs.

The greater portion of our effort has been directed at the establishment of a better balanced and more vigorous economy. It became apparent many years ago that greater diversity, especially in the field of agriculture, would be needed before real progress could be made. This need was clearly revealed, for example, in 1957 when acreage reductions, adverse weather conditions, and other factors caused a tobacco farm income loss of $137,313,000, or a drop of 27.1 per cent from the 1956 total.

In spite of the fact that we experienced a record-breaking industrial growth in 1957, our losses on our tobacco crop caused North Carolina to drop from forty-fourth to forty-fifth in the nation in per capita income. What better illustration could we have of the need for greater diversification and more industry?

The picture has been made brighter by the fact that 1958 was a good year for agriculture—and this fact has been reflected in the state's economy. Industrial growth has continued spectacularly, and livestock production and food processing have increased. We all hope that the threat of agricultural instability has been minimized, but it would be foolish to believe that it has been erased.

The threat, very definitely, remains, and it will continue to exist in some degree for many years to come. Our people can find great consolation, however, in the knowledge that they have, at least, established an economic trend that holds the promise of greater economic security and greater general prosperity in the years that lie ahead.

Sound economic development has been a major goal of my administration. In carrying out my duties and responsibilities as governor, I have suggested and offered encouragement to a variety of programs designed to accelerate state-wide progress. Since the nature of my overall responsibility makes it impossible for me to follow through in detail on all worthwile programs, it has been my policy to initiate programs and, whenever possible, leave the responsibility of carrying them out to capable individuals at the state, regional, and local levels.

This procedure has proved efficient and effective, and has, I am confident, contributed materially to the progress of our state. I am happy to say that most of the credit for the success of these programs goes to the thousands of men and women throughout North Carolina who have had faith in what we are trying to accomplish and have given their time and their support to these efforts.

One of the first and most important programs initiated by this administration was the effort to promote the establishment of small, local industries that would provide full and part-time jobs for surplus farm labor and, in the case of food processing plants, create a market for a variety of farm products. A Small Industries Study was completed in 1955 and its findings led to the establishment of the North Carolina Business Development Corporation. As of May 21, 1959, this privately-operated organization had approved seventy-eight loans, totalling $7,193,965. These loans, ranging from $2,000 to $475,000, in all parts of North Carolina, have been an important factor in helping small industries and firms get underway or expand their operations. Above all, these loans have helped create jobs and payrolls that were badly needed.

Another important chapter in the North Carolina Story was written by the 1957 General Assembly when it revised our tax allocation formula for multi-state corporations to place this state on a more competitive basis with other states in the bid for new industry. There can be no doubt that this farsighted legislative action has contributed immeasurably to North Carolina's continued industrial expansion. In 1957, a record-breaking $191,000,000 was invested in 170 new manufacturing plants and 143 plant expansions. During 1958, the investment figure rose to $253,074,000 and involved 423 new and expanded facilities. These investments created 21,757 new jobs with an annual payroll of $72,633,000. Figures compiled for the first quarter of 1959 indicate that the upward trend is continuing.

Closely related to this industrial growth has been the dramatic and tremendously exciting evolution of the Research Triangle—an evolution that was climaxed a few weeks ago with the announcement that a multi-million dollar research facility, employing more than 400 people, will be erected in the area by the Chemstrand Corporation. This is an example of the wonderful potential embodied in the Research Triangle, a major research park located in the center of the triangle formed by State College at Raleigh, the University of North Carolina at Chapel Hill, and Duke University at Durham. The growth of this great venture will bring far-reaching benefits to North Carolina and its people.

Another important part of the North Carolina Story has been the successful effort to promote the tourist trade from the mountains to the coast. Closely coordinated with the energetic and effective campaign to "Keep North Carolina Beautiful," this dual program has, in the past few years, given new meaning to this state's reputation as a "Variety Vacationland."

Good government has become a habit in North Carolina. State government has kept pace with the growth of North Carolina and is constantly striving to provide the citizens of the state with the services they need and require. We have not hesitated to improve or change old practices and procedures when it seemed advisable to do so. Some agencies of government—notably the highway and prison departments—have been reorganized to meet new needs and requirements. There is ample evidence to indicate that the state has benefited in a variety of ways from these conscientious efforts to provide a modern government for a modern state. The 1959 legislature has done its part in this regard. Certainly, all these efforts have served to enhance North Carolina's reputation as a progressive state.

This reputation has also been maintained in the field of education. There is much that remains to be done, many challenges that must be met, but the people of North Carolina have every reason to be proud of the progress that is being made in this vitally important field. This is true with respect to both public schools and higher education, whether privately-supported or state-supported colleges.

The people of North Carolina recognize the vital role that education must play in all their plans for the future—and they recognize their individual and collective responsibility in this connection. We know that this is a challenge that must be met, and we will meet it in the years ahead as we have met it in the past—with infinite faith in ourselves and in the things we are trying to accomplish for the benefit of this and future generations of North Carolinians.

I have tried here to tell only a part of the North Carolina Story. It would be impossible to put the whole story down in words, for much cannot be described. It must be felt. It is a dramatic and meaningful story—one that should have great significance to all who love North Carolina. It is a story of courage, determination, conviction, faith, and confidence. It is a story of people—more than four and one-half million of them—working together to make a better life for all. The future ahead is bright if we continue our great cooperation and keep our faith in North Carolina, one of the greatest states in this wonderful country of ours.

DESIGNATING A WEEK OF SPECIAL ATTENTION TO PROBLEMS OF THE AGING

June 27, 1959

The health, happiness, and welfare of North Carolina's aging citizens will be given special consideration during the period of July 12-18.

The state has more than 290,000 citizens sixty-five years of age or older, and many factors are producing a rapid increase in the size and proportion of this segment of population.

Increasing attention must be given to the needs of this group by state, county, municipal, and private agencies if these agencies are to discharge their moral and civic responsibilities. There is a growing need by this age group for housing, economic opportunity, medical and health care, welfare services, and recreation.

My attention has been called by the Governor's Coordinating Committee on Aging to the need for a wider and better understanding of these problems. Greater cooperation at both the state and local levels with respect to meeting the needs of this age group should bring beneficial results.

It is a pleasure, therefore, to designate the week of July 12-18, 1959, as a period for special attention to the interests, needs, and problems of the againg.

I urge all North Carolinians to observe this week in all appropriate ways which will bring added happiness, health, and welfare to the aging individuals in this segment of the state's population. It is my hope that individual citizens and organizations will show their special concern by expanding opportunities for the aged to participate in community affairs and becoming better informed themselves about available services for our aging citizens.

It is my further hope that city, county, and community leaders will take advantage of this special week to honor our aging citizens in suitable fashion. North Carolina and its citizens will add to the stature and sense of well-being of the state as a whole in recognizing these older citizens and giving them unmistakable evidence of sincere appreciation for their contributions.

DESIGNATING CITIZENSHIP DAY AND CONSTITUTION WEEK IN NORTH CAROLINA

August 10, 1959

North Carolina will proudly join the other states of the nation in the observance of Citizenship Day on September 17, and Constitution Week during the period September 17-23.

This annual observance, which has been officially designated by the President of the United States, commemorates the signing of the Constitution on September 17, 1787, and calls for reflection upon the historic events that are associated with that tremendously significant act. It is also appropriate that this occasion will serve to recognize all our citizens who have come to voting age or have been naturalized during the past year.

In these trying times, when freedom is being denied or threatened in many areas of the world, it is particularly fitting that Americans pay homage to their forebears who, with great vision and fortitude, created a charter designed "to form a more perfect union, establish justice, insure domestic tranquility, provide for the common defense, promote the general welfare, and secure the blessings of liberty" for themselves and the millions who would follow them as citizens of this nation.

In recognition of the need for strengthening our understanding of the rights and responsibilities of citizenship, I am glad to designate September 17, 1959, as Citizenship Day in North Carolina and the week of September 17-23, 1959, as Constitution Week in North Carolina and urge that every North Carolinian observe these occasions with appropriate ceremonies and activities in our schools and churches.

COMMENDING THE *SCOTLAND NECK* *COMMONWEALTH*

August 17, 1959

Again it is my privilege to commend the staff and management of the *Scotland Neck Commonwealth* on the effort that has gone into the preparation of the annual Fall Harvesting Edition which was published last week. This is an outstanding example of the service that a progressive, conscientious newspaper can perform when it is dedicated to the economic advancement of the people and the region it serves.

As indicated by the contents of this special edition, the area served by this newspaper is blessed with productive land and imaginative, forward-looking people. It is an area rich in the traditions of a people who know that the bountiful harvest is the result of planning, cooperation, dedication to hard work, and the

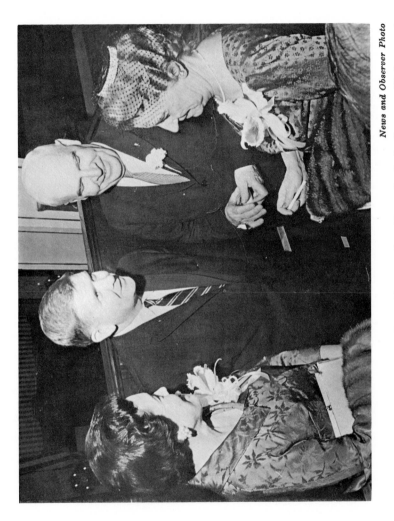

Left to right: Mrs. Terry Sanford, Governor-elect Terry Sanford, Governor Hodges, and Mrs. Hodges at a dinner honoring the out-going Governor, December 7, 1960.

Christmas at the Mansion, 1960. *Left to right:* Mrs. Hodges, Luther H. Hodges III, Governor Hodges, Luther H. Hodges, Jr., Mrs. Luther H. Hodges, Jr.

faith of a people in themselves and in their ability to capitalize on their opportunities.

Only in people of this caliber do we find the strength of character, the stamina, and the determination that enables us to face the uncertain future, meet its challenges with confidence, and reach out for the wonderful prosperity that our great potential offers.

I congratulate the people of your section on the progress they are making toward a better way of life for themselves and the generations of North Carolinians that will follow.

DESIGNATING BOYS HOME MONTH IN NORTH CAROLINA

August 26, 1959

In order to focus public attention on a tremendously important undertaking in our state and to stress the need for public support of this project, the month of September will be observed as Boys Home Month in North Carolina.

Sponsored by the North Carolina Junior Chamber of Commerce, the event is designed to familiarize the people of this state with the operation and purpose of the Boys Home of North Carolina and to solicit funds needed to continue and expand this commendable work.

The Boys Home, located at Lake Waccamaw, is a non-profit, non-sectarian corporation, established 1954 and licensed by the Department of Public Welfare as a home for underprivileged or neglected boys from throughout the state. The home is not sponsored by any one organization, but draws its support from various civic, church, and fraternal groups as well as individuals and business firms.

The present goal of the home is to expand its operation sufficiently to accommodate 100 boys and to provide, for those boys, a Christian environment, educational advantages, counsel, understanding supervision, religious training, and wholesome recreation.

In recognition of the importance of this undertaking, I am

glad to designate the month of September, 1959, as Boys Home Month in North Carolina and urge that all our citizens lend their enthusiastic support to this very worthwhile project.

EXPERIENCES WITH THE RUSSIAN NEWS MEDIA IN JULY, 1959

[Prepared for and published in *The Bulletin of the American Society of Newspaper Editors*, September 1, 1959.]

My experience with the Russian news media started at the airport of Moscow. They were there with their television cameras, their tape recorders for radio, and their notebooks as newspaper people. The television people were the more active. The newsmen seemed more controlled and less vigorous.

Although I didn't notice it at the time, there was a heavy-set cameraman of serious mien at the airport, without coat, open collar. I saw this man a hundred times later and found out that he had been assigned to us by Mr. Zhukov's department. Mr. Zhukov is head of the Soviet cultural exchange office. This cameraman was told to follow the governors the entire three and one-half weeks' tour and to make a documentary film. Incidentally, there will be nine copies of this film, with dubbed-in statements from each of the governors and each governor will receive, for his state, a complimentary copy of the film. This should be within the next few weeks and should be available for television and other use.

I found the newsmen, in my own experience, more cautious than our American newsmen. Maybe they were restrained or under orders. This was true not only in Moscow but in other cities like Leningrad, Kiev, etc. I was interviewed several times by the *Moscow News*. It was done in a quiet, guarded way, yet with seeming friendliness. The news media people seemed to be just as appreciative, as if they were an official or a citizen, if you praised the Soviet program or a special situation.

Generally speaking, I would suppose that their news media people followed the "line." However, down in one of the southern republics a Moscow radio man talked with me privately, and he was anxious to learn as much as he could about news media habits in America and some of the things about America. He did not do that when others were around.

I had an experience in Kiev with a Moscow radio man. He was asking the usual questions, "What do you think of this? Don't you feel that we have made great progress? Etc. Etc." He presumed he was asking a final question when he said, "You didn't find an iron curtain over here, did you?" I said to him, "I think your iron curtain may be a little rusty, but it is still there because you don't allow information through news media to come in from the United States of America and your people are kept in ignorance or are misled." He lost his balance somewhat and tried to regain composure by asking other questions.

I would say that the news media people whom we saw in the Soviet liked their association with the governors and with other people. They seemed to get quite a bang out of the freedom which we had and which we exhibited in our expressions and actions.

It is my understanding that their data was pretty carefully checked because some of our people who could read Russian found that some things that we gave, such as my own statement to Moscow radio in Kiev, were never carried.

Our own correspondents found that most of their stuff came through in good shape. This included a statement by one of the governors that Khrushchev was "a good alley fighter." None of our correspondents or governors felt that this expression would get through.

All in all, I would say that the news media people in the Soviet were well trained, more restrained and even disciplined, as compared to the people I have seen in the United States of America, particularly in the metropolitan areas.

DESIGNATING APPLE WEEK
IN NORTH CAROLINA

September 2, 1959

In order to call attention to the importance of the apple industry in the agricultural economy of our state, North Carolinians are being asked to observe Apple Week during the period September 1-7.

This event, sponsored by the North Carolina State Apple Growers Association, will be highlighted by the North Carolina Apple Festival which is held each year during this observance in Hendersonville. This festival is recognized nationally and reflects very favorably on our state and the quality of the apples we produce.

It is estimated that approximately 1,730,000 bushels of apples will be produced in North Carolina this year, principally in Henderson, Haywood, Wilkes, Mitchell, Yancey, Avery, Alexander, and Cleveland Counties.

In recognition of the importance of this industry to thousands of people in our state, I am pleased to designate the week of September 1-7, 1959 as Apple Week in North Carolina and urge that all our citizens support this industry by buying and promoting the sale of North Carolina apples at every opportunity.

ON KHRUSHCHEV'S VISIT TO THE UNITED STATES

September 11, 1959

I have been requested to give my reaction on the Khrushchev visit to the United States. First of all, let me repeat what I have said in some of the reports I wrote on my recent three and one-half week visit to the Soviet Union—namely, that I am more committed than ever to our American way of life, after having seen something of the Soviet system. I think our free enterprise system and our democratic insitutions mean more to me than ever before. At the same time, I feel that too many Americans take our liberties and freedoms for granted.

I favor the Khrushchev visit and the Eisenhower exchange visit to the Soviet Union. I said this directly to the President and to Mr. Khrushchev. The point that I made along with my fellow governors who took the trip to the Soviet Union was that such an exchange of visits between the leaders of the two strongest nations in the world had the possibility of doing a great deal of good and I didn't see where it would do any harm.

As to what the Khrushchev visit can achieve this may be a matter of opinion. It could be, as some people are saying, the turning point in history, certainly in the history of the cold war. As the President said in his message Thursday night, it will give Mr. Khrushchev a chance to see and know America and Americans. I think that if he sees our economic and military strength and if he understands the will of our people, it will make him pause and consider the future of his country and its part in a troubled world.

Certainly, this exchange of visits has the possibility of easing the tension that we have because the peoples of the two great nations do not want war and we saw at firsthand many evidences of that in the Soviet Union. I think that when Mr. Eisenhower goes to the Soviet Union he will be overwhelmed by his warm welcome. The Soviet people like America and Americans. The opposite of that is not so true. Russian leaders have not presented a clear picture of the Soviet people and their nature and intentions. Our own State Department at times has not contributed to any understanding of the Soviet people. Mr. Eisenhower will get a firsthand look at the average Soviet citizen.

As I see this important exchange, we ought to try it and make the most of it. Even though we don't like Mr. Khrushchev or his methods, he is a guest of the President of the United States and of the people of this great country. We must, therefore, be courteous. The alternative to the easing of tension through these exchange visits is what we have had for some years—namely, a continuation of the cold war of suspicion, of bitterness, of more costly military preparation, of possible atomic warfare. I am glad to see President Eisenhower take the initiative to try to do something about it. He was apparently unwilling to try it under Mr. Dulles.

I told a group of newspaper people last week that I felt that part of the great welcome accorded Mr. Eisenhower on his recent trip to Germany, England, and France was because of the great desire of the man in the street for peace and they saw in Mr. Eisenhower a representative of that desire. I believe the rest of the world is anxious to see these exchanges of visits between the leaders of the two nations.

CONGRATULATING RADIO STATION WPTF ON COMPLETION OF THIRTY-FIVE YEARS OF SERVICE

September 17, 1959

It is a pleasure to congratulate the staff and management of Radio Station WPTF upon the completion of thirty-five years of service to the people of its wide broadcast area.

As one of North Carolina's pioneer radio stations, WPTF has, during the past three and one-half decades, compiled an outstanding and enviable record in the news, entertainment, sports, and educational fields. Since its first broadcast on September 22, 1924, it has displayed a constant awareness of the radio station's position of leadership and responsibility at the community, regional, and state levels—proving itself ready at all times to contribute to the economic and cultural development of the people it serves.

I would especially like to commend the staff and management of WPTF for the manner in which they have cooperated with the various agencies of state government in efforts to promote North Carolina and make it a better and more prosperous place in which to live. Through this type of cooperation, the station has made a lasting contribution to the progress of our state. In so doing, it has measured up to the highest standards of the broadcasting profession.

I wish for WPTF every success in the years ahead.

ON A RECENT ADJUSTMENT IN WELFARE PAYMENTS BY THE STATE BOARD OF PUBLIC WELFARE

October 1, 1959

There seems to have been a misunderstanding in the press and by some people receiving welfare grants about my position in connection with the recent adjustment in welfare payments made by the State Board of Public Welfare. In fairness to everyone, I would like to clarify very briefly my position and the facts involved

1. I firmly believe in a good welfare program and am terribly sorry that any welfare grant has to be cut as our grants are already low.

2. The 1959 General Assembly, the State Welfare Board, and this office all believed that the welfare appropriation of approximately $17,670,000 was enough to keep grants at the 1958-59 average. Actually, this appropriation was almost 20 per cent more than was spent at the state level for welfare purposes during the previous biennium.

3. There is nothing the governor nor the board can do to raise the grants over last year's averages since there is no money available beyond the amount appropriated by the legislature. It is surprising to note that some people apparently believe that there is no limitation applied to funds available for welfare payments, as it is to all other agencies.

4. It was found during the past few months that the average welfare grants in old age assistance and for the disabled had risen above the level which had been discussed before the General Assembly, and above the amount appropriated by the legislature. In my press conference last week I said that the State Board of Public Welfare "was smart" to take its action at the time it did before the board got into real budgetary trouble later when it would be compelled to make drastic cuts. Some people apparently gained the impression that I said it "was smart to reduce grants." This was most unfortunate and unfair!

5. The State Board of Public Welfare had no choice other than to recommend a small reduction in welfare payments, and this had the sympathetic understanding of the Advisory Budget Commission and the Governor. Actually, the grants will continue to be equal to last year's average grant and that's what the General Assembly intended.

6. This administration wants to use wisely and effectively welfare funds appropriated by the General Assembly, but we cannot spend more than was appropriated. In fact, unless the funds are administered on a sound and realistic basis, we would not have enough available funds to last through the present biennium. However, we confidently expect that the state and county welfare boards will handle the matter properly and through

their many representatives in the state will see that the people understand this delicate problem.

May I express the hope also that the newspapers will help in this regard insofar as possible!

ON THE DEATH OF GENERAL JOHN VAN B. METTS

October 14, 1959

In the death last night of Major General John Van B. Metts, North Carolina loses a citizen who served the state with distinction, both in peace and in war. His long life was devoted to the National Guard. He was the gallant commander of the 119th Infantry Regiment of the Thirtieth Division in the First World War, and for thirty years, following his appointment in 1921, he was the adjutant general of North Carolina. Few men have served the state longer or with as great devotion.

IN SUPPORT OF THE PROPOSED 1959 BOND ISSUE

October 14, 1959

This is Luther H. Hodges, governor of North Carolina. On Tuesday, October 27, the people of North Carolina will vote in a state-wide bond election authorized by the 1959 General Assembly to provide greatly needed permanent improvements to many of our state governmental programs. There will be nine issues involved, including improvements to state educational institutions, state mental institutions, community colleges, hospitals, correctional and training schools, armories, blind rehabilitation centers, state ports, and historical sites and restoration.

I urge every citizen to go out on October 27 and vote *for* these bond issues to provide for most urgently needed facilities. I am confident that all nine issues will be passed by an overwhelming margin if all our voters take the time to go to the polls.

Vote for a better North Carolina! Vote for all nine bond issues on October 27!

DESIGNATING FISH AND SEAFOOD WEEK IN NORTH CAROLINA

October 19, 1959

In order to call public attention to the importance of the fish and seafood industries throughout the nation, and especially here in North Carolina, the people of the state are being asked to observe Fish and Seafood Week during the period, October 19-25.

This observance, endorsed by the Market Development Branch of the Fish and Wildlife Service, U. S. Department of the Interior, is designed to promote the increased consumption of seafood products, emphasize the fact that, historically, fishing is the nation's first industry, and draw attention to the thousands of people who depend upon this industry for their livelihood.

In North Carolina, where great emphasis has been placed on the economic significance of diversification in industry, agriculture, and other forms of business activity, we have a special responsibility to contribute whenever and wherever possible to the prosperity of our own sizeable seafood industry.

In recognition of these facts, I am glad to designate the week of October 19-25, 1959, as Fish and Seafood Week in North Carolina and urge that all our citizens observe this week in an appropriate manner.

DESIGNATING UNITED NATIONS DAY IN NORTH CAROLINA

October 20, 1959

North Carolinians are being asked to demonstrate their support of the United Nations and the principles upon which it was founded by joining all Americans in the observance of United Nations Day on Saturday, October 24—the fourteenth anniversary of the United Nations Charter.

In a courageous effort to save succeeding generations from the scourge of war, the United States joined the other nations of the world in founding the United Nations immediately following World War II. The action was taken in the belief that the best interests of freedom-loving people throughout the world would be served through such an organization.

The UN serves as a valuable forum for discussion and debate of crucial world problems and offers its machinery for conciliation, negotiation, and the peaceful settlement of international differences. It also helps many countries create the basic conditions for peace by encouraging greater production of food, better health, higher standards of living, and greater educational opportunities.

In North Carolina, special emphasis in being placed this year on civic club participation in this significant event. At the request of the Honorable Philip Whitley of Wendell, state chairman for the observance, I would like to urge all of our civic clubs, fraternal organizations, and other similar groups to cooperate in this noteworthy event.

In recognition of the great service performed by the United Nations during the past fourteen years and to call attention to the promise that its holds for the future, I am pleased to designate Saturday, October 24, 1959, as United Nations Day in North Carolina and urge that all our citizens use this occasion to develop a better understanding of the UN, its aims, achievements, and problems.

ON CONSERVING WATER RESOURCES

October 26, 1959

In order to call public attention to the importance of conserving and protecting our natural water resources, the people of the state are being asked to acquaint themselves with the water works system and the waste treatment plants in their respective communities.

This observance is being endorsed by the North Carolina Section of the American Water Works Association and the North Carolina Sewage and Industrial Wastes Association which are holding their Thirty-Ninth Joint Annual Convention in Durham, North Carolina, during November 9-11, 1959.

In North Carolina, where great emphasis is being placed on

the economic growth of our municipalities and industries, it is essential that we plan adequate supplies of safe drinking water and proper waste treatment facilities to protect the health and prosperity of our citizens and communities.

Our municipalities and industries are to be commended for their leadership in this field. Those which have not provided adequate water and waste treatment facilities to meet their present and anticipated needs are urged to initiate action to accomplish these objectives. All citizens should realize that water is one of North Carolina's greatest assets and should give their support to programs for its development and conservation.

ON THE VISIT OF PRESIDENT SEKOU TOURE TO NORTH CAROLINA

October 28, 1959

As is already generally known, President Eisenhower sometime ago invited President Sekou Toure of the Republic of Guinea to visit the United States. President Toure and his party arrived in this country Monday of this week, and I understand have been meeting with the President, Secretary of State Herter, and other American officials. Further, that his tour continues from North Carolina to other states during his sixteen-day stay in the United States.

Some weeks ago, I was informed that Mr. Toure would like to visit North Carolina and I was requested to assist in this visit. I, of course, am happy to cooperate with the President and the State Department in welcoming the head of a foreign nation who is on official visit to this country. (North Carolina's last presidential visitor from abroad, as will be recalled, was the President of Turkey, who visited North Carolina in 1954.)

President Toure and his party are scheduled to arrive at the Raleigh-Durham Airport this afternoon. They will visit Chapel Hill today, and visit in Durham tomorrow, leaving tomorrow afternoon, as I understand, for Chicago.

I am sure that all North Carolinians will join with me in saying that we welcome these visitors to North Carolina and we hope that President Toure, his cabinet ministers, and members of their families will all learn more of our great nation, its government, and its people.

NEWS ARTICLE FOR UNITED PRESS INTERNATIONAL

MUNICH, GERMANY
November 9, 1959

Our North Carolina Trade and Industry Mission to Europe is now at its mid-way point, and I am pleased to report that the trip has been most successful so far.

Our sixty-eight Tar Heels have been given a wonderful reception, and they are working hard in behalf of North Carolina. Since leaving our home state about a week ago, our mission, working in three separate groups, has visited London, Hamburg, Amsterdam, Rotterdam, Stuttgart, and Frankfurt before reassembling here this weekend.

In these European cities a total of 777 business and industrial leaders have been told the North Carolina story of economic opportunity through personal contacts, luncheons, and dinners. European industries contacted have included shipping lines, banking, electronics, heavy and light machinery, tobacco manufacturing, toys, food processing, chemicals, and automobile parts and assembly. We expect to contact at least 1,000 European businessmen by the time our tour has ended.

We are told by U. S. Government agencies that this is the first state-sponsored mission of its character and purpose to visit Europe. It has certainly made its impact here in Europe where we had really hoped primarily to obtain long range results—not immediate commitments. However, we have already been promised at least six visits by European industrialists who are interested in possible expansions of their plants in North Carolina. In addition, several firms and shipping companies have promised new trial shipments through our two North Carolina deep water ports at Morehead City and Wilmington.

The growth of European manufacturing and production has put industrialists here in a much more favorable trade position in world markets, and this should result in substantial business in and with the United States. We in North Carolina expect to be in on the ground floor of this development, and look forward to excellent long-range benefits from this mission to Europe.

We have found that European businessmen are interested and curious about our large group of North Carolina businessmen who have paid their own way to Europe to "sell" the state they love so much. They are impressed by patriotic citizens who are willing to give the time and money necessary to participate in this effort to improve our economy and the standard of living of all our people.

The exchange of information—especially person-to-person at luncheons and in personal visits—is most helpful to all concerned and certainly contributes to a better understanding of our common goals and objectives. Here in Germany we have found a much better understanding, for example, of the tremendous financial help which the United States has provided through the Marshall Plan and otherwise for this war-torn nation. I believe the average German now appreciates that American aid, implemented by German hard work and know-how, has made possible the great progress and growth of the past eight years.

Our mission has received excellent coverage in the European press, and this has made our efforts better known in each city and country visited. We are especially grateful to United Press International and the UPI coverage provided everywhere.

STATEMENT BY GOVERNOR HODGES UPON DEPARTURE FROM EUROPE AFTER TWO-WEEK TOUR WITH A SIXTY-EIGHT-MAN TRADE AND INDUSTRIAL MISSION

LE GRAND HOTEL
PARIS, FRANCE
November 15, 1959

I believe that the North Carolina Trade and Industry Mission to Europe has been a resounding success.

As we conclude our good-will tour of nine cities and five countries of Europe, I am convinced that this mission will result in stronger trade with Europe through our two state ports, will provide added industrial development for North Carolina through European-financed plants or European-controlled franchise agreements, and certainly will bring about a deeper and better understanding between our nations.

The three groups which made up our mission of sixty-eight men told the story of economic opportunity to more than 1,000 European business and industrial leaders through luncheons, dinners, and personal visits. While the basic purpose of our mission was long-range development for our state, I am delighted to report that six to eight Europeans have already made specific agreements to visit North Carolina in the months ahead.

We can expect additional inquiries, calls, and visits in the future as more businessmen over here look to America for production facilities and investment opportunities. Europe is definitely increasing its industrial activity, and the future holds great promise for increased and profitable trade between our countries if business and industrial leaders in each country will demonstrate the imagination, energy, and courage necessary to meet this challenge.

We in North Carolina and America need to know more about these expanding economies in Europe, and our European friends should do the same about our state and the great southeastern region in which it is located.

The common market and other developments have created great interest and change in the attitudes and outlook of many of the European businessmen whom we met. The rapid growth of competition from other areas of the world is causing Europeans to re-examine and analyze their own present operations as well as their plans for the future.

We believe the North Carolina Trade and Industrial Mission came here at a very timely moment and we should benefit greatly by these pioneering efforts in behalf of the people of North Carolina.

NEW YEAR'S STATEMENT

December 31, 1959

I greatly appreciate this opportunity to take a confident and enthusiastic look at 1960 in North Carolina. May I say that I have no reservations about predicting a great future for this state and its industrious people. This is not empty optimism, but genuine optimism based on an intimate knowledge of this state's limitless potential and supported by faith in the people of North Carolina to take full advantage of the opportunities that are available to them now and will be even more abundantly available in the months and years ahead.

This optimism in greatly strengthened by the development in recent years—and especially during the last twelve months—of a wonderful spirit of cooperation and unity of purpose among all our people. It is this spirit, manifested in a hundred different ways at local, regional, and state levels from the mountains to the coast, that has been principally responsible for bringing us to our present stage of economic and cultural development. And, it is this spirit that will stand us in good stead as we press on to even greater achievements in the future if we continue a state-wide point of view.

I am confident that 1960 will be a historic year for North Carolina. It will, I think, be a year in which many of the programs that we have worked on so diligently in the past will make contributions to our economic progress. It will, in many instances, be a year of maturity for many of these undertakings.

We have, in every year since 1956, bettered our records in industrial development—especially in the all important categories of new jobs and new and larger payrolls. I see no reason why this trend should not continue in 1960. Our efforts to encourage more diversification in agriculture have been increasingly successful, and I believe the benefits to be derived from this activity will become more and more apparent in the next twelve months.

I believe that a sound basis has been laid for future progress in the various activities of the state. A foundation has been established that will enable us to go forward in 1960 with confidence and faith in our ability to build a better way of life for our 4,500,000 North Carolinians.

DENYING THAT HE HAS ENDORSED ANY CANDIDATE FOR GOVERNOR

January 14, 1960

The rumors appearing in the press this morning have been brought to my attention, and I believe this sort of thing, because of its possible recurring nature, is of sufficient importance to require a formal statement from me, with the hope that everyone will know where I stand.

I would like to say as emphatically as possible, that I have not endorsed any candidate for governor, nor have I authorized anyone to speak for me in this connection. Further, I expect to continue this neutrality.

This does not mean that I shall not feel free to defend the policies of the administration during the last five years.

EXPLANATION OF A STATEMENT ABOUT EASTERN NORTH CAROLINA

January 19, 1960

[Governor Hodges had criticized eastern North Carolina for not showing more aggressiveness and a more purposeful leadership in the state's efforts to attract industry. His remarks, made at a meeting of the State Board of Conservation and Development in Raleigh on January 18, brought repercussions which this statement was designed to mitigate.]

I would like to refer to the statement appearing in the press concerning what I said about eastern North Carolina. I talked too vigorously yesterday, but I had good intentions. I feel as close to eastern North Carolina, its coast, and its people as I do to any section of our state. I do not believe there is anyone that has shown more interest in the development of the eastern part of the state than I have, but I do not think it is approaching its

Governor Hodges at the Raleigh-Durham Airport, December 4, 1960, returning from Florida where his appointment as Secretary of Commerce was announced by President-elect John F. Kennedy.

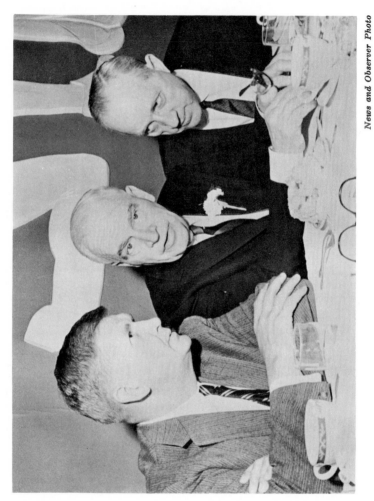

Governor-elect Terry Sanford (*left*), Governor Hodges, and Edward Scheidt, commissioner of motor vehicles (*right*), at a meeting of the Governor's Traffic Safety Council, December 6, 1960.

potential development. I have said this before and I say it again.

The thing that I am primarily interested in is the progress and development of this state, particularly eastern and western North Carolina where development has been slower and opportunities have been fewer. There have been many and notable exceptions in each section, of course.

In my statement yesterday I was talking about an excellent editorial appearing in the *Scotland Neck Commonwealth* on December 11, whose editor suggested that I call a meeting for the eastern part of the state to find out why they were not moving forward more rapidly. I favored the Eric Rodgers editorial and I favor the meeting he suggested. The only thought I had in mind when I made my statement, was to get the people of the eastern part of the state to realize the full possibilities which they have. I stand ready as I always have to help them in any way I can.

DESIGNATING AMERICAN MUSIC MONTH IN NORTH CAROLINA

January 25, 1960

The month of February will be observed in North Carolina and throughout the nation as "American Music Month"—a period set aside each year to honor our American composers and to express our appreciation for the contribution their music has made to the cultural life of the nation.

Sponsored by the National Federation of Music Clubs and supported in this state by the North Carolina Federation of Music Clubs, the event gives all citizens an opportunity to consider the important role that music has played in their individual lives. There can be no doubt that good music influences our lives in a beneficial way, and it is entirely appropriate that we honor those individuals who have the talent and dedication that is needed to compose this music.

In recognition of these facts, I am glad to designate the month of February as American Music Month in North Carolina and to urge that our music clubs and other groups interested in the cultural advancement of this state cooperate in the effort to make the people of North Carolina more aware of the beauty of composition by our own composers.

DESIGNATING AMERICAN HISTORY MONTH IN NORTH CAROLINA

January 29, 1960

In an effort to remind all Americans of their great heritage and to call their attention to the historical events and great sacrifices that gave us the priceless freedoms we enjoy today, North Carolina will join the other states of the nation in observing February as "American History Month."

This event, sponsored by the National Society, Daughters of the American Revolution of North Carolina, is especialy significant today at a time when the security of our nation is being threatened by strong international forces that seek to destroy the foundations of our freedom.

In recognition of the importance to each of us of learning more about our early history and of acquiring greater appreciation of the basic principles which underlie our democratic form of government, I am glad to designate February, 1960, as American History Month in North Carolina and to call upon all our organizations and schools to emphasize the study of American history during this period.

DESIGNATING NATIONAL CRIME PREVENTION WEEK IN NORTH CAROLINA

February 2, 1960

National Crime Prevention Week, a period set aside each year for the purpose of soliciting greater public interest in law enforcement, will be observed throughout North Carolina during the week, February 7-13.

This special nation-wide observance, sponsored by the National Exchange Clubs and supported by all local Exchange

Clubs, focuses attention on a serious state and national problem and, at the same time, stresses the importance of public interest and participation in law enforcement activities.

Respect for law and order is absolutely essential to the maintenance of our social structure, and it is the responsibility of every conscientious citizen to cooperate with law enforcement officers and agences in their efforts to curtail crime at local, state, and national levels.

In recognition of the importance of this occasion, I am glad to designate the week of February 7-13, 1960, as National Crime Prevention Week in North Carolina and to urge that all North Carolinians use this occasion to consider the part they can play in meeting this increasingly serious problem.

DESIGNATING HEART FUND MONTH IN NORTH CAROLINA

February 4, 1960

The increasing seriousness of cardiovascular diseases and the importance of public participation in efforts to conquer these diseases will be stressed in North Carolina during February with the observance of Heart Fund Month.

This state and nation continue to lose creative citizens to heart and blood vessel diseases, which today affect an estimated 10,000,000 Americans and account for more than half of all deaths. This, the number one health enemy in our society, causes widespread suffering and imposes serious economic and production hardships in industry and business.

Medical research has made dramatic progress in diagnosing, treating, and preventing heart diseases. Physicians today know how to check rheumatic fever, to control most cases of high blood pressure, to reduce the recurrences of heart ailments, to repair damaged heart valves and to correct in-born heart defects through surgery. North Carolinians can take pride in the fact that this state's medical institutions are contributing materially to this progress. Unfortunately, there is much work yet to be done before the battle is won.

In order to solicit the assistance needed to carry on this fight, the North Carolina Heart Association, in cooperation with the American Heart Association, conducts an annual fund drive to support research in this field. The fund also makes possible the dissemination of professional information to medical personnel and supports a broad program of public education which, undoubtedly, saves many lives each year.

In recognition of the importance of this work, I am glad to designate the month of February, 1960, as Heart Fund Month in North Carolina and urge that all our citizens give this campaign their enthusiastic support and cooperation.

DESIGNATING JOB SAFETY WEEK IN NORTH CAROLINA

February 22, 1960

In order to call attention to the President's Conference on Occupational Safety, to be held in Washington, D. C., March 1-3, and to stress the need for more effective methods of preventing occupational accidents, the week of February 28 - March 5 will be observed as "Job Safety Week" in North Carolina.

During 1959, a total of sixty-seven North Carolinians were killed and 122,318 injured in "on-the-job" accidents, resulting in much human suffering and incalculable production losses. The real tragedy is that none of these losses were inevitable; that methods exist or can be devised to eliminate almost all occupational accidents.

Because our workers are the pride and strength of this state and this nation, and because America needs the unmatched skill of all its citizens to meet the challenge of the future, I am glad to designate the week of February 28 - March 5, 1960, as Job Safety Week in North Carolina and to urge that all citizens of this state make job safety an increasingly important factor in their daily lives.

DESIGNATING ALSAC MONTH
IN NORTH CAROLINA

February 26, 1960

In order to call public attention to the nation-wide effort being made by the American Lebanese Syrian Associated Charities to combat the tragic and presently incurable disease, leukemia, North Carolinians are being asked to observe the month of March as "Aiding Leukemia Stricken American Children Month."

The primary purpose of this observance is to familiarize more Americans with this terrible disease and, at the same time, solicit public support in the campaign to raise funds for the erection and operation of the St. Jude Hospital in Memphis, Tennessee.

This hospital will concentrate exclusively on the care and treatment of children suffering from leukemia and related blood diseases. In addition to treatment facilities, the hospital will maintain a fully-equipped research laboratory in which three two-man teams of scentists will work twenty-four hours a day until a cure for leukemia has been discovered.

In recognition of the importance of this effort to conquer one of the world's most tragic diseases, I am glad to designate the month of March as ALSAC Month in North Carolina and urge that the people of North Carolina generously support this campaign.

DESIGNATING ALAMO DAY IN NORTH CAROLINA

March 1, 1960

In order to prepetuate the memory of the small band of couregeous men who gave their lives in the historic Battle of the Alamo, North Carolina—one of the eighteen states whose native sons died in the battle—will observe Alamo Day on March 6.

This observance, the first of its kind since the fall of the Alamo almost a century and a quarter ago, will remind present-day Americans of their great heritage and of the sacrifices made by our forefathers to give us that heritage.

Appropriately, it has been said, "Thermopylae had its messenger of defeat, the Alamo had none." The 185 heroic defenders stood against the 7,000 soldiers of the Mexican dictator, Santa Anna, until the last man fell. They destroyed 1,700 enemy troops and delayed the Mexican Army for thirteen days, sufficient time for General Sam Houston to assemble an army which forty-six days later defeated Santa Anna on the field of San Jacinto.

Certainly, of all the battles fought on American soil for the cause of freedom, the Battle of the Alamo stands foremost as a symbol of dedication, courage, and self-sacrifice.

I am glad, therefore, to commemorate this singularly historic event by designating March 6, 1960, as Alamo Day in North Carolina and urge that all North Carolinians use this occasion to reflect upon the glorious heritage that is theirs.

COMMENDING WILKES COUNTY CITIZENS FOR VOTE APPROVING DAM AND RESERVOIR BOND ISSUE

March 3, 1960

I would like to commend the citizens of Wilkes County and Winston-Salem on the progressive spirit and enthusiasm for the future they have demonstrated in voting overwhelming approval of the bond issue to facilitate construction of the much needed and long-awaited Wilkesboro Dam and Reservoir.

This pioneering venture, which for the first time incorporates a very desirable water storage feature in a flood control project, will greatly benefit both Wilkes County and the city of Winston-Salem while, at the same time, establishing a precedent that can be followed to tremendous advantage in other similar undertakings. The $1,200,000 that the county and city will invest in the project will be repaid many times in the form of new industrial sites, adequate water supplies, and recreational facilities.

The fact that the issuance of the bonds was approved is gratifying in itself, but the decisive nature of the vote in both areas is especially noteworthy and reflects considerable credit on the communities and their spirit of progress. This spirit was evident when I visited Wilkes County recently to join community leaders in urging a favorable vote in this vitally important referendum. It was even more evident this week when the citizens approved the bond issue by a vote of 10,032 to 263. This is a dramatic example of a people's faith in themselves.

REPLY TO A PETITION FOR RELOCATION OF CAMP POLK PRISON

[Camp Polk prison, located on the outskirts of Raleigh, was regarded as a menace by local residents who were demanding its removal elsewhere. These demands had been intensified by the murder of a prominent Raleigh resident by a man who had just been released from the prison in the summer of 1959.]

March 7, 1960

Mr. Marion Medlin
Box 166, Route 1
Cary, North Carolina
Dear Mr. Medlin:

Upon my recent return to the office I have seen the petition you sent to me, signed by several citizens in the Camp Polk area. As I stated at a recent press conference, I have not been actively negotiating for a relocation of the Camp Polk unit. I have received information as to a possible new site and have passed that on to the Prison Commission.

If there is anything that I can appropriately do to assist in resolving this matter to the satisfaction of all concerned, I will of course do it. I do not wish to mislead you however. The question of relocating a prison unit is not a simple one, by any means. In the specific case here, it comes down to a matter of a large expenditure of dollars—which the General Assembly would probably have to appropriate—as well as the question of finding another suitable location in which the citizens would not raise just as much objection as those where the unit is presently situated.

Ordinarily I would be glad to see your delegation but in view of the fact that the legal proceeding is now pending in the State Supreme Court, it would not be appropriate for me to discuss this matter with a group of citizens, as you requested, until the court case is decided one way or the other. The attorney general feels this way also.

Sincerely,

/s/ Luther H. Hodges

WHAT THE TEXTILE INDUSTRY HAS MEANT TO NORTH CAROLINA

March 8, 1960

The role played by the textile industry in the growth and development of North Carolina has been so significant that, in many respects, the history of this single dynamic industry has been the history of the state. As early as 1584, North Carolina was described by its first explorers as a land that might well relieve England of its dependence upon "infidels and doubtful friends" for such items as dyes, silk, flax, and hemp for textiles and cordage. England was to benefit little from this potential, but history has dramaticaly proven the validity of the appraisal.

Hand spinning and weaving operations began in North Carolina with the early colonists, and it is significant that the first water power-operated cotton mill to be located south of the Potomac River was erected in this state in 1813. By 1880, the forty-nine larger cotton mills of the state were producing goods valued at almost $2,500,000. At the turn of the century, this figure had risen to $30,000,000. In the next three decades, the value had increased fifteen times to $459,000,000. By 1939, the total had jumped to almost $550,000,000 and in 1958, according to *Industrial Development and Manufacturers Record,* the figure had risen to $2,586,000,000.

The industry continued to expand in 1959, increasing the value of its plants and machinery to approximately $1,000,000,000, while adding more millions to its sales volume. In recent years, as in decades past, the textile industry has demonstrated its ability to meet the challenge of changing times.

North Carolina today has 1,200 textile plants, most of them featuring the latest in modern equipment and desirable working conditions. These plants, which are distributed throughout our state, employ 222,300 people—more than 45 per cent of the state's total manufacturing work force—and provide annual payrolls amounting to $652,475,680. These productive workers man 93,209 looms, more than 7,000,000 spindles, and 49,728 knitting machines. In the hosiery field, alone, they account for better than half the nation's yearly production.

As late as 1954, North Carolina boasted the largest towel mill in the world, the largest hosiery mill, the largest denim mill, the largest damask mill, the largest men's underwear factory, and the world's "combed yarn capital." One of our counties has gone unchallenged in its claim to having more textile mills than any other county in the United States.

Still another factor that cannot be overlooked in assessing the value of the textile industry to North Carolina is the sizable contribution made annually by the industry in the form of corporate and individual income taxes, franchise taxes, sales taxes, and local property taxes. Reliable estimates place this figure at not less than $40,000,000 each year.

What has the textile industry meant to North Carolina and its people? It has meant a more stable economy by providing an industrial bulwark against the ever-present and unpredictable economic dangers that threaten a predominantly agricultural state. It has been a proving ground for the North Carolina worker—preparing him for the increasingly industrial society in which he must earn his livelihood while, at the same time, illustrating his capacity for work, his loyalty, his productive ability, and his desire to build a better way of life.

In so doing, the industry has provided employment for many thousands of our displaced farm people, while making it possible for many to remain on the land by providing a ready market for the cotton they produce. Even today, the industry consumes far more cotton than the state's farmers can provide.

Undoubtedly, the textile industry has earned a distinguished place in the history of our state and our region. From Colonial days, it has been a vital and energetic force in the economic life of our people, growing with them, suffering with them, sharing their hopes and dreams and their tremendous faith in the future.

The relationship between this industry and the people who have made it great has been a mutually beneficial one. And there is every indication that the future will be even more gratifying than the past. History has shown that the textile industry is capable of adapting, that it regards the rapid growth and development of the South in recent years, not as a threat, but as a challenge filled with opportunities—opportunities that can mean a stronger industry, a more dynamic state and regional economy, and a more abundant life for our people.

CORRECTING A NEWSPAPER ACCOUNT IN REGARD TO TAX CONCESSIONS TO INDUSTRY

March 21, 1960

[On March 17, 1960, William R. Henderson, head of the Commerce and Industry Division of the State Department of Conservation and Development had proposed to the Committee on Reorganization of State Government that a study of the subject of tax concessions to industry should be made in order to determine whether North Carolina was suffering by comparison with other states in this respect; and Governor Hodges had approved the proposal. This statement was issued to correct a newspaper headline of March 18 giving the impression that the Governor was favoring tax concessions to industry, which he had always opposed.]

On my return to the state from New Orleans where I had told the story of North Carolina's industrial progress, I saw some newspaper accounts which, unfortunately, gave a very misleading impression as to my own basic feelings on securing new industry. For example, in one of the newspapers Friday there was a front page headline which said, "Hodges, C & D—New Tax Concessions to Industry Proposed."

This prominent headline was erroneous as the detailed account in the same paper bears out, in which it was reported that Mr. Henderson was recommending a thorough study of the situation and at the same time expressed opposition to special tax concessions or favors. I have said throughout this country and in Europe that I do not favor tax concessions for industry.

I do not wish to be understood as unduly criticizing any newspaper for the interpretation it has put on this matter, but I do wish to make clear that there is a great distinction between my "proposing tax concessions for industry" (which I have not done) and my "proposing a *study* of the entire subject" (which I have done).

Our Department of Conservation and Development reports they have been getting increased competition in the past year from other states which reportedly make concessions, particularly to aid in financing buildings by way of long-term loans for industry coming into the state.

Instead of working on general statements or rumors as to what other states have been doing, I suggested that a "study" be made of what they are doing so that we would have the best factual information available. I think it is important to know as much as we can in complete detail on this subject.

DESIGNATING VERRAZZANO DAY IN NORTH CAROLINA

April 13, 1960

In order to provide an opportunity for appropriate recognition of the first known European explorer to visit the North Carolina coast, this state will join other states along the Atlantic seaboard in observing April 17 as Verrazzano Day.

Sponsored by the Italian Historical Society of America, the event will honor Giovanni da Verrazzano, the Florentine navigator who explored the Cape Fear region of the North Carolina coast during the spring of 1524 while sailing in the service of France.

It is entirely appropriate that North Carolinians should honor Verrazzano, for it is generally accepted as historical fact that this early explorer's glowing description of North Carolina, published in 1582, influenced Sir Walter Raleigh in his decision to attempt the establishment of a colony in this region of the New World. We are therefore indebted to the Italian explorer for the contribution he made, both directly and indirectly, to the exciting and unique early history of this state.

In recognition of these facts and in acknowledgement of the important role that history plays in our lives, I am glad to designate April 17, 1960, as Verrazzano Day in North Carolina and urge that all our citizens use this occasion to familiarize themselves with the exploits of this outstanding historical figure.

DESIGNATING JANE ADDAMS MONTH
IN NORTH CAROLINA

April 19, 1960

North Carolina has joined other states throughout the nation in observing the month of April as Jane Addams Month, honoring the 100th anniversary of the birth of this pioneer social worker.

Sponsored by the North Carolina Council of the National Association of Social Workers, this event is designed to give appropriate recognition to Miss Addams for her understanding of social problems and her effective work in combatting social injustice.

A winner of the Nobel Peace Prize, Miss Addams dedicated her life to the betterment of mankind. She campaigned effectively against child labor, inhuman working conditions, and disease, while at the same time devoting much time and effort to the cause of world peace.

In recognition of these noteworthy contributions to the improvement of man and his society, I am glad to designate April, 1960, as Jane Addams Month in North Carolina and urge that all our citizens support this observance by re-dedicating themselves to the preservation of the dignity of man.

URGING SUPPORT OF THE DEMOCRATIC TICKET
IN THE NOVEMBER 1960 ELECTION

April 28, 1960

We look forward to Tuesday, November 8, the date of our general election. On that day we Democrats must go to the polls in great numbers to give support to the Democratic party nominees at local, state, and national levels.

Never in the history of this country has the challenge to active citizenship been so great, so important. Our government is operated through political parties. You and I are Democrats and proud of it. Let's demonstrate our pride by our active work and our votes in the fall election.

The Democratic party has given to North Carolina a program befitting a modern, growing state. Under its leadership, the state has moved forward steadily and surely. Our state has been given a clean, honest government, and its people are united in a determination to build the state further—by raising the level of income of our citizens and by furnishing state services which are needed by a progressive state.

May I think you for your continued interest in and support of the Democratic party and our state's program.

ON THE NEW SALARY SCHEDULE FOR STATE EMPLOYEES

April 26, 1960

[This statement was prepared for and published in the May, 1960, issue of *Career*, a publication for personnel in North Carolina state government.]

I am very happy about the new salary schedule for state employees.

The Personnel Department and the Personnel Council have kept me advised of their studies and their proposals, and it is a great pleasure to me to endorse this significant change which should help state employees and make for better and fairer salary administration.

The new pay plan is an illustration of the fine, courageous job which the State Personnel Council and its staff have been doing for the state of North Carolina and its employees. The plan represents the biggest step forward in personnel administration in the eleven years of the council's existence.

Further, this reasonable and progressive step recognizes the outstanding performance consistently put forth by state employees in every line of duty. The employees richly deserve this reward and commendation for their continued efforts on behalf of a state government that has a long-standing reputation for honesty, integrity, and efficiency.

COMMENTS ON THE STATE'S REVENUE PICTURE FOR THE BIENNIUM 1959-1961

May 5, 1960

In the interest of clarification for the general public I want to make these comments about the state revenue picture as indicated by the recent report from the commissioner of revenue.

First, it appears definite that revenue collections for both years of this biennium will be sufficient to pay the 5 per cent contingent increase in school teacher salaries, authorized by the 1959 General Assembly to be paid at the end of this fiscal year and at the end of the next fiscal year. This 5 per cent bonus will require approximately $7,000,000 each of these two years, or a total of $14,000,000 extra in school teacher salaries for this beiennium.

Second, on the basis of present revenue collections, it is reasonable to estimate that under present tax schedules revenue collections for the next biennium, together with any credit balance remaining at the end of the current biennium, will be sufficient to cover the state's anticipated "A" Budget requirements for the next biennium (continuation of state services at present levels), *even though approximately $50,000,000 additional will be required the next biennium just for this purpose*—that is, continuing present level of state programs with no new programs or increased level of expenditures.

It is also apparent now, assuming continuing good economic conditions, that our biennial surplus of revenue collections over appropriations, together with a reasonably expected credit balance of unexpended appropriations by the end of this biennium, will be somewhat in excess of $30,000,000. This amount will more than offset the $27,500,000 non-recurring so-called income tax "windfall," and to me this is a clear-cut and strong answer to those few people who have criticized the adoption of the income tax withholding system and who have erroneously claimed that the state will start off the next biennium some $27,000,000 "in the hole."

Commissioner Currie has informed me that compared with the first ten months of the last fiscal year, there has been a substantial increase in the number of income tax returns filed with the Revenue Department. For example, the number of individual income tax returns (which report some tax due) has increased approximately 70,000—a 10 per cent gain over last year. There is no way to tell accurately at this time how many of the additional income tax returns have resulted from increased industrialization and improved economic conditions and how many may be attributed to the installation of the wtholding system and increased enforcement efforts. However, based upon the general improvement in the state's economy, Commissioner Currie estimates that probably 40,000 of the additional 70,000 individual taxpayer returns should be attributed to greater industrialization and improved economy and approximately 30,000 attributed to the withholding system and improved enforcement program.

As to appropriations for the next biennium, I think it is very important for us to keep in mind the large amount in *additional* appropriations which will be required for the next biennium merely to carry forward our state support of education, health, welfare, and other programs at the present level of salaries, etc. —which will amount to approximately $50,000,000 for the biennium, based on "A" budget requests which are running 5-10 per cent above last year. The large part of this $50,000,000 will be required for the support of the public schools. This is understandable when we remember that our schools will have some *25,000 additional pupils* entering *each* year of the next biennium!

As to revenue collections for the next biennium, on the basis of the most recent data it is reasonable to assume at this time that collections under present tax schedules for the next biennium will likely be sufficient to produce the additional $50,000,000 necessary for the state's "A" or continuation budget, but present revenue collection data does not indicate any amount over and above this figure under present tax schedules.

Our state's industrialization program, the benefits of the income tax withholding system, improved tax law enforcement, and general improvement in economic conditions are all reflected in the current optimistic revenue reports. I am glad that all present indications point to the reasonable conclusion that the next administration will have a sound fiscal base from which to continue a progressive program for North Carolina.

ON THE RESULTS OF THE MAY 1960 PRIMARY ELECTION

June 2, 1960

I am very pleased that we had a record vote in last Saturday's primary election, and trust we will have a much larger vote in the June 25 run-off election as there has never been a more vital election. I urge every qualified voter in the state to participate.

I am deeply interested in the future of North Carolina and its economic progress which is vital to our state. I am deeply interested in the preservation of our precious public schools and in the maintenance of peace and order which befits a great citizenry. Let's do all we can to preserve good government in North Carolina, and the pride and dignity of our people.

COMMENT ON GOVERNOR HOLLINGS' ALLEGED STATEMENT ON THE NORTH CAROLINA PRIMARY ELECTION

June 2, 1960

[Governor Ernest F. Hollings of South Carolina was reported in press dispatches to have said that "since Sanford has been described as a moderate in segregation, I naturally stand for Dr. Lake, who stands for segregation and our way of life." Hollings later repudiated this statement, denying that he had mentioned the name of any candidate and stating that he had only said that "were segregation or our way of life here in South Carolina at isue, I would necessarily favor the one who stood for segregation, as I do."]

I was surprised at what Governor Hollings is reported to have said, as it is most unusual for a governor of one state to comment on another state's primary election. As to any comment from me regarding Governor Hollings: I have for nearly six years refrained from making such comments, and I don't expect now to change my policy.

ON THE APPROACHING RUN-OFF PRIMARY ELECTION

June 23, 1960

Saturday, June 25, is the run-off primary elction—as I have said, one of the most important ever held in North Carolina—for governorship and other offices.

I want to urge, yes implore, every eligible voter to vote Saturday. This is important! If you are on vacation, come home to vote. If you plan to go away, vote before you go. This is your duty.

In the May 28 primary, over 650,000 of our citizens voted. There should be even more this time. Each of you who voted before, do it again Saturday and persuade another citizen to exercise his great privilege of voting.

Someone has said, "The punishment of wise men who refuse to take part in the affairs of government is to live under the government of unwise men."

STATEMENT FOR "VOICE OF AMERICA" PROGRAM

July 28, 1960

I consider it a distinct privilege to participate in this "Voice of Amerca" program—first, because its purpose is to create better understanding of the United States and its various regions, and, secondly, because it gives me an opportunity to tell you something about my state of North Carolina, its rich heritage, its unique scenic and historic attractions, and its unprecedented economic and cultural progress in recent years.

North Carolina boasts unexcelled geographical variety. A picturesque 300-mile shoreline on the Atlantic Ocean forms our eastern boundary. Moving to the west across the state we encounter first the rich agricultural Coastal Plain, then the rolling industrial Piedmont Plateau and, finally, the Appalachian Mountains, featuring the highest and most beautiful peaks in the eastern United States, including Mount Mitchell.

The first explorers came to this land early in the sixteenth century—the French led by the Florentine navigator Verrazzano and the Spanish led by the legendary de Soto. It was not, however, until 1585, when Sir Walter Raleigh's expedition arrived from England, that an attempt was made at settlement. It was here, on North Carolina's Roanoke Island, that the first English child was born and the first Protestant baptism performed in America. Today, these historic events are immortalized in a great outdoor drama—"The Lost Colony"—performed during the summer months on the exact site of the original settlement.

North Carolina's early settlers were Anglo-Saxons, Scotch-Irish, and German. They were hard-working and fiercely independent. They were proud of their new land and jealous of their freedom. They were simple men and women who gave our state the great heritage that we bear so proudly today.

We are proud of the fact that North Carolina took the lead in our nation's fight for independence. It was on April 12, 1776—more than a month before any of the other colonies acted—that North Carolina instructed its delegates to the Continental Congress to vote for freedom from England.

This same spirit of independent action has remained with us to this day. It is evident in the fact that North Carolina, in 1795, became the first state to open the doors of a state university. Today, the University of North Carolina is recognized as one of the leading educational institutions in the United States. Our people take pride in this fact and also in the knowledge that we were the first southern state, and one of the first in the nation, to estabilsh a public school system and public libraries.

North Carolina's interest in cultural development has continued. Our state legislature—with the enthusiastic endorsement of our people—established a state art museum. This museum today houses art treasures valued at several million dollars. Other examples of cultural activity include the North Carolina Symphony

Orchestra and the North Carolina Grass Roots Opera Company.

North Carolina is primarily an agricultural state, with tobacco our cash crop, but we are increasing our poultry and cattle and are extending our processing.

Our industrial growth has been phenomenal in the last five years. We lead the United States in the manufacture of textiles, tobacco products, and wooden household furniture. And we are gaining rapidly in such fields as electronics, metal working, and industrial research. New investments in industry are averaging over $200,000,000 a year.

There is a great deal more that I could tell you about North Carolina—past and present. I could tell you of the three Presidents and other great leaders we have given the nation. I could relate the fascinating exploits of fabled pirates who buried their treasures in the great sand dunes of our Outer Banks. I could tell you of the Wright Brothers, Orville and Wilbur, who came to those same sand dunes at Kill Devil Hill, just half a century ago, to give our state another proud "first" as the birthplace of aviation.

Yes, North Carolina has much to be proud of, but its greatest source of pride is its people. The motto of our state is "Esse Quam Videri"— "To be Rather Than to Seem." North Carolinians have, throughout their history, taken this motto seriously— translating it into a way of life that is unique in its simplicity, yet deeply profound in its meaning. There is an "esprit de corps" among our people that is born of confidence and humility and nurtured by the knowledge that deeds and not words are the true measure of accomplishment.

May I conclude by issuing a very warm and genuine invitation to each of you to visit North Carolina in the near future. Our state and our people will do everything possible to make it a most exciting and memorable experience.

ON THE FONTANA LAKE ROAD MATTER

May 12 and September 1, 1960

[Construction of the Fontana Dam reservoir by the Tennessee Valley Authority had caused the flooding of N. C. Route 288, which the U. S. Department of the Interior and the state of North Carolina had agreed in 1943 to replace, "as soon after World War II as possible," with another road along the north shore of Fontana Lake through the Great Smoky Mountains National Park. North Carolina had completed its section of the proposed road in June, 1959, and in the meantime had also built a road, N. C. Route 28, along the south shore of the lake. The Department of the Interior stood ready to fulfill its share of the obligation, but had met with opposition from the North Carolina Wildlife Federation on the ground that such a road would despoil a primeval wilderness area within the park. A request from the acting Secretary of the Interior, on April 26, 1960, for a statement from Governor Hodges as to the wishes of the state of North Carolina on the matter, elicited these two letters in which the Governor called for the Department of the Interior to honor its 1943 agreement to build the road.]

September 1, 1960

Honorable Fred Seaton
Secretary of the Interior
Department of the Interior
Washington, D. C.
Dear Mr. Secretary:

Last spring I received a letter dated April 26 from Acting Secretary Elmer F. Bennett, concerning the construction of a road along the north shore of Fontana Lake through the Great Smoky Mountains National Park in North Carolina.

For your convenience there is enclosed a copy of Mr. Bennett's letter and a copy of my response dated May 12, 1960, together with copy of press release from my office dated May 17, 1960, which describes the procedure I have followed in considering this matter.

I have received a brief in opposition to the proposed road from the North Carolina Wildlife Federation, Inc., and a brief from the Board of County Commissioners of Swain County supporting construction of the road. Copies of these briefs are enclosed.

In summary I wish to say that there is no question but that the Department of the Interior (Park Service) has a binding obligation to build the road, and I think it should fulfill its obligation.

You will note that the brief submitted to me by the North Carolina Wildlife Federation suggests that a compromise understanding should be reached on this matter and that the federal government should do various things which would be of benefit to Swain County and to the state of North Carolina in lieu of building the road through the park. I cannot pass judgment on these suggestions because the proper development of the National Park is a responsibility of the Department of the Interior, and the Department should promptly take the initiative in consulting with Swain County officials if it has any such suggestions or proposals to make.

Before reaching the summary conclusions which I express above, I read the briefs above referred to and discussed this matter with interested individuals and groups. As recently as August 14 through 17 I was in the area of Swain County and the National Park which would be involved in the construction of this road. On August 17 I flew in a light plane over the proposed route as described in the 1943 agrement. Also on August 17 I attended an open meeting in Bryson City, North Carolina, at the Swain County Court House and heard presentations from citizens of that county concerning the proposed road.

For your information I call particular attention to the following factors in connection with the road:

(1) The Department of the Interior almost seventeen years ago agreed to construction of the road in question, in a formal contract signed by the Secretary of the Interior, the governor of North Carolina, the chairman of the Board of Commissioners for Swain County, the acting chairman of the State Highway and Public Works Commission and the acting general manager of the Tennessee Valley Authority. This formal agreement recites in part that, "The Department regards a park standard road connection between Deals Gap and Bryson City as an important link in a planned 'around the park' road, has included the same as a part of a master plan for the development of the park (extended as aforesaid), and, subject to inclusion of the aforesaid additional acreage within the park area, is agreeable to initiating

construction of the park portion of such a road as soon as funds are made available therefor by Congress."

(2) So far as I know, the Department of the Interior has never informed anyone in this state of any official change in the master plan for the development of the National Park which was referred to in the 1943 agreement.

(3) The 1943 agreement sets forth in detail the route of the proposed road between Deals Gap and Bryson City, and in that agreement the Department of the Interior gives its unqualified promise and commitment that it would proceed with construction of this road as soon after World War II as possible, and the clear spirit and implication of the 1943 agreement is that the Department of the Interior will in good faith seek the necessary funds from Congress, to construct the road which the Department of the Interior "regards" as an important link in its planned "around the park" road. The state of North Carolina has already constructed its road from Bryson City to the park boundary as called for in the 1943 contract.

(4) Mr. Bennett's letter of April 26 refers to the "south shore road," which is North Carolina Route 28 running from Fontana to intersect with Route 19 south of Bryson City, as supplanting the need for a north shore route or the proposed road through the park described in the 1943 agreement. It is correct that North Carolina Route 28 has been constructed since 1943. However, it is my considered opinion that this road as now constructed is not an effective traffic artery between Fontana and Bryson City. This road is quite narrow, has many sharp winding curves, is not an attractive scenic route between Fontanta and Bryson City, and definitely needs rebuilding. It was not constructed nor intended to serve as a major traffic route nor a substitute for the anticipated north shore road.

(5) A major point of opposition to the proposed road is that it would have a great detrimental effect on a wilderness area which should be preserved. It is true that the area of the National Park which now extends to the north shore of Fontana Lake is no longer inhabited by private citizens. This area is now open only to citizens for hunting, fishing, and recreational purposes in accordance with National Park Service regulations. To

the extent that the area is now uninhabited, it might be described as a "wilderness" area. However, the area in question is not a virgin or primeval wilderness as apparently is assumed by a good many people who have expressed themselves on this question and who, because of their general interest in wildlife conservation, have more or less automatically taken a position opposing the construction of this road. Less than twenty years ago, approximately three thousand people lived in the area which was made a part of the National Park in accordance with the 1943 agreement. There were several substantial settlements in that area, including the town of Proctor. Of course, all of those settlements have now vanished and all of the people have now moved out of this area. There is an area much further north of Fontana Lake, included within the original boundary of the Smoky Mountains National Park, which can be classified as a true wilderness area. It is an area which has never been settled or inhabited, and it is an area with forests which have never been cut over.

(6) I conclude with respect to the "wilderness objection" that it is not correct that construction of the proposed road will despoil a virgin or primeval wilderness area within the Smoky Mountains National Park. The most that can be said for this argument is that the construction of the road will be through an area which is not now inhabited and which may be described as somewhat of a buffer zone for a truly wilderness area and to some people this would be objectionable.

(7) I cannot ignore the fact that Swain County, in its separate governmental capacity, is a formal party to the 1943 agreement no less than is the state of North Carolina. The county, therefore, holds contractual rights under that agreement in addition to and apart from those of the state itself. As the governor of the state could not in 1943 commit the county as such to become an individual party to the contract, neither can the state now, acting through the governor, unilaterally write off the county's standing as a separate bona fide party to the 1943 contract.

I am assuming that the road, if constructed, will be strictly limited to non-commercial traffic, and that no building or facility of any kind whatsoever can be constructed along the road without the approval of the Department of the Interior. I further assume that such approval would never be given unless the proposed construction or facility would be in keeping with the spirit and purposes of the Smoky Mountains National Park.

With respect to the specific issue put before me in the letter of April 26, I can only conclude, as I have indicated above, that the Department of the Interior should honor the contractual agreement which the Department itself entered into in 1943. I can make no distinction, in this respect, between the Department of the Interior and any private individual who puts his name to a prvate contract. I recognize that the 1943 agreement does not commit Congress to appropriate the necessary funds with which to construct the road. I believe, however, that Congress will certainly be disposed to do everything possible to see that the Department of the Interior is able to fullfill its contractual agreement, and I express the firm view that the Department of the Interior has an obligation to give more than lip service to the fulfillment of its contractual obligation.

Yours very truly,
/s/ Luther H. Hodges

May 12, 1960

Honorable Elmer F. Bennett
Acting Secretary of the Interior
United States Department of the Interior
Washington, D. C.
Dear Mr. Bennett:

This refers to your letter of April 26 concerning construction of a road along the north shore of Fontana Lake through the Great Smoky Mountains National Park.

As you stated in your letter, the Department of the Interior entered into an agreement in 1943 for the construction of this road. Parties to the 1943 contract included the Tennessee Valley Authority, the state of North Carolina, and Swain County. The state of North Carolina had agreed on its part to construct a road from Bryson City to a point on the eastern boundary of the National Park, and the Department of the Interior agreed to pick up at that point and construct a road along the north shore of Fontana Lake through the park area.

According to my understanding, both Swain County officials and state officials have always urged and insisted that the Department of the Interior comply with its 1943 contractual agreement. Furthermore, in 1958 the North Carolina State Highway Commission began construction of that portion of the road from Bryson City to the park line, which construction has now been completed and dead-ends at a point on the park boundary.

I frankly was surprised to receive your letter of April 26, which seemed to raise some question as to whether the state of North Carolina desired that the Department of the Interior carry out its commitment, in view of the well-known discussions through the years on this subject and the action of the State Highway Commission in building the portion of the road promised by the state.

Since receipt of your letter, I have learned that some individuals representing wildlife interests in North Carolina have raised some objection to the construction of this road and recently, upon representations made to the North Carolina Wildlife Resources Commission, that commission passed a resolution in opposition to the construction of this road by the Department of the Interior. I doubt that the North Carolina Wildlife Resources Commission, a state agency, was fully cognizant of the action taken over a period of years by another state agency—namely, the State Highway Commission.

In view of the history on this particular matter, and the prior position taken by the state, I probably would be justified in proceeding at this point and officially urge that your Department take immediate action to carry out your contractual commitment.

However, I have decided to defer an immediate decision on the question you have presented to me until I have had an opportunity to obtain from interested officials and others a full and complete statement of views concerning the construction of this road. I will give careful consideration to all representations made to me on this issue, and I am confident that if there presently exists any difference of opinion among citizens of this state on the construction of this road, these differences can be resolved satisfactorily.

I will be in a position within the near future to give you an unequivocal answer to your question which, as I stated above, I was surprised to have presented to me.

Yours very truly,

/s/ Luther H. Hodges

APPEAL FOR FEDERAL ASSISTANCE FOLLOWING HURRICANE DONNA
TELEGRAM

September 15, 1960

The Honorable Dwight D. Eisenhower
President of the United States
The White House
Washington, D. C.

On Sunday and Monday, September 11 and 12, 1960, Hurricane Donna struck the coast of North Carolina with such destructive force as to cause severe damage to public and private property in the coastal areas of the state reaching inland to depths yet undetermined.

It is now apparent that the damage, hardship and suffering are so extensive as to be beyond the capabilities of the state and local governments to alleviate and that federal assistance is required.

A detailed estimate of the damage will be made and furnished to you as expeditiously as possible. I have state engineers and other personnel in the affected areas at this time for the purpose of determining the amount of funds, personnel, equipment, and material required to alleviate conditions. A detailed estimate of the damage, together with a statement of the nature and extent of federal assistance required to supplement state and local efforts, will be furnished to you as soon as necessary information can be secured.

Although total damage and requirements cannot be determined at this time, certain measures requiring the full assistance of federal agencies within their authority and responsibility under the law are considered necessary to meet immediate problems.

Be assured that all available resources of the state and local governments will be committed to the foregoing purposes to the maximum extent possible. All state and local civil defense organizations and the American Red Cross are exerting maximum efforts. It is accordingly requested that a major disaster be declared covering the southeastern and coastal areas of North Carolina under authority of Public Law 875, 81st Congress, as amended, a specific request for an allocation of funds thereunder to await a detailed statement of damages and requirements together with state and local resources made available and committed.

Luther H. Hodges
Governor of North Carolina

IN FAVOR OF CONTINUING THE NICKELS FOR KNOW-HOW PROGRAM

September 23, 1960

Friday, September 30, is a very important day for North Carolina agriculture. On this day, the users of feed or fertilizer—which includes most of our farm citizens—will vote on whether to continue their unique Nickels for Know-How program.

In my opinion, the Nickels for Know-How program is an excellent example of a group of people using their own initiative and own resources to help solve their problems and increase their opportunities. Under the program, farm people voluntarily donate a nickel for each ton of feed and fertilizer they purchase to aid agricultural research and education at North Carolina State College.

Since the Nickels for Know-How program was launched in 1951, farmers have contributed $1,164,000. This amounts to about thirty cents annually per farmer. This money has helped State College conduct scores of needed projects. One project, for example, was a tobacco disease control program started in 1955. By 1959, tobacco losses from nematodes alone were down by 64 per cent, resulting in a $17,000,000 savings to tobacco growers over a four-year period.

The eagerness of North Carolina farm people to contribute to their own welfare is having other beneficial effects. State College officials tell me, for example, that agricultural industries are contributing more money to State College research as a result of this farm effort.

In past referendums, users of feed and fertilizer have voted twelve to one in favor of continuing the Nickels for Know-How program. I am sure that the vote in the September 30 referendum will be equally as favorable.

URGING CITIZENS TO REGISTER AND VOTE IN THE GENERAL ELECTION

September 29, 1960

Now is the time to make sure every eligible citizen in North Carolina is registered for voting in the general election.

Registration books will be open in ninety-four counties during the period October 15-29. In six counties—Cumberland, Forsyth, Guilford, Mecklenburg, Wake, and Wilson—where the loose-leaf permanent registration system is used, the final date for registration will be October 17.

There are over 2,500,000 citizens eligible to vote in North Carolina. However, only about one-half of these voted in the Presidential election in 1956. There are two reasons for this failure—failure to register and lack of concern for public affairs.

It has been estimated that there are approximately 500,000 unregistered voters in North Carolina. The registration of these citizens is a great civic challenge and responsibility. As governor, I wish that every citizen of this state could understand that one of the most precious privileges of American citizenship is voting by secret ballot in free elections. Vote for the party of your choice, but *vote*.

Four-fifths of the people of the world have no voice in the government under which they live. But when we Americans compare our voting record with that of other free countries, it comes as a shock to realize that our turnout at the polls is far below theirs. Fifteen free countries have voting percentages from 95 per cent to 67 per cent in recent elections in comparison to the United States' 51 per cent in 1948, 62 per cent in 1952 and 60 per cent in 1956.

To be able to cast a ballot, the potential voter *must be registered*. In the 1956 Presidential election, some forty million Americans did not register and were therefore unable to vote. Every vote is important—your vote does count. Elections have been won by less than one vote per precinct.

I urge each eligible citizen of North Carolina to study the true issues in this campaign—be informed, register, and vote.

CORRECTING A STATEMENT IN REGARD TO THE BAPTISTS
TELEGRAM

September 30, 1960

[Sommerkamp had called Governor Hodges earlier in the day in regard to a news item in the *Chicago Tribune* of September 20, quoting the Governor as saying in his Chicago speech in favor of the Kennedy-Johnson ticket on September 19, that the Baptists "usually are against anybody who is not one of them," but that Kennedy and Johnson would carry North Carolina "in spite of the fact that the state has 800,000 Baptists." The *Biblical Recorder,* official publication of the Baptist State Convention, which had expressed shock at the Governor's alleged statement, accepted this correction as having been made in good faith. (See issues of October 1 and 8, 1960.)]

Mr. Theo Sommerkamp
Assistant Director
Southern Baptist News Service
Nashville, Tennessee

This confirms telephone conversation regarding quotation attributed to me in the *Chicago Tribune* about Baptists. I definitely do not recall making the statement quoted. Many subjects were covered in hour press and TV conferences. I do recall discussing in jest with reporters the idea that one would certainly be in trouble politically in North Carolina unless Baptists liked him because there are at least 800,000 Baptists in our state. I am a Methodist, but some of my own family and many close friends and appointees of mine to jobs and boards in North Carolina are

Baptists. I deeply regret that anything I may have said in jest during a lengthy press conference could have been construed as criticism of any denomination.

Luther H. Hodges
Governor of North Carolina

DENYING EXECUTIVE CLEMENCY FOR THE DEFENDANTS IN THE VANCE COUNTY CONSPIRACY CASE
TELEGRAM

October 26, 1960

[Sent to William M. Nicholson, J. Glen Ledford, and James B. Ledford of Charlotte; James J. Randleman of Elkin; and Hill Yarborough of Louisburg—attorneys who represented the defendants in this case.]

I have given careful consideration to the petition for executive clemency in the Vance County conspiracy case. I have personally read the briefs and record of this case as submitted to the North Carolina Supreme Court.

Under the laws of North Carolina a conspiracy to commit a crime is in and of itself a criminal offense. This is not a new law. The extent to which the criminal laws of this state were violated in this case and by whom was a matter appropriately decided by the trial jury in the Vance County Superior Court in July, 1959.

In accordance with the rights available to all persons, the defendants in this case have, since the trial fifteen months ago, availed themselves of appeal to the North Carolina Supreme Court and then to the United States Supreme Court. The decisions of the appellate courts are to the effect that the defendants have had a fair and impartial trial free of prejudical error.

The petition for executive clemency does not present any new evidence or information which was not available at the time of the trial. Rather the petition for executive clemency seems to me to be based on the premise that I should substitute my judgment for that of a twelve-man jury, and that I should reach the conclusion that the court processes in this case have somehow failed to do justice. If information had been placed before me showing that the defendants had not received a fair and impartial trial or showing that the defendants had been wrongfully convicted, I would have had some basis for exercise of executive clemency.

In addition to my own study and following the usual custom, I have had the State Board of Paroles make an independent and thorough review of this case. In its report to me, the board said, "There seems to be no doubt of guilt and had arrests not been made by the State Bureau of Investigation, there is every reason to believe that the dynamiting which was planned would have taken place . . . After a close study of these cases the recommendation of the Board of Paroles to the Governor is that no executive clemency be granted. We are further of the opinion that parole should be considered as in other cases when a sufficient amount of time has been served to make the defendants eligible for parole consideration."

I have earnestly endeavored to give this matter a completely conscientious and prayerful review. I regret that I must inform you that I cannot act favorably on the petition for executive clemency.

Luther H. Hodges
Governor of North Carolina

APPOINTMENTS

APPOINTMENTS

[This list includes only the appointments made by Governor Hodges during 1959 and 1960, the two years of his administration covered by this volume. It does not contain all the persons who served on the various boards, commissions, and other appointive agencies during this period. These may be found in the *North Carolina Manual, 1959* (issued by the Secretary of State), pp. 285-338. The arrangement of the agencies here follows the order in which they appear in the *Manual.*

An asterisk by a name indicates that the person was appointed and re-appointed by Governor Hodges. A dagger indicates appointment during a previous administration and reappointment by Governor Hodges. A dagger followed by an asterisk indicates appointment during a previous administration and two or more reappointments by Governor Hodges.]

Name of Appointee	Address	Date Appointed	Date of Expiration
PRIVATE SECRETARY [1]			
Harold T. Makepeace [2]	Sanford	1-1-60	At pleasure of the governor
ATTORNEY GENERAL, SOLICITORS, AND JUDGES			
ATTORNEY GENERAL [3]			
T. Wade Bruton [4]	Raleigh	2-27-60	12-31-60
SOLICITORS, SUPERIOR COURT [5]			
James E. Walker [6]	Charlotte	6-20-59	12-31-60
John B. Regan [7]	St. Pauls	6-22-59	12-31-60
Kenneth R. Downs [8]	Charlotte	6-17-60	12-31-60
Edward K. Washington [9]	Jamestown	12-7-60	12-31-62
JUDGES, SUPERIOR COURT [10]			
Rudolph I. Mintz [11]	Wilmington	1-29-59	12-31-60
Kenneth A. Pittman [12]	Snow Hill	9-22-60	12-31-60
SPECIAL JUDGES, SUPERIOR COURT [13]			
Susie Sharp† *	Reidsville	6-19-59	6-30-63
J. Braxton Craven *	Morganton	6-19-59	6-30-63
George M. Fountain† *	Tarboro	6-19-59	6-30-63
William Reid Thompson *	Pittsboro	6-19-59	6-30-63
W. Jack Hooks [14]	Kenly	12-10-59	6-30-63
EMERGENCY JUDGES, SUPERIOR COURT [15]			
J. Paul Frizzelle	Snow Hill	9-23-60	For life
JUSTICES OF THE SUPREME COURT OF NORTH CAROLINA [16]			
Clifton L. Moore [17]	Burgaw	1-29-59	General Election, 1960

ADMINISTRATIVE OFFICERS

DEPARTMENT OF ADMINISTRATION[18]

————Raleigh————   8-22-60

David S. Coltrane, *Director*[19]   At pleasure of the governor

---

[1] The governor shall appoint a private secretary who shall enter in books kept for that purpose all such letters, written to and by the governor, as are official and important, and such other letters as the governor shall think necessary. *Public Laws of North Carolina*, 1868, *Ch. 270; General Statues of North Carolina*, Sec. 147-14. (Hereinafter the *Public Laws of North Carolina* will be cited as *P. L.*, and the *General Statues of North Carolina* as *G. S.*)

[2] Succeeded Edward L. Rankin, Jr., resigned.

[3] The attorney general is an elective official, but appointed by the governor when there is a vacancy during the term, as in this instance, *G. S.*, Sec. 147-4; Constitution of North Carolina, Art. III, Secs. 1, 13.

[4] Succeeded Malcolm B. Seawell, resigned to run for governor.

[5] Solicitors are elected by the qualified voters of the state for a four-year term and hold office until their successors are qualified. Vacancies are filled by appointment of the governor until the next general election. The Constitution of North Carolina, Art. IV, Secs. 23 and 25; *P. L., 1868-1869*, Ch. 270, Sec. 27-3.

[6] Newly created district.

[7] Newly created district

[8] Succeeded James E. Walker, resigned.

[9] Succeeded Horace R. Kornegay, elected to Congress.

[10] Resident judges of the Superior Courts are elected for terms of eight years beginning in January following the general election. Vacancies are filled by appointment of the governor to serve until the next general election. *G. S.*, Sec. 7-40; *Session Laws of North Carolina*, 1955, Sec. 129. (Hereinafter the *Session Laws of North Carolina* will be cited as *S. L.*)

[11] Succeeded Clifton L. Moore, resigned to accept appointment on the Supreme Court.

[12] Succeeded J. Paul Frizzelle, resigned.

[13] The law provides for four special judges, two from the eastern judicial division and two from the western judicial division of the state, to be appointed by the governor for four-year terms. *G. S.*, Sec. 7-54, 56; *S. L., 1955*, Ch. 1016.

[15] Succeeded W. Reid Thompson, resigned.

[15] Any judge of the Superior Court who has attained the age of sixty-five years and has served fifteen years on the Superior Court bench may retire and become an emergency judge of the Superior Court. Constitution of North Carolina, Art. IV, Sec. II; *G. S.* Sec. 7-51.

[16] The Supreme Court of North Carolina is composed of seven justices elected by the people for terms of eight years each. Vacancies are filled by appointment of the governor, and justices thus appointed serve until the next general election. The Constitution of North Carolina, Art. III, Secs. 21 and 25; *P. L., 1901*, Ch. 89, Sec. 4; *P. L., 1937*, Ch. 16.

[17] Succeeded Jeff D. Johnson, Jr., resigned.

[18] This department was created by the 1957 General Assembly for the purpose of consolidating various functions in the state's administrative system. The director is appointed by the governor and is removable at the governor's pleasure. *S. L.* 1957, Ch. 269.

[19] Succeeded Paul A. Johnston, resigned.

Name of Appointee	Address	Date Appointed	Date of Expiration
GENERAL ASSEMBLY, 1959 [20]			
SENATE			
Ernest W. Ross [21]	Marion	1-28-59	End, 1959 General Assembly
George K. Snow [22]	Mount Airy	4-20-59	End, 1959 General Assembly
Henry T. Stevens, III [23]	Warsaw	9-11-59	End, 1959 General Assembly
HOUSE OF REPRESENTATIVES			
Roscoe D. McMillan, Jr. [24]	Red Springs	8-8-59	End, 1959 General Assembly
GOVERNMENTAL BOARDS AND COMMISSIONS			
ADVISORY BUDGET COMMISSION [25]			
J. Kemp Doughton*	Sparta	2-11-59	At pleasure of the governor
Joseph C. Eagles, Jr. [26]	Wilson	8-7-59	At pleasure of the governor
BOARD OF DIRECTORS OF THE NORTH CAROLINA AGRICULTURAL HALL OF FAME [27]			
I. O. Schaub*	Raleigh	1-28-59	1-27-65
STATE BOARD OF AGRICULTURE [28]			
Hoyle C. Griffin†	Monroe	8-7-59	5-4-65
George Kittrell†	Corapeake	8-7-59	5-4-65
Charles F. Phillips†	Thomasville	8-7-59	5-4-65
STATE BOARD OF ALCOHOLIC CONTROL [29]			
J. Clifton Newton, Jr.*	Shelby	6-18-59	4-22-62

STATE DEPARTMENT OF ARCHIVES AND HISTORY EXECUTIVE BOARD [30]

J. Burch Blalock[31]	Yanceyville	6-18-59	3-31-63
Ralph P. Hanes[32]	Winston-Salem	8-25-59	3-31-63
Gertrude Carraway†	New Bern	6-18-59	3-31-65
McDaniel Lewis†	Greensboro	6-18-59	3-31-65
Daniel J. Whitener[33]	Boone	6-18-59	3-31-65

[20] The governor follows the recommendation of the county executive committee of the political party to which the vacating legislator belongs in appointing a successor. Constitution of North Carolina, Art. II, Sec. 13; G. S., Sec. 163-6.

[21] Succeeded Robert L. James, resigned.

[22] Succeeded Fred Folger, resigned.

[23] Succeeded Grady Mercer, resigned to accept appointment on the State Industrial Commission.

[24] Succeeded John B. Regan, resigned to accept appointment as Superior Court solicitor.

[25] Six members, of whom two are appointed by the governor and serve at his pleasure. The other four are the chairmen of the Appropriations and Finance Committees of the House and Senate. The governor is ex officio director. G. S., Sec. 143-4.

[26] Succeeded J. William Copeland.

[27] This board is composed of three members appointed by the governor for six-year terms and five ex officio members specified by the legislature: the commissioner of agriculture, the director of the North Carolina Agricultural Extension Service, the state supervisor of vocational agriculture, the president of the North Carolina Farm Bureau Federation, and the master of the State Grange. S. L., 1953, Ch. 1129.

[28] Composed of the commissioner of agriculture, who is ex officio, and ten members serving six-year terms, appointed by the Governor with confirmation by the Senate. The members are to be so distributed as reasonably to represent the different sections and agricultural interests of the state, and all must be practical farmers engaged in their occupation. G. S., Sec. 106-2.

[29] Consists of a chairman and two associate members, all appointed by the governor for three-year terms. G. S., Sec. 18-37, 38.

[30] Seven members appointed by the governor for six-year terms. G. S., 121-1.

[31] Appointed to succeed H. V. Rose, deceased, but did not qualify. Blalock was register of deeds in Yancey County. Acceptance of this appointment would have constituted double officeholding.

[32] Succeeded H. V. Rose.

[33] Succeeded William T. LaPrade.

Name of Appointee	Address	Date Appointed	Date of Expiration
DEPARTMENT OF ARCHIVES AND HISTORY, SPECIAL PEACE OFFICERS [54]			
Stanley A. South	Wilmington	1-20-60	At will of the governor
Helmuth J. Naumer	Mount Gilead	1-20-60	At will of the governor
Richard W. Sawyer	Durham	1-20-60	At will of the governor
Ava L. Honeycutt, Jr.	Raleigh	1-20-60	At will of the governor
Nicholas B. Bragg	Raleigh	1-20-60	At will of the governor
Robert O. Conway	Asheville	1-20-60	At will of the governor
Walter R. Wootten[35]	Burlington	7-21-60	At will of the governor
ARMORY COMMISSION [35]			
Edward F. Griffin[37]	Raleigh	5-1-59	At pleasure of the governor
STATE ART COMMISSION [38]			
Egbert L. Davis*	Winston-Salem	8-7-59	8-1-61
Edwin M. Gill†	Raleigh	8-7-59	8-1-61
Clemens Sommer†	Chapel Hill	8-7-59	8-1-61
BOARD OF DIRECTORS OF THE NORTH CAROLINA ART SOCIETY, INCORPORATED [39]			
Robert L. Humbert†	Greenville	6-19-59	5-1-63
Ralph C. Price*	Greensboro	6-19-59	5-1-63
Mrs. Charles Brantley Aycock[40]	Kinston	3-30-60	5-1-61
ATLANTIC STATES MARINE FISHERIES COMMISSION [41]			
Walton S. Griggs*	Point Harbor	7-7-60	6-20-63
ATOMIC ENERGY ADVISORY COMMITTEE			
Atwell Alexander	Stony Point	9-11-59	7-1-61
Fred C. Alexander	Charlotte	9-11-59	7-1-61
Killian Barwick	Elizabeth City	9-11-59	7-1-61

J. W. Bean	Raleigh	9-11-59	7-1-61
Wilbur H. Currie	Carthage	9-11-59	7-1-61
R. H. Goodman	Williamston	9-11-59	7-1-61
John I. Hopkins	Davidson	9-11-59	7-1-61
William M. Peck	Raleigh	9-11-59	7-1-61
B. J. Romeo	Hendersonville	9-11-59	7-1-61
Sheldon P. Smith	Charlotte	9-11-59	7-1-61
John C. Brauer	Chapel Hill	9-11-59	7-1-63
Emil T. Chanlett	Chapel Hill	9-11-59	7-1-63
Henry T. Clark, Jr.	Chapel Hill	9-11-59	7-1-63
J. C. Cowan, Jr.	Burlington	9-11-59	7-1-63
William F. Henderson	Raleigh	9-11-59	7-1-63
J. J. Hill	Charlotte	9-11-59	7-1-63
T. H. LeCroy	Rocky Mount	9-11-59	7-1-63

[34] Upon application of the director of the Department of Archives and History, the governor is authorized to commission as special peace officers, such of the employees of the department as the director may designate for the purpose of enforcing the laws, rules, and regulations adopted for the protection, preservation, and government of state historic or archeological properies under the department's control. G. S., Sec. 121-9; S. L., 1955, Ch. 543.

[35] Succeeded Ava L. Honeycutt, Jr.

[36] The commission is composed of five members, two of whom are appointed by the governor. The remaining three are ex officio members as follows: the governor, who is chairman, the attorney general, and the adjutant general. S. L., 1947, Ch. 1010.

[37] Succeeded Claude T. Bowers, resigned.

[38] Composed of five members appointed by the governor for two-year terms. G.S., Sec. 140-5.5.

[39] Sixteen members, four of whom are appointed by the governor for a term of four years, eight of whom are chosen by the members of the North Carolina State Art Society, Incorporated, and four of whom are ex officio members, as follows: the governor, the superintendent of public instruction, the attorney general, and the chairman of the Art Committee of the North Carolina Federation of Woman's Clubs, G. S., Sec. 140-1.

[40] Succeeded Mrs. Charles A. Cannon, resigned.

[41] Three members, appointed for three years, from each state which is represented on this commission. Of the members from North Carolina, two serve ex officio, one of whom is designated by the Board of Conservation and Development, and the other is a member of the legislature designated by the state Commission on Interstate Cooperation. The third member is appointed by the governor. S. L., 1949, Ch. 1086.

Name of Appointee	Address	Date Appointed	Date of Expiration
John D. Messick	Greenville	9-11-59	7-1-63
Robert J. Reeves	Durham	9-11-59	7-1-63
H. B. Robinson	Raleigh	9-11-59	7-1-63
E. Jack Story	Raleigh	9-11-59	7-1-63
William D. Carmichael, Chairman	Chapel Hill	9-11-59	7-1-65
C. C. Carpenter	Winston-Salem	9-11-59	7-1-65
D. W. Colvard	Raleigh	9-11-59	7-1-65
Frank Crane	Raleigh	9-11-59	7-1-65
Wilburt C. Davison	Durham	9-11-59	7-1-65
Paul Gross	Durham	9-11-59	7-1-65
Edwin L. Jones	Charlotte	9-11-59	7-1-65
A. C. Menius, Jr.	Raleigh	9-11-59	7-1-65
H. W. Oetinger	Charlotte	9-11-59	7-1-65
William P. Saunders	Raleigh	9-11-59	7-1-65
William M. Whyburn	Chapel Hill	9-11-59	7-1-65
William L. Wilson[43]	Raleigh	1-21-60	7-1-61
E. C. Fiss[44]	Charlotte	6-9-60	7-1-65
Leo W. Jenkins[45]	Greenville	6-24-60	7-1-63
H. Brooks James[46]	Raleigh	6-24-60	7-1-65

STATE ADVISORY COMMITTEE OF AVIATION[47]

Name of Appointee	Address	Date Appointed	Date of Expiration
Alexander B. Andrews	Raleigh	8-31-59	At pleasure of the governor
L. P. Broadfield	Rocky Mount	8-31-59	At pleasure of the governor
J. Tolliver Davis	Forest City	8-31-59	At pleasure of the governor
Thomas H. Davis	Winston-Salem	8-31-59	At pleasure of the governor
John C. Erwin	Charlotte	8-31-59	At pleasure of the governor
Carl Goerch	Raleigh	8-31-59	At pleasure of the governor
LeRoy Sossaman	Bryson City	8-31-59	At pleasure of the governor

CHARLES B. AYCOCK MEMORIAL COMMISSION [65]

B. F. Aycock†*	Fremont	6-18-59	5-24-65
Henry Belk†*	Goldsboro	6-18-59	5-24-65
William A. Dees, Sr.*	Goldsboro	6-18-59	5-24-65
Hugh Dortch†*	Goldsboro	6-18-59	5-24-65
Joseph C. Eagles, Jr.†*	Wilson	6-18-59	5-24-65
Frank P. Graham*	New York	6-18-59	5-24-65
Mrs. Fred Harrell†*	Goldsboro	6-18-59	5-24-65
Mrs. Ruth Pate Killette†*	Goldsboro	6-18-59	5-24-65
Emmett Robertson†*	Goldsboro	6-18-59	5-24-65
H. L. Stephenson†*	Smithfield	6-18-59	5-24-65
Hardy Talton*	Pikeville	6-18-59	5-24-65
Miss Gertrude Weil†*	Goldsboro	6-18-59	5-24-65

STATE BANKING COMMISSION [49]

Edwin P. Brown*	Murfreesboro	8-10-59	4-1-63
Edwin Duncan*	Sparta	8-10-59	4-1-63

---

[42] Thirty-five members, of whom thirty-two are appointed by the governor and three are ex officio: the commissioner of agriculture, the state superintendent of public instruction, and the state health director. Initial appointments were for two-, four-, and six-year terms. Reappointments are for six years. S. L., 1959, Ch. 48.

[43] Succeeded William M. Peck, resigned.

[44] Succeeded H. W. Oettinger, resigned.

[45] Succeeded John D. Messick.

[46] Succeeded D. W. Colvard.

[47] Seven members appointed by the governor to serve at his pleasure. S. L., 1959, Res. 79.

[48] Twenty-one members, three of whom, the director of the Department of Archives and History, the superintendent of public instruction, and the director of the Department of Conservation and Development, serve as ex officio members, and eighteen are appointed by the governor for six-year terms. S. L., 1949, Ch. 1021.

[49] Nine members appointed by the governor for four-year terms, plus the state treasurer (who serves as chairman) and the attorney general, who are ex officio. The commissioner is appointed by the governor with the approval of the Senate. G. S., Sec. 53-92; S. L., 1949, Ch. 372; S. L., 1953, Ch. 1209.

Name of Appointee	Address	Date Appointed	Date of Expiration
John P. Stedman*	Lumberton	8-10-59	4-1-63
G. Harold Myrick[50]	Lincolnton	8-10-59	4-1-63
Commissioner of Banks			
Ben R. Roberts*	Durham	4-1-59	4-1-63

HISTORIC BATH COMMISSION [51]

Name of Appointee	Address	Date Appointed	Date of Expiration
W. Harold Butt	Charleston, South Carolina	9-24-59	Term indefinite
Edmund Harding	Washington	9-24-59	Term indefinite
Grayson Harding	Edenton	9-24-59	Term indefinite
Mrs. Ernest L. Ives	Southern Pines	9-24-59	Term indefinite
Mrs. Edmund T. Knott	Washington	9-24-59	Term indefinite
Mrs. John W. Labouisse	Durham	9-24-59	Term indefinite
Mrs. Fred W. Morrison	Washington, D. C.	9-24-59	Term indefinite
Rev. A. C. D. Noe	Bath	9-24-59	Term indefinite
Dan M. Paul	Raleigh	9-24-59	Term indefinite
Wayland J. Sermons	Washington	9-24-59	Term indefinite
Mrs. Oscar Smith	Norfolk, Virginia	9-24-59	Term indefinite
Mrs. Wilton Smith	Bath	9-24-59	Term indefinite
Mrs. Mary Fowle Stearns	Raleigh	9-24-59	Term indefinite
Mrs. Rachel Tankard	Bath	9-24-59	Term indefinite
Lindsay C. Warren	Washington	9-24-59	Term indefinite

STATE COMMISSION FOR THE BLIND [52]

Name of Appointee	Address	Date Appointed	Date of Expiration
Sam Alford†*	Henderson	5-20-60	5-21-65
Sam M. Cathey†*	Asheville	5-20-60	5-21-65

NORTH CAROLINA BOARD OF BOILER RULES [53]

Name of Appointee	Address	Date Appointed	Date of Expiration
William W. Lloyd†	Greensboro	6-19-59	6-18-64

William M. Reading, Jr.*	Kinston	7-5-60	6-18-65
William C. Wallin[54]	Winston-Salem	10-28-60	6-18-64

BUILDING CODE COUNCIL [55]

Richard F. Booth*	Raleigh	8-7-59	7-31-65
Verne G. Moser*	Asheville	8-7-59	7-31-65
S. Warren Sanders, Jr.*	Wilmington	8-6-59	7-31-65
J. Sidney Kirk[56]	Raleigh	8-7-59	7-31-63
Jack H. Rogers[57]	Asheville	6-27-60	7-31-65

COMMISSION TO STUDY THE CAUSE AND CONTROL OF CANCER IN NORTH CAROLINA[58]

Ozmer L. Henry, *Chairman*	Lumberton	9-2-59	Report to the governor by Jan. 1, 1961
Dr. Rachel Davis, *Vice-Chairman*	Kinston	9-2-59	Report to the governor by Jan. 1, 1961
Mrs. H. L. Bacon	Bryson City	9-2-59	Report to the governor by Jan. 1, 1961

[50] Succeeded M. B. Fowler, resigned.

[51] Eighteen members, of whom fifteen are appointed by the governor and three are ex officio: the director of the Department of Archives and History, the chairman of the Beaufort County Board of Commissioners, and the mayor of Bath. S. L., 1959, Ch. 1005.

[52] Eleven members, of whom six are appointed by the governor to serve terms of five years. The superintendent of the State School for the Blind and Deaf, the state supervisor of vocational rehabilitation, the secretary of the State Board of Health, the director of the North Carolina Employment Service, and the commissioner of public welfare are ex officio members. G. S., Sec. 111-1, 2, 3.

[53] Six members, of whom five are appointed by the governor for terms of five years each. The sixth member is the commissioner of labor, who serves ex officio and is chairman of the board. Of the five appointive members one is a representative of the owners and users of steam boilers within the state, one a representative of the boiler manufacturers or boilermakers within the state, one a representative of a boiler inspection and insurance company licensed to do business in North Carolina, and one a licensed heating contractor. Any vacancy is filled with a representative of the same class. G. S., Sec. 95-54; S. L., 1953, Ch. 569.

[54] Succeeded William W. Lloyd, deceased.

[55] Nine members appointed by the governor for six-year terms. S. L., 1957, Ch. 1138.

[56] Succeeded R. E. Vick, resigned.

[57] Succeeded Verne G. Moser, deceased.

[58] Twenty members appointed by the governor. Successor to a similar commission authorized by the 1957 General Assembly. All members of the 1957 commission were reappointed by the governor and directed to report to him by January 1, 1961. S. L., 1957, Res. 34; S. L., 1959, Res. 78.

Name of Appointee	Address	Date Appointed	Date of Expiration
Mrs. Lucille Beasley	Colerain	9-2-59	Report to the governor by Jan. 1, 1961
Dr. D. H. Bridger	Bladenboro	9-2-59	Report to the governor by Jan. 1, 1961
Mrs. Alfonso Elder	Durham	9-2-59	Report to the governor by Jan. 1, 1961
Dr. J. Grady Faulk	Monroe	9-2-59	Report to the governor by Jan. 1, 1961
R. M. Kermon	Wilmington	9-2-59	Report to the governor by Jan. 1, 1961
Dr. John R. Kernodle	Burlington	9-2-59	Report to the governor by Jan. 1, 1961
Dr. Mark McD. Lindsey	Hamlet	9-2-59	Report to the governor by Jan. 1, 1961
Dr. James F. Marshall	Winston-Salem	9-2-59	Report to the governor by Jan. 1, 1961
Tom G. Maxwell	Hickory	9-2-59	Report to the governor by Jan. 1, 1961
Mrs. John C. Murrill	Jacksonville	9-2-59	Report to the governor by Jan. 1, 1961
Dr. Zack Owens	Elizabeth City	9-2-59	Report to the governor by Jan. 1, 1961
K. A. Pittman	Snow Hill	9-2-59	Report to the governor by Jan. 1, 1961
Dr. Hubert M. Poteat, Jr.	Smithfield	9-2-59	Report to the governor by Jan. 1, 1961
Dr. David L. Pressley	Statesville	9-2-59	Report to the governor by Jan. 1, 1961
Dr. James S. Raper	Asheville	9-2-59	Report to the governor by Jan. 1, 1961
Mrs. Grace Taylor Rodenbough	Walnut Cove	9-2-59	Report to the governor by Jan. 1, 1961
H. Fields Young, Jr.	Shelby	9-2-59	Report to the governor by Jan. 1, 1961

The North Carolina Cape Hatteras Seashore Commission [59]

Name of Appointee	Address	Date Appointed	Date of Expiration
Carlos D. Oden [60]	Hatteras	8-8-60	1-12-62
Eric W. Rodgers [61]	Scotland Neck	8-8-60	At pleasure of the governor

Governor Richard Caswell Memorial Commission [62]

Name of Appointee	Address	Date Appointed	Date of Expiration
W. Lamont Brown [63]	Southern Pines	6-20-59	11-30-65
Mrs. J. Roger Brooks*	Kinston	11-27-59	11-30-67
Mrs. Inglis Fletcher*	Edenton	11-27-59	11-30-67
Paul A. Rockwell*	Asheville	11-27-59	11-30-67
J. Carlyle Sitterson*	Chapel Hill	11-27-59	11-30-67

CAROLINA CHARTER TERCENTENARY COMMISSION [64]

Francis E. Winslow, *Chairman*	Rocky Mount	9-3-59
Henry Belk	Goldsboro	9-3-59
Winston Broadfoot	Hillsboro	9-3-59
Horace H. Cunningham	Elon College	9-3-59
Chalmers G. Davidson	Davidson	9-3-59
Lambert Davis	Chapel Hill	9-3-59
Mrs. Inglis Fletcher	Edenton	9-3-59
Paul Green	Chapel Hill	9-3-59
Grayson Harding	Edenton	9-3-59
Mrs. William Daniel Holmes, Jr.	Edenton	9-3-59
Mrs. Robert Grady Johnson	Burgaw	9-3-59
Mrs. Kauno A. Lehto	Wilmington	9-3-59
James G. W. MacLamroch	Greensboro	9-3-59
Mrs. Harry McMullan	Washington	9-3-59
Ben Dixon MacNeill	Buxton	9-3-59
Paul Murray	Greenville	9-3-59
Robert H. Spiro, Jr.	Black Mountain	9-3-59
George M. Stephens	Asheville	9-3-59

9-1-61 (appears for each row)

---

[59] Five members appointed by the governor for four-year terms and four ex officio members consisting of the director of the Department of Conservation and Development and three members of the Board of Conservation and Development designated by the governor and serving at his pleasure. *P. L., 1939, Ch.* 257.

[60] Succeeded Ben Dixon MacNeill, deceased.

[61] Succeeded Cecil Morris as ex officio member from the Board of Conservation and Development.

[62] Twenty members, sixteen appointed by the governor for eight-year terms and four ex officio (the director of the State Department of Archives and History, the state superintendent of public instruction, the mayor of Kinston, and the chairman of the Board of County Commissioners of Lenoir County). *S. L., 1955, Ch.* 977.

[63] Succeeded Ray Galloway, deceased.

[64] Twenty-two members appointed by the governor for two-year terms plus three ex officio members: the superintendent of public instruction, the director of the Department of Archives and History, and the director of the Department of Conservation and Development. *S. L., 1959, Ch.* 1238.

Name of Appointee	Address	Date Appointed	Date of Expiration
Gilbert T. Stephenson	Pendleton	9-3-59	9-1-61
David Stick	Kill Devil Hills	9-3-59	9-1-61
Mrs. J. O. Tally, Jr.	Fayetteville	9-3-59	9-1-61
J. E. Winslow	Hertford	9-3-59	9-1-61
D. Victor Meekins[65]	Manteo	7-29-60	9-1-61
North Carolina State Civil Air Patrol Agency [66]			
Lloyd Griffin*	Raleigh	9-15-59	9-1-61
Charles T. Hagan, Jr.*	Greensboro	9-15-59	9-1-61
Frank O. Sherrill*	Charlotte	9-15-59	9-1-61
North Carolina Civil Defense Agency [67]			
Edward F. Griffin, *Director*†[68]	Louisburg	8-7-59	At pleasure of the governor
Commercial Fisheries Advisory Board [69]			
A. Winfield Daniels*	Charlotte	8-18-59	7-1-63
Lewis J. Hardee*	Southport	8-18-59	7-1-63
Ralph Meekins[70]	Wanchese	8-18-59	7-1-63
Percy G. Grant[71]	Holly Ridge	8-16-60	7-1-64
Monroe Gaskill*	Cedar Island	8-16-60	7-1-64
North Carolina Confederate Centennial Commission [72]			
Hugh Dortch, *Chairman*	Goldsboro	9-11-59	9-1-61
Mrs. E. A. Anderson	Charlotte	9-11-59	9-1-61
W. H. S. Burgwyn	Woodland	9-11-59	9-1-61
Mrs. D. S. Coltrane	Raleigh	9-11-59	9-1-61
Mrs. G. W. Cover	Andrews	9-11-59	9-1-61
Burke Davis	Greensboro	9-11-59	9-1-61
Mrs. Bettie Sue Gardner	Reidsville	9-11-59	9-1-61

Robert R. Garvey, Jr.	Winston-Salem	9-11-59	9-1-61
W. S. Jenkins	Chapel Hill	9-11-59	9-1-61
Frontis W. Johnston	Davidson	9-11-59	9-1-61
Fitzhugh H. Lee	Goldsboro	9-11-59	9-1-61
Hugh T. Lefler	Chapel Hill	9-11-59	9-1-61
James S. Lewis, Jr.	Goldsboro	9-11-59	9-1-61
Mrs. Mary Jane McCrary	Brevard	9-11-59	9-1-61
Hector MacLean	Lumberton	9-11-59	9-1-61
R. Hunt Parker	Raleigh	9-11-59	9-1-61
John R. Peacock	High Point	9-11-59	9-1-61
R. F. Hoke Pollock	Southern Pines	9-11-59	9-1-61
William B. Rodman, Jr.	Raleigh	9-11-59	9-1-61
Reed Sarratt	Winston-Salem	9-11-59	9-1-61

[65] Succeeded Ben Dixon MacNeill, deceased.

[66] This agency is composed of three members appointed by the governor, and six ex officio members specified by the General Assembly: the adjutant general of the state of North Carolina and the deputy wing commander, the executive officer, the adjutant, the communication officer, and the co-ordinator of the civil defense of the North Carolina Wing of the Civil Air Patrol. Members serve a term of two years, and vacancies in the appointive membership are filled by the governor, who may also remove any member appointed by him. G. S., Sec. 167-1; S. L., 1953, Ch. 1231.

[67] One member appointed by the governor to serve at his will and six ex officio members: the governor, who acts as chairman; the commissioner of motor vehicles, who acts as executive vice-chairman; the executive secretary of the State Board of Health; the chancellor of North Carolina State College; the director of the State Bureau of Investigation; and the general counsel for the North Carolina League of Municipalities. G. S., Sec. 166-3, 4.

[68] Griffin had served as director since 1954, but was reappointed in consequence of changes in the law made by the 1959 General Assembly. S. L., 1959, Ch. 337.

[69] Composed of seven members, appointed by the governor for four-year terms: one from the Southport area; one from the New River Inlet area; one from the Morehead area; one from the Pamlico area; one from the Hatteras area; one from the Albemarle area; and one from the state at large, to be designated as chairman. S. L., 1955, Ch. 1031.

[70] Succeeded Arnold Daniels, resigned.

[71] Succeeded Eric Rodgers, appointed to Board of Conservation and Development.

[72] Twenty-five members appointed by the governor for two-year terms plus three ex officio members: the superintendent of public instruction, the director of the Department of Archives and History, and the director of the Department of Conservation and Development. S. L., 1959, Ch. 323.

Name of Appointee	Address	Date Appointed	Date of Expiration
James Stikeleather	Asheville	9-11-59	9-1-61
Henry S. Stroupe	Winston-Salem	9-11-59	9-1-61
Glenn Tucker	Flat Rock	9-11-59	9-1-61
Robert H. Woody	Durham	9-11-59	9-1-61
Thomas H. Wright, Jr.	Wilmington	9-11-59	9-1-61
H. Galt Braxton[73]	Kinston	9-2-60	9-1-61
Mrs. Charles U. Harris[74]	Raleigh	9-19-60	9-1-61

BOARD OF CONSERVATION AND DEVELOPMENT

Name of Appointee	Address	Date Appointed	Date of Expiration
D. G. Bell[76]	Morehead City	6-22-59	6-30-65
Orton A. Boren[77]	Greensboro	8-10-59	6-30-61
Edwin Pate[78]	Laurinburg	8-10-59	6-30-61
W. B. Austin†	Jefferson	8-10-59	6-30-65
Carl Buchan, Jr.†	North Wilkesboro	8-10-59	6-30-65
H. C. Kennett*	Durham	8-10-59	6-30-65
Hugh M. Morton†	Linville and Wilmington	8-10-59	6-30-65
T. Max Watson†	Forest City	8-10-59	6-30-65
Eric Rodgers[79]	Scotland Neck	7-21-60	6-30-65
B. C. Trotter[80]	Leaksville	7-21-60	6-30-61
John M. Akers[81]	Gastonia	11-11-60	6-30-65

SPECIAL PEACE OFFICERS FOR DIVISION OF PARKS, DEPARTMENT OF CONSERVATION AND DEVELOPMENT[82]

Name of Appointee	Address	Date Appointed	Date of Expiration
Paul T. Myers[83]	State Park Ranger	12-22-58	At pleasure of the governor
Myers G. Braxton[84]	Park Superintendent	12-23-58	At pleasure of the governor
Robert G. Stanley*[85]	Assistant Lake Warden	5-14-59-60	At pleasure of the governor
Henry T. Hood*	Lake Warden	5-14-59-60	At pleasure of the governor
Tracy R. Wallace*[86]	Lake Warden	5-14-59-60	At pleasure of the governor

Name	Position	Date	
Robert J. Spear*	Park Attendant	6-19-59	At pleasure of the governor
Purvis Stevens*	Assistant Lake Warden	6-22-59-60	At pleasure of the governor
Clyde Hopson	Park Ranger	7-20-59	At pleasure of the governor
Clyde H. Miller[87]	Park Ranger	9-8-59	At pleasure of the governor
Charles H. Milton	Park Ranger	4-5-60	At pleasure of the governor
Haywood L. Dillard*	Park Ranger	5-13-60	At pleasure of the governor
Rushian L. Gibson	Assistant Lake Warden	7-15-60	At pleasure of the governor
Philip L. Gray[88]	Park Ranger	7-15-60	At pleasure of the governor
Allen R. Conley, Jr.[89]	Park Ranger	11-17-60	At pleasure of the governor
James C. Johnson	Park Superintendent	11-17-60	At pleasure of the governor
Charles O. Lucas[90]	Park Ranger	11-17-60	At pleasure of the governor

[73] Succeeded Reed Sarratt, resigned.
[74] Succeeded Robert R. Garvey, Jr.
[75] Eighteen members appointed by the governor for six-year terms. G. S., Sec. 113-4, 5, 9; S. L., 1957, Ch. 1428.
[76] Succeeded Cecil Morris, resigned.
[77] Succeeded Robert M. Hanes, deceased.
[78] Succeeded Leo Harvey, deceased.
[79] Succeeded D. G. Bell, resigned.
[80] Succeeded Charles S. Allen, deceased.
[81] Succeeded Carl Buchan, Jr., deceased.
[82] These officers are employees of the Department of Conservation and Development, designated by the director of that department, and commissioned by the governor to serve at his pleasure. S. L., 1947, Ch. 577.
[83] Succeeded John D. Barnett.
[84] Succeeded Paul B. Berry.
[85] Succeeded Tracy R. Wallace.
[86] Succeeded Joshia C. Lamm.
[87] Succeeded James C. Gulledge.
[88] Succeeded John R. Wilson, resigned.
[89] Succeeded Philip L. Gray.
[90] Succeeded Raiford F. McKinley.

Name of Appointee	Address	Date Appointed	Date of Expiration
STATE BOARD OF CORRECTION AND TRAINING [91]			
Paul B. Bissette†	Wilson	8-12-59	7-1-65
M. S. Hayworth†	Rocky Mount	8-12-59	7-1-65
Clyde A. Dillon†	Raleigh	8-12-59	7-1-65
ADVISORY COMMITTEE ON EDUCATION [92]			
Thomas J. Pearsall, Chairman*	Rocky Mount	6-20-59	6-21-61
W. Lunsford Crew*	Roanoke Rapids	6-20-59	6-21-61
R. O. Huffman*	Morganton	6-20-59	6-21-61
William T. Joyner*	Raleigh	6-20-59	6-21-61
H. Cloyd Philpott*	Lexington	6-20-59	6-21-61
James G. Stikeleather*	Asheville	6-20-59	6-21-61
Edward F. Yarborough*	Louisburg	6-20-59	6-21-61
STATE BOARD OF EDUCATION [93]			
Charles E. Jordan*	Durham	8-26-59	4-1-67
George Douglas Aitken[94]	Charlotte	8-26-59	4-1-67
NORTH CAROLINA BOARD OF HIGHER EDUCATION [95]			
W. J. Kennedy, Jr.*	Durham	6-20-59	6-30-67
Oliver C. Carmichael*	Biltmore	6-20-59	6-30-67
William F. Womble[96]	Winston-Salem	5-6-60	6-30-63
John P. Kennedy, Jr.[97]	Charlotte	5-6-60	6-30-63
COMMISSION TO STUDY THE PUBLIC SCHOOL EDUCATION OF EXCEPTIONALLY TALENTED CHILDREN [98]			
C. D. Killian, Chairman	Cullowhee	9-1-59	Report to the 1961 General Assembly
Cecil Prince	Charlotte	9-1-59	Report to the 1961 General Assembly

Charles G. Reavis	Yadkinville	8-31-59	Report to the 1961 General Assembly
Henry G. Shelton	Speed	8-31-59	Report to the 1961 General Assembly
J. Raynor Woodward	Conway	8-31-59	Report to the 1961 General Assembly

STATE BOARD OF HEALTH [115]

B. W. Dawsey[116]	Gastonia	8-13-59	5-1-63
Jasper Carlton Jackson[117]	Lumberton	8-13-59	5-1-63

[102] Five members appointed by the governor for four-year terms. Not more than three of the members may be of the same political party, G. S., Sec. 173-8.

[103] Succeeded B. C. Trotter, resigned.

[104] Succeeded David M. McConnell, resigned.

[105] Succeeded Mrs. Charles W. Tillett, resigned.

[106] Seven members appointed by the governor for four-year terms. The governor designates the chairman. G. S., Sec. 96-3.

[107] The Advisory Council is composed of an equal number of employee representatives and such members representing the general public as the governor may designate. G. S., Sec. 96-4 (e).

[108] Succeeded W. A. Egerton.

[109] Five members, three of whom are appointed by the governor for four-year terms and two of whom are ex officio: the state insurance commissioner, who serves as chairman, and the state auditor. S. L., 1959, Ch. 1212.

[110] One member of this board is appointed by the director of agricultural extension or any other public official or commission, in this case the governor. G. S., Sec. 54-146 (b).

[111] Nine members appointed for two-year terms as follows: one each by the presidents of the North Carolina State Bar and North Carolina Bar Association; one each by the deans of the Law Schools of Duke, Wake Forest, and the University of North Carolina, one each by the president of the Senate and the speaker of the House of Representatives of the General Assembly, and two by the governor. G. S., Sec. 164-14 (a).

[112] Succeeded James H. Pou Bailey.

[113] Succeeded Buxton Midyette.

[114] Five members appointed by the governor to make recommendations to the 1961 General Assembly. S. L., 1959, Res. 65.

[115] Composed of nine members serving terms of four years, five of whom are appointed by the governor and four of whom are elected by the North Carolina Medical Society. G. S., Sec. 130-1, 7.

[116] Succeeded John P. Henderson, Jr.

[117] Succeeded H. C. Lutz.

Name of Appointee	Address	Date Appointed	Date of Expiration
STATE HIGHWAY COMMISSION [118]			
J. Melville Broughton, Jr., *Chairman**	Raleigh	8-19-59	6-30-61
Robert Bunnelle*	Asheville	8-19-59	6-30-63
James W. Mason*	Laurinburg	8-19-59	6-30-63
Lee White*	Concord	8-19-59	6-30-63
Robert T. Morris[119]	New Bern	8-20-59	6-30-61
Stanley R. Betts[120]	Henderson	8-2-60	6-30-61
NORTH CAROLINA HOSPITALS BOARD OF CONTROL [121]			
R. P. Richardson† *	Reidsville	8-13-59	4-1-63
Isaac D. Thorpe*	Rocky Mount	8-13-59	4-1-63
John W. Umstead† *	Chapel Hill	8-13-59	4-1-63
Dewey H. Bridger* [122]	Bladenboro	8-13-59	4-1-60-64
R. V. Liles[123]	Wadesboro	4-11-60	4-1-64
George R. Uzzell[124]	Salisbury	4-11-60	4-1-64
NORTH CAROLINA HOSPITAL BOARD OF CONTROL ADVISORY COMMITTEE [125]			
Robert J. Andrews	Roxboro	1-15-59	12-31-62
Harold L. Bacon	Bryson City	1-15-59	12-31-62
George W. Blair, Jr.	Burlington	1-15-59	12-31-62
D. H. Bridger	Bladenboro	1-15-59	12-31-62
E. W. Busse	Durham	1-15-59	12-31-62
Fred Falls	Shelby	1-15-59	12-31-62
John C. Foushee	Windsor	1-15-59	12-31-62
George C. Ham†	Chapel Hill	1-15-59	12-31-62
J. T. Llewellyn	Williamston	1-15-59	12-31-62
David A. Lockhart	Kannapolis	1-15-59	12-31-62

Robert M. McMillian	Southern Pines	1-15-59	12-31-62
A. C. Randolph	Winston-Salem	1-15-59	12-31-62
John C. Reese	Morganton	1-15-59	12-31-62
C. T. Smith	Rocky Mount	1-15-59	12-31-62
Winfield L. Thompson	Goldsboro	1-15-59	12-31-62
Graham B. Barefoot[216]	Wilmington	11-16-59	12-31-62

EASTERN CAROLINA REGIONAL HOUSING AUTHORITY [217]

W. Jack Hooks[218]	Kenly	8-18-59	4-10-60
Robert L. McMillan, Jr.*[219]	Raleigh	2-8-60	4-10-60-65

[118] Seven members appointed by the governor for four-year terms. The governor designates one member to be chairman for two years. S. L., 1957, Ch. 65.

[119] Succeeded E. L. White, deceased.

[120] Succeeded Fletcher H. Gregory, Jr., resigned.

[121] Consists of fifteen members appointed by the governor for four-year terms. There must be one member from each of the twelve Congressional districts and three at large. The institutions combined under this board are: The State Hospital, Raleigh; the State Hospital, Morganton; the State Hospital, Goldsboro; the State Hospital, Butner; and the Caswell Training School, Kinston. G. S., Sec. 122-7; S. L., 1943, Ch. 136; S. L., 1945, Ch. 925; S. L., 1947, Ch. 537.

[122] Succeeded Mrs. E. F. McCulloch, resigned; reappointed for four-year term on April 11, 1960.

[123] Succeeded John Ruggles.

[124] Succeeded Bedford W. Black.

[125] Fifteen members appointed by the governor for four-year terms. The committee is not statutory but was created by resolution of the Hospitals Board of Control in 1945.

[126] Succeeded D. H. Bridger, appointed to the Hospitals Board of Control.

[127] If the area of a regional housing authority consists at any time of an even number of counties, the governor of North Carolina shall appoint one additional commissioner to such regional housing authority, whose term of office shall be for five years, except that such term shall end at any earlier time that the area of operation shall be changed to consist of an odd number of counties. G. S., Sec. 157-36.

[128] Succeeded Martin Lee Black, resigned to accept appointment on Board of Certified Public Accountant Examiners.

[129] Succeeded W. Jack Hooks, resigned to become special judge of the Superior Court; reappointed for five-year term on April 28, 1960.

Name of Appointee	Address	Date Appointed	Date of Expiration
NORTH CAROLINA INDUSTRIAL COMMISSION [130]			
Grady Mercer[131]	Beulaville	8-27-59	5-1-63
INSURANCE ADVISORY BOARD [132]			
Robert G. Deyton[133]	Raleigh	9-15-59	9-1-63
H. P. Mobley*	Williamston	9-15-59	9-1-63
Max O. Welborn*	Yadkinville	9-15-59	9-1-63
NORTH CAROLINA COMMISSION ON INTERSTATE COOPERATION [134]			
Paul A. Johnston	Raleigh	8-25-59	6-30-61
Malcolm B. Seawell	Raleigh	8-25-59	6-30-61
George Randall	Raleigh	8-25-59	6-30-61
T. Wade Bruton[135]	Raleigh	3-4-60	6-30-61
David S. Coltrane[136]	Raleigh	9-9-60	6-30-61
JUDICIAL COUNCIL [137]			
Ike F. Andrews[138]	Siler City	8-13-59	6-30-61
John C. Kessler[139]	Salisbury	8-13-59	6-30-61
JOHN H. KERR RESERVOIR DEVELOPMENT COMMISSION [140]			
John P. Swain[141]	Raleigh	9-18-59	7-26-63
A. Leonidas Hux†	Roanoke Rapids	8-7-59	7-26-65
L. R. Taylor*	Jackson	8-7-59	7-26-65
STATE LEGISLATIVE BUILDING COMMISSION [142]			
A. E. Finley	Raleigh	8-24-59	Until completion of assigned duties
Edwin M. Gill	Raleigh	8-24-59	Until completion of assigned duties
Oliver R. Rowe	Charlotte	8-24-59	Until completion of assigned duties

BOARD OF TRUSTEES OF THE NORTH CAROLINA STATE LIBRARY [143]

Mark McD. Lindsey*	————————Hamlet	8-7-59	7-1-65
Clifford Peeler*	————————Salisbury	8-7-59	7-1-65

[130] Three members, including the chairman, appointed by the governor for six-year terms. G. S., Sec. 97-77.

[131] Succeeded Neros F. Ransdell, resigned.

[132] The board is composed of seven members, six of whom are appointed by the governor and one of whom, the commissioner of insurance, is an ex officio member and chairman. Appointments and reappointments are for four-year terms. The governor appoints members to fill any unexpired term of office, and may remove members when he feels the public interest requires such action. G. S., Sec. 58-27, 1.

[133] Succeeded J. Leslie Atkins, Jr.

[134] The 1959 General Assembly abolished the Governor's Committee on Interstate Cooperation and revised the membership of the North Carolina Commission on Interstate Cooperation. The new commission is composed of three administrative officials appointed by the governor for two-year terms, three senators designated by the president of the Senate, and three representatives designated by the speaker of the House. S. L., 1959, Ch. 137.

[135] Succeeded Malcolm B. Seawell, resigned to run for governor.

[136] Succeeded Paul A. Johnston, resigned.

[137] Fourteen members, of whom two are appointed by the governor for two-year terms. G. S., Sec. 7-448, 449, 45.

[138] Succeeded Fred B. Helms.

[139] Succeeded Howard Hubbard.

[140] Ten members, seven of whom are appointed by the governor from the general public and three of whom are ex officio members, also appointed by the governor from the membership of the North Carolina Recreation Commission, the Wildlife Resources Commission, and the Board of Conservation and Development, respectively. The seven regular members serve for terms of six years each. The three ex officio members serve only during their terms of office in the respective commissions which they represent. G. S., Sec. 143-284; S. L., 1953, Ch. 1312.

[141] Succeeded Tom Harrington, Sr.

[142] Seven members: three appointed by the governor to serve until completion of the duties assigned to the commission, two appointed by the president of the Senate, and two appointed by the speaker of the House. S. L., 1959, Ch. 938.

[143] Eight members, six of whom are appointed by the governor and two of whom are ex officio (the state superintendent of public instruction and the librarian of the University of North Carolina). The governor's appointees serve for six years. G. S., Sec. 125-29; S. L., 1955, Ch. 505.

Name of Appointee	Address	Date Appointed	Date of Expiration
LOCAL GOVERNMENT COMMISSION [144]			
S. Preston Douglas†*	Lumberton	9-18-60	9-1-62
C. W. Roberts†*	Leaksville	9-18-60	9-1-62
BOARD OF TRUSTEES, NORTH CAROLINA LOCAL GOVERNMENTAL EMPLOYEES' RETIREMENT SYSTEM [145]			
S. M. Gattis[146]	Hillsboro	4-28-60	4-5-64
C. L. Lineback[147]	Salisbury	4-28-60	4-5-64
NORTH CAROLINA MEDICAL CARE COMMISSION [148]			
H. Royster Chamblee*[149]	Raleigh	1-2-59	7-1-59-63
George Carrington†*	Burlington	8-7-59	7-1-63
Powell G. Fox[150]	Raleigh	8-7-59	7-1-63
Earl H. Tate*	Lenoir	8-7-59	7-1-63
Mrs. Roscoe Hunt[151]	Elizabeth City	12-17-59	7-1-61
Agnew H. Bahnson, Sr.*	Winston-Salem	8-22-60	7-1-64
Paul W. Bumbarger, Jr.[152]	Hickory	8-22-60	7-1-64
Sample B. Forbus†*	Durham	8-22-60	7-1-64
William Raney Stanford†*	Durham	8-22-60	7-1-64
MERIT SYSTEM COUNCIL [153]			
R. B. Justice†	Enka	6-18-59	4-8-65
Katherine Jocher[154]	Chapel Hill	6-18-59	4-8-65
NORTH CAROLINA MILK COMMISSION [155]			
W. W. Fitzpatrick†	Rougemont	8-26-59	8-6-63
I. B. Julian*	Fayetteville	8-26-59	8-6-63
William C. McIntire*	Greensboro	8-26-59	8-6-63
H. G. Strom†*	Asheville	7-29-60	8-6-64

JOHN MOTLEY MOREHEAD MEMORIAL COMMISSION [153]

Robert H. Frazier	Greensboro	9-10-59	7-1-65
Fielding L. Fry	Greensboro	9-10-59	7-1-65
Ralph C. Price	Greensboro	9-10-59	7-1-65
Lloyd C. Amos	Greensboro	9-10-59	7-1-63
Herman Cone, Jr.	Greensboro	9-10-59	7-1-68

---

[144] Nine members, five of whom are appointed by the governor for two-year terms, and four of whom are ex officio (the state treasurer, the secretary of state, the state auditor, and the commissioner of revenue). G. S., Sec. 159-3.

[145] The ten members of the Board of Trustees of the Local Governmental Employees' Retirement System consist of the eight members of the Board of Trustees of the Teachers' and State Employees' Retirement System, and two other persons appointed by the governor. Of the two other persons appointed by the governor, one must be a full-time executive officer of a city or town participating in the Retirement System, and one must be a full-time officer of the governing body of a county participating in the Retirement System. These are appointed for terms of four years each. G. S., Sec. 128-28 (2).

[146] Succeeded James A. Glover.

[147] Succeeded D. H. Umstead.

[148] Twenty members, of whom ten are appointed by the governor, and two are ex officio (the state health officer and the commissioner of public welfare). Of those nominated by the medical associations, three are from the North Carolina Medical Society, one from the North Carolina Hospital Association, one from the North Carolina Nurses Association, one from the North Carolina Dental Society, one from the North Carolina Pharmaceutical Association, and one from the Duke Foundation. Terms of office are four years. G. S., Sec. 131-117.

[149] Succeeded G. Fred Hale, resigned; reappointed for four-year term on August 7, 1959.

[150] Succeeded William M. Coppridge.

[151] Succeeded Mrs. Worth Yount, deceased.

[152] Succeeded Carl Cline.

[153] The council is composed of five members appointed by the governor for six-year terms. No member shall have held political office or have been an officer in a political organization during the year preceding his appointment, nor shall he hold such office during his term. G. S., Sec. 126-1.

[154] Succeeded J. B. Willis.

[155] The commission consists of nine members, eight of whom are appointed by the governor. The members represent: a producer, a producer-distributor, two distributors, three representatives of public interests, a retailer, and the ninth member is the commissioner of agriculture. Terms of office of the appointed members are for four years. G. S., Sec. 106-266.7; S. L., 1953, Ch. 1338; S. L., 1955, Ch. 406.

[156] Nineteen members, of whom nine are appointed by the governor. Initial appointments were for two-, four-, and six-year terms. Reappointments are for six years. S. L., 1959, Ch. 1308.

Name of Appointee	Address	Date Appointed	Date of Expiration
George H. Roach	Greensboro	9-10-59	7-1-63
Mrs. Huger S. King	Greensboro	9-10-59	7-1-61
Arnold A. Schiffman	Greensboro	9-10-59	7-1-61
A. Earl Weatherly	Greensboro	9-10-59	7-1-61

North Carolina National Park, Parkway, and Forest Development Commission [157]

Name of Appointee	Address	Date Appointed	Date of Expiration
Kelly E. Bennett†	Bryson City	6-19-59	7-1-65
William Medford†	Waynesville	6-19-59	7-1-65
Robert I. Presley†	Asheville	6-19-59	7-1-65

Board of Commissions of Navigation and Pilotage for the Cape Fear River [158]

Name of Appointee	Address	Date Appointed	Date of Expiration
Prince O'Brien[159]	Southport	5-29-59	4-15-61

New Bern 250th Anniversary Commission [160]

Name of Appointee	Address	Date Appointed	Date of Expiration
Graham A. Barden	New Bern	8-31-59	Term indefinite
Irwin Belk	Charlotte	8-31-59	Term indefinite
David Brinkley	New York City	8-31-59	Term indefinite
Gertrude Carraway	New Bern	8-31-59	Term indefinite
Beatrice Cobb	Morganton	8-31-59	Term indefinite
Thomas P. deGraffenried	Bayside, Long Island, New York	8-31-59	Term indefinite
T. C. Fitzgerald	New Bern	8-31-59	Term indefinite
William C. Friday	Chapel Hill	8-31-59	Term indefinite
Carl Goerch	Raleigh	8-31-59	Term indefinite
Jane Holland	New Bern	8-31-59	Term indefinite
Virginia Horne	Wadesboro	8-31-59	Term indefinite
Mrs. John A. Kellenberger	Greensboro	8-31-59	Term indefinite
Mrs. Thomas O. Moore	Winston-Salem	8-31-59	Term indefinite
R. A. Nunn	New Bern	8-31-59	Term indefinite

L. B. Pate	New Bern	8-31-59	Term indefinite
Robert L. Pugh	New Bern	8-31-59	Term indefinite
R. K. Rottet	Cherry Point	8-31-59	Term indefinite
James O. Simpkins	New Bern	8-31-59	Term indefinite
S. S. Wade	Camp Lejeune	8-31-59	Term indefinite
Sam Whitehurst	New Bern	8-31-59	Term indefinite
Romeo H. Guest[161]	Greensboro	9-15-59	Term indefinite

BOARD OF PAROLES [162]

Johnson Matthews*[163]	Durham	8-7-59	7-1-63
Howard Hepler[164]	Raleigh	3-15-60	7-1-61

STATE PERSONNEL COUNCIL [165]

Fred S. Royster, *Chairman*†*	Henderson	6-18-59	7-1-63
Mrs. Grace M. Hartzog[166]	Raleigh	3-31-60	7-1-61
Wade Barber†*	Pittsboro	7-7-60	7-1-64

[157] The commission is composed of seven members appointed by the governor for terms of six years. In addition, there are two ex officio members as follows: the chairman of the State Highway and Public Works Commission and the director of the Department of Conservation and Development. G. S., Sec. 143-255, 256.

[158] Five members appointed by the governor for four-year terms. G. S., Sec. 76-1.

[159] Succeeded M. R. Sanders, resigned.

[160] Twenty-five members, of whom twenty are appointed by the governor and five are ex officio: the superintendent of public instruction, the director of the Department of Archives and History, the director of the Department of Conservation and Development, the chairman of the Craven County Board of Commissioners, and the mayor of New Bern. S. L., 1959, Ch. 1321.

[161] Succeeded Beatrice Cobb, deceased.

[162] Three members appointed by the governor for four-year terms. G. S., 148-52; S. L., 1953, Ch. 17; S. L. 1955, Ch. 867.

[163] Succeeded George W. Randall as chairman on April 1, 1960.

[164] Succeeded George W. Randall, resigned to become director of prisons.

[165] The council consists of five members appointed by the governor for terms of four years each. At least one member is to be chosen from the field of personnel administration who is not an employee of the state, at least one member is to be engaged in the management of private business or industry, and not more than one member is to be chosen from the employees of the state. G. S., Sec. 143-35 (2); S. L., 1953, Ch. 1085.

[166] Succeeded Earl Crump, deceased.

Name of Appointee	Address	Date Appointed	Date of Expiration
NORTH CAROLINA PORTS AUTHORITY [167]			
Thomas M. Evins	Durham	9-9-59	6-1-61
Harvey C. Hines	Kinston	9-9-59	6-1-61
STATE PRISON COMMISSION [168]			
Edgar Gurganus* [169]	Williamston	8-27-59	6-30-63
James M. Parrott, Jr. [170]	Kinston	8-27-59	6-30-63
Harley C. Shands [171]	Chapel Hill	8-27-59	6-30-63
Director of Prisons			
George W. Randall [172]	Raleigh	3-15-60	7-1-62
SPECIAL OFFICERS, PRISON DEPARTMENT [173]			
William O. Upchurch [174]	Raleigh	9-2-59	At will of the governor
Holly R. Britt	Raleigh	7-19-60	At will of the governor
STATE PROBATION COMMISSION [175]			
William J. Bundy [176]	Greenville	1-30-59	5-28-62
John Anderson [177]	Brevard	6-18-59	5-28-64
Clarence H. Patrick*	Winston-Salem	5-20-60	5-28-65
Director of Probation			
C. Gordon Maddrey [178]	Ahoskie	6-8-59	
STATE BOARD OF PUBLIC WELFARE [179]			
Howard E. Manning [180]	Raleigh	9-17-59	4-1-65
Irving E. Carlyle†	Winston-Salem	10-5-59	4-1-65

North Carolina Recreation Commission [181]

Charles S. Hubbard†*	Chapel Hill	8-7-59	7-1-63
W. D. James*	Hamlet	8-7-59	7-1-63
Mrs. Harriet Pressly*	Raleigh	8-7-59	7-1-63
A. E. Weatherford*	Durham	7-25-60	7-1-64

[167] Consisted originally of seven members appointed by the governor for four-year terms. The 1959 General Assembly increased the number to nine and specified that the two new members should be appointed to serve until the expiration of the terms of the present members (1961) and thereafter for four-year terms. Evins and Hines were the two new members thus appointed. G. S., Sec. 143-216; S. L., 1953, Ch. 191; S. L., 1959, Ch. 523.

[168] Created by the 1957 General Assembly for the purpose of separating the prison system from the State Highway and Public Works Commission. The new prison commission consists of seven members appointed by the governor. Of the initial appointments, three were for two years and four for four years. Thereafter, all appointments would be for four-year terms. The governor designates one of the members of the commission as chairman. The director of prisons is appointed by the commission subject to the approval of the governor, initially for five years and thereafter for a four-year term. S. L., 1957, Ch. 349.

[169] Resigned on December 19, 1960, to serve as presidential elector; reappointed on December 22, 1960.

[170] Succeeded William McGehee, resigned.

[171] Succeeded T. R. Eller, resigned.

[172] Succeeded William F. Bailey.

[173] The governor is authorized to appoint officers for the purpose of transferring prisoners from place to place in the state, said officers to be commissioned specifically or generally to return escaped prisoners or other fugitives from outside the state. G. S., Sec. 148-4.

[174] Succeeded Andres J. Wilson, resigned.

[175] Five members appointed by the governor for five year terms, one member's term expiring each year. The director is appointed by the commission with the approval of the governor. G. S., Sec. 15-201.2.

[176] Succeeded Clifton L. Moore, resigned to become associate justice of the Supreme Court.

[177] Succeeded Martin Harmon.

[178] Succeeded Basil L. Sherrill, resigned.

[179] Seven members, at least one of whom must be a woman, appointed by the governor for six-year terms. The governor designates the chairman. G. S., Sec. 108-1; S. L., 1945, Ch. 43.

[180] Succeeded C. M. Vanstory, Jr.

[181] Eleven members, seven of whom are appointed by the governor for terms of four years and four of whom are ex officio as follows: the governor, the superintendent of public instruction, the commissioner of public welfare, and the director of the Department of Conservation and Development. Vacancies are filled by the governor for the duration of unexpired terms. G. S., Sec. 143-207.

NORTH CAROLINA RECREATION COMMISSION ADVISORY COMMITTEE [183]

Name of Appointee	Address	Date Appointed	Date of Expiration
Charles Milner Chairman*	Chapel Hill	9-4-59	7-1-61
Ruth Current†	Raleigh	9-4-59	7-1-61
Taylor Dodson*	Winston-Salem	9-4-59	7-1-61
Harold J. Dudley†‡	Raleigh	9-4-59	7-1-61
O. A. Fetch†‡	Fontana Village	9-4-59	7-1-61
Fred Fletcher†‡	Raleigh	9-4-59	7-1-61
Mrs. Josephine Gallagher*	Charlotte	9-4-59	7-1-61
Carlton Garrett†‡	Elizabeth City	9-4-59	7-1-61
J. B. Gillette*	Wilson	9-4-59	7-1-61
Mrs. Maurice Honigman†‡	Gastonia	9-4-59	7-1-61
Mrs. Miles A. Hughey†‡	Raleigh	9-4-59	7-1-61
C. Walton Johnson†‡	Winston-Salem	9-4-59	7-1-61
Ottis D. Mabe*	Greensboro	9-4-59	7-1-61
Blaine M. Madison*	Raleigh	9-4-59	7-1-61
Lucy Morgan*	Penland	9-4-59	7-1-61
I. E. Ready†‡	Roanoke Rapids	9-4-59	7-1-61
Ray Smith*	Roanoke Rapids	9-4-59	7-1-61
Mrs. Mildred Southern*	Raleigh	9-4-59	7-1-61
Mrs. Nancy Stamey*	Raleigh	9-4-59	7-1-61
Tully Blair[183]	Winston-Salem	9-4-59	7-1-61
Frances Cleary[184]	Chapel Hill	9-4-59	7-1-61
M. McRae Faison[185]	Roanoke Rapids	9-4-59	7-1-61
Hugh Hines[186]	Rocky Mount	9-4-59	7-1-61
Paul Lyman[187]	Raleigh	9-4-59	7-1-61
Alex McMahon[188]	Chapel Hill	9-4-59	7-1-61
Howard Pullen[189]	Raleigh	9-4-59	7-1-61

Arnold Peterson[190]	Wilmington	9-4-59	7-1-61
Richard Pierce[191]	Valdese	9-4-59	7-1-61
A. C. Snow[192]	Raleigh	9-4-59	7-1-61
Anne W. Tillinghast[193]	Fort Bragg	9-4-59	7-1-61

Commission on Reorganization of State Government[194]

David M. Britt	Fairmont	8-27-59	Report to governor by Nov. 15, 1960
Claude Currie	Durham	8-27-59	Report to governor by Nov. 15, 1960
H. Cloyd Philpott	Lexington	8-27-59	Report to governor by Nov. 15, 1960
Dwight M. Quinn	Kannapolis	8-27-59	Report to governor by Nov. 15, 1960
David J. Rose	Goldsboro	8-27-59	Report to governor by Nov. 15, 1960
Frank W. Snepp	Charlotte	8-27-59	Report to governor by Nov. 15, 1960
H. P. Taylor, Jr.	Wadesboro	8-27-59	Report to governor by Nov. 15, 1960
George R. Uzzell	Salisbury	8-27-59	Report to governor by Nov. 15, 1960
Fred H. Weaver	Chapel Hill	8-27-59	Report to governor by Nov. 15, 1960

[189] Thirty members appointed by the governor for two-year terms. The governor designates the chairman. G. S., Sec. 143-210.
[183] Succeeded Frank Pierson.
[184] Succeeded Edwin S. Lanier.
[185] Succeeded Marse Grant.
[186] Succeeded Edgar Johnson.
[187] Succeeded Donald Capstick.
[188] Succeeded Lloyd B. Hathaway.
[189] Succeeded John Parris.
[190] Succeeded W. G. Enloe.
[191] Succeeded Irvin Holmes.
[192] Succeeded William Smith.
[193] Succeeded Montgomery Hill.
[194] Successor to a commission authorized for the same purpose by the 1957 General Assembly; nine members appointed by the governor to study and make recommendations to him on or before November 15, 1960. S. L., 1959, Res. 71.

Name of Appointee	Address	Date Appointed	Date of Expiration
RESEARCH TRIANGLE REGIONAL PLANNING COMMISSION [195]			
E. K. Powe	Durham	9-10-59	7-1-63
Hubert C. Sears	Morrisville	9-10-59	7-1-63
George L. Simpson	Chapel Hill	9-10-59	7-1-63
ROANOKE ISLAND HISTORICAL ASSOCIATION BOARD OF DIRECTORS [196]			
David Stick[197]	Kill Devil Hills	1-15-59	12-1-59
NORTH CAROLINA RURAL ELECTRIFICATION AUTHORITY [198]			
Mrs. Fred Davis*	Stoneville	6-19-59	6-5-63
S. H. Hobbs, Jr.††	Chapel Hill	6-19-59	6-5-63
W. Avery Thompson[199]	Lake Waccamaw	12-9-59	6-5-61
NORTH CAROLINA RURAL REHABILITATION CORPORATION [200]			
Dudley W. Bagley*	Moyock	11-27-59	11-19-62
J. J. Hamlin, Jr.††	Rutherfordton	11-27-59	11-19-62
ADVISORY COMMITTEE OF THE SOUTHEASTERN INTERSTATE FOREST FIRE PROTECTION COMPACT [201]			
Ernest W. Ross, *Senate*[202]	Marion	8-25-59	Term indefinite
B. W. Thomason, *Senate Alternate*[203]	Brevard	8-25-59	Term indefinite
C. R. Crawford, *House*[204]	Whittier	8-25-59	Term indefinite
Leonard W. Lloyd, *House Alternate*[205]	Robbinsville	8-25-59	Term indefinite
NORTH CAROLINA STADIUM AUTHORITY BOARD OF DIRECTORS [206]			
George Watts Hill, Jr.	Durham	9-9-59	7-1-62
Add Penfield	Greensboro	9-9-59	7-1-62
Orville B. Campbell	Chapel Hill	9-9-59	7-1-62

Lewis R. Holding	Raleigh	9-9-59	7-1-63
J. S. Dorton	Raleigh	9-9-59	7-1-65
Joseph C. Eagles, Jr.	Wilson	9-9-59	7-1-65
J. W. York	Raleigh	9-9-59	7-1-65

STANDARDIZATION COMMITTEE [207]

Paul A. Johnston, *Chairman*	Raleigh	9-1-59	At pleasure of the governor
Ben H. Clarke	Chapel Hill	9-1-59	At pleasure of the governor
N. W. Conner	Raleigh	9-1-59	At pleasure of the governor
J. William Copeland	Murfreesboro	9-1-59	At pleasure of the governor
Clyde H. Harriss	Salisbury	9-1-59	At pleasure of the governor
J. L. Pierce	Raleigh	9-1-59	At pleasure of the governor
C. E. Proudley	Raleigh	9-1-59	At pleasure of the governor

---

[195] Fifteen members, three of whom are appointed by the governor for four-year terms. *S. L., 1959*, Ch. 642.

[196] The twenty-one members of this board are elected by the members of the association at regular meetings every two years. Vacancies are filled by the governor. G. S., Sec. 143-200.

[197] Succeeded Guy H. Lennon, deceased.

[198] Six members appointed by the governor for four-year terms. G. S., Sec. 117-1.

[199] Succeeded Harry L. Mintz, resigned.

[200] Nine members, five of whom are appointed by the governor for three-year terms. The remaining four members serve ex officio and are: the commissioner of agriculture, the director of the Co-operative Agricultural Extension Service of North Carolina State College, the director of the Division of Vocational Education, State Department of Public Instruction, and the North Carolina state director, Farmers Home Administration, U. S. Department of Agriculture, G. S., Sec. 137-31.3; *S. L., 1953*, Ch. 724.

[201] Consists of one member and one alternate from the State Senate, and one member and one alternate from the House of Representatives, and two others, one of whom shall be associated with forestry or forestry products industries. All are appointed by the governor for indefinite terms, but presumably from one General Assembly to the next. *S. L., 1955*, Ch. 803.

[202] Succeeded Roy Rowe.

[203] Succeeded Staton P. Williams.

[204] Succeeded Charles B. McCrary.

[205] Succeeded James G. Gaither.

[206] Seven members appointed by the governor. Initial appointments were for three-, four-, and six-year terms. Reappointments are for six years. *S. L., 1959*, Ch. 917.

[207] Seven members appointed by the governor to serve at his pleasure. G. S., Sec. 143-60.

Name of Appointee	Address	Date Appointed	Date of Expiration
J. Eugene Thompson, Jr.[208]	Raleigh	2-2-60	At pleasure of the governor
David S. Coltrane[209]	Raleigh	9-9-60	At pleasure of the governor

STATE STREAM SANITATION COMMITTEE [210]

Name of Appointee	Address	Date Appointed	Date of Expiration
J. Weldon Weir[211]	Asheville	1-29-59	7-11-63
P. Greer Johnson[212]	Asheville	3-9-59	7-11-63
Mrs. Karl Bishopric†	Leaksville	8-7-59	7-11-65
J. N. Vann†	Ahoskie	8-7-59	7-11-65

BOARD OF TRUSTEES OF THE NORTH CAROLINA SYMPHONY SOCIETY, INCORPORATED [213]

Name of Appointee	Address	Date Appointed	Date of Expiration
Mrs. Louis V. Sutton*	Raleigh	6-18-59	3-10-63
H. Patrick Taylor, Jr.*	Wadesboro	6-18-59	3-10-63
Cecil Hill[214]	Brevard	8-20-59	3-10-63
Holland McSwain[215]	Franklin	8-28-59	3-10-63

COMMISSION FOR THE STUDY OF TEACHER MERIT PAY AND IMPLEMENTATION OF A REVISED PUBLIC SCHOOL CURRICULUM [216]

Name of Appointee	Address	Date Appointed	Date of Expiration
E. E. Boyer	Statesville	9-2-59	Report to the governor by Dec. 1, 1960
J. L. Cashwell	Albemarle	9-2-59	Report to the governor by Dec. 1, 1960
Mrs. Hazel Curtright	Chapel Hill	9-2-59	Report to the governor by Dec. 1, 1960
Garland C. Garriss	Troy	9-2-59	Report to the governor by Dec. 1, 1960
W. C. Harris, Jr., *Chairman*	Raleigh	9-2-59	Report to the governor by Dec. 1, 1960
Mrs. Frank B. Meacham	Roanoke Rapids	9-2-59	Report to the governor by Dec. 1, 1960
Joseph S. Moye	Greenville	9-2-59	Report to the governor by Dec. 1, 1960
Frank N. Patterson, Jr.	Albemarle	9-2-59	Report to the governor by Dec. 1, 1960
Elbert S. Peel, Jr.	Williamston	9-2-59	Report to the governor by Dec. 1, 1960
S. Tom Proctor	Fuquay Springs	9-2-59	Report to the governor by Dec. 1, 1960
G. T. Profit	Lillington	9-2-59	Report to the governor by Dec. 1, 1960

C. Reid Ross	Fayetteville	9-2-59	Report to the governor by Dec. 1, 1960
Prince A. Simmons	Winston-Salem	9-2-59	Report to the governor by Dec. 1, 1960
Demint F. Walker	Edenton	9-2-59	Report to the governor by Dec. 1, 1960
Edward H. Wilson	Blanche	9-2-59	Report to the governor by Dec. 1, 1960

BOARD OF TRUSTEES, TEACHERS' AND STATE EMPLOYEES' RETIREMENT SYSTEM [217]

F. Kent Burns[218]	Raleigh	8-26-59	4-5-63
Withers Davis[219]	Fayetteville	8-26-59	4-5-63
Royal W. Sands[220]	Reidsville	8-26-59	4-5-60-64
Mrs. Annie Swindell†*	Durham	8-26-59	4-5-63
H. L. Stephenson†*	Smithfield	4-14-60	4-5-64

[208] Succeeded C. E. Proudley, resigned.

[209] Succeeded J. Paul Johnston, resigned.

[210] A permanent committee within the State Board of Health consisting of nine members, of whom seven are appointed by the governor for six-year terms. G. S., Sec. 143-213; S. L., 1957, Ch. 992.

[211] Appointed to succeed Walter Clark but failed to qualify.

[212] Succeeded Walter Clark, resigned.

[213] The board of trustees consists of not less than sixteen members, of whom four are named by the governor for four-year terms, ten are chosen by the North Carolina Symphony Society, and two serve ex officio as follows: the governor, and the superintendent of public instruction. G. S., Sec. 140-6; S. L., 1943, Ch. 755; S. L., 1947, Ch. 1049.

[214] Appointed to succeed H. Patrick Taylor, but did not accept.

[215] Succeeded H. Patrick Taylor, resigned.

[216] Fifteen members appointed by the governor plus two ex officio members: the superintendent of public instruction and the chairman of the State Board of Education. To report to the governor by December 1, 1960. S. L., 1959, Res. 8.

[217] The board is composed of eight members, six of whom are appointed by the governor with the consent of the Senate for four-year terms, and two of whom are ex officio as follows: the superintendent of public instruction and the state treasurer who is ex officio chairman. One appointee of the governor must be a member of the teaching profession, one must be an employee of the State Highway and Public Works Commission, and one a state employee. The remaining members must not be of the teaching profession or state employees. G. S., Sec. 135-6; S. L., 1947, Ch. 259.

[218] Succeeded Claude L. Love.

[219] Succeeded Thomas F. Royall.

[220] Succeeded Sam J. Burrow, Jr., resigned; reappointed for four-year term on April 14, 1960.

Name of Appointee	Address	Date Appointed	Date of Expiration
NORTH CAROLINA TEXTBOOK COMMISSION [221]			
Mrs. Dorothy Yarbrough Zimmerman[222]	Yanceyville	9-22-59	4-1-61
Chester N. Womack[223]	Spindale	10-8-59	4-1-61
COMMISSION FOR THE STUDY OF A TWELVE MONTHS' USE OF PUBLIC SCHOOL BUILDINGS AND FACILITIES FOR PUBLIC SCHOOL PURPOSES [224]			
Dan L. Drummond	Winston-Salem	8-31-59	Report to the 1961 General Assembly
W. G. Enloe	Raleigh	8-31-59	Report to the 1961 General Assembly
S. Glenn Hawfield	Monroe	8-31-59	Report to the 1961 General Assembly
John H. Kerr, Jr.,	Warrenton	8-31-59	Report to the 1961 General Assembly
Ernest W. Ross	Marion	8-31-59	Report to the 1961 General Assembly
NORTH CAROLINA COMMISSION ON UNIFORM STATE LAWS [225]			
J. Wilbur Bunn[226]	Raleigh	9-9-59	12-1-62
Ralph Moody[227]	Raleigh	6-23-60	12-1-62
UTILITIES COMMISSION [228]			
Richard G. Long*	Roxboro	1-29-59	2-1-65
Thomas R. Eller, Jr.[229]	Brevard	8-21-59	7-1-65
Clarence Noah[230]	Raleigh	8-21-59	7-1-61
NORTH CAROLINA VETERANS COMMISSION [231]			
Chris C. Fordham, Jr.[232]	Greensboro	8-29-59	5-16-64
J. Oscar Thomas*	Leaksville	5-20-60	5-16-65

SIR WALTER RALEIGH COMMISSION [233]

Jonathan Daniels[234]	Raleigh	4-14-60	Term indefinite
Mrs. Joseph C. Eagles[235]	Wilson	4-14-60	Term indefinite
Fred S. Royster[236]	Henderson	4-14-60	Term indefinite
Thomas J. White[237]	Kinston	4-14-60	Term indefinite

BOARD OF WATER COMMISSIONERS [238]

Dan K. Moore[239]	Canton	2-5-59	6-30-63

[221] Twelve members appointed for four-year terms by the governor and the superintendent of public instruction. S. L., 1945, Ch. 707.

[222] Succeeded Marie Haigwood, resigned.

[223] Succeeded Catherine Whitener, resigned.

[224] Five members appointed by the governor to report to the 1961 General Assembly. S. L., 1959, Res. 72

[225] The commission consists of three members appointed by the governor. There is no statutory authority for these appointments.

[226] Succeeded Robert E. Giles.

[227] Succeeded J. Wilbur Bunn, resigned.

[228] Five commissioners are appointed by the governor, with the consent of the Senate, three serving six-year terms and two serving four-year terms. The governor designates one member of the commission as chairman. G. S., Sec. 62-1, 4.

[229] Succeeded Edward H. McMahan, resigned.

[230] Succeeded R. Lee Whitmire, on leave.

[231] Five members, all of whom must be veterans, appointed by the governor for five-year terms. The director is elected by the commission with the approval of the governor. G. S., Sec. 165-5; S. L., 1945, Ch. 723.

[232] Succeeded W. W. Staton.

[233] Twenty-one members appointed by the governor for an indefinite term and two ex officio members: the governor and the superintendent of public instruction. The governor serves as chairman and the superintendent of public instruction as secretary S. L., 1947, Res. 26.

[234] Succeeded Lee B. Weathers, deceased.

[235] Succeeded William T. Polk, deceased.

[236] Succeeded J. Y. Joyner, deceased.

[237] Succeeded Mrs. W. T. Bost, resigned.

[238] Seven members, appointed by the governor. Of the initial appointments, two were for two years, two for four years, and three for six years. All subsequent appointments are for six years. S. L., 1955, Ch. 857. This board was abolished by the 1959 General Assembly.

[239] Succeeded David M. Hall, elected to Congress.

Name of Appointee	Address	Date Appointed	Date of Expiration
BOARD OF WATER RESOURCES [240]			
P. D. Davis	Durham	8-21-59	7-1-61
Ben R. Lewis	Goldsboro	8-21-59	7-1-61
S. Vernon Stevens, Jr.	Broadway	8-21-59	7-1-61
C. H. Pruden, Jr.	Windsor	8-21-59	7-1-63
Glenn Tucker	Carolina Beach	8-21-59	7-1-63
Dan K. Moore	Sylva	8-21-59	7-1-65
J. R. Townsend	Greensboro	8-21-59	7-1-65
NORTH CAROLINA WILDLIFE RESOURCES COMMISSION [241]			
James A. Connelly†	Morganton	1-26-59	1-24-65
R. Floyd Crouse†	Sparta	1-26-59	1-24-65
T. N. Massie*	Sylva	1-26-59	1-24-65
WRECK COMMISSIONERS [242]			
Alpheus W. Drinkwater†*	Manteo	1-21-60	2-21-62
Roy Eubanks†*	Beaufort	9-9-60	9-11-62
INSTITUTIONS			
APPALACHIAN STATE COLLEGE BOARD OF TRUSTEES [243]			
B. C. Brock†*	Mocksville	9-2-59	6-30-67
Mrs. J. Ed Broyhill*	Lenoir	9-2-59	6-30-67
William J. Conrad†*	Winston-Salem	9-2-59	6-30-67

ASHEVILLE-BILTMORE COLLEGE BOARD OF TRUSTEES [244]

E. B. Garrett[245]	Brevard	3-7-60	6-30-60-66
Louis Lipinsky, Sr.*	Asheville	8-10-60	6-30-66
Robert F. Phillips*	Asheville	8-10-60	6-30-66
Manly E. Wright*	Asheville	8-10-60	6-30-66

BOARD OF DIRECTORS OF THE STATE SCHOOL FOR THE BLIND AND DEAF [246]

Richard B. Ford[247]	Asheville	11-11-60	5-1-61

CHARLOTTE COMMUNITY COLLEGE BOARD OF TRUSTEES [248]

Thomas M. Belk*	Charlotte	7-28-60	6-30-66
C. A. McKnight[249]	Charlotte	7-28-60	6-30-66
Sheldon P. Smith*	Charlotte	7-28-60	6-30-66
Thomas J. Watkins, Sr.*	Charlotte	7-28-60	6-30-66

---

[240] Seven members appointed by the governor. Initial appointments were for two-, four-, and six year terms. Reappointments are for six years. G. S., Sec. 143-353; *1959*, Ch. 779.

[241] This commission is composed of nine citizens informed on wildlife conservation and restoration problems and appointed by the governor for terms of six years. Vacancies are filled by appointment of the governor for the duration of unexpired terms. G. S., Sec. 143-241; *S. L., 1947*, Ch. 263.

[242] Whenever necessary, the governor appoints wreck commissioners for the various districts in the state's coastal counties to serve for two-year terms. Each commissioner is to live in the district for which he is appointed. G. S., Sec. 82-2.

[243] Twelve members appointed by the governor for eight-year terms. The terms are so staggered that three vacancies occur every two years. *S. L., 1957*, Ch. 1142.

[244] Twelve members, four of whom are appointed by the governor for six-year terms. *S. L., 1957*, Ch. 1098.

[245] Succeeded Laurence C. Merchant, resigned; reappointed for six-year term on August 10, 1960.

[246] Eleven members appointed by the governor for four-year terms. G. S., Sec. 116-106.

[247] Succeeded James L. Penland, resigned.

[248] Twelve members, four of whom are appointed by the governor for six-year terms. *S. L., 1957*, Ch. 1098.

[249] Succeeded Cecil Prince, deceased.

J. Fred Rippy, Jr.*	———— Wilmington	8-12-60	6-30-66
Eugene B. Tomlinson*	———— Southport	8-12-60	6-30-66

AGRICULTURAL AND TECHNICAL COLLEGE BOARD OF TRUSTEES [268]

Murray Davis†	———— High Point	9-1-59	6-30-63
Robert P. Holding*	———— Smithfield	9-1-59	6-30-63
W. L. Reed[269]	———— Kannapolis	9-1-59	6-30-65
J. Mack Hatch[270]	———— Charlotte	9-1-59	6-30-67

[250] Twelve members appointed by the governor. The 1957 General Assembly lengthened the terms of members of this board from six to eight years and provided that the terms should be staggered so that three vacancies occur every two years. S. L., 1957, Ch. 1142.
[251] Succeeded Luther Hamilton.
[252] Succeeded I. H. O'Hanlon.
[253] Succeeded Arthur L. Tyler.
[254] Succeeded Ralph H. Hodges.
[255] The 1957 General Assembly increased the size of this board from eleven to twelve members and lengthened the terms from four to eight years, the terms to be staggered so that three vacancies occur every two years. S. L., 1957, Ch. 1142.
[256] Succeeded James A. Sampson.
[257] Succeeded John L. Carter.
[258] Succeeded Purnell Swett.
[259] Succeeded D. F. Lowery.
[260] Succeeded James R. Lowery, deceased.
[261] Seven members, six of whom are appointed by the governor for four-year terms. The director of vocational education serves ex officio. G. S., Sec. 115-255.1; S. L., 1945, Ch. 806.
[262] Succeeded A. W. Bell.
[263] Twelve members appointed by the governor for eight-year terms, the terms to be staggered so that three vacancies occur every two years. S. L., 1957, Ch. 1142.
[264] Succeeded Frank H. Watson.
[265] Succeeded Mrs. Robert Russell.
[266] Twelve members of whom four are appointed by the governor for six-year terms. S. L., 1957, Ch. 1098, Sec. 4 (a) and (b).
[267] Succeeded Howard A. Ponton, deceased; reappointed for six-year term on August 12, 1960.
[268] The 1957 General Assembly reduced the size of this board from fifteen to twelve members and lengthened the terms from six to eight years, the terms to be staggered so that three vacancies will occur every two years. S. L., 1957, Ch. 1142.
[269] Succeeded J. Wilson Alexander.
[270] Succeeded E. R. Merrick.

Name of Appointee	Address	Date Appointed	Date of Expiration
ELIZABETH CITY STATE TEACHERS COLLEGE BOARD OF TRUSTEES [271]			
Roger R. Jackson, Jr.[272]	Harrellsville	9-1-59	6-30-67
A. J. Jones*	Tillery	9-1-59	6-30-67
Clifford Jones*	Elizabeth City	9-1-59	6-30-67
Lunsford Long[273]	Warrenton	6-27-60	6-30-61
FAYETTEVILLE STATE TEACHERS COLLEGE BOARD OF TRUSTEES [274]			
C. J. Barber[275]	Garner	9-1-59	6-30-67
Gurney E. Edgerton†*	Fayetteville	9-1-59	6-30-67
Albert J. Ellis*	Jacksonville	9-1-59	6-30-67
NORTH CAROLINA COLLEGE BOARD OF TRUSTEES [276]			
Welch Harris*	High Point	9-2-59	6-30-67
Clyde A. Shreve*	Summerfield	9-2-59	6-30-67
Clarence Watkins[277]	Reidsville	9-2-59	6-30-67
WINSTON-SALEM TEACHERS' COLLEGE BOARD OF TRUSTEES [278]			
Sam J. Burrow, Jr.[279]	Asheboro	8-28-59	6-30-67
Thomas B. Rice*	Winston-Salem	8-28-59	6-30-67
Paul Wallace[280]	Troy	8-28-59	6-30-67
BOARD OF DIRECTORS FOR THE NORTH CAROLINA CEREBRAL PALSY HOSPITAL [281]			
Mrs. Kenneth W. Cuyler*	Durham	8-10-59	7-10-65
George Hughes†	Pollocksville	8-10-59	7-10-65
W. M. Roberts†	Gastonia	8-10-59	7-10-65
Mrs. B. V. Hedrick[282]	Salisbury	7-20-60	7-10-63

NORTH CAROLINA ORTHOPEDIC HOSPITAL BOARD OF TRUSTEES [283]

James E. McKnight[284]	Mooresville	8-25-59	4-4-63
Willis Frank Dowd†	Charlotte	8-25-59	4-4-65
Mrs. C. Gordon Maddrey*	Raleigh	8-25-59	4-4-65
Frank Phillips*	Charlotte	8-25-59	4-4-65

BOARD OF DIRECTORS OF THE NORTH CAROLINA SANATORIUMS FOR THE TREATMENT OF TUBERCULOSIS [285]

Charles A. Cannon†	Concord	8-27-59	4-29-65
Carl C. Council†	Durham	8-27-59	4-29-65
Gordon Greenwood[286]	Black Mountain	8-27-59	4-29-65
M. A. Pittman†	Wilson	8-27-59	4-29-65

[271] The 1957 General Assembly increased the size of this board from nine to twelve members and lengthened the terms from four to eight years, the terms to be staggered so that three vacancies occur every two years. S. L., 1957, Ch. 1142.

[272] Succeeded Herbert Hardy, resigned.

[273] Succeeded J. W. Davis, resigned.

[274] The 1957 General Assembly increased the size of this board from nine to twelve members and lengthened the terms from four to eight years, the terms to be staggered so that three vacancies occur every two years. S. L., 1957, Ch. 1142.

[275] Succeeded C. W. Furlong.

[276] Twelve members. The General Assembly lengthened the terms of members of this board from four to eight years and provided that the terms should be staggered so that three vacancies should occur every two years. S. L., 1957, Ch. 1142.

[277] Succeeded Mrs. Ida Duncan.

[278] The 1957 General Assembly increased the membership of this board from nine to twelve and lengthened the terms from four to eight years, the terms to be staggered so that three vacancies occur every two years. S. L., 1957, Ch. 1142.

[279] Succeeded Rufus S. Hairston.

[280] Succeeded Fleet L. Gobble.

[281] Established in 1945 as the North Carolina Hospital for Treatment of Spastic Children; name changed in 1953 to North Carolina Cerebral Palsy Hospital. The board is composed of nine members appointed by the governor for six-year terms. G. S., Sec. 131-127, 128; S. L., 1945, Ch. 504; S. L., 1953, Ch. 893.

[282] Succeeded John D. Messick, resigned.

[283] Consists of nine members appointed by the governor for six-year terms. G. S., Sec. 131-1.

[284] Succeeded George Blanton, deceased.

[285] Twelve members appointed by the governor and confirmed by the Senate for terms of six years. The secretary of the North Carolina State Board of Health is an ex officio member. Vacancies are filled by appointment of the governor and confirmed by the next succeeding session of the Senate. G. S., Sec. 131-62, 63, 64.

[286] Succeeded L. L. Love.

Name of Appointee	Address	Date Appointed	Date of Expiration
BOARD OF DIRECTORS OF THE CONFEDERATE WOMAN'S HOME [287]			
Henry C. Doby[288]	Albemarle	9-3-59	6-30-61
J. Henry Hill, Jr.[289]	Hickory	9-3-59	6-30-61
John R. Jenkins, Jr.[290]	Aulander	9-3-59	6-30-61
Mrs. E. R. MacKeithan†*	Fayetteville	9-3-59	6-30-61
Charles G. Rose, Jr.†*	Fayetteville	9-3-59	6-30-61
J. H. Ross[291]	Lincolnton	9-3-59	6-30-61
Mrs. H. L. Stevens, Jr.†*	Warsaw	9-3-59	6-30-61

EXAMINING BOARDS

Name of Appointee	Address	Date Appointed	Date of Expiration
STATE BOARD OF CERTIFIED PUBLIC ACCOUNTANT EXAMINERS [292]			
Richard Killian Worsley[293]	Greenville	8-12-59	6-30-62
Martin L. Black, Jr.[294]	Durham	8-12-59	6-30-62
NORTH CAROLINA BOARD OF ARCHITECTURE [295]			
John E. Ramsey†	Salisbury	6-18-59	4-8-64
F. Carter Williams[296]	Raleigh	4-14-60	4-8-65
STATE BOARD OF BARBER EXAMINERS [297]			
J. Marvin Cheek†	High Point	8-11-59	7-1-65
STATE BOARD OF CHIROPRACTIC EXAMINERS [298]			
W. Dillon Chambers[299]	Asheville	6-9-59	5-5-62
C. H. Peters†*	Rocky Mount	6-9-60	5-5-63

STATE LICENSING BOARD FOR GENERAL CONTRACTORS [300]

Jesse P. Phifer[301]	.... Rockingham	2-5-59	12-31-63
R. D. Beam†*	.... Raleigh	12-11-59	12-31-64

BOARD OF COSMETIC ART EXAMINERS [302]

James A. Henderson*	.... Winston-Salem	8-7-59	7-1-62
Mrs. Charles B. Noe*	.... Beaufort	8-7-59	7-1-62
Mrs. Eleanor Register Wallace*	.... Durham	8-7-59	7-1-62

[287] Composed of seven members appointed by the governor for two-year terms. The state treasurer is the treasurer of the board. G. S., Sec. 112-2.

[288] Succeeded Mrs. J. Y. Gatewood.

[289] Succeeded Mrs. Robert Grady Johnson.

[290] Succeeded Mrs. J. F. McGill.

[291] Succeeded Mrs. John D. Boyd.

[292] Consists of four members appointed by the governor for a term of three years and until their successors are appointed G. S., Sec. 93-12.

[293] Succeeded R. Glenn Snipes.

[294] Succeeded Sydney H. Shaw.

[295] Five members appointed by the governor for five-year terms. G. S., Sec. 83-2, 10. Originally called the State Board of Architectural Examination and Registration; name changed by the 1957 General Assembly. S. L., 1957, Ch. 794.

[296] Succeeded Leon McMinn, resigned.

[297] Consists of three members to be appointed by the governor for six-year terms. Each member must be an experienced barber. G. S., Sec. 86-6.

[298] Consists of three members appointed by the governor for three-year terms. Members must be practicing chiropractors of integrity and ability and residents of the state. No more than two members shall be graduates of the same school or college of chiropractic. G. S., Sec. 90-140, 141.

[299] Succeeded Wilfred O. Briens.

[300] Composed of five members appointed by the governor for five-year terms. Vacancies are filled by appointment of the governor. G. S., Sec. 87-2, 4.

[301] Succeeded Roy L. Goode.

[302] Consists of three members appointed by the governor for three-year terms. G. S., Sec. 88-13.

Name of Appointee	Address	Date Appointed	Date of Expiration
STATE BOARD OF DENTAL EXAMINERS [303]			
Wade H. Breeland*	Belmont	6-16-59	7-31-62
S. W. Shaffer*	Greensboro	6-16-59	7-31-62
G. Shuford Abernethy*	Hickory	7-21-60	7-31-63
S. L. Bobbitt*	Raleigh	7-21-60	7-31-63
BOARD OF EXAMINERS OF ELECTRICAL CONTRACTORS [304]			
C. H. Gudger[305]	Asheville	6-20-59	4-15-61
Elwood C. Peele†	Burlington	6-20-59	4-15-62
Robert J. Pearsall*	Raleigh	4-28-60	4-15-63
STATE BOARD OF REGISTRATION FOR ENGINEERS AND LAND SURVEYORS [306]			
George S. Rawlins[307]	Charlotte	9-8-59	1-31-59-64
BOARD OF NURSE REGISTRATION AND NURSING EDUCATION [308]			
Mrs. Bessie Perry Burges[309]	Durham	1-2-59	1-1-63
Mrs. W. D. James, Sr.†*	Hamlet	1-2-59	1-1-63
Moir S. Martin†*	Mount Airy	1-2-59	1-1-63
J. Grayson Brothers*	Morganton	1-7-60	1-1-64
Mrs. Eloise R. Lewis[310]	Chapel Hill	1-7-60	1-1-64
John K. Lockhart[311]	Mount Airy	1-7-60	1-1-62
John Gilmer Mebane[312]	Rutherfordton	1-21-60	1-1-63
NORTH CAROLINA STATE BOARD OF OPTICIANS [313]			
Everett H. Stamper[314]	Greensboro	6-28-59	7-1-64
Frank McBryde†*	Fayetteville	6-27-60	7-1-65

STATE BOARD OF EXAMINERS IN OPTOMETRY [315]

| John D. Costabile† | —————— | Wilson | 6-16-59 | 5-1-64 |
| John T. High* | —————— | Rocky Mount | 6-9-60 | 5-1-65 |

STATE BOARD OF OSTEOPATHIC EXAMINATION AND REGISTRATION [316]

| Guy T. Funk* | —————— | Winston-Salem | 6-16-59 | 5-1-64 |
| Walter C. Eldrett[317] | —————— | Hendersonville | 5-26-60 | 5-1-65 |

[303] The board consists of six members of the North Carolina Dental Society, elected by the society at its annual meeting and commissioned by the governor for three-year terms of office. G. S., Sec. 90-22.

[304] The board consists of three members appointed by the governor for three-year terms, and ex officio members as follows: the state electrical engineer who is also the chairman, and the secretary of the Association of Electrical Contractors of North Carolina. G. S., Secs. 87-39.

[305] Succeeded W. A. Darden, deceased.

[306] Five members appointed by the governor for five-year terms, the terms so staggered that one expires each year. G. S., Sec. 89-4; S. L., 1957, Ch. 1060.

[307] Succeeded Louis E. Wooten, Sr., resigned; reappointed for five-year term on December 11, 1959.

[308] The board consists of nine members. Five members are to be registered nurses, two are to be physicians, and two are to be representatives of hospitals operating nursing schools, who are not physicians, all of whom are appointed and commissioned by the governor for terms of four years. Vacancies are filled for the remainder of unexpired terms by the governor from a list of two nominees filed by the organization which previously nominated the member creating the vacancy, or by the appointment of the governor if such member was not a nominee of any organization. G. S., Sec. 90-158; S. L., 1953, Ch. 1199.

[309] Succeeded Miss J. Elizabeth White.

[310] Succeeded Miss Willie Louise Harkey.

[311] Succeeded J. Lyman Melvin.

[312] Succeeded Moir S. Martin, deceased.

[313] Consists of five members appointed by the governor from a list of names submitted by the North Carolina Opticians Association. Terms of office are for five years. The governor appoints members to fill unexpired terms. G. S., Sec. 90-238; S. L., 1951, Ch. 1089.

[314] Succeeded Robert L. Albertson.

[315] Composed of five members elected by the North Carolina State Optometric Society and commissioned by the governor for five-year terms. Vacancies are filled by the governor for unexpired terms. G. S., Sec. 90-116.

[316] Composed of five members appointed by the governor for terms of five years. The membership is selected from a number of not less than five practioners of osteopathy recommended by the State Osteopathic Society. The governor fills vacancies for unexpired terms in the same manner and may request an increase in the number recommended by the society. G. S., Sec. 90-130.

[317] Succeeded Monroe E. Beverly.

Name of Appointee	Address	Date Appointed	Date of Expiration
STATE BOARD OF PHARMACY [318]			
Norfleet Owen McDowell, Jr.*	Scotland Neck	4-23-59	4-28-64
Robert Neal Watson†	Sanford	6-9-60	4-28-65
STATE EXAMINING COMMITTEE OF PHYSICAL THERAPISTS [319]			
Anne Parrish*	Raleigh	1-28-59	1-1-62
Oliver Wortman[320]	Salisbury	8-10-59	1-1-61
G. Erick Bell*	Wilson	1-5-60	1-1-63
Rachel L. Nunley[321]	Chapel Hill	1-5-60	1-1-63
STATE BOARD OF EXAMINERS OF PLUMBING AND HEATING CONTRACTORS [322]			
Ralph Henry Haley†	Charlotte	6-19-59	4-25-66
W. H. Sullivan, Jr.[323]	Greensboro	8-27-59	4-25-61
Finley Lee[324]	Kinston	2-8-60	4-25-62
L. L. Vaughan†	Raleigh	4-28-60	4-25-67
COMMITTEE ON POSTMORTEM MEDICOLEGAL EXAMINATIONS [325]			
Holt McPherson*	High Point	11-27-59	11-29-63
NORTH CAROLINA REAL ESTATE LICENSING BOARD [326]			
Peter Hairston*[327]	Mocksville	8-27-59	7-31-60-63
Henry V. Koonts[328]	High Point	8-27-59	7-31-62
D. Russell Foster*	Kinston	8-27-59	7-31-62
J. Bart Hill*	Belmont	7-28-60	7-31-63
STATE BOARD OF REFRIGERATION EXAMINERS [329]			
C. V. Stevens*	Salisbury	1-15-59	1-1-65

| John C. Lumsden | ——— | Raleigh | 9-9-59 | 1-1-66 |
| P. B. Mayo* | ——— | Asheville | 1-7-60 | 1-1-67 |

318 Five members, elected by the North Carolina Pharmaceutical Association and commissioned by the governor for five-year terms. G. S., Sec. 90-55.

319 Five members, including at least one doctor and four physical therapists, appointed by the governor from a list submitted to him by the North Carolina Physical Therapy Association, Inc. Members are appointed triennially for three-year terms. The governor appoints persons to fill unexpired terms and no member is allowed by law to serve more than two successive three-year terms. G. S., Sec. 90-257.

320 Succeeded Miss Routh P. Dixon, resigned.

321 Succeeded Margaret Moore.

322 Composed of seven members, each appointed by the governor for a seven-year term with the term of one member expiring each year. Among those appointed there must be one member from the Engineering School and one member from the Division of Public Health of the Greater University of North Carolina, one from the State Board of Health, one plumbing inspector from some city of the state, one licensed master plumber, one heating contractor, and one licensed air conditioning contractor. Vacancies are filled by appointment of the governor for the remainder of the unexpired term. G. S., Sec. 87-16.

323 Succeeded W. H. Sullivan, Sr., deceased.

324 Succeeded C. C. Davis, deceased.

325 This committee was created within the State Board of Health by the 1955 General Assembly. It consists of seven members, six ex officio and one appointed by the governor. The ex officio members are: the state health officer, the attorney general or his representative, the director of the State Bureau of Investigation or his representative, and the heads of the Departments of Pathology at the University of North Carolina, Wake Forest, and Duke University Medical Schools, or their respective representatives. The ex officio members serve during the tenure of their respective offices or that of the officer they represent. The governor's appointee serves for four years. G. S., Sec. 130-293; S. L., 1955, Ch. 972.

326 Five members appointed by the governor, initially for one-, two-, and three-year terms and thereafter for three years. Not more than two of the members may be licensed real estate brokers or salesmen. S. L., 1957, Ch. 744.

327 Succeeded W. B. Harrison, Jr., resigned; reappointed for three-year term on July 28, 1960.

328 Succeeded Harry E. Isenhour, resigned.

329 Seven members, all appointed by the governor: one from the State Board of Health, one from the Engineering School of the Greater University of North Carolina, one from the Division of Public Health of the Greater University of North Carolina, one wholesaler of refrigeration equipment, one manufacturer of refrigeration equipment, and two licensed refrigeration contractors. The terms of office were to be so designated by the governor that one should expire each year. S. L., 1955, Ch. 912. The governor was advised that appointment of a member of the State Board of Health would create a condition of double officeholding, which is forbidden under the state constitution, and therefore this appointment was left vacant. This situation was remedied by action of the 1959 General Assembly specifying an "employee of the State Board of Health" instead of a member of this board S. L., 1959, Ch. 1206. John C. Lumsden was appointed in consequence of the revised legislation.

Name of Appointee	Address	Date Appointed	Date of Expiration
STATE BOARD OF SANITARIAN EXAMINERS [330]			
Robert W. Brown	Asheville	12-23-59	12-15-60
James N. Fulp	Roxboro	12-23-59	12-15-61
Walter C. Lackey	Murfreesboro	12-23-59	12-15-62
Fred C. Pegg	Winston-Salem	12-23-59	12-15-62
Marley M. Melvin	Raleigh	12-23-59	12-15-63
E. R. Spruill	Wilkesboro	12-23-59	12-15-63
STRUCTURAL PEST CONTROL COMMISSION [331]			
J. A. Harris[332]	Raleigh	8-26-59	7-1-60
David L. Goforth[333]	Greensboro	6-24-60	7-1-63
John L. Reitzel*	Raleigh	7-7-60	7-1-63
NORTH CAROLINA BOARD OF VETERINARY MEDICAL EXAMINERS [334]			
C. B. Randall	Kinston	8-7-59	7-1-64
J. G. Martin[335]	Boone	6-27-60	7-1-65

STATE OWNED RAILROADS

Name of Appointee	Address	Date Appointed	Date of Expiration
ATLANTIC AND NORTH CAROLINA RAILROAD [336]			
DIRECTORS			
W. G. Crawford*	Charlotte	8-7-59	8-5-60
W. E. Gladding	Kinston	8-7-59	8-5-60
George Akers Moore, Jr.*	Raleigh	8-7-59	8-5-60-61
J. F. Oglesby*	Kinston	8-7-59	8-5-60
Robert L. Stallings, Jr.*	New Bern	8-7-59	8-5-60
Hugh G. Swan*	New Bern	8-7-59	8-5-60-61

Name	Location		
Dan E. Taylor* ——— Sealevel and West Palm Beach, Florida	8-7-59	8-5-60
George R. Wallace* ———Morehead City	8-7-59	8-5-60-61
John M. Belk ———Charlotte	8-5-60	8-5-61
Leo Brody ———Kinston	8-5-60	8-5-61
J. E. Ragan, Jr. ———Oriental	8-5-60	8-5-61
Arthur L. Tyler ———Rocky Mount	8-5-60	8-5-61
Frank C. Williams ———Roanoke Rapids	8-5-60	8-5-61

OFFICERS

Name	Location		
George Akers Moore, *President** ——— Raleigh	8-7-59	8-5-60-61
G. Paul La Roque, *Secretary-Treasurer*†* ——— Kinston	8-7-59	8-5-60-61
R. M. Kermon, *Attorney* ——— Wilmington	8-7-59	8-5-60
Malcolm B. Seawell, *Attorney* ——— Chapel Hill	8-5-60	8-5-61

---

[380] Nine members, six appointed by the governor and three ex officio: the state health director or his representative, the dean of the School of Public Health at the University of North Carolina or his representative, and the director of the Division of Sanitary Engineering of the State Board of Health. Initial appointments were for one-, two-, three-, and four-year terms. Reappointments are for four-year terms. S. L., 1959, Ch. 1271.

[381] Five members, appointed by the governor: one from the Division of Entomology faculty of North Carolina State College, one from the State Department of Agriculture, and two from the pest control industry at large but not from the same company. Original appointments were: **one for a one-year term, two for two-year terms, and two for three-year terms. All subsequent appointments** for three years. S. L., 1955, Ch. 1017.

[382] Succeeded D. L. Wray.

[383] Succeeded Walter H. Wilson.

[384] Composed of five members of the North Carolina Veterinary Medical Association appointed by the governor for five-year terms and until their successors are appointed and qualified. One term expires each year. G. S., Sec. 90-180.

[385] Succeeded George R. Armstrong.

[386] The board of directors is composed of twelve members, eight of whom the governor appoints annually. The governor also nominates the officers and the inspector and appoints the finance committee and the proxy. P. L., 1852, Ch. 136; P. L., 1858-1859. Resolution (p. 99); P. L., 1891, Ch. 483; P. L., 1925, Ch. 157.

Name of Appointee	Address	Date Appointed	Date of Expiration
EXECUTIVE COMMITTEE			
W. G. Crawford	Goldsboro	8-7-59	8-5-60
George Akers Moore, Jr.	Raleigh	8-7-59	8-5-60-61
Hugh G. Swan	New Bern	8-5-60	8-5-61
FINANCE COMMITTEE			
Vinton E. Fountain*	Tarboro	8-7-59	8-5-60
Charles F. Gold	Raleigh	8-7-59	8-5-60
Robert L. Stallings, Jr.*	New Bern	8-7-59	8-5-60
E. L. Scott	Kinston	8-5-60	8-5-61
Robert W. Taylor	Morehead City	8-5-60	8-5-61
Arthur L. Tyler	Rocky Mount	8-5-60	8-5-61
INSPECTOR			
Albert R. Bell†*	New Bern	8-7-59	8-5-60-61
PROXY			
Charles F. Gold	Raleigh	8-7-59	8-5-60
E. N. Richards	Raleigh	8-5-60	8-5-61
NORTH CAROLINA RAILROAD [387]			
DIRECTORS			
W. G. Alligood	Mount Holly	7-9-59	7-9-60
J. A. Babcock	Raleigh	7-9-59-60	7-9-60-61
Charles E. Brady	Salisbury	7-9-59	7-9-60
John M. Morehead	New York	7-9-59-60	7-9-60-61
Robert H. Nutt	Greensboro	7-9-59	7-9-60
R. E. Price	Rutherfordton	7-9-59	7-9-60

Name	Location		
Ralph H. Scott	Haw River	7-9-59-60	7-9-60-61
Harry Vanderlinden*	Hickory	7-9-59	7-9-60
Stacy Budd	Sanford	6-27-60	6-27-61
N. K. Dickerson, Jr.	Monroe	6-27-60	6-27-61
Huber Hanes, Jr.	Winston-Salem	6-27-60	6-27-61
W. Trent Ragland, Jr.	Raleigh	6-27-60	6-27-61
Smith Richardson, Sr.	New York	6-27-60	6-27-61

OFFICERS

Name	Location		
John M. Morehead, *President*	New York	7-9-59-60	6-27-60-61
Edwin S. Pou, *Secretary-Treasurer*	Raleigh	7-9-59-60	6-27-60-61
Harley B. Gaston, *Attorney*	Belmont	7-9-59-60	6-27-60-61
Ray Byerly, *Expert*	Sanford	7-9-59	7-9-60
Charles Heath, *Expert*	Shelby	6-27-60	6-27-61

FINANCE COMMITTEE

Name	Location		
James H. Glenn	Charlotte	7-9-59	7-9-60
George L. Hundley	Thomasville	7-9-59	7-9-60
Harris Nelson, Sr.*	Spray	7-9-59-60	7-9-60-61
J. G. Northcott, Jr.	Black Mountain	6-27-60	6-27-61
Irving R. Squires	Greensboro	6-27-60	6-27-61

PROXY

Name	Location		
Edwin M. Gill*	Raleigh	7-9-59-60	6-27-60-61

[887] The board of directors consists of twelve members, eight of whom are appointed by the governor with the advice and consent of the Council of State. See the bylaws of the North Carolina Railroad Company, and charter and amendments thereto. *P. L., 1854-1855,* Ch. 32. *P. L., 1873-1874,* Ch. 33, 54; *P. L., 1879,* Ch. 138; *P. L., 1891,* Ch. 392; *P. L., 1925,* Ch. 157.

Name of Appointee	Address	Date Appointed	Date of Expiration
MISCELLANEOUS			
DAVIDSON COUNTY COURT [338]			
Charles E. Williams, Jr., *Judge* [339]	Lexington	12-2-60	12-3-62
Thomas H. Suddarth, Jr., *Solicitor**	Lexington	12-2-60	12-3-62
DURHAM COUNTY SMALL CLAIMS COURT [340]			
Oscar G. Barker, *Judge**	Durham	7-31-59	8-5-61
Dan K. Edwards, *Assistant Judge*	Durham	9-4-59	8-5-61
TOWN OF LONG BEACH [341]			
A. H. Cromer [342]	Long Beach	5-19-59	6-1-63
E. F. Middleton*	Long Beach	5-19-59	6-1-63
W. L. Simmons [343]	Long Beach	5-19-59	6-1-63
COMMISSIONERS OF THE TOWN OF OCEAN ISLE BEACH [344]			
Watt Huntley	Ocean Isle Beach	11-16-59	6-1-61
Homer L. Johnston	Ocean Isle Beach	11-16-59	6-1-61
N. F. Meggs	Ocean Isle Beach	11-16-59	6-1-61
George Sloane	Ocean Isle Beach	11-16-59	6-1-61
Odell Williamson	Ocean Isle Beach	11-16-59	6-1-61
W. T. Wimbish	Ocean Isle Beach	11-16-59	6-1-61
TOWN OF SURF CITY [345]			
R. T. Batts, *Mayor**	Surf City	6-9-59	6-30-61
M. J. Blizzard*	Surf City	6-9-59	6-30-61
A. H. Ward [346]	Surf City	6-9-59	6-30-61

THOMASVILLE RECORDER'S COURT [347]

L. Roy Hughes, *Judge*†* ——— Thomasville   3-20-59   4-1-61
E. W. Hooper, *Solicitor** ——— Thomasville   3-20-59   4-1-61

TAX COLLECTOR, TRANSYLVANIA COUNTY [348]

Margaret Whitmire Guilkey[349] ——— Brevard   11-11-60   12-5-60

TOWN OF WHITE LAKE [350]

Jack Womble, *Mayor*[351] ——— White Lake   6-12-59   7-5-61

---

[338] The judge and the solicitor are appointed by the governor to hold office for two years or until their successors are appointed. *Public Local Laws, 1933*, Ch. 82. (Hereinafter cited as *P. L. L.*)

[339] Succeeded Joe H. Leonard.

[340] A special county court, created by the Board of County Commissioners under authority of G. S., Sec. 7-405-7. The governor appoints the judge for a two-year term.

[341] Six commissioners appointed by the governor for four-year terms. The commissioners elect the mayor from among their number for a two-year term. *S. L., 1955*, Ch. 1067.

[342] Succeeded C. C. Carr.

[343] Succeeded G. S. Sherrod.

[344] The governor appoints the six persons receiving the highest number of votes in an election. Initial appointments were for two years. At the end of this period the three persons receiving the highest number of votes would be appointed for four years and the other three for two years. Thereafter all appointments are for four years. *S. L., 1959*, Ch. 887.

[345] In the second week of June, 1953, and at that time every two years, a mayor, who also serves as a commissioner, and two other commissioners are appointed by the governor from persons recommended to him as having had the highest number of votes in the general election. Vacancies are filled by the remaining commissioners for the duration of unexpired terms. *S. L., 1949*, Ch. 512, Sec. 12.

[346] Succeeded J. R. Hubbard.

[347] The judge and solicitor are appointed by the governor for two-year terms upon the recommendation of the city of Thomasville. *P. L. L., 1933*, Ch. 245.

[348] Officials of the county make recommendations to the governor. *P. L. L., 1925*, Ch. 8, as amended by *P. L. L., 1933*, Ch. 30.

[349] Succeeded C. M. Douglas, deceased.

[350] The mayor and four commissioners are appointed by the governor from a list of the five persons who received the highest number of votes in the biennial election. The law recommends that the person with the highest number of votes be appointed mayor and the other four be appointed commissioners. Any vacancies are filled by appointment of the governor upon the recommendation of the remaining commissioners. *S. L., 1951*, Ch. 511.

[351] Succeeded James R. Nance as mayor.

Name of Appointee	Address	Date Appointed	Date of Expiration
William Corbett, Jr.[852]	White Lake	6-12-59	7-5-61
Gordon W. Love*	Garland	6-12-59	7-5-61
Rodney Marshburn*	White Lake	6-12-59	7-5-61
Hiram R. Melvin†*	White Lake	6-12-59	7-5-61
TOWN OF WRIGHTSVILLE BEACH [853]			
Lawrence C. Rose[854]	Wrightsville	6-4-59	7-5-63
Robert M. Williams[855]	Wrightsville	6-4-59	7-5-63
TOWN OF YAUPON BEACH [856]			
Kay L. Dixon	Yaupon Beach	5-20-59	6-1-61
Wesley E. Garner	Yaupon Beach	5-20-59	6-1-61
Clarence E. Murphy	Yaupon Beach	5-20-59	6-1-61
C. E. Bellamy	Yaupon Beach	5-20-59	6-1-63
Robert C. Sellers	Yaupon Beach	5-20-59	6-1-63
E. G. Sinclair	Yaupon Beach	5-20-59	6-1-63

[852] Succeeded Jack Womble.
[853] The governor appoints five aldermen for four-year terms. The aldermen choose one of their number as mayor. *S. L., 1951*, Ch. 687; *S. L., 1955*, Ch. 772.
[854] Succeeded R. S. Dunlea, Sr.
[855] Succeeded Robert R. Bellamy.
[856] The commissioners are elected by the qualified voters and appointed by the governor. Initial appointments were for two- and four-year terms; reappointments for four years. *S. L., 1957*, Ch. 899.

INDEX

DATE DUE

GAYLORD			PRINTED IN U.